EXPLAINING COMMUNICATION

Contemporary Theories and Exemplars

LEA's COMMUNICATION SERIES

Jennings Bryant / Dolf Zillmann, General Editors

Selected titles in the Communication Theory and Methodology Subseries (Jennings Bryant, series advisor) include:

Berger • *Planning Strategic Interaction: Attaining Goals Through Communicative Action*

Dennis/Wartella • *American Communication Research: The Remembered History*

Ellis • *Crafting Society: Ethnicity, Class and Communication Theory*

Greene • *Message Production: Advances in Communication Theory*

Heath/Bryant • *Human Communication Theory and Research: Concepts, Contexts, and Challenges, Second Edition*

Jensen • *Ethical Issues in the Communication Process*

Potter • *An Analysis of Thinking and Research About Qualitative Methods*

Reese/Gandy/Grant • *Framing Public Life: Perspectives on Media and Our Understanding of the Social World*

Riffe/Lacy/Fico • *Analyzing Media Messages: Using Quantitative Content Analysis in Research, Second Edition*

Salwen/Stacks • *An Integrated Approach to Communication Theory and Research*

For a complete list of titles in LEA's Communication Series, please contact Lawrence Erlbaum Associates, Publishers at www.erlbaum.com

EXPLAINING COMMUNICATION

Contemporary Theories and Exemplars

Edited by

Bryan B. Whaley
University of San Francisco

Wendy Samter
Bryant University

Routledge
Taylor & Francis Group
New York   London

First published by Lawrence Erlbaum Associates, Inc., Publishers
10 Industrial Avenue
Mahwah, New Jersey 07430

Transferred to digital printing 2010 by Routledge

Routledge

270 Madison Avenue
New York, NY 10016

2 Park Square, Milton Park
Abingdon, Oxon OX14 4RN, UK

Cover design by Tomai Maridou

Library of Congress Cataloging-in-Publication Data

Explaining communication : contemporary theories and exemplars /
edited by Bryan B. Whaley, Wendy Samter.
    p. cm. — (Lea's communication series)
Includes bibliographical references and index.
ISBN 978-0-8058-3959-3

    1. Communication. I. Whaley, Bryan B. II. Samter, Wendy.
P90.E88 2006
302.2—dc22

                          2006028670

This book is dedicated to
Stephen W. Littlejohn
Those who know … know why

Contents

Preface

There are numerous books about interpersonal communication theory and research authored by respected colleagues in the field. As such, making the case for another was a challenge. However, we believed that missing from this collection of texts for undergraduates was a book that presented the explanation of theory *by the theorists themselves*, or by scholars doing the bulk of research within a particular theoretical perspective. We view the approach taken in this volume as unique—and advantageous—for several reasons. First, in most other books, fundamental theoretical principles and research findings are naturally filtered through the perceptual lenses of various authors and editors. Thus, the foundations and contributions of different theories—and, in many ways such basic notions as where the theory fits in the field—are interpreted by others. This is important and legitimate but, in this text, the authors offer their own view of the core ideas and findings of a given theoretical perspective, what that perspective is best equipped to explain, how it fits within the field, where future efforts are best placed, and the like. Second, scholars of interpersonal communication rarely have the chance to directly address an undergraduate audience. We believed it was important to give some of the foremost "theory builders" in interpersonal communication a chance to tell the story of their own journey—to speak, in untranslated words, to the coming generations of communication scholars. Finally, we have asked our authors to include information that is not normally present in other treatments of interpersonal communication. Namely, we requested that they not only include a review of their most current research findings but also provide a developmental framework for the reader—in other words, we asked them to outline the roots of theory as well as the directions they believe future research should take. We see this as one way in which undergraduate students can begin to learn about and appreciate not just various theories themselves but also the difficult process of theory *development*.

Obviously, the scope of this book precluded the inclusion of every theory of interpersonal communication ever written. Those presented here represent, in our minds, (a) some of the most active, (b) some that have demonstrated "traction" in terms of generating a substantial body of knowledge across a relatively long period of time, and (c) some that have yet to be articulated in detail elsewhere. The book is not exhaustive, and it should not in any way be seen as such. In addition, the reader will notice that absent from this volume are organizational sections or groupings of works. This is because we were hesitant to provide false divisions for the theories covered in the text. However, one could make the case that the first five chapters deal with the nature of theory as well as fundamental concepts in interpersonal communication (and the theories that attempt to explain them). Chapters 6 through 11 might be viewed as loosely centered on accounting for individual differences in message production—particularly individual differences in skilled message production. Attempts to explain human communication from dyadic, relational, and cultural levels are addressed by chapters 12 through 20. The last chapter, by Bryant and Miron, provides an excellent history of the roots of communication theory in general. These are very basic ways to think about how to organize the corpus of information in this book—and, as we said earlier, we are hesitant to provide false groupings.

Finally, there are many people who lent their expertise and support to this project. First and foremost, we would like to thank the contributors to this volume both for agreeing with us that this work would be unique from other treatments of interpersonal communication and for sticking with us throughout the long and sometimes arduous process of putting the text together. Great appreciation is also extended to Linda Bathgate, Karin Wittig Bates, and the production staff at Lawrence Erlbaum Associates, Inc. for their sound advice and unwavering enthusiasm. We thank Marissa Michaels and Natalie Jeha for reviewing initial drafts of sample chapters in an effort to ascertain undergraduates' perspective and Jeff Hunter for providing a much needed "outsider's" view on the manuscript.

It is our hope that this text is read and received as intended. It is meant to add to the already rich, but different, array of theory books produced by colleagues within the field (some of which have graciously agreed to write for us). It presents explanations of interpersonal theory and research written by the scholars themselves and thus provides a unique and tremendously accurate picture of the field. We hope you find the book as rich and informative as we do.

—Bryan B. Whaley
Wendy Samter

1

The Nature and Evaluation of Theory

Stephen W. Littlejohn
Public Dialogue Consortium

NATURE AND EVALUATION OF THEORY

Raúl and Taisha emerged from their history class shaking their heads and feeling disappointed. They wandered out of the building and down to the duck pond, where they sat on a bench to talk.

"How could any professor be that bad?" Raúl asked and then added, "He is so disorganized and dull, and you can't really understand what he's trying to say."

"Hard to figure," Taisha mused. "I'm upset because I was really looking forward to this course. I think he just can't connect with the subject. I think he hates it. They probably forced him to teach the class."

"Well, I don't know," Raúl responded, "I think he's just shy and doesn't like students very much. You know, I get the impression that he just doesn't like to teach."

"Or he's afraid of people," Taisha added.

"That may be the case," Raúl surmised, "but how do you explain that dense language he's always using? I can't make sense of it."

"Oh, professors just talk like that. They seem to get some false sense of importance out of using hard words," Taisha replied.

"Well, my English prof doesn't," Raúl said. "He's so cool. I mean, he really clicks with students, and he can explain stuff really clearly. Plus he's super interesting. He's an Assistant Professor, and he seems to just love coming to class. Everything seems really fresh and new to him. I think that matters. When you haven't taught the same thing 800 times, it's easier and more fun to share with others."

"If that's so," Taisha wondered, "how come some of the older profs do such a great job showing the relevance of what they teach? I think experience can help teachers see more angles and ways of understanding their subject."

Taisha and Raúl were repeating a pattern heard just about everywhere we go. They were trying to explain a communication experience. In this case, they wanted to get an idea of why their professor communicated in certain ways. These students did what we all do. They took turns proposing possible explanations.

We are able to explain our experience because we have a variety of theories about how things work. Normally, such theories are implicit, or not spoken. Sometimes they are even subconscious. We may believe people are more nonverbally engaging when they are interested in the subject than when they are not. We may think that personal traits such as shyness affect individuals' interaction styles. We could say that people are more curious about things they know less about and that experience leads to familiarity and lower enthusiasm, or we could suggest just the opposite—that experience leads to commitment, which in turn leads to enthusiasm.

In addition, we have certain implicit theories of language. For example, we might believe that people use certain forms of talk to identify themselves as a community, or that we use language in certain ways to build our image in social situations. Each of these explanations surfaced in Raúl and Taisha's conversation.

Human beings seem to have a strong need to interpret, understand, and explain their experience in the world. We want to be able to make sense out of things, and when it comes to human social life, we are especially compelled to create meaning for the patterns of interaction we experience.

What Is a Theory?

A theory is a set of related propositions used to classify and explain aspects of the universe in which we live (Littlejohn, 1999, p. 21). *Theory* is normally taken as an academic term, because we associate it with science, but really everyone operates by theory most of the time. We put patterns of experience together in ways that help us make sense of our lives, predict what is going to happen, and help us respond and react to situations as they come up. We use terms—words, symbols, and numbers—to identify what we experience and to connect things together. When we have a way to talk about what we experience and explain things systematically, then we are using a theory.

Notice that we take our theories to be true, or at least we act as if they were true. However, you will also notice that people change their theories from moment to moment, as new explanations become necessary. Most important for ordinary people is that their theories work, that they are useful, that they make appropriate responses possible. When our understanding helps us see things clearly, then our theories are taken as true. When our ideas fail us—as they often do—we continue our search for a better way to understand.

Our theories provide us with two things that help us interpret experience. First, we have *concepts*, which are categories of things identified with a term. Look at the concepts that surfaced in Raúl and Taisha's conversation—boredom, shyness, liking, fear, dense language, self-importance, clear explanation, interest, experience, age, and others. Each of these is a set of perceptions that Raúl or Taisha group together, categorize, and distinguish from other perceptions. *Boring* experiences are different from *interesting* ones. So boredom and interest are concepts. *Clear explanation* is different from *unclear explanation*, which makes these concepts. Taisha and Raúl are able to communicate because these concepts mean more or less the same things to them.

But Taisha and Raúl are doing more than listing concepts. They are connecting them, or relating them to one another, which is the second thing that theories do. So Taisha and Raúl imply such things as, *Shyness causes a feeling of boredom in listeners* and *Language density corresponds with comprehension.* Of course much of the theory behind these conclusions remain unstated, but they could be articulated if Raúl and Taisha needed to do so. If they had to explain why they draw these conclusions, they would probably present a whole string of connections that justify the final conclusion about shyness, language, or clarity. It is the system of connections lying behind their conclusions that constitute Raúl and Taisha's theory-in-use.

In this chapter we will explore the nature of theory with a special emphasis on scholarship. First, we will take a look at how scientific theory is different from ordinary, implicit theory. Next, we will see how theory is created. Following that, we will discuss the role of research and publication in the production of theory and the similarities and differences among different types of theory and then look at various bodies of theory. We will conclude the chapter by learning about how to evaluate communication theories.

Scientific Theory

Given this tendency in human nature to seek clear and useful explanations, it is not surprising that scientists and scholars formalize theories. Scholars typically go about theorizing in a more systematic manner than do people in ordinary life. Scholars call their conceptual connections *propositions*, which are statements that associate or connect a concept to one or more other concepts. Here are some examples of propositions from various communication theories you will learn about in this book:

- Immediacy is correlated positively to eye contact.
- Cognitive dissonance causes attitude or behavior change.
- Well-defined roles found in working class families bring about the use of restricted codes, which reinforce the closed role system of the family.
- People control the impression they make on others by how they present themselves.

Let's take a closer look at these propositions.

The first statement claims that *immediacy* is associated with *eye contact* (Mehrabian, 1972). In ordinary language, this means that you give more eye contact to people you like than to people you do not like. This proposition has two concepts—immediacy (liking) and eye contact. The connection between these two is called a *correlation*, meaning that the two concepts are associated, though one does not necessarily cause the other. A positive correlation means that when one variable goes up, the other one also goes up. When one goes down, the other goes down. A negative correlation means that when one variable goes up, the other goes down. This proposition is simply saying that there is a positive correlation between liking and eye contact. It doesn't say that liking causes greater eye contact, or that greater eye contact causes liking, only that the two are associated with one another.

The second proposition deals with *cognitive dissonance*, which means *awareness of being inconsistent*. If you are a vegetarian for health reasons, but eat a lot of butter and cream, you might suffer cognitive dissonance. You value a healthy diet, but eat unhealthy, saturated fats. According to this proposition, once you become aware of this inconsistency, you will undergo either attitude or behavior change (Festinger, 1957). This is a *causal relationship*: Dissonance causes change. Notice, however, that a causal proposition can never stand on its own because other propositions are required to help explain the causal relationship. In this case, the explanation goes something like this:

When you are aware of an inconsistency in your thinking, you become stressed and feel tense, which is uncomfortable. In an attempt to relieve the tension and return to a more comfortable state of balance, you will change an attitude so that the cognitive dissonance disappears.

The third proposition states that well-defined roles found in working class families bring about the use of restricted codes, which reinforce the closed role system of the family (Bernstein, 1971). To translate,

> Members of working class families behave in pre-defined ways and have little individuality. Such families use simple language that does not allow family members to elaborate very much on what they want to say. This restricted language will tend to keep the family members' behavior within the prescribed roles.

You can see that this is a circular connection. Limited roles leads to limited language, and limited language leads to limited roles. This kind of connection is called a *causal loop*, or *mutual causation*.

The fourth proposition has a different ring to it: People control the impression they make on others by how they present themselves (Goffman, 1959). The two concepts connected by this proposition are impression and presentation, and these are connected by personal choice. This is called an *action connection*. The action one takes leads to a goal or outcome. Unlike the first two types of proposition, which are more or less determined, an action statement suggests that people can choose to do various things to reach certain goals.

Propositions are the building blocks of theory, but no proposition by itself makes a theory. A theory is an organized set of propositions that together form a way of explaining or understanding something. The propositions of a theory paint a picture of how something works. *Elaboration likelihood theory* is a good illustration of what a theory looks like (Petty & Cacioppo, 1986); it is typically used to understand how persuasion works. Notice in the following paragraph, that this theory (presented in simplified form) is nothing more than an interconnected set of propositions that forms *a picture of how information processing affects attitude change*:

> An individual sometimes evaluates a message in an elaborate, or critical, way, which is called *central processing*. In contrast, individuals sometimes treat a message in a noncritical way, which is *peripheral processing*. If a person is motivated and able, he or she will use central processing. When this is done, attitude change is less likely to occur, but when it does occur, it will be more enduring. If a person lacks motivation or ability, he or she will process the information peripherally, in which case attitude change will be more likely, but less enduring. Motivation is created by personal relevance of the message, the diversity of arguments in the message, or one's personal tendency to like critical thinking. Ability is associated with such factors as prior knowledge and message clarity.

For example, if you care deeply about the environment and pride yourself on knowing a lot about the natural world, you will probably process information on this subject in a *central* way, meaning that you would pay close attention to the details of environmental messages. If someone tried to persuade you that the Endangered Species Act caused harm to the environment, you would probably be pretty resistant to the idea, even though the speaker is quite credible in other ways. However, if you looked closely and found that there is some merit to the argument, you might change your mind a little, and this would probably be a fairly durable change.

How Theory Is Created

Most people will tell you that a theory is an educated guess about how something works. The common idea about theories goes something like this: *A well informed person creates a theory about a phenomenon, not knowing whether the theory is true or false. By careful research, the theory is tested to determine whether it is correct or incorrect. If it proves false, it is discarded, and a new theory is created. If it proves correct, the theory is no longer a theory, but a picture of reality.*

In this book, you will learn to understand theory in a way that is different from this. Very few contemporary scholars would distinguish between theory and reality. Rather, a theory is a way of packaging reality, a way of understanding it (Deetz, 1992, p. 66). You cannot understand reality without a theory. Reality in any realm of life can be represented in a variety of ways, so a number of theories could be useful. Because human beings always represent reality symbolically, they are always operating in the realm of theory. A theory is a system of thought, a way of looking at things. We can never "view" reality purely. Instead, we must use a set of concepts and symbols to define what we see, and our theories provide the lenses with which we observe and experience the world. In the chapters that follow, you will read many theories that utilize different concepts and symbols—and thus provide different lenses—for understanding the phenomenon of interpersonal communication.

Theories, then, are made. They are constructed by scholars for particular purposes (Pearce, 1991). People name concepts in the theory, they decide what connections or relationships to feature, they determine how to organize the theory, and they give the theory a title. They then use the theory to talk about what they experience.

Does this mean that anything goes, that you can "make up" any theory and assume it is as good as any other theory? No, it does not. Theories must have fit and utility (Brinberg & McGrath, 1985). *Fit* is the degree to which the categories and relations in a theory explain our experience of events. Do the categories and connections in the theory make sense in terms of our experience? Many theories are rejected because they do not seem to hold up in this way. However, a number of theories may fit; a number of theories may make sense in light of our experience. This is a good thing, because multiple theories expand our ability to describe and explain things from various perspectives.

The second way in which theories are tested is *utility*. Do they help us do things? Theories guide practice. Teachers like certain theories because they help explain things and organize a learning experience. Researchers like certain theories because they point to what should be observed and guide methods of observation. Physicians, psychologists, economists, managers, and architects all follow certain principles derived from theory to guide their work.

There is a circular relation between theory and practice. Theory drives practice, but practice drives theory. In other words, our theories influence what we do, and what we do influences our theories. We will change what we do based on new ideas about how things work, and we change our ideas about how things work based on what we experience. Once this circle becomes fairly stable, so that practice and theory are relatively predictable, then we would say that the theory is showing sustained utility. It seems to be working as a way of both understanding and guiding experience.

But how are fit and utility established? There is no standard against which all theory must be measured. The creation and development of theory is a *human social activity* (Krippendorff, 1993). As a *human* activity, it is subjectively determined. Human beings create it, test it, and evaluate it. As a *social* activity, theory making is done within communities of scholarship that share a way of knowing and a set of common practices. In the end, the community of scholars or practitioners decides what works for them and what theories prevail. Because the communities of practice vary tremendously, they will differ in what they consider to be valuable theories. A theory widely adopted by one community may be rejected entirely by another. For example, theorists in the "critical" school generally mistrust theories based on experimental research, and theorists in the "experimental" tradition often say that critical theorists are off base.

So creating a theory is largely a question of persuading some community that the theory has fit and utility within that community. In the academic world, this is done by research and publication.

Research and Publication

Raúl and Taisha's concern about their professor began with observations they made in class. They *saw* certain things happening and then *talked* about what they observed. Scholars do the same thing: They "observe" and they "talk." Their observations are more formalized than those of Raúl and Taisha, and their "talk" is both informal and formal. Scholars constantly discuss their observations and ideas with colleagues, and these informal conversations are an extremely important part of the work. But scholarship is never considered complete without formal presentation such as papers, convention presentations, journal articles, and books.

These formal communications provide the means by which scholarly work is "tested." There is no scale that can be applied objectively to scholarship, so it must be judged subjectively by peers. Although scholars apply well-worked standards in the evaluation of one another's work, this evaluation is always a matter of judgment, and consensus about the value of a piece of scholarship is rare. Just as a group of students might disagree as to why their professor is a poor communicator, scholars also disagree about the merits of particular research and theory.

Although standards vary from one academic community to another, scholars follow a fairly predictable pattern of production. First, a scholar or group scholars becomes curious about a topic. Sometimes the topic relates to something personal in the scholar's own life. Sometimes it is an extension of what he or she has been reading in the literature. Often a conversation with mentors or colleagues will provoke interest in a particular subject. Also, professors are often challenged by questions that come up when they are preparing lectures or having class discussions.

Scholars are usually motivated to investigate interesting subjects because their professional advancement may depend on it. They cannot get a PhD without developing scholarly curiosity that leads to research on a topic of their choice. They often will not be able to get pay raises, tenure, or promotion without doing this kind of work. There are many other incentives as well, including the ability to get grant money, travel, be recognized as a leader, get awards, and so forth. For Raúl and Taisha, observing and theorizing happen informally, but for scholars, this kind of work is a way of life.

So the process starts with curiosity about a topic. Next, the scholar will begin to do some kind of research on the topic. This almost always includes a survey of literature to see what others have done on this subject. It will also include some kind of systematic observation. What the scholar observes and how he or she collects data depend on the tradition of research and theory being used. There is tremendous variation in research practice from one community to another. Some focus on words, sentences, and meanings. Some criticize by applying values. Some do experiments and use sophisticated statistics. Some conduct interviews. Some observe behavior in natural settings.

Because scholarship is never a solitary activity, the results of reading, observing, and thinking must be shared with others. On the most informal level, scholars often share their work with students. They may bring some of their latest work into the classroom as a lecture or basis for discussion; this can be helpful in refining ideas. Ultimately, however, a scholar's work must go out for peer review. One of the first formal "tests" a scholar may use is the convention paper. The researcher writes a paper and submits it to a professional association to be presented at a regional, national, or international meeting. Most of these papers are reviewed by a panel of peers. This review itself is a level of evaluation that can help a scholar determine if he or she is on the right track. Universities usually encourage professors to submit papers by agreeing to pay their travel expenses if they have a paper accepted by a professional association.

Whether a paper is reviewed for acceptance before the convention or not, the presentation permits at least two other forms of peer assessment. One—more informal—consists of the comments that colleagues make after hearing the presentation. This kind of feedback may come in the bar, hallway, or airport. Colleagues may even enjoy phone calls or e-mail exchanges about one another's work. More formally, there is often a designated critic who delivers comments about several papers to the audience right after they are presented.

Conventions are very valuable for scholars as an initial testing ground for ideas. Not only do the convention-goers have the opportunity to hear the most recent research, but the presenters can refine their work based on the reactions they receive. Often a group of researchers will present various iterations of their work several times at conventions before the work is submitted to publication.

There are two forms of publication most valued in the academic community. The first is a journal article, and the second is a monograph, or book. There are literally thousands of academic journals around the world, and every field, no matter how small, will have at least one—and usually several—journals. The members of the field subscribe to these journals, use their contents as background for their own research, and learn about the latest and best developments in the field from the articles. Usually, the articles in a journal are refereed, meaning that they are formally reviewed and judged by a panel of peers for quality. Because only the best articles are published, the majority of papers submitted to journals do not end up appearing in print. This rigorous form of review is the primary force establishing what is taken seriously within an academic community.

Many research and theory projects find their way to another level of publication—the scholarly monograph, or book. After a group of scholars develops a line of research and theory in some detail—usually after a number of convention presentations and journal articles—they may write it all up in a book manuscript. These books are not the same thing as a textbook. Textbooks are written primarily to help students learn the content of certain courses. Scholarly treatises are published for the benefit of the field, as a convenient way to "house" the results of a major research program. Mostly graduate students and other scholars use these books, and many professors use scholarly books as a basis for their lectures in classes. Again, peers review manuscripts submitted for publication as a book, and only a few manuscripts are deemed good enough for publication. Having a scholarly book is considered a great honor in most fields.

Through this process of presentation and publication, the scholarship considered most interesting, profound, useful, or progressive will "bubble up" and form the corpus of recognized work within the community of scholars. As this work develops, those responsible, along with their colleagues, begin to develop more formal explanations that tie the work together. Initially, these explanations may be mere interpretations of research findings, but as they give more convention papers and publish more articles on their work, the scholars' explanations become more formal, and that is where we see theory emerging. Once a theory, or emerging theory, is identified, other scholars may use it to guide additional research, which in turn adds to the body of research and theory taken as standard within the community.

Now you can begin to see how theory development is a social activity. Once you live through several years of producing research, positing theory, being reviewed, revising your work, publishing, and using the published work of others, you cannot deny that theories are social constructions that are only as valuable as the collective wisdom of the scholarly community.

Reading the various chapters of this book will give you a glimpse of this world. The authors of the chapters in this book are all established scholars in the communication field. All of them have given numerous convention papers, published many journal articles, and some have even produced books. Keep in mind that the theories selected for this book have been judged to be important ways of understanding communication by at least one of the academic communities within the field of communication.

Notice that the theories here vary in terms of how they were generated, the kind of research used, the style in which they are presented, and the aspect of communication they address. The theories are different because they come from various academic communities within the field. Each academic community has its own standards of excellence, some of which will be explained in a later section. What is judged as valuable within one community may not be considered very interesting or rigorous within another. That's just the way it is in the world of scholarship. Indeed, huge debates rage about which community's methods and standards should prevail, but these debates will never be settled. In the end we need to realize two things: (a) Theory is the product of human judgment and social interaction, and (b) we live in a multivalued world in which different people prefer different ways of knowing. Do not take this state of affairs as a problem. Instead, treat differences as a rich resource for developing a more thorough and complex understanding of your communication experience.

Similarity and Difference Among Theories

Imagine several objects in a box. They are of different sizes, colors, and shapes. They are made out of different materials. Now imagine that there are magnetic fields in the box that can be turned on and off. When one field is turned on, the objects will be drawn together according to color so that when you look in the box you will see all the red objects together, all the blue ones together, and so on. Now you turn the color switch off and turn the size switch on, and a new magnetic field draws the objects into different clusters by size. By activating different switches, you can recluster the objects in a variety of ways depending on their many similarities and differences.

Using the box of objects as an analogy, we can better understand similarities and differences among theories. The box represents a field or discipline such as communication, and the objects represent theories. There are several dimensions, "magnetic fields" if you will, that draw theories together in different ways. The scholarly communities mentioned earlier are often formed around such magnetic fields. Let's look at several of these (Littlejohn, 1999, pp. 30–35).

The Focus Field: Individuals, Social Relations, and Texts. When theories are clustered by focus, you will notice three general groups. Some communication scholars are fascinated by individual human behavior. These researchers wonder why people behave as they do, and they are preoccupied with predicting—and in some cases—controlling communication behavior. The scholars interested in individual behavior spend a lot of time observing and measuring behavior, and their theories tend to classify behavior according to type and to establish causal links between ways of thinking and ways of behaving. Argumentativeness theory (Rancer & Nicotera, chap. 7, this volume) is an example of this type of theory.

Other scholars are more interested in how people act together interpersonally, the nature of their relationships with one another. These researchers look at connections among people in dyads, groups, organizations, and other collectives. Scholars interested in social relations tend to distinguish between different types of relationships, look at ways that the persons' behaviors are connected to one another, and theorize about how human systems work. Dialectical theory (Baxter & Braithwaite, chap. 15, this volume) is an example.

The third broad group focuses on texts, or messages and discourse. These people want to examine language and look at how language is used. The scholars who value texts like to look carefully at the way messages are put together, the structure of messages, and how discourse is used in various settings. Conversation analysis (Beach, chap. 18, this volume) illustrates this.

The Value Field: Description Versus Critique.   Another way to cluster theories is to group them according to those that are primarily descriptive and those that are primarily critical. Many scholars believe that their job is to describe and explain communication, whereas others believe it is their job to attach values to what they observe. Descriptive theories tell us how things work, but critical theorists tell us what is wrong with how things work. Descriptive theories take a more scientific approach in explicating the world, whereas critical theories take a political approach to show how people are disadvantages or oppressed in the world. This distinction is not benign. Indeed, it divides theorists on the question of the whole purpose of scholarship—to describe without comment or to raise consciousness of value dimensions. Although critical theories are important, this book concentrates on descriptive theories.

The Methods Field: Objective Measurement and Subjective Interpretation.   This clustering reflects another obvious and important difference among theories. You will see this difference in the "look" of a theory—how it is reported—but the difference really lies at a deeper level in terms of *how the scholar works* and *what counts as valid data*. Many scholars use a scientific approach and work out ways to minimize subjective judgment in observation. These researchers use objective categories and scales to measure what they see and to do so in a way that is valid and reliable. *Validity* involves a set of procedures designed to make sure that what you see is what you really wanted to see, that you are measuring what you intended to measure. *Reliability* involves a set of procedures designed to make sure that your method of observation is consistent, or accurate across cases and time. Scientific researchers want to use protocols by which different observers would all report seeing the same thing. They also use statistical and experimental procedures that eliminate error in testing the connections and causal relations among variables. This is the type of theory emphasized in this book.

Another group of scholars work in a rather different way, relying more on their own wits as observers and interpreters to "give a reading" to what they see. These scholars value individual subjective judgment and develop sophisticated ways of interpreting what is observed so that interesting and useful insights emerge.

The Scope Field: Broad and Narrow.   Yet another way in which theories can be clustered according to similarity and difference is in scope or generality. Some theories are designed to cast a broad net and capture many varieties of fish. Other theories are like hooks designed to catch just one species of fish. Some theories try to explain communication in general, others try to explain some narrower aspect of communication, and some focus on very specific types of behavior. Some of the theories in this book are quite broad, whereas others are rather narrow in focus.

Bodies of Theory

The communication discipline consists of many subfields, and each of these has its own body of theory available to the members of a scholarly community. Although the boundaries between the communities of scholarship are fuzzy and bodies of theory overlap, most scholars can name the theories they most trust and use. They may not agree on which theories are most important or useful, but they will agree that theories are available to guide their work.

A body of theory is really just a snapshot in time. It provides a brief glance at a moment in the evolving history of ideas within a community of scholars. This is like looking at the Cadillac of the 1950s with big fins, which really does not look much like the Cadillac of today. The metaphor of "body" is good because it captures the qualities of growth, change, development, aging, and renewal. A community of scholars, like any community, changes over time, and one way to see this change is to note what happens to its theories during particular periods (Littlejohn, 1999, pp. 28–30).

One period involves *incremental growth*, a process of adding new theories. At some points in the development of a field, theories seem to proliferate with lots of alternative approaches to the same thing. In the 1950s, many brands of American cars, not just the Cadillac, had fins. Sometimes these compete with an ensuing struggle to resolve which theory is best, just like the competition among automobiles. Often, however, the theories are not really competitive. They offer complementary explanations of the process, or they address different aspects of the subject. To continue our analogy, all General Motors cars of the 1950s were really variations on the same theme.

Another period involves *developmental growth*, a process of elaborating or improving existing theories. When this kind of change is happening, the field puts a lot of effort into developing existing theories by making them more complex, improving their fit, extending their utility. Of course, it is entirely possible for incremental and developmental growth to be happening at the same time. Staying in our analogy of cars, the 1960s was a time of tremendous automotive engineering development. Engines became more complex, fuel efficiency was added, and emissions technology came to the fore. The same thing happened in the 1980s, when computers were added to car engines.

A third period involves *canonical development*. At these times, certain standard theories emerge as the "canon" of the community. Canonical periods tend to be stable and may go on for a period of time. The canon will eventually come into question, however, as formerly favored theories become passé. Actually, in many fields such as communication, theories are rather trendy. Perfectly good theories are set aside and fade away as new ones come into favor. As foreign cars became very popular in the United States, American motor companies had to struggle to maintain a position in the marketplace.

A fourth kind of period involves *revolution* (Kuhn, 1970). After periods of incremental and developmental growth occur, a canon is established. The canonical period is one of relative stability in which scholars come to depend on a certain way of understanding their subject. This state is a model for what we might call "normal science." In general, the scholars within a community pretty much agree theoretically, or at least they agree which theories are most powerful and useful. At some point, however, the canon is called into question. This may happen because events can no longer be very well explained by the standard theory or theories in use. It may happen because critics have shown the standard theories to be lacking in some fundamental way, or it may happen because society itself changes, new social trends emerge, and old ideas no longer look very appealing. These are moments of revolution in which the field may be turned on its head as entirely new ways of understanding come into being. We may be at a revolutionary moment in the development of the motorcar, as the hybrid engine (electric and gas) may move us eventually into a new form of fuel.

Over time, then, in almost every field, you will see the body of theory change. What a scholar came to respect and use in graduate school will not be the same set of theories he or she uses in midcareer, and that will probably not resemble very closely what is most valued within the community late in one's career. Scholars are often bemused by these changes at moments when they read old journal articles, cull their library, or prepare to teach new courses.

Still, some body of theory will always exist at any point in time, and this is always a vital force. The body of theory provides shape and meaning to the discipline. It offers a set of tools for research, practice, and teaching. The body of theory helps members of the community identify their primary foci and interests, it pulls them together as a community, and it provides a set of standards for how scholarly work should proceed. In general, theories fulfill several functions (Littlejohn, 1999, p. 30).

1. Theories help us organize and summarize knowledge. Because a theory is a way to package reality, it has useful categories and relations that provide a framework for connecting and separating different areas of knowledge.
2. Theories help us focus on important things. They call some variables into attention for special observation and thought. They allow us to "view" the ways in which certain things relate to other things.
3. Theories help clarify what is observed. How do we know what you are looking at? How can we understand the relation of one thing to another thing? Theories help in this regard.
4. Theories tell us how to look, how to observe. They reveal pathways from one point to another, a series of connections that can be followed.
5. Theories help us predict. They posit causal connections that allow us to anticipate what will happen when two or more things are brought together.
6. Theories help us learn more by suggesting fruitful new avenues for research.
7. Theories help us communicate ideas by providing a vocabulary and organizational framework with which we can express what we see and think.
8. Theories help us control our environments. They provide "handles" with which we can grab hold of otherwise abstract concepts and behaviors, and they suggest "levers" by which we can manipulate outcomes.
9. Finally, theories can help us think critically about our experience. They can lead us to find the powers and limits of social structures and behavioral patterns.

As you study the theories in this book, you will need to consider their powers and limits. Let's look next at evaluation.

How to Evaluate Theories

There is not one standard way to evaluate a theory. As we have explored in this chapter, different communities of scholarship evaluate theories in different ways. However, this is not a very satisfying answer for students trying to figure out how to orient to many theories encountered in their studies. When you look at a theory, it may be helpful to ask several questions about it (Littlejohn, 1999, pp. 35–37).

How Far Does the Theory Allow Me to Generalize?   One of the characteristics of theory is that it is general. In other words, the theory should allow you to reason beyond the individual case. You should be able to apply the theory to a range of experiences. The scientifically ideal theory consists of *covering laws*, which explain all instances of a happening regardless of when or where it occurs. In the social sciences these days, we do not place a lot of faith in covering laws because behavior is too situational. But is human life so situational that we cannot have theories at all? Some scholars believe so, but most think that some level of theorizing is possible and desirable. Theories vary widely in how much ground they cover. Some are limited to just a few situations, and others cover more. It is fair to say that a theory that covers too much is probably missing rich detail and ignoring the fabric of human life, but a theory that covers too little is so narrow as to be useless. You can decide for yourself when you read a theory whether it has sufficient generality to help you understand your experience.

In What Realms of Life Is the Theory Appropriate?   Appropriateness is an important criterion in evaluating theory because it draws your attention to a theory's assumptions and methods. Certain kinds of data are appropriate for certain purposes, and other types of data are appropriate for entirely different purposes. For example, if you need to know how people are different from one another, it would make sense to establish some personality traits and count numbers of people in each category using statistics. If you wanted to know about the experience of oppression, that approach would not work very well, and you would need to rely on political theories. For a purpose of evaluation, then, the question is, how do I want to use a theory and what is the best kind of theory for that purpose?

Does the Theory Stimulate Me to Think of Interesting Questions?   Good theories should do that. They should stimulate creative, inquisitive thinking. They should suggest interesting lines of inquiry. They should make you eager to learn more. So when you read a theory, ask not only what answers it provides but what questions it brings to mind. And what would become possible for you if you were to pursue answers to those new questions?

Does the Theory Seem to Fit My Experience?   Does it make intuitive sense? The question here is not whether the theory merely repeats what you already know but whether it provides an "aha" experience. In other words, your reaction is something like this: "I hadn't thought of it that way before, but it does make sense." The theory seems to fit your experience while also helping to explain your experience and expand your awareness. It is consistent with how things seem to you, but it provides new perspectives and insights that seem valid.

Does the Theory Say a Lot in a Simple and Logical Way?   A theory should not be simplistic, or overly simple, but it should be logically parsimonious. In other words, the theory should reduce the explanatory mechanism down to a manageable set of ideas. Most scholars believe that explaining something well in 10 steps is better than explaining it in 100 steps. In other words, the theory has a lot of power. It leverages a relatively small set of ideas into a useful explanation by powerful logic.

Is the Theory Open to Improvement and Change?   Can you see places where the theory could be expanded or modified? Is the theory a stepping-stone toward increasingly powerful ways of seeing the world, or is it dogmatically closed or so narrow that new pathways are not suggested?

Have Fun

You may not associate theory with fun, but if you look at the exploration of theory as an intriguing journey, it is indeed fun. All of the authors in this book would say that they have enjoyed working with their theories. This does not mean that every moment was fun, but looking back, developing theories can be very rewarding.

So, as you work your way through this book, have fun! Enjoy looking at your own implicit theories of communication and comparing these with the more formal approaches you will encounter in this book. Think about the different kinds of claims theorists make and what they accomplish by these. Notice how theories are made, and relax a little bit when you realize that theories are a product of social interaction among scholars. Think about the important of research, and when you read the literature on communication, realize that it fulfills an important publishing function, not so much to report theory, but to take a step in developing it. Play with theoretical similarities and differences. Don't be daunted by these differences but consider them rich resources by which you can enrich your understanding of communication. When you read through the chapters of this book, don't get stuck on *individual* theories but consider that each is part of a community of scholars struggling to understand their own experience. Finally, enjoy evaluating theories. Don't think that you have to pick the one correct or true theory but value each for the contribution it makes.

REFERENCES

Bernstein, B. (1971). *Class, codes, and control: Theoretical studies toward a sociology of language*. London: Routledge & Kegan Paul.

Brinberg, D., & McGrath, J. E. (1985). *Validity and the research process*. Beverly Hills, CA: Sage.

Deetz, S. A. (1992). *Democracy in an age of corporate colonization: Developments in communication and the politics of everyday life*. Albany, New York: SUNY Press.

Festinger, L. (1957). *A theory of cognitive dissonance*. Palo Alto, CA: Stanford University Press.

Goffman, E. (1959). *The presentation of self in everyday life*. Garden City, NY: Doubleday.

Krippendorff, K. (1993). Conversation or intellectual imperialism in comparing communication (theories). *Communication Theory, 3,* 252–266.

Kuhn, T. S. (1970). *The structure of scientific revolutions*. Chicago: University of Chicago Press.

Littlejohn, S. W. (1999). *Theories of human communication* (7th ed.). Belmont, CA: Wadsworth Publishing.

Mehrabian, A. (1972). *Nonverbal communication*. Chicago: Aldine-Atherton.

Pearce, W. B. (1991). On comparing theories: Treating theories as commensurate or incommensurate. *Communication Theory, 2,* 159–164.

Petty, R. E., & Cacioppo, J. T. (1986). *Communication and persuasion: Central and peripheral routes to attitude change*. New York: Springer-Verlag.

QUESTIONS TO PONDER

1. Think of a situation in your life that has been a challenge to you, something with which you have struggled. Become conscious of how you explain or account for this

problem. Now turn your implicit theory into an explicit one. What kinds of correlations and causal relations are you assuming? How might you pursue this "folk" theory to make it more valid and complete?

2. Select three or four chapters from this book and compare the theories? What do they share, and how are they different? In your answer, use the categories from this chapter.

3. How well do the authors of these chapters explain the history and development of their theories? To what extent do you get a sense of how these theories are a product of a scholarly community? In addressing this question, do not look only at the text, but examine the citations and references for clues as well.

4. After reading through the chapter of this book, what are you curious about? What topics related to communication would you like to learn more about? How could you develop knowledge about these areas of curiosity.

2

Discourse and Identity: Language or Talk?

Karen Tracy
University of Colorado, Boulder

In a class I teach that focuses on understanding how discourse and identities link, I begin by defining the focal terms and then playing two telephone conversations. Discourse is a name we give to units of writing or speaking longer than a single sentence; identities refers to the multiple layers of who a person is, including who he or she wants to be seen as in a given situation. After listening to the calls I ask students to tell me what they think they know about the people. Can they tell if the callers are old or young? Male or female? American? If so, from what region of the country? What kinds of jobs do the people have? Do the conversationalists know each other well? What kind of relationship do the parties have? Are the speakers considerate or rude? In addition to telling me what they think they know, I ask students to describe how they know: What particulars of these exchanges (i.e., the discourse) are leading to their conclusions? Consider the two telephone calls.[1]

Call 1

A: Hello?
B: Hello, may I speak to Mrs. Maret?
A: Yeah, hold on (10 seconds)
C: Hi
B: Hello, this is Miss Rodriguez from Valley High school calling
C: uh huh

---

[1]These calls were made available to me by Anita Pomerantz. My thanks to her.

B: Was Ryan home from school ill today? (1 second)
C: ((off phone)) Ryan wasn't home ill was he? (½ second)
A: ((off phone)) not at all
C: No

Call 2

D: Hello?
E: Hi,
D: Hi.
E: How are you?
D: Fine, how are you?
E: Okay.
D: Good. (½ second)
D: What's doing?
E: Oh nothing,
D: You didn't go meet Todd?

In the discussion about the calls, students in my classes routinely advance the following claims: All five of the speakers are described as American and presumed to be from the Midwest or West. Nobody thinks the conversationalists are from the Northeast or Southern United States. Students' conclusions about geographic regions are anchored in something that you as readers do not have—the sound of the speakers' talk. Based on the cadence of speech and the way words are pronounced, the five people are presumed to be native English speakers, American, and living outside of the South and East. No speaker's accent is taken to sound "Southern" or "New Englandish." Using the sound of each speaker's voice, students also infer that Speaker A is a man and all the rest are women. In the first call, though, other features than the pitch of each speaker's voice are identified as providing evidence why listeners are quite certain that B and C are women. In particular, students identify how Speaker B uses the titles Miss and Mrs. to refer to self and to address the other person.

In terms of jobs and relationships, the following inferences are usually made. For Call 1, it is assumed that Miss Rodriguez is an attendance clerk at a local high school and that she and Mrs. Maret are not friends. Furthermore, it is assumed that the purpose of Miss Rodriguez's call is to see if Ryan is playing hooky from school and that in performing her task Miss Rodriguez is taken to be a "polite" person. Mrs. Maret is assumed to be Ryan's mother and Ryan, a high school student. For Call 2, it is inferred that D and E are close female friends, probably in their teens or early 20s and that in all likelihood E is dating Todd.

In creating these portraits—that is, in making these particular inferences—listeners are drawing on extensive knowledge about how people in American culture talk to and about each other. People are able to construct these elaborate portraits because there are ways of talking that routinely "go with" being a certain kind of person, doing particular activities, and having certain relationships.

Probably, you are aware of features of these telephone conversations that contribute to some of these inferences; probably there are other facets of the call that you have not thought about. That Miss Rodriguez is likely to be the clerk at a high school arises from the fact that persons in certain institutional roles are expected to perform certain kinds of actions and not others. The most likely person in a high school to request information about attendance is an office staff person, not the maintenance person and not the principal. Although it is possible to imagine circumstances where a principal would initiate such a phone call, it is more likely that a principal would explicitly mention her role in the call ("This is Miss Rodriguez, the principal at Valley High") rather than merely mentioning the school. That the two women do not know each other well is cued by the absence of reference to prior calls ("This is Miss Rodriguez from Valley High calling again"), the last name address forms, the full institutional identification, and the absence of a friendly inquiry. Compare, for instance, how we would make different inferences about the relationship between the two women if Miss Rodriguez had said the following: "Hi Jane, this is Rita from the school, I hate to be calling you about this but was Ryan … ."

That Ryan is likely to be a high-school-age son of Mrs. Maret, rather than her husband or an adult son who teaches at the school, is linked to two other facets of talk: the forms of address and reference selected and which people are presumed to be able to speak for others. If Ryan were Mrs. Maret's husband or an adult son who was a teacher at the high school, it is much more likely that she would have referred to Ryan as "Mr. Maret." Given Miss Rodriguez selected last name plus title reference forms (Miss, Mrs.) for herself and Mrs. Maret, but used a first name to refer to Ryan, it is unlikely they are equals. Nonreciprocal forms of address where speaker uses a title and last name for self, but a first name for the other, usually is done when the speaker is higher ranking or older than the person being asked about is. In addition, if Ryan were an adult rather than a teen, it is unlikely that Mrs. Maret would have been asked to speak for him. Rather, Miss Rodriguez would have asked to speak to Ryan (Mr. Maret) directly and not asked someone answering the phone to provide work-related information about him (e.g., "This is Miss Rodriguez from Valley High, is Mr. Maret there?").

Finally, Miss Rodriguez is assumed to be polite rather than rude because of the conversational style of her request. Instead of asking, "Is Ryan playing hooky today?" (what she in fact was trying to find out) she said, "Was Ryan home from school ill today?" Simply put, Miss Rodriguez formulated a question about Ryan's absence that offered a legitimate reason why Ryan was absent. This does not mean that she actually thought that illness was the reason for Ryan's absence but it did offer a nonaccusatorial, "polite" explanation, leaving it up to the mother to volunteer the more damaging answer. Her question form avoids suggesting that the mother is a "bad" parent, not adequately monitoring her child. Importantly, though, the mother is expected to understand that Miss Rodriguez's question is really about hooky and not about illness. For instance, if Ryan were doing a college visit on that day and the mother had just said, "No, he's not sick," and nothing else, people would likely judge the mother as "dense," "not very smart." If Ryan has another legitimate reason for his absence, Mrs. Maret is expected to understand the intended meaning of the illness question and say something like, "No he's not sick but he is visiting a college."

In Call 2, it is the absence of name identification, as well as any interactional trouble by doing so, that cue students that D and E must be close friends. To recognize a person by voice within less than a second of speech is one of the ways people routinely perform "being close." It is not possible to do this without extensive familiarity with another. In addition, D's query, "You didn't go meet Todd?" is a question that not only suggests that D is familiar with E's everyday activities, but presumes the reasonableness and desirability of asking about these activities, a topical "right" that goes with friendship but not necessarily with acquaintanceship. Moreover, the informality of their greetings ("Hi" "What's doing?") rather than ("Hello," "How are you today?") pointed toward an attitudinal stance more typical of young people than middle-aged or older friends. Finally, although people were uncertain of who Todd was in relation to E, it seemed likely to many students that he was a romantic interest rather than an impersonal coworker. The conversational topic of "relationships with men" is a frequent and favored subject for talk among young, heterosexual, women friends. Given the other conversational clues of a close friendship, that E was interested in or already seeing Todd seemed a reasonable, albeit not a certain, inference.

Language and *talk* are the main theoretical frames communication theorists have for understanding discourse. In this chapter, I explain what is meant by each of these frames, arguing why talk is the more useful one for communication analysis. Then, in the chapter's second part I work within the talk frame to explain several particularly important components. Finally, I describe how talk can be linked with identities, suggesting why a two-way linkage is needed.

LANGUAGE VERSUS TALK: THE TWO FRAMES

The Language Frame

In the early years of the 20th century, Ferdinand De Saussure, A Swiss linguist, made a distinction that significantly shaped the way we approach discourse. He distinguished between *langue,* the grammatical, structural system of a language and *parole* or speech, its spoken manifestation (Saussure, 1966). For Saussure, as well as Chomsky (1957, 1965), a person many have regarded as the most prominent linguistic thinker of the 20th century, *langue* (i.e., language) was the preferred frame. Speech, what we now refer to as *talk,* was considered too chaotic and messy to study. According to Saussure and others, what was important was language as a code, the abstract and systematic knowledge base, separate from any instance of actual expression.

Language, then, refers to a code that resides in people's heads and is what enables them to construct sentences and convey meanings. This code involves rules that pertain to a variety of features, often conceived as "levels" of the code. First, people need to learn the code's basic sounds, what physical movements of the mouth will count as official sounds in a particular language, and what sound differences matter for making an expression a different word. Japanese and English, for instance, do not have the same basic sound units or *phonemes*. In English it is important to distinguish *r* from *l* sounds, but this is not a distinction made in Japanese. How long one holds a vowel sound changes what phoneme will be heard in many languages but not so much in English. *Phonology,* then, refers to study of the sound system of a language.

A second area for language rules concerns *semantics*. Words of a language are comprised of different meaning units, and speakers and listeners need to learn what the units mean and how to string them together. "Jumped," for instance has two main meaning units (*morphemes*). The first morpheme is the word stem, "jump" meaning something like to move with a bob or bounce; the second morpheme, "ed," transforms this jump action (and others) to mean that the referred-to action happened in the past. Although a person's tone of voice and facial expression may function as a *sign*, cuing certain kinds of emotional meaning, most words are *symbols*—arbitrary but conventionally shared ways of referring to something in the world. "Dog," for instance, is the symbol in English for the four-legged creature that so many of like to have as a pet; in other languages this critter has different words to reference it.

A third area of language, one considered especially important by linguists, is the code's syntax. *Syntactics* (grammar) is the study of the rules about how to sequence words into meaningful sentences. In English, for instance, speakers could say, "The kids jumped off the bench," but they could not say, "The bench, off, kids, the, jumped." A language's syntax specifies what kinds of word and phrase units (e.g., verbs, adjectives, prepositional phrases) may or must occur in what order.

A final area of language is *pragmatics*. Pragmatics refers to the rules about how to use language in different communicative situations. For instance, when should a speaker say "Hi, whaz up?" versus "Hello, how are you doing?" Pragmatics seeks to spell out the ways the phonological, semantic and syntactic rules are transformed or altered when they occur in particular contexts. The semantic meaning of the word, "sorry," for example is an expression of regret. In actual exchanges between people, however, its pragmatic meaning may be to ask for someone to repeat what she just said or it may be a mild rebuke, as is likely if a person said, "I'm sorry you feel the need to be so legalistic." Just about all the identity inferences I flagged in the opening brief exchanges could be considered a matter of pragmatics. From a linguistic point of view, then, just about everything that communication theorists are interested in could be considered to be in this one small area of linguistic specialization.

The frame of *language* is highly useful for learning to read, write, and speak a new language; it is also helpful for developing certain kinds of expertise in oral and written expression. Yet the *language* frame has limitations that make it less than ideal for students of communication. In a nutshell, *language* maps discourse, and the communicative world in a way that gives little space to those issues in which communication theorists are most interested, and gives lots of attention to issues that communication theorists find less engaging.

To provide an analogy, using language to understand discourse is a bit like observing a New York city inhabitant's mental mapping of the United States, memorialized in an old cover of *The New Yorker* magazine. The cover, which has found its way onto many posters, showed a detailed map of the central streets of Manhattan with a little bit of space given to the other boroughs of New York city (Queens, Brooklyn, etc.). Toward the map's edge was the Hudson River dividing New York from New Jersey. On the other side of the Hudson was New Jersey, the Midwest, and California, all crammed into a tiny inch or so at the map's margin.

The language map does provide a category for all the parts of discourse. Yet in treating pragmatics as that little bit of territory on the domain's fringe, a communication student may feel a bit like a person from Pittsburgh, Houston, or Seattle viewing the New Yorker's map of the United States. A better map for communication students is likely to be a view of discourse through a *talk* frame.

The Talk Frame

The language frame leads to a minimizing of those features of discourse that are responsive to the particular conversational partner, the physical and social scene within which talk is occurring, and to the national, social class, and ethnic communities with which exchanges are always situated. An early critic of Saussure was a Russian scholar named Mikhail Bakhtin (Morson & Emerson, 1990). According to Bakhtin, rather than focusing on language and treating the sentence as the basic unit, speech communication, what I call talk, should be. Talk is what social life is all about; it refers to what's said by people to others at specific places and times. Talk is what people do; it is always sensitive to particularities of the situation. Units of talk, then, are units of activity between people.

The smallest unit of talk is the *utterance*. In contrast to sentences that exist apart from particular contexts, an utterance is always responding to something and said to someone. In the opening telephone calls there are 10 utterances in each call. The first utterance in each call, the single word, "Hello," uttered with an upward intonation, can be understood as a response to a summons that was initiated by the phone ringing. An utterance may be a single word ("no," "okay"), a short phrase ("will do," "tomorrow at 4"), or one or more sentences, perhaps including person's name ("Tiffany, could you hold the door open for me?" or, "I was thinking, Tom, well, I'm gonna skip out of the meeting. I hope that won't cause trouble but I'm feeling awful").

When we view discourse through a talk frame we highlight the features of talk that accomplish social actions. Perhaps the most obvious function of talk is to convey information. Yet even in situations where this function is central (giving directions, in classrooms), other activities are getting done. Especially important in communicative life is the ongoing way talk is doing identity-work: *Identity-work* is how talk both reflects who people are and builds who they want to be. Viewing discourse as talk makes visible that people's communication will suggest not only who they are, but also how they see the others to whom they are talking.

Altercasting references the work a person's talk does to maintain, support, or challenge the conversational partner's identities. Altercasting involves how the way we talk to and act toward others (alter) puts them in roles (casts them). For instance, consider how the following two forms of a question, asked by a student during his teacher's office hour, altercast the teacher:

Example 1

"Excuse me Dr. Trintash, I was wondering if you could go over the systems perspective with me again. I wasn't feeling well in class the other day and didn't listen as closely as I should have."

Example 2

"Hi Jean, how's it goin? I was getting lost in class when you're were talking about the system perspective. Could you explain it to me one more time?"

The student's talk in Example 1 altercasts the teacher as being in a more distant, formal relationship than that implied by Example 2. In not only using a title as the selected form of address, but prefacing the request for a repeat of information with an apology and an account that blames self, the talk of Example 1 supports the teacher as a competent and able explainer. In addition, the talk from Example 1 casts the teacher as someone in a superior role relative to the student, and one deserving a fair amount of respect. In contrast, the talk in Example 2 altercasts the teacher in a much less distant and formal relationship, one having, perhaps, a certain amount of friendliness. By using the teacher's first name, expressing personal interest in her, albeit perfunctory, before getting down to the business at hand, and using vocabulary that creates a breezy style ("How's it goin?" "I was getting lost"), the speaker in Example 2 altercasts the other as far less superior and much closer to a peer. In addition, it is possible that the comment about "getting lost" may have been heard by the teacher as a criticism of her ability to explain ideas clearly. Whether it was intended or not, the comment may have had this meaning for the teacher. This highlights a complexity of meaning in actual occasions of talk: Speakers and recipients may have different understandings of what was meant.

When people share a common language it is relatively unproblematic to identify the semantic meaning of what was said. The semantic meaning of what's said is its literal meaning, the dictionary-level meaning of the words and phrases. More challenging than the literal meaning is to figure out the interactional meaning of utterances. Interactional meaning is what separates *talk* from *language*. The *interactional meaning* refers to the meaning(s) intended by a speaker or taken by a listener. Interactional meanings involve an utterance's implications, where the implications may be about who people must be, what kind of social action is being performed, the character of the interactional situation, or the kind of relationship a speaker and recipient must have. In most communicative situations, it is aspects of the interactional meaning that are crucial. It is mix-ups related to interactional meanings that frequently cause problems.

Interactional meaning involves layers. A first layer is the *speech act* that is being done. That is, if a speaker says "excuse me," is the action performed by those words apologizing or reprimanding? In the opening phone calls, for instance, we heard three different kinds of speech acts: greetings, requests, and answers. A second layer of meaning available in communicative exchanges is the situation frame—the kind of talk occasion that is happening. *Frames* are broader than speech acts and are the everyday names we give to occasions: a therapy session, two friends chatting, an interview, having coffee, an advising session, a prayer group, a team meeting, and so on. In the telephone calls the frame in the first exchange was a business call and in the second one it was a friendly chat. In the comments just analyzed, the frame is a teacher–student "office hour exchange."

Frames typically go unnamed, seeming self-evident to participants.[2] It is only when people have different understandings that the frame gets noticed. For instance, if a person set up a meeting to talk to a fellow worker about a joint project, the taken-for-granted frame would be work meeting. However, if in the course of the meeting the colleague commented positively about the person's appearance, touched the person's hand a couple times, asked about the other's past weekend, and held the person's gaze for slightly longer than is normal, the person might wonder if the other is flirting. Frames are suggested by the physical context (meeting in a teacher's office versus a coffee shop), but are modified and redefined through ways of talking.

Besides the speech acts being performed and the situational frame—each of which has an implication for communicators' identities—a third and the most abstract layer relates directly to identity. The *identity-work* accomplished by communication highlights how any of a large array of communicative particulars, as was seen in the teacher–student office visit chats, will have implications for who people are and who they are taken to be.

Every utterance, then, can be analyzed in terms of its literal content (what's said) and its interactional meaning. Arriving at the interactional meaning of an utterance requires examining what was said (the words) in light of how it was said, the people who said it, the situation, and what had previously been uttered. Put another way, the multiple meanings of an utterance arise from the content of a message in combination with the context. *Context*, then, references all the background kinds of information that shape how interactional meanings get assigned to what is said. Talk cannot be understood without looking closely at its context. Thus the particular setting and identities of the participants (are they friends, teacher and student, strangers on the street?) as well as a speaker's tone of voice, facial expression, prior

---

[2]Tannen (1993) reviewed the different meanings of frame. The one developed here is most strongly tied to Bateson's (1972) notion.

TABLE 2.1
Differences in Looking at Discourse as "Language" Versus "Talk"

	Language	*Talk*
Definition	A rule-governed symbols system (code) for expressing meaning	The fundamental activity that occurs between people
Highlights	Stable aspects of the meaning-making process	Aspects of meaning that depend on who said what, when, and where (context)
Central unit	Sentence	Utterance
Focal discourse type	Writing	Speaking
Key concepts	Phonology Semantics Syntax Pragmatics	Interactional Meaning Speech Acts Frame Identity-work

utterances, and so on will shape the situated meaning of an utterance. These factors, what Gumperz (1982) referred to as *contextualization cues,* include the features of a communicative situation that people use to arrive at the meaning of an utterance.

When people use the same contextualization cues—a likely state when people come from the same sociocultural background—a speaker's intended meaning is usually the one that a listener assigns. However, if people do not share contextualization cues, a problem can arise. For instance, in American English a central way that speakers convey interest in a person or enthusiasm about an issue is through their tone of voice. Thus, if in responding to an invitation a speaker said in a very monotone voice, "Thank you for asking, perhaps another time," a different meaning would be attached than if he emphasized the phrase "thank you" and had a strong upward vocal inflection at the end of the phrase "another time." In the former case, the American English-speaking listener is likely to infer that the person is just trying to be polite but does not really want to spend time with her. In the latter, the listener may feel that the other really does want to spend time but cannot make this particular occasion. The use of voice inflection to signal attitude is a contextualization cue. But voice inflection, as well as other contextualization cues, are not universal. A consequence of this is that if speakers come from communities that use different contextualization cues, they may very well misinterpret each other.[3]

Talk both reflects who people are and is the instrument through which people build who they want to be. Yet while talk reflects and builds, it is a delicate, somewhat uncertain process. Features of talk are *cues,* not absolute indicators. In the telephone calls, Miss Rodriguez was

---

[3]See Gumperz (1982).

a high school attendance clerk; D and E were close female friends. However, the talk features that cued these identities do not straightforward "mean" that someone is a high school attendance clerk, or that two people are close. The context could change what these cues mean, or in a particular instance the cue may misfire. Not mentioning your name at the start of a telephone call and assuming the sound of your voice will be sufficient to make your identity clear may mean closeness, but it may not. If E's estimation of the closeness of her relationship to D were wrong, rather than simply returning a "Hi" (line 3) in a way that acknowledged that D knew to whom she was talking, she may have said to E "Who is this?" causing a moment of discomfort, making E aware that she had misjudged the closeness of their relationship, altercasting D inappropriately.

When we conceptualize discourse as "talk" rather than "language," then, the key issue shifts from trying to identify the rules that govern different facets of the code (i.e., phonological rules, syntactic rules) to considering which aspects of communicative exchanges accomplish social actions, and, particularly, how the social meanings are constructed. That is, we are led to ask, "How do packages of talk features in a context do identity-work?" Table 2.1 summarizes key differences between the language and talk frames.

TWO ASPECTS OF TALK THAT DO IDENTITY-WORK

Person-Referencing Practices

Much of our everyday talk is about people. In talking to or about people, including ourselves, we need to select some set of terms. *Person-referencing practices* is the name for a family of communicative choices about how to address or refer to people, including ourselves.[4] When the person-referencing decision involves what to call another directly, we are dealing with *forms of address*. The two phone calls illustrated some of the identity implications of selecting either a first name or a title plus last name. In general, the forms a person picks to address another and refer to self, convey something about the two people's perceived closeness or distance, and whether a speaker sees self and other as relatively equal or not. In selecting person-referencing terms, it is always possible to offend someone. To call someone by a first name may be judged inappropriately chummy or disrespectful; to address someone with a title and last name may be regarded as overly formal and distancing. Choice of address forms implicates a set of desired or disdained identities.

To make matters more complex, it is also the case that persons from different countries or regions use address forms differently. Southerners, for instance, are known for using the polite forms, "Sir," and "Ma'am," more than people from other regions of the United States. This tendency to use polite forms of address more frequently is part of how a person talks like a Southerner. In general, Americans address others they have just met by first names in situations that other nationalities would not. Around the world this taken-for-granted American practice causes offense.

Besides address forms, talk regularly requires us to reference others. In performing this task, communicators need to choose among terms that mark an individual person or a group of people in terms of their gender, sexual orientation, ethnicity, or other identities. These

---

[4]Fitch (1998) offered a nice review of the different forms of address and the complexity in interpreting their meaning.

choices of terms altercast the person being referred to, but they also convey identity information about the person speaking. Contrast choice (a) with choice (b) in the three examples below.

Example 3

(a) "I was walking down the street and this Oriental guy stopped me to ask"
(b) "I was walking down the street and this Asian guy, probably Korean stopped me to ask … ."

Example 4

(a) "There's a homosexual group that has a meeting scheduled in that room."
(b) "There's a gay group that has a meeting scheduled in that room."

Example 5

(a) "If a student wants to go over the exam, he should stop by the TA's office"
(b) "If a student wants to go over the exam, he or she should stop by the TA's office."

In terms of the semantic meaning, (a) and (b) in each of the examples have virtually the same meaning. However, their interactional meaning is far from the same. This is the case because many terms used in referring to others' ethnicity, gender, and sexual orientation are socially contested. In each of the three examples, persons of the referred-to category have argued that the (a) term is distasteful to them—it is disrespectful or conveys something negative—and members of these groups have suggested why the (b) term is preferred. Many women, for instance, have indicated that they do not feel included in the generic he (5a) and like to hear the more explicit inclusion that is accomplished when a speaker uses a "he or she" formulation. Although for any single comment, a speaker's choice of terms is not highly consequential, across occasions it becomes so. Using terms of reference that many members of less powerful and marginalized groups in U.S. society would use for themselves, rather than the terms that many in the group do not like, imply a speaker's likely social–political stance. Using the (a) terms enacts a more conservative political identity; using the (b) terms implies a more liberal political identity.

Person-referencing practices are informative in another way. In what identities a speaker *marks* or leaves *unmarked*, a speaker conveys what is taken to be the usual and normal identity pairings.[5] For instance, imagine that a friend is recounting his observations of a small claims court. He might begin his story as follows, "It was noisy in the courtroom. Then the judge walked into the room." If the judge was a White man, it is quite likely that nothing else would be said. However if the judge is not, the friend is likely to use marked forms. He might say something like the following, "It was noisy in the courtroom. Then the lady judge walked in," or "the Black judge walked in." Because judges in U.S. society are less commonly African American and female than they are White or male, a speaker is likely to note this. It

---

[5]The notion of marked and unmarked is a basis idea in linguistics. Levinson (1983, pp. 306–307) briefly explained this and contrasted it with the conversation analytic idea of "preference."

is not the case that being non-White or female is what is always marked—it depends on the identity. A communicator, for example, is much more likely to mark a nurse's gender if the nurse were male rather than female. Marking, then, is a way speakers convey that the taken-for-granted identities expected for a specific interactional one (e.g., judge, nurse, friend) do not apply. Marked forms are longer and more elaborated than are unmarked forms. Moreover, in marking an identity that is typically left unmarked, communicators can convey a challenging stance toward an existing social arrangement. For instance is analyzing Call 2, I wrote that the conversational topic of relationships with men is a favorite subject for talk among "young, heterosexual, women friends." In my person-referencing, I marked a number of features about the kind of friends that give attention to talking about relationships with men, making visible that not all friendship pairs favor this subject as a topic. What I especially want to draw attention to is my inclusion of the women's sexual orientation. I could have written, "young women friends," omitting reference to their sexual orientation altogether. If I had chosen to express myself this way, the content meaning of the sentence would have been pretty much the same. That is so because heterosexuality is assumed to be what most people are; it is usually unmarked. The most usual case in which sexual orientation is mentioned is when a person is not heterosexual. In including the women's sexual orientation in my sentence, where it was unnecessary, my phrasing choice conveyed something about me. What exactly it conveyed is not straightforward. But by marking something that is usually left unmarked, it conveys a mild challenge of what society takes to be "normal." In listing heterosexuality in the description, it treated sexual orientation as another kind of identity, similar to age and sex, that affects people's topic preferences.

Finally, consider one other feature of person-referencing terms. The terms that people use to refer to self and others do strategic work. A person can be referred to in terms of any number of categories. The most frequently used categories are those of sex and race, but others can be selected. People can be referred to in terms of their age (kid, young man, teen), size (fat, skinny), appearance (disheveled, neat), or emotional and relational distance from self (stranger, acquaintance, friend, brother). These sets of terms Harvey Sacks (1992) labeled *membership categorization devices* (MCD). The selection of one category set rather than an other, and the particular term within a set shape the inferences a conversational partner is likely to make. What exactly the inferences will be depends on the contextual particulars. Consider the potential interactional meanings of the term, *friend.* As Donald Anderson and I discuss elsewhere (Tracy & Anderson, 1999) the term *friend* can be a polite way to refer to an acquaintance or it may be used in intimate relationships to mark enjoyment of and close emotional connection ("He's not only my husband but my best friend"). Its most common usage in American English, though, is as a contrast category with intimate. A referred-to-other is a boyfriend, girlfriend, a significant other, a spouse, or "just a friend."

Let us examine the strategic reasons for, and the identity implications of, using the term *friend* in a telephone call in which a woman tried to get help from the police to retrieve her missing car. The caller initially stated her problem to the police operator as, "my car has been taken." When the operator probed, inquiring if the car had been stolen, the woman replied, "Well a friend borrowed it and he never brought it back." She went on to explain that a friend had come to visit her but she had had to go into the hospital. When she got out of the hospital, her friend and her car were gone. At this point in the exchange, the police operator transfers her to auto fraud where she explained her story to a second police operator. This second operator, however, was less sympathetic and asked her for more specific information about her "friend." After retelling the story of how her car and friend were gone when she got out of the hospital the following exchange occurred:

Police Call Excerpt

PO: Okay a friend of yours, meaning an acquaintance friend? or a friend? a boyfriend?
C: He was staying with me.
PO: Pardon?
PO: A boyfriend?
C: Yeah.
PO: Okay. So it's a boyfriend and he stayed with you for how long?
C: Pardon?
PO: How long has he stayed with you?
C: About a month.
PO: Okay, so you're together as boyfriend and girlfriend.

In the first part of the call, although the caller did not state so explicitly, she strongly implied that the man who had taken her car was not a sexual intimate. This implication was set in motion though her selection of the term, friend, as well as several other particular wording choices she made. The reason the woman initially referred to the man as a "friend" rather than a "live-in boyfriend" is fairly easy to imagine. Most likely she thought the police might be more sympathetic, find her problem more serious, and see her as more deserving of help if her car was taken by someone to whom she was not intimately connected. Moreover, in terms of the literal meaning of the term, friend, the woman was not lying. Nonetheless her usage of the term set in motion understandings of her relationship and the event that were quite different than what later came out in the exchange with the second operator. If two people living together as sexual intimates have a dispute, and one goes off with the car that is officially the other's, we might be less quick to see it as an instance of "stealing." The membership term the woman used initially sought to downplay her closeness to the man who had caused the problem.

There are other reasons for using the term, friend, than to get help. An aspect of personal identity that is always at stake in everyday life is how reasonable people are in their judgments about close partners. If a woman selects a man as an intimate who acts in a nasty and malicious manner—such as stealing her car—she is more likely to be judged harshly (naive, foolish, even stupid) than if her car was taken by just a friend. Stated simply, people care about how others see them. They use their talk to construct a version of themselves that is as positive as possible in the circumstances they face. Consider a second facet of talk that both reflects and builds identities.

Speech Acts

Some years ago philosopher J. L. Austin (1962) noted that people use words for more than describing and representing the world. Words are used to criticize, praise, request, account, beg, warn, threaten, and so on. The social act that a segment of talk performs is one aspect of communicative meaning; it is the answer to the question: "What is a person doing in saying X?" The number of potential speech acts a person could perform is huge. Austin suggested that there are as many different speech acts as there are verbs in a language. In English, for instance, we distinguish between a person ordering, demanding, suggesting, requesting, hinting, pleading, begging, and so on. While these acts are clearly related—each is an attempt to direct the actions of another—they involve a host of subtle differences.

Consider the following short exchange, recorded by one man talking with a coworker, that later becomes the focus of a criminal trial. Tyner was an Oklahoma horse breeder who had been charged with extortion. Hyde believed he had bought a share in a horse; Tyner denied that this had happened. Prior to the dispute about the horse, the two men had been on friendly terms. Tyner had occasionally taken Hyde's son, David, on outings with him. Once the dispute began, Hyde began taping his telephone calls in the hope of showing clearly that Tyner had extorted money from him.

Recorded call used in a trial (Shuy, 1993, pp. 108–109)

Tyner: How's David?
Hyde: Do what?
Tyner: How's David?
Hyde: You mean my son?
Tyner: Yep
Hyde: Don't threaten my son. Do a lot of things but don't ever threaten my son.
Tyner: I didn't threaten anybody. I just said, "How's David?"

During the trial, the prosecution and defense attorneys claimed radically different speech acts were being performed by the utterance, "How's David?" The prosecution argued, drawing on an FBI expert witness, that the utterance was intended as a threat, with a meaning something like, "If you don't drop this matter, something could happen to David." The defense stated that this utterance was not intended as a threat. It was meant as a request for information whose purpose was to rebuild a pleasant connection with the coworker. Drawing on studies of everyday talk, the attorney showed that one of the ways friends close down conflicts they are having with each other is to switch to small talk topics. Acquaintances and friends disengage from conflicts by moving to a topic where they can be pleasant to each other. In this trial Tyner was acquitted, but a context in which a question about a person's son might be intended as a threat is not hard to imagine. Threats packaged as benign questions, in fact, are a staple of television shows and movies.

Speech acts and identities are tied in multiple ways, each both affecting and being affected by the other. Relationships, for instance, change over time. Strangers become acquaintances, bosses and employees become friends, acquaintances or friends become sexual intimates, intimates become ex's (ex-girlfriend, ex-boyfriend, ex-spouse), and so on. In large measure, relational change is accomplished through beginning to do, or refraining from doing, particular speech acts. A request for help can change a pair of acquaintances into people in the beginning stage of a friendship; invitations and compliments of certain types can transform a friendship into a love relationship; refraining from polite chit-chat or voicing one's criticisms may bring about a new level of relational intimacy, and not inviting someone to go on a vacation may signal a demotion from friend to acquaintance.

Identities related to distance or intimacy are especially open to negotiation and renegotiation. But while intimacy-related identities are particularly fluid and constructed through talk, status-linked identities also are modified this way. For instance, it is through different ways of talking that parents and children move from relationships in which parents are authorities to ones in which children and parents are equal or near-equal. It is as parents refrain from asking for reports, offering advice, and ordering actions, and themselves disclose their feelings and fears, and as children stop asking for help or for permission, and themselves provide support and advice, that the parent–child relationship becomes one between equals.

Besides the selection of a type of speech act, the particular form that a speaker selects is also consequential. Most importantly, a communicator can perform a speech act directly or indirectly.[6] A *direct speech act* is one in which the speaker's intended meaning is captured in the content of the message. An *indirect speech act* is one where a listener needs to do a good amount of conversational inferencing to arrive at the speaker's meaning. Although some amount of conversational inferencing is required to arrive at any interactional meaning, for some utterances, the distance between what is said and what is meant is considerably larger. Indirect speech acts are those acts in which what is meant is a good distance from what is said. In the first telephone call, we heard Miss Rodriguez performing an indirect request. Although she wanted to find out if Ryan had cut class, she asked if he was home ill. By phrasing her request in the way she did rather than more directly, she displayed herself as a "polite" staff person. Indirectness in speech is a central way communicators show themselves to be "considerate," "thoughtful," "tactful," or "polite" (see chap. 12, this volume).

If performing acts indirectly always led to positive impressions, being an effective communicator would be an easy job. Unfortunately, the job is not that easy. In some contexts, the choice to perform a speech act indirectly can lead others to attribute personally negative identities. Indirectness in response to a question may be seen as evasive and deceptive rather than considerate; indirectness in giving an order may be seen as evidence of a person's discomfort with leadership and an inability to "take responsibility" rather than evidence of her tactfulness. This interpretive picture is complicated even more by a second fact.

Speech communities evolve ways of talking that are prized within a community, and distinctive to it. For instance in Australia working-class speakers of both genders, but especially men, have a practice of saying something bad about their conversational partner as a way of having fun. This speech act, which Australians call chyacking, is "one of their favorite national pastimes and forms of entertainment"; "usually the men speak one at a time, making negative remarks about the addressee, while the other men are laughing, so that a group of 'mates' constitutes both a group of participants and an audience." Examples of statements referring to this speech act would be, "They whooped, they made ribald noises, they chyacked one another," and "I was always civil to the chaps, for all the chyacking they gave me" (Wierzbicka, 1991, pp. 166–168).

Chyacking, Wierzbicka (1991) suggested, has similarity to a speech act common to African American men that has been extensively studied. The act, alternately called "playing the dozens" or "sounding" involves men and boys making insulting-sounding comments, often about the conversational partner's mother, for the purposes of having fun, displaying self's verbal skill, and jointly enacting a rejection of society's values about "proper behavior." While sounding shares chyacking's goal of promoting fun through potentially hostile remarks about the other, sounding differs in its valuing of verbal virtuosity; sounding is an individual performance and gives weight to verbal skill. In contrast, chyacking involves group-created commenting and allows for minimal verbalizations and grunts or other nonspeech sounds. Besides some speech acts being distinctive to a national or ethnic group, people from different communities, and men and women within them, also differ in their preferred directness style.

Katriel (1986) noted that direct expression is understood differently for Israelis than for other nationalities. *Dugri,* a term originating in Arabic and now colloquial in Hebrew, is an

---

[6]In an edited volume of essays, Blum-Kulka, House, and Kasper (1989) developed the means of direct and indirect and some cross-cultural variation.

TABLE 2.2
Valuing and Use of Directness

	American	Malagasy	Arab	Israeli
Women	−	+	−	+
Men	+	−	−	+

important symbol of Zionist socialism. It is the name for an honest person who speaks straight to the point, and it also is the name of an act (doing dugri) that involves speaking straight to the point. Dugri entails speaking plainly and without adornment or softening ("This is not a good plan to follow," "You shouldn't treat your grandmother that way."). A prototype act of dugri is where a subordinate speaks out to someone of higher rank and expresses a negative opinion at some risk to self. To do so is seen as a courageous and valued kind of expression. To speak dugri is to show self to care about another or to display one's commitment toward an issue. Other societies that Katriel documents contrast in interesting ways with this Israeli ideal. Table 2.2 displays these differences.

Among men and women in Israeli society, expressing opinions directly is valued for both sexes. In American society, this style is used and valued less for women than men. Similar to Israeli culture, in Arab society, there is a similar ideal for both sexes. However, Arab women and men are expected to "do musayra"—work to make relations harmonious. The communicative ideal is to go along, to humor and accommodate others so that an interaction may proceed smoothly. The ideal of musayra also goes with a valuing of hierarchy. Among Arab interactants, it is the person who is lower ranking that is expected to do musayra. Finally, in Malagsay, similar to the United States, valuing and expectation of directness is linked to gender. The gender linkage, however, is the opposite of that expected in the United States. In Malagasy men are regarded as the subtle communicators, the ones who can handle sensitive situations. In contrast, women are seen as direct in their speech style, lacking subtlety. Women may be able to handle a direct confrontation in the marketplace, but they cannot be counted on to manage diplomatically sensitive scenes among people. In sum, the likelihood of performing particular speech acts, as well as the preferred directness in so doing, is shaped by a person's national, ethnic, and gender identity.

Speech acts and person-referencing practices are not the only features of talk that do identity-work. The connection (or lack thereof) between one speaker's utterance and the next one is crucially important, as is who takes turns, how often, and whether one person overlaps and interrupts the other (see chap. 18, this volume). If a communicator speaks more than one language, which he uses, or how and when the two languages are mixed conveys a whole range of things. The stories people tell are also highly informative about who they are, and who the other is to whom they are talking; talk has a sound and it is embodied. The way a person uses her voice—the loudness, rate of speech, how she varies intonation, the words that are stressed (and so on) convey important information about the people and the feelings they are experiencing at the moment. At the same time, talk is enacted with hand gestures and facial expressions (see chap. 3, this volume). Table 2.3 identifies the facets of talk we have taken up in this chapter as well as the most important other facets that contribute to establishing interactional meaning.

TABLE 2.3
Facets of Talk Contributing to Interactional Meaning

Talk Practices	*Description*
Talk's building blocks	
Person referencing practices	Terms to address or refer to people
Speech acts	Social acts performed through talk
Sounds of speech	Speakers' dialects, ways of using voice (loudness, rate, pitch quality)
Language selection	The meaning of choosing or switching between English, Spanish, Vietnamese, etc.
Complex discourse practices	
Interaction structures	Speech act units, turn-taking
Directness style	The relative directness of language choice, speech acts, etc.
Narratives	Structure, content and style of stories
Stance indicators	Linguistic, vocalic, and gestural means of conveying in-the-moment attitude

Note. Adapted from *Everyday Talk: Building and Reflecting Identifies* (p. 22), by K. Tracy, 2002, New York: Guilford. Copyright 2002 by Guilford. Reprinted with permission.

Cultural and Rhetorical Lenses

In seeking to understand how talk and identities link, I have drawn on two perspectives. The first perspective is a cultural one. When using a *cultural lens*,[7] identities are in the foreground. The focal concern becomes "How do we account for the differences we observe in talk?" The cultural perspective answers this question by showing the myriad ways talking practices reflect communicators' identities. Persons of different identities will talk and interpret in systematically different ways: Israeli differing from American, men from women, teachers from students, older from younger speakers, and so on. In adopting a cultural perspective, we treat identities as relatively stable things, existing prior to particular conversational moments, best thought of as "brought to" interaction, and as capable of explaining patterns we see in talk.

The second perspective used in this chapter has been a *rhetorical lens*[8]. Rather than explaining talk by appealing to identity differences, we explain identity differences by showing how they tie to choices about how to talk. Choosing to compliment someone and use her first name, versus apologizing for bothering her and using her last name is how communicators do "being friendly" or "being respectful." A woman describing a man who took her car as a "friend" versus a "boyfriend with whom she is living" is how a person works to get institutional help and minimize others seeing her as unreasonable. In taking a rhetorical perspective we recognize how talk is strategic, chosen and designed to accomplish certain ends and avoid others. Talk is morally and practically consequential and a person may talk well or poorly.

---

[7]For discussion of the cultural perspective see Philipsen (1992), Fitch (1998), and Katriel (1986).

[8]A rhetorical perspective is adopted in mych of my own research (see Tracy, 2001) as well as in discursive psychology (Potter, 1996).

The linkage between talk and identities is a reciprocal one, and it is important to keep these two perspectives in an ongoing tension with each other. In adopting a rhetorical perspective, weight is given to one truth—that each person's choices about how to talk build his or her unique identity. Each of us can become what we want to be through reflecting about talk and choosing wisely. In adopting a cultural perspective, weight is given to an alternative truth: that how people talk is stable and not easily changed. People are shaped, one could even say, imprinted, by the communities in which they are born, spend time, and acquire beliefs about how to be a reasonable person. Recognizing these contradictory truths, I would suggest, is an essential part of understanding communication.

ADDITIONAL READING

This chapter includes sections from *Everyday Talk: Building and Reflecting Identities* (Tracy, 2002). A more in-depth discussion of discourse, identities, and talk is available there. Nice discussions of language, with a focus on its pragmatic aspects, can be found in review chapters by the communication theorist, Jacobs (1985, 1994), and in books by Levinson (1983) and Clark (1992).

Books arguing for the study of discourse, including methodological suggestions about how to do so, have become especially prominent. Two book-length sources I would especially recommend are Cameron (2001) and Wood and Kroger (2000). In a recent handbook of discourse analysis that features primarily linguistic contributions (Schiffrin, Tannen, & Hamilton, 2001), there is a chapter (Tracy, 2001) that overviews the different traditions of discourse that are especially visible in the field of communication.

The notion of identity extends Goffman's (1959, 1967) ideas about face and interaction (see chap 12, this volume). Fitzgerald (1993) developed how identity links to culture groups, and Ochs (1993) considered how it shapes ways of talking.

REFERENCES

Austin, J. L. (1962). *How to do things with words*. Oxford, England: Oxford University Press.

Bateson, G. (1972). *Steps to an ecology of mind*. New York: Ballantine.

Blum-Kulka, S., House, J., & Kasper, G. (Eds.). (1989). *Cross-cultural pragmatics: Requests and apologies*. Norwood, NJ: Ablex.

Cameron, D. (2001). *Working with spoken discourse*. London: Sage.

Chomsky, N. (1957). *Syntactic structures*. The Hague, The Netherlands: Mouton.

Chomsky, N. (1965). *Aspects of the theory of syntax*. Cambridge, MA: MIT Press.

Clark, H. H. (1992). *Arenas of language use*. Chicago: University of Chicago Press.

Craig, R. T., & Tracy, K. (Eds.). (1983). *Conversational coherence: Form, structure and strategy*. Beverly Hills, CA: Sage.

Fitch, K. L. (1998). *Speaking relationally: Culture, communication and interpersonal connection*. New York: Guilford.

Fitzgerald, T. K. (1993). *Metaphors of identity: A culture communication dialogue*. Albany: State University of New York Press.

Goffman, E. (1959). *The presentation of self in everyday life*. New York: Anchor Books.

Goffman, E. (1967). *Interaction ritual*. Garden City, NY: Anchor.

Gumperz, J. J. (1982). *Discourse strategies*. Cambridge, England: Cambridge University Press.

Jacobs, S. (1985). Language. In M. L. Knapp & G. R. Miller (Eds.), *Handbook of interpersonal communication* (pp. 313–343). Beverly Hills, CA: Sage.

Jacobs, S. (1994). Language and interpersonal communication. In M. L. Knapp & G. R. Miller (Eds.), *Handbook of interpersonal communication* (2nd ed., pp. 199–228). Thousand Oaks, CA: Sage.

Katriel, T. (1986). *Talking straight: Dugri speech in Israeli Sabra culture*. Cambridge, England: Cambridge University Press.

Levinson, S. C. (1983). *Pragmatics*. Cambridge, England: Cambridge University Press.

Morson, G. S., & Emerson, C. (1990). *Mikhail Bakhtin: Creation of a prosaics*. Palo Alto: Stanford University Press.

Ochs, E. (1993). Constructing social identity: A language socialization perspective. *Research on Language and Social Interaction, 26,* 287–306.

Philipsen, G. (1992). *Speaking culturally: Exploration in social communication*. Albany: State University of New York Press.

Potter, J. (1996). *Representing reality: Discourse, rhetoric and social construction*. London: Sage.

Sacks, H. (1992). *Lectures on conversation* (2 vols., G. Jefferson, Ed.). Cambridge, MA: Blackwell.

Saussure, F., de (1966). *Course in general linguistics* (C. Bally & A. Sechehaye, Eds., & W. Baskin, Trans.). New York: McGraw Hill.

Schiffrin, D., Tannen, D., & Hamilton, H. (Eds.). (2001). *Handbook of discourse analysis*. Oxford, England: Blackwell.

Shuy, R. W. (1993). *Language crimes: The use and abuse of language evidence on the courtroom*. Malden, MA: Basil Blackwell.

Tannen, D. (Ed.). (1993). *Framing in discourse*. New York: Oxford University Press.

Tracy, K. (2001). Discourse analysis in communication. In D. Schiffrin, D. Tannen, & H. Hamilton (Eds.), *Handbook of discourse analysis* (pp. 725–749). Oxford, England: Blackwell.

Tracy, K. (2002). *Everyday talk: Building and reflecting identities*. New York: Guilford.

Tracy, K., & Anderson, D. L. (1999). Relational positioning strategies in calls to the police: A dilemma. *Discourse Studies, 1,* 201–226.

Wierzbicka, A. (1991). *Cross-cultural pragmatics: The semantics of human interaction*. Berlin, Germany: Mouton de Gruyter.

Wood, L. A., & Kroger, R. O. (2000). *Doing discourse analysis: Methods for studying action in talk and text*. Thousand Oaks, CA: Sage.

QUESTIONS TO PONDER

1. When you reflect about communicative situations, in what kinds of situations are you more likely to use a cultural lens to understand the situation? Which ones a rhetorical lens? In which ones do you find yourself moving back and forth between the two?

2. Students of communication are often asked to explain how what they study differs from some other field. A common one that this is asked about is psychology. In this chapter I highlighted the points of commonality and difference with linguistics. In your own words explain how a communication approach differs from a linguistic one. Can you think of any other differences between viewing communication (and a piece of discourse) as language versus talk?

3. Analyze the B–K exchange in the appendix from a talk perspective. Note that colons in the transcript indicate that the speaker is prolonging a sound and hyphens indicate that a speaker began a word but cut it off. Double parentheses (( )) describe how talk was spoken or other sounds that were hearable in the exchange.

    (a) What do you think you know about the two people's identities? Are they male or female? Teens, middle-aged, or older? What kinds of roles are they in? What type of people are they? (Consider all the personality and character labels we use to describe people.) How close or distant are they to each other?

    (b) Consider how features of the talk contribute to the inferences you make. Which ones are you certain about and which ones do you feel quite tentative in making? What kinds of speech acts can you identify in this exchange? What would you say is the situational frame? What other aspects of talk are doing identity-work?

(c) Find utterances in this exchange that illustrate the notion that the interactional meaning depends on the content and its particular context.

APPENDIX: TRANSCRIPT OF THE B-K CONVERSATION[9]

01 B: It's alright.

02 K: So how are you doing? ((pause, rustling sound))

03 B: ((laugh)) As well as can be expected this time of the semester. How about you.

04 K: ((animated)) Umm good.

05 B: Are you sure that you don't want half? This is huge.

06 K: No. Thanks, I've finally got my apple,

07 B: Umm, alright. (pause)

08 K: I didn't think I'd have time for lunch at all, so this is a real treat!

09 B: Umm (pause) a bonus, ((extended laugh)) (pause)

10 K: Wha:t?

11 B: A bonus. (pause)

12 K: Oh. What kind of sandwich is that,

13 B: Turkey.

14 K: Very Thanksgiving of you!

15 B: Appropriate.

16 K: ((barely audible)) Yes, (pause)

---

[9] This is a segment of a longer conversation analyzed in its entirety in Craig and Tracy (1983). B and K are female college students. K is in her early 20s and B is in her late 20s. The two had worked together for a class project most of the semester and were on friendly terms. B and k are both European Americans. A copy of the audiotape may be requested from me (Karen.Tracy@Colorado.edu) for instructional purposes.

17   B: K (pause) what are you giving ((laughing)) people be Christmas this year? ((both laughing)) I've started thinking about it'n my ability to be inventive without spending much ((laughing)) money is very very small.

18   K: oh

19   K: Like family? Friends?

20   B: Family mostly.

21   K: Family hhhoh: (pause) What do you buy men in your family for Christmas.

22   B: My father is the main problem.

23   K: Yes. I have that same problem. I finally resorted to saying ((louder, mock exasperation)) "Dad? What do you want." ((high pitch, comical)) "I don't need anything."

24   B: That's exact- I think we've got the same father ((laugh))

25   K: I think everybody's father must be like that at some point

26   B: Hmm

27   K: y'na. he doesn't so you end up buying him something that he really doesn't need or want.

28   K: Um hmm?

29   K: But (pause)

30   B: I mentioned that problem to my father on his birthday. He said "I don't want anything, I don't need anything save your money," so I did and I just sent him a card and he was tremendously hurt and upset. ((laugh))

31   K: Um hmm? (pause) I don't think my dad would be hurt. Cuz he really doesn't, he enjoys Christmas and birthdays just as a family activity.

32   B: Um Hmm

33   K: And he'd ra- much rather give. (pause) But (pause) it's just not the same.

34   B: Are you going home for Christmas?

35   K: Oh yeah, (pause) hhh. Is there any other choice?

36   B: You'll be up in Illinois?

37 K: ((laugh)) um hm?

38 B: Sure there's another choice. Some folks don't go home for Christmas!

39 K: Oh where's your mom living. (pause)

40 B: ((laugh))

41 K: You weren't supposed to take a bite right ((laughing)) then, (pause)

42 B: My mother lives in Minneapolis.

43 K: Hmm::

44 B: Which is easy and I visit her on vacations a lot.

45 K: Um hmm? And your dad lives in Philadelphia but he's now in Florida?

46 B: Um hmm Well he'll be in Florida by the time I get there.

47 K: What's he going t- does- Is this part of his business?

48 B: No, uhm, he works he's a lawyer but he works part time as n assistant district attorney. And for that job he gets. I think it's three weeks or a month or something of vacation every year.

49 K: Hmm

50 B: He hates winter.

51 K: Ah:::. So you leave!

52 B: He does. This is the first time I'll have been to Florida.

53 K: Hmm:: I meant to ask you the other day, are you flying down?

54 B: Um hm, and I hate planes.

55 K: I:: know you said that. (pause)

56 B: Yup

57 K: Are you going to be gone long?

58 B: It seems like long. It's gonna be two weeks.

59 K: Hmm:

60   B: My father and I haven't spent two weeks together in quite some time. ((snicker))

61   K: A real challenge? (pause) Or will it be fun.

62   B: He's a challenging person. ((laugh)) He um, he's a lawyer so he only listens to as much as he needs to of what you're saying to make an argument against it. And if there is no argument going at the time he provokes one.

63   K: Ah:::

64   B: Every once in a while you have to just sit down and tell him to back off. ((snicker)) That's done if you're willing t'either burst into tears or duck. ((laugh))

65   K: Oh::h

66   B: He uh. he doesn't like being told things like that. After ten or fifteen minutes he cools down and listens but- the first few minutes are difficult. ((laugh)) (pause) How bout you. You have brothers and sisters, don't you?

67   K: Brothers, two brothers. y'nger.

68   B: Ah. So they're still at home?

69   K: Well, no, one is in college. He's- he'll be home though too- and the other one's little yet.

70   B: ((slight laugh))

71   K: In my estimation I bought him a tee-shirt. Ahm, every year. It seemed like, my other brother goes to a small college and, we always bring him home a shirt from our school? Each of us? So he's got a collection of Wisconsin shirts that he's outgrown cuz he's thirteen so he's in the growing stage, and he's got a collection of Northwestern shirts that he's outgrown over the years.

72   B: I know

73   K: So I got him one the other day an' ma, I showed my mom it, an' she said ((raised pitch, animated)) well what size did you get'em, An'I just I picked it up and looked at it sa- Oh! A medium. I got him one to fit me. She wha::::t? Well by summer he'll be wearing the same size I am. He wears the same size shoes.

74   B: And then when he outgrows it you'll have it.

75   K: Uh huh

76   B: Um hmm

77 K: I'm getting to that stage where if I go home and need a- a sweater to wear or a grubby shirt to wear I w' jus' go rummaging through his closet and see what's: a little big for him an' dig it out.

78 B: ((slight laugh))

79 K: ((cough))You don't have any brothers d- and sisters do you?

80 B: No I have uh two stepbrothers and a stepsister. But (pause) my father divorced their mother, so we don't see each other too much.

3

Nonverbal Communication

Walid A. Afifi
Pennsylvania State University

Sayings that attest to the importance of nonverbal communication in our lives vary from "A picture is a worth 1,000 words" to "Appearances are deceiving." But what are we talking about when discussing nonverbal elements of communication? Many people think of "body language" when discussing nonverbal messages. However, thinking of nonverbal only as body language ignores several important elements. For our purposes, nonverbal communication will be defined as "those behaviors other than words themselves that form a socially shared coding system" (Burgoon, 1994, p. 231). Two primary aspects of this definition are worth noting: First, it includes a wide variety of behaviors besides "body language." Second, it assumes people recognize the meaning of these behaviors within their social or cultural setting. These two aspects of nonverbal will become very clear by the end of this chapter.

Scholars often claim that nonverbal messages are more important than verbal ones (see Burgoon, Buller, & Woodall, 1996). Their claim is based on several arguments. First, studies suggest that nonverbal messages make up a majority of the meaning of a message (see Andersen, 1999). Think of the times you've watched people from a distance, not being able to hear what they're saying but being able to see them. Based only on their nonverbal messages, you are able to understand a lot about their relationship and their interaction. You may be able to determine whether they are friends or dating partners, whether they are having a pleasant or unpleasant interaction, and whether they are in a hurry or not; all these interpretations occur without hearing a word. Although the importance of nonverbal messages for the meaning of an interaction varies, they play at least some role in every interaction. Second, nonverbal communication is omnipresent. In other words, every communication act includes a nonverbal component; nonverbal behavior is part of every communicative message. From how we say something to what we do and how we look when saying it, nonverbal messages are constant influences on our interpretation of what others are communicating to us. Third, there are nonverbal signals that are understood cross-culturally. Unlike verbal messages, which carry meaning strictly within the relevant language culture, nonverbal messages can be used as a communication tool among individuals from vastly different language cultures. For example, individuals from a wide variety of cultures recognize smiles to indicate happiness or recognize hunger from the act of putting fingers to your mouth. Finally, nonverbal messages are trusted over verbal messages when those two channels of information conflict. Because we (somewhat erroneously) believe that nonverbal actions are more subconscious than verbal messages, we tend to believe the nonverbal over the verbal. All these arguments for the importance of nonverbal messages will be defended by the end of this chapter.

In part because nonverbal behaviors are an important aspect of every communication message, this chapter will be organized somewhat differently than some others in this book. Rather than focus on one theory or one concept, the primary goal of this chapter is to make you aware of the many aspects of our behavior that fall under the rubric of nonverbal communication. As part of that goal, several theories will be briefly reviewed when they seem to apply particularly well to a type or function of nonverbal behavior. However, it is important to keep in mind that all theories described in this book are behaviorally represented through nonverbal messages; the theories noted in this chapter are simply a small sampling of the many theories that could be used as illustrations of nonverbal messages "in action."

The chapter is divided into roughly two sections. The first section overviews the various types of nonverbal messages (i.e., codes), starting with body movements (i.e., kinesics) and ending with physical aspects of the environment that affect behavior (i.e., artifacts). You should have a good sense for the breadth and importance of nonverbal communication by the end of that section. The next part of the chapter overviews the ways we use nonverbal messages (i.e., functions). Nonverbal messages can be used to accomplish a wide variety of outcomes, from allowing the smooth flow of an interaction to deceiving others. Theories will be applied throughout the chapter but will be concentrated in the discussion of functions.

NONVERBAL CODES

As noted earlier, nonverbal behaviors include a lot more than "body language." Although scholars disagree on the exact number, there are seven codes (or categories) of nonverbal behavior that will be reviewed in this chapter: kinesics, haptics, proxemics, physical appearance, vocalics, chronemics, and artifacts. I will define each code in turn and discuss some of the associated behaviors.

Kinesics

What do you think of when you ponder nonverbal behavior? If you're like many people who have not studied nonverbal communication, you think of gestures, body movements, eye contact and the like. In other words, you think of only one of the seven codes that exist to describe nonverbal behavior. The kinesic code includes almost all behaviors that most people believe make up nonverbal ways of expression, including gestures, eye contact, and body position. Burgoon et al. (1996) defined kinesics as referring to "all forms of body movement, excluding physical contact with another" (p. 41). As you can imagine, these movements number in the hundreds of thousands, but there are classifications of kinesic activity that help us better place the movements into discrete categories. Perhaps the most widely used is Ekman and Friesen's (1969) distinction among emblems, illustrators, regulators, affect displays, and adaptors. This typology describes kinesic behaviors according to their intended purpose.

Emblems are body movements that carry meaning in and of themselves. Emblems stand alone, without verbal accompaniment, and still convey a clear message to the recipients. Common examples of emblems include a thumbs-up gesture, "flipping someone the bird," using the thumb and index finger to signal "OK," and moving two fingers across your throat to signal someone to stop. In fact, sports are often an arena where celebratory emblems are displayed or become a part of our cultural fabric. An example is the "raise the roof" signal, an emblem signaling celebration that quickly caught on among sports players and is now understood relatively widely in this culture. The historical development of emblem form and meaning is fascinating and varies dramatically from culture to culture. Certain cultures (e.g., Italy, France, Egypt) rely on emblems for the delivery of meaning much more so than other cultures, but all cultures include emblems as part of their communication channel.

Unlike emblems, *illustrators* do not carry meaning without verbal accompaniment. Instead, illustrators are body movements that help receivers interpret and better attend to what is being said verbally. The sort of "nonsense" hand gestures that often accompany a person's speech, especially when speaking publicly, are one form of illustrators. Yet these "nonsense" gestures actually serve important functions: They help focus the receiver's attention on what is being said, they help the sender emphasize a part of his or her speech, they help the sender clarify what is being said, and so on. A father who scolds his child may accentuate the seriousness of the message by waving a finger in the youngster's face, or a traveler may clarify a description of her lost luggage by drawing a "picture" of its shape in the air as she describes it; these are simply two examples of how we use illustrators to assist the verbal component.

Regulators are body movements that are employed to help guide conversations. They may be used to help signal a desire to speak, or a desire not to be called on, or to communicate to the speaker that you are or are not listening. Perhaps the most common example of a regulator is the head nod. We consistently use head nods during conversation to signal to speakers that we are listening, a sign that encourages them to continue. Other behaviors that function as regulators of our conversation include maintaining eye contact, turning our bodies toward or away from the speaker, and looking at our watch.

Adaptors are body movements that "satisfy physical or psychological needs" (Burgoon et al., 1996, p. 42). These movements are rarely intended to communicate anything, but they are good signals of the sender's physiological and psychological state. There are three categories of adaptors: self-adaptors, alter-directed adaptors, and object adaptors. *Self*-adaptors are movements that people direct toward themselves or their bodies; examples include biting fingernails, sucking on a thumb, repeatedly tapping a foot, adjusting a collar, and vigorously rubbing an arm to increase warmth. *Alter-directed* adaptors include the same sorts of behaviors found among self-adaptors except that they are movements people direct to the bodies of others; examples include scratching a friend's back itch, caressing a partner's hair, adjusting a partner's collar, or dusting off a friend's rarely worn jacket. Alter-directed adaptors often signal to the target person or to the audience the level of attachment between the individuals in the exchange. *Object* adaptors are movements that involve attention to an object; common examples include biting on a pen, holding a (sometimes unlit) cigar, or circling the edge of a cup with a finger.

Finally, *affect* displays are body movements that express emotion without the use of touch. Like emblems, affect displays often do not require verbal accompaniment for understanding. In fact, several studies have shown that people across cultures understand certain nonverbal facial expressions as reflective of particular emotions (see Ekman & Oster, 1979; Izard, 1977). By manipulating three facial regions (the eyes and eyelids, the eyebrows and forehead, and the mouth and cheeks), people can create affect displays that are recognizable world wide. For example, sadness is expressed by somewhat constricting the eyes and forehead region, while flattening the cheeks and displaying a slight downward curvature of the mouth.

Although Ekman and Friesen's category system captures most gestural movements, it doesn't describe all kinesic behaviors. Perhaps most importantly, it gives short shrift to the types and functions of eye contact. A popular saying exults that "the eyes are the window to the soul." Research on eye behavior supports these beliefs. Eye contact has been shown to vary dramatically in form and to differ significantly in function (for review, see Grumet, 1983). It clearly occupies a central place as a channel for message transmission and will emerge in studies reviewed throughout the chapter.

One concept that captures several aspects of our kinesic activity and has received considerable research attention is *immediacy*. Included as part of the cluster of immediacy behaviors are the kinesic behaviors of eye contact, body orientation (i.e., the degree to which the interactant's body is oriented toward or away from the other), body lean (i.e., the degree to which the person's body is leaning forward or back), head nods, interpersonal distance (part of the proxemic code), and touch (part of the haptic code). Together, this set of behaviors communicates the degree to which an individual is involved in the interaction. Studies have shown that changes in immediacy behavior strongly affect the outcome of interactions, from having important consequences for the success of job interviews to influencing the attentiveness of patients during interactions with physicians (Buller & Street, 1992; Forbes & Jackson, 1980).

Haptics

A second general category of nonverbal behavior is labeled haptics and refers to all aspects of touch. Perhaps no other code has stronger communicative potential than does touch. Research has shown that individuals place considerable weight on the meaning of touch and that touch has important developmental benefits (see Jones & Yarbrough, 1985). In fact, several studies have found that the absence of touch from parents has serious consequences for children's growth (for review, see Montagu, 1978). Close, physical contact with the caregiver seems to give children the critical sense of protection and security that cannot be attained in other ways. As such, it is not surprising that holding babies is often the behavior that can best calm them and that physicians spend some time explaining baby-holding techniques to new parents.

Touch does not only play an important role during early childhood, it is a critical part of our life as we age as well (see Barnard & Brazelton, 1990). Indeed, the elderly may be most affected by the harmful consequences of touch deprivation (see Montagu, 1978). When lifelong partners pass away, the elderly often lose the one source of affectionate touch on which they have relied for much of their lives. Although certain associations (e.g., long-time neighbors, family members) may help alleviate some potential for loneliness, it is unlikely that their needs for touch will be fully satisfied by these connections.

As with kinesics, haptic behaviors may be classified in multiple ways, some focused on type and others focused on function. Among the type of haptics discussed, scholars have distinguished between the form of touch and its qualities. On the one hand, the form of the touch sends an important communicative message. For example, we could easily separate nuzzles from kisses, rubs from hugs, pokes from hits, pushes from punches, and so on. In fact, Morris (1971) observed 457 different types of touch that seemed to signal the presence of a relationship between the parties. He then categorized the touches into 14 categories of what he labeled tie signs. Among these tie signs are hand-holding, patting, arm-linking, several types of embraces, and kissing. Afifi and Johnson (1999) compared dating partners and male–female friends in their use of these tie signs in college bars. Interestingly, they found more similarities than differences in the frequency that the tie signs were used across the two relationship types. Specifically, all types of tie signs were used in both dating relationships and friendships. However, daters were more likely than friends to lean against one another, use shoulder and waist embraces, and to kiss. Given the relative similarity between daters and friends of the opposite sex in their use of tie signs in bars, it is no wonder that young adults often report confusion about the status of their cross-sex friendships (see Monsour, 2002). Although not assessed by Afifi and Johnson, qualities of the touch, such as the duration and intensity (e.g., amount of pressure) undoubtedly play an important role in their meaning. Both friends and daters may exchange kisses, but a "peck" is different from a longer and more intense kiss. Similarly, a hug can differ dramatically in duration and intensity, aspects that are much more meaningful than simply recognizing that a hug occurred. In other words, both the type of touch and its characteristics serve to define its meaning and affect its outcome.

A final way that touches have been categorized is by their intended purpose. Heslin (as cited in Andersen, 1999) differentiated between five purposes of touch, each increasing in intimacy. *Functional/professional* touches have a specific task-related purpose. They are considered the least intimate forms of touch. Although the type and quality of touch may be considered intimate in other contexts, the receiver of the touch recognizes the function of the touch as being necessary for the task at hand. For example, physicians sometimes touch us in highly intimate areas, but the touch is not considered an intimate one because its function is recognized as being part of the required task of health maintenance. The next function of touch is labeled *Social/polite* and is characterized by relatively formal touches that accompany greetings and departures. A common example of social/polite touches is the handshake. Although other cultures utilize more intimate sorts of greetings (e.g., kisses), the context again defines the otherwise intimate touch as functioning as a polite expression rather than an intimate one. *Friendship/warmth* touches are the sort typically exchanged between friends. The formality of social/polite touches is gone and replaced with qualities of touch that signal increased bondedness. Examples of friendship/warmth touches include partial embraces, full embraces, and pats. *Love/intimacy* touches function to signal elevated closeness and are less likely to be enacted publicly. Touches such as a kiss or a prolonged embrace may serve the love/intimacy function. Finally, touches that function to increase *Sexual* arousal are the most intimate types of touch. The sort of touch that occurs during sexual activity is the most common example of this function. In sum, rather than consider touches as differing by type, this category scheme focuses on their function. The same type of touch (e.g., a backrub) may serve a functional/professional purpose when conducted by a masseuse or sports therapist but act to increase sexual arousal when conducted by a romantic partner. Unfortunately, the existing categorization schemes do not adequately capture the many types of more harmful touches or the more negative purposes of touch (e.g., to harm, to intimidate).

Proxemics

The proxemic category of nonverbal behavior captures the way we use space. From analyses of overpopulation in certain nations, to the impact of small dorm room space, to overcrowding in prisons, studies consistently show harmful effects of limited space. Although cultures differ dramatically in the amount of space that is typically given, we are all born with at least minimum needs for space. Threatening those space needs, especially for prolonged periods, produces high stress that, in turn, affects our psyche and behavior dramatically (see Edwards, Fuller, Vorakitphokatorn, & Sermsri, 1994). It is not surprising then, that confinement in a very small and dark room is commonly used as a method of torture (www.amnesty.org) and that such torture has devastating psychological impact. Indeed, Lester (1990) found an increase in suicide rates associated with overcrowding in prisons. Donoghue (1992) reported overcrowding as a factor contributing to stress among teenagers in the Virgin Islands. Curiously, he noted that sexual activity (sometimes leading to pregnancy) was one of consequences. Also, Gress and Heft (1998) showed that the number of roommates in college dorms negatively affected the residents both emotionally and behaviorally. One way in which this need for space is expressed is through our behavior around territories.

Territories are physically fixed areas that one or more individuals defend as their own (Altman, 1975). To maintain the spatial needs provided by these territories, we set up markers so that others know the territory's boundaries (Buslig, 1999). For example, students may put books on the seat next to them to ensure that the seat is not taken, or spread their belongings across a wide area of a table to indicate the area as their own. Fences around property, "Keep Away" and "Do Not Disturb" signs, and markers around beach blankets are other common examples of signaling territory. Interestingly, locations where space is limited are particularly prone to markers of territory. Roommates often send very clear signals about the boundaries of their territory by hanging unique posters or signs that mark the area as their own. The importance of these territories to our well being is evident in the way individuals react to their violation. Intrusions into territory have been shown to produce elevated stress, and behavioral responses varying from withdrawal to confrontation (for review, see Lyman & Scott, 1967).

Unlike territories, which are fixed physical entities, *personal space* is a proxemic-based need that moves along with the individual. It is an "invisible bubble" that expands and shrinks according to context, but follows each individual, protecting him or her from physical threats (Hall, 1966). Violation of that personal space bubble produces responses similar to those found for the violation of territory. In North America, typical personal space has a circumference of approximately 3 ft, but the size of that space varies dramatically and is influenced by a variety of factors, from the target of your conversation to its location (see Burgoon et al., 1996). For example, you would likely feel much more uncomfortable standing 2 ft away from someone in a relatively empty elevator than in a crowded elevator. We recognize that certain contexts necessitate the temporary violation of our personal space, but we also keenly anticipate extracting ourselves from that context and restoring the security that comes with maintaining those personal space needs. A behavior that is commonly used both to violate personal space and restore it is eye contact. Have you ever felt that your personal space has been violated by someone simply staring at you, even from a distance? Many people report such a sensation. Have you ever looked away from someone who got too close physically? That sort of behavior is a common response to the violation of personal space in elevators, for example (see Rivano-Fischer, 1988).

Physical Appearance

The physical appearance category of nonverbal behavior includes all aspects related to the way we look, from our body type, to body adornments (e.g., tattoos, rings), to what we wear. Perhaps no other category of nonverbal behavior has a stronger effect on initial impressions than our physical appearance. The two general types of physical appearance that will be addressed in this chapter are body type and attire.

Researchers have identified three general body types: ectomorphs, mesomorphs, and endomorphs (see Burgoon et al., 1996). *Ectomorphic* bodies are characterized by thin bone structures and lean bodies, *mesomorphic* bodies have strong bone structures, are typically muscular and athletic, and *endomorphic* bodies have large bone structures, and are typically heavy-set and somewhat rounded. An individual's body type is partly based on genetic elements such as bone structures and partly based on other elements such as diet and levels of activity. Regardless of the source of one's body structure or the degree to which it has any actual effect on behavior, research has clearly shown that people have strong impressions of others based on their body type. Specifically, ectomorphs are perceived to be timid, clumsy, and anxious, but also intelligent; mesomorphs are seen as outgoing, social, and strong; and endomorphs are considered lazy, jolly, and relatively unintelligent (Burgoon et al., 1996). Some factors may affect these perceptions. For example, women ectomorphs and male mesomorphs may be perceived more favorably than their other-sex counterparts. Unfortunately, research has not sufficiently addressed these possibilities. However, one pattern that has been well documented is that, regardless of actual body size, women are more likely than men to perceive their bodies negatively (for review, see Cash & Pruzinsky, 1990). Such "body image disturbances" have devastating consequences, affecting self-esteem, leading to eating disorders, and even increasing suicide rates (e.g., Phillips, 1999; Stice, Hayward, Cameron, Killen, & Taylor, 2000). Why do many women have such dislike for their bodies? Although the answer to this question is not at all simple, it is undoubtedly based, at least in part, on a cultural obsession with images of overly thin women (see Botta, 1999).

However, body shape is not the only aspect of physical appearance that has been shown to affect people's perceptions of us. Another strong influence on perceptions is height. Taller men and women are more likely to be seen as competent, dominant, and intelligent (see Boyson, Pryor, & Butler, 1999). Interestingly, however, the advantage of height does not extend to perceptions of women's attractiveness. Instead, shorter women are perceived as more attractive and date more frequently than taller women (Sheppard & Strathman, 1989). Men and women who fall well above or below this preferred standard encounter lifelong difficulties, including a diminished likelihood of relational success and struggles with perceptions of credibility across a wide range of evaluative contexts (see Martel & Biller, 1987). To combat these perceptions, short people sometimes change their environment to hide their height. For example, Robert Reich, who served on three presidential administrations and is under 5 ft tall, would speak behind a podium and use a step stool, making media viewers unaware of his short stature.

One explanation for the strong perceptions associated with body type and height comes from Evolutionary Theory. Evolutionary theorists (otherwise called sociobiologists) argue that our attraction to others is based in large part on our perceptions of their genetic makeup (see Buss, 1994). They suggest that, much like other mammals, the strongest members of our species receive the greatest attention and are considered the most attractive. For us, signs of health, wealth, and intelligence are the primary determinants of "strength." As such, it is not surprising to these scholars that people's body type (which may be associated with health) and height (which often translates to physical superiority) affect their life success.

Finally, the clothes we wear are a part of our physical appearance that also affects people's perceptions of us. The clothes we wear strongly influence perceptions of credibility, status, attractiveness, competence, and likability (e.g., Kaiser, 1997). This should come as no surprise to anyone who has seen students proudly display their *Abercrombie & Fitch* shirts, observed the respect often afforded to those wearing their military uniforms, or shook their head in frustration at someone who leaves for an interview in completely disheveled clothes. Indeed, individuals wearing formal clothes are seen as more credible and more persuasive than those wearing informal clothes, affecting their success across a range of interaction contexts, from job interviews to dates. Other aspects of physical appearance that relate to people's judgments include tattoos, rings, and hair styles. In sum, studies unequivocally demonstrate that physical appearance, both things under individuals' control (e.g., attire) and those not (e.g., height), strongly influence perceptions.

Vocalics

Vocalics, a category that people sometimes have difficulty recognizing as a nonverbal component, reflect all aspects of the voice, including loudness, pitch, accent, rate of speech, length of pauses between speech, and tone, among many others. Vocalic elements carry much of the meaning of a message and communicate a lot about the sender. Its importance can be reflected by a simple exercise. Try saying the same words (e.g., "Come over here") with slightly different vocalic qualities. Depending on how we say these words, we could communicate anger, passion, sadness, love, or a variety of other emotions. Indeed, studies have shown that we make relatively accurate judgments about a person's sex, age, height, and cultural background based on vocal cues alone (see Argyle, 1988). Like many of the codes discussed so far, vocalic elements also affect perceptions of attractiveness and competence (Semic, 1999). Deeper voices among men, like that of Barry White for example, are considered sexual and romantic, whereas high-pitched voices among men are considered feminine and weak. Other vocal qualities such as accent and speech rate are also associated with intelligence. For example, certain accents (e.g., British accents) may be considered sophisticated whereas others may not (e.g., thick Boston accents). This difference in the attractiveness of accents is illustrated in the movie *My Fair Lady* which is based on the premise that individuals sometimes must change their accent to affect judgments of their credibility.

One theory that has been applied to understand vocalic shifts is Communication Accommodation Theory (CAA, see chap. 16, this volume). Central to CAA is the belief that we converge our speech toward the style of individuals with whom we want to be associated and diverge away from that of individuals with whom we do not want association (see Giles, Mulac, Bradac, & Johnson, 1987). Examples of this behavior can be found across a wide range of contexts, including interactions between individuals of different ages (e.g., adults and the elderly), individuals from different cultures, individuals with different levels of status, even individuals of different sexes (see Gallois, Giles, Jones, Cargile, & Ota, 1995). So, if you were from the eastern United States and were to spend considerable time in the South, you would likely develop somewhat of a Southern accent, at least when around your friends from the South. That accent accommodation is a way of signaling connectedness with the South. Not surprisingly, the degree to which you are willing to accommodate others in your language has also been shown to significantly affect their perceptions of you. Failure to accommodate your vocalic patterns to others implicitly signals to them that you are not interested in joining their cultural group. On the other hand, a willingness to accommodate communicates attraction.

Chronemics and Artifacts

Chronemics and artifacts are the last two categories of nonverbal behavior that we will discuss in this chapter. Rarely considered when discussing nonverbal messages, these codes nevertheless play a strong role in our interactions. The chronemic code captures our use and perception of time, including (among other things) our perception of the "appropriate" duration of an event, the number of things we do at once, the importance of punctuality, our use of time in our language, and the desired sequencing of events (Andersen, 1999). The North

American culture is preoccupied with the notion of time; life is fast-paced and individuals are seemingly always struggling against time constraints. Two hours seems to be the maximum time that one expects to allot for entertainment or food events; movies are typically 2 hr or less, plays may go 3 hr but will have a prolonged recess to affect the perception of time, and guests often start getting anxious when meals take longer than 2 hr. Other countries differ dramatically from this North American norm. Although we rarely think of these time norms, they become very evident when we visit other countries. For example, Mediterranean countries often take 3 to 4 hr for a meal, making it as much as a social event as it is time for nourishment. This chapter will focus on three chronemic elements: duration, punctuality, and the distinction between polychronism and monochronism.

The expectations surrounding event duration are captured in part by the example provided previously. For every event or interaction, we have culturally and socially based expectations about its duration (Gonzalez & Zimbardo, 1999). Whether it be the amount of time a professor spends in an office meeting with a student, the amount of time set aside for a lunch date, or the amount of time before contact is made following a successful first date, these expectations strongly affect our perceptions of others' competence or attractiveness. Imagine if you had strong expectations that someone not call you back until 2 or 3 days after a first date but the person calls you within minutes after dropping you off. That violation of your chronemic expectations would undoubtedly affect your perceptions of him or her. In a similar vein, perceptions associated with punctuality vary according to the context and have important consequences. Punctuality is held with relatively high esteem in the North American culture, especially for more formal engagements. Arriving late to an interview, even if 5 min, is considered inexcusable, but 5 min late for a lunch date may be acceptable. However, even informal occasions have relatively strict punctuality expectations; arriving 30 min late for a lunch date is not appropriate, for example. In other cultures, however, there is a recognition that the time set for an appointment is rarely adhered to, and expectations are that the appointment may begin 30 to 45 min following the originally set appointment time. Failing to meet these culturally and contextually driven expectations have important implications for assessments of individuals (see Burgoon & Hale, 1988).

A final concept related to chronemics that will be considered in this chapter is the distinction between polychronism and monochronism (Hall & Hall, 1999). Polychronism reflects the act of doing multiple activities at once, whereas monochronism characterizes a focus on one activity at a time. For example, interacting with someone while you are cleaning your apartment, or watching TV while talking to someone reflects polychronistic behavior. Although sometimes necessary, such behavior is often considered a reflection of (dis)interest in the conversation. Of course, certain careers (e.g., secretarial work, CEOs) require that individuals are adept at polychronistic activity, and some cultures consider polychronism a sign of importance, so monochronism is not universally preferred.

The final nonverbal code is *artifacts*, a category that includes "the physical objects and environmental attributes that communicate directly, define the communication context, or guide social behavior in some way" (Burgoon et al., 1996, p. 109). Hall (1966) classified artifacts into two main types: fixed-feature elements and semifixed-feature elements. Fixed features include aspects of our surroundings that are not easily movable and are unlikely to change. Among these features is the structure of our surroundings, including the architectural style, the number and size of windows, and the amount of space available. Studies have shown that such architectural features directly impact the sort of communication that occurs (see Sundstrom, Bell, Busby, & Asmus, 1996). For instance, people who work in small cubicles are much less productive and less satisfied than people who work in their own office space, especially when the office space includes windows. Semifixed features are defined as aspects of our surroundings that are somewhat easily movable. Examples include rugs, paintings, wall color, the amount of lighting, and the temperature, among others. Considerable evidence suggests that these features also strongly affect both psychological health and communication outcome (for review, see Sundstrom et al., 1996). For example, research has shown that the semifixed aspects of a hospital affect the speed of patient recovery (Gross, Sasson, Zarhy, & Zohar, 1998).

In sum, nonverbal messages affect our interactions in hundreds of ways, from movement in our face, to our body posture, our gestures, the space between us, the ways we touch, the intonations in our voice, the way we use time, and the surroundings in which we find ourselves. Together, these nonverbal features inescapably guide the way we act and the outcome of our interactions. However, noting the population of nonverbal message types is only part of the equation. Each of these nonverbal behaviors can serve a variety of functions or purposes.

FUNCTIONS OF NONVERBAL CODES

There are three assumptions about nonverbal behavior that shape the research reviewed in the remainder of this chapter (for review, see Cappella & Street, 1985). First, all behavior is motivated by particular goals. In other words, all behavior is functional in some way. You gesture to someone with a specific purpose in mind, you look at someone to get his attention, you touch someone to let her know you're here, you yell at someone to communicate your anger, and so on. Second, each function or purpose can be achieved in multiple ways. For instance, you are not limited to only one way that you can show affection to people. You may hug them, kiss them, hold their hand, or take them out to a fancy restaurant. The third assumption related to this perspective on nonverbal messages is that a single behavior can serve multiple functions. For example, a hug can show someone you care, while simultaneously signaling to others that you and the recipient of the hug are in a committed relationship. These three assumptions are an inherent part of almost all studies of nonverbal communication and guide our understanding of nonverbal messages and their use.

Although scholars disagree on the exact number of functions served by nonverbal behaviors, there are six functions that seem to emerge in most discussions on this issue and that will be highlighted in this chapter. These six functions are (a) structuring and regulating interaction, (b) creating and managing identities, (c) communicating emotions, (d) defining and managing relationships, (e) influencing others, and (f) deceiving others.

Structuring and Regulating Interaction

Each of the nonverbal codes serves to shape the quality of the interactions in which we find ourselves. By so doing, they structure and regulate these encounters. For example, Robinson's (1998) analysis of physician–patient interaction reveals the way in which the kinesic behaviors of eye gaze and body orientation signal to patients the physician's willingness to begin the interaction. Patients learn to stay silent until the physician kinesically signals that he or she is ready to start the interaction. Indeed, as noted earlier, many studies of immediacy reach similar conclusions, with varying levels of nonverbal involvement strongly affecting the quality of the interaction. Research on our use of vocalics also demonstrates the many ways that we nonverbally structure interactions. Conversations are typically considered a series of turns at talk. Each turn is requested, given, and ended in subtle, but clearly understood, nonverbal ways. For example, turns at talk are requested by such behaviors as establishing eye contact with the speaker, abruptly and noticeably inhaling a short breath, and starting to gesture toward the speaker (Wiemann & Knapp, 1975). In contrast, we communicate that our turn is ending by subtly changing the rhythm, loudness, and pitch of our voice (Boomer, 1978). In another interesting study on the potential of nonverbal message to structure interactions, Eaves and Leathers (1991) compared the physical layouts of McDonald's and Burger King to determine whether they affected interactions. Their study demonstrated that customers at McDonalds showed considerably higher levels of nonverbal involvement than did Burger King customers. Given these differences within two relatively similar fast-food chains, you can imagine how more noticeable differences in the level of restaurant formality affect our interactions.

One of the clearest signs that nonverbal behavior serves to structure the flow of interactions comes from examining how people adapt behavior during interaction. Indeed, a long history of research has shown that we react and adapt to one another's nonverbal expressions during interaction (for review, see Burgoon, Stern, & Dillman, 1995). Interaction Adaptation Theory (Burgoon, Stern, & Dillman, 1995) argues that people carry certain nonverbal needs for affiliation, recognize societal expectations for levels of affiliation, and have preferences for particular levels of affiliation from each interaction partner. The levels of these components differ in each context. For example, you may be may upset 1 day and feel the *need* for some autonomy. You *expect* your roommate to greet you and welcome you home. But, your *preference* is that your roommate not interact with you at all for the next few hours. The combination of these three elements produces what is called the *Interaction Position*, a concept that reflects the amount of distance you anticipate from your roommate. The argument in this theory is that your needs and preferences act together with your general social expectations to affect what behavior you anticipate from your interaction partner (i.e., the interaction position, the IP). In the previous example, the IP may be that your roommate will greet you but recognize your mood and give you some space. This IP is then compared to the actual behavior you receive (A). The theory argues that the comparison between your IP and the A determines how you will nonverbally adapt. If the actual behavior (i.e., the A) is better than you anticipated (i.e., the IP) you will converge toward the person's behavior, but if the actual behavior is worse than you anticipated, you will diverge away from that behavior. This "dance" is perhaps the greatest example of concerning the effect of nonverbal behavior on the structure of interactions.

Creating and Managing Identities and Impressions

Another general function of nonverbal messages is to communicate to others the groups to which we belong and to convey particular impressions of ourselves to others. I will review two theoretical frameworks that apply this function. Social Identity Theory (Tajfel & Turner, 1979) focuses on our identity as group members, whereas theoretical work on self-presentation (e.g., Goffman, 1959) focuses on our identity as individuals. Together, these theories help explain the way in which we use nonverbal behavior to achieve the function of creating and managing identities and impressions.

Communicating Group Identities.   The main premise of Social Identity Theory is that we develop and maintain our self-concept in large part from the social groups with which we affiliate or to which we belong (e.g., ethnicity, sports team, club membership, department, organizational unit).The importance of these group memberships vary according to context (e.g., the importance of your status as a member of a particular fraternity decreases when with your parents), but each group has specific ways through which membership is communicated to others. So, when group membership becomes relevant, we act in ways that convey to others that we are a part of that group, while also letting people who are not in that group become more aware of their out-group status. Not surprisingly, the primary method of communicating these group memberships is nonverbal.

Take membership in a high school clique, for example. Members of a particular clique are likely to dress in relatively similar ways (physical appearance), and often have specific gestures they use to greet one another or that they use during conversation (kinesics). Individuals can indicate group membership by standing close to one another or by sitting next to each other at the lunch table (proxemics). Group members may spend a significant portion of their day with others in their clique (chronemics), place indicators of affiliation (signs, letters, etc.) on their lockers (artifacts), and may whisper to one another in the presence of an outgroup member (vocalics). Given the importance of group membership (Worschel & Austin, 1986), it is not surprising that we go to such lengths to identify with groups that we consider enhancing to our self concept.

It is also the case that we distance ourselves nonverbally from groups with which we want to remain independent. A look around college campuses shows a lot of the ways that people accomplish this distancing. Individuals often make little effort to include members of ethnic groups other than their own in their conversations. Eder's (1985) study of behavior among midadolescent females showed that group members communicated distance from group outsiders by avoiding interaction, body contact, or eye contact with nonmembers. Although these are examples of interpersonal ways in which we send group-related identity messages, there are ways in which societies or cultures communicate outgroup status to entire groups. Certainly laws discriminating against where particular cultural groups can gather—let alone eat, sit, or stand—are examples of such societal messages that become translated through nonverbal means. Everything from kinesics gestures (e.g., lack of eye contact) to proxemic decisions (e.g., maintaining large distances) to artifacts (e.g., signs indicating that entrance is prohibited to certain groups) communicate exclusion. For example, laws prohibiting the homeless from loitering in certain parks or communities are violations of public territorial rights that reflect one of many ways through which the homeless are shown their status as a societal "outgroup."

Communicating Individual Identities.   Besides communicating our identity as members of particular groups, we also send nonverbal messages that are intended to convey our individual identities. Several theories have been advanced to capture this aspect of our behavior. The labels of these frameworks include Politeness Theory (Brown & Levinson, 1987), the Theory of Self-Identification (Schlenker, Britt, & Pennington, 1996), and Facework (Tracy, 1990). Within each of these theories are such concepts as self presentation, impression management, and identity management. In general, they all refer to the idea that we are motivated by a desire to maintain a positive impression of ourselves in the eyes of others. In other words, we generally want others to see us in a positive light. DePaulo (1992) defined *self-presentation* as "a matter of regulating one's own behavior to create a particular impression on others, of communicating a particular image of oneself to others, or of showing oneself to be a particular kind of person" (p. 205). For many reasons, we often manage our impression in front of others nonverbally (see DePaulo, 1992). For example, Albas and Albas (1988) examined ways in which students reacted after receiving graded exams. They found that individuals who received good grades smiled (kinesics), displayed an open body posture (kinesics), and left their exams open with the grade showing, whereas those who received poor grades displayed a closed body posture (kinesics) and left immediately following the class (chronemics).

The use of nonverbal methods to manage impressions is obviously not limited to students' reactions to exam scores; evidence for other applications can be found across a whole host of contexts. Daly, Hogg, Sacks, Smith, and Zimring (1983) reported that people in early stages of relationships spend more time adjusting their clothes, fixing their hair, and attending to their physical appearance than those in later stages. In a similar vein, Montepare and Vega (1988) showed that women's vocalic cues communicated greater approachability and sincerity, among other characteristics, when talking over the phone with men with whom they had an intimate relationship, as compared to those with whom they had no relationship. Finally, Blanck, Rosenthal, and Cordell (1985) reported that judges were more likely to display nonverbal cues associated with warmth, professionalism, and fairness when facing older, more educated jurors than younger, less educated jurors. In sum, the function of creating and managing identities is a common purpose of our nonverbal activity and involves actions from all codes.

Communicating Emotions

Another common purpose of nonverbal behavior is to communicate emotion. In fact, as noted earlier, the majority of emotion messages are communicated through facial cues (i.e., kinesically). Particularly impressive is the evidence that some of these expressions are recognized cross-culturally. The argument underlying the Universality Hypothesis on emotion expression is that humans are innately equipped to decode certain expressions of emotion (for review, see Ekman, 1978), leading to cross-cultural recognition of these emotions. Initially, several studies supported that claim (e.g., Ekman, 1973; Izard, 1977). However, when researchers improved their studies, they found dramatic differences in individuals' nonverbal responses. To reconcile the differences in the research and to help account for both cultural-specific and universal patterns of expression, Ekman and colleagues developed the Neurocultural Theory of emotion expression (Ekman & Friesen, 1969). The theory argues that there is an element of biological innateness in our expression of emotion that accounts for the consistency across cultures in recognition of emotion expressions. For example, an experience of joy produces an upward curvature of the mouth and lips. However, differences in actual expression of emotion occur across cultures due to (a) cultural differences in the association between events and the experience of particular emotions and (b) culturally learned and context-based rules about the appropriateness of expressing particular emotions (labeled *display rules*). The first of these two factors makes sense once you consider the way that cultures shapes the emotions we experience (for review, see Nussbaum, 2000). For instance, some cultures emphasize individuality and are likely to encourage intense emotional responses to events that threaten individuality, whereas other cultures emphasize the collective and are likely to shape emotional responses accordingly. In other words, the same events are unlikely to produce the same emotions across cultures. However, researchers have devoted much more energy toward understanding the second of these factors: display rules. *Display rules* are defined as "socially learned habits regarding the control of facial appearance that act to intensify, deintensify, mask, or qualify a universal expression of emotion depending on the social circumstance" (Kupperbusch et al., 1999, p. 21).

Studies have shown that infants' emotional expressions abide by cultural, gender, and familial display rules before their first birthday (e.g., Malatesta & Haviland, 1982). These rules are communicated by parents from infancy but reinforced throughout life by the media, family members, peers, and even strangers. Common examples of these display rules are those generally discouraging overt public displays of affection, or those directing people on appropriate methods of emotional expression in movie theatres, funeral homes, classrooms, concerts, and so on. Display rules also direct people regarding the appropriateness of emotion expression in close relationships. Considerable evidence demonstrates that "negative" emotions (e.g., anger, jealousy) are considered inappropriate to express in early stages of relationships (for review, see Aune, 1997). Moreover, studies show the way that these display rules affect our expression of emotion even in our most intimate relationships. For example, Cloven and Roloff (1994) found that one fifth of relational irritations were not expressed in couples at the most advanced relational stages, and Aune, Buller, and Aune (1996) found that positive emotions were considered more appropriate to express than negative emotions, regardless of relationship stage.

Defining and Managing Relationships

Another important function of nonverbal messages is to help people negotiate and express the quality or status of the relationship they have with others. These relational messages vary along five dimensions (see Burgoon & Hale, 1987). Labeled the topoi (themes) of relational communication, the five dimensions along which nonverbal messages can differentially communicate relational qualities are (a) the amount of dominance, (b) the level of intimacy, (c) the degree of composure or arousal, (d) the level of formality, and (e) the degree to which the interaction is focused on task or social elements. Evidence associated with how each of these dimensions is communicated nonverbally will be briefly summarized.

Dominance. Nonverbal messages help indicate the degree to which one member of the interaction is powerful, dominant, and controlling. The way in which men and women communicate power nonverbally has been examined frequently, most notably by Henley (1977). Behavior from each nonverbal code can be applied to study how dominance is conveyed (see Burgoon et al., 1996). For example, people communicate dominance by refusing to engage in eye contact (kinesics), by initiating touch (haptics), by arriving late for a meeting (chronemics), by having access to large office space or by displaying awards (artifacts), by demanding large personal space needs or unilaterally changing the amount of space between themselves and their interactants (proxemics), by speaking loudly and in a lower pitch (vocalics), and by emphasizing their body size or dressing in formal attire (physical appearance).

Intimacy. Nonverbal messages help communicate the amount of affection, inclusion, involvement, depth, trust, and similarity there is between interactants. As noted earlier in this chapter, several studies have shown the benefits of expressing nonverbal involvement in interactions. Displays such as gestural activity, direct body orientation, forward body lean, and close (but socially acceptable) conversational distance increase the success of job interviews, increase liking, and produce perceptions of personality warmth (Burgoon et al., 1996). Whereas expressing involvement is one method of communicating relational intimacy and interest, more intimate messages are communicated in other ways, such as the use of tie signs and an increase in the frequency and intimacy of touch. Interestingly, the eyes are often the best indicator of attraction (Grumet, 1983). Establishing eye contact is typically the first way individuals communicate attraction and people who are attracted to one another look into each other's eyes more than others do. Also, our pupils involuntarily increase in size when we are talking to someone to whom we are attracted, a fact that, in turn, subconsciously seems to make us more attractive to others (Hess, 1975). In sum, the nonverbal methods for communicating intimacy are numerous.

Composure and Arousal.   The degree to which individuals are relaxed and calm in an interaction has also been shown to communicate qualities of their relationship. As a general rule, people in close relationships are more likely to be relaxed around one-another than acquaintances. In fact, people sometimes manipulate their levels of composure to send messages about their comfort in the interaction or the relationship. For example, job candidates or people on first dates usually do their best to hide the amount of anxiety being felt in part because they want to show a level of relational comfort. In other words, we make efforts to appear composed in certainty situations precisely because we know what anxiety communicates about relationships.

Formality.   Another way in which individuals can communicate qualities of the relationship is through the degree of casualness conveyed in their nonverbal behavior. Although relatively few studies have examined it, the level of formality, like other dimensions of relationship quality, can be communicated in many different ways. Three common methods of indicating the formality of the relationship are through the formality of the attire, through kinesic rigidity, and through conversational distance (Burgoon, 1991; Burgoon et al., 1996). The more casual the clothing, the more relaxed the body posture, the more frequent the hand gesturing, and the greater the distance between interactants, the greater the perception that the interaction is an informal one. Not surprisingly, studies have shown that the likelihood of communicating formality differs across status and that these differences affect people's perceptions. For example, Lamude and Scudder (1991) reported that upper level managers are more likely to be formal than lower or middle-level managers. Interestingly, research has also shown that college teachers are perceived as more effective when they dress informally (Butler, & Roesel, 1991; Lukavski, Butler, & Harden, 1995), whereas physicians and interview candidates are perceived as less effective when behaving or dressing informally (Burgoon et al., 1987; Gifford, Ng, & Wilkinson, 1985).

Task or Social Orientation.   Nonverbal messages reflecting the degree to which the interaction is one focused on a task constitute the final dimension through which people communicate qualities of their relationships nonverbally. This dimension is typically communicated through the chronemic code and, again, the desirability of communicating a focus on task is strongly affected by context. On the one hand, managers who focus on task, to the exclusion of relational maintenance behaviors, receive the lowest ratings of satisfaction by subordinates (Lamude, Daniels, & Smilowitz, 1995). On the other hand, teachers whose in-class behavior focuses on task produce better student outcomes (Harris, Rosenthal, & Snodgrass, 1986). In general, the communication of a task orientation has been shown to convey lower levels of relational connectedness than socially oriented messages (Burgoon & Hale, 1987).

Influencing Others

A long history of research has examined the methods we use to attempt to change someone's attitudes or behavior or to strengthen already established attitudes or behaviors (see O'Keefe, 1990). In general, studies find that we are most influenced by people who we find attractive (i.e., likeable), credible, or powerful (see O'Keefe, 1990).

Social Attractiveness or Liking.   Scholars have shown many ways in which individuals can increase their attractiveness to others. For example, studies demonstrate that establishing eye contact increases the likelihood of influencing others in a wide variety of situations including persuading strangers to give a dime for a phone call, donate to a charity, take pamphlets, or pick up a hitchhiker (for review, see Segrin, 1999). Also, light touching is linked to bigger tips, an increase in petition signings, and a greater willingness to sign up for volunteer work (e.g., Goldman, Kiyohara, & Pfannensteil, 1985). Physical appearance cues also strongly affect perceived attractiveness and the potential to influence others. In one study, a confederate gave the same speech to two different audiences but varied her physical appearance through differences in the messiness of her hair and the fit of her clothes (Mills & Aronson, 1965). Results showed that she was more convincing when she was dressed more neatly. In a similar vein, physically attractive political candidates are more likely to get elected for office and physically attractive defendants are less likely to be found guilty (Mazzella & Feingold, 1994; Sigelman, Thomas, Sigelman, & Ribich, 1986). However, other studies suggest that the advantage of physical attractiveness depends at least somewhat on context. Juhnke, Barmann, Cunningham, and Smith (1987) found that strangers were more willing to give detailed directions to college students who were poorly dressed and asking about the location of a lower status location (i.e., a thrift shop) than students who were well dressed or asking for directions to a higher status location (e.g., the Gap). In sum, physical appearance has repeatedly been shown to be a nonverbal signal that functions to increase or decrease the success of social influence attempts.

Credibility.   Besides physical attractiveness, research has shown that our perceptions of someone's credibility affect the degree to which they influence us. The notion of credibility refers to "the judgments made by a perceiver (e.g., a message recipient) concerning the believability of a communicator" (O'Keefe, 1990, pp. 130–131). Kinesic behaviors that are related to perceptions of credibility include eye contact, moderate amounts of gesturing, use of supportive head nods, facial expressiveness, and moderately forward leans, all indicators of conversational immediacy (see Burgoon, Birk, & Pfau, 1990). For example, Badzinski and Pettus (1994) showed that jurors determined a judge's credibility by attending to his or her kinesic behavior. Equipped with this knowledge, many lawyers approach the bench of jurors during opening and closing remarks, establish eye contact with each juror, and use other kinesic behaviors that are known to increase credibility ratings.

Besides kinesic elements, vocalic cues also affect perceptions of credibility. Among the most common findings is that nonfluencies in speech strongly decrease credibility ratings and the potential for successful persuasion. Nonfluencies include pauses in speech (e.g., "Auh," "Aummm"), repetition of "nonsense" words (e.g, "like"), and difficulty in articulation (O'Keefe, 1990). Besides the absence of nonfluencies, credible speakers use more varied intonation, speak more loudly and with more intensity, and talk faster (see Burgoon et al., 1996). But perhaps no other nonverbal code has received more attention for its effect on perceptions of credibility than physical appearance. For example, studies have shown that women who have specific eye shapes, short hair, appear older (although not elderly), wear a moderate amount of makeup, and are conservatively dressed were rated as more credible than their counterparts (Dellinger & Williams, 1997; Rosenberg, Kahn, & Tran, 1991). The final aspect known to increase persuadability is the perceived power of the speaker.

Power.   Power will be defined in this chapter as a perception that the speaker holds a position of authority. Like most assessments, this perception of authority is primarily established through nonverbal means. Again, perhaps the most common method of affecting perceptions of power is through physical appearance. Attire and physical size go a long way toward establishing a speaker's authority. For example, individuals wearing suits or uniforms, and those standing tall, as opposed to those with a slumped posture, are immediately afforded greater perceptions of power than their counterparts (see Andersen & Bowman, 1999). An extreme example of the effect of physical appearance on the success of influence came from Milgram's (1974) research program on obedience. In his studies, he showed that individuals dressed in lab coats were able to convince research participants to administer what participants believed to be fatal levels of electric shock to others. The result of Milgram's research program starkly demonstrated the degree to which people will obey others who they perceive to hold power positions, a perception primarily guided by nonverbal cues.

Deceiving Others

The last purpose of nonverbal messages that will be reviewed in this chapter is to deceive others. Deception is defined as "a message knowingly transmitted by a sender to foster a false belief or conclusion by a receiver" (Buller & Burgoon, 1996, p. 205). Although people assume that most interactions involve truth-telling, some studies suggest that a majority actually involve some element of deception (e.g., O'Hair & Cody, 1994). So, how is it that we get away with so much deception and when is it that we're likely to be caught? The answer to both questions lies in our manipulation of nonverbal behavior.

Interpersonal Deception Theory (Buller & Burgoon, 1996) is a framework that combines several perspectives to help explain the process of deception in interactions. Although the theory is quite complex, it relies primarily on the idea that deception is an interactive activity and that its detection is a process affected by the behavior of both sender and receiver, as well as contextual and relational factors. In other words, whether you are successful at lying is partly based on your nonverbal cues, but it is also affected by the receiver's behavior, the relationship you have with him or her, and the context surrounding the interaction, among other elements. Given the emphasis of this chapter, I will focus on the nonverbal behaviors that have been shown to affect the success of the deceiver.

Research suggests that successful liars are those who maintain eye contact, display a forward body lean, smile, and orient their bodies toward the other person (for review, see Buller & Burgoon, 1994). That is, people who can display elevated levels of immediacy are more likely to get away with a lie (Burgoon, Buller, Dillman, & Walther, 1995). Burgoon and colleagues offer at least two explanations for this finding. First, the high immediacy by receivers may produce an adaptational response by the deceiver—increased immediacy. That response, in turn, makes the deceiver appear honest. So, the receiver's immediacy "pulls" the liar into that behavioral pattern and causes him or her look more honest. Another possibility is that the receiver's immediacy makes the deceiver feel better about the success of his or her deception and lessens the anxiety cues that often "leak" from deceivers. In addition to the previously noted cues, successful liars display vocalic fluency and kinesic composure, while also being generally expressive nonverbally and avoiding extended pause rates during conversation. In contrast, unsuccessful liars "leak" their anxiety nonverbally through heightened pitch, greater nonfluencies, negative expressions, nervous behaviors, and generally lowered immediacy levels (for review, see Burgoon, Buller, & Guerrero, 1995).

Although the research on deception is vast and includes much more detailed analysis of factors affecting deception success and failure, among other aspects of the deception episode, the previously noted cues seem to capture some of the essential elements of deceiver behavior.

CONCLUSION

The research reviewed in this chapter leaves no doubt as to the impact of nonverbal messages on our lives. To summarize, nonverbal actions are often considered more important than verbal messages for determining message meaning. One reason for their importance is that they are omnipresent—an inherent part of every communication act. Indeed, there are seven codes of nonverbal behavior that could be simultaneously sending messages. For example, one could be communicating attraction by dressing nicely (physical appearance), maintaining eye contact (kinesics), interacting at a close distance (proxemics), lightly touching the other (haptics), varying vocal intonation (vocalics), extending the conversation (chronemics), and setting up the interaction to be in an intimate setting (artifacts). Relatedly, many of these cues could be serving multiple functions, from interaction management to emotion expression to relational management to influence. As such, it is important to keep nonverbal behaviors in mind when assessing the application of all communication theories; they undoubtedly play a critical role in explaining interaction outcomes.

ADDITIONAL READING

Given the breadth of the research on nonverbal communication, it is difficult to summarize the literature well. Nevertheless, there are very good texts available. Textbooks that do an exceptional job of summarizing the research in the area include Burgoon et al. (1996) and Andersen (1999). Another resource for interested readers is Guerrero, DeVito, and Hecht (1999), an edited volume that includes excellent readings from across the spectrum of nonverbal research, each written by some of the best scholars in the area.

Recommended readings within specific areas of nonverbal messages include Burgoon, Stern, et al. (1995) for nonverbal adaptation, DePaulo (1992) for research on nonverbal self-presentation strategies, and Henley (1977) for an extended discussion of dominance and sex differences in the use of touch.

REFERENCES

Afifi, W. A., & Johnson, M. L. (1999). The use and interpretation of tie signs in a public setting: Relationship and sex differences. *Journal of Social and Personal Relationships, 16,* 9–38.

Albas, D., & Albas, C. (1988). Acers and bombers: Post-exam impression management strategies of students. *Symbolic Interaction, 2,* 289–302.

Altman, I. (1975). *The environment and social behavior.* Monterey, CA: Brooks/Cole.

Andersen, P. A. (1999). *Nonverbal communication: Forms and functions.* Mountain View, CA: Mayfield.

Andersen, P. A., & Bowman, L. L. (1999). Positions of power: Nonverbal influence in organizational communication. In L. K. Guerrero, J. A. DeVito, & M. L. Hecht (Eds.), *The nonverbal communication reader: Classic and contemporary readings* (2nd ed., pp. 317–334). Prospect Heights, IL: Waveland.

Argyle, M. (1988). *Bodily communication* (2nd ed.). London: Methuen.

Aune, K. S. (1997). Self and partner perceptions of the appropriateness of emotions. *Communication Reports, 10,* 133–142.

Aune, K. S., Buller, D. B., & Aune, R. K. (1996). Display rule development in romantic relationships: Emotion management and perceived appropriateness of emotions across relationship stages. *Human Communication Research, 23,* 115–145.

Badzinski, D. M., & Pettus, A. B. (1994). Nonverbal involvement and sex: Effects on jury decisions making. *Journal of Applied Communication Research, 22,* 309–321.

Barnard, K. E., & Brazelton, T. B. (Eds.). (1990). *Touch: The foundation of experience.* Madison, CT: International Universities Press.

Blanck, P. D., Rosenthal, R., & Cordell, L. H. (1985). The appearance of justice: Judges' verbal and nonverbal behavior in criminal jury trials. *Stanford Law Review, 38,* 89–164.

Botta, R. A. (1999). Televised images and adolescent girls' body image disturbance. *Journal of Communication, 49,* 22–41.

Boomer, D. S. (1978). The phonemic clause: Speech unit in human communication. In A. W. Siegman & S. Feldstein (Eds.), *Nonverbal behavior and communication* (pp. 245–262). Hillsdale, NJ: Lawrence Erlbaum Associates, Inc.

Boyson, A. R., Pryor, B., & Butler, J. (1999). Height as power in women. *North American Journal of Psychology, 1,* 109–114.

Brown, P., & Levinson, S. (1987). *Universals in language usage: Politeness phenomena.* Cambridge, England: Cambridge University Press.

Buller, D. B., & Burgoon, J. K. (1994). Deception: Strategic and nonstrategic communication. In J. A. Daly & J. M. Wiemann (Eds.), *Strategic interpersonal communication* (pp. 191–223). Hillsdale, NJ: Lawrence Erlbaum Associates, Inc.

Buller, D. B., & Burgoon, J. K. (1996). Interpersonal Deception Theory. *Communication Theory, 6,* 203–242.

Buller, D. B., & Street, R. L., Jr. (1992). Physician-patient relationships. In R. S. Feldman (Ed.), *Applications of nonverbal theories and research* (pp. 119–141). Hillsdale, NJ: Lawrence Erlbaum Associates, Inc.

Burgoon, J. K. (1991). Relational messages interpretations of touch, conversational distance, and posture. *Journal of Nonverbal Behavior, 15,* 233–259.

Burgoon, J. K. (1994). Nonverbal signals. In M. L. Knapp & G. R. Miller (Eds.), *Handbook of interpersonal communication* (2nd ed., pp. 229–285). Thousand Oaks, CA: Sage.

Burgoon, J. K., Birk, T., & Pfau, M. (1990). Nonverbal behaviors, persuasion, and credibility. *Human Communication Research, 17,* 140–169.

Burgoon, J. K., Buller, D. B., Dillman, L., & Walther, J. B. (1995). Interpersonal deception: IV. Effects of suspicion on perceived communication and nonverbal behavior dynamics. *Human Communication Research, 22,* 163–196.

Burgoon, J. K., Buller, D. B., & Guerrero, L. K. (1995). Interpersonal deception: IX. Effects of social skill and nonverbal communication on deception success and detection accuracy. *Journal of Language and Social Psychology, 14,* 289–311.

Burgoon, J. K., Buller, D. B., & Woodall, W. G. (1996). *Nonverbal communication: The unspoken dialogue* (2nd ed.). New York: McGraw-Hill.

Burgoon, J. K., & Hale, J. L. (1987). Validation and measurement of the fundamental themes of relational communication. *Communication Monographs, 54,* 19–41.

Burgoon, J. K.,& Hale, J. L. (1988). Nonverbal expectancy violations: Model elaboration and application to immediacy behaviors. *Communication Monographs, 55,* 58–79.

Burgoon, J. K., Pfau, M., Parrott, R., Birk, T., Coker, R., & Burgoon, M. (1987). Relational communication, satisfaction, compliance-gaining strategies, and compliance in communication between physicians and patients. *Communication Monographs, 54,* 307–324.

Burgoon, J. K., Stern, L. A., & Dillman, L. (1995). *Interpersonal adaptation: Dyadic interaction patterns.* Cambridge, England: Cambridge University Press.

Buslig, A. L. S. (1999). 'Stop' signs: Regulating privacy with environmental features. In L. K. Guerrero, J. A. DeVito, & M. L. Hecht (Eds.), *The nonverbal communication reader: Classic and contemporary readings* (2nd ed., pp. 241–249). Prospect Heights, IL: Waveland.

Buss, D. M. (1994). *The evolution of desire.* New York: Basic Books.

Butler, S., & Roesel, K. (1991). Students perceptions of male teachers: Effects of teachers' dress and students' characteristics. *Perceptual and Motor Skills, 73,* 943–951.

Cappella, J. N., & Street, R. L. (1985). A functional approach to the structure of communicative behavior. In R. L. Street & J. N. Cappella (Eds.), *Sequence and pattern in communicative behavior* (pp. 1–29). London: Edward Arnold.

Cash. T. F., & Pruzinsky, T. (Eds.). (1990). *Body images: Development, deviance, and change.* New York: Guilford.

Cloven, D. H., & Roloff, M. E. (1994). A developmental model of decisions to withhold relational irritations in romantic relationships. *Personal Relationships, 1,* 143–164.

Daly, J. A., Hogg, E., Sacks, D., Smith, M., & Zimring, L. (1983). Sex and relationship affect social self-grooming. *Journal of Nonverbal Behavior, 7,* 183–189.

Dellinger, K., & Williams, C. L. (1997). Makeup at work: Negotiating appearance rules in the workplace. *Gender and Society, 11,* 151–177.

DePaulo, B. M. (1992). Nonverbal behavior and self-presentation. *Psychological Bulletin, 111,* 203–243.

Donoghue, E. (1992). Sociopsychological correlates of teenage pregnancy in the United States Virgin Islands. *International Journal of Mental Health, 21,* 39–49.

Eaves, M. H., & Leathers, D. G. (1991). Context as communication: McDonald's vs. Burger King. *Journal of Applied Communication, 19,* 263–289.

Eder, D. (1985). The cycle of popularity: Interpersonal relations among female adolescents. *Sociology of Education, 58,* 154–165.

Edwards, J. N., Fuller, T. D., Vorakitphokatorn, S., & Sermsri, S. (1994). *Household crowing and its consequences.* Boulder, CO: Westview.

Ekman, P. (1973). *Darwin and facial expression: A century of research in review.* New York: Academic.

Ekman, P. (1978). Facial expression. In A. W. Siegman & S. Feldstein (Eds.), *Nonverbal behavior and communication* (pp. 96–116). Hillsdale, NJ: Lawrence Erlbaum Associates, Inc.

Ekman, P., & Friesen, W. V. (1969). The repertoire of nonverbal behavior: Categories, origins, usage, and coding. *Semiotica, 1,* 49–98.

Ekman, P., & Oster, H. (1979). Facial expression of emotion. *Annual Review of Psychology, 30,* 527–554.

Forbes, R. J., & Jackson, P. R. (1980). Nonverbal behavior and the outcome of selection interviews. *Journal of Occupational Psychology, 53,* 67–72.

Gallois, C., Giles, H., Jones, E., Cargile, A. C., & Ota, H. (1995). Accommodating intercultural encounters: Elaborations and extensions. *International and Intercultural Communication Annual, 19,* 115–147.

Gifford, R., Ng, C. F., Wilkinson, M. (1985). Nonverbal cues in the employment interview: Links between applicant qualities and interviewer judgments. *Journal of Applied Psychology, 70,* 729–736.

Giles, H., Mulac, A., Bradac, J. J., & Johnson. P. (1987). Speech Accommodation Theory: The first decade and beyond. In M. McLaughlin (Ed.), *Communication Yearbook* (Vol. 10, pp. 13–48). Newbury Park, CA: Sage.

Goffman, E. (1959). *The presentation of self in everyday life.* Garden City, NY: Doubleday.

Goldman, M., Kiyohara, O., & Pfannensteil, D. A. (1985). Interpersonal touch, social labeling, and the foot-in-the-door effect. *Journal of Social Psychology, 125,* 143–147.

Gonzalez, A., & Zimbardo, P. G. (1999). Time in perspective. In L. K. Guerrero, J. A. DeVito, & M. L. Hecht (Eds.), *The nonverbal communication reader: Classic and contemporary readings* (2nd ed., pp. 227–236). Prospect Heights, IL: Waveland.

Gress, J. E., & Heft, H. (1998). Do territorial actions attenuate the effects of high density? A field study. In J. Sanford & B. R. Connell (Eds.), *People, places, and public policy* (pp. 47–52). Edmond, OK: Environmental Design Research Association.

Gross, R., Sasson, Y., Zarhy, M., & Zohar, J. (1998). Healing environment in psychiatric hospitals. *General Hospital Psychiatry, 20,* 108–114.

Grumet, G. W. (1983). Eye contact: The core of interpersonal relatedness. *Psychiatry, 48,* 172–180.

Guerrero, L. K., Devito, J. A., & Hecht, M. L. (Eds.). (1999). *The nonverbal communication reader: Classic and contemporary readings* (2nd ed.). Prospect Heights, IL: Waveland.

Hall, E. T. (1966). *The hidden dimension* (2nd ed.). Garden City, NY: Anchor/Doubleday.

Hall, E. T., & Hall, M. R. (1999). Monochronic and polychronic time. In L. K. Guerrero, J. A. DeVito, & M. L. Hecht (Eds.), *The nonverbal communication reader: Classic and contemporary readings* (2nd ed., pp. 237–240). Prospect Heights, IL: Waveland.

Harris, M. J., Rosenthal, R., & Snodgrass, S. E. (1986). The effects of teacher expectations, gender, and behavior on pupil academic performance and self-concept. *Journal of Educational Research, 79,* 173–179.

Henley, N. M. (1977). *Body politics: Power, sex, and nonverbal communication.* Englewood Cliffs, NJ: Prentice-Hall.

Hess, E. H. (1975). The role of pupil size in communication. *Scientific American, 233,* 110–119.

Izard, C. E. (1977). *Human emotions.* New York: Plenum.

Jones, S. E., & Yarbrough, A. E. (1985). A naturalistic study of the meanings of touch. *Communication Monographs, 52,* 19–56.

Juhnke, R., Barmann, B., Cunningham, M., & Smith, E. (1987). Effects of attractiveness and nature of request on helping behavior. *Journal of Social Psychology, 127,* 317–322.

Kaiser, S. B. (1997). *The social psychology of clothing: Symbolic appearances in context* (2nd ed.). New York: Fairchild.

Kupperbusch, C., Matsumoto, D., Kooken, K., Loewinger, S., Uchida, H., Wilson-Cohn, C., et al. (1999). Cultural influences on nonverbal expressions of emotion. In P. Philippot, R. S. Feldman, & E. J. Coats (Eds.), *The social context of nonverbal behavior* (pp. 17–44). Cambridge, England: Cambridge University Press.

Lamude, K. G., Daniels, T. D., & Smilowitz, M. (1995). Subordinates(satisfaction with communication and managers' relational messages. *Perceptual and Motor Skills, 81,* 467–471.

Lamude, K. G., & Scudder, J. (1991). Hierarchical levels and type of relational messages. *Communication Research Reports, 8,* 149–157.

Lester, D. (1990). Overcrowding in prisons and rates of suicide and homocide. *Perceptual and Motor Skills, 71,* 274.

Lukavsky, J., Butler, S., & Harden, A. J. (1995). Perceptions of an instructor: Dress and students' characteristics. *Perceptual and Motor Skills, 81,* 231–240.

Lyman, S. M., & Scott, M. B. (1967). Territoriality: A neglected sociological dimension. *Social Problems, 15,* 236–249.

Malatesta, C. Z., & Haviland, J. M. (1982). Learning display rules: The socialization of emotion expression in infancy. *Child Development, 53,* 991–1003.

Martel, L. F., & Biller, H. B. (1987). *Stature and stigma: The biopsychosocial development of short males.* Lexington, MA: Lexington.

Mazzella, R., & Feingold, A. (1994). The effects of physical attractiveness, race, socioeconomic status, and gender of defendants and victims on judgments of mock jurors: A meta-analysis. *Journal of Applied Social Psychology, 24,* 1315–1344.

Milgram, S. (1974). *Obedience to authority: An experimental view.* New York: Harper & Row.

Mills, J., & Aronson, E. (1965). Opinion change as a function of the communicator's attractiveness and desire to influence. *Journal of Personality and Social Psychology, 1,* 74–77.

Monsour, M. (2002). *Women and men as friends: Relationships across the life span in the 21st century.* Mahwah, NJ: Lawrence Erlbaum Associates, Inc.

Montagu, A. (1978). *Touching: The human significance of the skin* (2nd ed.). New York: Harper & Row.

Montepare, J. M., & Vega, C. (1988). Women's vocal reactions to intimate and casual male friends. *Personality and Social Psychology, 14,* 103–113.

Morris, D. (1971). *Intimate behavior.* New York: Random House.

Nussbaum, M. C. (2000). Emotions and social norms. In L. P. Nucci & G. B. Saxe (Eds.), *Culture, thought, and development* (pp. 41–63). Mahwah, NJ: Lawrence Erlbaum Associates, Inc.

O'Hair, H. D., & Cody, M. J. (1994). Deception. In W. R. Cupach & B. H. Spitzberg (Eds.), *The dark side of interpersonal communication* (pp. 181–214). Hillsdale, NJ: Lawrence Erlbaum Associates, Inc.

O'Keefe, D. J. (1990). *Persuasion: Theory and research.* Newbury Park, CA: Sage.

Phillips, K. A. (1999). Body dysmorphic disorder and depression: Theoretical considerations and treatment strategies. *Psychiatric Quarterly, 70,* 313–331.

Rivano-Fischer, M. (1988). Micro territorial behavior in public transport vehicles: A field study on a bus route. *Psychological Research Bulletin, 28,* 18.

Robinson, J. D. (1998). Getting down to business: Talk, gaze, and body orientation during openings of doctor-patient consultations. *Human Communication Research, 25,* 97–123.

Rosenberg, S. W., Kahn, S., & Tran, T. (1991). Creating a political image: Shaping appearance and manipulating the vote. *Political Behavior, 13,* 345–367.

Schlenker, B. R., Britt, T. W., & Pennington, J. (1996). Impression regulation and management: Highlights of a theory of self-identification. In R. M. Sorrentino & E. T. Higgins (Eds.), *Handbook of motivation and cognition: The interpersonal context* (Vol. 3, pp. 118–147). New York: Guilford.

Segrin, C. (1999). The influence of nonverbal behaviors in compliance-gaining processes. In L. K. Guerrero, J. A. DeVito, & M. L. Hecht (Eds.), *The nonverbal communication reader: Classic and contemporary readings* (2nd ed., pp. 335–346). Prospect Heights, IL: Waveland.

Semic, B. (1999). Vocal attractiveness: What sounds beautiful is good. In L. K. Guerrero, J. A. DeVito, & M. L. Hecht (Eds.), *The nonverbal communication reader: Classic and contemporary readings* (2nd ed., pp. 149–155). Prospect Heights, IL: Waveland.

Sheppard, J. A., & Strathman, A. J. (1989). Attractiveness and height: The role of stature in dating preference, frequency of dating, and perceptions of attractiveness. *Personality and Social Psychology Bulletin, 15,* 617–627.

Sigelman, C. K., Thomas, D. B., Sigelman, L., & Ribich, F. D. (1986). Gender, physical attractiveness, and electability: An experimental investigation of voter biases. *Journal of Applied Social Psychology, 16,* 229–248.

Stice, E., Hayward, C., Cameron, R. P., Killen, J. D., & Taylor, C. B. (2000). Body-image and eating disturbances predict onset of depression among female adolescents: A longitudinal study. *Journal of Abnormal Psychology, 109,* 438–444.

Sundstrom, E., Bell, P. A., Busby, P. L., & Asmus, C. (1996). Environmental psychology 1989–1994. *Annual Review of Psychology, 47,* 482–512.

Tajfel, H., & Turner, J. C. (1979). An integrative theory of group conflict. In W. G. Austin & S. Worchel (Eds.), *The social psychology of intergroup relations* (pp. 33–47). Monterey, CA: Brooks-Cole.

Tracy, K. (1990). The many faces of facework. In H. Giles & W. P. Robinson (Eds.), *Handbook of language and social psychology* (pp. 209–226). Chichester, England: John Wiley & Sons.

Wiemann, J. M., & Knapp, M. L. (1975). Turn-taking in conversation. *Journal of Communication, 25,* 75–92.

Worschel, S., & Austin, W. G. (Eds.). (1986). *The social psychology of intergroup relations.* Chicago: Nelson Hall.

QUESTIONS TO PONDER

1. Given the research reviewed in this chapter, which code would you argue is the one that most affects our daily lives? Provide evidence for why the one you choose is significantly more important than other codes.

2. There were several studies discussed that had implications for people's performance on job interviews or other important interactions. What nonverbal behaviors would you recommend to someone going on a job interview? What nonverbal behaviors should this person avoid at all costs?

3. In this chapter, nonverbal research was applied to a few theories and I argued that many other theories have been applied to explain nonverbal behaviors. Think of three theories discussed in the book (but not in this chapter) and apply them to the nonverbal arena.

4. QVC and other home shopping channels make hundreds of millions of dollars by persuading viewers to make purchases they may otherwise not consider making. Nonverbal messages play a very important role in their success. Watch these channels carefully and review the ways they use nonverbal messages to influence viewers.

5. Watch Sunday morning political talk and interview shows. Closely examine how the nonverbal messages of both the interviewer and the person being interviewed affect their credibility. Pay especially close attention to kinesics, vocalics, and physical appearance. How does the interviewee recover from a possible threat to their credibility? What does he or she do nonverbally in these cases?

4

Impression Formation

Charles Pavitt
University of Delaware

INTRODUCTION

Imagine the following circumstance: We are at a party at a friend's house. One of the party-goers is a person whom we have never previously met, introduced by our friend as Joe Schmo. Over the course of the party, we observe Joe at different times spill his drink on the floor, knock over a bowl of popcorn, and step on people's feet as he walks around the house. Suppose that at the end of the party, a stranger walks in the door, introduces himself as Professor Nosey, and gives us a survey that asks the following 10 questions about Joe Schmo:

1. Does Joe pause a lot when he is speaking?
2. Does Joe listen well to others when they talk?
3. Does Joe act awkwardly?
4. Does Joe smile a lot?
5. Is Joe an honest person?
6. Is Joe a clumsy person?
7. Is Joe a friendly person?
8. Is Joe a stubborn person?
9. How much do you think you would like Joe?
10. How much would you want Joe as a friend?

Surely, having a Professor Nosey give us a survey at the end of a party is a very implausible event. However, it is plausible that, at some time, we might ask ourselves some of these same questions about Joe Schmo. They are questions that reflect the process of *impression formation*. An impression is an image that we form of people we meet. The image consists of a set of beliefs that describes the person. The process of forming an impression consists of four stages. First, we observe a person's behavior. Next, we attribute a cause for the behavior.

Third, if we believe the person to be the cause for that behavior (in a sense of the word *cause* that I will describe in a moment) we form an impression of her or him. Finally, based on this impression, we make an evaluation, or like versus dislike judgment, of the person.

In this chapter, I will discuss the four stages that occur when we form an impression of someone we meet. Next, to show that the impression formation process occurs not just at parties but in many different types of situations, I will describe its impact in a much different circumstance: group leadership. Finally, I will describe some additional factors that are present when we learn about people second-hand, through communication with a third person. But before any of this, I wish to answer the following question: What is the function performed by impressions?

THE "NAIVE SCIENTIST" METAPHOR

The most influential thinking about impression formation appeared in a book published in 1958 by a psychologist named Fritz Heider. As is often the case in theorizing about people, Heider adopted a particular metaphor as the foundation of his work. It has come to be known as the "naive scientist" metaphor. According to this metaphor, when people communicate with one another, their activities can be compared to those of scientists at work. The main goal of scientists is the formulation of theories. The task of a theory is to provide the scientist with four capabilities:

1. To describe relevant phenomena. A meteorologist, for example, might want to form a description of the important characteristics of a hurricane.
2. To explain this phenomena. The meteorologist would want to provide an explanation for how hurricanes form and sustain themselves.
3. To predict this phenomena. The meteorologist would want to predict when and where hurricanes will form.
4. To control this phenomena. Although it is not possible at this time, the meteorologist would like to be able to influence hurricane formation and movement so as to keep people out of harm's way.

The order in which I have listed these four capabilities is not random. The scientist cannot do anything without a description of what she is studying. With that description of what something is like, the scientist can then formulate an explanation for how that something got to be that way. At this point, the scientist knows what she needs to know to make predictions about it and, if it is at all possible, to control the way it acts.

Let us adopt this metaphor for the human communicator. When we meet another person, we act like scientists, even though most of us have not had scientific training (this is why we call the metaphor the "naive" scientist, using "naive" in the sense of "unsophisticated"). First, we try to describe how that person acts. Then, we attempt to explain why that person acts that way. Armed with this explanation, we can now try to predict how that person will act in the future. Finally, although we cannot control people's actions the way that, for example, a chemist can control the composition of some material he is making, we can perhaps influence them. To reach these goals, we form a theory about what the person is like. That theory is our impression of that person.

As I describe the four stages in the impression formation process in the upcoming sections, I will relate these stages to the "naive scientist" metaphor. In addition to those theories I will discuss, others have adopted this metaphor. One of these is uncertainty management theory, and Brasher (chap.11, this volume) describes some strategies people use to gain information and thus form impressions about other people.

STAGE 1: OBSERVING BEHAVIOR

The first stage in the impression formation process is the observation of a person's behavior. Of course, whenever we are observing people, we are observing their behavior. This is because, as Watzlawick, Beavin, and Jackson (1967) reminded us, behavior has no opposite. In other words, people are behaving in some way at all times. Some of this behavior is verbal, but much of it is nonverbal, and, as Afifi describes (chap. 3, this volume), people are always observing and making judgments about one another's nonverbal behaviors. In fact, even sleeping can be considered a type of nonverbal behavior that people can observe that can enter into the impression formation process. Further, behavior occurs in a never-ending stream, sometimes changing quickly, at other times varying slowly over time. As observers of people's behavior, we are prone to try to make sense of it. This sense-making process consists of two parts: *unitizing* and *labeling*.

When we unitize, we divide our observations of behavior into manageable sections. These sections can be of various sizes, depending on what we wish to do with our observations. Most of the time, we are satisfied with relatively coarse-grained observations. For example, we might consider "starting a car" as one unit of behavior. Sometimes, however, we have a reason to divide our observations into more finely grained units. Suppose we were teaching someone who has never driven how to start a car. We would have to describe it in a number of steps, including putting the key into the ignition, releasing the emergency brake, stepping just a little bit on the gas pedal as we turn the key, moving the stick from neutral into gear, and so on. Research by Newtson and Engquist (1976) suggested that people with similar goals concerning what they are doing with their observations divide up a stream of behavior into similar units. Going back to the party, we would probably agree that Joe is "talking to someone," and then "walking across the room," and then "sitting in a chair."

But would we agree on what to call these units? Maybe not, because different people, and even the same person in different situations, might use different terms to describe the same behavior. For example, one person might use a relatively neutral description, such as "Joe talked loudly," whereas others might use more positive ("Joe spoke with enthusiasm and energy") or negative ("Joe yelled and screamed") terminology for the same behavior. One type of factor that will affect a behavior's label is the context in which the behavior occurs. We are more likely to label Joe's loud talking as "yelling and screaming" if we see Joe engaged in an argument than if we see Joe is fooling around with his friends. The characteristics of the person making the observation are another type of factor that affects behavior labeling. Just for one example, we are more likely to see Joe as "yelling and screaming" if we are in a bad mood than if we are feeling good.

The behaviors we have seen Joe perform might, as a set, be labeled as "acting awkwardly." Therefore, there is a good chance that we might have given Joe a high rating for the third question on Professor Nosey's survey. So we, as "naive scientists," now have a description of Joe's behavior. But the impression formation process has only begun.

STAGE 2: ATTRIBUTING THE CAUSE OF THE BEHAVIOR

Why did Joe act awkwardly? We could perhaps think of several different reasons. Some of these reasons are circumstantial; Joe may have had a bit too much to drink tonight, or perhaps he has had a long week and is particularly tired. Other reasons are not so incidental; perhaps Joe characteristically acts awkwardly. In the second stage of the impression formation process, we attempt to explain the behavior by deciding which of these reasons is correct.

Most important here is the distinction between attributing the cause of the behavior to *circumstance* and attributing it to Joe's *character* or *personality*. If we believe that Joe's behavior is due to circumstance, then we do not see it as indicating anything about Joe. In this case, the impression formation process ends at this point. If, instead, we believe that acting awkwardly is characteristic of Joe, then we accept it as indicative of what type of person Joe actually is. It is in this case that we begin building our impression of Joe, by assigning Joe a *trait* that we believe to be indicated by a particular behavior.

A "trait" is a label we give to designate what we believe to be a characteristic of a person's personality. As such, we expect it to influence that person's behavior in many different circumstances. Going back to the "naive scientist" metaphor, we use traits to explain what we have seen people do in the past, to predict what they are likely to do in the future, and sometimes to try to influence their behavior. In Professor Nosey's survey, there is a trait that is related to Joe's party behavior: "clumsy." If we decided that Joe's behavior is the result of his personality, we are likely to have given him a high rating on that question. We are then using this trait, clumsiness, to explain why Joe acted as he did. We would also use this trait to predict that Joe is likely to make an expensive mess if he went to an expensive china shop and, if the situation arose, to try to persuade him not to go.

It is important to keep in mind the distinction between traits and behaviors. Behaviors are things we can see. We saw Joe spilling his drink and stepping on feet. Traits are things we *cannot* see. We cannot see "clumsy." What we *can* see are behaviors that we believe indicate clumsiness. There is a simple way that usually works to tell traits and behaviors apart. Descriptions of traits normally require the use of some form of the verb *is* ("is clumsy"). Descriptions of behaviors normally require the use of an action verb ("spills a drink"). One reason for keeping the contrast between behaviors and traits in mind is that, if we want people to change their behavior, it will only work if we can describe to them the behavior we want them to change. If we say to Joe "don't be so clumsy," he has the right to ask us "how do I do that?" If, instead, we say to Joe "think about where your feet and hands are going," then we have told him what he needs to know to change the way he acts.

How, then, do we decide whether a behavior is the result of a person's character rather than mere circumstance? Various "attribution theories" have attempted to provide an answer to this question. According to Jones and Davis (1965), we are likely to consider a behavior as due to someone's personality to the extent that the behavior is unusual and extreme. In most situations, there are types of behavior that are socially acceptable. It is not too hard to come up with a list of the sorts of things one expects people to do at weddings, funerals, job interviews, and the like. When a person's actions are consistent with those expectations, then we usually do not see the actions as telling us very much about the person. When actions are inconsistent with our expectations, however, we often consider them as indicative of the *real* person. One is not supposed to act awkwardly at parties, and so we may take Joe's unusual behavior to mean that he is a clumsy person.

Sometimes, we have the opportunity to compare a person's behavior with that of other people, or even with that of the same person at other times. Kelley (1967) claimed that, when comparisons are possible, we use three types of information to help us decide whether or not the person's character or the circumstance is responsible. Imagine the behavior we want to explain is Joe's stepping on Phil Thrill's foot during the party. According to Kelley we would ask three questions about that behavior. First, is there *distinctiveness* in that behavior; in other words, does the person act the same way when interacting with the same people over time? For example, does Joe step on Phil's foot in other situations? Second, is there *consistency* in that behavior; in other words, does the person act the same way when interacting with other people? We saw Joe step on Phil's foot during the party; did he also step on Sue Blue's? Third, is there *consensus* in that behavior; in other words, does everyone step on Phil Thrill's foot?

We combine the answers to these three questions when we decide whether the person's character or the circumstance is responsible for a behavior. There are several possible combinations that lead to differing decisions about responsibility. If the behavior is high on consistency but low on distinctiveness and consensus (Joe is the only person stepping on people's feet, and he does it to everyone all the time), then we are likely to assign responsibility to the person (in this case, conclude that Joe is clumsy). If consensus and consistency is high but distinctiveness is low (not just Joe but everyone is stepping on everyone else's feet during the party, but not in other situations), then the situation is likely to be seen as responsible (perhaps we decide that the room is too crowded). If consensus and distinctiveness is high but consistency is low (not only Joe but everyone steps on Phil, and Joe does not step on other people), then the "target" of the behavior (in this case, Phil) is to blame. Finally, if consistency and distinctiveness is high and consensus is low (Joe always steps on Phil's feet but nobody else's, and nobody else steps on Phil), then there is something unique about the interaction between the two people that leads to this behavior.

The ideas proposed by Jones and Davis (1965) and by Kelley (1967) make a lot of sense. However, we are not always so sensible when trying to explain the cause of a behavior. We are prone to various *biases* in the process. I need to make it clear what the term *bias* means. A bias is a nonrandom error. In other words, it is an error that tends toward one direction rather than another. When error is random, it is impossible to predict the direction the error will take, whereas when error is nonrandom we would generally be able to guess the error's direction. Let us imagine that a group of us were trying to guess how many marbles are in a bottle. About half of us guess a number that is too high, while the other half of us guesses a number that is too low. This would reflect random error. If, instead, almost all of us guess a number that is too high, then there would be a bias in our guessing.

In terms of attributions, we tend to overestimate the extent to which other people's character is responsible for their behavior. However, we tend not to make that error when judging our actions. This bias has come to be known as the *fundamental attribution error*. The main reason why the fundamental attribution error exists appears to be the *salience* of other people in our perceptions. In other words, people tend to be the most interesting things around us, so we normally pay attention to what they are doing, rather than to what other objects in that field are doing, including ourselves. Because our attention tends to be directed toward other people, it is natural for us to give responsibility to those people when explaining their actions. We are not as likely to have our attention directed toward other things in the situation that could be influencing the person's actions. In particular, we cannot see ourselves, so we tend to ignore the effect that our own behavior has on others. Yet, we are conscious of the effect that other things in the situation, including other people, have on our own actions.

This bias is accentuated when the behavior we are trying to explain is one we would evaluate as undesirable or bad. To protect our self-esteem, we are prone to take responsibility for good things and try to blame others for things that are bad. Therefore, if something bad happens between us, we tend to blame the other person for it, rather than ourselves. This tendency has come to be known as the *self-serving motivational bias*. Sillars (1980) discussed how the self-serving motivational bias tends to aggravate conflicts between people. If two people are angry at one another about something that happened between them, each is likely to blame the other for it and to see their own behavior as merely a reasonable reaction to what the other did. Unless these people can overcome this tendency, their conflict is likely to continue and worsen.

To return to our initial example, we are likely to see Joe's awkward behavior as indicative of Joe's inherent clumsiness, even though if *we* were to perform the same behavior we would be prone to attribute it to happenstance. We are now ready to form the rest of our impression of Joe.

STAGE 3: FORMING THE IMPRESSION

Let us presume that we have concluded that Joe is acting awkwardly because he is an inherently clumsy person. Therefore, we have given him a high rating for "clumsy" along with "acts awkwardly" on Professor Nosey's survey. But what about the questions on the survey about other behaviors and traits? Did we give Joe a high rating for "pauses a lot when he is speaking" and for "stubborn?" Or did we assign him low grades for "smiles a lot" and for "friendly"? Research findings suggest that we are likely to have made those judgments. In the third stage of the impression formation process, we form our impression of the person we have observed. In so doing, we tend to include in that impression other behaviors that we believe to be related to the behavior we saw and other traits that we believe to be related to the trait we chose as the cause of the observed behavior.

An insight into the process by which we form impressions is one of the first contributions made by social scientists to our understanding about interpersonal communication. Back in 1920, Thorndike discovered the *halo effect*, or tendency for people to presume that if someone has a trait that we think of as "good," the person also has other "good" traits. Therefore, if we believe Sue Blue to be "intelligent," we are also likely to believe that she is "honest" and "hard-working." Just 2 years later, Rugg (1922) discovered the analogous *horns effect*, or the tendency for people to see one "bad" trait as implying other "bad" ones. This is why there is a tendency for us to presume that "clumsy" Joe is also "stubborn." In 1931, Newcomb found that our judgments of behaviors work similarly. Joe "acting awkwardly" suggests to us that he must "pause a lot when he is speaking," and Sue "listening well to others" means that she also "smiles a lot."

You might think that this inclination makes no sense, because there is no logical reason why, for example, clumsiness has anything to do with stubbornness. There may indeed be no *logical* reason for these assumptions, but people do make them more often than not, so there must be a *psychological* reason behind the tendency. In 1954, Bruner and Tagiuri proposed such a reason: the existence of *implicit personality theories* in our mind. An implicit personality theory is an image we have of the traits possessed by, and behaviors performed by, various "types" of people. In the following 20 years, researchers found that people have distinctly different ideas about the characteristics of some of these types. Research by Beilin (1963) found people to consider policeman to be reliable, honest, and persistent; librarians to be intelligent, disciplined, and serious; and lawyers to be confident, shrewd, and argumentative.

My research in impression formation has been concerned with implicit personality theories that are relevant to communication and how these implicit theories are used to form impressions of communicators that we have observed (Pavitt, 1989; Pavitt & Haight, 1986). Let us suppose, as my research suggests, that people have an implicit theory relevant to the characteristics of the "ideal communicator." We begin using this implicit theory in situations in which we have observed a communicator's behavior and attributed the cause of the behavior to the person's character. We then use the implicit theory as a mold from which we form the impression. If, for example, we watch Sue Blue "smiling a lot" and attribute the cause of that behavior to the trait "friendly," we then subconsciously examine our implicit theory of the "ideal communicator" for other characteristics relevant to these characteristics. If our implicit theory includes the beliefs that "smiles a lot" and "is friendly" are *positively* related to "listens well to others" and "is honest" (in other words, if Sue is high on the first two, then she will be high on the second two), then these latter attributes will be included in our just-formed impression of Sue. If our implicit theory includes the beliefs that "smiles a lot" and "is friendly" are *negatively* related to "pauses a lot before speaking" and "is stubborn" (in other words, if Sue is high on the first two, then she will be low on the second two), then our impression of Sue will include the information that she does *not* pause a lot and is *not* stubborn.

The impact of our implicit theory on our impression of Joe works similarly, except that it begins with a behavior and trait that the ideal communicator does not have. Joe "acts awkwardly" and "is clumsy," both of which are positively related to "pauses a lot" and "is stubborn," and negatively related to "smiles a lot" and "is friendly," in our implicit theory of the ideal communicator. Therefore, our impression of Joe is likely to include this information, and we are prone to making judgments about Joe's pausing, friendliness, and the other questions on Professor Nosey's survey. Note that the presence of implicit theories accounts for the early research findings we described earlier. Our judgments of Sue were subject to the halo effect, and our judgments of Joe to the horns effect, as a consequence of the workings of implicit theory.

One final, but important, issue remains before we move on. Our implicit theories are partly formed as a result of our observation of other people. If we have seen people who "pause a lot before speaking" also "act awkwardly" much of the time, then we are bound to learn that these two behaviors are associated. However, the bulk of the information in our implicit theories is not based on direct observation but is learned from others. This is particularly the case for various person "types." Most of us have not had a great deal of experience observing the behaviors of bank managers and gardeners, but we have learned from others a *culturally shared image* of what these types of people are supposed to be like. Such culturally shared implicit theories are often called *stereotypes*. Although it can be argued that we need stereotypes to make sense of the people we see around us, they are often incorrect, and throughout human history, stereotypes have had disastrous effects on the way people treat other people. Far too many of us believe, for no good reason, that Blacks are lazy, that Southerners lack intelligence, that Asians are untrustworthy, that Arabs are religious fanatics, and so forth. Because stereotypes are so natural to us, it may be too much to ask that we discard them, but it is *not* asking too much of us to be aware of their negative effects and to work actively to disregard them when making judgments about people.

There are still two questions unanswered on Professor Nosey's survey: First, how much would we think that we would like Joe, and second, how much would we want him as a friend. I turn to these questions, and the final stage of the impression formation process, next.

STAGE 4: MAKING AN EVALUATION

At this point in the impression formation process, we have a newly formed picture of Joe. We have labeled his behavior as "acting awkwardly," attributed the reason for this behavior to being "clumsy," and formed an impression with related characteristics such as "pauses a lot before speaking" and "stubborn." One feature that all of these behaviors and traits share is that most of us would tend to evaluate them negatively. We are likely to believe that it is bad to act awkwardly and pause a lot before speaking, that it is bad to be clumsy and stubborn, and that we would tend to dislike a person with those attributes and not want to become friends with them. Therefore, our ratings for Joe on the last two questions in Professor Nosey's survey are likely to be low. These last two questions reflect the last stage of the impression formation process, our evaluation (or judgment of liking or disliking) of the relevant person.

This evaluation is based on the extent to which we think that each of the characteristics in our impression is positive or negative. There is, in fact, research showing that people have very definite and consistent opinions about the favorability of particular traits (Anderson, 1968). Sincere, honest, understanding, loyal, and dependable rank among the most positive; cruel, mean, phony, and deceitful are among the least. Research has also shown that our overall evaluation of a person can be estimated pretty well if we take the average evaluation of the traits in our impression of that person (Anderson, 1965). Therefore, Joe would be evaluated negatively. If we think Sue Blue is "friendly" and "honest," our evaluation of her would be positive. An impression of someone including both positive and negative traits would be somewhere in the neutral range.

There are, however, exceptions to this averaging rule. Sometimes the evaluation of a combination of traits cannot be predicted by averaging the evaluations of the traits making up that combination. This seems to occur when a combination of traits reminds us of a relevant stereotype. For example, people evaluate "irresponsible" negatively, whereas "father" tends to be judged positively. The evaluation of the combination of the two, "irresponsible father," is not the average of the two alone; rather, it tends to be even more negative than "irresponsible" alone. One can imagine that the description "irresponsible father" calls up images of starving children and a broken home, leading to particularly negative feelings. Analogously, whereas "dishonest" is rated negatively and "generous" positively, their combination reminds at least some people of a Robin Hood type of person, leading to a positive overall evaluation.

Going back to our example, we have finished the process of forming an impression of Joe. Referring back to the "naive scientist" metaphor, we have completed our theories of Joe that we can use to describe, explain, and predict his behavior. We have what you need to make a decision whether or not we want to interact with Joe in the future, and if we do, under what circumstances and in what ways. At least for the time being, our "scientific" work is complete.

From what I have described thus far in this chapter, it should be obvious that the process of impression formation is a central part of the manner by which we make friends and acquaintanceships with other people. It is, in addition, also important on other circumstances. In the following section, I will describe the part that the impression formation process plays in group leadership.

APPLICATION TO GROUP LEADERSHIP

If I were to ask you the attributes of a good group leader, what would you tell me? When I asked some students to list a few of these characteristics, several traits and behaviors stood out. For instance, they believed that a good leader should be intelligent, enthusiastic, and organized, that a good leader should encourage group member participation, facilitate group discussion, and manage conflict among group members. Clearly, people have beliefs about what a good leader is and does. Could these beliefs act as an implicit personality theory specifically about leadership, and influence group members' impressions and evaluations of their group's leadership? Along with three other researchers, I performed a study to find out (Pavitt, Whitchurch, McClurg, & Petersen, 1995).

Even before our research, there was reason to believe that people have implicit theories of leadership. Several studies (e.g., Eden & Leviatan, 1975) have shown that when people are asked to rate fictitious organizational leaders ("the manager of a plant you do not know, that makes food products and is located in the central region of the country"), their answers are comparable to ratings people make of real organizational leaders. These studies seem to demonstrate that, through experience and education, people have acquired a set of beliefs about the characteristics shared by successful leaders. Other research, reviewed by Lord (1985), has suggested that these beliefs affect people's judgments of leaders when they have the opportunity to observe those leaders in action.

In our study, students answered a survey designed to measure their implicit theories of leadership. About a month later, groups of these students who did not previously know one another participated in a discussion, during which they talked about possible solutions to a personnel problem faced by an imaginary organization. After the discussion, they judged one another's leadership-relevant traits and behaviors and evaluated one another's leadership performance during the discussion. The results showed very strong relationships among the students' implicit theories about leadership, their impressions of one another's leadership-relevant characteristics, and their evaluations of one another's leadership performance. In other words, the students formed impressions and made evaluations of one another as group leaders using the same type of process that we used in forming our impression and evaluation of Joe.

Findings such as these are important, because they help us understand why some groups are successful at meeting their members' goals and others fail. For a group to be successful, it needs effective leaders. However, leaders can only be effective if they have the trust and support of the rest of the group. If the members of a group judge their leaders negatively, then it is almost impossible for their leaders to be effective, and the group is sure to fail. Effective leadership can only occur when the members of a group believe in their leader's ability. If it is the case that group members use their implicit theories of leadership when making judgments about their leaders' ability, then these theories can act as a standard that leaders need to reach in order to gain the members' trust, do their job effectively, and help their group reach its members' goals. In other words, if a leader performs those behaviors that their group's members expect (such as encouraging participation and facilitating discussion), then the members will form a good impression of the leader (as, e.g., enthusiastic and organized), have positive feelings toward that leader, and are more likely to work effectively with that leader to reach their group's goals.

INDIRECT IMPRESSION FORMATION

Thus far, I have described the process of impression formation under circumstances in which people have the opportunity to observe and communicate with the person they are interested in learning about. In our imaginary example, we watched Joe's behavior at a party, and in my own research, people interacted with other members of their discussion group. There are times, however, when we wish to learn about a person that we cannot observe or with whom we cannot communicate. Suppose that we did not get to our imaginary party, but when we ask about it, our friend tells us something like the following: "I invited a guy I met in class named Joe Schmo, and it was a mistake. He kept stepping on people's feet, he knocked over a bowl of popcorn, and he kept spilling his drinks. We had to keep cleaning up after him." Would our process of impression formation work the same way as if we had actually seen Joe? Would we attribute the cause of his behavior to inherent clumsiness, form an impression with related characteristics, and evaluate Joe negatively? Research described by Hewes and Graham (1988) suggested that we might not. Particularly when we think that it is important for us to make an accurate judgment, we sometimes think about the possibility that what we heard about somebody from a third person might not be entirely reliable. In those circumstances we are likely to *second-guess*. Second-guessing occurs when we assume that there is some bias in the third person's report and that we should reinterpret it in light of that bias.

The research described by Hewes and Graham (1988) sheds light on the second-guessing process. In one study, people answered survey questions about how they interpreted third-person messages about people. About 70% of the survey respondents reported that they often second-guessed those messages. Further, they claimed to be aware of several of the types of biases that can lead to inaccurate third-person messages about people. Almost all of the respondents who second-guessed believed that third persons sometimes distort information for their own benefit (in other words, are susceptible to the self-serving motivation bias) and sometimes do not know the circumstances that caused the person they are describing to behave as they did (in other words, are prone to the fundamental attribution error). Finally, the respondents said that they took those biases into consideration when interpreting messages. This would mean, for example, that if we heard our friend describe Joe Schmo's behavior at the party in a particularly negative way, and we thought that our friend was doing this to make himself look better in comparison, then we might imagine a somewhat more positive description of Joe to be accurate. Similarly, if our friend were to blame Joe's personality for this behavior ("He's a really clumsy guy"), we would attempt to come up with a situational reason for the actions ("Maybe he was just tired that day").

It is important to keep in mind that, just because people reported in a survey that they second-guess, it does not necessarily mean that they actually do so. However, other research reported by Hewes and Graham (1988) suggested that people may actually do as the surveys suggested. When given particularly negative descriptions of behaviors and clues that the descriptions might be biased in some way, research participants tended to interpret those behaviors in a more positive manner than the description implied. Thus, there is evidence that second-guessing might be a significant part of the impression formation process when that process is based on indirect information.

CONCLUSION

In this chapter, I have discussed a model of the four stages in the impression formation process: observing a person's behavior, attributing the cause of that behavior, forming the impression, and making an evaluation of the person. As an example, I used a fictional, but potentially realistic, example of a situation in which impressions are normally formed—observing people at a party. To show its generality, I have applied this model to a substantially different situation, group leadership. I also described how second-guessing may be an additional stage when the impression formation process is indirect.

It is important to remember that this model is particularly relevant to *initial interactions*, or situations in which we meet people for the first time. We generally have very little information to work with in these circumstances. Usually, this information consists only of the behaviors we see to begin the impression formation process and of our implicit theories of personality to complete it. As a result, our first impressions of people are generally pretty simple. Because of halo and horns effects, the traits and behaviors we attribute to people we have just met tend to be unrealistically consistent; they are either all good or, as with our example of Joe, all bad, and our evaluations follow suit. However, if we have the opportunity to interact with a person repeatedly over time, in different situations, we come to learn more and more about that person, and one thing we usually find out is that the person is not so simple after all. Perhaps we were correct in thinking that Joe is clumsy and stubborn, but we also see behaviors that imply Joe is sincere and loyal and not so bad after all. Similarly, our first impression of Sue as friendly and honest may turn out to be too good to be true, because we later observe behaviors that imply she is lazy and greedy too. In other words, real people are rarely as simple and consistent as our stereotypes and our implicit theories of personality imply. As a consequence, our relationships with them enter a different phase; they become *personal*. Although our impressions of others are always critical to our feelings about them, at this point we have left the impression formation process behind, and the types of processes described in other chapters in this book (e.g., chap. 15, this volume, on social dialectics) become critical.

ADDITIONAL READING

Anybody wishing to delve into what is known about impression formation will be well served if they read two books; Fiske and Taylor (1984) and Schneider, Hastorf, and Ellsworth (1979). The latter book has a particularly good discussion of behavioral observation and of implicit personality theory. Another good book on impression formation that is somewhat simpler than these two is Wegner and Vallacher (1977). Nisbett and Ross (1980) is a superb discussion of the impact that biases have in many of the judgments we make, with practical implications that go far those for impression formation I described here.

In addition, many of the readings cited in this chapter are now considered classics and should be read by anybody with an interest in their topics. For example, Jones and Davis (1965) and Kelley (1967) are essential reading for people with an interest in attribution theory. Bruner and Tagiuri (1954) introduced the concept of "implicit personality theory" and, for that reason, became a very influential essay. Anderson's (1965) work started an important debate about the way in which people combine information to form evaluations, not only of people, but of any object or idea.

REFERENCES

Anderson, N. H. (1965). Adding versus averaging as a stimulus combination rule in impression formation. *Journal of Experimental Psychology, 70,* 394–400.

Anderson, N. H. (1968). Likableness ratings of 555 personality-trait words. *Journal of Personality and Social Psychology, 9,* 272–279.

Beilin, H. (1963). Impression formation under varied set and stimulus-trait conditions. *Journal of Social Psychology, 60,* 39–55.

Bruner, J. S., & Tagiuri, R. (1954). The perception of people. In G. Lindzey (Ed.), *Handbook of social psychology* (vol. 2, pp. 634–654). Reading, MA: Addison-Wesley.

Eden, D., & Leviatan, U. (1975). Implicit leadership theory as a determinant of the factor structure underlying supervisory behavior scales. *Journal of Applied Psychology, 60,* 736–741.

Fiske, S. T., & Taylor, S. E. (1984). *Social cognition.* Reading, MA: Addison-Wesley.

Griffin, E. (1991). *A first look at communication theory.* New York: McGraw-Hill.

Heider, F. (1958). *The psychology of interpersonal relations.* New York: Wiley.

Hewes, D. E., & Graham, M. (1988). Second guessing theory: Review and extension. In J. Anderson (Ed.), *Communication yearbook 12* (pp. 213–248). Newbury Park, CA: Sage.

Jones, E. E., & Davis, K. E. (1965). From acts to dispositions: The attribution process in person perception. In L. Berkowitz (Ed.), *Advances in experimental social psychology* (Vol. 2, pp. 220–266). New York: Academic.

Kelley, H. H. (1967). Attribution theory in social psychology. In D. Levine (Ed.), *Nebraska symposium on motivation* (Vol. 15, pp. 192–238). Lincoln: University of Nebraska Press.

Lord, R. G. (1985) An information processing approach to social perceptions, leadership, and behavioral measurement in organizations. In L. L. Cummings & B. M. Staw (Eds.), *Research in organizational behavior* (pp. 87–128). Greenwich, CT: JAI Press.

Newcomb, T. M. (1931). An experiment designed to test the validity of a rating technique. *Journal of Educational Psychology, 22,* 279–289.

Newtson, D., & Engquist, G. (1976). The perceptual organization of ongoing behavior. *Journal of Experimental Social Psychology, 12,* 436–450.

Nisbett, R., & Ross, L. (1980). *Human inference: Strategies and shortcomings of social judgment.* Englewood Cliffs, NJ: Prentice-Hall.

Pavitt, C. (1989). Accounting for the process of communicative competence evaluation: A comparison of predictive models. *Communication Research, 16,* 405–433.

Pavitt, C., & Haight, L. (1986). Implicit theories of communicative competence: Situational and competence level differences in judgments of prototype and target. *Communication Monographs, 53,* 221–235.

Pavitt, C., Whitchurch, G. G., McClurg, H., & Petersen, N. (1995). Melding the objective and subjective sides of leadership: Communication and social judgments in decision-making groups. *Communication Monographs, 62,* 243–264.

Rugg, H. (1922). Is the rating of human character practicable? *Journal of Educational Psychology, 13,* 30–42.

Schneider, D. J., Hastorf, A. H., & Ellsworth, P. C. (1979). *Person perception* (2nd ed.). Reading, MA: Addison-Wesley.

Sillars, A. L. (1980). Attributions and communication in roommate conflicts. *Communication Monographs, 47,* 180–200.

Thorndike, E. L. (1920). A constant error in psychological ratings. *Journal of Applied Psychology, 4,* 25–29.

Watzlawick, P., Beavin, J. H., & Jackson, D. D. (1967). *Pragmatics of human communication.* New York: Norton.

Wegner, D. M., & Vallacher, R. R. (1977). *Implicit psychology: An introduction to social cognition.* New York: Oxford University Press.

QUESTIONS TO PONDER

1. Most important activities, such as the "starting the car" example used in this chapter, require a set of sequential steps to perform successfully. Consider some similar activity about which you are very knowledgeable. When you are performing this activity, how do you think about the steps in the process? Is your unitizing relatively coarse- or fine-grained? How would this change if you were teaching somebody how to do this activity?

2. In his textbook, Griffin (1991) likened the attributional process of assigning responsibility for the cause of a behavior to the legal problems involved in assigning guilt or innocence to someone accused of a crime. One of the important factors in the legal circumstance is deciding whether the accused person's behavior was intentional, in other words, whether it was purposeful rather than accidental. What role does intentionality play in the attributional process? Do we only assign causal responsibility to the person's character when we believe their behavior to be purposeful, or might we assign causal responsibility when we believe their behavior is accidental?

3. Write a list of the behaviors and traits you believe describe the stereotypical politician. How many of them are positive, and how many are negative? Do you believe that you use these characteristics when you form impressions of specific politicians, such as candidates for President or Governor of your state? Do you use these characteristics in evaluating their election campaigns, or judging their performance if elected?

4. Think about your own second-guessing. Do you find yourself doing it? What are the biases that you believe you look for when interpreting people's descriptions of other people, and how do you think you compensate for these biases in your final interpretation?

5. Scientists wish for their theories to be disconfirmable; in other words, capable of being shown false. For example, the attributional theorists such as Kelley (1967) and Jones and Davis (1965) would want to be able to tell if their ideas about assigning responsibility for behaviors are wrong. What can the "naive scientist" do to discover whether or not his or her formed impression of another person is inaccurate?

5

Communication Theory and the Concept of "Goal"

Steven R. Wilson
Purdue University

> *The assumption that communicative action is strategic and goal-oriented is virtually a given starting point of communication research.*
>
> —Tracy (1991, p. 1)
>
> *There are few properties of human communication more frequently noted than that interpersonal messages function in the service of multiple, social goals.*
>
> —Greene and Lindsey (1989, p. 120)
>
> *Few would dispute the postulate that social interaction is a goal-directed activity.*
>
> —Berger (2002, p. 181)
>
> *The concept of goal has become a centerpiece in theorizing about message production*
>
> —Wilson (1995, p. 4)

This chapter begins with a seemingly obvious, but important, observation about human communication—people engage in social interaction for a reason. Whether you are trying to convince your roommate to clean up his or her half of the shared living space, comfort a friend who was dumped recently by a romantic partner, or explain to your family what someone can do with a "communication major," your words and actions are guided by an underlying purpose. Even when you engage in "small talk," you probably do so for reasons such as to maintain a sense of community or fellowship with others and to fill what otherwise might be awkward silence (Knapp & Vangelisti, 1996). In most cases, your words and actions are designed to pursue multiple goals: You want to get your roommate to clean up without alienating him or her, comfort your friend without spending all day listening to the same sad

This chapter is adapted from chapter 5 in *Seeking and Resisting Compliance: Why People Say What They Do When Trying to Influence Others*, by Steven R. Wilson, 2002, Newbury Park, CA: Sage Publications. Copyright 2002 by Sage Publications. Adapted with permission.

stories, or explain what one can do with a "communication major" without appearing overly defensive (Clark & Delia, 1979).

Goals help explain not only what we say but also how we comprehend messages from others (Berger, 2002). If someone asks what you are doing this weekend, you might wonder about the purpose behind this question—is the speaker going to ask you out on a date, checking to see if you might take his or her shift at work, or simply looking for a topic to extend the conversation? The meaning of the question depends, in part, on what you infer about the speaker's underlying goal.

As the quotes at the beginning of this chapter make clear, most communication scholars presume that people pursue goals during social interaction. This assumption, however, raises a number of important yet puzzling questions about human communication. Do people typically think about their goals while participating in everyday conversation? If not, how do they pursue goals without keeping them in mind? If people often pursue multiple goals at the same, what happens when the best thing to say in terms of accomplishing one goal is the worst thing to say with regards to another goal? Can people always anticipate what will be the purpose(s) of a conversation? If not, how do they form goals as a conversation unfolds? Do individuals ever conceal the "real" purpose of their talk? If so, how do we make inferences about their actual goals? Can a conversation ever take on a "life of its own" independent of the participants' goals?

To address such questions, I explore how communication scholars have conceptualized the nature and substance of goals. Initially, I define the concept of goal and review several research programs that have focused on two different classes or types of goals. Following this, I address common criticisms of the notion that "communication is goal oriented."

Before moving forward, let me clarify two points. First, it is important to recognize that the concept of "goal," in and of itself, is not a theory. Goals are something that can be theorized in many ways. Scholars have developed theories to explain how people form goals during conversation (Fishbach, Friedman, & Kruglanski, 2003; Wilson, 1990, 1995), how people translate goals into actions (Berger, 1997; Greene, 1997), how roles and situations can make particular goals relevant to pursue (O'Keefe, 1988), how what already has been said during a conversation sets limits on which goals are now relevant to pursue (Sanders, 1987, 1991), and so forth. Rather than review all these theories, I explore how most communication theorists have viewed the concept of "goal". Second, my focus in this chapter is largely on goals pertaining to interpersonal influence. As I noted at the start, people engage in social interaction for all sorts of reasons—to persuade, explain, comfort, and so forth. A good deal of theory and research on goals, however, has focused on interpersonal influence, and many important lessons learned from this work can be translated to other communicative functions as well. Keeping these points in mind, I turn to how communication scholars have conceptualized goals.

CONCEPTUALIZING "GOALS"

Nature of Interaction Goals

Goals are future states of affairs that an individual desires to attain or maintain (Dillard, 1997). Desired end states become *interaction goals* when we must communicate and coordinate with others to achieve those states (Clark & Delia, 1979). As an example, my spouse and I often take turns in the evening—so that one of us drives our younger children to activities while the other cleans up after dinner. Getting the kitchen clean is a goal that, in principle, I can accomplish myself. Convincing my spouse to both drive our children and to clean up, so that I can return to my office late on a specific evening, is a goal that can be achieved only through interaction.

Although pursued through communication, interaction goals are part of the *cognitive* (i.e., mental) rather than the behavioral domain. Imagine that a stranger approached and said "Excuse me, can you tell me how to get to the library?" Even though the goal underlying this question seems obvious at first glance, literally, you can observe the stranger's behavior but you must infer his or her goal. It is possible, for instance, that the stranger is using this question as an opening line to strike up a conversation, rather than, or in addition to, a means of obtaining directions. Goals motivate and explain behaviors, but they are not behaviors themselves. Goals and behaviors share a complex and indeterminate relationship (Craig, 1986; Tracy, 1991).

Interaction goals are end states desired by individuals. People pursue goals in situations, but, as conceptualized here, *individuals have goals whereas situations do not* (Benoit, 1990). People possess vast stores of knowledge about goals that typically might be pursued in situations; however, people only possess those goals when they desire to reach those end states. Put differently, you may know about an interaction goal without adopting it as your own.

Most communication theorists assume that interaction goals are *proactive*; that is, people strive to accomplish goals (Tracy, 1989; Wilson & Putnam, 1990). As Kellermann (1992) argued,

> communication is goal-directed … .We don't communicate (i.e., engage in symbolic exchange) randomly. Symbols are not selected like poker chips by reaching one's hand into a bag and drawing them out in random combinations. Symbols are selected and structured. Symbols are also not cast willy-nilly for whomever might wish to grab one going by. Even when we beam symbols into outer space in a search for extraterrestrial intelligence, these symbols are organized and transmitted for a purpose. (p. 289)

It is true that individuals at times invent goals, after the fact, to make sense of their actions (see Donohue, 1990). Even some cases of retrospective sense-making, however, are motivated proactively by goals.[1] Throughout this chapter, I explore how people's actions of exerting and resisting influence are motivated, explained, shaped, and constrained by interaction goals.

Saying that interaction goals are proactive does not mean that: (a) people are highly conscious of their goals, (b) people consciously plan how to accomplish goals in advance, or (c) people's goals are static. To illustrate these points, imagine that I received a telephone call from a teacher saying that my stepdaughter, Lisette, was earning a grade of D in her English class. Given these circumstances, I might set up a time to discuss the issue with Lisette and plan the general nature of my remarks in advance. On the other hand, if Lisette showed me a D on her report card without any prior warning, I might launch into my remarks about why she needed to earn a better grade immediately, without advance planning and without much thought about exactly what I hoped to accomplish. Imagine that you stopped me in the middle of the conversation and asked, "what are you doing?" Regardless of whether my remarks were rehearsed or spontaneous, I would reply, "I am trying to convince Lisette that she needs to improve her performance in English." My remarks, in either case, are motivated proactively by this goal. Finally, imagine that I have mistakenly read the grade on Lisette's report card, such that I thought it said D when actually her grade was a B. My goals would change quickly after Lisette informed me of my mistake, but my behavior at that point still would be motivated proactively by goals (e.g., wanting to reduce my embarrassment and

---

[1]As one example, negotiators at times attempt to maintain a positive impression with their own constituents by claiming, after the fact, that serendipitous events actually were part of their plans for achieving their constituents' goals. But a negotiator's objective in such instances is not simply to make sense of prior experience; rather, it is to persuade constituents that the "sense" he or she has made is a valid interpretation of prior events. Such impression-management objectives are examples of interaction goals (see Wilson & Putnam, 1990).

make amends with Lisette). As shown in this example, people have greater awareness of their interaction goals under certain conditions, such as when their expectations are violated, their initial attempts to accomplish goals are thwarted, or their goals come into conflict (Motley, 1986). In general, however, people often have only limited and fleeting awareness of their interaction goals (Greene, 2000; Kellermann, 1992; Wilson & Putnam, 1990).

TWO CLASSES OF GOALS: PRIMARY AND SECONDARY

Individuals often pursue multiple goals while exerting and resisting influence (Dillard, Segrin, & Harden, 1989; Saeki & O'Keefe, 1994; Schrader & Dillard, 1998). According to Dillard (1990), participants define conversational episodes on the basis of the goal or objective that accounts for their interaction. When we try to influence another person, this *primary goal,* by definition, is a desire to modify the target person's behavior. The primary goal exerts a "push" force that motivates us to speak; hence, it also helps explain why the interaction is taking place. The primary goal "brackets the situation. It helps segment the flow of behavior into a meaningful unit; it says what the interaction is about" (Dillard et al., 1989, p. 21). The primary goal offers a "frame" by which participants recognize "what is going on" and thus signals expectations about each party's identity, rights, and obligations (Goffman, 1959).

To illustrate the concept of primary goal, consider the following hypothetical scenarios:

Scenario 1:   You've known your friend, Chris, for 3 years. Chris has spent one semester at a community college. Chris is thinking about quitting school and working full-time. In your opinion, a college education is essential for career opportunities. You believe that if Chris quits school now, he wouldn't finish any more college course work. You want Chris to stay in school. You speak to Chris.

Scenario 2:   You've known your friend, Chris, for 3 years. You are going to Florida over spring break and do not want to leave your car at the airport for a week while you are gone. You want Chris to take you to the airport for your flight, which takes off at 8:00 a.m. this Saturday morning. You'd also like Chris to pick you up when you return next week. You speak to Chris.

What is "going on" in each of these scenarios? Does it seem likely that you are about to offer Chris advice and hope that he will take it into consideration in the first scenario, whereas you are about to ask Chris a favor and hope that he will grant it in the second? Notice that it would seem sensible for you to lead up to the second scenario, but not the first, by saying, "Chris, can I ask you a big favor?" Similarly, it would make sense for you to lead into the first scenario, but not the second, by saying, "Chris, can I give you some advice?"[2] In each scenario, the primary goal (i.e., giving advice or asking a favor) is what motivates you to speak. It also provides a culturally viable explanation of why, for the moment, each interaction is taking place.

---

[2]My point here is not that every friend would offer Chris advice in this situation. Some friends, despite their desire for Chris to stay in school, might feel it was not their place at that moment to offer advice. In such a case, the interaction, for the moment, would be defined by some primary goal other than giving advice. As will become clear, my point also is not that giving advice would be the friend's only goal or even the friend's most important goal. People frequently offer advice in indirect ways, for instance, to avoid looking "too pushy" (Goldsmith & Fitch, 1997). Rather, my point here is that "giving advice" provides one recognizable frame for what may be about to unfold in this situation. If the friend's behavior can be construed as "giving advice", then both participants, for the moment, are likely to orient to it as such.

Although the primary goal defines an influence interaction, it often is not the speaker's only goal. In the first scenario, you may want to give advice without (a) appearing to be butting into Chris' affairs, (b) making Chris defensive, or (c) damaging your relationship. In the second scenario, you may want to ask your favor without (a) appearing to lack the ability to handle your own problems, (b) imposing too much on Chris, or (c) making Chris feel like he is being used. These latter concerns are *secondary goals*, or objectives "that derive from more general motivations that are recurrent in a person's life" (Dillard et al., 1989, p. 20). Whereas the primary goal exerts a "push" towards action, secondary goals exert a "pull" force that acts to "shape, and typically to constrain, the behaviors whose overriding purpose is to alter the behavior of the target" (Dillard et al., 1989, p. 21).

The labels primary and secondary may seem to imply that the desire to exert, or resist, influence always is more important than other goals (Shepherd, 1992, 1998), but that is not what these labels are intended to convey.[3] Primary and secondary refer to the function and directional force rather than to the importance of goals. Influence goals are primary only in the sense that, for a point in time, they may frame what an interaction is about and energize the actors.

Having explained the concepts of primary and secondary goals, I now review research on the nature of people's influence (primary) and secondary goals.

Defining the Situation: Research on Influence Goals

Several studies have proposed typologies of influence goals, or lists of specific reasons why individuals seek to influence others. Three investigations have used diverse methods to identify influence goals commonly pursued by college students. Rule, Bisanz, and Kohn (1985) asked male and female Canadian undergraduates, "What kinds of things do people persuade _____ to do?" (p. 1129). Participants initially listed as many responses as they could when the target individuals were specified as "other people," then again when the targets were "their friends," and finally when the targets were either "their fathers" or "their enemies." Based on previous research and responses from their participants, the researchers developed a list of 12 specific influence goals.

Dillard (1989) used a three-step procedure to develop a typology of influence goals. Dillard (1989) initially asked American college undergraduates and employees of retail and service businesses to provide a written description "of a situation in which they tried to persuade someone to do something and to describe their goal in that influence attempt" (p. 296). Participants were instructed that the target should be someone they knew well, that the influence attempt should have involved trying to change the target's behavior, and that the situation should be one in which they were either successful (N = 87 participants) or unsuccessful (N = 104 participants) at getting the target to comply. After analyzing the goal descriptions for topical content (e.g., health matters, entertainment), structure (i.e., who benefitted from

---

[3]To be fair, Dillard has been somewhat vague on this point. He is clear that primary goals vary in strength across people and situations (Dillard et al., 1989, p. 20) and he has maintained that actors may understand episodes to be about influence (e.g., asking a favor) even when they rate other goals (e.g., not imposing too much on the target) as more important (Dillard & Schrader, 1998, p. 302). However, he also has written that, for researchers, the primary goal is "the chief purpose of an interaction [that] distinguishes that communication event from other areas of inquiry" (Dillard et al., 1989, p. 21), and this could be taken to mean that a goal must be an actor's most important concern to be labeled as primary. In this chapter, "primary" refers to the goal that, for the moment, frames the interaction; it is not to intended to convey whether that goal is a speaker's most important concern.

the request), and clarity, three coders identified a total of 59 unique goal statements in these written descriptions.

In Phase 2 of Dillard's (1989) study, 100 additional undergraduates each were given a deck of 59 index cards, one goal statement per card. These participants sorted his or her cards into piles so that all of the goal statements in each pile were alike and different from statements in other piles (Q-sort task). In Phase 3, 240 additional undergraduates each rated a subset of the 59 goal statements in terms of a number of dimensions along which compliance-gaining situations can differ (e.g., benefit of compliance to the message source, benefits to the target, specificity of the source's request). These dimensional ratings were used to help interpret the clusters of goal statements identified in Phase 2. Using these procedures, Dillard (1989) proposed a typology of six influence goals that are common in close, personal relationships.

Taking a different approach, Cody, Canary, and Smith (1994) asserted that influence goals could be thought of as different points at which the multiple dimensions of compliance-gaining situations intersect. Favors, for example, are requests that benefit primarily the message source, rather than the target. Typically we do not ask favors of complete strangers. Hence, situations defined by the influence goal "obtaining a favor" should share the qualities of having high source benefits, low target benefits, and at least moderate relational intimacy. To test this reasoning, Cody et al. examined undergraduates' recall of a compliance-gaining episode from his or her own life and then rated the situation along seven situational dimensions (e.g., rights to request, perceived resistance, source benefits). A variety of message targets were included in these recalled situations, including parents, friends, romantic partners, roommates, and professors. Upon analyses, Cody et al. proposed a typology of 12 influence goals. Cody et al.'s undergraduate participants seemed to distinguish two types of situations defined by the influence goal of giving advice: one cluster involving advice to friends, and a second involving advice to parents.

Aside from studies with college students, two studies have asked organizational managers about specific goals that motivate their upward, lateral, or downward influence attempts at work (Kipnis, Schmidt, & Wilkinson, 1980; Yukl & Falbe, 1990). Kipnis et al. asked 165 U.S. American managers (75% male) from engineering and technical organizations to "describe an incident in which they actually succeeded in getting either their boss, a co-worker, or a subordinate to do something they wanted" (p. 441). After reading these descriptions, the authors proposed a list of five general categories of influence goals. Subsequent studies have used slight variations on this typology, often grouping the five to six specific influence goals into the larger categories of "personal goals" (i.e., those that primarily benefit the employee him or herself, such as asking for a raise) versus "organizational goals" (i.e., those that potentially benefit the larger organization, such as advocating a procedural change to improve coordination between different departments; Schmidt & Kipnis, 1984).

Based on previous research on the nature of managerial work as well reports from 197 employed MBA students on how frequently they pursued various objectives at work, Yukl and Falbe (1990) initially proposed a typology of eight influence goals. After conducting a subsequent pilot study in which they analyzed diaries and critical incidents, Yukl, Guinan, and Sottolano (1995) further grouped their initial typology into five categories of influence goals.

In sum, these studies have (a) included college student and nonstudent participants, (b) investigated episodes with a variety of target persons, (c) used different stimuli to elicit data about goals, and (d) used both quantitative and qualitative methods to establish goal categories. Despite this diversity, these studies have produced a number of similar findings. In particular, eight specific influence goals have been identified in at least two of the five studies just reviewed (see Table 5.1). The influence goals of "gaining assistance" (e.g., favors) and "giving advice" have emerged in all five studies. Four goals (obtain permission, enforce obligations, share activity, escalate or deescalate relationship) appear in three of the five studies, and the final two (obtain personal benefit, elicit support for third party) were detected in two studies. Although students and managers in some cases report different influence goals (e.g., obtain personal benefits versus share activity), in many cases they report similar goals (e.g., gain assistance, enforce obligations).

The fact that these studies have produced similar findings is important for three reasons. First, these findings help explain why we are able to define influence episodes in terms of the underlying primary goal. For individuals to make sense of an unfolding influence episode based on the primary goal, it seems necessary that at least some primary goals should be common within a given culture. As Dillard (1990) explained,

> it is important to emphasize that these investigations are not simply exercises in list making. Rather, illumination of the substance of goals provides some clues as to what constitutes culturally viable explanation and to the ways that compliance seekers conceive of their own actions. (p. 46)

A second, related reason these findings are important is that people appear to organize their knowledge about exerting and resisting influence around primary goals. People not only share an understanding about which specific influence goals are common, they also appear to associate a wide range of information with each influence goal. This information includes the following:

1. Situational dimensions: The goal of asking a favor is associated with high self benefits, low target benefits, and relational intimacy, whereas the goal of giving advice typically involves high target benefits and moderate perceived resistance (Cody et al., 1994; Dillard, 1989; Rule et al., 1985).
2. Message targets: People typically think about pursuing the goal of seeking permission from targets such as parents and bosses rather than from friends or coworkers (Cody et al., 1994; Rule et al., 1985; Yukl et al., 1995).
3. Threats to identity: People are more likely to worry that they could appear to be "nosy" when they pursue the goal of giving advice than when they ask a favor. In turn, people are more likely to worry that they could appear too "lazy" to handle their own problems when they ask a favor than when they give advice (Cai & Wilson, 2000; Wilson, Aleman, & Leatham, 1998; Wilson & Kunkel, 2000).
4. Emotions: People associate the emotion of anger more strongly with the goal of having to enforce unfulfilled obligations than with most other influence goals (Cody et al., 1994; Wilson, 1990).

Given this wealth of information, several scholars suggest that persons develop "schemas" about exerting influence, organized around primary goals (Meyer, 2000; Rule et al., 1985; Smith, 1982). A *schema* is "a cognitive structure that represents knowledge about a concept or type of stimulus, including its attributes and the relations among those attributes" (Fiske & Taylor, 1991, p. 98). In other words, *schemas* refer to our knowledge about social roles (e.g., college professors), categories of people (e.g., "extroverts") or situations (e.g., job interviews), stages of relationships (e.g., "going steady," "breaking up"), or types of conversational episodes (e.g., a "favor" episode; Berger, 2002). In each case, schemas refer to both the attributes we associate with a category (e.g., professors often are bright but longwinded; favors typically are asked by people we know) as well as relationships we perceive among the attributes (e.g., professors who are especially bright also tend to be especially longwinded;

TABLE 5.1

A Comparison of Five Studies on Types of Influence Goals

| | | *Research Study* | | |
Cody, Canary, and Smith (1994)	Dillard (1989)	Kipnis, Schmidt, and Wilkinson (1980)	Rule, Bisanz, and Kohn (1985)	Yukl, Guinan, and Sottolano (1995)
1. Gain assistance (friend, prof.)	Gain assistance	Obtain assistance	Agency/assist	Get assistance
2. Share activity (friend)	Share activity	—	Activity	—
3. Give advice (friend, parent)	Give advice (lifestyle, health)	Initiate change	Change habit (health)	Change work (procedures)
4. (De)escalate relationship	Change relationship	—	Change relationship	—
5. Enforce obligation	—	Get others to do their job	—	Change work (follow rules)
6. Obtain permission (parent, prof.)	—	—	Get permission	Get support (approval)
7. —	—	Obtain benefits	—	Get benefit
8. Elicit support for 3rd party	—	—	Help 3rd party	—

asking a question such as "Are you going to be around later today?" is one way of leading up to a favor). We develop schemas based on repeated experience, be it direct or indirect, with groups of people, objects, or events. Schemas serve numerous functions during conversation, including the following: They set up expectations about what is, and is not, likely to occur; direct attention towards specific pieces of information; suggest inferences about other persons that go beyond what we literally have observed; and help integrate large amounts of information into a coherent picture (Fiske & Taylor, 1991). Like any type of generic knowledge, schemas can create problems. By relying too rigidly on a schema, we may make inaccurate inferences based on nothing that we have directly observed about another party, fail to remember evidence contradicting a schema, fail to modify our schema in light of contradictory evidence, or communicate our expectations about others in ways that set off self-fulfilling prophecies. Despite such risks, schema play a vital during communication, for without them we would perpetually be like aliens from another universe who know nothing about the circumstances of human life.

The research reviewed earlier suggests that people do not develop a single schema for "trying to influence others." Instead, people appear to organize their knowledge about interpersonal influence in a more differentiated fashion; that is, we develop schemas around more specific influence goals such as wanting to "give advice," "ask a favor," or "share an activity." This may occur because there are important differences in how we would try to go about influencing another person in these different types of situations.

A third reason studies of influence goals are important is that people do indeed vary how they attempt to exert or resist influence depending on the underlying primary goal. Research shows that people, depending on their specific influence goal, report being more or less likely to (a) confront and actually attempt to influence the target person; (b) be direct about what they want; (c) provide explicit reasons to support their request; (d) anticipate that the target will raise particular obstacles; (e) persist in the face of initial resistance by the target; (f) use particular compliance-seeking strategies, both before and after encountering resistance; and (g) succeed at getting the target to comply (Cai & Wilson, 2000; Cody et al., 1994; Dillard, 1989; Kipnis et al., 1980; Wilson et al., 1998; Wilson & Kunkel, 2000; Yukl et al., 1995).

In sum, individuals share similar understandings about what are common reasons for trying to influence others. Individuals also appear to organize their own knowledge about interpersonal influence around primary goals. Although people decide what to say when exerting or resisting influence, due in part to qualities of the primary goal, they also orient to other concerns during compliance-gaining interactions.

MULTIPLE GOALS AS CONSTRAINTS: RESEARCH ON SECONDARY GOALS

Participants define influence interactions in terms of primary goals, but they often pursue additional objectives when exerting or resisting influence. Four groups of scholars have explored how goals shape and constrain the way that individuals exert influence.

Hample and Dallinger's Cognitive Editing Standards

When trying to influence another, participants are faced with decisions about what to say, but also about what not to say. Hample and Dallinger (1990) have conducted a program of research investigating this issue. As these authors explained,

In the course of producing an argument, people must do two analytically distinct things. They must generate messages which might possibly be said, and then must decide whether or not to utter them.... Rather than studying the whole process of argument production, we have concentrated on the editing phrase. By "editing," we refer to the simple decision to say or suppress a possible argument. (Hample & Dallinger, 1990, p. 153)

These authors have attempted to identify "cognitive editing standards," or grounds on which people might decide to reject arguments that could be used to influence a target person, and have explored individual-difference factors that predict people's choice of editing standard.

Throughout their studies, Hample and Dallinger (1987, 2002; Dallinger & Hample, 1994) employed a "strategy rejection" procedure. Participants in each study have read multiple hypothetical influence scenarios, as well as a list of possible messages that might be used in each scenario (derived from Marwell & Schmitt's, 1967, typology of 16 "compliance-seeking" strategies). Hample and Dallinger typically have written three concrete messages (utterances) to instantiate each of the 16 compliance-seeking strategies in each scenario, that is, three examples of the "promise" strategy, three examples of a "threat" strategy, and so forth within each situation. In their early studies, participants indicated which compliance-seeking messages they would, and would not, be willing to use in each situation. For each rejected message, participants then wrote out why they would not be willing to use that message in the given situation.

Drawing on written rationales for rejected compliance-seeking messages, Hample and Dallinger (1990) developed a category system of eight cognitive editing standards (see Table 5.2). Participants rejected messages based on *effectiveness*; that is, they perceived that some messages would not convince the target to comply, and might even make the target more resistant (Standard 2). Effectiveness reflects concern about accomplishing the influence, or primary, goal. Participants also rejected messages on *principled grounds*; that is, some persons objected to specific strategies due to the nature of those strategies (Standard 3). Participants also rejected compliance-seeking messages due to *concern for oneself* (i.e., the message would project an undesirable self image; Standard 4); *concern for the other* (i.e., the message would make the target look or feel bad; Standard 5); and *concern for the relationship* (i.e., the message might damage the participant's relationship with the target; Standard 6). Standards 4 to 6 all reflect "person-centered" concerns about supporting identities and relationships. Finally, participants rejected compliance-seeking messages due to concerns about *truthfulness* (i.e., the message is false or is not logical in the situation; Standard 7) and *relevance* (i.e., the message does not fit the topic or situation; Standard 8). Standards 7 and 8 both reflect "discourse competence" concerns about meeting fundamental expectations for conversation (see Grice, 1975). In sum, people edit influence messages not only out of a concern for what will or will not work, but also in light of whether the message makes sense within the situation, whether it is an appropriate or ethical form of action, and whether it will have desirable interpersonal consequences.

Aside from identifying cognitive editing standards, Hample and Dallinger (1987; Dallinger & Hample, 1994) also investigated individual differences in people's preference for specific standards. Findings suggest that people's personalities (i.e., argumentativeness, construct differentiation, interpersonal orientation, self monitoring, social desirability, verbal aggressiveness) influence whether they typically prioritize primary or secondary goals when responding to hypothetical influence scenarios.

As noted previously, Hample and Dallinger have included multiple scenarios in their studies to assess whether the effects of personality variables generalize across situations. Given this purpose, they have not selected scenarios that differ systematically in terms of the influence goal defining the situation or the perceptual dimensions along which influence

TABLE 5.2
Hample and Dallinger's (1990) Cognitive Editing Standards
for Compliance-Seeking Messages

Editing Standard	Description
1. I would use this one.	This means that you would be willing to say or do whatever is indicated. You may accept as many of the 48 messages as you wish.
2. No: This would not work.	You reject this approach because it would fail, or perhaps even backfire.
3. No: This is too negative to use.	You prefer not to use this one because it is too high pressure—a distasteful threat or bribe, perhaps.
4. No: I must treat myself positively.	You might later regret using this approach, or it doesn' match your self image.
5. No: I must treat the other positively.	You feel that this approach might hurt the other's feelings—perhaps make him/her feel guilty or mad.
6. No: I must treat our relationship positively.	You reject this approach because it might injure the relationship between you and the other person.
7. No: This is false.	You consider that this approach is false or impossible or easily refuted.
8. No: This is irrelevant.	The approach seems irrelevant, either to you or to the other person.
9. No: Other.	You wouldn't use this approach, but for reasons other than numbers 2 through 8.

Note. From "Arguers as Editors," by D. Hample and J. M. Dallinger, 1990, *Argumentation, 4*, pp. 157–158. Copyright 1990 by Kluwer Academic Publishers. Reprinted with permission.

situations can vary (Cody et al., 1986). Nevertheless, subsidiary analyses have revealed that individuals do vary their use of specific criteria for editing compliance-seeking messages across situations, and that personality traits often exert different effects on editing criteria in different situations (Hample & Dallinger, 2002).

Explanations for cognitive editing also must include relational factors. Although the participants in Hample and Dallinger's research usually have been college students, one of their studies (Hample, Dallinger, & Meyers, 1989) explored how married couples edit compliance-seeking messages. A married person's preference for specific editing criteria was predictable, in part, from his or her partner's preferences. For example, if Partner A selected "concern for one-self" (Standard 4) frequently, Partner B tended not to select "concern for the other party" (Standard 5) as a criteria for editing his or her messages (and vice versa). In addition, some partners both selected the "other" category frequently (Standard 9), perhaps indicating that these couples had developed their own, idiosyncratic editing criteria. In sum, people's preferences for specific editing criteria appear to develop within and reflect their close personal relationships.

DILLARD'S SECONDARY GOALS

At the same time that Hample and Dallinger were developing a list of cognitive editing standards, Dillard and his colleagues were conducting an independent series of studies to specify

TABLE 5.3
Dillard, Segrin, and Harden's (1989) Content Analysis of Reasons for Rejecting
Compliance-Seeking Messages

Goal Category	Frequency	Proportion	Exemplar Statements
Influence	865	44%	It wouldn't work. It's irrelevant.
Identity	672	34%	It's immoral. Not my style.
Interaction	180	9%	That would make me look bad. This is inappropriate for the situation.
Resource	98	5%	This would cost me our friendship. I'd suffer for it.
Arousal	8	1%	This would make me apprehensive. Makes me too nervous.
Uncodable	136	7%	This is stupid. You must be kidding.
Total	1959	100%	

Note. From "Primary and Secondary Goals in the Production of Interpersonal Influence Messages," by
J. P. Dillard, C. Segrin, and J. M. Harden, 1989, *Communication Monographs, 56*, p. 24. Copyright 1989 by the
Speech Communication Association. Reprinted with permission.

the content of secondary goals, or recurrent motivations in one's life that shape and constrain attempts to influence others. Based on a review of the literature, Dillard et al. (1989) initially proposed a typology of four secondary goals:

1. Identity goals: objectives related to the self concept, that focus on internal standards of behavior, and that derive from one's own moral standards or preferences for conduct.
2. Interaction goals: objectives concerned with social appropriateness, such as to manage one's own public impression, to avoid threatening the other party's face, and to produce messages that are relevant and coherent.
3. Resource goals: objectives related to increasing or maintaining valued assets, such as one's own physical or material assets as well as the rewards of participating in a relationship with the target.
4. Arousal management goals: objectives related to maintaining a state of arousal that falls within comfortable boundaries for the individual, such as reducing excessive apprehension.

To evaluate their typology, Dillard et al. (1989, Study 1) used a strategy rejection procedure. One hundred undergraduates each read 2 hypothetical influence scenarios, drawn from a larger pool of 10 scenarios. For each scenario, participants decided whether they would (or would not) use each of 14 messages (Schenk-Hamlin, Wiseman, & Georgacarakos' 1982 typology), and then wrote out their reasons for each rejected message. Across situations and strategies, the 100 students generated a total of 1959 written reasons for rejecting specific compliance-seeking messages. As is apparent in Table 5.3, nearly half of these reasons reflected concern about accomplishing the influence (primary) goal, while most of the remaining reasons reflected concerns about one of their four secondary goals.

In a second study, Dillard et al. (1989) asked a new sample of 604 undergraduates to recall a recent interpersonal influence episode from their own life, and then rated how important each goal statement was in their situation. Based on a series of statistical analyses, Dillard et al. measured the importance of the influence goal, as well as each secondary goal. In addition, the authors divided the original "resource goals" category into two separate goals: relational resources versus personal resources. Table 5.4 shows a sampling of items that measure the influence goal and five secondary goals.

To illustrate how goals guide people's planning and action, Dillard et al. (1989) conducted yet a third study. Three hundred four undergraduates recalled a recent episode from their own life in which they attempted to influence a target person, describing the interaction in response to the alternating prompts: "First, you said," "then she said," "next, you said," and so forth. Coders then analyzed each participant's own turns from the recalled conversation, as a set, along three dimensions: (a) *explicitness*, or the degree to which the participant made his or her intentions apparent to the target; (b) *positivity*, or the degree to which the participant highlighted positive consequences if the target complied, as opposed to highlighting negative consequences if the target did not comply; and (c) *argument*, or the degree to which the participant offered explicit reasons why the target should comply with his or her request, regardless of the quality of those reasons. After recalling their conversation, participants also rated the degree to which they had thought about how to persuade the target in advance (*planning*) and had tried hard to persuade the target (*effort*). Finally, participants completed the closed-ended goal scales shown in Table 5.4 for their situation.

Given the conceptual distinction between primary and secondary goals, Dillard et al. (1989) predicted that the importance of the influence goal would determine how motivated participants were to seek compliance (i.e., planning and effort), whereas secondary goals would predict how participants actually went about trying to influence the target (i.e., explicitness, positively, and argument elaboration). As the influence goal became more important, participants reported that they had planned more in advance and had exerted more effort; in addition, they included more reasons in their recalled attempts to gain compliance. Regarding secondary goals, participants were (a) less likely to be explicit about what they wanted as their concern about both identity and arousal management goals increased, (b) more likely to emphasize positive consequences as their concern about both interaction and relational goals increased and as their concern about arousal management goals decreased, and (c) more likely to provide reasons as their concern about identity goals increased and as their concern about arousal management goals decreased. Dillard et al. (1989) concluded, "while the pattern [of results] is not a perfect dichotomy, it does support our distinction between primary and secondary goals; the primary goal serves to initiate and maintain social action, while the secondary goals act as a set of boundaries which delimit verbal choices available to sources" (p. 32).

KELLERMANN'S AND KIM'S CONVERSATIONAL CONSTRAINTS

In a third research program, Kellermann (1992) and Kim (1994) both explored constraints on strategic communication. Kellermann distinguished *primary goals* such as seeking a target person's compliance, "that are impermanent and can be achieved at particular moments in time," from *constraints*, or "ongoing regulators of behavior" (p. 289). Kellermann analyzed the nature of and relationship among conversational constraints with middle-class, European-American samples, whereas Kim has explored conversational constraints across cultures.

TABLE 5.4
Dillard et al.'s (1989) Scales for Measuring Influence and Secondary Goals

Goal Type	Sample Scale Items
Influence	1. It was very important for me to convince this person to do what I wanted him or her to do.
	2. I really didn't care that much whether he or she did what I asked (R).
Identity	3. In this situation, I was concerned with not violating my own ethical standards.
	4. I was concerned about being true to myself and my values.
Interaction socially	5. In this situation, I was careful to avoid saying things which were inappropriate.
	6. I didn't want to look stupid while trying to persuade this person.
Relational resource	7. I was not willing to risk possible damage to the relationship in order to get what I wanted.
	8. I didn't really care if I made the other person mad or not (R).
Personal resource	9. This person could have made things very bad for me if I kept bugging him/her
	10. I was worried about the threat to my safety if I pushed the issue.
Arousal management	11. This situation did not seem to be the type to make me nervous (R).
	12. I was afraid of being uncomfortable or nervous.

Note. From "Primary and Secondary Goals in the Production of Interpersonal Influence Messages," by J. P. Dillard, C. Segrin, and J. M. Harden, 1989, *Communication Monographs, 56*, p. 27. Copyright 1989 by the Speech Communication Association. Adapted by permission. Only 12 of the 25 total goal scales are shown. A 5-point Likert scale ranging from 1 (*strongly disagree*) to 5 (*strongly agree*) accompanied each item. (R) = an item that was reverse scored.

Explicating Two Conversational Constraints

According to Kellermann (1992; Kellermann & Park, 2001), communication is regulated by two overarching constraints: social appropriateness and efficiency. *Appropriateness* refers to whether a message is "nice, civil, pleasant, proper, and courteous" as opposed to "rude, uncivil, nasty, improper, and ill-mannered" (Kellermann & Shea, 1996, p. 161). This first constraint is reminiscent of Hample and Dallinger's (1990) "person-centered" editing criteria, as well as Dillard et al.'s (1989) interaction and relational resource categories of secondary goals. *Efficiency* refers to whether a message is "direct, immediate, and to the point, wasting neither time, energy, steps, or effort" as opposed to "roundabout, indirect, and wasteful, consuming time, energy, and/or effort" (Kellermann & Shea, 1996, p. 161). This second constraint corresponds, loosely, to Dillard et al.'s (1989) personal resource secondary goal. Keep in mind that this second constraint is labeled efficiency, and not effectiveness. Effectiveness refers to whether a compliance-seeking strategy will succeed at gaining the target's compliance, whereas efficiency refers to whether a strategy will require the expenditure of time or effort. Hints, for instance, are inefficient because the message target must infer the source's actual intent, but hints are seen as a very effective compliance-seeking strategy in some cultures (Kim & Wilson, 1994).

Appropriateness and efficiency are constraints in that they set limits on people's choices during influence interactions. As Kellermann (1992) explained,

> Communication is selected, fashioned, edited, enacted, and evaluated on these grounds ... This is not to say that individuals always will be (or want their behavior to be) appropriate and efficient; rather, it is saying that individuals are constrained by the level of appropriateness and efficiency expected in particular situations (which could call for high, moderate, or low levels). (pp. 289–290)

Expectations about proper levels of appropriateness or efficiency during influence episodes vary depending on many factors, including the type of primary goal being pursued (Cody et al., 1994; Wilson et al., 1998); the urgency of the requested action (Kellermann & Park, 2001); and participants' gender, culture, and relationship (Kim & Wilson, 1994; Metts, Cupach, & Imahori, 1992). Individuals can feel pressure to meet social expectations when attempting to exert or resist influence, since violating expectations can undermine one's credibility and persuasiveness (Burgoon & Burgoon, 1990). In sum, Kellermann (1992) asserted that people always orient to these two conversational constraints.

Aside from defining two conversational constraints, Kellermann also explored the perceived relationship between them. Kellermann and Shea (1996) argued that appropriateness and efficiency are separate dimensions and that the relationship between them takes different forms depending on the type of primary goal that defines the interaction. According to these authors, however, many scholars mistakenly assume that appropriateness and efficiency form opposite ends of a single dimension. As one example, she cites the "rebuff hypothesis," which predicts that message sources, on encountering resistance, typically use less polite and more direct strategies in their subsequent influence attempts. If the assumption of a single dimension were correct, then knowing whether a compliance-seeking strategy was efficient also would tell us whether it was appropriateness (and vice versa). Assuming a single dimension, if the strategy of "hint" was seen as inefficient then it also would be seen as appropriate; moreover, if "hint" were seen as less efficient than the strategy of "direct request," then "hint" would also have to be more appropriate than "direct request."

To rebut such "single dimension" thinking, Kellermann and Shea (1996) had 169 undergraduates rate the appropriateness and efficiency of five specific compliance-seeking strategies (direct request, suggestion, hint, promise, and threat). To ensure generalizability, participants each rated one of three different sets of examples of these five strategies. Findings indicate that U.S. American students do make separate, and largely independent, judgments about the appropriateness and efficiency of compliance-seeking strategies. For instance, examples of the "direct request" strategy always were rated as much more efficient than examples of the "hint" strategy, and yet examples of "direct request" and "hint" were rated almost equally appropriate. Kellermann and Shea concluded that "[Communication] researchers treat nice strategies as inefficient and nasty strategies as expedient and hinge their theoretical thinking on such supposition. The available evidence suggests that this supposition is simply incorrect (p. 157)."

Although Kellermann clarified the concept of conversational constraints, her work, like most research on interpersonal influence, has been conducted exclusively with European American participants. Kim and her colleagues (e.g., Kim, 1994; Kim et al., 1996) compared the importance of appropriateness and efficiency, as well as the perceived relation between these two constraints, across individualistic and collectivistic cultures.

Culture and Conversational Constraints

According to Triandis (1993), culture can be defined as "shared attitudes, beliefs, categorizations, expectations, norms, roles, self-definitions, values, and other such elements of subjective culture found among individuals whose interactions were facilitated by shared language, historical period, and geographic region" (p. 156). When elements of a subjective culture are organized around a theme, a cultural syndrome is present. Individualism and collectivism are examples of cultural syndromes. "In the case of individualism, the organizing theme is the centrality of the autonomous individual; in the case of collectivism, it is the centrality of the collective—family, tribe, work organization, consumer group, state, ethnic group, or religious group" (Triandis, 1993, p. 156). Thus, individualistic cultures emphasize autonomy and independence, self deter- mination, and concern for one's own interests, while collectivistic cultures emphasize intercon- nectedness, conformity to group norms, relational harmony, and concern for ingroup interests (see Hofstede, 2001; Schwartz, 1990). Collectivistic cultures place greater emphasis than indi- vidualistic cultures on status and legitimate authority, and distinguish more clearly between ingroups and outgroups (Gudykunst et al., 1992). Australia, Great Britain, and the United States are places where individualism is the predominate cultural syndrome, whereas Columbia, Japan, South Korea, and Pakistan are countries in which collectivism is predominant (Hofstede, 2001).

As widely shared sets of beliefs and values, cultural syndromes are transmitted "though socialization, modeling, and other forms of communication from one generation to another" (Triandis, 1993, p. 156). Thus, an individual's sense of self reflects, in part, the cultural syndrome into which he or she is born (Kim et al., 1996). Markus and Kitayama (1991) suggested persons within individualistic cultures tend to develop *independent* self construals; that is, they view themselves primarily in terms of internal, psychological qualities that distinguish them from others and that remain constant across situations. In contrast, persons within collectivistic cultures tend to develop *interdependent* self construals; that is, they think of themselves primar- ily in terms of the social relations (e.g., family, workplace, community) of which they are a part. Interdependent self construals do not draw sharp boundaries between self and others, and vary more in content across situations involving different relationships. Remember, independent and interdependent self construals are qualities of individuals, whereas individualism and collec- tivism are cultural syndromes. Although members of individualistic cultures, on average, develop more independent self construals than members of collectivistic cultures, not every person within an individualistic culture will form a highly independent sense of self (and vice versa). The pre- dominate cultural syndrome is but one factor influencing a person's self construal.

In a recent series of studies, Kim and her colleagues (Kim, 1994; Kim & Bresnahan, 1994, 1996; Kim et al., 1996; Kim & Sharkey, 1995; Kim, Shin, & Cai, 1998; Kim & Wilson, 1994) examined similarities and differences in conversational constraints within individualistic and collectivistic cultures. Similar methods have been used throughout these studies. With one exception (Kim & Sharkey, 1995), each study has compared undergraduate college students studying in the mainland United States (a predominately individualistic culture) with students studying in South Korea or Japan (both predominately collectivistic cultures) and Hawaii (whose local culture has been influenced by both cultural syndromes). Participants have read one or more hypothetical influence situations, defined by different primary goals and containing different levels of source-target dominance.

After reading a hypothetical scenario, participants have completed one of two tasks. In one set of studies (Kim, 1994; Kim & Bresnahan, 1996; Kim et al., 1996; Kim & Sharkey, 1995), participants have rated the importance of satisfying four conversational constraints in the sce- nario: (a) concern for clarity; (b) concern to avoid hurting the other's feelings; (c) concern for

TABLE 5.5
Kim's (1994) Scales for Measuring Four Conversational
Constraints, Plus Effectiveness

Type of Constraint	Scale Items
Clarity	1. In this situation, it is very important to make my point as clearly and directly as possible. 2. In this situation, I want to directly come to the point while conveying my message.
Feelings	1. In this situation, I feel it is very important to avoid hurting the other's feelings. 2. In this situation, being considerate toward the other's feelings is a major\concern to me.
Avoiding negative evaluation	1. In this situation, it is very important that the other person does not see me in a negative light. 2. In this situation, it is very important that my message does not cause the other person to dislike me.
Avoiding imposition	1. In this situation, it is very important not to intrude on the other person. 2. In this situation, it is very important to avoid inconveniencing the other.
Effectiveness (influence goal)	1. In this situation, it is very important to get the other person to do what I want. 2. In this situation, making the other person to comply with my request is very important.

Note. From "Cross-Cultural Comparisons of the Perceived Importance of Conversational Constraints," by M. S. Kim, 1994, *Human Communication Research, 21,* p. 139. Copyright 1994 by the International Communication Association. Reprinted with permission. A 7-point Likert scale ranging from 1 (*strongly disagree*) to 7 (*strongly agree*) accompanied each item.

avoiding negative evaluation by the hearer; and (d) concern for minimizing imposition. Aside from these four conversational constraints, participants also have rated the importance of being effective at accomplishing the influence (primary) goal. Table 5.5 displays the scales that have been used to measure each constraint, plus effectiveness. As is apparent, concern for clarity is synonymous with Kellermann's (1992) efficiency constraint, while the latter three concerns each tap a more specific aspect of Kellermann's social appropriateness constraint.

In the second set of studies (Kim & Bresnahan, 1994; Kim et al., 1998; Kim & Wilson, 1994), participants have read a hypothetical scenario plus 12 different strategies for requesting compliance in that scenario. The 12 request strategies have been organized into three larger strategy clusters:

1. Direct statements: requests in which the message source's intent is stated explicitly (e.g., "You must repay the loan");
2. Queries: conventionally indirect requests, which make reference to the logical pre-conditions for requesting (e.g., "Could you repay the loan?"); and
3. Hints: nonconventionally indirect requests, in which the message source's intent is left implicit (e.g., "I have run out of cash").

TABLE 5.6

Kim and Sharkey's (1995) Scales for Measuring Two Types of Self Construals

Scale Items	Type of Self Construal

Independent self

1. I don't change my opinions in conformity with those of the majority.
2. I don't support my group when they are wrong.
3. I assert my opposition when I disagree strongly with members of my group.
4. I act the same way no matter who I am with.
5. I enjoy being unique and different from others in many respects.
6. I am comfortable with being singled out for praise or rewards.
7. Speaking up in a work/task group is not a problem for me.
8. I value being in good health above everything.

Interdependent self

1. I will sacrifice my self interest for the benefit of the group I am in.
2. I act as fellow group members would prefer.
3. I stick with my group even through difficult times.
4. It is important for me to maintain harmony with my group.
5. It is important to me to respect decisions made by the group.
6. I will stay in a group if they need me, even when I am not happy with the group.
7. Even when I strongly disagree with group members, I avoid an argument.
8. I respect people who are modest about themselves.
9. I often have the feeling that my relationship with others is more important than my own accomplishments.
10. My happiness depends on the happiness of those around me.

Note. From "Independent and Interdependent Construals of Self: Explaining Patterns of Interpersonal Communication in Multi-Cultural Organizational Settings," by M. S. Kim and W. F. Sharkey, 1995, *Communication Quarterly, 43*, p. 38. Copyright 1995 by the Eastern Communication Association. Reprinted with permission. A 7-point Likert scale ranging from 1 (*strongly disagree*) to 7 (*strongly agree*) accompanied each item.

Participants typically have rated the degree to which each request strategy meets the four conversational constraints. As an example, for the "clarity" constraint, participants were instructed to "Please rate each statement in terms of the degree to which it communicates your intention in a clear, explicit, and unambiguous manner" (Kim & Wilson, 1994, p. 221). Aside from the four conversational constraints, participants also judged the perceived effectiveness, as well as their likelihood of using, each request strategy in the scenario.

In their earlier studies, Kim and her colleagues (Kim, 1994; Kim & Bresnahan, 1994, Kim & Wilson, 1994) simply compared how students from individualistic and collectivistic cultures completed these tasks. In more recent studies (Kim et al., 1996; Kim & Sharkey, 1995; Kim et al., 1998), however, participants also have completed scales that measure the degree to which they possess an independent or interdependent sense of self. Measures of independent and interdependent self construals are shown in Table 5.6. By including these scales, Kim and her colleagues have been able to assess whether (a) individuals from different countries of origin tend to possess different self construals, as well as (b) individuals who possess different self construals, whatever their country of origin, differ in their perceptions of conversational constraints.

Five major findings about conversational constraints have emerged from Kim et al.'s research. First, similarities exist between individualistic and collectivistic cultures. Students from the mainland United States and South Korea, for example, rate the three clusters of request strategies quite similarly in terms of the relative degree to which they meet the four conversational constraints (Kim & Wilson, 1994). As one example, direct statements, on average, are seen by both cultures as being clearer (i.e., more efficient) than queries, which in turn are seen as clearer than hints. Students from the mainland United States, Hawaii, and South Korea also do not differ in their importance ratings for effectiveness at gaining compliance (the primary goal), because all three cultures place a high degree of importance on being effective (Kim, 1994).

A second finding is that individualistic and collectivistic cultures differ dramatically in which specific request strategies they view as most effective. South Korean students, on average, rate hints as a more effective strategy for gaining a target person's compliance than queries, which in turn are rated as more effective than direct statements. Just the opposite pattern occurs for U.S. American students (Kim & Wilson, 1994). Regardless of country of origin, the degree to which students possess an independent sense of self is inversely related with the degree to which they view hints as effective means of responding to target resistance (Kim et al., 1998). Not surprisingly, then, students from South Korea and the United States also see different conversational constraints as important for being effective. For South Korean students, the degree to which a request is sensitive to the other's feelings and avoids creating disapproval are the two most important determinants of whether it is perceived as effective, whereas clarity and avoiding imposition are unrelated to effectiveness. For U.S. American students, the degree to which a request is clear is the most important determinant of whether it is perceived as effective. Being sensitive to the other's feelings is a less important determinant, whereas avoiding disapproval and imposition are unrelated to effectiveness (Kim & Bresnahan, 1994).

A third finding is that individualistic and collectivistic cultures hold different perceptions of the relations between conversational constraints. Replicating Kellermann and Shea's (1996) findings, mainland United States students make separate, and only moderately related, judgments of a request strategy's appropriateness (i.e., the degree to which it avoids hurting the other's feelings, negative evaluation, and imposition) and that strategy's efficiency (i.e., the degree to which it is clear). On the other hand, students from South Korea treat appropriateness and efficiency more as a single dimension, in that their average ratings of a request strategy's appropriateness is highly predictable from their average ratings of that strategy's efficiency (Kim & Wilson, 1994).

Fourth, individualistic and collectivistic cultures differ in the importance they place on meeting specific conversational constraints. The most striking cross-cultural differences involve clarity (i.e., efficiency). Mainland United States students, on average, place greater importance on being clear than do students from Hawaii, and both groups place much greater emphasis on being clear than do South Korean students (Kim, 1994). South Korean students, in turn, place significantly greater emphasis on avoiding hurting the other's feelings and avoiding imposing than do students from Hawaii or the mainland United States. Cultural differences in importance ratings for these two constraints, however, are smaller than the differences for clarity. These cultural differences hold up for both female and male participants (Kim & Bresnahan, 1996).

Fifth and finally, cultural differences in importance ratings for conversational constraints are mediated, in part, by differences in self construal. According to Kim and Sharkey (1995), different self construals should lead individuals to prioritize different conversational constraints:

> Individuals with the predominant tendency towards independent self construals tend to assert their needs with direct, clear, and non-ambiguous forms of communicative strategies that make the speaker's intention more or less transparent to the hearer. Such discourse functions to express

or assert the individual needs of the self…. Unlike the self-contained and consistent independent self, the interdependent self does not exist except in relation to the actors and situations around it … Thus, in choosing a communicative strategy, the person with a tendency towards interdependence will be concerned about the other's evaluation of him or her and not hurting the other's feelings. (pp. 25–26)

Kim et al. (1996) reported that college students from the mainland United States, on average, score higher on level of independent self construal than do students from Hawaii, Japan, or South Korea, although students from these four cultures differ much less in their average level of interdependent self construal (also see Levine et al., 2003). As expected, persons with higher levels of independent self construal, regardless of their country of origin, rate efficiency (i.e., concern for clarity) as a more important constraint; those with higher levels of interdependent self construal rate appropriateness (i.e., concerns for not hurting the other's feelings, not imposing, and avoiding negative self evaluation) as more important (Kim et al., 1996; Kim & Sharkey, 1995). Finally, cultural differences in the importance of conversational constraints are significantly smaller once the effects of culture on self construal have been controlled (Kim et al., 1996).

In sum, the research program by Kim and her colleagues reveals several cross-cultural differences in perceived constraints during compliance-gaining episodes. The most striking difference pertains to efficiency. Persons from individualistic cultures, who tend to have more independent self construals, place greater value on being clear and direct than do persons from collectivistic cultures. Persons from individualistic cultures also view efficient request strategies as being an effective means for gaining compliance, whereas those from collectivistic cultures view request efficiency as irrelevant to effectiveness or even counterproductive.

According to Kim (1994; Kim & Wilson, 1994), these cross-cultural differences in conversational constraints increase the possibility of misunderstanding during *intercultural* interactions. As one example, both Chinese (Ma, 1996) and Greek (Tannen, 1981) adults are significantly more likely than U.S. Americans to interpret unelaborated, unenthusiastic agreement with a request (e.g., "OK") as indirect resistance. During an intercultural influence episode, a Chinese message target, who expects people to be sensitive to others' feelings, may be resentful if an U.S. American interprets his or her "OK" as signaling a willingness to comply with a request. The U.S. American message source, who in turn expects people to "say what they mean" rather than "beating around the bush," may be frustrated when a Chinese target does not communicate his or her reluctance to comply directly. As this example illustrates, intercultural competence requires knowledge of cultural differences in conversational constraints. Aside from cultural differences, however, individuals within a culture also differ in their propensity for recognizing and attending to multiple concerns during compliance-gaining episodes.

O'KEEFE AND DELIA'S ANALYSIS OF GOAL AND BEHAVIORAL COMPLEXITY

Research programs by Hample and Dallinger (1990), Dillard et al. (1989), and Kim (1994) all confirmed that individuals frequently pursue multiple goals when attempting to influence others. Why is this the case? In one attempt to address this issue, O'Keefe and Delia (1982) analyzed the potential "complexity" of interpersonal influence situations. However, they claimed that individuals also differ in their likelihood of recognizing and addressing this complexity.

At the outset, O'Keefe (1988) distinguished two senses of the term goal: "Goals as generalized constraints defined and activated by social structures and goals as they are recognized and pursued by individuals" (p. 82). O'Keefe's first sense of the term goal referred to general problems posed by a social situation, given its constituent features (e.g., the focal task, the participants' roles and relationship). In this sense, goals are demands implicit within the nature of social situations themselves. Goals in this sense are identified through an analysis of "the predefined activities of human cultures and the general norms of consideration, self-respect, cooperation, and so on, that govern group life" (p. 82). They are "the central elements of socially codified representations of situations" (p. 82); hence, goals in this first sense exist independent of the desires of any specific individual. O'Keefe provided the following example:

> For any situation, some possible goals are intrinsically relevant and some are not. For instance, in a committee meeting any goal related to the accomplishment of committee business is naturally relevant and a committee member can be held accountable for meeting such a goal whether or not that particular member identities with the committee and its objectives. (p. 82)

O'Keefe's second sense of the term *goal* refers to those future states of affairs that an individual wants to attain or maintain. Goals in this second sense refer to an individual's mental states, and, as such, they are identified by asking the individual what she is trying to accomplish, or by inferring the individual's purposes from her behavior. It is in this second sense that I have used the term *goal* throughout this chapter. Hence, to avoid confusion, from this point forward I will refer to O'Keefe's first sense of goal as "situationally relevant objective," and limit my own use of the word *goal* to her second sense of the term.[4]

Drawing on the concept of situationally relevant objective, O'Keefe and Delia (1982) distinguished "complex" and "simple" communicative situations. A situation is complex when (a) its constituent features create multiple situationally relevant objectives, as well as (b) significant obstacles to achieving those objectives are present, or (c) actions that accomplish one objective conflict with those that accomplish other relevant objectives. To illustrate the concept of a complex situation, consider a pharmacist who hopes to convince a patient to continue taking her antihypertensive (high blood pressure) medication regularly (Lambert & Gillespie, 1994). The patient often is late in refilling her prescription, and frequently complains about the medication's side effects. In this situation, would we hold the pharmacist accountable for trying to (re)gain the patient's commitment about controlling her high blood pressure? Given the pharmacist's role and the patient's condition, this is one situationally relevant objective. Should the pharmacist also discuss the medication's side effects, as well as acknowledge the patient's ultimate control over decisions regarding her own health? Given the patient's comments and the value placed on autonomy and personal responsibility within individualistic cultures such as the United States, these also are situationally relevant objectives. All three criteria for complex situations are present in this example: (a) the pharmacist reasonably could be held accountable for meeting multiple objectives, (b) obstacles (e.g., the medication's side effects) to achieving these objectives are present, and (c) actions that help accomplish one objective (e.g., acknowledging that side effects are not uncommon) could undercut other objectives (e.g., gaining this patient's compliance).

---

[4]For discussions similar to O'Keefe's (1988) two senses of goals, see Craig's (1986) distinction between "functional" and "intentional" goals, and Donohue's (1990) distinction between goals from "restricted" versus "generalized" subject-meaning perspectives.

According to O'Keefe and Delia (1982), interpersonal influence situations, by their nature, contain the potential for complexity. How many situationally relevant objectives are present in each of the following examples?

1. A parent wants to advise her spouse about the best ways to get their three-year-old daughter to "listen."
2. An office manager wants to convince an employee, who occasionally is 5 to 10 min late returning from lunch but otherwise performs well, to arrive back at work on time.
3. A college student wants to convince the person he has been seeing for 2 months that they should stop dating and "just be friends."
4. An adult son wants to convince his mother to take care of his children for 5 days, while he and his spouse both are away at a professional conference.

As you can see, many influence situations, including those defined by the influence goals of giving advice (Goldsmith & Fitch, 1997), enforcing obligations (Wilson, 1990), redefining relationships (Cupach & Metts, 1994), and asking favors (Wilson et al., 1998) contain potential complexity. Influence situations also can be complex from the perspective of the message target, because the target may be accountable to multiple demands such as opposing the request clearly, providing a rationale for his or her refusal, and not communicating disapproval of the message source (Kline & Floyd, 1990; Metts et al., 1992; Saeki & O'Keefe, 1994).

Although influence episodes typically contain multiple situationally relevant objectives, individuals do not always form and pursue multiple goals when attempting to exert or resist influence. According to O'Keefe and Delia (1982), people with higher levels of *interpersonal construct differentiation* are more likely than their less differentiated counterparts to define influence situations in a manner that makes salient multiple situationally relevant objectives. Persons with high construct differentiation are those who spontaneously rely on a larger number of abstract, psychological dimensions to interpret others' actions, and hence are more skilled than less differentiated persons at taking the perspective and inferring the emotional states of others (see Burleson, 1987). Given these differences in person perception, O'Keefe and Delia (1982) argued that highly differentiated individuals also are more likely than less differentiated persons to form multiple interaction goals during influence episodes, as well as to use "behaviorally complex" communication strategies that address multiple goals.

O'Keefe and Delia (1982) proposed three strategies for managing multiple, conflicting goals. *Selection* involves giving priority to one goal, either the primary or a secondary goal, while ignoring other goals. Our pharmacist, for example, could prioritize the primary goal of getting the patient to comply by saying "Hypertension is a serious disease" and hence "Don't stop taking the medication," with no attention to the patient's concerns about side effects or the patient's role in decision making. *Separation* involves addressing multiple goals in temporally or behaviorally distinct aspects of a message. A pharmacist who says "I understand the medication has some unpleasant side effects," but then counsels the patient that "the medication is worth the cost" starts by addressing secondary goals, followed by the primary goal. *Integration* means attempting to address multiple goals simultaneously. A pharmacist who says "One of us should contact your doctor and see if a more effective alternative can be found" simultaneously is trying to keep the patient's hypertension controlled and to involve the patient in decision making about her health. Separation and integration are more "behaviorally complex" than selection, in that they reflect greater concern about accomplishing multiple goals (Burleson, 1987). In a nutshell, O'Keefe and Delia predicted that highly differentiated persons will use behaviorally complex strategies.

Consistent with this thinking, several studies have shown that adults high in construct differentiation are more likely than less differentiated adults to use persuasive strategies that address multiple goals when exerting or resisting influence (Kline & Floyd, 1990; O'Keefe, 1988; O'Keefe & Shepherd, 1987). O'Keefe and Delia's (1982) "goal complexity/behavioral complexity" analysis has made two valuable contributions. First, their work highlights the central role that goals play in explaining why people say what they do during influence interactions. People with more sophisticated social-perception skills (e.g., those who are better perspective takers) are more likely to form multiple goals when attempting to exert influence, and this in turn leads them to generate qualitatively different influence messages. O'Keefe and Delia explained:

> social cognitive processes might be involved at many different stages in the process of producing a message; in particular, representations of listeners and social situations might generate the communicative intentions out of which messages originate … .[Our] model suggests that the [central] processes in message production are the generation or reconciliation of message objectives. (pp. 51–52)

Even when faced with the "same" influence situation, two individuals still may form different goals if one person recognizes several situationally relevant objectives whereas the other does not.

A second contribution is that O'Keefe and Delia's (1982) model highlights key components of communication competence (Wilson & Sabee, 2003). People who address multiple goals when seeking to exert or resist influence are judged, in general, as more "competent" than those whose messages address only the primary goal (Bingham & Burleson, 1989; Kline & Floyd, 1990; O'Keefe & McCornack, 1987; but not Waldron & Applegate, 1998). People judged as highly competent, in comparison to those judged less competent, also report having had more goal-relevant thoughts, and fewer self-focused thoughts, when asked to recall their thoughts immediately after an informal conversation (Cegala & Waldron, 1992). Based on O'Keefe and Delia's (1982) framework, communication competence seems to mean (a) being able to identify when you may be held accountable for meeting multiple objectives and (b) being able, when faced with such situations, to produce messages that coordinate seeking or resisting compliance with secondary goals (Tracy, 1989; Wilson & Sabee, 2003).

SUMMARY OF RESEARCH ON SECONDARY GOALS

Four research programs on multiple goals during influence interactions have been reviewed. Three important conclusions can be drawn from these studies. First, people's attempts to exert and resist influence are shaped and constrained by multiple goals. People decide what to say, and what not to say, during influence interactions based on concerns such as being true to themselves; looking favorable in the eyes of significant others; protecting others' self esteem; maintaining desired relationships; meeting the norms for cooperative interaction; and not wasting time, energy, or other valued resources (Dillard et al., 1989; Hample & Dallinger, 1987; Kim, 1994; O'Keefe & Shepherd, 1987). We are unlikely to have all of these goals within any specific interaction, and the goals we do possess typically are prioritized such that some are more important than others (Wilson et al., 1998). Still, people's influence messages typically reflect their concern about multiple goals (e.g., Dillard et al., 1989).

A second conclusion is that people's concern about multiple goals varies across individuals, situations, relationships, and cultures. Individuals differing in personality attributes such as argumentativeness or interpersonal construct differentiation place differing importance on primary or secondary goals (e.g., Hample & Dallinger, 1990; O'Keefe & Shepherd, 1987). Situational and relational factors such as intimacy or benefits to self also affect the importance that people, in general, place on primary or secondary goals (Hample & Dallinger, 2002; Smith, 1982; Wilson et al., 1998). Individuals from diverse ethnic and cultural backgrounds also conceptualize and prioritize secondary goals differently (Kim, 1994; Tracy, 1989). Interaction goals are "heuristic" in the sense that they help explain how a host of factors affect what individuals say during influence interactions.

A third conclusion is that a focus on multiple goals highlights the potential complexity of influence interactions (O'Keefe & Delia, 1982; Schrader & Dillard, 1998). Primary and secondary goals frequently conflict, such that the actions one might take to accomplish the influence goal seem to jeopardize secondary goals (and vice versa). A goals perspective highlights why interpersonal influence episodes can be complicated to manage, suggests competencies needed to coordinate complex episodes (O'Keefe, 1988; Tracy, 1989), and highlights how judgments about communication competence can vary across culture (Kim, 1994).

Despite these contributions, the trend towards studying interaction goals is not without its critics. The rest of this chapter reviews and addresses criticisms of the assumption that people engage in social interaction to accomplish goals. One set of criticisms focus on ideological assumptions underlying the concept of interaction goals, whereas a second set questions whether interaction goals can explain the emergent nature of influence interactions.

CRITICISMS OF A GOALS PERSPECTIVE

Ideological Criticisms

The term *ideology* refers to a set of issues regarding the interrelationships between knowledge, meaning, and power (Lannamann, 1991; Parks, 1995). Ideological critics challenge scholars to make explicit their own underlying, taken-for-granted, assumptions about individuals, relationships, and communication and to recognize that these assumptions are not the only ways of understanding the world. Ideological critics draw attention to how scholars' taken-for-granted assumptions reflect the larger cultures and political systems in which they live. Ideological analyses push scholars to explore what questions about communication they do (and do not) typically ask and how their understandings of communication may be influenced by what they do (and do not) typically look for when conducting research. Ideological critics argue that current theorizing about goals is based on several Western and masculine perspectives.

For instance, Lannamann (1991) argued that the concept of "interaction goal" is central to the ideology that underlies contemporary research on interpersonal communication. According to Lannamann, most studies of interpersonal communication, including those on influence, share four ideological tendencies: (a) individualism (studies typically examine the "individual" as their unit-of-analysis, and thereby ignore the social origins of the self and fail to explore how individuals are constrained by power relations within the larger society); (b) subjectivism (studies rely heavily on self-report measures that capture people's subjective perceptions of interaction, and thereby fail to analyze how social and material conditions shape those perceptions); (c) intentionality (studies rely on the goals and desires of individuals to explain their behavior during interpersonal communication, and thereby ignore how individuals' goals and desires are shaped and constrained by larger social forces as well as downplay the unintended consequences of interpersonal behavior); and (d) ahistoricism (studies rely primarily on experimental rather than historical methods, and thereby reifying current social practices as if they were timeless generalizations). In response to these four tendencies, Lannamann called for research that illuminates, and challenges, how everyday interactions both reflect and are constrained by historical, societal-level values and relations of power.

Lannamann's (1991) characterization of ideological tendencies underlying mainstream interpersonal communication research, although exaggerated, is largely accurate. As seen in this chapter, scholars rely heavily on goals and desires to explain what people say, and do not say, when trying to exert and resist influence. Scholars have relied heavily on various self-report procedures to identify the types of goal that are commonly pursued during influence interactions. And, historical analyses of societal-level forces are rare. Studies comparing individualistic and collectivistic cultures, for instance, have examined how individuals from different countries of origin perceive and prioritize conversational constraints (Kim, 1994; Kim & Wilson, 1994), but they have ignored the historical and economic forces that helped create those cultural syndromes (see Triandis, 1993). Research that explored whether conversational constraints are changing within different segments of collectivistic cultures in response to economic and technological developments would compliment current studies (Rao, Singhal, Ren, & Zhang, 2001).

Having said this, I believe that Lannamann's (1991) ideological critique can be appreciated without devaluing current research on interaction goals. Individuals are not automons buffeted about by historical and economic forces. Individuals do pursue goals and make choices, albeit within circumstances that are not totally of their own choosing. Rawlins (1992) put it nicely when he wrote, "the human communicator [is] an ongoing producer and product of his or her choices within an encompassing cultural matrix" (pp. 7–8). As shown in this chapter, one promising feature of the concept of "interaction goal" is that it can highlight both choice *and* constraint. We can learn a great deal about influence interactions as well as our larger society by studying people's goals. The level of the "individual" is not the only valid vantage point from which communication can be studied, but it is one useful vantage point (Hewes & Planalp, 1987).

In a second ideological critique, Shepherd (1992, 1998) argued that the concepts of primary and secondary goals, which serve as an organizing framework for this chapter, are part of a masculine and egoistic bias that pervades the communication discipline. Initially, Shepherd (1992) argued that

> From humanistic definitions of rhetoric in the 1930's, through social scientific conceptions of communication in the 1960's, to critical considerations of discourse in the 1990's, interaction processes have typically been characterized essentially and primarily in terms of persuasion, influence, and power. The history of communication as a field of study coalesces around this traditional conceptualization of communication as social influence. (p. 204)

Shepherd claimed that this historical tradition is masculinely biased, in that it prioritizes qualities such as "being able to get one's way" and "controlling one's environment" that stereotypically are viewed as important for men in our society (see Bem, 1993; Buzzanell, 1994). This historical tradition also deemphasizes alternative feminine views that define communication "in terms of relations, concern, caring, and responsibility, rather than influence" (Shepherd, 1992, p. 206).

According to Shepherd (1992, 1998), the conception of influence goals as "primary" and relational concerns as "secondary" represents one example of masculine bias. Taking issue with Dillard's (1990) description of primary goals, Shepherd (1992) wrote that communication as the realization of a desire to influence, however, may be an explanation for a given interaction but it is not the explanation for any interaction. There is no "influence interaction," there are only interactions that we, as theorists and researchers, label. The field's masculine definitional bias has simply led to a corresponding bias in labeling. If we had long-assumed a feminine definition of communication, our collective theories and corpus of research might look very different. Goal-based approaches, for example, would probably have theorized relational desires as typically primary in communication situations, with influence conceived as a secondary, sometimes constraining concern (pp. 210–211).

There is some merit to Shepherd's criticism here. As you will recall, studies of influence goals often have instructed women and men to describe an interaction from their own lives in which they attempted to alter another person's behavior and then classified common reasons why behavior change is sought (e.g., Dillard, 1989; Kipnis et al., 1980). Put differently, these studies have simply assumed, rather than verified, that both women and men (or feminine and masculine individuals) actually defined what was going on in their recalled interaction as "an attempt to influence the target person." More recent research has found that participants in general, when asked to imagine or recall a situation defined by an influence (primary) goal, often still rate one or more secondary goals as more important than gaining compliance (Schrader & Dillard, 1998; Wilson et al., 1998).

Although these points suggest that scholars should take care in studying primary and secondary goals, to my mind they do not undermine the utility of Dillard's (1990) conceptual distinction. Primary and secondary goals differ in function and directional force but not necessarily importance. Participants may define an interaction, for the moment, as one in which a message source is offering a target advice (primary) even though both participants have cross-situational concerns that are more important than giving and receiving advice (secondary goals). In addition, primary goals do not inevitably involve influence; relational desires can become primary in the sense of defining, for the moment, what is going on in an interaction (Dillard & Schrader, 1998, pp. 301–302). Participants may understand the "same" interaction to be about influence, then about relational maintenance, and then about influence again over short periods of time.

Finally, the question of whether women and men actually define interactions differently in terms of underlying goals is an *empirical* question. No study, to my knowledge, has addressed this question directly to date. Several recent findings, however, raise doubt about whether women and men differ substantially in how they frame interactions. Shepherd (1992, p. 208), drawing on Hample and Dallinger's (1987) research on cognitive editing, claimed that men in general are more likely to adopt a task orientation that emphasizes effectiveness during interaction, whereas women in general are more likely to adopt a relational orientation that emphasizes concern for others. Although it is true that Hample and Dallinger report sex differences in these cognitive editing standards, the *magnitude* of the differences are extremely small. After reanalyzing data from several early studies, that involved a total of 1,471 college students, Dallinger and Hample (1994) found that biological sex at most explained only 1% of the difference in people's choice of particular cognitive editing standards. In a similar vein, Kim and Bresnahan (1996) detected no significant differences in Hawaiian, Japanese, South Korean, or mainland U.S. women's and men's importance ratings for the conversational constraints of efficiency and appropriateness, either within each culture or across cultures. Findings such as these suggest that college-aged women and men actually are more similar than different in terms of how they frame interactions in terms of primary and secondary goals.

Criticisms of the Explanatory Potential of Goals

Communication theories attempt to explain relevant phenomena, such as why individuals say what they do when seeking to exert or resist influence. Aside from ideological critiques, some scholars also question whether the concept of "goal" really can help explain what occurs during influence episodes. One group of scholars emphasizes that goals, in and of themselves, are insufficient to generate communicative *action* (Berger, 1997; O'Keefe, 1988). Aside from goals, people also must possess "procedural knowledge" about potential means by which they might accomplish their goals (Berger, 2002). Without procedural knowledge, we would live in a constant state of confusion, wanting things but having no idea what to say in order to achieve what we want. O'Keefe (1988) explained the necessity of procedural knowledge nicely:

> We know that messages are designed to serve goals ... but it is transparently clear that goals alone cannot generate messages. Simply wanting some end or effect to be brought about does not specify or mark out ways of bringing about the end or effect. Therefore, a message producer must have some process or principle that is used in constructing the verbal expressions that will serve goals. (p. 96)

Thus, individuals can differ not only in terms of how they weight influence and secondary goals, but also in the amount and type of knowledge they possess about pursuing and coordinating multiple goals, as well as in their ability to actually put their procedural knowledge into practice. Theories of plans and planning processes (Berger, 1997), action assembly theory (Greene, 1997), and message design logics (O'Keefe, 1988) all have been developed to help understand how people move from forming goals to actually speaking words, gesturing, and so forth.

A second group of scholars argue that goals may not be well-suited for explaining communicative *interaction* (for debate on this point, cf. Bavelas, 1991, with Hewes & Planalp, 1987). Speakers do not attempt to exert influence in a vacuum, but rather during conversation with a target person who has his or her own set of goals. Neither party may behave exactly as the other anticipates, and both will adapt what they say depending on what the other says. Goals may explain how a message source and target initiate an influence interaction but do people really continue to pursue goals as their interaction unfolds? Do conversations develop a momentum of their own, independent of the participants' goals? Can goals explain the emergent nature of influence interactions? Bavelas posed the problem in this fashion:

> The essential nature of a mental goal, however, is monadic: It refers to some process, disposition, or awareness in an individual. Yet, if such goals are then connected with face-to-face interaction, a fundamental disparity of units arises. Goals as a construct located in an individual mind might explain monologue, but even the cleverest and bravest reductionist does not have the alchemy to produce the creative spontaneity of dialogue out of two goals, in separate minds ... Mentally driven theories can hypothesize a start to the interaction, but they also must account for the reciprocity and accommodation that characterize face-to-face interaction. Otherwise, the goals of the two individuals would run parallel, never affecting each other. (p. 122)

The issues that Bavelas (1991) raised here are important. Identifying the content of primary and secondary goals is not an end in itself. Primary and secondary goals are useful only to the degree to which they help explain people's messages during influence interactions. It is my belief, however, that a goals perspective can account for the dynamic, emergent nature of influence interactions. Unlike static personality traits, interaction goals are dynamic forces that can change quickly over time. For example, Waldron (1997) asked research participants to watch videotapes immediately after they had completed a 10-min get acquainted conversation with a stranger. Participants' rated the importance of Dillard et al.'s (1989) five secondary goals at each and every 30-sec interval over the course of their 10-min conversation. Interestingly, the rated importance of specific goals often varied dramatically from one interval to the next. During an influence interaction, the message source's and target's goals may change, and new goals may emerge, whenever (a) initial attempts to exert or resist influence are thwarted, (b) assumptions about the other party or the situation prove false, or (c) one or both parties feel attacked and become defensive (Sanders, 1991; Wilson & Putnam, 1990). Presuming that we can track such changes in goals on a moment-to-moment basis, goals can help explain the emergent, dynamic nature of influence interactions.

Scholars also have highlighted obstacles to developing reliable and valid measures of interaction goals (Donohue, 1990; Greene, 2000). If a speaker often has only limited awareness of his or her goals, and goals can change quickly, then how can anyone (including the speaker) really know whether he or she is pursuing a goal? Researchers are using a variety of techniques to address these potential obstacles to measuring goals (e.g., inferring participants' goals from examples of their discourse, interpreted in context; O'Keefe & Shepherd, 1987; Tracy, 1991; having participants report their goals after they watch a videotape of themselves interacting with others; Waldron, 1997). Evidence regarding the reliability and validity of these techniques is reviewed elsewhere (Craig, 1986; Greene, 1988; Waldron & Cegala, 1992; Wilson & Putnam, 1990); hence, I will not do so in detail here. Each method has strengths and limits; for example, some methods are better suited for capturing how goals change quickly during conversation, whereas others are better suited for making people aware of interaction goals that typically remain implicit or tacit. Despite these differing strengths and limits, my contention is that research using a variety of these methods is providing a consistent picture of people's goals during interpersonal influence episodes.

CONCLUSION

Although communication scholars are aware of such criticisms, most still view communication as a goal-driven process. This view offers a number of important insights, including that participants in any influence interaction (a) actively define what is going on in terms of underlying primary goals; (b) may not always agree about which goal defines, or ought to define, their current interaction; (c) have shifting, momentary, and often limited awareness of their primary and secondary goals; (e) differ in their ability to draw on strategic and pragmatic means for pursuing and coordinating multiple goals; and (e) often alter the importance or drop old goals and pursue new ones as their interaction unfolds. Given these insights, it seems likely that the concept of "goal" will continue to figure prominently in our theories of communication.

REFERENCES

Bavelas, J. B. (1991). Some problems with linking goals to discourse. In K. Tracy (Ed.), *Understanding face-to-face interaction: Issues linking goals and discourse* (pp. 119–130). Hillsdale, NJ: Lawrence Erlbaum Associates, Inc.

Bem, S. (1993). *The lenses of gender: Transforming the debate on sexual inequality.* New Haven, CT: Yale University Press.

Benoit, P. J. (1990). The structure of interaction goals. In J. A. Anderson (Ed.), *Communication yearbook 13* (pp. 407–416). Newbury Park, CA: Sage.

Berger, C. R. (1997). *Planning strategic interaction: Attaining goals through communicative action.* Mahwah, NJ: Lawrence Erlbaum Associates, Inc.

Berger, C. R. (2002). Goals and knowledge structures in social interaction. In M. L. Knapp & J. A. Daly (Eds.), *Handbook of interpersonal communication* (3rd ed., pp. 181–212). Thousand Oaks, CA: Sage.

Bingham, S. G., & Burleson, B. R. (1989). Multiple effects of messages with multiple goals: Some perceived outcomes of responses to sexual harassment. *Human Communication Research, 16,* 184–286.

Burgoon, M., & Burgoon, J. K. (1990). Compliance-gaining and health care. In J. Dillard (Ed.), *Seeking compliance: The production of interpersonal influence messages* (pp. 161–188). Scottsdale, AZ: Gorsuch Scarisbrick.

Burleson, B. R. (1987). Cognitive complexity. In J. C. McCroskey & J. A. Daly (Eds.), *Personality and interpersonal communication* (pp. 395–349). Newbury Park, CA: Sage.

Buzzanell, P. M. (1994). Gaining a voice: Feminist perspectives in organizational communication. *Management Communication Quarterly, 7,* 339–383.

Cai, D., & Wilson, S. R. (2000). Identity implications of influence goals: A cross-cultural comparison of interaction goals and facework. *Communication Studies, 51,* 307–328.

Cegala, D. J., & Waldron, V. R. (1992). A study of the relationship between communicative performance and conversation participants' thoughts. *Communication Studies, 43,* 105–123.

Clark, R. A., & Delia, J. G. (1979). Topoi and rhetorical competence. *Quarterly Journal of Speech, 65,* 187–206.

Cody, M. J., Canary, D. J., & Smith, S. W. (1994). Compliance-gaining goals: An inductive analysis of actors' goal types, strategies, and successes. In J. Daly & J. Wiemann (Eds.), *Strategic interpersonal communication* (pp. 33–90). Hillsdale, NJ: Lawrence Erlbaum Associates, Inc.

Cody, M. J., Greene, J. O., Marston, P. J., O'Hair, H. D., Baaske, K. T., & Schneider, M. J. (1986). Situation perception and message strategy selection. In M. McLaughlin (Ed.), *Communication yearbook 9* (pp. 390–420). Beverly Hills, CA: Sage.

Craig, R. T. (1986). Goals in discourse. In D. G. Ellis & W. A. Donohue (Eds.), *Contemporary issues in language and discourse processes* (pp. 257–274). Hillsdale, NJ: Lawrence Erlbaum Associates, Inc.

Cupach, W. R., & Metts, S. (1994). *Facework.* Newbury Park, CA: Sage.

Dallinger, J. M., & Hample, D. (1994). The effects of gender on compliance gaining strategy endorsement and suppression. *Communication Reports, 7,* 43–49.

Dillard, J. P. (1989). Types of influence goals in personal relationships. *Journal of Social and Personal Relationships, 6,* 293–308.

Dillard, J. P. (1990). A goal-driven model of interpersonal influence. In J. P. Dillard (Ed.), *Seeking compliance: The production of interpersonal influence messages* (pp. 41–56). Scottsdale, AZ: Gorsuch Scarisbrick.

Dillard, J. P. (1997). Explicating the goal construct: Tools for theorists. In J. O. Greene (Ed.), *Message production: Advances in communication theory* (pp. 47–69). Mahwah, NJ: Lawrence Erlbaum Associates, Inc.

Dillard, J. P., & Schrader, D. C. (1998). On the utility of the goals-plans-action sequence. *Communication Studies, 49,* 300–304.

Dillard, J. P., Segrin, C., & Harden, J. M. (1989). Primary and secondary goals in the production of interpersonal influence messages. *Communication Monographs, 56,* 19–38.

Donohue, W. A. (1990). Interaction goals in negotiation: A critique. In J. A. Anderson (Ed.), *Communication year-book 13* (pp. 417–427). Newbury Park, CA: Sage.

Fishbach, A., Friedman, R. S., & Kruglanski, A. W. (2003). Leading us not unto temptation: Momentary allurements elicit overriding goal activation. *Journal of Personality and Social Psychology, 84,* 296–309.

Fiske, S. T., & Taylor, S. E. (1991). *Social cognition* (2nd ed.). Reading, MA: Addison-Wesley.

Goffman, E. (1959). *The presentation of self in everyday life.* New York: Doubleday.

Goldsmith, D. J., & Fitch, K. (1997). The normative context of advice as social support. *Human Communication Research, 23,* 454–476.

Greene, J. O. (1988). Cognitive processes: Methods for probing the black box. In C. H. Tardy (Eds.), *A handbook for the study of human communication: Methods and instruments for observing, measuring, and assessing communication processes* (pp. 37–66). Norwood, NJ: Ablex.

Greene, J. O. (1997). A second generation action assembly theory. In J. O. Greene (Ed.), *Message production: Advances in communication theory* (pp. 151–170). Mahwah, NJ: Lawrence Erlbaum Associates, Inc.

Greene, J. O. (2000). Evanescent mentation: An ameliorative conceptual foundation for research and theory on message production. *Communication Theory, 10,* 139–155.

Greene, J. O., & Lindsey, A. E. (1989). Encoding processes in the production of multiple goal messages. *Human Communication Research, 16,* 120–140.

Grice, H. P. (1975). Logic and conversation. In P. Cole & J. L. Morgan (Eds.), *Syntax and semantics: Vol. 3. Speech acts* (pp. 41–58). New York: Academic Press.

Gudykunst, W. B., Gao, G., Schmidt, K. L., Nishida, T., Bond, M. H., Leung, K., et al. (1992). The influence of individualism—collectivism, self monitoring, and predicted outcome value on communication in ingroup and outgroup relationships. *Journal of Cross-Cultural Psychology, 23,* 196–213.

Hample, D., & Dallinger, J. M. (1987). Individual differences in cognitive editing standards. *Human Communication Research, 14,* 123–144.

Hample, D., & Dallinger, J. M. (1990). Arguers as editors. *Argumentation, 4,* 153–169.

Hample, D., & Dallinger, J. M. (2002). The effects of situation on the use or suppression of possible compliance-gaining appeals. In M. Allen & R. W Preiss (Eds.), *Interpersonal communication research: Advances through meta-analysis* (187–209). Mahwah, NJ: Lawrence Erlbaum Associates, Inc.

Hample, D., Dallinger, J. M., & Meyers, K. A. (1989, November). *Marital argument.* Paper presented to the annual meeting of the Speech Communication Association, San Francisco.

Hewes, D. E., & Planalp, S. (1987). The individual's place in communication science. In C. R. Berger & S. H. Chaffee (Eds.), *Handbook of communication science* (pp. 146–183). Newbury Park, CA: Sage.

Hofstede, G. (2001). *Culture's consequences: Comparing values, behaviors, institutions and organizations across nations* (2nd ed.). Thousand Oaks, CA: Sage.

Kellermann, K. (1992). Communication: Inherently strategic and primarily automatic. *Communication Monographs, 59,* 288–300.

Kellermann, K., & Park, H. S. (2001). Situational urgency and conversational retreat: When politeness and efficiency matter. *Communication Research, 28,* 3–47.

Kellermann, K., & Shea, B. C. (1996). Threats, suggestions, hints, and promises: Gaining compliance efficiently and politely. *Communication Quarterly, 44,* 145–165.

Kim, M. S. (1994). Cross-cultural comparisons of the perceived importance of conversational constraints. *Human Communication Research, 21,* 128–151.

Kim, M. S., & Bresnahan, M. (1994). A process model of request tactic evaluation. *Discourse Processes, 18,* 317–344.

Kim, M. S., & Bresnahan, M. (1996). Cognitive bases of gender communication: A cross-cultural investigation of perceived constraints in requesting. *Communication Quarterly, 44,* 53–69.

Kim, M. S., Hunter, J. E., Miyahara, A., Horvath, A. M. Bresnahan, M., & Joon, H. J. (1996). Individual- vs. cultural-level dimensions of individualism and collectivism: Effects on preferred conversational styles. *Communication Monographs, 63,* 28–49.

Kim, M. S., & Sharkey, W. F. (1995). Independent and interdependent construals of self: Explaining cultural patterns of interpersonal communication in multi-cultural organizational settings. *Communication Quarterly, 43,* 20–38.

Kim, M. S., Shin, H. C., & Cai, D. (1998). Cultural influences on the preferred forms of requesting and re-requesting. *Communication Monographs, 65,* 47–66.

Kim, M. S., & Wilson, S. R. (1994). A cross-cultural comparison of implicit theories of requesting. *Communication Monographs, 61,* 210–235.

Kipnis, D., Schmidt, S. M., & Wilkinson, I. (1980). Intraorganizational influence tactics: Explorations in getting one's way. *Journal of Applied Psychology, 65,* 440–452.

Kline, S. L., & Floyd, C. H. (1990). On the art of saying no: The influence of social cognitive development of messages of refusal. *Western Journal of Speech Communication, 54,* 454–472.

Knapp, M. L., & Vangelisti, A. L. (1996). *Interpersonal communication and human relationships* (3rd ed.). Boston: Allyn & Bacon.

Lambert, B. L., & Gillespie, J. L. (1994). Patients' perceptions of pharmacy students' hypertension compliance-gaining messages: Effects of message design logic and content themes. *Health Communication, 6,* 311–325.

Lannamann, J. W. (1991). Interpersonal communication as ideological practice. *Communication Theory, 1,* 179–203.

Levine, T. R., Bresnahon, M. J., Park, H. S., Lapinski, M. K., Wittenbaum, G. M., Shearman, S. M., et al. (2003). Self-construal scales lack validity. *Human Communication Research, 29,* 210–252.

Ma, R. (1996). Saying "yes" for "no" and "no" for "yes": A Chinese rule. *Journal of Pragmatics, 25,* 257–266.

Markus, H. R., & Kitayama, S. (1991). Culture and the self: Implications for cognition, emotion, and motivation. *Psychological Review, 98,* 224–253.

Marwell, G., & Schmitt, D. R. (1967). Dimensions of compliance-gaining behavior: An empirical analysis. *Sociometry, 30,* 350–364.

Metts, S., Cupach, W. R., & Imahori, T. T. (1992). Perceptions of sexual compliance-resisting messages in three types of cross-sex relationships. *Western Journal of Communication, 56,* 1–17.

Meyer, J. R. (2000). Cognitive models of message production: Unanswered questions. *Communication Theory, 10,* 176–187.

Motley, M. T. (1986). Consciousness and intentionality in communication: A preliminary model and methodological approaches. *Western Journal of Speech Communication, 50,* 3–23.

O'Keefe, B. J. (1988). The logic of message design: Individual differences in reasoning about communication. *Communication Monographs, 55,* 80–103.

O'Keefe, B. J., & Delia, J. G. (1982). Impression formation and message production. In M. E. Roloff & C. R. Berger (Ed.), *Social cognition and communication* (pp. 33–72). Beverly Hills, CA: Sage.

O'Keefe, B. J., & McCornack, S. A. (1987). Message design logic and message goal structure: Effects on perceptions of message quality in regulative communication situations. *Human Communication Research, 14,* 68–92.

O'Keefe, B. J., & Shepherd, G. J. (1987). The pursuit of multiple objectives in face-to-face persuasive interaction: Effects of construct differentiation. *Communication Monographs, 54,* 396–419.

Parks, M. R. (1995). Ideology in interpersonal communication: Beyond the couches, talk shows, and bunkers. In B. R. Burleson (Ed.), *Communication yearbook 18* (pp. 480–497). Thousand Oaks, CA: Sage.

Rao, N., Singhal, A., Ren, L., & Zhang, J. (2001). Is the Chinese self-construal in transition? *Asian Journal of Communication, 11,* 68–95.

Rawlins, W. K. (1992). *Friendship matters: Communication, dialectics, and the life course.* New York: Adline de Grutyer.

Rule, B. G., Bisanz, G. L., & Kohn, M. (1985). Anatomy of a persuasion schema: Targets, goals, and strategies. *Journal of Personality and Social Psychology, 48,* 1127–1140.

Saeki, M., & O'Keefe, B. J. (1994). Refusals and rejections: Designing messages to serve multiple goals. *Human Communication Research, 21,* 67–102.

Sanders, R. E. (1987). *Cognitive foundations of calculated speech: Controlling understandings in conversation and persuasion.* Albany, New York: SUNY Press.

Sanders, R. E. (1991). The two-way relationship between talk in social interaction and actors' goals and plans. In K. Tracy (Ed.), *Understanding face-to-face interaction: Issues linking goals and discourse* (pp. 167–188). Hillsdale, NJ: Lawrence Erlbaum Associates, Inc.

Schenk-Hamlin, W. J., Wiseman, R. L., & Georgacqrakos, G. N. (1982). A model of the properties of compliance-gaining strategies. *Communication Quarterly, 30,* 92–100.

Schmidt, S. M., & Kipnis, D. (1984). Managers' pursuit of individual and organizational goals. *Human Relations, 37,* 781–794.

Schrader, D. C., & Dillard, J. P. (1998). Goal structures and interpersonal influence. *Communication Studies, 49,* 276–293.

Schwartz, S. H. (1990). Individualism—collectivism: Critique and proposed refinements. *Journal of Cross-Cultural Psychology, 21,* 139–157.

Shepherd, G. J. (1992). Communication as influence: Definitional exclusion. *Communication Studies, 43,* 203–219.

Shepherd, G. J. (1998). The trouble with goals. *Communication Studies, 49,* 294–299.

Smith, M. J. (1982). Cognitive schemata and persuasive communication: Toward a contingency rules theory. In M. Burgoon (Ed.), *Communication yearbook 6* (pp. 330–362). Beverly Hills, CA: Sage.

Tannen, D. (1981). Indirectness in discourse: Ethnicity as conversational style. *Discourse Processes, 3,* 221–238.

Tracy, K. (1989). Conversational dilemmas and the naturalistic experiment. In B. Dervin, L. Grossberg, B. J. O'Keefe, & E. Wartella (Eds.), *Rethinking communication: Volume 2, Paradigm exemplars* (pp. 411–423). Newbury Park, CA: Sage.

Tracy, K. (1991). Introduction: Linking communicator goals with discourse. In K. Tracy (Ed.), *Understanding face-to-face interaction: Issues linking goals and discourse* (pp. 1–20). Hillsdale, NJ: Lawrence Erlbaum Associates, Inc.

Triandis, H. C. (1993). Collectivism and individualism as cultural syndromes. *Cross-Cultural Research, 27,* 155–180.

Waldron, V. R. (1997). Toward a theory of interactive conversational planning. In J. O. Greene (Eds.), *Message production: Advances in communication theory* (pp. 195–220). Mahwah, NJ: Lawrence Erlbaum Associates, Inc.

Waldron, V. R., & Applegate, J. L. (1998). Person-centered tactics during verbal disagreements: Effects on student perceptions of persuasiveness and social attractiveness. *Communication Education, 47,* 53–66.

Waldron, V. R., & Cegala, D. J. (1992). Assessing conversational cognitions: Levels of cognitive theory and associated methodological requirements. *Human Communication Research, 18,* 599–622.

Wilson, S. R. (1990). Development and test of a cognitive rules model of interaction goals. *Communication Monographs, 57,* 81–103.

Wilson, S. R. (1995). Elaborating the cognitive rules model of interaction goals: The problem of accounting for individual differences in goal formation. In B. R. Burleson (Ed.), *Communication Yearbook 18* (pp. 3–26). Thousand Oaks, CA: Sage.

Wilson, S. R., Aleman, C., & Leatham, G. (1998). The identity implication of influence goals: A revised analysis of face-threatening acts and application to seeking compliance with same-sex friends. *Human Communication Research, 25,* 64–96.

Wilson, S. R., & Kunkel, A. W. (2000). Identity implications of influence goals: Similarities in face threats and facework across sex and close relationships. *Journal of Language and Social Psychology, 19,* 195–221.

Wilson, S. R., & Putnam, L. L. (1990). Interaction goals in negotiation. In J. A. Anderson (Ed.), *Communication yearbook 13* (pp. 374–406). Newbury Park, CA: Sage.

Wilson, S. R., & Sabee, C. M. (2003). Explicating communicative competence as a theoretical term. In J. O. Greene & B. R. Burleson (Eds.), *Handbook of communication and social interaction skills* (pp. 3–50). Hillsdale, NJ: Lawrence Erlbaum Associates, Inc.

Yukl, G., & Falbe, C. M. (1990). Influence tactics in upward, downward, and lateral influence attempts. *Journal of Applied Psychology, 75,* 132–140.

Yukl, G., Guinan, P. J., & Sottolano, D. (1995). Influence tactics used for different objectives with subordinates, peers, and superiors. *Group & Organizational Studies, 20,* 272–296.

QUESTIONS TO PONDER

1.   At the beginning of this chapter, I claim that we always communicate with others for a reason or a purpose. Clearly, we are pursuing goals in some situations; for example, if you attended a job fair and talked with company representatives, then you might want to create a good impression and learn about companies who are hiring. But is this always true—are we always pursuing goals when we talk with others? If you run into an acquaintance that you have not seen for a while and stop to talk for a few minutes, is your communication goal oriented? After reading this chapter, what might someone who argued "yes" say to support his/her position? What might someone who argued "no" say? What do you think?

2.   Look at the list of influence (primary) goals in Table 5.1. Can you think of real situations from your own life in which you were pursuing each of the eight types of influence goals with someone else? Can you think of real situations in which someone else was pursuing each of these eight types of influence goals with you?

3.   Imagine that you are working on a group presentation for a class that is worth 25% of your final course grade. Everyone in the group will be assigned the same grade on the presentation. One of your group members, Ron, has been really late for a couple of the group's prior meetings without explanation. Your group is scheduled to meet again tomorrow, which is only two days before the class presentation. Ron phones you and says he's not going to be able to attend the group meeting tomorrow because he's got to work, but he can drop off the research he's done so far so that you can share it with the group. What would you say to Ron in this situation? In saying this, what is your primary goal? What secondary goals might you also have during this phone conversation with Ron? (For a list of five secondary goals, see Table 5.4).

4.   Read the independent and interdependent self construal scales in Table 5.6. Do you agree or disagree with the first set of questions—that is, would you say that you are high, medium, or low in terms of the concept of "independent" self construal? Do you agree or disagree with the second set of questions—that is, would you say that you are high, medium, or low in terms of the concept of "interdependent" self construal? How might your answers to these questions reflect your own family background as well as the larger culture in which you grew up? How might your answers help explain why you tend to communicate with others as you do?

5.   Think again about the situation described in Question 3, including various things you could say to Ron. O'Keefe and Delia discuss three strategies for managing multiple, competing goals (selection, separation, integration). Can you generate an example of what O'Keefe and Delia would call a "selection" strategy for this situation? What about examples of separation and integration strategies? What might be the advantages and disadvantages of using each of these strategies in the Ron situation? Which do you think is the best strategy for this situation? Why?

6

Constructivism: A General Theory of Communication Skill

Brant R. Burleson
Purdue University

INTRODUCTION

This chapter is about communication skills and one particular theory of these skills—constructivism. As you've probably discovered in your reading of this book, communication is a broad term that encompasses lots of different things. So, I will begin by presenting some examples of what I mean by "more and less skilled communication."

Consider two young adults, each of whom is trying to comfort a friend who has recently been "dumped" by a long-term dating partner:

Mary: Ben broke up with you? He's an idiot! But, this isn't the end of the world, you know. I mean, it's not the worst thing that could happen to you, and to be honest, I think you'll be better off without Ben. Anyway, there are tons of cute guys on this campus, you know, lots of fish in the sea. You just gotta get out there and catch another one! Keep in mind that no guy is worth getting all worked up about. I mean, it's just not that big a deal, not at this point in life. You can do a lot better than Ben. Just remember that Ben isn't worth any heartache and you'll stop being so depressed about the whole thing.

Michael: Barb broke up with you? Oh man! I'm really sorry; I know you must be hurting right now. Do you want to talk about it? You were together a long time and were really involved with her, so you must have some real heartache. This just sucks; I'm really sorry, man. The same thing happened to me last year, and I remember how rotten it makes you feel. It's especially tough when it's sudden like that. It's probably gonna take some time to work through it—after all, breaking up is a really hard thing. I know it may not mean very much right now, but keep in mind that you've got some good friends here—people who really care about you. I'm here whenever you want to talk about things.

Who does the better job of comforting their distressed friend, Mary or Michael? Why?

The second instance represents what most of us intuitively recognize as a more sensitive, sophisticated, and effective performance—in a word, more skillful communication. Why do most of us regard the second instance as more skillful conduct? That is one of the questions this chapter seeks to answer.

Across a broad set of situations, some people consistently communicate more skillfully than do others. You probably know some really skillful communicators—people who with great regularity are able to recognize quickly what is going on in social situations, who can understand the meanings and messages of others, who are able to convey their ideas to others in effective and appropriate ways, and who can smoothly enter and manage conversations. You also almost certainly know people who seem clueless about the social situations they enter, who never seem to get the point of another's message, who can't convey their own ideas in ways understandable by others, and who always seem abrasive, if not rude, in conversation.

What is it that some people know that enables them to be highly successful and effective communicators? What qualities, abilities, and knowledge do they have? And how did they come by or acquire these qualities and abilities? These are some of the other questions this chapter tries to answer.

I begin this chapter by previewing different kinds of communication competencies and describing in some detail the type of competency with which this chapter is most concerned—*functional communication competence*. I then present a brief overview of the theory that will guide our exploration of different kinds of functional communication competence, a theory known as *constructivism*. Most of the chapter examines skilled behavior with respect to three major communication processes: social perception, message production, and message reception.[1] For each of these processes, we will explore two questions: (a) What counts as skilled behavior with respect to this process? (b) Why are some people more skilled than others with respect to this process? In the last part of the chapter, I describe some of the background factors that lead some people to emerge "naturally" as highly skillful communicators and others as less skilled. Overall, this chapter should help you think about your own communication skills, why you communicate as you do in various situations, and what you can do if you want to improve your functional communication skills.

SKILLFUL FUNCTIONAL COMMUNICATION: ITS NATURE, SIGNIFICANCE, AND CONCEPTUALIZATION

Types of Communication Competence

Successful communication is a complicated matter that requires the mastery of several different types of knowledge or competencies (Clark & Delia, 1979). First, to communicate

---

[1]Due to space limitations, a fourth skill—conversational management—is not discussed in this chapter. The ability to manage face-to-face conversations is an essential skill that involves such components as allocating conversational turns, directing the topic of the conversation, and adjusting one's own plans for the conversation to take account of other participants' plans. Unfortunately, comparatively few theoretical models of skill in conversational management have been proposed to date. A brief review of research on individual differences in conversational management skill is presented by Burleson and Caplan (1998).

successfully, people must know the linguistic or grammatical rules that enable them to produce and comprehend sentences in a particular language (such as English or Chinese). Such knowledge is referred to as *linguistic competence*; this kind of competence is studied mostly by linguists and psycholinguists (psychologists who are especially interested in how people generate and process grammatical sentences).

Second, successful communicators must know the social rules that govern the appropriate use of language for different situations and groups of people. Knowing how to use and interpret expressions in socially correct or appropriate ways (as determined by the rules of a relevant community or group) is referred to as *sociolinguistic competence.* This kind of competence is studied mostly by sociologists and anthropologists who try to identify the rules for "correct speaking" in various groups.

Third, successful communicators must know how to generate and process messages in ways that enable them to accomplish their personal and social goals efficiently and effectively. Skillful communicators must know how to produce messages that inform others clearly, persuade others convincingly, and comfort others sensitively. Skillful communicators must also be able to appreciate the nuances in others' messages and must even be capable of "reading between the lines" to extract intended (and sometimes unintended) meanings. Knowing how to produce messages and interpret the messages of others in ways that enable you to accomplish your goals is referred to as *functional* or *rhetorical competence.* This kind of competence is studied mostly by researchers in the communication discipline and is the kind of competence with which this chapter is concerned.

Functional communication competence includes more than the ability to produce messages that effectively achieve personal goals. Successful functional communication requires mastering skills associated with several distinguishable communication processes, including interpreting people and social situations (*social perception*), producing messages (*message production*), and receiving and processing messages generated by others (*message reception*). Skillful communicators do all of these things well. But why should you care about these skills?

The Personal and Social Significance of Functional Communication Skills

There are several good reasons why you should care about functional communication skills. First, skillful functional communicators are more likely to achieve success both personally and professionally. At work or in professional life, skillful communicators are upwardly mobile—they are more likely to earn promotions, raises, and professional advancement (e.g., Sypher & Zorn, 1986; Zorn & Violanti, 1996). At home or in private life, skillful communicators enjoy higher quality personal relationships, including more satisfying friendships (Burleson & Samter, 1994) and marriages (Burleson & Denton, 1997).

Second, skilled functional communicators usually are sensitive to the personal characteristics and goals of others. Thus, they often communicate in ways that contribute to other people being able to achieve their goals (including identity and relationship goals). As you might imagine, this can contribute to enhanced liking for skilled communicators; people generally like those who help them achieve their goals (e.g., B. J. O'Keefe & Shepherd, 1989). This can also lead to enhanced personal relationships with others.

Third, skillful functional communication can contribute to the physical health of others. For example, skillful communicators can effectively present information regarding healthy behaviors and lifestyles. They may also be more effective at persuading people to comply with treatment regimens (Lambert & Gillespie, 1994) or reduce risky behaviors (e.g., smoking, drinking, drug use, unprotected sexual activity). Other research has found that people who regularly receive sensitive, skillful, emotional support from caring others suffer less from life stress and, as a result, exhibit better physical and emotional health (Burleson, 2003).

Finally, skillful functional communicators may indirectly (and probably unintentionally) enhance the communication skills of others. They may do this by exhibiting or modeling skilled forms of communicative behavior that others can then imitate (Burleson & Kunkel, 2002). In addition, the skilled communication behaviors of those such as parents may "exercise the mind" of the child, thereby fostering the development of psychological abilities and motivational orientations required for effective social interaction (Hart, Newell, & Olsen, 2003).

I hope you are convinced that functional communication skills are important and that you should be interested in learning more about them as a first step toward improving your own skills. What do you need to help you learn more about the nature of these skills, how they work, and how they can be improved? You need the same thing that professional researchers and educators who are interested in learning about these skills need: *a good theory*. Good theories help scientists explain, predict, and control the things that interest them. Let's get acquainted with one theory of functional communication skills.

Constructivism: A Brief Overview

Constructivism is a communication theory that seeks to explain individual differences in the ability to communicate skillfully. Jesse Delia and his associates at the University of Illinois initially developed the theory of constructivism in the communication discipline during the 1970s (see Delia, O'Keefe, & O'Keefe, 1982). I am one of those "associates"—I was a graduate student at the University of Illinois in 1970s and worked closely with Delia and several others who contributed to the development of constructivism. Those of us who developed the constructivist approach to human communication were interested in understanding how people's interpretations of the social world influenced their communicative behavior. Much of our early theorizing was influenced by scholars such as the Swiss psychologist, Jean Piaget (1896–1980), and the American philosopher, George Herbert Mead (1863–1931), both of whom believed that effective communication depended on the ability to "take" (or imaginatively construct) the perspective of others. Because we viewed communication as a skill—as a practical art for accomplishing social purposes—we were particularly interested in understanding how individual differences in the perception of people and social events were related to the use of more and less effective forms of communication.

Constructivist theory has been applied successfully to a great many communication events and behaviors during the past 30 years and has generated one of the largest bodies of empirical findings in the communication discipline (see reviews by Burleson & Caplan, 1998; Coopman, 1997). Today, constructivist theory continues to be refined and applied in new settings, leading to improved understandings of many communication events and behaviors. For example, in recent years the constructivist framework has served as a foundation for theories of relationship development and maintenance, cultural influences on communication, language acquisition and communicative development, socialization processes, and communication instruction, as well as examinations of communication processes in business, educational institutions, health care contexts, the mass media, and political settings.

Despite its many elaborations and extensions, at base constructivism remains a general theory of communication skill. That is, constructivism aims to provide descriptions and explanations of individual differences in communication skill. It does this by presenting models or accounts of several things. First, constructivism identifies what counts as skillful conduct with respect to several processes, including *social perception* (the ability to acquire, retain, manipulate, and use information about the social world), *message production* (the ability to generate verbal and nonverbal messages that efficiently and effectively accomplish various personal and social goals), and *message reception* (the ability to fully comprehend the meaning of others' messages and, when appropriate, go beyond those messages to understand the source's intentions and motives). Second, constructivism explains why there are individual differences in these communication skills. That is, constructivism specifies the characteristics and qualities people must possess if they are to communicate in a skillful way. Third, constructivism explains the source or origin of individual differences in the characteristics that lead some people to be more skillful communicators than others. The rest of this chapter explores the explanations of communication skill generated by constructivist theory. Because constructivism maintains that the interpretive or perceptual processes of individuals play a central role in all communicative conduct, I first examine social perception skill.

SOCIAL PERCEPTION SKILL

Perception, Social Perception, and Social Perception Skills

Perception is the mental process of noticing, identifying, and interpreting things in the world. Perception is an active process. That is, we do not passively receive information about the world; the world does not directly impose itself on our senses and brain. Rather, we actively make sense out of the world: We selectively direct our attention to particular aspects of the world at any given time; we classify the things we notice in terms of the mental categories we have acquired; we retrieve information about similar experiences from memory and view current experiences in terms of those memories; and we make inferences (guesses) about the nature of a current experience, its causes, and its possible consequences. Even though we are rarely consciously aware of these mental activities, they are quite real and absolutely necessary; they keep us connected to the world.

Social perception refers to the process through which we make sense of the human or social world, including our experiences of ourselves, other people, social relationships, and social institutions (for an overview of research on social perception, see Barone, Maddux, & Snyder, 1997). In most social encounters, the actions and qualities of other people are especially important, so much of our mental energy and attention is focused on them. Quite spontaneously, we seek answers to a range of questions about the others around us: who they are, how they stand in relation to us, the type of situation they currently occupy, what they are doing, their intentions and motivations, and their personal qualities.

Social perception is particularly important for communication because (as shown in other sections of this chapter) people base their communicative behaviors on their perceptions of others' conduct, qualities, roles, intentions, and dispositions. Put another way, much of your own communicative conduct toward others, as well as your understanding of others' communicative efforts, is grounded in your perceptions of these others.

Researchers have examined many different *social perception processes*, including affect recognition (identifying the emotional states experienced by others), causal attribution (inferring the causes for another's behavior), nonverbal decoding (determining the meaning of nonverbal behaviors), impression formation (organizing diverse information about others into an overall impression), information integration (recognizing and reconciling potentially inconsistent information about others), social evaluation (making evaluative judgments about others), and social perspective taking (inferring the thoughts and feelings of another). These are all "input-oriented" cognitive activities through which we define and make sense of social situations and the qualities, thoughts, and behaviors of others.

People can engage in these processes more or less well; thus, social perception represents a *skill* (or, more precisely a set of skills) on which people *differ*. You know that some people have more developed athletic skills than others, some have more developed musical or artistic skills than others, and some have more developed mathematical skills than others. Quite similarly, some people have more developed *social perception skills* than others.[2] For example, people differ in the richness and organization of the impressions they form of others. Consider the impressions that Beth and Brian formed of their partners, "Chris" and "Jamie":

Beth: My partner, Chris, is a generally happy person. I think Chris has a great smile. Chris works hard in school and I really admire that. I think Chris is concerned about physical appearance and is really good-looking. Chris is caring and a good friend. We have lots of fun together. One of my favorite things to do with Chris is to go out to dinner and a movie. Chris likes to be the center of attention, but also has a good sense of humor. I think Chris' jokes are really funny. Chris treats people with respect. We are a lot alike in many ways.

Brian: My partner, Jamie, is self-confident, outgoing, friendly, and curious about the world in general. Jamie is open-minded and is always willing to learn new things. Jamie has a definite sense of what's right and wrong and sticks to beliefs that have been well thought out. However, Jamie is open to constructive criticism and new ways of thinking. Sometimes Jamie gets frustrated and tends to show some temper, but usually manages to channel that negative energy into a positive form of expression. Jamie gets along well with others due to a caring and supportive nature. Overall, Jamie is an independent and compassionate individual.

Each of these impressions contains about the same number of words. However, while the impression of Chris is rather superficial, fragmented, and unorganized, the more systematically organized impression of Jamie strikes most people as more revealing and insightful.

Here's another example of individual differences in a social perception process: Some people have difficulty understanding and explaining the apparently inconsistent actions of others; others can explain these actions relatively easily. Let's say a fellow named Walt displays both some positive behaviors (befriending a new kid in the dorm, preventing panic when a fire breaks out at a party) and some negative behaviors (making fun of a friend's low grades the previous semester, indicating a willingness to cheat on exams if he has to). How can we explain the kind of person Walt is? Some people will explain Walt by deciding that he is either a good guy or bad guy, essentially ignoring half of the information about him (the behaviors that don't "fit" with the overall judgment). Some people will use all the information, but not be able to really explain what leads Walt to act in such different ways, and conclude that Walt must be very "moody." Still other people will make use of all the information about Walt and be able to explain the variations in his behavior, perhaps in terms of an underlying trait such

---

[2]Some writers use the term emotional intelligence when referring to the abilities this chapter calls social perception skills (Goleman, 1995). I am not favorably disposed toward the emotional intelligence terminology because it is vague (see Russell & Barchard, 2002) and, for some, connotes a genetically based ability (see Zeidner, Matthews, Roberts, & MacCann, 2002). In contrast, the term skill denotes an acquired ability, and this better corresponds with my understanding of the character of individual differences associated with social perception (i.e., that such differences result largely from learning and experience rather than genetics).

as "insecurity" ("Walt is a pretty insecure guy, and this means that he always is trying to look good to others. So sometimes he does positive, helpful things but sometimes he cuts others down or takes short cuts just so he looks good by comparison"). Accounts that consider all the information about Walt and explain variations in his behavior are more complete and satisfying than accounts that ignore some of the information or fail to explain the variability in this behavior (Press, Crockett, & Delia, 1975). These accounts do a better job of integrating information about others than do the less sophisticated accounts.

There are many other examples of individual differences in social perception skills. For instance, some people have difficulty understanding another person's point of view on a situation, especially when that point of view is different from their own. Dealing with such people can be difficult, especially if you need them to appreciate the perspectives of others. Or, when it comes to making attributions about the causes of another's behavior, some people only focus on the personality traits or dispositions of the actor whereas other people not only consider the actor's personal qualities but also assess how characteristics of the situation may have influenced the actor's behavior. Generally speaking, the more sources of information people consider, the more accurate their attributions will be (Wilson, Cruz, & Kang, 1992).

Interpersonal Constructs, Cognitive Complexity, and Social Information Processing Capacity

What makes some people more skilled than others at social perception? According to constructivist theory, all social perception processes occur through the application of the cognitive elements termed *interpersonal constructs*. Interpersonal constructs are cognitive schemes or mental templates that apply to the thoughts, behaviors, characteristics, and qualities of people. It might be useful to think of interpersonal constructs as analogous to muscles in the body. Our muscles are flexible structures that enable us to engage in a variety of different physical activities (running, jumping, throwing, dancing, cycling). Similarly, interpersonal constructs are flexible mental structures that enable us to engage in a variety of cognitive activities—the various social perception processes discussed previously (e.g., attribution, impression formation, information integration, perspective taking).

As you know, certain properties of the muscular system (strength, flexibility, stamina) determine an individual's general level of athletic skill. Similarly, three properties of the interpersonal construct system are particularly important in determining our general level of social perception skill: differentiation, abstractness, and integration. *Differentiation* refers to the number of interpersonal constructs in a person's cognitive system; people with more differentiated interpersonal construct systems have more schemas available for use as they interpret the activities of others. *Abstractness* refers to the conceptual quality of a construct. Some constructs are comparatively concrete, focusing on the more superficial aspects of others such as their physical characteristics (e.g., body size, hair color), specific behaviors (e.g., smiles a lot, takes walks in the evenings), and particular social roles (e.g., part-time bartender, graduate student in English). Other constructs are comparatively abstract in character, focusing on deeper, underlying psychological qualities such as traits and dispositions (e.g., intelligent, compassionate). *Integration* refers to the extent to which the constructs in a system are organized, interconnected, and hence, easily accessible.

Systems of constructs that are more differentiated, abstract, and integrated are considered to be more complex. Thus, people who have lots of constructs (high differentiation) that are well organized (high integration) and typically reference psychological characteristics of others (high abstractness) are considered to have a high level of *interpersonal cognitive complexity*.

A common method of assessing cognitive complexity is via the Role Category Questionnaire (Crockett, 1965), where people generate impressions of others they know; these impressions are then scored by trained coders for qualities such as construct system differentiation, abstractness, and organization (for details concerning RCQ, see Burleson & Waltman, 1988).

Because interpersonal constructs are the basic cognitive structures through which we perceive and understand the social world, people with higher levels of cognitive complexity are better able than those with lower levels of complexity to acquire, store, retrieve, organize, and generate information about other persons and social situations. For example, when researchers have compared people having more and less complex systems of constructs, they have found that those with complex systems of interpersonal constructs (a) form detailed and organized impressions of others, (b) are better able to remember impressions of others, (c) are better able to resolve inconsistencies in information about others, (d) learn complex social information quickly, (e) use multiple dimensions of judgment in making social evaluations, and (f) are better able to "take" or understand the perspective of others (see review by Burleson & Caplan, 1998). These findings suggest that it is useful to view people with a high level of interpersonal cognitive complexity as having a greater *capacity to process social information* than do people with lower levels of interpersonal cognitive complexity. This is why people with a high level of interpersonal cognitive complexity are better able to carry out various social perception processes and exhibit higher levels of social perception skill. In a very important sense, people with high levels of interpersonal cognitive complexity are experts when it comes to understanding people and events in the social world; they know more, understand more, and can do more with their knowledge of the social world than less complex perceivers.

Summary

Social perception skill refers to the ability to acquire, retain, manipulate, and use information about aspects of the social world, especially other people. There are many different social perception processes and, hence, many different social perception skills. However, because all social perception processes make use of the individual's interpersonal constructs, we can get a general idea about someone's social perception skill by examining the complexity of his or her interpersonal construct system. People with high levels of interpersonal cognitive complexity have a greater capacity to acquire and process social information; thus, they are also particularly good at producing effective messages.

MESSAGE PRODUCTION SKILL

Message production is the process of generating verbal and nonverbal behaviors that are intended to obtain a desired response from those to whom they are directed. When successful, the message production process enables individuals to smoothly and effectively accomplish various personal and social goals. Message production is a complicated process and, just as there are many different social perception skills, so there are many different message production skills (for review, see Berger, 2003). Here, I am concerned with only one general message production skill: the ability to produce *highly person-centered messages*.

Some of our communicative efforts are directed at accomplishing simple, routine tasks (saying hi to an acquaintance, asking or answering straightforward questions about the time or the weather, etc.). When communicating to accomplish these simple, routine tasks we do not typically give much attention to the unique characteristics of the specific person or audience with whom we are communicating. Rather, we can rely on standard, "scripted" message forms that fit the occasion.

However, in many other circumstances the successful accomplishment of our communicative goals requires that we produce messages that show awareness of, and accommodation to, the particular psychological characteristics of our specific target audience and features of the specific social situation. Comforting someone upset about a recent loss, disciplining an employee about a rule violation, persuading a romantic partner to accept our ideas concerning future joint actions, entertaining a family gathering through jokes and stories, or explaining how some machine or drug works to someone with little background are all fairly complicated communicative tasks that require (among other things) that we carefully consider the goals, traits, feelings, knowledge, and desires of our audience.

The Nature of Person-Centered Messages

Person-centered messages take into account and adapt to the subjective, emotional, and relational aspects of communicative contexts (for a detailed discussion of the person-centered construct, see Burleson, 1987), . Person centeredness is an important quality of functional communication; such messages are more responsive to the aims and utterances of an interactional partner, are tailored to the characteristics of the partner and situation, attend to the identity-relevant features of communicative contexts, and may encourage reflection about persons and social situations.

Person-centeredness is a general quality of messages that takes on a somewhat different form depending on the primary communicative goal pursued (e.g., persuading, comforting, informing). For example, highly person-centered persuasive messages exhibit greater concern with the goals and desires of the persuasive target than do less person-centered persuasive messages. Consider the following persuasion efforts by two teenagers, both aimed at securing parental permission to host an overnight party:

Albert: Hey mom, can I have an overnight party this weekend? Please! Oh, please say yes! I really want to have my friends over! Please, mom! Is it OK? A party would be so cool! That's what I really want this weekend, OK?

Angela: Hey mom, you know how you've been saying how you want to get to know my friends better—you know, get to know the kids I hang out with? Well, I've been thinking about that, and I think you're right. It's really important that you know who my friends are. Plus, I have some really cool friends, and I'd like for you to get to know them, and them to know you. So, I've been thinking that maybe I could have an over-night party this weekend for some of my friends. That way, they'd be here in the house for a while and you'd have a chance to see them and talk to them and get to know them. Does that sound like a good idea?

Notice that Albert's message focuses only on his goals and wants. His message shows no consideration of the concerns or interests of his audience (here, his mother). Rather, he merely emphasizes how much he wants the party. In contrast, Angela cleverly frames her request so that the goals and interests of her audience (her mother) are given priority; Angela presents hosting the party as a means of achieving her mother's goal of getting to know her daughter's friends.

When disciplining or regulating the behavior of others, highly person-centered messages seek to induce the other's understanding of and compliance with behavioral rules by getting the other to reflect on and reason through the consequences of the problematic behavior. In contrast, less person-centered regulative messages seek compliance by threatening punishment or engaging in other exercises of power. For example, consider the disciplinary efforts of two mothers, each of whose 7-year-old child misbehaved by calling another child a hurtful name:

Donna: Amy, you are a naughty little girl! We don't ever call other children bad names, not ever, and not for any reason. That's wrong, and you are going to be punished. I won't tolerate that kind of behavior from a child of mine. Do you understand me? Now, you march right over to William and apologize to him and then go to your room. Children who don't play nice don't get to play at all.

Susan: Alice, what happened here? Can you tell me why you called Bonnie a name? When you get upset with someone, does that make it OK to hurt them? Do you remember how you felt last week when you got called names at school? Pretty bad, huh? How do you think Bonnie feels right now? Pretty bad, too? Do you really want her to feel bad? Do you want Bonnie to be your friend and play with you again sometime? Well, what do you think you should do here? Do you need to say something to Bonnie or apologize to her? What are you going to do next time you get upset with someone?

Both of these messages are likely to get a child's compliance in the immediate situation (in the sense of getting the misbehaving child to apologize to the victim). However, Donna's message implicitly teaches her child that "name calling" is bad behavior because she says so. It further creates a negative identity for her daughter, implying that Amy is a bad person for engaging in bad behavior. In contrast, Susan's message encourages her child to focus on the social consequences of bad behavior but does not imply that Alice is a bad person for having acted inappropriately. Susan's message also invites her child to reason through what should be done to "repair" the situation whereas Donna's message directly tells her child what must be done. Donna's message implicitly teaches her child that certain behavior is wrong when authorities say it is wrong and are present to detect and punish bad behavior. Susan's message implicitly teaches her child that certain behavior is wrong because of how it affects others, so we need to be sensitive to the effects of our behavior on others. Whose child is least likely to engage in "name calling" when parents (or other adults) are *not* present to keep the peace? And, in the long term, whose child is most likely to develop an internalized moral code for social relations with others?

In the context of providing comfort to those experiencing emotional upset, highly person-centered messages acknowledge, elaborate, and legitimize the feelings of distressed others and encourage them to express and explore their feelings. Look back at the comforting effort by Michael at the beginning of this chapter. He acknowledges his friend's feelings and legitimizes them by stating that they are understandable. Michael lets his friend know that it is OK to be upset in this situation; he further invites his friend to talk about his upset feelings when he is ready to do so. In contrast, less person-centered comforting messages challenge the legitimacy of the distressed other's feelings and perspective (at least implicitly), often telling the other how he or she *should* feel about or act in the troubling situation. Look back at the comforting effort by Mary at the beginning of this chapter. Mary is sympathetic, but her message largely tells her friend how she should feel and act in this situation. Further, whether she intends it or not, Mary is implicitly critical of her friend's feelings (and her taste in boyfriends), telling her that she didn't lose much in losing Ben. However true that may be, it is not a particularly relevant or helpful observation in this immediate situation.

These are some of the many ways in which person-centeredness is exhibited in the messages people produce. However, it is important to realize that highly person-centered messages are not necessarily "nicer" or always more prosocial; for example, some highly person-centered messages are designed to be particularly effective at hurting or embarrassing others (see Adams, 2001). Overall, highly person-centered messages are comparatively sophisticated forms of behavior in that they respond to a relatively large number of features in the communicative situation (e.g., the goals of the audience as well as the goals of the speaker), more subtle features of the situation (e.g., "face" concerns such as maintaining personal autonomy and the regard of others), and more fundamental features of the situation (e.g., the other's perceptions and feelings about a situation rather than "objective" aspects of the situation).

Beyond being comparatively sophisticated forms of conduct, there are several reasons for regarding person-centered messages as more *skillful* forms of communicative behavior. First, the use of person-centered message forms increases steadily with age over the course of childhood and adolescence (e.g., Burleson, 1982; Delia, Kline, & Burleson, 1979). This suggests that person-centered messages are more developed, mature forms of behavior. Second, people who have a lot of experience at pursuing a particular communication goal (e.g., comforting upset others) are more likely to use highly person-centered messages whereas those with less experience are more likely to use messages exhibiting a low level of person-centeredness (MacGeorge, Clark, & Gillihan, 2002). Third, people are more likely to use highly person-centered messages when they are strongly motivated to achieve their communicative goals (Samter & Burleson, 1984). This suggests that many people intuitively sense that person-centered message forms are comparatively effective at attaining desired communicative outcomes. Fourth, and perhaps most important, quite a bit of research indicates that highly person-centered messages are, in fact, more effective than less person-centered messages with respect to several different outcomes. Studies indicate that highly person-centered messages are more likely to attain desired goals than less person-centered messages in contexts such as comforting (e.g., Jones & Guerrero, 2001), persuading (e.g., B. J. O'Keefe & Shepherd, 1989), and disciplining or regulating (e.g., Adams & Shepherd, 1996). Moreover, the use of person-centered messages has been found associated with such long-term outcomes as social acceptance (e.g., Burleson, Delia, & Applegate, 1992) and professional success (e.g., Sypher & Zorn, 1986). For all these reasons, it makes good sense to view highly person-centered messages as more advanced, sophisticated, and skillful forms of behavior.[3]

Factors Influencing the Production of Person-Centered Messages

What enables people to produce highly person-centered messages? You probably won't be surprised to learn that one of the most important factors contributing to the use of highly

---

[3]It is important to keep in mind that most of the communicative situations we routinely encounter do not call for highly person-centered messages. Rather, person-centered messages are most appropriate and effective in comparatively challenging communicative situations, such as comforting a distraught friend, persuading a romantic partner who has his or her own agenda and ideas, or reprimanding an employee who also happens to be a friend. Even in these challenging circumstances, a highly person-centered message may not always be the most effective way of handling the situation. For example, a teenager seeking his or her mother's permission to host an overnight party may know that all he or she needs to do is make a simple request such as, "Hey mom, can I have a few of the girls over for a sleepover this weekend?" Such simple requests can be quite effective under the right circumstances; as one teen explained: "This is my last year at home; I'll be leaving for college in the fall. So, right now, I'm getting pretty much whatever I want from my parents, as long as it isn't too outrageous. It's cool, all I have to do is ask." Although the message strategy used by this teen was quite simple, note that the reasoning leading to the use of the simple message form was quite sophisticated, and reflected a good understanding of the psychological state of the audience.

person-centered messages is social perception skill. Scores of studies have found that people with advanced social perception skills, and the complex systems of interpersonal constructs that underlie these skills, are considerably more likely than those with less advanced social perception skills (and less complex systems of interpersonal constructs) to use highly person-centered messages in a variety of settings (for review, see Burleson & Caplan, 1998).

Complex interpersonal constructs contribute to the production of highly person-centered messages in several ways. First, and probably most important, people with high levels of interpersonal cognitive complexity are more sensitive to varied aspects of communicative situations than are people with less advanced social perception skills. In particular, people with complex systems of interpersonal constructs are more likely to recognize and appreciate what others are thinking and feeling, what their goals are, how they see themselves in relation to others in the situation, and how they want to be viewed and treated by others in the situation. In a very real sense, people with high levels of interpersonal cognitive complexity form more detailed, complex views of social situations than do those with less advanced construct systems.

Cognitively complex people also frequently have deeper insights into the dynamics of human thought, feeling, and behavior. For example, complex perceivers appear to understand intuitively that they cannot help emotionally distressed people feel better about a significant loss just by telling them that they should feel better or distracting them from the loss. Rather, complex perceivers appear to know that people will generally feel better about a loss only after they have had the chance to work through their feelings about that loss, often talking about the loss and their feelings at length. Complex perceivers also better understand how to hurt and embarrass others; for example, studies have found that cognitively complex communicators are more skilled at inducing guilt in others (Bacue & Samter, 2001) and making them unhappy (Burleson & Denton, 1997).

Because people with high levels of interpersonal cognitive complexity see more features of social situations as potentially relevant to their communicative efforts, and further have deeper and richer understandings about human nature and behavior, they tend to develop more complex and sophisticated goals for many social situations, especially those that appear challenging or demanding. Thus, having a comparatively complex system of interpersonal constructs helps people to perceive social situations more acutely, which, in turn, leads them to formulate more complex and sophisticated goals for these situations. But how does having such goals for social situations contribute to the production and use of highly person-centered messages? One must have some way of putting advanced goals and knowledge into words. How does this happen?

Scholars of the message production process assume that all people have a *procedural memory system* (e.g., see chap. 9, this volume). Procedural memories are recollections about how to do something; they are the building blocks of complex actions, like messages. Each procedural memory connects recollections about an action, outcomes of that action, and situations in which that action has been used in the past. Procedural memories are "activated" (retrieved from long-term memory) when a person's current goals and features of the current situation match those stored in the memory. These activated memories are then sorted, selected, and assembled to generate an "output representation," which you can think of as a message plan or behavioral program.

Some people have larger, better organized sets of procedural memories pertinent to certain communicative goals than do others. For example, people who get lots of practice with a particular communicative goal (e.g., a teacher informing, a salesman persuading, a counselor comforting) are likely to develop more numerous and richer sets of procedural memories relevant to the goal than people who rarely engage in these activities.

Having a large set of procedural memories relevant to a particular communicative goal facilitates the production of highly person-centered messages. People who can generate a lot of different ideas about how to achieve a communicative goal (i.e., display a large procedural memory) are more likely to use highly person-centered messages when pursuing that goal (e.g., Delia et al., 1979; Kline, 1991). This finding makes sense: Highly person-centered messages are complicated forms of behavior that do a lot of work; they reflect the integration of many distinguishable goals. Typically, highly person-centered messages pursue a primary goal (such as informing, persuading, or comforting a target) while also addressing many secondary goals (e.g., letting the target know that he or she is liked, that he or she is respected, that the speaker sees the target as an equal, that the speaker would like to deepen his or her relationship with the target). In contrast, a message low in person-centeredness may pursue only a primary goal. Accomplishing the larger set of goals associated with highly person-centered messages is assisted by having a larger and more interconnected system of relevant procedural memories.

As we have seen, however, if our procedural memories are to contribute to the messages we produce, those memories must be activated or recalled from long-term storage. This is where a person's perceptions and goals come into play. Goals and perceptions of relevant situation features activate procedural memories, so the more goals generated and features noticed in a given episode, the greater the number of procedural memories that are likely to be activated. And the larger the number of relevant procedural memories that are activated, the more likely it is that the speaker will generate and use highly person-centered messages (see Kline, 1991; Waldron & Applegate, 1994; Wilson, 1990).

Summary

Message production is the process of generating verbal and nonverbal behaviors designed to obtain a desired response from those to whom they are directed. Many of our everyday communicative efforts don't require much skill; they are routine and comparatively simple. However, some of our efforts require messages that show awareness of, and accommodation to, the particular psychological characteristics of our specific target audience. In such instances, highly person-centered messages have been found particularly effective.

Figure 6.1 summarizes the linkages that lead to the production of person-centered messages. Complex construct systems facilitate skilled social perception processes which generate rich, detailed representations of social situations. These more comprehensive, multifaceted views of social situations lead to the development of more complex communicative intentions and goals. Goals activate procedural memories. If a sufficient number and the right type of procedural memories are activated, they will be assembled into a representation or plan for a highly person-centered message strategy, and when that plan is executed, we see a highly person-centered message.

MESSAGE RECEPTION SKILL

As you have seen, constructivism has quite detailed theories of social perception and message production. Another core communication process, message reception, has thus far been given less theoretical and research attention by constructivist scholars. Thus, this section of the chapter contains more speculation, and less hard evidence, than the two preceding sections. If the ideas presented here interest you, perhaps you will help conduct some of the research needed to improve our understanding of the process of message reception.

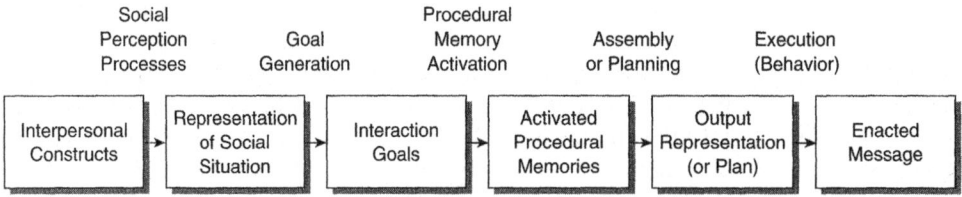

Fig. 6.1.   A model of the goal formation and message production process. (Note: Rectangles represent structures; arrows represent processes.)

The Nature of Message Reception

Message reception (what some call "decoding") is the process of interpreting the communicative behavior of others in the effort to understand the meaning and implications of that behavior.[4] Message reception is a special kind of social perception process that focuses on comprehending and contextualizing what we take to be the intentional communicative expressions of others. Skill in message reception is evidenced by grasping the meaning of another's messages and, when appropriate, going beyond these messages to understand more fully the other's intentions and motivations.

Like message production, message reception is a complex process that is made up of several distinguishable components (for reviews, see Wyer & Adaval, 2003). Typically, when people receive and interpret a message from another, they seek to understand the *meaning* of the other's words (what the other said), the *intention* associated with those words (what the other was trying to do in saying what he or she did), and the *motive* underlying the other's intention (why the other was trying to accomplish what he or she was trying to do). For example, suppose your roommate asks you, "Hey, do you want to walk to the library with me tonight?" You understand the words here; you know what a library is and the particular library to which your roommate is referring; you know what it is to walk to some place; you know that "tonight" refers to a time later in this day, probably after sunset; and you know that your roommate is asking you a question about your interest in accompanying him or her to the library. You also understand your roommate's intention; by speaking these words, your roommate is, in effect, inviting you to accompany him or her to the library. And you probably have an adequate understanding of the motives underlying your roommate's invitation; for example, you know that your roommate enjoys your company or enjoys engaging in light exercise (such as walking) with you, and that's why he or she invited you to join him or her for a walk.

Usually, our interpretations of the other's meanings, intentions, and motives are accomplished very quickly and automatically with little conscious awareness on our part. It feels like we almost immediately grasp what the other is saying, doing, and wanting. Most of the time, this is all the understanding we need; if we understand this much, we will be able to communicate smoothly with others and engage in cooperative actions with them.

---

[4]The analysis of message reception developed in this section has not been presented previously. As will become apparent, my analyses of message reception and message processing owe much to several sources, including Habermas's (1998) explication of the conditions underlying the possibility of communicative action and discourse, Hewes's (1995) discussion of the processing of "problematic messages," and dual process theories of responses to persuasive messages (see Chaiken & Trope, 1999).

What I have described to this point might be characterized as *standard, surface-level processing* of messages. In such processing, the receiver assumes that the source's messages can be accepted at "face value" and that an adequate understanding of these messages (and the source) does not require searching for deeper, underlying meanings. More specifically, when engaged in standard, surface-level message processing, the receiver takes for granted that the source (a) is engaged in straightforward, honest communication; (b) wants his meanings, intentions, and motives to be transparent to the recipient; and (c) will readily provide any clarifications or explications needed to ensure such transparency. When such assumptions can be made—and they routinely *are* made in the vast majority of the cases in which we receive messages—then message reception is not a particularly challenging task. Surface-level processing of messages proceeds automatically and makes comparatively small demands on our cognitive system. Almost everyone possesses a reasonable level of skill when it comes to standard, surface-level processing of messages.

Of course, we do not always immediately and fully understand the other's meanings, intentions, or motives. On occasion, we do not understand what the other has said; we either do not hear or do not comprehend a particular word, phrase, or statement. This kind of problem is usually easy to fix; we can ask the other to repeat the message or clarify it.

However, the "rough and ready" understanding of the other's words generated by standard surface-level processing may not always be adequate for the purpose at hand. Sometimes, we may feel a need to have a very thorough understanding of the other's statements, including all the nuances and fine shades of meaning. Then, there are those occasions when we have a perfectly adequate understanding of what the other has said, but do not understand what the other is trying to do in saying certain things to us (the other's intentions) or why the other is seeking to realize these intentions (the other's motives). Something about the message, the source, or the situation is peculiar, special, or just doesn't "feel right" to us. For example, some aspect of the message content may strike us as untrue or may contradict what we already believe. Or perhaps the situation and what gets said in it is of great consequence to us (e.g., we are negotiating a deal for an expensive new car or trying to resolve a serious conflict with our long-term romantic partner).

On these special occasions, we may engage in *depth processing* of the messages we receive. Depth processing involves a motivated, systematic, and mindful scrutiny of the message, the source of the message, or the communicative situation, the aim of which is answering some concern. The specific concerns directing this systematic, mindful scrutiny will vary with the occasion. For instance, if the recipient senses that the message reflects source bias or contains questionable (i.e., false) information, the depth processing may be directed at "unbiasing" the message (i.e., adjusting the content of the message to correct for the suspected bias or untruth). This unbiasing process involves generating one or more alternative interpretations of the message, each of which adjusts the message for the perceived bias or deception; the alternative interpretations are then assessed and a candidate alternative is selected (for a detailed description of this unbiasing process, see Hewes, 1995). When bias or deception is suspected, depth processing may also aim at developing explanations about why the source appears to be biased or acting deceptively in this situation. The recipient may seek to infer the motives of the source, an understanding of which may provide guidance about how to view the source and his or her messages in the current situation, as well as other situations (past, present, and future). Thus, depth processing may generate one or more hypotheses about the "real" intentions and motivations of the source (for details, see McCornack, 1992).

There are occasions when, although we do not suspect the message source of bias or deception, the intentions or motivations of the source will not be clear to us: We may understand what has been said to us but be uncertain about how we should take the message (the source's intention) or the character of the source's underlying motivations. For example, consider the following conversation between two acquaintances:

Ashley: Hi Laura! It's been a while since I've seen you. What's new?
Laura: Hi Ashley. Yes, it has been a while. Well, the big news is that Mark T. and I started dating a couple of weeks ago. Everything is going great so far.
Ashley: Oh yeah, I know Mark. He really likes women.

Just how should Laura take Ashley's statement that Mark "really likes women?" Is this statement intended as an encouragement or a warning? In either case, is Ashley's statement motivated by concern for Laura's welfare or does it reflect some other motive? In cases such as these, depth processing aims at resolving the intentional or motivational ambiguity associated with a source's message. In the effort to resolve such ambiguity, the recipient typically generates and then assesses several alternative interpretations of the source's intentions or motivations. In this process, the recipient will likely give scrutiny not only to the source's message and conduct in the current context but also to recalled interactions with the source.

On still other occasions, depth processing may be triggered by the recipient's concern with the content or topic of the message (rather than by some ambiguity or cue emitted by the source). In such cases, processing focuses on the significance or implications of what has been said. For example, when thoughtfully processing persuasive messages about a matter of personal import, we typically carefully scrutinize the merits of the arguments in the message and generate many distinct thoughts about that message (see Petty & Wegener, 1999). If processing regulative messages disciplining us or correcting some action of ours, we may scrutinize the message for the fairness of the invoked regulation and the degree of respect we are shown by the regulator. If processing comforting messages intended to console us about an emotionally upsetting situation, we may scrutinize them for the extent to which they help us more fully understand or make sense of the hurtful situation (see Burleson & Goldsmith, 1998). In each case, depth processing is indicated by the extensiveness and detail of the thoughts generated by the message.

Depth processing is a cognitively demanding activity, so we do not always expend the effort needed to deeply process another's message, even when that might be appropriate. Sometimes we ignore cues inviting depth processing, assuming that the "problem" we have sensed is not very significant or will be resolved in the course of further routine communication. Sometimes our ability to engage in depth processing is limited by other demands on our attention and information processing capacity. And sometimes we act directly to resolve the matter concerning us, perhaps asking the source to clarify his or her intentions and motivations.

We are most likely to engage in depth processing of a message when (a) multiple cues in the message, the source's conduct, or other aspects of the situation suggest that the message should not be taken at face value, (b) the matter addressed in the message has great personal relevance, or (c) we strongly desire accurate information about or a full understanding of the matter at hand (Hewes, 1995; Petty & Wegener, 1999).[5] Although depth processing is a

---

[5]An addition to increasing the likelihood of engaging in depth processing, personal relevance of the topic and the desire for accurate information may also increase the message recipient's sensitivity to cues that the message should not be accepted at face value (see Hewes, 1995).

cognitively "expensive" activity, it has some real payoffs. Research indicates that depth processing is often quite effective at correcting for source bias and deception, can resolve puzzling ambiguities, assists with determining the strength of arguments, and results in more informed, optimized decisions (see Chaiken, Liberman, & Eagly, 1989; Hewes, 1995).

Factors Influencing the Ability to Deeply Process Messages

As you might guess, depth processing of messages is a mentally demanding activity that places a significant load on a person's attention, memory, and other cognitive resources. Although everyone can engage in depth processing to an extent, some people can do so better (more easily, elaborately, and thoroughly) than others. What factors contribute to differences in the ability to engage in depth processing?

Both situational and personal factors influence the ability to engage in depth processing. Distraction and other forms of interference in the communication situation have been shown to undermine the ability to process messages deeply; if one's attention is being distracted by noise, flashing lights, or another task, the ability to process a message deeply will suffer (see D. J. O'Keefe, 2002). Another factor influencing the ability to process a message deeply is preexisting knowledge about the message topic or source. Put simply, the more you already know about the topic or source of a message, the easier it is to deeply process new information about that topic or source made available in the current message or communicative situation (Hewes, 1995; D. J. O'Keefe, 2002).

Research showing that preexisting knowledge influences the ability to engage in depth processing suggests that individual differences in the ability to *acquire* knowledge about the message topic or source from the ongoing communicative situation might contribute to skillful depth processing. We are already familiar with one factor that influences the individual's ability to acquire information about other people and social situations: *interpersonal cognitive complexity*. The advanced social perception skills enabled by a complex system of interpersonal constructs provide the individual with a basis for extracting comparatively large amounts of information from messages, the conduct of the source, and other features of the communicative situation. The information so acquired should facilitate the depth processing of messages.

So far, no studies have directly examined whether interpersonal cognitive complexity underlies the ability to deeply process messages. However, several lines of research indirectly suggest a connection between cognitive complexity and skillful depth processing. First, some studies have found a statistical association between measures of cognitive complexity and listening comprehension. In one such study, Beverly Sypher and her colleagues (Sypher, Bostrom, & Seibert, 1989) had employees from various ranks in a business organization complete a measure of interpersonal cognitive complexity (the Role Category Questionnaire) and the Kentucky Comprehensive Listening Test, an instrument assessing five aspects of listening. Cognitive complexity was associated with better performance on three of the five listening measures.

Second, deeply processed messages are more likely to be remembered than messages that receive only surface-level processing. Consistent with the idea that cognitive complexity facilitates depth processing, Stacks and Murphy (1993) found that people with high levels of cognitive complexity reported that they had better memories for conversations than did people with low levels of complexity. More directly, Neuliep and Hazelton (1986) found that people with high levels of interpersonal cognitive complexity were better able than those with low complexity levels to recall details of a conversational interaction they had recently witnessed.

Third, sophisticated, complex messages (like highly person-centered messages) that pursue multiple goals may be most effective at attaining their various aims when they are deeply processed by recipients. Depth processing of these message forms may be needed to maximally extract their multiple meanings and nuances. Several studies have found that although highly person-centered messages tend to be more effective than low-person-centered messages with all recipients, cognitively complex recipients get more information from and respond more favorably to highly person-centered messages than do less complex recipients (see review by Burleson & Caplan, 1998). These findings suggest that cognitively complex recipients are processing highly person-centered messages more deeply than are less complex recipients.

Summary

Message reception is the process of interpreting the communicative behavior of others in the effort to understand the meaning and implications of that behavior. Most of the messages we receive in everyday life can be taken at face value, and thus are adequately understood when subjected to standard, surface-level processing. However, some of the messages we receive demand deeper processing, either because of our personal concerns or because we detect cues that suggest the source is biased or acting deceptively. Depth processing involves (a) subjecting the message and other elements of the communicative situation (such as the conduct of the source) to intense scrutiny, (b) generating multiple thoughts about or interpretations of the message, and (c) reaching some decision about the truth, significance, or implications of the message.

Several motivational factors affect the likelihood of engaging in depth processing; several ability factors influence the skillfulness of depth processing. In particular, some research suggests that having a high level of interpersonal cognitive complexity contributes to skill in the depth processing of messages. However, more research is needed that directly examines the connection between cognitive complexity and depth processing.

BECOMING A SKILLED COMMUNICATOR: ANTECEDENTS AND TRAINING

By now, you may be convinced that having a high level of interpersonal cognitive complexity is a pretty good thing, especially if communicating effectively is important to you. People with comparatively high levels of cognitive complexity have more acute social perception skills, can produce more effective messages in challenging circumstances, and appear to process others' messages more deeply when needed, getting more out of these messages.

Two questions have probably occurred to you as you have read this chapter: (a) How do people get to be more or less cognitively complex to begin with? That is, what are the *antecedents* of interpersonal cognitive complexity and the skills associated with it? (b) What can you do to improve your own level of cognitive complexity? What kind of *training* facilitates the growth of interpersonal cognitive complexity and the skills associated with it? Our current knowledge permits a more complete answer to the first question than the second, so I initially discuss antecedents of cognitive complexity and functional communication skills.

Antecedents of Social-Cognitive and Communicative Development in Childhood

Cognitive complexity and communication skills increase naturally over the course of childhood and adolescence (just as body size and intellectual skills do). Thus, young adults typically have much higher levels of interpersonal cognitive complexity and communication skills than do children. However, at every stage of the life cycle, some people possess higher levels of cognitive complexity and communication skills than do others (just as some people are physically stronger than others at every stage of the life cycle). Thus, there are both developmental and individual differences in cognitive complexity and associated communication skills. Why do these differences exist?

Growing evidence indicates that the social environment in which a youngster is raised has an important influence on the development of social skills across childhood, adolescence, and into adulthood. Two caregiver practices appear particularly important: (a) the use of language that explicitly mentions intentions, feelings, and other internal states and (b) the use of person-centered messages when disciplining and nurturing the child.

Explicit talk with young children about feelings, intentions, and related internal states appears to contribute substantially to the development of complex interpersonal constructs and sophisticated social perception skills (Dunn, 1998). Such talk helps make the child aware of the nature and range of internal states, leads to an appreciation of the circumstances that motivate various states, and implicitly teaches the child that internal states are significant and need to be taken into account. This is important because young children spontaneously think about others in concrete, physical, and behavioral terms. Explicit talk about internal states thus draws the child's attention to "invisible" features of others, makes them a more prominent part of the child's world, and thereby helps create the interpersonal constructs that children come to use in interpreting and acting upon their world. Caregivers may talk to children about the internal states of others in a wide variety of contexts, including while playing, observing others, reading stories, regulating behavior, and watching television.

Caregiver use of highly person-centered message forms when disciplining (regulating) and nurturing (comforting) also has been shown to contribute to the development of complex interpersonal constructs and advanced social perception skills (for review, see Burleson & Kunkel, 1996). Highly person-centered disciplinary and comforting efforts typically involve a good deal of emotion talk which, as just discussed, can foster the development of interpersonal constructs. These message forms also model the use of social perception skills such as perspective taking (e.g., "What do you think Billy felt when you took his toy?") and situation-based causal attributions (e.g., "Did something happen before that to make Jill mad?"). Additionally, caregiver use of highly person-centered messages appears to foster the child's own communication skill development, especially the use of comparatively person-centered messages (Applegate, Burleson, & Delia, 1992). Children regularly exposed to person-centered messages may learn how to use them by observing and imitating their caregiver models.

In addition to these caregiver practices, frequent social interaction with peers appears to facilitate the child's development of complex construct systems, social perception skills, and sophisticated communication skills (e.g., Strayer & Mashal, 1983). Peer interactions create opportunities for children to exercise their social perception and communication skills; these peer interactions also provide feedback to children about the effectiveness of their skills (Buhrmester, 1996). In addition, some research (e.g., Burleson & Kunkel, 2002) indicates that children may use peers as models for the messages they produce. This suggests that children who interact with highly skilled peers are more likely to develop a high level of communication skills themselves; of course, this also implies that regular interaction with low-skilled peers may suppress the child's skill development. There is a tendency for children (as well as adults) to befriend peers who have skill levels similar to their own (Burleson, 1998); this tendency may further foster skill development by relatively advanced children and slow skill development by less advanced children. Thus, teachers and other caregivers may find it desirable to create contexts where highly skilled children regularly interact with their less skilled peers.

Many other factors probably influence the development of construct systems and communication skills over the course of childhood and adolescence. Much more research is needed to better understand the antecedents of interpersonal cognitive complexity and associated social perception, message production, and message reception skills.

Training Programs Designed to Enhance Cognitive Complexity, Social Perception, and Communication Skills

Studying the antecedents of cognitive complexity and related abilities helps us understand why some people "naturally" emerge as more (or less) skilled communicators. But past childhood, what can people do to improve their communication skills? What can YOU do to become a more skilled communicator? Unfortunately, only a little research has directly addressed these questions.

Professional counselors, therapists, and other clinicians who work with people that have problems should benefit from having their levels of cognitive complexity enhanced. Two recent studies (Brendel, Kolbert, & Foster, 2002; Duys & Hedstrom, 2000) found that students enrolled in basic counseling skills-training courses developed significantly higher levels of cognitive complexity than did similar students in a control condition. Thus, certain counseling education programs appear to be somewhat successful at increasing the cognitive complexity levels of counselor trainees. Of course, counselor trainees represent a rather specialized group and we don't yet know whether the training programs effective with them also help increase cognitive complexity in other, more diverse populations.

Several training programs have been developed to enhance the social perspective-taking skills of children (e.g., Marsh, Serafica, & Barenboim, 1980), but most of these programs have met with only mixed success. Few programs aimed at enhancing the social perspective-taking skills of adults have been developed (for one example, see Pelias, 1984), and little is known about whether these programs achieve any lasting improvements in skill levels. Similarly, only a few studies have evaluated specific programs for teaching message production skills to children (Clark, Willihnganz, & O'Dell, 1985) or adults (Rowan, 1984), and the results of these studies are far from conclusive. On the whole, then, we know little about the best ways to systematically enhance social perception, message production, and message reception skills through training programs and educational interventions.

As a communication researcher and educator, I find this situation embarrassing and unacceptable. We researchers now know a lot about cognitive complexity and advanced social perception and communication skills, but thus far there have been few efforts to translate what we know into *proven* programs that effectively enhance these skills. Clearly, *much* more research is needed in this area.

Until the necessary research is completed, we must make do with some educated guesses about how best to improve your functional communication skills. The research on childhood antecedents of social skills suggests several ways that adults may be able to improve their skills:

1. Expose yourself to as many different types of people and social experiences as you can. Embrace diversity. Travel broadly if you can, and mix as much as possible with others, especially those different from you. View unexpected events as opportunities to learn something new about yourself and others.

2. Focus on the internal states of others (their thoughts, feelings, motives, etc.). Try to figure people out—what they want, why they want the things they do, and what will happen if they get the things they want. Share your ideas with others and talk often about people and their motivations.

3. Try to understand others' moods and feelings. Pay attention to the circumstances associated with certain emotional reactions and the thought patterns about these circumstances that result in specific emotional reactions. Try to understand why different people may have very different emotional reactions to similar events.

4. Spend as much time as you can with people you think are really effective communicators. Pay attention to what they say and do. If you can, talk with them about how they handle various social situations and problems. Ask their advice about how you might handle challenging communication problems.

5. Think before you talk, especially in important or "high stakes" situations. Focus not only on what you feel and want, but also on what others are likely to be feeling and wanting. Try to imagine how others will respond if you say certain things. Imagine how their responses would change if you said something different.

6. Try to process messages you receive from the viewpoint of the source, especially when those messages are problematic in some way. Generate alternative interpretations about what the source might mean and think carefully about the criteria you should use to select among the alternative interpretations.

7. Cultivate complexity in your thinking about people, social situations, and messages. Internalize the idea that in many important situations, messages are (or should be) constructed in the effort to achieve multiple goals. Try to identify the various goals that people should pursue in challenging communication situations and think about alternative ways in which these goals can be achieved efficiently and effectively.

Although none of these self-improvement methods has yet been shown by research to be effective at enhancing skills, each is consistent with what is known about the nature and acquisition of communication skills, so each holds at least some promise of helping you develop your skills.

CONCLUSION

This chapter has provided an overview of one theory of communication skill, constructivism. Constructivism is largely focused on functional communication skills, which concern producing messages and interpreting the messages of others in ways that facilitate goal achievement. Functional communication skills are very important in everyday life, and mastery of these skills leads to several forms of personal and professional success.

Constructivism maintains that people actively interpret their experiences, and these interpretations are the major influence on their behavior. People differ in the complexity of their interpretive schemes (or constructs), and these differences in cognitive complexity have important implications for social perception skills, message production skills, and message reception skills. In general, people with higher levels of interpersonal cognitive complexity possess more advanced social perception and communication skills, but the connections between cognitive complexity and various skills can be quite complicated (review Figure 6.1). Researchers have learned quite a bit about childhood socialization factors that influence the development of cognitive complexity and associated communication skills. Unfortunately, much less is known about how adults can reliably improve their levels of cognitive complexity and communication skills. Much more research is needed on communication skill training; perhaps some of you will make contributions in this area some day.

REFERENCES

Adams, C. H. (2001). Prosocial bias in theories of interpersonal communication competence: Must good communication be nice? In G. J. Shepherd & E. W. Rothenbuhler (Eds.), *Communication and community* (pp. 37–52). Mahwah, NJ: Lawrence Erlbaum Associates, Inc.

Adams, C. H., & Shepherd, G. (1996). Managing volunteer performance: Face support and situational features as predictors of volunteers' evaluations of regulative messages. *Management Communication Quarterly, 9,* 363–388.

Applegate, J. L., Burleson, B. R., & Delia, J. G. (1992). Reflection-enhancing parenting as antecedent to children's social-cognitive and communicative development. In I. E. Sigel, A. V. McGillicuddy-Delisi, & J. J. Goodnow (Eds.), *Parental belief systems: The psychological consequences for children* (2nd ed., pp. 3–39). Hillsdale, NJ: Lawrence Erlbaum Associates, Inc.

Bacue, A., & Samter, W. (2001, July). *The dark side of cognitive complexity, II: The production of guilt-inducing messages.* Paper presented at the third annual joint conference of the International Network on Personal Relationships and the International Society for the Study of Personal Relationships, Prescott, AZ.

Barone, D. F., Maddux, J. E., & Snyder, C. R. (1997). *Social cognitive psychology: History and current domains.* New York: Plenum.

Berger, C. R. (2003). Message production skill in social interaction. In J. O. Greene & B. R. Burleson (Eds.), *Handbook of communication and social interaction skills* (pp. 257–289). Mahwah, NJ: Lawrence Erlbaum Associates, Inc.

Brendel, J. M., Kolbert, J. B., & Foster, V. A. (2002). Promoting student cognitive development. *Journal of Adult Development, 9,* 217–227.

Buhrmester, D. (1996). Need fulfillment, interpersonal competence, and the developmental contexts of early adolescent friendship. In W. M. Bukowski, A. F. Newcomb, & W. W. Hartup (Eds.), *The company they keep: Friendship in childhood and adolescence* (pp. 158–185). New York: Cambridge University Press.

Burleson, B. R. (1982). The development of comforting communication skills in childhood and adolescence. *Child Development, 53,* 1578–1588.

Burleson, B. R. (1987). Cognitive complexity. In J. C. McCroskey & J. A. Daly (Eds.), *Personality and interpersonal communication* (pp. 305–349). Newbury Park, CA: Sage.

Burleson, B. R. (1998). Similarities in social skills, interpersonal attraction, and the development of personal relationships. In J. S. Trent (Ed.), *Communication: Views from the helm for the 21st Century* (pp. 77–84). Boston: Allyn & Bacon.

Burleson, B. R. (2003). Emotional support skills. In J. O. Greene & B. R. Burleson (Eds.), *Handbook of communication and social interaction skills* (pp. 551–594). Mahwah, NJ: Lawrence Erlbaum Associates, Inc.

Burleson, B. R., & Caplan, S. E. (1998). Cognitive complexity. In J. C. McCroskey, J. A. Daly, M. M. Martin, & M. J. Beatty (Eds.), *Communication and personality: Trait perspectives* (pp. 230–286). Cresskill, NJ: Hampton.

Burleson, B. R., Delia, J. G., & Applegate, J. L. (1992). Effects of maternal communication and children's social-cognitive and communication skills on children's acceptance by the peer group. *Family Relations, 41,* 264–272.

Burleson, B. R., & Denton, W. H. (1997). The relationship between communication skills and marital satisfaction: Some moderating effects. *Journal of Marriage and the Family, 59,* 884–902.

Burleson, B. R., & Goldsmith, D. J. (1998). How the comforting process works: Alleviating emotional distress through conversationally induced reappraisals. In P. A. Andersen & L. K. Guerrero (Eds.), *Handbook of communication and emotion: Research, theory, applications, and contexts* (pp. 245–280). San Diego, CA: Academic.

Burleson, B. R., & Kunkel, A. W. (1996). The socialization of emotional support skills in childhood. In G. R. Pierce, B. R. Sarason, & I. G. Sarason (Eds.), *Handbook of social support and the family* (pp. 105–140). New York: Plenum.

Burleson, B. R., & Kunkel, A. W. (2002). Parental and peer contributions to the emotional support skills of the child: From whom do children learn to express support? *Journal of Family Communication, 2,* 79–97.

Burleson, B. R., & Samter, W. (1994). A social skills approach to relationship maintenance: How individual differences in communication skills affect the achievement of relationship functions. In D. J. Canary & L. Stafford (Eds.), *Communication and relational maintenance* (pp. 61–90). San Diego, CA: Academic.

Burleson, B. R., & Waltman, M. S. (1988). Cognitive complexity: Using the Role Category Questionnaire measure. In C. H. Tardy (Ed.), *A handbook for the study of human communication: Methods and instruments for observing, measuring, and assessing communication processes* (pp. 1–35). Norwood, NJ: Ablex.

Chaiken, S., Liberman, A., & Eagly, A. H. (1989). Heuristic and systematic information processing within and beyond the persuasion context. In J. S. Uleman & J. A. Bargh (Eds.), *Unintended thought: Limits of awareness, intention, and control* (pp. 212–252). New York: Guilford.

Chaiken, S., & Trope, Y. (Eds.). (1999). *Dual-process theories in social psychology.* New York: Guilford.

Clark, R. A., & Delia, J. G. (1979). *Topoi* and rhetorical competence. *Quarterly Journal of Speech, 65,* 187–206.

Clark, R. A., Willihnganz, S., & O'Dell, L. L. (1985). Training fourth graders in compromising and persuasive strategies. *Communication Education, 34,* 331–342.

Coopman, S. Z. (1997). Personal constructs and communication in interpersonal and organizational contexts. In G. Neimeyer & R. Neimeyer (Eds.), *Advances in personal construct psychology* (Vol. 4, pp. 101–147). Greenwich, CT: JAI Press.

Crockett, W. H. (1965). Cognitive complexity and impression formation. In V. B. A. Maher (Ed.), *Progress in experimental personality research* (Vol. 2, pp. 47–90). New York: Academic.

Delia, J. G., Kline, S. L., & Burleson, B. R. (1979). The development of persuasive communication strategies in kindergartners through twelfth-graders. *Communication Monographs, 46,* 241–256.

Delia, J. G., O'Keefe, B. J., & O'Keefe, D. J. (1982). The constructivist approach to communication. In F. E. X. Dance (Ed.), *Human communication theory: Comparative essays* (pp. 147–191). New York: Harper & Row.

Dunn, J. (1998). Siblings, emotion, and the development of understanding. In S. Braten (Ed.), *Intersubjective communication and emotion in early ontogeny* (pp. 158–168). Cambridge, England: Cambridge University Press.

Duys, D. K., & Hedstrom, S. M. (2000). Basic counselor skills training and counselor cognitive complexity. *Counselor Education & Supervision, 40*(1), 8–18.

Goleman, D. (1995). *Emotional intelligence.* New York: Bantam Books.

Habermas, J. (1998). *On the pragmatics of communication.* Cambridge, MA: MIT Press.

Hart, C. H., Newell, L. D., & Olsen, S. F. (2003). Parenting skills and social-communicative competence in childhood. In J. O. Greene & B. R. Burleson (Eds.), *Handbook of communication and social interaction skills* (pp. 753–799). Mahwah, NJ: Lawrence Erlbaum Associates, Inc.

Hewes, D. E. (1995). Cognitive processing of problematic messages: Reinterpreting to "unbias" texts. In D. E. Hewes (Ed.), *The cognitive bases of interpersonal communication* (pp. 113–138). Hillsdale, NJ: Lawrence Erlbaum Associates, Inc.

Jones, S. M., & Guerrero, L. A. (2001). The effects of nonverbal immediacy and verbal person centeredness in the emotional support process. *Human Communication Research, 27,* 567–596.

Kline, S. L. (1991). Construct differentiation and person-centered regulative messages. *Journal of Language and Social Psychology, 10,* 1–27.

Lambert, B. L., & Gillespie, J. L. (1994). Patient perceptions of pharmacy students' hypertension compliance-gaining messages: Effects of message design logic and content themes. *Health Communication, 6,* 311–325.

MacGeorge, E. L., Clark, R. A., & Gillihan, S. J. (2002). Sex differences in the provision of skillful emotional support: The mediating role of self-efficacy. *Communication Reports, 15,* 17–28.

Marsh, D. T., Serafica, F. C., & Barenboim, C. (1980). Effect of perspective-taking training on interpersonal problem solving. *Child Development, 51,* 140–145.

McCornack, S. A. (1992). Information manipulation theory. *Communication Monographs, 59,* 1–16.

Neuliep, J. W., & Hazelton, V., Jr. (1986). Enhanced conversational recall and reduced conversational interference as a function of cognitive complexity. *Human Communication Research, 13,* 211–224.

O'Keefe, B. J., & Shepherd, G. J. (1989). The communication of identity during face-to-face persuasive interactions: Effects of perceiver's construct differentiation and target's message strategies. *Communication Research, 16,* 375–404.

O'Keefe, D. J. (2002). *Persuasion: Theory and research* (2nd ed.). Thousand Oaks, CA: Sage.

Pelias, R. J. (1984). Oral interpretation as a training method for increasing perspective-taking abilities. *Communication Education, 33,* 143–151.

Petty, R. E., & Wegener, D. T. (1999). The elaboration likelihood model: Current status and controversies. In S. Chaiken & Y. Trope (Eds.), *Dual-process theories in social psychology* (pp. 41–72). New York: Guilford.

Press, A. N., Crockett, W. H., & Delia, J. G. (1975). Effects of cognitive complexity and perceiver's set upon the organization of impressions of others. *Journal of Personality and Social Psychology, 32,* 865–895.

Rowan, K. E. (1984). The implicit social scientist and the implicit rhetorician: An integrative framework for the introductory interpersonal course. *Communication Education, 33,* 351–360.

Russell, J. A., & Barchard, K. A. (2002). Toward a shared language for emotion and emotional intelligence. In L. F. Barrett & P. Salovey (Eds.), *The wisdom in feeling: Psychological processes in emotional intelligence* (pp. 363–382). New York: Guilford.

Samter, W., & Burleson, B. R. (1984). Cognitive and motivational influences on spontaneous comforting behavior. *Human Communication Research, 11,* 231–260.

Stacks, D. W., & Murphy, M. A. (1993). Conversational sensitivity: Further validation and extension. *Communication Reports, 6,* 18–24.

Strayer, J., & Mashal, M. (1983). The role of peer experience in communication and role-taking skills. *Journal of Genetic Psychology, 143,* 113–122.

Sypher, B. D., Bostrom, R. N., & Seibert, J. H. (1989). Listening, communication abilities, and success at work. *Journal of Business Communication, 26,* 293–303.

Sypher, B. D., & Zorn, T. E. (1986). Communication-related abilities and upward mobility: A longitudinal investigation. *Human Communication Research, 12,* 420–431.

Waldron, V. R., & Applegate, J. L. (1994). Interpersonal construct differentiation and conversational planning: An examination of two cognitive accounts for the production of competent verbal disagreement tactics. *Human Communication Research, 21,* 3–35.

Wilson, S. R. (1990). Development and test of a cognitive rules model of interaction goals. *Communication Monographs, 57,* 81–103.

Wilson, S. R., Cruz, M. G., & Kang, K. H. (1992). Is is always a matter of perspective? Construct differentiation and variability in attributions about compliance-gaining. *Communication Monographs, 59,* 350–366.

Wyer, R. S., Jr., & Adaval, R. (2003). Message reception skills in social communication. In J. O. Greene & B. R. Burleson (Eds.), *Handbook of communication and social interaction skills* (pp. 291–355). Mahwah, NJ: Lawrence Erlbaum Associates, Inc.

Zeidner, M., Matthews, G., Roberts, R. D., & MacCann, C. (2003). Development of emotional intelligence: Towards a multi-level investment mode. *Human Development, 46,* 69–96.

Zorn, T. E., & Violanti, M. T. (1996). Communication abilities and individual achievement in organizations. *Management Communication Quarterly, 10,* 139–167.

QUESTIONS TO PONDER

1. What is cognitive complexity? What is the connection between cognitive complexity and various social perception skills? Why should theories of communication skill be concerned with social perception processes?

2. What is person-centeredness and how is person-centeredness manifested in different types of messages? Why are highly person-centered messages viewed as more skilled forms of behavior? What factors influence the ability to produce highly person-centered messages?

3. What is involved in the depth processing of messages? What costs and benefits are associated with depth processing? When and why are people likely to engage in depth processing? What factors contribute to skill at depth processing?

4. Why are some people more cognitively complex and socially skilled than others? If you want to raise children who are cognitively complex and have good functional communication skills, what should you do?

5. Suppose you get a job in the human resources division of a large corporation. Management wants you to develop a training program designed to enhance the social perception and communication skills of employees. What exercises would you include in your program?

7

Aggressive Communication

Andrew S. Rancer
University of Akron

Anne Maydan Nicotera
Howard University

INTRODUCTION

In a world of diverse attitudes, opinions, and values, differences between persons over issues both large and small are inevitable. When engaging in a controversial issue, individuals vary in their levels of aggressiveness. Social scientists have taken numerous approaches to the ways in which individuals manage difference and disagreement. One of the problems encountered in social science is that scholars from many disciplines are interested in studying the same processes. Although we may all be interested in the same phenomenon—aggression, for example—we typically are not interested in studying the same elements of the phenomenon. Even when we are interested in the same elements, we may be using very different approaches. For example, psychologists are generally interested in individual cognitive processes and the ways in which they affect individual behavior; clinical psychologists are interested in applying this knowledge therapeutically in helping relationships with persons in distress. Sociologists are generally interested in broad societal patterns of behavior. Communication scholars are generally interested in the processes that unfold when people interact (Nicotera, 1996).

This chapter will explain what is meant by "communication predispositions," provide important definitions, explain the theory of aggressive communication predispositions, describe how these communication traits are measured in research, and discuss the ways in which these communication traits are related theoretically. Following this preliminary explanation, the chapter will provide a review of research conducted in this area. The chapter will close with a discussion of the limitations of our knowledge and the importance of thinking critically about the research.

WHAT ARE COMMUNICATION PREDISPOSITIONS?

Communication predispositions are personality traits that influence individuals to communicate in particular ways across situations. A communication predisposition is an individual's natural inclination to communicate in a certain fashion. Theorists and researchers who utilize the concept of communication predispositions assume that an individual will often tend to respond to a variety of situations with similar behavioral patterns (Nicotera, 1993, 1994). Most scholars assume that these tendencies are rooted in personality. Although we can categorize people according to their predispositions, we cannot predict with certainty that their behaviors will follow those tendencies. The specific characteristics of each situation have an impact on how individuals choose to act. People with aggressive personality traits are predisposed to communicate aggressively, but their actual aggressive communication will vary in its intensity from situation to situation. Still, they have a general tendency, or predisposition, to use aggressive communication.

It is important to understand that we cannot predict an individual's behavior solely through an understanding of communication predispositions. Communication researchers who take this psychological approach generally do not intend to specify or predict the behavioral patterns of a single individual. Rather, measurements of individual's psychological traits or communication predispositions are aggregated—grouped—with the scores of other individuals. The resulting group is commonly called an aggregate sample. By examining the ways in which psychological measures correspond to or vary with other measures (of behaviors, other traits, or specific outcomes) across an aggregate sample, researchers can draw general conclusions about patterns in human communication. These general patterns can sometimes be used to design training programs and other such interventions to aid people in improving their communication in a variety of settings.

For example, research has shown that the most favorable conditions for organizational communication exist when superiors and subordinates are high in argumentativeness (constructive aggression, as explained later), low in verbal aggressiveness (destructive aggression, also explained later), and communicate in an affirming style (relaxed, friendly, and attentive; Gorden & Infante, 1987a; Infante & Gorden, 1987, 1989, 1991). Under these conditions morale, productivity, commitment, and goal-achievement are high. By examining personality traits, communication patterns, and outcomes, scholars were able to identify particular ways to help organizational superiors and subordinates to improve their communicative lives. Such conclusions can only be drawn, however, by examining aggregate samples.

DEFINITION OF AGGRESSIVE COMMUNICATION PREDISPOSITIONS

Communication scholars who take a psychological approach assert that personality traits and predispositions can provide valuable insight into communication behaviors. One of the most widely researched sets of communication predispositions has been predispositions toward aggressiveness. Infante (1987a; Infante & Wigley, 1986) contended that aggression, though widely studied in various social science disciplines, had traditionally been regarded in a generic sense. In conceptualizing aggressive communication predispositions, Infante's (1987a) intent was to come to an understanding of aggression in interpersonal relations. Although it is distinctly psychological, his specific approach allows for situational determinants to play a role in influencing behavior; in other words, it is assumed that traits can be learned.

THE THEORY OF AGGRESSIVE COMMUNICATION PREDISPOSITIONS

The theory of aggressive communication predispositions is based upon a general definition of aggression in interpersonal communication:

> An interpersonal behavior may be considered aggressive if it applies force physically and/or symbolically in order, minimally, to dominate and perhaps damage or, maximally, to defeat and perhaps destroy the locus of attack. The locus of attack in interpersonal communication can be a person's body, material possessions, self-concept, position on topics of communication, or behavior. (Infante, 1987a, p. 158)

Aggression is not one, but several traits. The first distinction made in categorizing aggression is physical versus symbolic. Physical aggression involves the aggressor's forceful use of his or her body (roughly handling or striking objects or others). Symbolic aggression involves the aggressor's forceful use of his or her communication (words, gestures, vocal tone, etc.). It is this latter set of behaviors which the theory of aggressive communication predisposition seeks to explain.

Symbolic aggression can be divided into two categories: constructive and destructive. Constructive symbolic aggression is subsumed under the heading "assertiveness." One facet of assertiveness is *argumentativeness*, defined as a stable trait that predisposes an individual to defend a position on an issue and verbally attack the positions of others (Infante & Rancer, 1982). Moreover, "Argumentativeness may be considered a subset of assertiveness, in that all arguing is assertive, but not all assertiveness involves arguing" (Infante, 1987a, p. 164). According to Infante and Rancer (1982), a person with high argumentativeness enjoys arguing and will eagerly engage in verbal debate. In addition, "the individual perceives this activity as an exciting intellectual challenge, a competitive situation which entails defending a position and 'winning points'" (p. 72). Furthermore, individuals are more likely to score highly on Infante and Rancer's (1982) argumentativeness scale, which is explained later, and more likely to actually engage in argument when they hold positive beliefs about arguing (Rancer, Baukus, & Infante, 1985). A person low in argumentativeness feels uncomfortable about arguing before, during, and after the event that calls for argument (Infante & Rancer, 1982).

Here is a good example of argumentativeness. In a disagreement about what movie to see together, Linda might say to her boyfriend John, "I understand that you enjoy action films, but I don't like them. I've read the reviews of 'Death Force 8000,' and they said it was really gory, so you'll love it, but I'll hate it. I don't think it's fair for you to insist that I go with you. If we're going to see a movie together, I think it makes more sense for us to see the kind of movie we can both enjoy, like a comedy. I think it's important that we both enjoy ourselves." Here, Linda respectfully states her understanding of his position; she does not "put him down" for his position, and she provides evidence to support her own position. She attacks his position—but not his person—and constructively asserts her own point of view. Most importantly, she does not back away from defending her own viewpoint and attacking his; this is what reveals her argumentativeness.

Destructive symbolic aggression is classified as hostility. One facet of hostility is *verbal aggressiveness,* defined as "the tendency to attack the self-concepts of individuals instead of, or in addition to, their positions on topics of communication" (Infante, 1987a, p. 164). These attacks most commonly take the form of competence attacks, teasing, and nonverbal emblems (i.e., "flipping the bird"). Other less common forms of verbal aggressiveness include character attacks, background attacks, physical appearance attacks, maledictions (i.e., wishing someone harm, as when we say to someone "drop dead"), teasing, swearing, ridicule, and threats (Wigley, 1998). Thus, the essential difference between argumentativeness and verbal aggressiveness is in the locus of the attack. In argumentativeness the attack is on the adversary's *position* on the controversial issue; in verbal aggressiveness, the attack is on the adversary's *self-concept*.

Verbally aggressive behavior is more common in exchanges where the topic is of great importance and the consequences are very meaningful to those involved. Infante, Trebing, Shepherd, and Seeds (1984) identified four primary reasons individuals are verbally aggressive, including psychopathology (repressed hostility), disdain for the other person, social learning of aggression, and argumentative skill deficiency (not knowing how to argue constructively). Infante, Riddle, Horvath, and Tumlin (1992) found that verbally aggressive individuals view threats, competence attacks, character attacks, maledictions, nonverbal emblems, and ridicule as less hurtful than those who are low in verbal aggressiveness. They also found that such individuals reported their reasons for being verbally aggressive as follows: trying to appear "tough"; rational discussions degenerate into verbal fights; wanting to be mean to the other; and wanting to express disdain for the other. In another study, Martin, Anderson, and Horvath (1996) observed that highly verbally aggressive individuals often perceive that their aggression is justified.

Let's see how different the conversation between Linda and John might look if Linda were verbally aggressive rather than argumentative. "I cannot understand why you enjoy action films. They're stupid and childish, and so is anybody who wastes their money to see them. Gory movies like 'Death Force 8000' are just garbage. I really don't want to see it, and I think you're a jerk to insist that I go with you. Anybody with a brain could see that it makes more sense for us to see the kind of movie we can both enjoy, like a comedy, you selfish pig." Ouch. Here, Linda makes her point by both directly and indirectly attacking John's self-concept.

To review, symbolic (or communicative) aggression is divided into constructive and destructive types. Constructive aggression is assertiveness, which includes argumentativeness—the tendency to defend one's position on a controversial issue and attack the positions of others. Destructive aggression is hostility, which includes verbal aggressiveness—the tendency to attack others' self-concepts. The distinction between argumentativeness and verbal aggressiveness is the locus of attack (Infante, 1987a; Infante & Wigley, 1986). In argumentativeness, the aggressor is attacking the other's position on an issue, while maintaining respect for the other person. In verbal aggressiveness, the individual is attacking the other person's self-concept.

MEASUREMENT OF AGGRESSIVE COMMUNICATION PREDISPOSITIONS

Like other personality traits, argumentativeness and verbal aggressiveness are measured with paper-and-pencil self-report questionnaire instruments. Each is a 20-item scale, though they are scored somewhat differently as will be explained later. These measurement instruments are not intended to result in individual scores in the same way that psychological tests (such as IQ) are. In other words, scores on the argumentativeness and verbal aggressiveness scales are not meant to provide conclusive information about individuals filling out the forms; rather, they are intended to allow researchers to develop an understanding of how these personality traits are related to other traits and to communication behaviors and outcomes for aggregate samples of persons.

Argumentativeness

The Argumentativeness Scale (Infante & Rancer, 1982) is based on Atkinson's (1957, 1966) theory of achievement motivation. This theory posits that individuals weigh their likelihood of failure and success; this judgment determines their motivation to succeed at a given task. In conflict situations, individuals respond based on their judgments of likely failure or success. Atkinson' s (1957, 1966) terminology is "excitation-inhibition"; in other words, there are competing approach and avoidance motivations for engaging in argument. These motivations are based on both personality (trait) and situational (state) factors.

Based on this assumption of coexisting motivations to engage in argument (approach) and to withdraw from argument (avoidance), Infante and Rancer (1982) designed subscales to measure both. Thus, general trait argumentativeness (ARGgt) equals the predisposition to approach argument (ARGap) minus the predisposition to avoid argument (ARGav).

$$ARGgt = ARGap - ARGav \qquad \text{[ARG Formula 1]}$$

The ARGgt scale thus measures trait argumentativeness, the predisposition to engage in argument that is embedded in personality.

To link argumentativeness as a predisposition (ARGgt) more closely to a prediction of argumentative behavior embedded in a particular situation, Atkinson's theory was again drawn on to include situational factors. In a real situation that might require argument, as explained previously, Atkinson's theory tells us that an individual's motivation to argue is based on judgments of the likelihood of succeeding and failing. In addition, Infante and Rancer (1982) assumed that motivation to argue is impacted by the individual's feelings about the importance of success or failure in a particular situation. Thus, four situational factors were identified: probability of success (Ps), probability of failure (Pf), importance of success (Is), and importance of failure (If). That is, including these four situational factors should enhance our ability to predict how argumentative an individual might be in a given situation.

An individual's tendency to approach an argument (Tap) in a situation is equal to his or her predisposition to approach argument (ARGap) multiplied by his or her perceptions of the probability and importance of success (Ps and Is) in that situation.

$$Tap = ARGap \times Ps \times Is \qquad \text{[ARG Formula 2]}$$

Similarly, a person's tendency to avoid argument (Tav) is equal to his or her predisposition to avoid argument (ARGav) multiplied by perceptions of the probability and importance of failure (Pf and If) in that situation.

$$Tav = ARGav \times Pf \times If \qquad \text{[ARG Formula 3]}$$

Finally, the resultant motivation for argument (RMArg), which would predict the argumentativeness of an individual in a specific situation, is calculated as follows:

$$RMArg = Tap - Tav \qquad \text{[ARG Formula 4]}$$

Resultant motivation for argument (RMArg), which predicts the likelihood of argumentative behavior in a specific situation, is a combination of state (situational) and trait factors. Adding situational perceptions should enhance our prediction of resultant motivation to argue in a given situation. For example, let's say that you are preparing to ask your boss for a raise. Since the budget for salary increases is "tight" this year, you recognize that this request will likely result in an argumentative encounter with your boss (i.e., you will provide data to support your request while the boss is likely to engage in refutation and counterarguing).

To more accurately predict your resultant motivation to argue (RMArg) in that particular situation, we would need to obtain several measures. First, we would need to assess your general tendency (i.e., trait) to argue. This is obtained by administering the Argumentativeness Scale that will provide us with a measure of your general motivation to approach (ARGap) and your general motivation to avoid (ARGav) argumentative situations (see ARG Formula 1). In addition, we would need to measure your perceptions of the probability and importance of success and failure (Ps, Is, Pf, If) for that particular argumentative encounter.

To measure Ps, we would ask you to respond this item, "I believe me *winning* this argument would be:" (*likely–unlikely, probable–improbable, possible–impossible*). To measure Pf, we would ask you to respond this item, "I believe me *losing* this argument would be:" (*likely–unlikely, probable–improbable, possible–impossible*). To measure Is, we would ask you to respond to this item, "If I *win* this argument, it would be:" (*important–unimportant, significant–insignificant, meaningful–meaningless*). To measure If, we would ask you to respond to this item, "If I *lose* this argument, it would be:" (*important–unimportant, significant–insignificant, meaningful–meaningless*). All responses would be measured on a 7 space scale format. Thus, a quantitative score for all components in Formulas 2 and 3 above have now been obtained, allowing us to predict your resultant motivation to argue in that situation.

Let's return to the "asking for a raise" example. Suppose that you score in the moderate level for both ARGap and ARGav, that is, you are neither high or low in the general trait. Let us further suppose that while your probability of success (Ps) for arguing with your boss is also in the moderate range (i.e., you think you have a 50–50 chance of winning), your importance of success (Is) is quite strong (i.e., you see it as extremely important that you "win" the argument and receive the raise). Further, while your probability of failure (Pf) is also moderate (i.e., you think you have a 50–50 chance of losing), your importance of failure (If) is very strong (i.e., if you lose the argument and don't receive the raise you will need to get a second job to pay your expenses). By obtaining all of these measures, we would expect your resultant motivation to argue (RMArg) in that situation to be higher than it would have been if we predicted it on the basis of your general tendency (trait; ARGgt) to argue alone (which you recall was in the moderate range). Thus, adding situation perceptions can enhance the precision in our ability to predict how motivated a person will be to argue in any given situation. This assumption has been supported by research (Infante, 1987b).

The scale described in this next section is a measure of argumentativeness as a personality trait, your generally tendency to argue (ARGgt). The Argumentativeness Scale was developed in a series of three studies reported by Infante and Rancer (1982). The first administered to 141 undergraduate students a questionnaire consisting of 45 items designed by the authors to tap into argumentativeness approach, argumentativeness avoidance, and verbal aggressiveness. The students were asked to rate their agreement with each statement using a Likert scale from 1 (*strongly disagree*),2 (*disagree*), 3 (*neither agree nor disagree*), 4 (*agree*), 5 (*strongly agree*). A statistical procedure known as factor analysis was conducted on these data. Factor analysis allows a researcher to discover which items on such a scale are most closely related to one another. The results of factor analysis consist of a set of factors, or clusters, of items. Each item receives a score or "loading" on each factor; using these factorial loadings, the researcher determines which items are the best measures of each factor.

Other studies helped to confirm and refine this factor structure. Today, the Argumentativeness Scale is composed of 10 items assessing the extent to which individuals approach (or endorse) argumentativeness and 10 items tapping the extent to which they avoid it. Examples of items that measure ARGap include "I am energetic and enthusiastic when I argue," "I enjoy a good argument over a controversial issue," and "I enjoy defending my point of view on an issue." Examples of items that measure ARGav include "Arguing with a person creates more problems for me than it solves," "I get an unpleasant feeling when I realize I am about to get into an argument," and "I am happy when I keep an argument from happening." Responses for ARGap items are added together (summed) to achieve an ARGap score; responses for ARGav items are summed to achieve an ARGap score; ARGav is then subtracted from ARGap. ARGgt scores can range from –40 to 40.

Verbal Aggressiveness

Infante and Wigley (1986) recognized that aggressive communication is controlled by destructive traits as well. Thus, they set out to develop a scale designed to measure the other form of attacking communication, the tendency of people to engage in delivering messages that attack another person's *self-concept*. Thus, the Verbal Aggressiveness Scale (Infante & Wigley, 1986) was developed in a similar fashion as the Argumentativeness Scale. A questionnaire consisting of 30 items designed to tap into verbal aggressiveness was administered to 209 undergraduate students. The 30 items were written to reflect the definition of verbal aggressiveness developed by Infante (1987a)—the tendency to attack the self-concept of others instead of (or in addition to) their positions on issues. To avoid defensiveness in students' responses three steps were taken. First, the existence of verbal aggressiveness is assumed, so some items asked where, how, and when it is expressed, rather than whether it is expressed. Second, in some items justification for the behavior was provided to legitimize the expression of verbal aggressiveness. Finally in some items, the verbally aggressive response was made to appear benevolent. These strategies are consistent with research revealing that aggressive individuals often provide justification to themselves for their socially undesirable aggressive behavior (Infante et al., 1992). The same students also completed the Argumentativeness Scale to be sure the two scales were measuring different things.

The result of these investigations was a 20-item scale consisting of 10 positively worded items (e.g., "I refuse to participate in arguments when they involve personal attacks," "When people criticize my shortcomings, I take it in good humor and do not try to get back at them," and "When I try to influence people, I make a great effort not to offend them") and 10 negatively worded items (e.g., "If individuals I'm trying to influence really deserve it, I attack their character," "When individuals are very stubborn, I use insults to soften the stubbornness," and "When individuals insult me, I get a lot of pleasure out of really telling them off"). Responses to each item range from 1 (*strongly disagree*), 2 (*disagree*), 3 (*neither agree nor disagree*), 4 (*agree*), 5 (*strongly agree*). Agreement with the negatively worded items indicates verbal aggressiveness; disagreement with positively worded items also indicates verbal aggressiveness. This is another strategy that controls for defensiveness; respondents might be reluctant to express agreement with items that cast them in a negative light. In fact, Infante and Wigley (1986) found that individuals were slightly more likely to admit to positively worded items than they were to negatively worded items. Verbal aggressiveness scores can range from 20 to 100.

RELATIONSHIP BETWEEN ARGUMENTATIVENESS
AND VERBAL AGGRESSIVENESS

Theoretically, argumentativeness and verbal aggressiveness are completely separate constructs, or phenomena. An individual may be neither argumentative nor verbally aggressive, skirting controversy altogether ("See you later"). An individual may be both argumentative and verbally aggressive, attacking both the viewpoint and the self-concept of the other ("Your idea does not consider all the facts, you idiot"). Alternatively, an individual may be argumentative but not verbally aggressive ("Your idea does not consider all the facts, but you had no way of knowing. Let me explain"). Finally, an individual may be verbally aggressive but not argumentative ("You're a moron").

Without knowledge of other factors (such as a person's history, other personality traits, causes for their development of these traits, etc.), we cannot predict a relation between argumentativeness and verbal aggressiveness. However, there is some evidence, which will be discussed in the last section of this chapter, that the relation between argumentativeness and verbal aggressiveness varies between cultures, between genders, and between age groups. Furthermore, there may be patterns in a relation between argumentativeness and verbal aggressiveness that vary according to combinations of culture, gender, and generation.

When faced with a situation where he or she disagrees with another person and where success in persuading the other person is perceived as important and probable, a highly argumentative individual is quite likely to actively and forcefully defend his or her point of view while attacking the other's. Highly argumentative people are predisposed to engage in argument to convince others to change their positions on controversial issues. When faced with a situation where he or she disagrees with another person, a verbally aggressive individual is quite likely to actively and forcefully attack the self-concept of the other. Highly verbally aggressive people are predisposed to verbally "go for the jugular." Furthermore, a highly verbally aggressive person is unlikely to consider his or her comments as hurtful to the degree that the recipient of those comments might. Regarding the relation between argumentativeness and verbal aggressiveness, it is conceivable that an individual may be predisposed to attack both the other person's ideas and feelings or neither.

LITERATURE REVIEW ON AGGRESSIVE COMMUNICATION

Over the last 20 years, a great deal of research has been conducted on the aggressive communication traits of argumentativeness and verbal aggressiveness (Infante & Rancer, 1996; Rancer & Avtgis, 2006). It has been estimated that this line of research has produced almost 200 published articles, convention papers, and dissertations! In this section we would like to present you with a sense of the types of studies conducted on argumentativeness and verbal aggressiveness, as well as provide you with some findings that we can glean from this rather large body of research. We shall be quite selective in our examples and presentation. However, we hope to provide enough information to give you a sense of the impact of these traits on a wide variety of behaviors and perceptions, while not overwhelming you with vast amounts of detail and studies.

Thus, this section will describe some of the research on aggressive communication that has been conducted in several of the major communication contexts: family communication, organizational communication, instructional communication, and intercultural communication. We must be careful to note here that the vast majority of research in the field of communication, including the research reviewed later, has been conducted with respondents who are predominately White, middle-class Americans. As such, summary comments about "Americans" are usually limited to Americans of European descent. We know little about argumentativeness and verbal aggressiveness for Americans of African, Asian, Native American, Middle Eastern, or Hispanic descent. In addition, it must be noted that such cultural groups have vast internal diversity. The research reviewed here is valuable in terms of what it can tell us about White Americans; however, we should use caution when attempting to generalize these findings to other American cultural groups.

FAMILY COMMUNICATION

Family communication shapes much of how we communicate in many other contexts, and influences how we communicate on the job and with romantic partners (Infante, Rancer, & Womack, 1997, p. 429). Consequently, a great deal of attention in recent years has been paid to this context. Recently, a number of researchers have begun to examine the influence of aggressive communication in the family. Much of this work has explored the impact of parents' aggressive communication on their children's behavior, and some research has even explored how similar children are to their parents on the aggressive communication traits.

First, we shall explore the role of the parents' aggressiveness on children. In a seminal study in this area, Beatty, Zelley, Dobos, and Rudd (1994) found that the more the fathers were perceived as using criticism, sarcasm, and verbal aggression, the higher their fathers were in verbal aggressiveness. Beatty, Burant, Dobos, and Rudd (1996) extended this study and examined the effectiveness and appropriateness of fathers' verbal plans for interacting with a young son who disobeyed a father's orders. Verbal plans were defined as that which fathers intend to say or do in response to a son's verbal behavior. Fathers' levels of verbal aggressiveness was measured by the Verbal Aggressiveness Scale (Infante & Wigley, 1986). The fathers were then asked to respond to a situation (a young son disobeyed his order to shut a television set off and return to studying) by selecting from several tactics in response to their sons' disobedience. The results indicated that the appropriateness and effectiveness of the plans fathers said they would use deteriorated as the interaction with the resistant son progressed. That is, as the son continued to resist the father's requests, the tactical choices got more destructive moving from supportive tactics (such as doing homework together with the son, talking about the importance of school, and negotiating with the son) to coercive tactics (such as yelling, whipping, slapping, spanking, and threatening to spank). In addition, the fathers' level of verbal aggressiveness was related to plan appropriateness and effectiveness, with the higher the fathers' verbal aggressiveness yielding lower effectiveness and appropriateness scores.

This study was replicated (Rudd, Beatty, Vogl-Bauer, & Dobos, 1997) by asking fathers to indicate how appropriate each tactic was in gaining compliance from his son. Again, the higher the trait verbal aggressiveness, the lower the ratings of supportive tactics, and the higher the ratings of coercive tactics. Another study (Rudd, Vogl-Bauer, Dobos, Beatty, & Valencic, 1998) examined the relation between parents' verbal aggressiveness and the anger they experienced when interacting with their children. Results indicated that parents' trait verbal aggressiveness was more strongly related to anger under highly frustrating conditions than under mildly frustrating conditions, and that the higher parents' levels of verbal aggressiveness, "the more easily frustration is converted to anger" (Rudd et al., 1998, p. 7).

Weber and Patterson (1997) observed that children (both boys and girls) who were exposed to verbally aggressive messages from their mothers became more verbally aggressive themselves. As these children entered adult romantic relationships, they tended to use more verbally aggressive messages with romantic partners. Weber and Patterson suggested that this may set up a cycle of reciprocity in that the partners then use verbal aggression to defend themselves, which, in turn, begets more verbal aggression. This cycle of verbal aggression leads to less satisfying and less productive interpersonal relationships.

Booth-Butterfield and Sidelinger (1997) found that parents who rated themselves high on verbal aggressiveness had children who saw their family communication as being "closed." Children growing up in such families were hesitant to discuss issues, hesitant to share opinions, and felt much less free to communicate in the family. Thus, the researchers conclude that "verbal aggression closes the communication between the parent and child" (Booth-Butterfield & Sidelinger, 1997, p. 415).

Research on the impact of aggressive communication in the family has also looked at the role of parenting style. Parents with an "authoritative" style (e.g., used reasoning with children, encouraged a give-and-take) were found to be lower in verbal aggressiveness and higher in argumentativeness (Bayer & Cegala, 1992). Conversely, parents with an "authoritarian" style (e.g., low in emotional display, discouraged verbal responses from their children) were higher in verbal aggressiveness and lower in argumentativeness.

Studies have explored the role of aggressive communication in family sibling relationships. Martin, Anderson, Burant, and Weber (1997) found that people who report being verbally aggressive with their siblings are less satisfied with that sibling relationship, and have less trust in their siblings when they saw them as being verbally aggressive. Being verbally aggressive was also related to teasing of siblings, that is, those reporting higher levels of verbal aggressiveness, also reported greater amounts of teasing. Teven, Martin, and Neupauer (1998) also found that the more verbally aggressive messages people received from their siblings, the less satisfied they were with that relationship.

Another line of research has also explored the role of the aggressive communication traits in understanding marriages troubled by violence. Much of this research supports what has been called the *argumentative skill deficiency* explanation for intrafamily violence (Infante et al., 1989). The argumentative skill deficiency model suggests that individuals low in motivation to argue, and weak in argumentative skill quickly "run out of things to say" (i.e., arguments) when they are engaged in an argument with someone. In other words, these low argumentative individuals do not have much ability to generate arguments as they are needed, and quickly use up their rather meager store of arguments during a conflict. They may present one or two very weak arguments in support of their position, but these arguments are usually refuted very quickly and easily by their adversary. If the conflict continues, this "attack-and-defend" mode may still exist causing individuals to feel the need to continue to defend themselves and attack their adversary. If they cannot attack their adversary's position on the issue with arguments (i.e., engage in argumentativeness), they may redirect their attack to the person's self-concept (i.e., engage in verbal aggressiveness). Infante, Chandler, and Rudd (1989) tested this model in a study with abused wives and abusive husbands. They found that the abused wives and abusive husbands were lower in argumentativeness and higher in verbal aggressiveness than a control group of nonviolent wives and husbands. This finding suggests that verbal aggressiveness might be a catalyst for interspousal violence.

In another study, Sabourin, Infante, and Rudd (1993) examined three types of married couples (violent couples; couples in therapy-distressed, nonviolent; and nondistressed–nonviolent couples) with respect to aggressive communication. Among other things, Sabourin et al. observed that (a) spouses in violent marriages reported the greatest number of verbally aggressive messages exchanged between the partners, (b) violent couples reported higher levels of verbally aggressive reciprocity than any other couple type, and (c) character attacks (e.g., "you are a no good liar") and threats (e.g., "I'm going to hit you") differentiated the violent couples from both nonviolent groups (Sabourin et al., 1993).

Rudd, Burant, and Beatty (1994) also explored the role of compliance-gaining messages (i.e., messages designed to get someone to do something you want) as a function of the aggressive communication traits. The participants were women who resided in protective housing for domestic abuse victims. The women evaluated themselves on argumentativeness and verbal aggressiveness, and then indicated the frequency which they employed 16 different compliance-gaining messages (e.g., threat, guilt, direct request, etc.). Battered women who were higher in verbal aggressiveness and lower in argumentativeness tended to use guilt, bargaining, debt, and aversive stimulation (e.g., pouting, sulking, crying) more often as compliance-gaining strategies. However, battered women who were higher in argumentativeness and lower in verbal aggressiveness reported using strategies such as allurement (i.e., charming their spouse by telling them how complying would make other people respect him), hinting, and direct requests more often as compliance-gaining strategies (Rudd et al., 1994).

The results indicated that, in general, the abused women tended to favor indirect compliance-gaining messages over direct strategies. The researchers suggested that while these women tried to "pacify their husbands or accommodate them in any way possible" in order to prevent the abuse, these strategies did not prevent the violence (Rudd et al., 1994, p. 17). The researchers argue that the use of these indirect compliance-gaining strategies are most likely the result of power inequities in the relationship. That is, because the women studied were generally unemployed with young children who relied heavily on their spouses for financial support, they felt that they had little direct power in the relationship. This suggests some degree of relationship power equity (at least in the domain of financial independence) may be needed in order for these women to use more direct compliance-gaining strategies.

Collectively, this group of studies demonstrates the impact that argumentativeness and verbal aggressiveness has on parents' and children's behaviors and perceptions, as well as on feelings of openness in family interaction. The research underscores the destructive nature of verbal aggression in family communication and suggests that more constructive and positive family outcomes may result when individuals have higher motivation and greater skill in argumentative communication and lower levels of verbal aggressiveness.

ORGANIZATIONAL COMMUNICATION

A great deal of research has examined the role of aggressive communication in the organization. For example, Infante and Gorden (1985) found that if subordinates saw their bosses as higher in argumentativeness and lower in verbal aggressiveness, they expressed more satisfaction with their superior, saw their employee rights as being protected, and expressed greater satisfaction with their career. Conversely, Infante and Gorden (1991) found that when superiors were seen as verbally aggressive, subordinates tended to express lower levels of organizational commitment, and were less satisfied with their work (and with their supervisor).

A theory, the Independent-Mindedness Theory of Organizational Communication (Infante & Gorden, 1987), has grown out of this work on the impact of aggressive communication in the workplace. Independent-mindedness is the tendency of employees to have their own thoughts and opinions rather than to passively accept the opinions of their supervisors. A basic tenet of this theory is that employees want the values held by society to be reflected and affirmed in the workplace. Thus, American organizations, the theory holds, should encourage freedom of speech and promote individualism and independent-mindedness. The Theory of Independent-Mindedness suggests that when superiors encourage this freedom of speech among their employees and promote individualism and independent-mindedness, more favorable organizational outcomes should result including promoting stronger commitment to the organization.

The most favorable conditions for organizational communication are when superiors and subordinates are high in argumentativeness, low in verbal aggressiveness, and communicate with an *affirming* communicator style (Norton, 1978, 1983). Communicator style is seen as a cluster of traits (e.g., dramatic, animated, open, contentious, friendly, attentive, relaxed) that influence how a message is communicated (Norton, 1983). An affirming communicator style involves communicating in a highly relaxed, highly friendly, and highly attentive manner by using a great deal of eye contact, relaxed and composed gestures, smiling, head nods and other positive facial expressions. In fact, Infante, Anderson, Martin, Herington, and Kim (1993) found that subordinates' levels of satisfaction with their superiors increased as the superiors were seen as higher in argumentativeness, lower in verbal aggressiveness, and were more affirming (relaxed, friendly, attentive) in communicator style.

Some studies have explored the role of aggressive communication traits in fostering or dampening organizational dissent. It was thought that *dissent* (the expression of disagreement or contradictory opinions in the workplace) should be related to both employee voice and aggressive communication traits. For example, Nicotera and DeWine (1991) found that employees who are more nonconfrontational and avoidant in their conflict management styles are less willing to discuss controversial issues in the workplace. Kassing (1998) distinguished between three types of dissent behaviors: articulated dissent, latent dissent, and displaced dissent. Articulated dissent involves expressing dissent openly and clearly within the organization so as to influence the organization positively. Latent dissent occurs when employees want to voice their opinions but lack the avenues to do so and hence, become frustrated and then complain to those around them in an aggressive fashion. Displaced dissent involves expressing dissent only to external audiences (e.g., friends, spouses, strangers, family). Kassing and Avtgis (1999) found that those employees who were higher in argumentativeness and lower in verbal aggressiveness use more articulated dissent. In addition, they found that lower organizational status and verbal aggressiveness were associated with the latent dissent behavior.

While Infante, Myers, and Buerkel (1994) suggested that workplace factors such as fear of economic reprisal may inhibit the use of verbal aggression, a constellation of studies (Infante & Gorden, 1987, 1989, 1991) supported the contention that argumentativeness is a constructive communication trait when coupled with an affirming communicator style in the organizational context, whereas verbal aggressiveness, when exhibited, remains destructive.

INSTRUCTIONAL COMMUNICATION AND TRAINING

This line of research has produced investigations that can be separated into two distinct types: studies that focus on training students to become more argumentative and less verbally aggressive and studies that focus on perceptions of aggressive communication in instructors. We will first look at the research that focuses on the teachers.

It should come as no surprise to you that the influence of an instructor's communication behavior can have a measurable effect on students' actual learning and motivation. Kearney, Plax, Hays, and Ivey (1991) found that several behaviors that clearly fit within the domain of verbal aggression (i.e., putdowns, sarcasm, verbal abuse) had a negative impact on student learning. Rocca and McCroskey (1999) examined the relation of verbal aggression and teacher immediacy (behaviors that draw people closer such as closer distance, greater use of gestures, greater eye contact). They hypothesized a negative relation between teacher immediacy and teacher verbal aggression, and the results of their study supported this prediction. Teachers who are more immediate (smile, stand closer, use more gestures, and more eye contact) were seen as less verbally aggressive, and teachers who are more verbally aggressive were also seen as less immediate.

An instructor's communicator style is another factor that can promote or decrease student learning and motivation (Nussbaum, 1992). Rocca and Myers (2000) studied the relations among perceived instructor communicator style, instructor argumentativeness, instructor verbal aggressiveness, and instructor use of certain verbally aggressive messages. They found that when instructors are seen as argumentative they are also seen as leaving a positive impression, being more open, relaxed, attentive, animated, precise, dramatic, and dominant. However, when instructors are seen as verbally aggressive, they are also seen as unfriendly, inattentive, and low on impression-leaving.

Myers (1998) also investigated the relation between students' perceptions of a college instructor's competence and their perceptions of that instructor's argumentativeness and verbal aggressiveness. Among other things, Myers drew two major conclusions regarding this relation: (a) Competent instructors are rated higher in argumentativeness, and (b) noncompetent instructors are rated higher in verbal aggressiveness. Johnson and Johnson (1979) found that being argumentative in the classroom is associated with increased problem-solving ability, greater creativity, and increased perspective-taking. Rancer et al. (1985) suggested that arguing is a positive behavior in that individuals who engage in argumentative practices learn about issues and problems. On the other hand, instructors who use verbal aggression are not seen as being responsive to students.

Among students, training in argumentation has been found to increase critical thinking and the ability to recognize strong from weak arguments (Sanders, Wiseman, & Gass, 1994). Thus, the numerous positive outcomes associated with being argumentative and the number of negative outcomes associated with being verbally aggressive (see Infante & Rancer, 1996; Rancer & Avgtis, 2006) underscores the need to train students to enhance their argumentativeness while reducing their levels of verbal aggression. A number of efforts have begun to address these concerns. Rancer, Whitecap, Kosberg, and Avtgis (1997) first tested whether Infante's (1988) Inventional System (a method of helping people generate arguments) could be employed to train adolescents to be more motivated to argue and to generate more arguments. Seventh-grade students were presented with a week-long program designed to do just that. The results demonstrated that after the training, students increased their motivation to argue and were able to develop a greater number of arguments than before the training. Indeed, approximately 1 year after the training, the researchers went back to test the same students (now in 8th grade), and found that students maintained their increased levels of argumentativeness (Rancer, Avtgis, Kosberg, & Whitecap, 2000). Unfortunately, modifying students' levels of verbal aggressiveness has been found to be more difficult (Rancer et al., 2000). However, Infante (1995) offered several suggestions designed to understand and control verbal aggression, including "anger management" training, teaching students to dismiss verbally aggressive attacks, and teaching students that verbally aggressive messages can be treated as "arguments" which could be refuted.

INTERCULTURAL COMMUNICATION

Over the last two decades, interest in intercultural communication has blossomed. Accompanying this has been an increase in research attention focused on intercultural and cross-cultural communication. Some of this research has explored the role of aggressive communication as it manifests itself in the context of intercultural communication. In particular, differences in aggressive communication predispositions and conflict styles across and between cultures have been identified. To facilitate this research, the Argumentativeness (Infante & Rancer, 1982) and Verbal Aggressiveness Scales (Infante & Wigley, 1986) have been translated into several languages including Japanese, Chinese, Korean, Finnish, German, and Slovakian, (among others).

A number of studies have examined whether Americans are similar to, or different from, members of other cultures on the aggressive communication traits. One classification scheme identifies cultures as being either "high-context" or "low-context" (Hall, 1966, 1981). In a "high-context" culture, most of the information in a message is contained in the physical context or in the culture's rules. Communication in high-context cultures is generally formal (Infante et al., 1997). In a "low context" culture, most of the information in a message is contained in the explicit or verbal message (Infante et al., 1997). Communication in low-context cultures tends to be direct and informal. Aggressive communication traits have been studied in both types of cultures. For example, Prunty, Klopf, and Ishii (1990a, 1990b) found that Americans are higher than the Japanese on argumentativeness. Americans were also found to be higher than Koreans in argumentativeness, but this result seems to be due to the significant difference between U.S. and Korean women, rather than between U.S. and Korean men (Jenkins, Klopf, & Park, 1991).

Suzuki (1998) speculated that people coming from a high-context culture, such as Japan, may not be very motivated to engage in argumentative communication. Because the context itself provides much information, people may understand each other without having to engage in the give-and-take of opinions as is often done in argumentative communication. The same explanation may hold true for differences found between high- and low-context cultures on verbal aggressiveness. That is, because a great deal of information is already "programmed" into the context and understood by the participants, there may be less need to be verbally aggressive as well.

Cross-cultural differences in aggressive communication between low-context cultures has also been studied. For example, both the Norwegian and Finnish cultures have been found to be higher than the U.S. culture in argumentativeness (Klopf, Thompson, & Sallinen-Kuparinen, 1991; Rahoi, Svenkerud, & Love, 1994). Although some research exists on the influence of culture on aggressive communication, more research from cultures other than North American, Scandinavian, and Asian needs to be investigated if we are to understand more fully what factors contribute to cross-cultural conflict.

DISCUSSION: THINKING CRITICALLY ABOUT THIS RESEARCH

This review is but a sample of the vast literature on argumentativeness and verbal aggression. Because of these, and many other research efforts, we have learned a great deal about the influence of aggressive communication in several communication contexts. The distillation of this body of research allows us to underscore one major conclusion, that argumentativeness is a constructive communication trait while verbal aggressiveness is destructive. This conclusion appears to hold true regardless of the context in which we are communicating.

In addition to the contextual research cited throughout this chapter, we have discovered other trends regarding aggressive communication traits. For example, findings from studies suggest that gender differences exist in both argumentativeness and verbal aggressiveness. That is, men have been found to score higher than women on both argumentativeness (Infante,

1985; Nicotera & Rancer, 1994; Schultz & Anderson, 1984) and verbal aggressiveness (Infante, Wall, Leap, & Danielson, 1984; Infante & Wigley, 1986; Nicotera & Rancer, 1994). In addition, sex-based stereotyped perceptions of aggressive communication traits have emerged. Specifically, there is a tendency to see highly argumentative individuals of the opposite sex as also highly verbally aggressive (Nicotera & Rancer, 1994). Still, there is much to learn regarding the development of these gender differences and how we can best sensitize individuals to sex stereotyping in aggressive communication.

In addition, cultural issues have only begun to be understood. True, there have been numerous studies comparing Americans to other nationalities. But, as noted previously, the studies of "Americans" have essentially been studies of "White Americans." For instance, we do not know how aggressive communication functions in African American families, for African American organizational members, or for African American instructors and students. There is evidence to predict that the constructs might operate similarly to the way they do in American groups of European descent. African American norms for appropriate conflict management include such similar things as making well-constructed, credible arguments, engaging in polite communication, being assertive, and using directness (Hecht, Collier, & Ribeau, 1993). This would suggest that argumentativeness might be seen as positive and verbal aggression might be seen as negative. Similarly, there is evidence to predict how the constructs of argumentativeness and verbal aggressiveness might operate for Asian Americans depending on their levels of acculturation. However, these predictions need to be confirmed with actual research. In addition, of course, we must study other U.S. cultural groups as well.

We must remember that the American culture also varies regionally, and such differences have not been sufficiently addressed in research on aggressive communication. In one study, however, Geddes (1992) found northerners were higher in verbal aggressiveness than midwesterners and southerners. Finally, we need to examine intercultural interactions (i.e., actual dialogue during conflict) rather than just make comparisons between cultures on the levels of each trait. Even with the extensive number of studies of aggressive communication in (White) American culture, what we do not know outweighs what we know.

Also of concern theoretically are the assumptions we make regarding the relation between the two constructs (argumentativeness and verbal aggression). Certainly, in an abstract sense we can separate the two and define them as different things. However, European-based cultures, such as European American culture, are more likely than African- or Asian-based cultures (for instance) to view a position on an issue as distinct from one's self concept. This is because many non-European-based cultures view such things more holistically. To separate the issue from the person may not make as much sense to individuals from non-European-based cultures as it does to White Americans.

In general, the relation between argumentativeness and verbal aggressiveness across cultural groups is largely unexplored. Although it is theoretically conceivable that a person could be high on one, high on both, or low on both (as we explained at the beginning of the chapter), we do not know if there are cultural patterns to this within the United States or in comparison to cultures abroad.

The relationship between argumentativeness and verbal aggression may be developmental. The studies of adolescents cited previously (Rancer et al., 2000; Rancer et al., 1997) suggested that argumentativeness and verbal aggressiveness may be closely related for that age group. We do not know whether the relation between a person's argumentativeness and verbal aggressiveness changes as the person ages.

In conclusion, the study of aggressive communication is very important. Through such careful research, we come to understand the ways in which individuals' behavior in dealing with controversial issues impacts their relationships with others—in families, organizations, schools, and across cultures. As in any area of social research, we still have much to learn. It is crucial that we critically consider what research has discovered—to examine just how far results should be applied and to generate questions for future research. Among you, the students reading this book, there are present and future spouses, parents, workers, managers, leaders, teachers, and even communication researchers. Regardless of the ways in which you might use the information in this chapter and the other chapters in this book, you would do well to use it with a critical mind.

ADDITIONAL READING

Readers with an interest in aggressive communication traits should read the original work by Infante and Rancer (1982) on argumentativeness, and Infante and Wigley (1986) on verbal aggressiveness. These seminal works will provide you with an understanding of the theoretical development of each trait, and provide you with the original conceptualization and the actual scales used to measure argumentativeness and verbal aggressiveness. Those interested in the motivational theory that underlies the argumentativeness trait should consult the work of Atkinson (1957, 1966).

In addition, Infante and Rancer (1996) and Rancer and Avgtis (2006) provide a comprehensive review of research on aggressive communication from the early efforts in the 1980s to the present. They offer several conclusions about the influence of these aggressive communication traits that emerged from the many research studies during that period.

REFERENCES

Atkinson, J. W. (1957). Motivational determinants of risk-taking behavior. *Psychological Review, 64,* 359–372.

Atkinson, J. W. (1966). *An introduction to motivation.* New York: Van Nostrand.

Bayer, C. L., & Cegala, D. J. (1992). Trait verbal aggressiveness and argumentativeness: Relations with parenting style. *Western Journal of Communication, 56,* 301–310.

Beatty, M. J., Burant, P. A., Dobos, J. A., & Rudd, J. E. (1996). Trait verbal aggressiveness and the appropriateness and effectiveness of fathers' interaction plans. *Communication Quarterly, 44,* 1–15.

Beatty, M. J., Zelley, J. R., Dobos, J. A., & Rudd, J. E. (1994). Fathers' trait verbal aggressiveness and argumentativeness as predictors of adult sons' perceptions of fathers' sarcasm, criticism, and verbal aggressiveness. *Communication Quarterly, 42,* 407–415.

Booth-Butterfield, M., & Sidelinger, R. J. (1997). The relationship between parental traits and open family communication: Affective orientation and verbal aggression. *Communication Research Reports, 14,* 408–417.

Christophel, D. M. (1990). The relationships among teacher immediacy behaviors, student motivation, and learning. *Communication Education, 39,* 323–340.

Frymier, A. B. (1994). A model of immediacy in the classroom. *Communication Quarterly, 42,* 133–144.

Geddes, D. S. (1992). Comparison of regional interpersonal communication predispositions. *Pennsylvania Speech Communication Annual, 48,* 67–93.

Gorden, W. I., & Infante, D. A. (1987). Employee rights: Context, argumentativeness, verbal aggressiveness, and career satisfaction. In C. A. B. Osigweh (Ed.), *Communicating employee responsibilities and rights* (pp. 149–163). Westport, CT: Quorum.

Hall, E. T. (1966). *The hidden dimension.* New York: Random House.

Hall, E. T. (1981). *Beyond culture.* New York: Doubleday.

Hecht, M. L., Collier, M. J., & Ribeau, S. A. (1993). *African American communication: Ethnic identity and cultural interpretation.* Newbury Park, CA: Sage.

Infante, D. A. (1982). The argumentative student in the speech communication classroom: An investigation and implications. *Communication Education, 31,* 141–148.

Infante, D. A. (1985). Inducing women to be more argumentative: Source credibility effects. *Journal of Applied Communication Research, 13,* 33–44.

Infante, D. A. (1987a). Aggressiveness. In J. C. McCroskey & J. A. Daly (Eds.), *Personality and interpersonal communication* (pp. 157–192). Newbury Park, CA: Sage.

Infante, D. A. (1987b). Enhancing the prediction of response to a communication situation from communication traits. *Communication Quarterly, 35,* 308–316.

Infante, D. A. (1988). *Arguing constructively.* Prospect Heights, IL: Waveland.

Infante, D. A. (1995). Teaching students to understand and control verbal aggression. *Communication Education, 44,* 51–63.

Infante, D. A., Anderson, C. M, Martin, M. M., Herington, A. D., & Kim, J. (1993). Subordinates' satisfaction and perceptions of superiors' compliance-gaining tactics, argumentativeness, verbal aggressiveness, and style. *Management Communication Quarterly, 6,* 307–326.

Infante, D. A., Chandler, T. A., & Rudd, J. E. (1989). Test of an argumentative skill deficiency model of interspousal violence. *Communication Monographs, 56,* 163–177.

Infante, D. A., & Gorden, W. I. (1985). Superiors' argumentativeness and verbal aggressiveness as predictors of subordinates' satisfaction. *Human Communication Research, 12,* 117–125.

Infante, D. A., & Gorden, W. I. (1987). Superior and subordinate communication profiles: Implications for independent-mindedness and upward effectiveness. *Central States Speech Journal, 38,* 73–80.

Infante, D. A., & Gorden, W. I. (1989). Argumentativeness and affirming communicator style as predictors of satisfaction/dissatisfaction with subordinates. *Communication Quarterly, 37,* 81–90.

Infante, D. A., & Gorden, W. I. (1991). How employees see the boss: Test of an argumentative and affirming model of superiors' communicative behavior. *Western Journal of Speech Communication, 55,* 294–304.

Infante, D. A., Myers, S. A., & Buerkel, R. A. (1994). Argument and verbal aggression in constructive and destructive family and organizational disagreements. *Western Journal of Communication, 58,* 73–84.

Infante, D. A., & Rancer, A. S. (1982). A conceptualization and measure of argumentativeness. *Journal of Personality Assessment, 46,* 72–80.

Infante, D. A., & Rancer, A. S. (1996). Argumentativeness and verbal aggressiveness: A review of recent theory and research. In B. R. Burleson (Ed.), *Communication yearbook 19* (pp. 319–351). Beverly Hills, CA: Sage.

Infante, D. A., Rancer, A. S., & Womack, D. F. (1997). *Building communication theory* (3rd ed.). Prospect Heights, IL: Waveland.

Infante, D. A., Riddle, B. L., Horvath, C. L., & Tumlin, S. A. (1992). Verbal aggressiveness: Messages and reasons. *Communication Quarterly, 40,* 116–126.

Infante, D. A., Trebing, J. D., Shepherd, P. E., & Seeds, D. E. (1984). The relationship of argumentativeness to verbal aggression. *Southern Speech Communication Journal, 50,* 67–77.

Infante, D. A., Wall, C. H., Leap, C. J., & Danielson, K. (1984) The relationship of argumentativeness to verbal aggression. *Communication Research Reports, 1,* 33–37.

Infante, D. A., & Wigley, C. J. (1986). Verbal aggressiveness: An interpersonal model and measure. *Communication Monographs, 53,* 61–69.

Jenkins, G. D., Klopf, D. W., & Park, M. S. (1991, July). *Argumentativeness in Korean and American college students: A comparison.* Paper presented at the annual meeting of the World Communication Association, Jyvaskyla, Finland.

Johnson, D. W., & Johnson, R. T. (1979). Conflict in the classroom: Controversy and learning. *Review of Educational Research, 49,* 51–70.

Kassing, J. W. (1998). Development and validation of the organizational dissent scale. *Management Communication Quarterly, 12,* 183–229.

Kassing, J. W., & Avtgis, T. A. (1999). Examining the relationship between organizational dissent and aggressive communication. *Management Communication Quarterly, 13,* 100–115.

Kearney, P., Plax, T. G., Hays, E. R., & Ivey, M. J. (1991). College teacher misbehaviors: What students don't like about what teachers say and do. *Communication Quarterly, 39,* 309– 324.

Klopf, D. W., Thompson, C. A., & Sallinen-Kuparinen, S. (1991). Argumentativeness among selected Finnish and American college students. *Psychological Reports, 68,* 161–162.

Martin, M. M., Anderson, C. M., Burant, P. A., & Weber, K. (1997). Verbal aggression in the sibling relationship. *Communication Quarterly, 45,* 304–317.

Martin, M. M., Anderson, C. M., & Horvath, C. L. (1996). Feelings about verbal aggression: Justifications for sending and hurt from receiving verbally aggressive messages. *Communication Research Reports, 13,* 19–26.

McCroskey, J. C., Richmond, V. P., Sallinen, A., Fayer, J. M., & Barraclough, R. A. (1995). A cross-cultural and multi-behavioral analysis of the relationship between nonverbal immediacy and teacher evaluation. *Communication Education, 44,* 281–291.

Myers, S. A. (1998). Instructor socio-communicative style, argumentativeness, and verbal aggressiveness in the college classroom. *Communication Research Reports, 15,* 141–150.

Nicotera, A. M. (1993). Beyond two dimensions: A grounded theory model of conflict handling behavior. *Management Communication Quarterly, 6,* 282–306.

Nicotera, A. M. (1994). The use of multiple approaches to conflict: A study of sequences. *Human Communication Research, 20,* 592–621.

Nicotera, A. M. (1996). The management of conflict communication in groups. In L. Frey & K. Barge (Eds.), *Managing group life: Communicating in decision-making groups.* Boston: Houghton Mifflin.

Nicotera, A. M., & DeWine, S. (1991). Understanding entry into controversy at work and at home. *Communication Research Reports, 8,* 89–99.

Nicotera, A. M., & Rancer, A. S. (1994). The influence of sex on self-perceptions and social stereotyping of aggressive communication predispositions. *Western Journal of Communication, 58,* 283–307.

Norton, R. W. (1978). Foundation of a communicator style construct. *Human Communication Research, 4,* 99–112.

Norton, R.W. (1983). *Communicator style: Theory, applications, and measures.* Beverly Hills, CA: Sage.

Nussbaum, J. F. (1992). Communicator style and teacher influence. In V. P. Richmond & J. C. McCroskey (Eds.), *Power in the classroom: Communication, control, and concern* (pp. 145–158). Hillsdale, NJ: Lawrence Erlbaum Associates, Inc.

Prunty, A. M., Klopf, D. W., & Ishii, S. (1990a). Argumentativeness: Japanese and American tendencies to approach and avoid conflict. *Communication Research Reports, 7,* 75–79.

Prunty, A. M., Klopf, D. W., & Ishii, S. (1990b). Japanese and American tendencies to argue. *Psychological Reports, 66,* 802.

Rahoi, R., Svenkerud, P., & Love, D. (1994). *Searching for subtlety: Investigating argumentativeness across low-context cultural boundaries.* Unpublished manuscript, Ohio University.

Rancer, A. S., & Avtgis, T. A. (2006). *Argumentative and aggressive communication.* Thousand Oaks, CA: Sage.

Rancer, A. S., Avtgis, T. A., Kosberg, R. L., & Whitecap, V. G. (2000). A longitudinal assessment of trait argumentativeness and verbal aggressiveness between seventh and eighth grades. *Communication Education, 49,* 114–119.

Rancer, A. S., Baukus, R. A., & Infante, D. A. (1985). Relations between argumentativeness and belief structures about arguing. *Communication Education, 34,* 37–47.

Rancer, A. S., Whitecap, V. G., Kosberg, R. L., & Avtgis, T. A. (1997). Testing the efficacy of a communication training program to increase argumentativeness and argumentative behavior in adolescents. *Communication Education, 46,* 273–286.

Rocca, K. A., & McCroskey, J. C. (1999). The interrelationship of student ratings of instructors' immediacy, verbal aggressiveness, homophily, and interpersonal attraction. *Communication Education, 48,* 308–316.

Rocca, K. A., & Myers, S. A. (2000, April). *The relationship between perceived instructor communicator style, argumentativeness, and verbal aggressiveness.* Paper presented at the annual meeting of the Eastern Communication Association, Pittsburgh, PA.

Rudd, J. E., Beatty, M. J., Vogl-Bauer, S., & Dobos, J. A. (1997). Trait verbal aggressiveness and the appropriateness and effectiveness of fathers' interaction plans II: Fathers' self- assessments. *Communication Quarterly, 45,* 379–392.

Rudd, J. E., Burant, P. A., & Beatty, M. J. (1994). Battered women's compliance-gaining strategies as a function of argumentativeness and verbal aggression. *Communication Research Reports, 11,* 13–22.

Rudd, J. E., Vogl-Bauer, S., Dobos, J. A., Beatty, M. J., & Valencic, K. M. (1998). Interactive effects of parents' trait verbal aggressiveness and situational frustration on parents' self- reported anger. *Communication Quarterly, 46,* 1–11.

Sabourin, T. C., Infante, D. A., & Rudd, J. E. (1993). Verbal aggression in marriages: A comparison of violent, distressed but nonviolent, and nondistressed couples. *Human Communication Research, 20,* 245–267.

Sanders, J. A., Wiseman, R. L., & Gass, R. H. (1994). Does teaching argumentation facilitate critical thinking? *Communication Reports, 7,* 27–35.

Schultz, B., & Anderson, J. (1984). Training in the management of conflict: A communication theory perspective. *Small Group Behavior, 15,* 333–348.

Suzuki, S. (1998). *Argumentativeness and verbal aggressiveness: Effects of gender and low- and high-context communication.* Unpublished manuscript, Hokkaido Tokai University.

Teven, J. J., Martin, M. M., & Neupauer, N. C. (1998). Sibling relationships: Verbally aggressive messages and their effect on relational satisfaction. *Communication Reports, 11,* 179–186.

Weber, K., & Patterson, B.R. (1997). The effects of maternal verbal aggression on the adult child's future romantic relationships. *Communication Research Reports, 14,* 221–230.

Wigley, C. J., III (1998). Verbal aggressiveness. In J. C. McCroskey, J. A. Daly, M. M. Martin, & M. J. Beatty (Eds.), *Communication and personality: Trait perspectives* (pp. 191–214). Cresskill, NJ: Hampton Press.

QUESTIONS TO PONDER

1. Recall an instance of argumentative communication and an instance of verbally aggressive communication in your family. Compare these two events. How did each feel? What were the outcomes? What could have been done differently?

2. Why might an individual develop argumentative or verbally aggressive communication predispositions? How much of this do you think is inborn? What kind of experiences early in life might lead to one behavior pattern or another?

3. What kinds of positive results might one expect from argumentative communication when used in the workplace? In what situations might argumentativeness be most appropriate?

4. What kinds of negative results might one expect from verbally aggressive communication when used in the workplace? In what situations might verbal aggressiveness be most damaging?

5. Can you think of any situations in which argumentative communication might have negative results? Can you think of any situations in which verbal aggressiveness might have a positive result?

8

Plans, Planning, and Communication Effectiveness

Charles R. Berger
University of California, Davis

INTRODUCTION

There are two fundamental questions about how human communication works. The first of these is how people are able to give meaning to the patterns of light, sound, and thermal energy that other people give off. These patterns of energy that impinge on our senses include the sights and sounds that make up the verbal and nonverbal messages we receive from others and the actions in which others are engaged; they also include information provided by the physical and social context within which these verbal and nonverbal messages and actions originate. When we speak with others face-to-face, we not only hear what they say, we see what they are doing and how they are responding to others in the situation, including ourselves. The problem for us, as perceivers of all of these inputs, is to make sense out of them. What enables us to understand others' words and actions?

A second fundamental question about human communication is how people are able to take their ideas and concepts and encode them in such a way that others can understand their intended meaning. More often than not it is a waste of time and energy to attempt to communicate about highly complex concepts using English when the person with whom one is speaking is utterly unfamiliar with the English language code. The idea that words are like vessels that carry meaning from the head of one person to the head of another has been abandoned (Berlo, 1961; Reddy, 1979). Words and the actions that accompany them do not have intrinsic meaning. In order for individuals to attain mutual understanding, they must share common codes and arrive at a common set of meanings.

But making oneself understood to another is not merely a matter of using a vocabulary and a grammar that are commonly understood. Behind every utterance lurks intent. We don't use language merely to use language. We use language for practical purposes, that is, to get things done (Austin, 1962; Clark, 1994; Wittgenstein, 1953). As Clark observed,

People engage in discourse not merely to use language but to accomplish things. They want to buy shoes or get a lost address or arrange a dinner party or trade gossip or teach a child improper fractions. Language is simply a tool for achieving these aims. (p. 1018)

The problem for us as message producers is to organize our verbal and nonverbal messages and actions in such a way that we achieve our intended goals. How are we able to get from intentions to the production of messages and actions that get the things we want done?

The communication processes to which these two fundamental questions refer mutually influence each other. To produce effective messages and actions, communicators must understand each other's intentions, and verbal and nonverbal messages and actions reveal intentions. The answers to these two fundamental questions about human communication are each very long, quite complex, and still incomplete. However, the answers do have certain elements in common. These common elements include the notions of plans and planning. These two concepts may help provide a partial answer to both questions.

The remainder of this chapter is devoted to explaining the nature of plans and the planning processes that produce them. After these two concepts are discussed in some detail, their relationships with communication effectiveness are then explored. As will become apparent, the kinds of plans that individuals develop both before and during their interactions with others are vital in determining the degree to which people will be successful in attaining their interaction goals. When individuals engage in nonoptimal planning and use ineffective plans to guide their interactions with others, they tend to experience undesirable outcomes. Thus, by the conclusion of this chapter you should have a fair idea of how to avoid various planning pitfalls.

The Nature of Plans

When we use the term *plan*, we are referring to mental representations of action sequences that people use to achieve their goals. For example, a plan to achieve the goal of asking someone out on a date might include such abstract types of actions as striking up a conversation, obtaining background information from the person, assessing common interests, determining whether the person seems interested in going out and then maybe asking the person out. These mental plans are organized in hierarchies with abstract action types at the top and successively more concrete actions nested below them. In the date-request example, there are many alternative ways that one might strike up a conversation or obtain background information from a person. In general, these hierarchically organized cognitive plans represent our knowledge about how to achieve goals, and because we pursue many different goals in our everyday lives, we must have a very large repertoire of plans available in our long-term memory.

With respect to the first of our two fundamental questions—that is, how we comprehend others' intentions—a number of researchers have argued that cognitive plans are vital for achieving an understanding of others' verbal messages and actions. This point of view is quite well illustrated by Green (1996) when she observed, "Understanding a speaker's intention in saying what she said the way she said it amounts to inferring the speaker's plan, in all of its hierarchical glory, although there is room for considerable latitude regarding the details" (p. 13). Knowledge about the goals people pursue and the plans they typically use to pursue them is critical to our understanding of their actions and their verbal and nonverbal messages. And, with respect to the second fundamental question concerning guidance of action and discourse toward goals, other theorists have contended that it is plans that do most of the work (Berger, 1995, 1997). Plans enable us to realize our goals and intentions in both spoken and written discourse and in the actions we take to achieve goals. Plans provide the blueprints for the messages we generate and the actions we take to achieve our goals.

You might have noticed that in describing what plans are and what they do for communicators, I have stressed that plans not only guide the interpretation and production of spoken discourse, but they also guide our interpretations of others' actions and the generation of our own actions. Unfortunately, it is quite common for communication theorists to focus their attention exclusively on the verbal aspects of communication and to some extent on certain aspects of nonverbal communication such as eye gaze, facial expressions, and gestures. However, scholars often ignore the fact that verbal and nonverbal communication occur within the context of complex ongoing sequences of action. Communication and action work together to enable people to reach their goals, but the relative mix of communication and action may vary from situation to situation. Sometimes when people individually set out to achieve common, everyday goals, some of these mundane goals require little, if any, verbal communication for their successful attainment, for example, buying gas for one's car, obtaining money from a bank teller, or buying groceries. In fact, because the successful achievement of these goals usually demands so little in the way of verbal interaction, these commercial transactions are becoming automated using interactive communication technologies (e.g., automatic teller machines and paying for gasoline at the pump). Moreover, even in some nonroutine communication situations, actions may assume a more important role than talk. Such well-known aphorisms as "talk is cheap" and "actions speak louder than words" signify such situations. For example, as a romantic encounter progresses, there is usually a point where words may only serve "to get in the way" of the ongoing event sequence; similarly, in escalating conflict situations individuals may reach the point of having to "put-up, or shut-up."

By contrast, when people pursue other goals, discourse may assume a primary role. For example, in persuading a friend to go to a movie or presenting an argument in a courtroom, the focus may be almost entirely on words and how they are used. However, in most cases it is a mistake to separate discourse and action. In many if not most social interaction situations, talk and action are bundled together in patterns designed to get things done. The important point is that plans provide simultaneous guidance to both the interpretation and production of discourse and action. If plans to achieve goals are to be useful, they have to organize knowledge about both actions and discourse.

The Nature of Planning

People often fail to distinguish clearly between the concepts of plan and planning. We have already examined the plan concept in considerable detail. Planning is a concept that refers to the processes that produce plans as their end result. As Wilensky (1983) put it, "Planning concerns the process by which people select a course of action—deciding what they want, formulating and revising plans, dealing with problems and adversity, making choices, and eventually performing some action" (p. 2). Clearly, however, when people are involved in face-to-face interactions in which back-and-forth exchanges of speaking turns may take place rapidly, there may be only minimal amounts of time for them to engage in highly conscious and elaborate deliberative planning. While planning opportunities during conversations are usually limited, there is some evidence to suggest that silent pauses in speech, those times when people silently hesitate before making their next utterance, are sometimes indicative of linguistic planning activity (Berger, 1997; Goldman-Eisler, 1968). That is, speakers may use silent pausing time to plan their future utterances.

Even though we can employ silent pauses and conversational listening turns as opportunities to plan future messages, the cognitive demands associated with speech production and listening may preclude extensive planning during conversations. To compensate for reduced planning opportunities during conversations, we rely on old plans stored in long-term memory to understand others' discourse and actions and to guide the production of our own messages. As noted earlier, many social interactions in which we participate in everyday life are highly routine. Grocery shopping, obtaining money from a bank or automatic teller machine, ordering food at a restaurant, and even some daily interactions with friends and family are highly routinized. Successful execution of such routine encounters requires little if any conscious planning either before they begin or while they are underway; by the time most people reach adulthood, they have developed a large collection of canned plans stored in long-term memory that can be activated automatically when the routine situation calls for them (Hammond, 1989). That is, once a goal has been activated, for example, obtaining gas for one's car, a plan to procure gas is automatically activated outside of conscious awareness and implemented without a great deal of careful monitoring.

The idea that people use canned plans to achieve routine goals and to recognize the routine actions of others does not mean that canned plans will necessarily be completely appropriate for a given situation. Even similar situations may show some variations; so, canned plans may have to be altered to meet the requirements of a specific situation (Alterman, 1988). For instance, although the process of obtaining money from a bank teller is essentially the same across banks and tellers, various banks may use slightly different withdrawal slips that force customers to vary the actions necessary to complete them, and tellers may differ in what they say to customers. It is also true that in spite of the cognitive demands associated with speech production and listening, people show evidence of planning during their conversations with others (Waldron, 1990, 1997; Waldron & Applegate, 1994). Some of this planning activity during conversations is directed toward anticipating the future moves of conversational partners and how such moves might be countered (Waldron, 1990, 1997; Waldron & Applegate, 1994). Planning activity is necessary during some conversations because social interactions are sometimes highly dynamic and somewhat unpredictable. Canned plans may not fit these novel situations very well because they do not include unique actions that are taking place in the current situation. Thus, when this happens, conversational participants may be faced with the task of generating new plans to cope with the unpredictable or unanticipated events. However, in the heat of conversation, there may be only limited time to formulate and implement such plans.

Although people usually do not engage in extensive planning before most conversations, and planning opportunities during conversations may be limited by the cognitive processing demands of conversations, there are certain communication contexts in which people can and do engage in extensive planning efforts before they disseminate messages. Sometimes people may spend time imagining interactions before they take place (Honeycutt, 1989, 1991). Job interviews and other interactions with potentially important consequences may be imagined and, to some degree, planned before they occur. Public speeches and presentations are usually planned well before they are executed. Within the context of marketing, advertising, public-information campaigns, and the mass media, much time, effort and money is spent planning and implementing messages to accomplish such goals as persuading and informing large audiences. Thus, even though many of our everyday social interactions with others are not planned before they are carried out (probably because many of these daily interactions are highly routine), advanced message planning is a ubiquitous activity in many public and mass communication contexts.

As we have seen, plans and planning are vital both to understanding the discourse and actions of others and to guiding the production of our own actions and messages. Without knowledge about goals and plans, we would find it extremely difficult to make sense out of others' speech and actions, and we would find it equally difficult to know what to say and how to act in order to achieve our goals. In the absence of goal-plan knowledge, it would be difficult if not impossible to bridge the gap between ideas on the one hand and speech and actions on the other. The remainder of this chapter will focus on the roles plans and planning play in the production of messages. Specifically, the relations between plan effectiveness and communication effectiveness will be explained. In pondering these relations, you should keep in mind that plan-based knowledge is also vital for understanding others' messages and actions. When you observe people pursuing everyday activities such as studying, watching television, and listening to a lecture, you understand what you are witnessing because of your knowledge of the typical goals people seek to attain and the plans they characteristically use to achieve them. Unfortunately, plan-based understanding by itself is such a vast topic that it cannot be examined further here. Now that the crucial roles plans and planning play in social interaction has been established, we now turn to the question of how plan effectiveness is related to communicative success.

PLAN EFFECTIVENESS AND COMMUNICATION EFFECTIVENESS

When we watch other people pursue their goals during social encounters, we can usually identify those who are apparently very effective in getting what they want. Some people appear to be very talented and successful in face-to-face selling situations, whereas others may excel in influencing others in less formal communication contexts such as borrowing someone's class notes. By contrast, other people pursuing these same goals may experience chronic failure. Why are some individuals seemingly able to achieve goals that require social interaction with great ease while others who pursue the same goals flounder and frequently fail?

Communication Competence and Communicative Performance

Before answering this question of communication effectiveness, it is useful to distinguish between communication competence on the one hand and communicative performance or communicative skill on the other (Berger, 1997).

Communication Competence.   Communication competence involves the degree to which individuals are knowledgeable about other people and social-interaction procedures. Communication competence includes knowledge about goals and plans as well as knowledge about people's personalities and beliefs. This knowledge may be general or specific. General knowledge is concerned with what we know about people in the abstract and about the goals, plans, actions, and discourse that people typically manifest in their social interactions with others. For example, we may know that certain persuasive message appeals may be highly effective with people in general. Appeals that involve the welfare of family members might be effective across a wide spectrum of the public. "Buy this insurance policy to ensure the financial future of your loved ones" might be such an appeal. As we observe the talk and actions of strangers interacting with other people, we may be able to determine the degree to which the strangers are outgoing, sociable, and extroverted or quiet, reserved, and introverted. It is our knowledge of the actions and talk that is associated with extroversion and introversion that enables us to make inferences about complete strangers' personalities. These inferences can be made even though we do not talk directly with the strangers. Thus, if we notice that as a stranger speaks he or she avoids eye contact, talks in a soft voice, and says that he or she would rather study alone in the library on weekends than attend parties, our general knowledge of people would lead us to infer that the stranger is probably quite introverted.

Repeated observations of the same people or frequent interactions with them enable us to acquire more specific knowledge about them. As we gain more detailed knowledge about specific people, we may come to understand the individuals' particular preferences, beliefs, and attitudes. By interacting with a person, we may discover that in some situations he or she is extroverted whereas in other situations the same individual is quiet and reserved. We may also acquire specific information about the person's interaction style. The person may speak rapidly, loudly, and interrupt others often in some situations but be quite quiet in others. This kind of specific knowledge enables us to understand the person more completely and to fashion more effective plans for attaining goals that involve the person. Knowing that a friend is very fond of chocolate may serve as the basis of a promised reward for compliance with a request, for example, "If you loan me your class notes, I'll give you this box of chocolate candy." As relationships become closer, generally we acquire more knowledge about others; however, there may be upper limits to this knowledge. Sillars (1998) reported that in some studies of married couples, no significant relation has been found between the number of years the couple has been married and the degree to which they exhibit mutual understanding. Apparently, in the initial stages of close relationship development, individuals acquire large amounts of knowledge about each other and mutual understanding increases sharply; however, if the close relationships continue over a long period, mutual understanding shows little additional increase. This is probably because even people involved in close relationships develop canned plans and routinize their daily interactions with each other the longer they are together.

Communicative Performance.   It is one thing to have general and specific knowledge or communication competence, but it is quite another thing to be able to utilize that knowledge to one's advantage while pursing one's goals during face-to-face interaction. To realize this knowledge in action, performance skills are necessary. This distinction between communication competence and performance skills is reflected in the division of roles between speech writers and politicians and between screen writers and actors. Speech writers may have the competence to plan effective speeches, but may lack the performance skills necessary to deliver their speeches effectively. Conversely, politicians may have high levels of performance skills, but lack the knowledge necessary to be communicatively competent. Speech writers are planners, whereas politicians are performers. Of course, the same holds for screen writers and playwrights on the one hand, and actors on the other. In the case of everyday social interaction, some individuals may be able to develop highly effective interaction plans for dealing with others but not be able to carry them out successfully because they have odd vocal characteristics or a quirky interaction style. Parents may have perfectly effective plans for inducing their children to do their homework; however, if the plan is implemented using an angry tone of voice because the planner cannot successfully control his or her emotions, it may well fail.

In most daily social encounters, people must simultaneously play the roles of planner and performer. Pulling off this act can be very difficult. Of course, prior to some interactions individuals may consult with others to seek help in formulating their interaction plans. These consultants may know a great deal about the persons with whom interaction is anticipated; thus, such consultants are able to expand people's knowledge bases along these lines. Or, people who are especially talented at achieving the kinds of goals that individuals are seeking to attain in their anticipated interactions may be consulted. These interaction-procedure consultants may be able to provide people with valuable plan-relevant information concerning how to go about achieving their goal or goals in the interaction, for example, how to ask someone out for a date, how to persuade someone to marry one, or how to induce someone to propose marriage to one.

Plans not only guide the actions and messages that people generate in order to attain their goals, plans, and planning also affect communicative performance. With respect to communicative performance, most of us would find the task of suddenly being asked to give an impromptu speech in front of a large audience to be at least somewhat distressing. A few years ago, less than 1 hr after landing in Seoul, South Korea, after a 12-hr flight from San Francisco, I was asked to make a few remarks to a large group of journalists attending a dinner at a downtown hotel. Before arriving at the dinner I had no idea I would be called on to make these remarks, and I did not know I would be asked to make them in Korean, a language with which I have only some familiarity. The combination of jet-lag induced fatigue, the limited amount of time during which to "tune into" the Korean language, as well as the complete lack of opportunity to plan, conspired to undermine my performance significantly.

Without the opportunity to engage in any planning—or even limited planning before speaking—we fully expect to be less verbally fluent than if we are given the opportunity to plan before appearing in front of an audience. In the absence of planning, we would probably speak more slowly, utter more vocalize pauses (um's and ah's) and display more frequent and longer silent pauses. Moreover, without the opportunity to plan, our message would probably be less well organized than it would be if we had the opportunity to plan, and in the absence of planning we might well forget to include important points or arguments in our message. By contrast, if we had made these remarks many times in the past, as a politician might during a political campaign, we could rely on a canned message plan and our performance might not suffer as a result. In any case, these examples suggest that plans and planning are critical for producing skilled communicative performances.

It is now time to consider the evidence that planning and plans have a real impact on the degree to which people are successful in achieving their goals in social interaction situations. Not all of the research to be discussed involves social interaction directly, but much of it will, and those studies that do not will have obvious relevance to social interaction effectiveness. First the effects of planning on communicative performance will be examined, and then how plans affect performance will be discussed.

Planning and Social-Interaction Effectiveness

There is considerable evidence to support the idea that the opportunity to plan before engaging in certain tasks improves performance once the task is undertaken. For example, in one study, individuals who were given the chance to plan before trying to solve a traveling salesman problem, a problem that required them to schedule a series of client calls, produced more efficient routes for making their client calls than did those who did not plan before making their schedules (Battman, 1989). Planning before undertaking the scheduling task produced more efficient schedules. In another study by Pea and Hawkins (1987), elementary school children were given the task of scheduling a series of classroom chores such as cleaning blackboards, feeding classroom pets, and putting away books. Youngsters devised progressively more efficient plans when they were given the opportunity to revise their chore schedules. With each revision, the chore schedules became more efficient. These researchers suggested that good planners engage in cycles of plan revision and simulation to develop and test increasingly efficient plan organizations. They also observed that the children generally revised more concrete elements of their plans rather than completely reorganizing them at higher levels. One reason plans may become more efficient when individuals are given the opportunity to revise them is that replanning may enable planners to recognize previously unseen opportunities for improving their plan's efficiency and perhaps its effectiveness. Some researchers have suggested that this kind of opportunistic planning is more the rule than the exception in everyday planning situations (Hayes-Roth & Hayes-Roth, 1979).

Although such studies show that planning and replanning may result in improved performance, they do not directly demonstrate that planning improves communicative performance. However, there is considerable evidence that planning before speaking increases verbal fluency as measured by speech rate, that is, the number of words or syllables per minute individuals utter (Berger, 1997; Berger, Knowlton, & Abrahams, 1996, Experiment 2; Greene, 1984; Greene & Lindsey, 1989). Those who speak more rapidly are generally judged by others to be more verbally fluent (Berger, 1997). Berger et al. (1996, Experiment 2) found that people who planned geographic directions before giving them to another person spoke more quickly when they actually gave the directions than did direction-givers who did not plan before giving their directions. However, when the direction-givers were asked to provide their directions a second time, those who planned spoke no more quickly than those who did not plan when providing the second rendition of their directions. Thus, the initial facilitating effects of planning on communicative performance may be nullified by events that occur as the interaction progresses beyond its initial stages. In related research, Allen and Honeycutt (1996) found that individuals who planned before an interaction displayed fewer object adaptors than did those who were distracted from planning before their interactions. Object adaptors are such behaviors as fooling with a pen, pencil, or a watch and they are sometimes indicative of the degree to which an individual is experiencing anxiety (see chap. 3, this volume, on nonverbal communication for a complete explanation of object adaptors).

Some researchers have examined the relation between planning and the success with which people lie to others. The questions here is whether planned lies are any more convincing than are unplanned or spontaneous lies. This question has at least two parts. First, when people tell planned lies are they any more verbally fluent than people who tell spontaneous lies? For this question the evidence seems to be clear. One study reported that those perpetrating planned lies began to speak more quickly when engaging in deception than did those who told spontaneous lies (Cody, Marston, & Foster, 1984). Another study found that individuals telling planned lies responded more quickly than did those who told the truth. In addition, individuals telling planned lies displayed significantly fewer leg and foot movements, affirmative head nods, and head adaptors than did truth-tellers (Greene, O'Hair, Cody, & Yen, 1985). Individuals who plan lies appear to be more verbally fluent than those who tell unplanned lies or even those who tell the truth.

The second question concerns whether planning lies makes them more difficult to detect. Given this evidence, one might suppose that planned lies are more difficult to detect than are spontaneous lies because those who tell planned lies are more verbally fluent and less fidgety than those who tell spontaneous lies. However, the evidence here is mixed. Sometimes planned lies are more difficult to detect than spontaneous lies but sometimes they are not (DePaulo, Davis, & Lanier, 1980; Littlepage & Pineault, 1982; Miller, deTurck, & Kalbfleisch, 1983; Miller & Stiff, 1993).

It is one thing to show that those who engage in planning before they interact are more fluent or efficient than those who do not engage in planning; however, it is quite another thing to show that various features of plans themselves influence the degree to which people are effective in attaining their social interaction goals. The following studies have examined these relations.

Plans and Social-Interaction Effectiveness

Some of the research that has explored relations between plan effectiveness and interaction effectiveness has asked people to devise interaction plans outside of ongoing social interactions. Such investigations might be thought of as studies of preinteraction plans. Other studies have attempted to examine the plans that people formulate while they are conversing with others and to link characteristics of these plans with effectiveness during the interaction. These two types of studies will be considered in turn.

Preinteraction Plans.   One way to determine whether plan effectiveness is related to social-interaction effectiveness is to try to measure both kinds of effectiveness and see whether those people who have effective plans are also more effective in achieving their goals during social interactions with others. This is what we tried to do in two similar studies (Berger & Bell, 1988; Berger & diBattista, 1992). In both studies, college men and women were each asked to write two different plans. In one of these plans (date request), they were asked to describe how they would go about asking someone they had seen at a party out for a date. In the other (roommate ingratiation), students were asked to describe how they would get a new roommate to like them. After completing these two plans, under the guise of participating in another study, the students completed the UCLA loneliness scale (Russell, 1982). This scale taps feelings of loneliness and has been related to various conversational behaviors. For example, those who scored high on the UCLA loneliness scale tended to be less talkative, less attentive, and less involved when conversing with others than did those who were less lonely (Bell, 1985). Thus, the UCLA loneliness scale indirectly measures social-interaction effectiveness.

The date-request and roommate-ingratiation plans written by the students were given to separate groups of college student judges who had not participated in the study. The judges each sorted all of the plans into 11 piles that represented a continuum ranging from *extremely effective* at one end to *extremely ineffective* at the other end, with the middle pile representing *average effectiveness*. Even though the judges were not told what constituted "*effective*" or "*ineffective*" plans before sorting them, the judges showed high levels of agreement in the way they sorted the same plans. Thus, there seems to be a tacit or implicit social consensus about what constitutes an effective way to ask someone out for a date and how to get a roommate to like one. The averages of the judges' ratings were used to measure plan effectiveness.

The two studies showed very similar results. Men whose plans for requesting a date that were judged as more effective showed lower levels of loneliness than men whose date-request plans were judged to be less effective. In sharp contrast, among women, date-request plan effectiveness was not correlated with loneliness. Women whose date-request plans were deemed more effective by the judges were no less lonely than women whose date-request plans were judged to be less effective. Both studies revealed that men are usually the date requesters whereas women are usually the date request receivers; thus, the difference between women and men makes considerable sense. Because men are more likely than women to initiate date requests, their plan effectiveness in this domain of social interaction is critical to their social success. However, because women are less likely to request dates, their date-request plan effectiveness in this domain is much less consequential to their social success.

In contrast to the findings for the date-request plans, plan effectiveness in the roommate-ingratiation situation showed similar relations with loneliness for both women and men. Students whose plans for getting a new roommate to like them were judged to be more effective reported less loneliness than did students whose plans were judged to be less effective. In the case of roommate ingratiation, one would not expect the kinds of differences between men and women as those observed in the case of date requests. College students of both genders are faced with the situation of having to live with new roommates at one time or another during their college career. Thus, one would expect plan effectiveness and social-interaction effectiveness to be similarly related for both women and men.

These studies also showed that plan effectiveness in the date-request domain was not strongly related to plan effectiveness in the roommate-ingratiation domain. That is, people whose date-request plans were judged to be highly effective did not necessarily write highly effective roommate-ingratiation plans. Conversely, people who devised ineffective date-request plans did not necessarily develop ineffective roommate-ingratiation plans. The lack of generalizability across these two different domains suggests that social-interaction competence may be specific to particular goals. The level of effectiveness of people's plans for specific goals may be strongly influenced by the amount of experience they have in pursuing that goal. The more experience they have, the more competent they are likely to be. This line of thinking is supported by the results of a study in which college men arranged two different sets of cards on which were printed various actions that were each part of a sequence of actions for reaching two different goals. The two action sequences examined were asking someone out on a date and the actions that would be taken on a first date (Pryor & Merluzzi, 1985, Study 4). The cards on which the actions were printed were randomly ordered. The task required the men to arrange the actions in the order in which they would normally occur. In a previous study, the students had indicated the number of different people they had dated during the previous year.

This investigation showed that men who had more different dates during the previous year performed the two card-sorting tasks significantly more quickly than did men who reported that they had been on only a few dates. However, the ways in which these dating experts and dating novices sorted the cards did not differ. Both groups generally placed the actions in the same order; however, the experts performed the sorting tasks more quickly in both cases. These results suggest that experts and novices in the dating domain do not differ very much with respect to the content of their knowledge about the actions involved in getting dates and going out on dates, but the knowledge of dating experts is organized in such a way that the experts have faster access to it when they need it. Other research indicates that the knowledge of experts is more likely than the knowledge of novices to be organized in a hierarchical fashion (McKeithen, Reitman, Rueter, & Hirtle, 1981). Thus, it may be that dating experts' plans for getting dates and going out on dates are more likely to display a hierarchical structure.

Although the results of this study revealed no evidence that the knowledge levels of experts and novices differed, one can imagine many domains of human endeavor in which there should be large differences between experts and novices with respect to the amount of knowledge each group possesses. For example, one would expect large knowledge gaps between experts and novices in such domains as baseball, tennis, politics, computer programming, and brain surgery. However, when it comes to social behavior and interpersonal communication, something that we do everyday, most of us receive daily instruction. We make mistakes, for example, unintentionally embarrassing or offending people, and then we correct these errors and try not to make them again. When we are children, our parents correct these mistakes. Thus, within the domain of social behavior and social interaction, by the time most people are adults, they have acquired the requisite knowledge about people and social interaction. Because this knowledge about social interaction tends to be widely shared, what may differentiate between experts and novices in the social-interaction domain is not the amount of knowledge each group has but the way it is organized and how easily it can be accessed when it is needed.

Conversational Plans. As pointed out earlier, individuals may engage in planning during their conversations with others. Although these opportunities may be somewhat limited under most conditions, thoughts about goals and plans appear to be frequent during some conversations. In one study, after strangers participated in information-seeking interactions, they individually reviewed a videotape of their just-completed conversation and noted those points during the conversation when they could recall what they were thinking (Waldron, 1990). Of the some 2,273 thoughts that the participants were able to recall, 44% of them were concerned with the goals individuals were pursuing in the conversation and the plans they were using to attain their goals. A later study yielded similar results (Waldron, Caughlin, & Jackson, 1995). The 44% figure may actually underestimate the extent to which goals and plans exert influence during conversations because people may not be able to recall all of their thoughts after their interactions have ended. Nonetheless, these results support the view that individuals actively think about goals and plans while they are in the process of conversing with others; however, such findings by themselves do not shed light on the relation between planning activity during conversations and social-interaction effectiveness. Studies that have sought to reveal relations between attributes of plans developed during conversations and social interaction effectiveness can answer this question.

Waldron (1990) used the videotape recall or "cued recall" procedure described previously to determine whether the plans of people who were given the goal of obtaining sensitive information from their conversation partners affected their performance on the information-seeking task. This study showed that people who reported using simple and direct plans (e.g., just asking for the information) were more likely to be judged as socially inappropriate than people whose information-seeking plans were less direct (e.g., gradually steering the conversation in the desired direction and seeing if the person volunteers the information). However, although those who employed this indirect strategy for obtaining information were perceived to be more socially appropriate, they failed to achieve their goal of obtaining the desired information more often than those who were more direct. In a similar study, Waldron and Applegate (1994) videotaped individuals discussing an issue on which they disagreed. After the discussion, each person individually viewed the videotape using the cued-recall procedure. The videotapes were also analyzed to determine how competent each person was in using various disagreement tactics. The plans that people developed during the conversation were scored in terms of their complexity, specificity, and sophistication. Plan complexity was determined by the number of distinct actions contained in the plan, more actions indicated greater complexity. Plan specificity was determined by the degree to which planned actions were abstract or concrete. For example, the action "giving help" is more abstract than the specific actions involved in performing the helping act. Plan sophistication concerned the degree to which planners relied solely on canned plans versus their propensity to accommodate their plans to the current situation. Highly sophisticated planners took into account the actions of their conversational partners, and they anticipated future conversational moves that might help them to achieve their goals. Waldron and Applegate found that people who developed more complex, specific, and sophisticated plans used more effective disagreement tactics than did those whose plans were simple, general, and less sophisticated.

Later studies have shown similar results. For example, in one investigation interviewers were given the task of eliciting as much AIDS-related information as they could from another person (Waldron et al., 1995). Again, the cued-recall procedure was used to determine the kinds of plans the information seekers developed while they conducted their interviews. This study demonstrated that interviewers whose plans were specific acquired more AIDS-related information from their interviewees than did interviewers whose plans contained more general actions. In this context, a specific action would be "ask about using latex condoms," whereas a general action might be "ask about using protection." Thus, it appears that plans specifying concrete actions may be more effective than plans that contain only general and abstract actions. Moreover, this research also suggests that people who are able to look ahead during the conversation and plan for future moves are more likely to be successful than those who are unable to anticipate and plan for such future moves (Waldron, 1997).

The plans of individuals who are able to look ahead in a conversation are likely to be more complex because their plans will probably include more contingencies than the plans of those who do not anticipate the future. As noted earlier, contingencies represent alternative actions that can be taken depending on the events that occur in the interaction; for example, a conversational plan contingency might read something like "If he refuses my large request, I will make the smaller request. But, if he grants the larger request, I will make an even larger request." As the number of contingencies in a plan increases, by default the plan becomes more complex. Because some research has shown that people who develop more complex plans during their interactions with others use more effective tactics to achieve their goals (Waldron & Applegate, 1994), it is tempting to jump to the general conclusion that complex plans are more effective than simple plans. However, this conclusion may not be warranted.

Some research has shown that when people with very simple or very complex plans fail to reach their goal and are forced to undertake alternative actions, their verbal fluency is reduced relative to people whose plans are only moderately complex (Berger, 1997; Berger, Karol, & Jordan, 1989; Berger, Knowlton, & Abrahams, 1996; Knowlton & Berger, 1997). When people's planned actions fail and they have no contingencies or alternative actions available in their plans, they must pause to try to generate an alternative course of action, thus reducing their verbal fluency. When people who have highly complex plans fail, their problem is that they may have many alternative planned actions from which to choose. Because it takes more time to choose among many alternatives, their fluency is also reduced. Consistent with this idea, one study found that when people involved in a persuasion task failed to convince their partners, persuaders whose plans contained no alternative arguments and persuaders whose plans contained six alternative arguments took longer to resume speaking than did persuaders whose plans contained three alternative arguments (Knowlton & Berger, 1997, Experiment 3). Those whose plans contained three alternative arguments recovered more quickly from the failure.

These studies suggest that there may be an optimal level of plan complexity for approaching specific communication tasks on which one may experience failure. When the communication task is relatively simple, it may make no sense to develop highly complex plans that contain many contingencies and alternative actions. By contrast, complex communication tasks, in which failure is more likely to occur, may require more complex plans for successful goal achievement. Whether plans need to be more or less complex also depends on the degree to which the environment in which the plan will be carried out is predictable. When uncertainty is relatively low, simple plans may suffice, but as uncertainty increases, more complex plans with many contingencies may be required (Berger, 1997). However, it is possible that if the amount of uncertainty is extremely high and the environment is highly dynamic and unpredictable, it may be neither possible nor wise to plan at all. Attempting to achieve goals in a cultural milieu about which one has little knowledge, including knowledge of the language spoken, might be one such highly uncertain environment. In extremely uncertain situations like these the best course of action might be first to gather information to try to reduce uncertainty, and once uncertainty is reduced somewhat, to engage in planning efforts.

CONCLUSION

Plans organize knowledge about the actions and verbal and nonverbal messages that are necessary for reaching goals. Plans serve both to guide the production of actions and verbal messages and to enable people to understand the actions and verbal and nonverbal messages of others. That is, plans provide answers to the questions of what others' goals are and how they are pursuing them during social encounters. Much of the time, individuals are not consciously aware of their plans. When people pursue very important goals or when plans fail to bring about desired goals, they may become more aware of their plans and alter them in some way.

When individuals interact with each other, their plans also interact. In some situations social actors may find themselves trying to second-guess each other's goals and plans (Waldron, 1997). This second-guessing may occur without exchanging any words about plans and intentions. Such interactive planning itself may be a kind of communication in which people mutually try to guess each other's future planned moves (Bruce & Newman, 1978; Waldron, 1997). At this point, researchers are far from understanding how these interactive planning dialogues play themselves out during social encounters and how they affect what is said and done during such encounters. Exploring the interplay between planning dialogues and verbal dialogues is the next step to understanding more clearly the vital roles that plans and planning play in goal-directed social interaction.

ADDITIONAL READING

Much of the work on planning and natural language processing has been carried out by artificial intelligence researchers and cognitive scientists interested in developing conversational computers (Carberry, 1990; Hammond, 1989) and a deeper understanding of how humans produce and comprehend language (Green, 1996; Levelt, 1989). This work has influenced communication researchers who study conversations and social interaction, especially those concerned with how individuals achieve their goals during social encounters. Useful overviews of this planning work can be found in Berger (1995, 1997) and Waldron (1997). Kellermann's (1995) review of her work on the organization of conversation is similar to the planning perspective presented in this chapter. Some researchers have raised several important general questions about these cognitive approaches to social interaction (McPhee, 1995).

REFERENCES

Allen, T. H., & Honeycutt, J. M. (1996). *An analysis of the effects of imagined interactions and planning on the use of object adaptors.* Unpublished paper, Department of Speech Communication, Long Beach State University, Long Beach, CA.

Alterman, R. (1988). Adaptive planning. *Cognitive Science, 12,* 393–421.

Austin, J. L. (1962). *How to do things with words.* Oxford, England: Oxford University Press.

Battman, W. (1989). Planning as a method of stress prevention: Will it pay off? In C. D. Spielberger, I. G. Sarason, & J. Strelau (Eds.), *Stress and anxiety: Volume 12* (pp. 259–275). New York: Hemisphere Publications.

Bell, R. A. (1985). Conversational involvement and loneliness. *Communication Monographs, 52,* 218–235.

Berger, C. R. (1995). A plan-based approach to strategic communication. In D. E. Hewes (Ed.), *The cognitive bases of interpersonal communication* (pp. 141–179). Hillsdale, NJ: Lawrence Erlbaum Associates, Inc.

Berger, C. R. (1997). *Planning strategic interaction: Attaining goals through communicative action.* Mahwah, NJ: Lawrence Erlbaum Associates, Inc.

Berger, C. R., & Bell, R. A. (1988). Plans and the initiation of social relationships. *Human Communication Research, 15,* 217–235.

Berger, C. R., & diBattista, P. (1992). Information seeking and plan elaboration: What do you need to know to know what to do? *Communication Monographs, 59,* 368–387.

Berger, C. R., Karol, S. H., & Jordan, J. M. (1989). When a lot of knowledge is a dangerous thing: The debilitating effects of plan complexity on verbal fluency. *Human Communication Research, 16,* 91–119.

Berger, C. R., Knowlton, S. W., & Abrahams, M. F. (1996). The hierarchy principle in strategic communication. *Communication Theory, 6,* 111–142.

Berlo, D. K. (1961). *The process of communication.* New York: Holt, Rinehart & Winston.

Bruce, B., & Newman, D. (1978). Interacting plans. *Cognitive Science, 2,* 195–233.

Carberry, S. (1990). *Plan recognition in natural language dialogue.* Cambridge, MA: MIT Press.

Clark, H. H. (1994). Discourse in production. In M. A. Gernsbacher (Ed.), *Handbook of psycholinguistics* (pp. 985–1021). San Diego, CA: Academic.

Cody, M. J., Marston, P. J., & Foster, M. (1984). Deception: Paralinguistic and verbal leakage. In R. N. Bostrom (Ed.), *Communication yearbook 8* (pp. 464–490). Beverly Hills, CA: Sage.

DePaulo, B. M., Davis, T., & Lanier (1980, April). *Planning lies: The effects of spontaneity and arousal on success in deception.* Paper presented at the annual meeting of the Eastern Psychological Association, Hartford, CT.

Goldman-Eisler, F. (1968). *Psycholinguistics: Experiments in spontaneous speech.* New York: Academic.

Green, G. M. (1996). *Pragmatics and natural language understanding* (2nd ed.). Mahwah, NJ: Lawrence Erlbaum Associates, Inc.

Greene, J. O. (1984). Speech preparation processes and verbal fluency. *Human Communication Research, 11,* 61–84.

Greene, J. O., & Lindsey, A. E. (1989). Encoding processes in the production of multiple-goal messages. *Human Communication Research, 16,* 120–140.

Greene, J. O., O'Hair, H. D., Cody, M. J., & Yen, C. (1985). Planning and control of behavior during deception. *Human Communication Research, 11,* 335–364.

Hammond, K. J. (1989). *Case-based planning: Viewing planning as a memory task.* New York: Academic.

Hayes-Roth, B., & Hayes-Roth, F. (1979). A cognitive model of planning. *Cognitive Science, 3,* 275–310.

Honeycutt, J. M (1989). A functional analysis of imagined interaction activity in everyday life. In J. E. Shorr, P. Robin, J. A. Connelia, & M. Wolpin (Eds.), *Imagery: Current perspectives* (pp. 13–25). New York: Plenum.

Honeycutt, J. M. (1991). Imagined interactions, imagery and mindfulness/mindlessness. In R. Kunzendorf (Ed.), *Mental imagery* (pp. 121–128). New York: Plenum.

Kellermann, K. (1995). The conversation MOP: Model of patterned and pliable behavior. In D. E. Hewes (Ed.), *The cognitive bases of interpersonal communication* (pp. 181–221), Hillsdale, NJ: Lawrence Erlbaum Associates, Inc.

Knowlton, S. W., & Berger, C. R. (1997). Message planning, communication failure, and cognitive load: Further explorations of the hierarchy principle. *Human Communication Research, 24,* 4–30.

Levelt, W. J. M. (1989). *Speaking: From intention to articulation.* Cambridge, MA: MIT Press.

Littlepage, G. E., & Pineault, M. A. (1982). *Detection of deception of planned and spontaneous communications.* Unpublished paper, Department of Psychology, Middle Tennessee State University, Murfreesboro.

McKeithen, K. B., Reitman, J. S., Rueter, H. H., & Hirtle, S C. (1981). Knowledge organization and skill differences in computer programmers. *Cognitive Psychology, 13,* 307–325.

McPhee, R. D. (1995). Cognitive perspectives on communication: Interpretive and critical responses. In D. E. Hewes (Ed), *The cognitive bases of interpersonal communication* (pp. 225–246), Hillsdale, NJ: Lawrence Erlbaum Associates, Inc.

Miller, G. R., deTurck, M. A., & Kalbfleisch, P. J. (1983). Self-monitoring, rehearsal, and deceptive communication. *Human Communication Research, 10,* 97–117.

Miller, G. R., & Stiff, J. B. (1993). *Deceptive communication.* Newbury Park, CA: Sage.

Pea, R. D., & Hawkins, J. (1987). Planning in a chore-scheduling task. In S. L. Friedman, E. K. Skolnick, & R. R. Cocking (Eds.), *Blueprints for thinking: The role of planning in cognitive development* (pp. 273–302). New York: Cambridge University Press.

Pryor, J. B, & Merluzzi, T. V. (1985). The role of expertise in processing social interaction scripts. *Journal of Experimental Social Psychology, 21,* 362–379.

Reddy, M. J. (1979). The conduit metaphor-A case of frame conflict in our language about language. In A. Ortony (Ed.), *Metaphor and thought* (pp. 284–324). London: Cambridge University Press.

Russell, D. (1982). The measurement of loneliness. In L. A. Peplau & D. Perlman (Eds.), *Loneliness: A sourcebook of current theory, research and therapy* (pp. 81–104). New York: Wiley.

Sillars, A. L. (1998). (Mis)Understanding. In B. H. Spitzberg & W. R. Cupach (Eds.), *The dark side of close relationships* (pp. 73–102). Mahwah, NJ: Lawrence Erlbaum Associates, Inc.

Waldron, V. R. (1990). Constrained rationality: Situational influences on information acquisition plans and tactics. *Communication Monographs, 57,* 184–201.

Waldron, V. R. (1997). Toward a theory of interactive conversational planning. In J. O. Greene (Ed.), *Message production: Advances in communication theory* (pp. 195–220). Mahwah, NJ: Lawrence Erlbaum Associates, Inc.

Waldron, V. R., & Applegate, J. L. (1994). Interpersonal construct differentiation and conversational planning: An examination of two cognitive accounts for the production of competent verbal disagreement tactics. *Human Communication Research, 21,* 3–35.

Waldron, V. R., Caughlin, J., & Jackson, D. (1995). Talking specifics: Facilitating effects of planning on AIDS talk in peer dyads. *Health Communication, 7,* 249–266.

Wilensky, R. (1983). *Planning and understanding: A computational approach to human reasoning.* Reading, MA: Addison-Wesley.

Wittgenstein, L. (1953). *Philosophical investigations.* Oxford, England: Basil Blackwell.

QUESTIONS TO PONDER

1. Some researchers have objected to plan-based approaches to communication on the grounds that social interaction is highly dynamic and ever-changing and plans are static entities that cannot "keep up" with rapidly changing circumstances. As a nascent planning theorist, how would you respond to such critics?

2. Recall a recent instance when you experienced "plan failure" during a conversation with someone; that is, when you implemented actions and talk to try to achieve a goal but failed to do so. How did it feel when you discovered you were failing? What did you do in response to the failure? Why?

3. Some theorists have argued that we learn more when our plans fail than when they succeed. Why is it that this kind of learning may indeed be "failure-driven"?

4. When it comes to social interaction with others, are you a better communication strategist (planner) or a better performer (actor)? Why do you think this is so? In what communication domains do you have strengths? In which domains are you particularly weak?

5. Have you ever had the experience of having a wordless "planning dialogue" with someone? One in which your plans interacted in such a way that you both acted together in a mutually understandable way without using any words? How did you know you mutually understood each other's plans? Did you talk about the experience with the person afterward?

9

Formulating and Producing Verbal and Nonverbal Messages: An Action Assembly Theory

John O. Greene
Purdue University

This chapter is about processes that lie at the very heart of human communication—processes so central and so fundamental that theories failing to address these phenomena ultimately seem somewhat lacking because they miss so much of what we experience and know to be involved when we communicate with others. Consider how much of what takes place when we interact with others falls into the two broad categories of "thinking things" and "doing things." When you converse with your roommates, parents, professors, and that special "main squeeze," innumerable thoughts go through your mind—thoughts about yourself, about what you're doing and saying, about the other person, or even about something far away and unconnected to the moment. And at the same time that you're experiencing this shifting hodgepodge of *thoughts*, you're also *doing* things—selecting and constructing things to say that might be sensible to the other, actually producing verbal utterances that reflect your meanings and your understanding of the interaction as it unfolds, and enacting all the facial expressions, gestures, and other nonverbal behaviors that arise from, and tell something about, your thoughts, emotions, and even your physiological state.

When we delve into issues such as these we're cutting close to the core of what we experience when we communicate with our coworkers, friends, and loved ones. This chapter is concerned with a theory that focuses squarely on these essential processes of *thinking* and *doing*. Action assembly theory[1] is the product of an effort to understand some of the most

---

[1]Action assembly theory has undergone a number of refinements and revisions, both subtle and substantial, over the last 25 years. The characterization presented in this chapter is an amalgam of various versions of the theory, written expressly for this book, with the intention of making the action assembly framework readily available to an undergraduate audience. As such, it should not be taken to reflect any specific instantiation of the theory (either of the "first" or "second" generation), and it does not attempt to explicate the more complex and nuanced features of any version of the action assembly framework.

complex and fascinating questions confronting scholars of human communication: Where do the thoughts and ideas that run through your mind come from? How can you think something that you (or anyone else for that matter) have never thought before? How is it possible for you and me to have any conscious experience of thoughts at all? How are you able to formulate a conception of what you might say to another person? How are you able to express some idea or understanding in what you say and do? How is it possible that your overt verbal and non-verbal behavior express some aspect of what you intended and yet also manifest more than even you understood? How can things in the recesses of your mind that you're *not* aware of impact in some way your verbal and nonverbal actions? And, as one final example, how is it possible that without any conscious effort to suppress them, you can think things and *not* say them?

Obviously any characterization of human communication that failed to tackle issues such as these would leave some pretty serious gaps in our understanding, but it is precisely these fundamental processes of thinking and doing that action assembly theory was developed to address. Action assembly theory (AAT) is a *cognitive theory*—meaning simply that it seeks to explain the phenomena of interest by describing the mental mechanisms that produce those phenomena. In essence, then, AAT attempts to explain how people formulate meanings and produce verbal and nonverbal behaviors that bear some relation to those meanings by describing how the mind carries out these activities. Along the way, AAT sheds light on a whole host of problems that are of interest to people who study human communication, including the nature of the "self" and the role of the self in guiding our behavior, the development of communication skill and reasons that we sometimes perform poorly in interactions with others, the sources of both stability and change in our behavior from one situation to the next, the processes involved when we experience anxiety about interacting with others, and, as just one more illustration out of many, the mechanisms that link deception to changes in overt behavior. In fact, if it has to do with the way people produce thoughts and actions in their conversations with others, AAT probably has something to say about it.

LAYING THE FOUNDATION: SOME BASIC OBSERVATIONS ABOUT HUMAN BEHAVIOR

I think that one of the best ways to understand AAT is to start with four simple observations that played a key role in the theory's development—in essence, much like a detective working from a set of clues to solve a crime, we can place ourselves in the role of the theorist and reason along with him in seeing how a "solution" emerges. Our four observations, or "clues," are as follows:

- *Behavior is simultaneously patterned and repetitive, yet novel and creative.* Human behavior is comprised of repetitive elements of various sorts. For example, your verbal behavior is made up of sets of words, phrases, syntactic patterns, topics, and so on, that you use over and over again. You also have a repertoire of nonverbal behaviors—gestures, facial expressions, and other mannerisms—that crop up in your behavior again and again. But, at the same time that your behavior reflects these repetitive elements, it is also constantly new and creative. Your speech behavior may be made up of a repetitive set of words, but any particular utterance is probably going to be novel—something that you've never said before. Nonverbally, you make use of your own repertoire of mannerisms, but any particular gesture, or facial expression, or what have you, is probably one that you've never enacted in just that way before. The problem in developing AAT, then, was to account for the simultaneous repetitive and creative nature of human behavior. In other words, what is the nature of the mental system that could give rise to these properties?

- *People act on the basis of the meanings that they assign to stimulus inputs, and not the raw inputs themselves.* In many ways this idea is a simple one, but it presents some complex problems for theories of behavioral production. Perhaps the best way to explicate this second observation about human behavior is with an example. Suppose you were walking down the sidewalk and saw one of your friends approaching. You smile and wave, but your friend continues on without acknowledging you. Now, what meaning might you assign to your friend's behavior? One possibility would be to interpret her behavior as a deliberate snub. Another possibility would be to decide that she was deep in thought and simply didn't see you. The key point here is that your response would be determined by your interpretation of her actions. If you thought she had snubbed you, you'd likely respond in a very different way than if you thought she hadn't seen you. Notice that in either case the raw stimulus event is the same: Your friend walked by without acknowledging you. What matters in determining how you'll respond, then, is the meaning you assign to the event. The issue for theories of behavioral production is one of how it is possible for meanings to influence behavior. Or, to put it another way, what is the link between interpretations given to inputs and behavioral production?

- *There are times when we must carefully monitor and control what we're doing and saying, but in other cases our actions run off automatically, without any conscious awareness.* The idea here is that sometimes our behavior is very conscious and deliberate—times when we focus on the details of what we're doing; at other times, though, we seem to go along on "automatic pilot"—we don't have to think about what we're doing in order to produce our behaviors. Take the example of driving a car. If you're like most of us, there was a time when driving was a very deliberate process: It took all your concentration just to steer, brake, and change gears. Now, however, driving is probably pretty automatic; you don't need to think about what you're doing in order get around. In this same way, much of our communication behavior is automatic: We don't have to monitor our facial expressions, for example. Further, even when *some* aspects of our behavior are deliberate and carefully controlled, choosing just the right words for expressing some idea, for example, other aspects of that same behavior (e.g., pronouncing those words), can run off automatically. The essential problem for theories of behavioral production suggested by this observation, then, is to understand what is going on when we're deliberately monitoring our actions and when they seem to be running off automatically.

- *Behavior ultimately consists of a very large number of efferent commands, and yet our phenomenal experience of behavior and behavioral control consists of abstract action specifications.* The language for expressing this last observation may make it seem like the most difficult of the four to understand, but, in fact, when you cut through the language, this idea turns out to be pretty straightforward. Let's start with another example. Think about a simple behavior like reaching for the "page down" key on your computer keyboard. Carrying out even a simple action like this involves the coordination of a very large number of muscle, or "efferent," commands: You have to contract certain muscles in your upper arm and relax others, you have to rotate your wrist and extend your finger, and so on. Thus, there is a complex coordination of efferent commands involved in even the simplest sort of action.

At the same time, what is your conception of what you're doing when you reach for the "page down" key? Are you thinking "I've got to relax the triceps" or "flex the wrist"? No, of course not. Your conception of what you were doing (your "phenomenal experience" of your behavior) was likely some abstract act specification like "go on to the next page" or even "I'll keep reading until the pizza comes." The essence of Observation 4, then, is that production of behavior involves the specification and coordination of a very large number of muscle commands, but our experience of what we're doing when we produce such behaviors doesn't consist of these muscle commands at all; instead, we understand what we're doing in much more abstract terms. For theories of message production, the general problem, then, is one of the relationship between our abstract conceptions of what we're doing and the efferent commands that make up that behavior. Even more to the point, consider that it is possible to control behavior (at least to some extent) by specifying abstract conceptions of action. For example, if you decide to page down on your computer screen, then in some way, your hand actually reaches to push the "page down" key. How is it, then, that these abstract conceptions of action can exert influence on the efferent commands that make up that action, or even more simply, how do my thoughts influence my overt behaviors?

Well, there you have the "clues"—the basic observations, each one pretty simple on the surface and yet indicative of some complex problems lurking below. Now put yourself in the role of theorist—if you wanted to develop a theory that could account for these facts, what kind of theory would it be? What kinds of concepts and processes would you include to make sense of, or explain, these phenomena? In fact, rather than peeking ahead to see what happens in the end, you might take a little time right now to formulate your own solution, just to see whether your approach ends up being similar to AAT or whether you're able to come up with an alternative and creative account.

AN ACTION ASSEMBLY THEORY

As we've already noted, cognitive theories are concerned with the nature of the mind—they seek to provide scientific explanations of various processes (processes like *understanding* what another person is saying, *remembering* the major points of a lecture, or, as in the case of AAT, *formulating* and *enacting messages*) by describing the mental system that allows those processes to be carried out.

To be more specific, the descriptions of the mind found in cognitive theories usually focus on two sets of concerns: representation and processing. When cognitivists talk about "representation" they're dealing with questions about how information is stored in the mind—that is, *what* information is held in the mental system, and how is that information *coded* and *structured?* If that seems a little obscure, just think about the same questions applied not to the mind, but to another information repository you're familiar with: your telephone book. What information is represented in the telephone book?—names, addresses and telephone numbers; How is that information coded?—as strings of letters and digits; How is the information structured?—in groupings of three related items: a name, an address, and a number (and these also have an overarching alphabetical structure as well). Cognitive theorists, then, seek to answer these same questions about the mind—what is stored there, what kind of code is used to represent this information, and how is that information structured or organized?

Apart from problems of representation, the other big concern for cognitive theorists is "processing"—that is, what kinds of operations and transformations are carried out on the information held in the mind? Common conceptions of cognitive processes would include things like *attending* to a radio ad as you drive to work, storing some new piece of information in long-term memory, mentally *rehearsing* a telephone number, *planning* what you'll say to your boss when you arrive late, and *retrieving* your mental list of the grocery items you need to pick up on the way home.

Taken together, cognitive science's concern with representation and processing boils down to two, interrelated, questions: What information is held in the mental system and how is that information used to produce the phenomena of interest? Because the "phenomena of interest" for AAT are those involved, and manifested, in message production, the whole thrust of the theory comes down to an attempt to specify what information is represented in the mind and what processes operate over that information such that we are able to conceive and enact verbal and nonverbal messages.

Representation: How Is Message-Relevant Information Coded and Structured?

One of the most important features of AAT, and one of the things that makes it different from other theories of message production that have been developed in the field of Communication, is the idea that message-relevant information is represented in multiple code systems. One of these code systems corresponds to our everyday language—that is, some of the information we draw on in producing our messages is expressed in the mental equivalent of words. At the same time, though, message-relevant information is held in other formats. For example, some information is represented as abstract concepts rather than as words or sentences, other information exists in the mind in a form that is essentially image-like, and still other information is coded as the muscle-movement programs that are involved in speaking, gesturing, facial expressions, and so on.

Turning to questions of structure, AAT posits that the information used in message production is stored in long-term memory as little packets, or units, called "procedural records." Just like the earlier example of an entry in the telephone book that contains three interrelated pieces of information (name, address, and number), each procedural record also contains three types of information: features of action, outcomes, and situations.

The notion of "features of action" is crucial to AAT, but it's also one of those ideas that would probably register as a blank until we unpack a little bit more of the theory. From the perspective of AAT, your behavior at any moment is made up of a very large number of action features. For example, when you answer a question in a job interview, you might employ action features like "say something relevant," "say something friendly," "say something that allows you to demonstrate your expertise," "specialized language will allow you to demonstrate your expertise," "express the concept HOMEOSTASIS," "the concept homeostasis can be expressed by the word *balance*," "the concept homeostasis can be expressed by the word *equilibrium*," "the concept homeostasis can be expressed by the word *homeostasis*," "*equilibrium* is a singular noun and requires a singular verb," "the word *equilibrium* can be pronounced by enacting movement programs $a, b, c \ldots$," "gestures that are related to the expression of the concept HOMEOSTASIS are given by movement programs x, y, z," "movement program x can be implemented in this situation by modifying sub-programs x_1, x_2, and x_3 to accommodate the fact that your arms are restricted (by your dress shirt)," and, well, you get the idea. At any moment there are probably hundreds, or more likely thousands, of these action features comprising the configuration of our thoughts and outward behavior—and the vast majority of these features we're not even aware of, and most we couldn't describe or articulate even if we *were* aware of them.

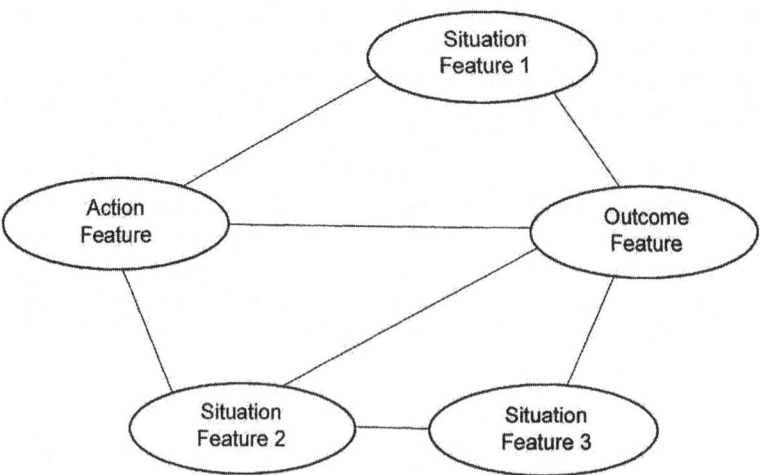

FIG. 9.1. *Structure of a procedural record.*

In the same way that memory stores these tiny features of action, it also stores similar features of outcomes that tend to be associated with those actions. So, when you engage in action feature *x,* outcome feature *y* tends to occur—like the action feature "telling a joke" is associated with the outcome feature "makes other people laugh." In AAT, procedural records serve a very important function because, just like the entries in your phone book that relate names to numbers, procedural records relate what we do to what tends to happen as a result of those actions.

The simplest way to think about procedural records, then, is that they are the records of what we've learned about the connections between actions and outcomes, but there's a little bit more to the story than this. The fact that procedural records store relations between actions and outcomes is a really good thing, but it is also the case that an action that tends to result in a particular outcome in one situation, may not have the same effect in a different context. As an example, think about the young child who has learned that the action feature "grab toy" is associated with the outcome feature "possess object," and this relation works fine at home with her parents and younger brother. However, on the first day of kindergarten she discovers that "grab toy" results in being pushed down and loss of the toy. In the same way, "chugging a six pack" may impress someone's fraternity brothers, but probably wouldn't have the same impact on his pastor. The moral of the story again is that actions that result in a particular outcome in one context may not result in the same outcome in a different situation. What procedural records do, then, is preserve relations between action features, outcome features, and situational features. The bottom line, as you can see in Figure 9.1, is that procedural records are just *action—outcome—in situation* memory packets.

Processes in AAT: Activation and Assembly

You can probably already see that a concept like that of procedural records would be an important piece of the puzzle in understanding how people produce messages, but procedural records, by themselves, can't *do* anything—until some sort of processes are applied to the information in procedural records, they're just sitting there in long-term memory. In one sense, your mind is like a huge warehouse of procedural records—records about how to ride a bike, type, speak English, take turns in conversations, and on and on—but just like crates stored in a warehouse, those procedural records are just going to sit there until some processes kick in and start making things happen. The question, then, is what kinds of processes must be involved in "making things happen" when it comes to message production?

We can gain an important clue for answering this question by considering another analogy. Imagine a kid playing with Lego blocks—he's got all these pieces of different sizes, shapes, and colors, but to build something, he's got to *choose certain ones* and then *put them together* in a particular way. In a sense, the problems facing message producers are the same: When you and I encode messages we've got to select certain procedural records from among all those stored in memory, and once certain records have been selected, there's got to be some way of fitting together their action features to form patterns of verbal and nonverbal cues. These processes of *selecting* and *combining* action features fall at the very heart of AAT, and we need to give them a closer look.

Activation.   Think again about the problem we've posed for ourselves: Each of us possesses hundreds of thousands of procedural records, but from this huge warehouse, we draw on a relatively small subset to guide our actions at any given moment. So for example, assuming you know how to swim, you've got records pertaining to swimming, but you're not using them right now, are you? Assuming you can drive a car with a stick shift, you've got records about how and when to use the clutch, gear-shift lever, and gas pedal, but, again, unless this chapter has found it's way onto "books on tape," or someone in the car is reading this to you while you drive (both highly unlikely events), the records for shifting gears probably aren't playing a role in what you're doing at this moment. As these examples illustrate, each of us has innumerable procedural records, but the vast majority of them aren't involved in what we're doing at any particular time. Just like the child playing with plastic blocks, then, we confront the problem of selection: If we've got this huge assortment of "building blocks," then how are only certain ones (say, 1000 or 10,000, just to put a number on it) brought to bear on what we're doing right now?

AAT approaches this selection problem in a very simple way. The theory states that each procedural record has an *activation level*, something like an energy level, that varies from moment to moment. So, just like light bulbs controlled by dimmer switches, you can think about some procedural records having such a low level of activation that you can't even tell that they're on, others will be glowing softly, and still others, the ones that are most highly activated, will be blazing brightly. AAT solves the problem of selection, then, by positing that the records that are most highly activated are the ones most likely to be used in message production.

Now, chances are that at this moment something like this is going through your mind: "Whoa—not so fast there—you're saying that certain records are selected because they're highly activated, but doesn't that amount to nothing more than replacing the word 'selected' with 'activated'? Unless you can explain *why* those records are highly activated, you haven't really solved the selection problem at all." You are indeed a perceptive student, Grasshopper! We're going to have to push this one small step further: What causes the activation level of a procedural record to increase?

We can fill in this crucial piece of the activation puzzle by thinking again about what is stored in procedural records: features of action, outcomes, and situations. One of the key conceptual moves of AAT, then, is to suggest that the activation level of a particular procedural record will be increased when a person has a goal, or faces some sort of functional requirement, that matches the outcome feature stored in that record. Thus, if you want to ask your roommate to turn down the stereo or you need to construct an utterance that will be understood as a request, then the procedural records relevant to those ends will become more highly activated. In exactly the same way, procedural records will become more highly activated when the situational features stored in those records are matched by current situational conditions, as occurs, for example, in the case of the procedural records governing word choice when speaking to a child versus an adult. The upshot of all this is that the procedural records that tend to be most highly activated at any particular time are those that are relevant to our goals and the context in which we find ourselves.

Assembly.   The picture we've painted to this point is of an enormous store of procedural records represented in a variety of code systems. From this store, at any given moment, a certain subset (perhaps numbering in the thousands, but maybe far more), will be activated well above their resting levels because they are relevant to a person's goals and ongoing activities and the situational features perceived to be present at that moment. Think about the pictures you've seen of people clamoring in the trading pit at the New York Stock Exchange—everyone shouting their bids amid the noise and confusion. That's something like the situation caused by the activation process—you've got all these activated features shouting their presence. This, then, is where the second process in AAT, *assembly*, comes in—assembly serves to organize the clamoring action features into a (fairly) coherent configuration of verbal and nonverbal cues. Returning to our analogy of the kid playing with Legos, the activation process corresponds to selecting which blocks to use, but assembly is the mental equivalent of putting those blocks together to form a structure (in this case, the structure of features that make up our message behavior).

Assembly, then, is exactly what it sounds like—fitting together, or integrating, action features, and just like a wall of Legos, it has both a vertical and a horizontal dimension. When we speak about the "vertical" dimension of assembly, we're referring to integrating action features represented in different symbolic code systems, as for example when the abstract-concept-code feature(s) for HOMEOSTASIS is fit with the word-code feature "*equilibrium*," which, in turn, is fit with the muscle-code programs for pronouncing that word. The "horizontal" dimension of assembly, in contrast, refers to combining and sequencing features *within* a code system, as might occur when you attempt to get your roommate to do you a favor by linking the abstract concept MAKE REQUEST with the concept GIVE REASON, when you follow the first event in a story about what you did last night with the second event in that story, when you couple a noun phrase with a verb phrase, or the word "*Jim's*" with the word "*Harley.*"

The result of the assembly process is called the *output representation,* and this is nothing more or less than the entire configuration of action features that constitute your behavior at any split second. And this output representation is being revised every instant as new behavioral features are activated and integrated into the unfolding pattern of your actions. If this seems a little slippery, it may help to visualize the output representation as a puzzle that is constantly being expanded into the future, as is illustrated in Figure 9.2. The "puzzle pieces," then, correspond to activated action features that are being fit within the output representation as it unfolds.

Because assembly involves the integration of a great many behavioral features, it should be obvious that it normally runs off pretty smoothly—any process that occurs as often as assembly does in a single second must be humming along pretty well. At the same time, there are occasions when assembly hits a snag—situations where two action features simply don't mesh very well or where action features that would fill in gaps in the output representation aren't available. For example, with respect to the horizontal dimension of assembly, we may have problems combining an abstract action feature like "be honest" with another feature like

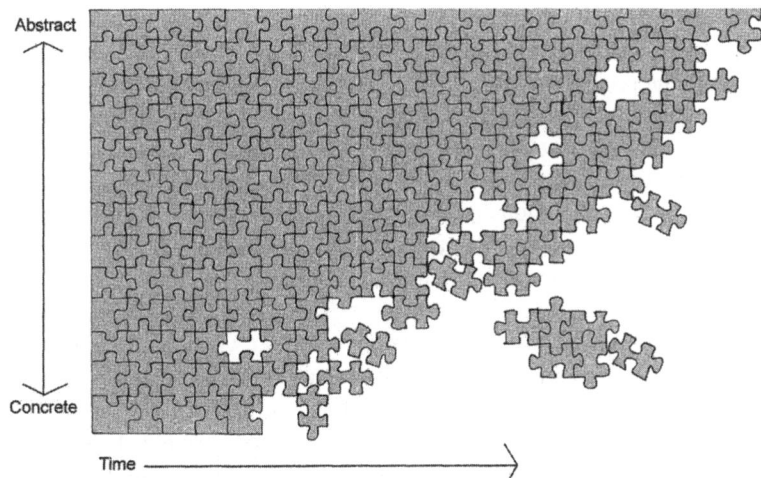

FIG 9.2.   Assembling the output representation.

"don't hurt the other person's feelings." In the vertical dimension we may have an idea and simply can't find the words to express it.

When we encounter these sorts of difficulties in assembly a number of important things can occur. *First*, our behavior tends to slow down—we may not be able to go on until we find some way around the impasse. *Second*, what we might think of as the "quality" of our performance may suffer. For example, our behavior may not reflect all the features or characteristics that would be relevant in that situation (in essence, some things get "left out" because we can't find a way to integrate them with other features of our behavior). Conversely, behavioral features that we'd like to suppress may actually find their way into our verbal and nonverbal messages because the action features relevant to suppressing them create assembly problems. And, as yet one other example of the ways in which the quality of our performance might suffer, our behavior may lack coherence, or appear disjointed, conveying conflicting meanings due to the lack of an overarching integration of relevant action features. A *third* phenomenon associated with difficulties in assembly is that we may become consciously aware of the assembly problem. In fact, according to AAT, one of the chief functions of consciousness is to help us deal with snags in the assembly process by bringing the problem to awareness where we can attempt to resolve it.

In many cases, glitches in assembly are resolved pretty quickly—the word we need pops into mind in just a second and we go on, but in other cases the assembly process starts to spin its wheels and we experience real difficulty in formulating our messages. If you've ever struggled to come up with the "right" thing to say to cheer someone up, to win an argument, to ask someone for a date, or to give bad news, then you've had experiences with some difficult assembly problems. One of the interesting features of AAT, however, is that it specifies a couple of ways that we may be able to avoid the slow, error-prone responses that stem from assembly difficulties. One of these is to plan what you're going to say in advance. Of course, you already have an intuitive and practical grasp of this idea: If you're facing a difficult communication situation like having to explain to your professor why your assignment is late, then planning the account of how the dog ate your homework before you get to her office may help you to speak more fluently than if you tried to formulate your story on the spot. What is important for our purposes here is to recognize that what's happening when we engage in such advance message planning is that we're doing some of the necessary assembly prior to the interaction. By advance planning, then, you can work out potential assembly problems before you get to the professor's office, the employment interview, or the witness stand.

Early in this chapter we made the distinction between cognitive structures and cognitive processes; recall that "structure" involves the way information is organized in the mind, and "process" concerns the operations by which that information is transformed and used. The idea that behavioral manifestations of problems in assembly can be alleviated by advance planning is a process-based notion. However, AAT suggests a second, structurally based, conception of how we might overcome difficulties in assembly.

Think again about the concept of "procedural records." These structures are formed through experience as people come to link certain features of action with various results, or outcomes. Now consider that just as memory can preserve relations between features of action and outcomes, it could also store links between groups of action features. AAT suggests that when a particular set of action features is repeatedly activated and assembled they become linked together, in effect, they become a single unit in memory. These macrostructures are called "unitized assemblies," and they work just like procedural records, except that they represent combinations of action features that have already been integrated. The advantage of unitized assemblies, then, is that they can serve as preformed solutions to various assembly problems—things like riding a bike, reciting the alphabet, or greeting a coworker in the hallway.

Model car and airplane kits are pretty common toys, and they provide a useful analogy for illustrating the way unitized assemblies work. If you've ever built a model, you know that in the process of assembling all the pieces you're bound to run into a problem here and there—missing pieces, pieces that don't quite fit, things that need to be done in a different order, and so on. As a result, putting the model together can be slow going. However, once you've got it all together, you don't have to reassemble it every time you want to play with it. Unitized assemblies are a lot like that model—they're already put together, so when we need them we can just pull them off the shelf and put 'em to work.

Summary

At the beginning of this chapter we noted that AAT is a theory about *thinking* and *doing*—about how it is that people are able, on one hand, to formulate thoughts and, on the other, to produce their verbal and nonverbal messages. Clearly, then, the theory stakes a claim on a pretty big chunk of territory, but it is noteworthy that AAT seeks to explain a wide array of complex phenomena in a relatively simple way. In fact, the theory proposes just two fundamental processes, *activation* and *assembly*, and three structures: *procedural records* and *unitized assemblies*, which are stored in long-term memory, and the *output representation*, which is just an organization of activated action features. That's about all there is to it; in fact, if you've got a pretty good handle on these five ideas, then you're well on your way to understanding AAT.

THE FOUR BASIC OBSERVATIONS REVISITED

Now that we've gone through the major points of the theory, let's look again at the four observations about human behavior that were introduced earlier to see how AAT addresses these fundamental phenomena.

Recall that our first observation was that behavior is simultaneously patterned and repetitive, yet novel and creative, thus raising the question of how we are to account for the simultaneous repetitive and creative character of human action. From the perspective of AAT, the repetitive and patterned property of behavior stems from the content of procedural records and unitized assemblies—these are the basic building blocks of action, and we draw on them again and again in formulating our messages. At the same time, the novel, creative property of action stems from assembling new configurations of action features to meet the demands of the moment. As an analogy, consider a piano keyboard—it has just 88 keys, but from this finite set, an infinite number of musical compositions can be assembled. The same sort of thing occurs in the case of message behavior, except that we've got far more than 88 procedural records and, unlike the keys of a piano, our procedural records reflect many different code systems.

Our second observation was that people act on the basis of the meanings they assign to stimulus inputs, thus raising the question of how it is possible for our interpretations of what's going on around us to influence our actions. The key to this one lies in the AAT conception of procedural records. If you check Figure 9.1 again to refresh your memory you'll see that in addition to action features and outcome features, procedural records also contain situational features that we've learned are relevant to that particular action—outcome relation. In effect, these situational features correspond to aspects of our interpretation of what's transpiring around us. So, if you understand some event in one way, a particular set of procedural records will be activated, but if you have a different interpretation of that event, then the records activated in that situation will also be different.

The next observation was that there are times when our behavior is very conscious and deliberate and others when our actions run off automatically. This observation suggests the problem of understanding what's going on when we must consciously monitor what we're doing and when we're running on "auto pilot." Based on our discussion of difficulties in assembly, you can probably see that the AAT approach to this one is pretty straightforward. Our actions can proceed without the need for conscious monitoring when the assembly process is humming along (due to the availability of unitized assemblies or to action features that are readily integrated). On the other hand, as we saw earlier, when assembly hits a snag, conscious awareness is brought to bear in order to help solve the problem.

Finally, we noted that, in the end, our behavior consists of muscle commands for moving and speaking, but our phenomenal experience of what we're doing doesn't consist of muscle commands at all; instead, we tend to have much more abstract conceptions of our activities that, in some way, exert influence on lower level efferent (i.e., muscle) commands. The AAT approach to this phenomenon involves the idea that the output representation is made up of action features represented in code systems that vary in level of abstraction. As you'll recall from Figure 9.2, the output representation is hierarchical, with abstract, conceptual features of action at the top, and efferent-command features at the bottom. Lower level activities relevant to speaking and nonverbal behavior are typically well practiced and tend to run off smoothly so that they're often outside our awareness (but think about situations like trying to pronounce a difficult and unfamiliar word or trying to suppress or control some habitual gesture). Our phenomenal experience of what we're doing, then, tends to be filled by the contents of the more abstract levels of the output representation. And, finally, because of the way the assembly process works to integrate action features that "fit" with each other, low-level activities usually bear some resemblance to the higher order conceptions of action operating at the moment.

AAT AND STUDIES OF MESSAGE PRODUCTION

One of the most important features of a scientific theory is its ability to generate research questions and hypotheses, a feature referred to as the "heuristic power" of the theory. From the perspective of science, theories that lack heurism are not very desirable. In this regard, AAT has fared pretty well because the theory has provided the conceptual foundation for studies of a wide variety of communication phenomena. To give you a feel for the kind of research generated by AAT it's useful to take a look at a few of these studies, particularly some of the ones that have focused on verbal message production.

Cognitive scientists rely on a variety of techniques and cues to draw conclusions about how the mind works. For example, they examine people's ability to recall word lists or to recognize faces in order to make inferences about how information is stored in memory. Another particularly valuable cue is *time*; by examining the time required to complete a task or generate a response, investigators can test ideas about how those activities are carried out. If the slice of human behavior we wish to study is message production, then we can examine a variety of time-based measures. All of these measures are related in one way or another to the speed or fluency with which people can produce their messages. For example, *speech-onset latency* is a measure of how long it takes a person to actually begin speaking. Other measures are related to the amount of silent pausing a person does once he or she has started talking. These silent-pause measures include *speech rate* (e.g., words per second), *average pause duration*, and *pause–phonation ratio* (i.e., the total time spent in silent pauses divided by the total time spent speaking). Again, one of the things that makes these measures important is that they provide us with a window on what's going on when people formulate their messages. But, there's even more to the story of the significance of these types of measures: In a sense, they lead a "double life" because although they do tell us something about cognitive processes, they also have *social significance* in that they play a role in how the speaker is perceived by others. It would probably come as no surprise to you to learn that slower, hesitant speech is associated with less positive impressions, so when we exhibit a halting speech pattern, people may question our knowledge, preparation, or competence.

Encoding Multiple-Goal Messages

One of the issues that has been explored extensively from the perspective of AAT involves the production of messages aimed at accomplishing multiple social goals. As you probably know from your reading and coursework in communication, scholars commonly recognize that it is a rare occasion when a message is designed with just one goal in mind. It is much more likely that if you've got a goal, say, of conveying a certain piece of information to someone else (e.g., telling your boss that you'll be late for work), then you'll also have some other social objectives as well—objectives, for example, related to what the other person may think of you and to maintaining a good relationship with that person.

From the perspective of AAT, these multiple-goal situations are very interesting because they raise the potential for assembly problems due to the fact that the action features associated with one goal may not mesh very well with features relevant to other objectives. Have you ever struggled over how to say something because you didn't want to sound "mean"? Or to answer a question without seeming like a "know-it-all"? Or to talk about your accomplishments without sounding like you were bragging? Or to tell everyone that you'd been accepted into a sorority without making someone else feel bad? These, and countless other situations that we encounter every day, are examples of cases where encoding is made difficult because the actions associated with one goal may be incompatible with the pursuit of other goals.

To study these multiple-goal situations in a systematic way, a number of experiments have been conducted in which the speech performance of people given a single message objective is contrasted with that of people who are assigned two goals (see Greene, 1995b, for a review). As an example, in one study (Greene, Lindsey, & Hawn, 1990), undergraduate participants reviewed the job file for an employee (John Stevens) whose performance over the last year had been very poor. After they had taken a few minutes to familiarize themselves with the file, participants in the "single goal" condition were given the following instructions:

> Your task is to report on the job performance of John Stevens to his superiors. Assume that Mr. Stevens will not be aware of your comments. Please try to be as clear and direct as possible.

In contrast, people in the "multiple goal" condition were given a different set of message instructions:

> Your task is to report on the job performance of John Stevens to Mr. Stevens himself. Please try to be clear and direct while also showing concern for his feelings and self-esteem.

Again, the hypothesis derived from AAT is that people in the multiple-goal condition would be more likely to experience assembly difficulties, and this would be manifested in lower levels of speech fluency. Although the results vary somewhat from study to study, the results of these experiments generally support the theory: People attempting to accomplish multiple goals tend to exhibit longer speech-onset latencies and more silent pausing than their counterparts pursuing a single message objective.

Although these studies indicate that multiple-goal messages are associated with more hesitant speech, an important caveat is in order here because AAT suggests that the pursuit of multiple goals should not *necessarily* lead to slower message encoding. In the studies showing that people are less fluent when seeking to meet multiple objectives, the goals are always *incompatible* in some sense (e.g., conveying negative evaluations while trying to show concern for the other person). As a result, it is reasonable to expect that people will experience the sort of assembly problems thought to slow their speaking. But what about situations where a person is given two, *compatible* objectives? AAT would lead us to expect that assembly problems would be less likely to occur under these conditions. Studies examining this question have shown that people attempting to accomplish multiple, compatible goals are significantly more fluent than those pursuing similar, but incompatible, goals (Greene, McDaniel, Buksa, & Ravizza, 1993). This pattern of results is consistent with the idea that when we pursue compatible goals we're less likely to encounter assembly difficulties that slow our speech.

Effects of Planning and Practice

As we've already noted, encoding multiple-goal messages presents an interesting application of the action assembly framework because such situations often give rise to difficulties in assembly. However, as you'll recall from our discussion of the assembly process, according to the theory, *prior planning* and *practice* allow us to reduce the effects associated with assembly difficulties. A number of studies generated by AAT, then, have focused on the impact of these factors on message encoding.

Some of the experiments that have examined the impact of multiple versus single goals have also looked at the impact of advance preparation, either in the form of time to plan, opportunity to repeat the message, or even jotting down what one intends to say. So, for example, in one study (Greene & Lindsey, 1989), participants played the role of a university administrator who had to convey the information that a student would not receive a scholarship for which she had applied. Some of the participants were asked to communicate this message to other members of the scholarship committee. The other participants, though, were asked deliver this information to the student herself. As you can probably imagine, when people were asked to produce these messages with no advance preparation, those who were asked to speak directly to the scholarship applicant had much longer speech-onset latencies than those who were giving their message to other members of the scholarship committee. However, when participants in this study were given 60 sec to think about their messages, there was virtually no difference in speech-onset latency for those speaking to the student and those speaking to the other committee members.

Like the multiple-goal studies we've already mentioned, then, the studies looking at the effects of advance preparation show that when participants give multiple-goal messages spontaneously, they are significantly more hesitant than people pursuing a single goal. However, when people are given the chance to prepare multiple-goal messages in advance they tend to be as fluent as people with a single goal. This, of course, is exactly what we would expect if advance planning gives us the opportunity to resolve assembly problems.

Beyond the experiments involving multiple-goal messages, another group of studies has examined the impact of using an organizational sequence to structure what one wishes to say. If you've had a public speaking class, no doubt you learned various patterns for organizing a speech, patterns like the problem–solution sequence, the temporal sequence, or maybe even Monroe's Motivated Sequence. These sorts of organizing patterns are relevant to AAT because they help us to overcome certain types of assembly problems (i.e., deciding what to say and in what order to say it); as a result, they should help us to speak more fluently. Some of the very first studies conducted within the AAT framework (Greene, 1984b) showed that people who had learned a simple organizing sequence were more fluent when discussing an assigned topic than their counterparts who hadn't learned an organizing sequence, even though they did not know in advance what topic they'd be asked to discuss! In other words, just knowing the sequence, without knowing the topic, helped people to assemble their messages when the topic was presented (Can you see ways that prior attention to patterns for structuring your responses in an employment interview might help you come across as more knowledgeable and prepared?). Other experiments have shown that the more practice one has with an organizing sequence, the greater its impact on speech fluency (e.g., Greene, 1984b, Study 2). In fact, one set of studies (Greene, Sassi, Malek-Madani, & Edwards, 1997) showed that even after hundreds of practice trials using a simple organizing sequence, people were still improving from trial to trial!

CONCLUSION

As we noted at the beginning of this chapter, the focus here is on fundamental and ultimately inescapable questions about thinking and doing: How it is that you and I are able to "think" things, and how is it that these thoughts—these remembrances, these creations, these conceptions of who we are, of others, of situation, of propriety—bear some relation to our words, facial expressions, and gestures?

The bulk of this chapter has been devoted to laying out one approach to these questions, but there is an imbalance in the chapter because it has focused almost exclusively on explaining the gist of AAT. If the reader walks away with a firm grasp of the details of the theory, a big chunk of what the action assembly project has been about will still be missing. Just as important as the concepts and claims of the theory is the *spirit* of the theory—the sense of wonder, of exploration, of pushing the boundaries to think in different ways about how things might be working.

In the end, science is fundamentally a process—a process of arriving at more complete and complex descriptions of phenomena, of developing more sophisticated theoretical accounts of those phenomena, and of posing ever more probing questions. Action assembly theory has always been a "work in progress," and in that spirit I would leave the reader with an invitation to take part: Where would you take it? What would you change?

ADDITIONAL READING

Interested students should investigate the original statement of AAT (Greene, 1984a), as well as more recent developments in the theory (e.g., Greene, 1997, 2000). Other treatments explore the philosophical foundations of AAT (e.g., Greene, 1990, 1994, 1995a). Readers interested in studies of message production and speech fluency from an action assembly perspective should see Greene's (1995b) review.

In addition to studies of message production, AAT has been applied to the analysis of a number of other communication-relevant phenomena, including the nature of the self and the role of the self in guiding behavior (Greene & Geddes, 1988), social skill (Greene & Geddes, 1993) and skill acquisition (Greene, 2003), and the interaction of individual and situational factors in guiding behavior (Greene, 1989).

REFERENCES

Greene, J. O. (1984a). A cognitive approach to human communication: An action assembly theory. *Communication Monographs, 51,* 289–306.

Greene, J. O. (1984b). Speech preparation processes and verbal fluency. *Human Communication Research, 11,* 61–84.

Greene, J. O. (1989). The stability of nonverbal behavior: An action-production approach to problems of cross-situational consistency and discriminativeness. *Journal of Language and Social Psychology, 8,* 193–220.

Greene, J. O. (1990). Tactical social action: Toward some strategies for theory. In M. J. Cody & M. L. McLaughlin (Eds.), *The psychology of tactical communication* (pp. 31–47). Clevedon, England: Multilingual Matters.

Greene, J. O. (1994). What sort of terms ought theories of human action incorporate? *Communication Studies, 45,* 187–211.

Greene, J. O. (1995a). An action assembly perspective on verbal and nonverbal message production: A dancer's message unveiled. In D. E. Hewes (Ed.), *The cognitive bases of interpersonal communication* (pp. 51–85). Hillsdale, NJ: Lawrence Erlbaum Associates, Inc.

Greene, J. O. (1995b). Production of messages in pursuit of multiple social goals: Action assembly theory contributions to the study of cognitive encoding processes. In B. R. Burleson (Ed.), *Communication yearbook 18* (pp. 26–53). Thousand Oaks, CA: Sage.

Greene, J. O. (1997). A second generation action assembly theory. In J. O. Greene (Ed.), *Message production: Advances in communication theory* (pp. 151–170). Mahwah, NJ: Lawrence Erlbaum Associates, Inc.

Greene, J. O. (2000). Evanescent mentation: An ameliorative conceptual foundation for research and theory on message production. *Communication Theory, 10,* 139–155.

Greene, J. O. (2003). Models of adult communication skill acquisition: Practice and the course of performance improvement. In J. O. Greene & B. R. Burleson (Eds.), *Handbook of communication and social interaction skills* (pp. 51–91). Mahwah, NJ: Lawrence Erlbaum Associates, Inc.

Greene, J. O., & Geddes, D. (1988). Representation and processing in the self-system: An action-oriented approach to self and self-relevant phenomena. *Communication Monographs, 55,* 287–314.

Greene, J. O., & Geddes, D. (1993). An action assembly perspective on social skill. *Communication Theory, 3*, 26–49.

Greene, J. O., & Lindsey, A. E. (1989). Encoding processes in the production of multiple-goal messages. *Human Communication Research, 16*, 120–140.

Greene, J. O., Lindsey, A. E., & Hawn, J. J. (1990). Social goals and speech production: Effects of multiple goals on pausal phenomena. *Journal of Language and Social Psychology, 9*, 119–133.

Greene, J. O., McDaniel, T. L., Buksa, K., & Ravizza, S. M. (1993). Cognitive processes in the production of multiple-goal messages: Evidence from the temporal characteristics of speech. *Western Journal of Communication, 57*, 65–86.

Greene, J. O., Sassi, M.S., Malek-Madani, T. L., & Edwards, C. N. (1997). Adult acquisition of message-production skill. *Communication Monographs, 64*, 181–200.

QUESTIONS TO PONDER

1. If you asked a friend to describe her behavior at some particular instant she'd probably respond that she was "driving," "eating," "having a conversation," "talking on the phone," or something similar. By way of contrast, how would a person speaking from the perspective of AAT describe (as opposed to explain) behavior?

2. A remarkable feature of human behavior is that it tends to be relevant to our purposes and the present context. How does AAT explain this fact?

3. One of the frustrating facts of social interaction is that we sometimes can't come up with the perfect thing to say when we need it, but then we realize afterward what we should have said. How would AAT account for both of these observations?

4. One of the important functions of self-concept is that we use it in regulating and guiding our behavior. For example, a person who thinks of himself as "honest" may consider this personal trait in deciding whether to cheat on an exam or not. How might our perceptions of personal characteristics and abilities be incorporated into AAT, and how might they play a role in regulating our behavior?

5. Why do abstract conceptions of action tend to be those we're aware of? Are there situations were lower-level processes might become conscious?

6. The act of lying is often accompanied by what appear to be discrepancies in what is being communicated in various nonverbal channels (e.g., facial expression and posture). How might AAT be used to explain the presence of such discrepancies?

7. An interesting feature of human behavior is that we sometimes exhibit great consistency in what we do in two situations, and at other times we behave very differently from one situation to the next. From the perspective of AAT, what factors might be important in determining the degree of consistency in a person's behavior in two different situations?

10

Problematic Integration Theory

Austin S. Babrow
Purdue University

SETTING THE STAGE

To begin this chapter on a theory that is very likely to be brand new to you, it will help to establish some common understandings. Let's do this with an example. If you are reading this book, you are probably a college student. If so, have you ever wondered why you are in college? This thought might have crossed your mind if you read in the newspaper about computer-savvy high school drop-outs making big salaries working for dot.com companies. Perhaps you wondered why you are here when you heard about a friend with little college experience who has been making good money teaching English in Japan, or when you learned that 1 year of college expenses would fund perhaps 2 years of travel around South America or 3 to 4 years in other exotic parts of the world. Such musings become particularly meaningful during the end-of-semester crush of final exams and term projects, or when you find out that, once again, the university has fouled up your fees, class schedule, or both. In short, you may ask, "Why am I here? Why aren't I doing something else?"

Students' answers to these questions are quite varied. Even so, if we were to look carefully across a wide range of answers to questions such as these, we would discover important underlying characteristics or themes. You might want to see these themes for yourself. You can do this simply by taking a few moments to answer the question "What does my being in college mean to me right now?" Go ahead, make a list of answers. To really test the truth of what I have to say, ask some friends to list their answers to the question, too, and gather all these answers so you can examine them together.

If you take this little project seriously, your list may include items like the following: Being in college now means learning skills that will qualify me for a fulfilling job, maximizing future earning potential, having fun, delaying the start of full-time work, becoming an educated person, learning things I'll never have the time to study once I start working, satisfying my parents or guardians, I don't know what else I want to do right now, and so on.

What are the important underlying characteristics in this diverse set of thoughts about college attendance? First, and most obviously, each thought associates college attendance with something else: learning skills, maximizing earning potential, having fun, delaying full-time work, and so on. Second, and a bit less obviously, you "believe" in these associations; you think that they are true, with greater and lesser degrees of certainty or assurance. For instance, you may believe with *certainty* that attending college is a way of postponing full-time work. By contrast, you may believe it is *very likely* that going to college will teach you skills necessary for a good job. And as one more contrast, you may believe that it is only *fairly likely* that going to college will satisfy your folks (maybe they want more, maybe they are hard to satisfy). In short, you associate college attendance with various things, with experiences, outcomes, and you believe in these associations with varying levels of belief strength.

A third characteristic of your list is that each of your associations with college attendance has some evaluative meaning for you (although the evaluation may be neutral). For example, you may value learning the skills, for a good job quite positively, satisfying your family somewhat less positively, and postponing full-time work neutrally or perhaps even somewhat negatively (perhaps you are tired of poverty).

In summary, your list is characterized by beliefs about college. Each belief is held with some degree of strength, and each implies some evaluative meaning (it associates college attendance with something good, bad, or neutral). These basic characteristics will be present no matter how long your list or how many other students' answers you gather. Indeed, these are basic characteristics of human thought and communication. They are so fundamental that they are the focal point of an enormous range of scholarship across the social sciences and humanities.

COMMON IDEAS

What I mean by the foregoing statement is that theories and research in a wide variety of fields are concerned with the characteristics of human thought and communication that we noted moments ago. For example, a major branch of philosophy, called *epistemology*, has to do with the nature of human knowledge: what we can know, how we know it, and so on. From the perspective sketched here, we might say that this area of philosophy is concerned with the nature of human *belief*. Other branches of philosophy have to do not with knowing but with *evaluation*. For example, ethics is the study of the good in human action: the nature of goodness, the modes and ends of human conduct that are most desirable or worthy. As another example, axiology or value theory is an area of philosophy concerned with the nature of value and valuation.

Rhetoric, the mother of communication studies, is traditionally concerned with establishing belief or persuading people on matters about which knowledge is uncertain. Hence much scholarly thinking about rhetoric concerns the classic issue of how we use communication to establish the probable truth of a factual claim. However, some aspects of rhetorical theory are concerned with what we might consider evaluation. For instance, rhetoricians have long studied arguments that seek to establish the importance of some specific value (e.g., protecting the environment, eradicating world hunger) and the value of a proposed policy (e.g., fostering organic farming, encouraging genetic engineering). Still other aspects of rhetorical scholarship consider ways of establishing and fostering a shared, communal sense of social values; called epideictic rhetoric, speeches and other forms of discourse that praise or celebrate a society's heroes and that vilify its enemies serve the vital societal purpose of identifying, clarifying, and reinforcing a people's shared values.

In addition to traditional concerns in rhetorical scholarship, interest in what we here have been calling beliefs and evaluations also pervades corresponding conceptual frameworks across the more recently developed social and behavioral sciences, such as communication studies, psychology, sociology, political science, economics, marketing, and advertising. These many areas are home to innumerable theories dealing either with the way that people come to form beliefs (also called expectations, opinions, attributions, schemata, etc.) and thereby understand the structure of their world, and theories of how we come to form our likes and dislikes (attitudes, values, morals, prejudices, wishes, desires, hopes, dreams, etc.). There also are some theories that try to grapple with the nature of both beliefs and evaluations and their interrelations. Problematic integration (PI) theory is of this latter sort.

THE SUBSTANCE OF PI THEORY

Probabilistic Orientations

PI theory shares with many other theories two basic assumptions about human beings (see Babrow, 1992, 1995, 2001c). One is that *humans form probabilistic orientations to their world.* By "probabilistic orientation" I mean a belief or expectation that associates some object of thought with another object of thought. The term *object* is used in the most generic sense to stand for any focus of perception or thought (e.g., person, thing, place, event, idea). Probabilistic orientations answer questions like the following: What does this (object) seem to be? What are its characteristics? What seems to have caused this? How will it behave?

More concretely, you have illustrated probabilistic orientations to "attending college now" with beliefs about how you got here, what it is like to attend college, what college attendance has done for you already, what it will do for you in the future, and so on. Notice from these examples that probabilistic orientations form our understandings of the past, present, and future.

When students learn new theories, a common reaction is to wonder why the theorist used uncommon and often difficult, polysyllabic words. Wouldn't it have been wiser to use common and often simpler words that seem just as fitting and are a lot easier to remember? For example, to refer to these foundational understandings of the world, I have chosen the phrase *probabilistic orientation* rather than a number of more common terms, such as *belief, opinion, assumption, viewpoint, perspective, frame of reference, schema,* and the like. There are several reasons for this choice of terms. One is that I wanted a general term to encompass all of the ways that people associate and thereby come to understand aspects of their world (whether concrete or abstract). I also wanted a somewhat uncommon term so that it would make people stop and think about this very basic aspect of human being rather than continuing to take it for granted like the proverbial fish taking for granted the water that sustains its life.

One other reason I chose the term probabilistic orientation was that it brings to the foreground the inherent uncertainty in human knowledge. To appreciate the importance of this third reason for my choice of terms, it is vital to note that many of our probabilistic orientations are experienced as certainties. In other words, "probabilistic orientations" are often held as basic assumptions about life and the world. For instance, have you ever questioned the expectation that the sun will rise tomorrow? That you will survive the next minute? That your best friend truly likes you? That you can pass strangers in the street without fear of assault? By choosing the term probabilistic orientation, I mean in part to encourage students to reflect on the idea that any such assumption, no matter how apparently well warranted, can be called into question and experienced as uncertain. For example, a mugging victim looks with new eyes at all strangers. Even the most honored beliefs of science, those called "laws," are forever open to dispute; this openness to new evidence, to new belief, is an essential element of science. So, in short, from the most taken for granted to the most tentative, probabilistic orientations are foundational aspects of our understanding of the world.

Evaluative Orientations

It is clear on reflection that probabilistic orientations are basic features of being human, but it also is clear that they are not our only foundation. This vital point is often missed or neglected. For example, a number of my professors in graduate school at University of Illinois emphasized the important idea that humans have what some termed a "rage for order." My instructors noted that, without the general belief that the world is ordered and predictable, as well as more specific ideas about how the physical and social world are put together, we would be unable to act. For example, one of my professors asserted convincingly that we would not get out of bed in the morning without assuming that the floor would support the weight of our standing body. But this example captures only part of what is necessary for human understanding and action. We also need some evaluative understanding of the potential consequences of action. In other words, getting out of bed in the morning, if it is to be a free and thoughtful action, requires not only that we can anticipate the consequences (e.g., the floor supporting our weight; reaching the kitchen for our food and first cup of coffee; going to school, work, or play). Rising from bed also requires that we value the consequences. Hence, a second most basic idea of PI theory is that *humans form evaluative orientations to concrete and abstract features of their world.* Evaluative orientations answer the following question: Is this object, characteristic, event, or outcome good or bad?

Here PI theory is compatible with an enormous range of social science perspectives that posit evaluation as a basic element in human psychological and social being. For instance, some anthropologists and ethicists believe that human beings are distinguished from other life forms by the fact that we evaluate, form value judgments, and develop moral and ethical codes. In a related vein, one major approach to defining and differentiating among cultures is in terms of the distinctive sets of values espoused by groups of people.

Among the largest bodies of theory and research in the social sciences, the study of attitudes provides one more powerful illustration of the significance of evaluative orientations (Babrow, 2001c). Although the scholarly meaning of the term *attitude* was vague and disputed up through the first 75 to 80 years of the last century, the consensus evolving over the past couple of decades holds that attitudes are evaluative orientations that arise from and are in turn manifested in cognition, affect (mood and emotion), and behavior (Eagly & Chaiken, 1993). Consistent with the PI framework, the attitude literature has demonstrated the pervasiveness of evaluative orientations in three kinds of research findings. One is the ease with which people report evaluative reactions to a wide variety of objects. A second relevant finding is the difficulty of identifying categories of objects within which evaluative distinctions are *not* made. Third, scholars have observed the pervasiveness of an evaluative component in judgments of meaning (paraphrased from Greenwald, 1989, p. 2).

In short, PI theory holds that human beings cannot orient to their world based solely on probabilistic orientations (beliefs, assumptions, and so on) no matter how well warranted. To orient ourselves thoughtfully, meaningfully, reasonably, we must consider not only what any object or issue might be associated with; we also must determine the evaluative meanings these associations hold for us (e.g., for our survival, well-being, happiness). Together, these two ideas form the theory's foundation: *People form probabilistic and evaluative orientations to concrete and abstract features of their world.*

Before proceeding to other theoretical claims, I want to note again that the ideas that make up PI theory's most basic propositions are not unique to this framework. However, they are not always recognized or appreciated as fully as they ought to be. Moreover, although an enormous number and variety of perspectives share one or the other of these notions, only a smaller subset of theories recognize and fully appreciate the significance of both sorts of orientations and their interrelations. The wonderfully thoughtful stress researchers Lazarus and Folkman (1984) offered one such view that was quite influential in the development of PI theory. Writing in 1991, Lazarus offered the following clarification of the importance of and distinction between probabilistic orientations (what he calls "knowledge") and evaluative orientations ("appraisals" in his terms): "People are continually seeking *knowledge* (that is, beliefs about how things work in general and in the specific adaptational encounter) and *appraisals* of the significance of the person-environment relationship for personal well-being, whether about a specific encounter or life as a whole" (p. 127). In addition to Lazarus and Folkman's stress appraisal theory, concepts quite compatible with my understanding of "probabilistic" and "evaluative orientations" are basic constituents in a variety of descriptive and prescriptive theories of human communication, decision making, motivation, and action.

Integration

PI theory builds on the notions of probabilistic and evaluative orientations in several ways. It recognizes that probabilistic and evaluative orientations are not merely separate phenomena that occur at the same time. A central claim in PI theory is that *probabilistic and evaluative orientations are integrated in experience* (Babrow, 1992, 1995).

In part "integration" means that expectations and evaluations (e.g., desires, dreads) related to any one object or issue are interdependent; they affect one another in complex ways. On the one hand, the probability of obtaining an object can increase its value (see the discussion of scarcity in Cialdini, 2000). Note, for example, how commodities from baseball cards to oil become more valuable as they become more scarce or rare (assuming some basic level of demand; Babrow, 2001c). Alternatively, we may choose to devalue objects because the probability of obtaining or realizing them is low. "Why spend time and energy on what is likely to be a fruitless search or quest?" we reason. "Surely the object of desire isn't all that valuable!" In short, perceived probabilities affect evaluations.

On the other hand, evaluation can influence the perceived and actual probability of obtaining or achieving what we desire. Evaluative judgments affect our subjective or personal probability estimates. For example, evaluation can trigger optimism; we commonly overestimate the odds of obtaining what we want and underestimate the chances of negative events occurring. Theorists have named this very human phenomenon "wishful thinking," "optimistic bias," and "perceived unique invulnerability" (for a review, see Babrow, 1991). In other words, we commonly think that we are less likely than most other people to experience some negative event. Of course, we all can't be less likely to experience misfortune than are most other people!

Aside from affecting subjective probability estimates, evaluative orientations often motivate behaviors that alter objective probabilities. This is precisely what we do when we decide to study very hard for a test; we are trying to increase our chances of achieving a desired (positively evaluated) outcome (Babrow, 1991, 1992). So, in summary, integration means in part that our probabilistic and evaluative orientations to any given object influence one another in a variety of ways. With a bit of thought, you can easily illustrate all of these ideas in the context of your beliefs about being in college: How might your belief in the likelihood of getting a particular job related to your college major affect your evaluation of that job? How might the value of that job affect your view of, and efforts to influence, the chances of landing that position?

Beyond the integration or synthesis of probabilistic and evaluative orientations to any given object, such orientations also are integrated with orientations to other objects. In other words, these orientations to a given object or focus of thought are integrated with one another and with broader complexes of knowledge, feelings, and behavioral intentions. The probability and value of obtaining (or avoiding) a given object (or experience) affect other life possibilities, values, intentions, plans, and ongoing behavior. For example, your sense of the value and odds of obtaining a particularly desirable job will influence your identity ("I'm an aspiring journalist, lawyer, politician, entrepreneur"). It also will influence your relationships with others, such as your views about whether and when to marry. For example, depending on your career aspirations, you might be more or less interested in marrying soon after graduation. Similarly, job-related expectations and evaluations will influence your views about friendship. For instance, these orientations will shape the sorts of people you are likely to befriend, and whether you would be willing to relocate anywhere the desired job opportunity arises or you are committed to staying in the area where you have many, significant, established friendships. And, of course, your expectations and evaluations related to career will influence your thoughts and feelings about the natural environment, politics, economics, culture, leisure, and the like.

In summary, probabilistic and evaluative orientations to any given object of thought or perception do not simply arise at the same time but largely independently of one another. Rather, they are integrated in various significant ways. Such orientations to any one object or issue influence one another, and they both shape and are shaped by encompassing systems of beliefs, values, intentions, plans, and ongoing action.

Problematic Integration

Another basic claim in the theory is that *integration of probabilistic and evaluative orientations is often problematic*. Such difficulty arises in the integrative processes noted previously. To begin, because probabilities and evaluations influence one another, they can make one another change again and again. For example, both the perceived probability and value of a particular romantic relationship may shift repeatedly, each influencing the other in turn, during the course of a relational break-up. When one person broaches the topic of breaking up with her or his partner, this prospect can make the relationship seem more dear to one or both parties; this might in turn stimulate optimism, and so on (see Babrow, 1995). Alternatively, when one person initiates a break-up with another, that other person might engage in self-defensive thinking by appraising the relationship as less desirable. In turn, and further defending the self against sorrow, the new evaluation of the relationship might result in pessimism. In either case, the point is that integration of expectation of desire can result in a shifting to and fro of probabilities and evaluations as one orientation in turn destabilizes another.

Integration can be problematic in a second sense. As suggested previously, PI entails difficulty in forming and maintaining other probabilistic and evaluative orientations associated with the initial dilemma (also see Hines, 2001). Continuing the previous example, unstable evaluation of the romance and subjective estimates of the chances of maintaining the romantic relationship make it difficult for the partners to interpret messages (e.g., judge the honesty of expressed feelings). In turn, this instability can make it difficult to sustain a particular outlook (e.g., maintain optimism), make decisions (e.g., choose between shifting from an exclusive dating relationship to more open dating or to a complete break-up), and act consistently with prior decisions (e.g., to date nonexclusively). So, in summary, problematic integration is the difficulty we experience when probabilistic and evaluative orientations to a particular object, person, thing, event, or idea destabilize one another and unsettle such orientations to related objects. But when is integration most likely to be straightforward and untroubled? When is it most likely to be problematic?

Integration of probabilistic and evaluative orientations occurs instantaneously when associations appear to be crystal clear and when there is no divergence: situations in which positively evaluated associations are assured or negatively valued associations are apparently impossible. If you think about all that you take for granted in the physical and social world (e.g., the workings of your body, established relationships with family and friends), it becomes clear that integration is often nonproblematic. Juxtaposing these two ideas, that integration can be instantaneous or problematic, we can understand an important longstanding debate about the nature of human beings: whether or to what extent humans are essentially thoughtful, reflective, rational, willful actors.

Some scholars and thinkers have emphasized our apparent thoughtfulness and capacity for rational action. Indeed, some thinkers see this capacity as a defining feature of humanity, an element of our being that separates us from, and some believe elevates us above, other life forms. Ethicists who take this point of view argue that communication should foster mindfulness and avoid any strategies that undermine reasoned action (e.g., propaganda that arouses our most rudimentary fears and biases). Others have emphasized our pervasive and apparently necessary inclination toward habit: scripted, automated, or otherwise mindless behavior. A large body of accumulated research has demonstrated our strong inclinations to follow simple behavioral cues without much thought.

For instance, in a widely read textbook on social influence that is by turns delightful and disturbing, Cialdini (2000) argued that we quite often behave automatically or mindlessly. He illustrated our powerful and relatively unreflective tendencies to (a) comply with authority; (b) follow the herd; (c) say "yes" to people we like; (d) repay debts; (e) maintain consistency in thoughts, feelings, and behavior; and (f) value items perceived to be scarce simply because of their scarcity. Cialdini argued that these habitual responses are necessary because of the impossibility of thinking carefully about every stimulus. He also maintained that they are powerful because they are usually beneficial. However, Cialdini also recognized that these very qualities of habitual response make them useful tools for human manipulation.

PI theory suggests that we act relatively mindlessly, guided by habit, to the extent that probabilistic orientations are experienced as certainties (or impossibilities), evaluative orientations are uniformly positive (or negative), and expectations and desires converge (good things are certain; bad things are impossible). By contrast, PI fosters mindfulness[1]. From the standpoint of communication theory, and particularly PI theory, we must consider what conditions bring about mindlessness and what brings about mindfulness in the form of PI. Communication in any ethical sense is possible only to the extent that people are mindful (or

---

[1]I do not mean to equate PI and mindfulness, for the latter is a broader concept. For instance, it is useful to understand the distinction between PI and another form of mindfulness: what Csikszentmihalyi (1975, 1990) termed "the psychology of optimal experience," or what people more commonly refer to as the experience of "flow" You experience "flow" when absorbed in a situation in which your goals and abilities are closely matched by the demands of the situation. That is, the situation demands that you use your abilities to their fullest to achieve your goals. In a state of flow you lose track of time and lose any sense of self-consciousness (particularly doubts about your ability to meet the situational demands). By contrast, PI is a state of consciousness marked by doubt, reconsideration of goals, reflection on related belief, values, plans, and so on. Csikszentmihalyi saw flow as an optimal state of being, and, therefore, a state that should be fostered by re-engineering social structures like school and the workplace to produce flow-enhancing opportunities. Although these aims are attractive, we also should be wary of the dark side of flow: exclusive absorption in a particular task, the loss of a sense of self, and particularly the loss of mental space for critical reflection.

in a state of flow (again, see endnote 1) arising out of their absorption in communication, as opposed to, say, playing basketball, studying for a test, riding a motorcycle, or playing chess).

Original View of PI Forms.   The initial statement of the theory (Babrow, 1992) analyzed four main forms of PI. These four forms continue to be the focus of reviews, theorizing, and research based on the theory (e.g., Egbert, 2000; Ford et al., 1996; Littlejohn, 1999; McPhee & Zaug, 2001; Miller, 2002). The first of these forms was termed *divergence.* These are situations made difficult because probabilities and values diverge in the sense that something good is uncomfortably unlikely or something bad is unpleasantly likely. For instance, we experience PI retrospectively when we believe that something bad seems to have happened. Various signal emotions mark the occurrence of retrospective PI: anger, frustration, disappointment, worry, sorrow, embarrassment, regret, remorse, guilt, shame, and the like. We can also experience PI in relation to current events or as we think about the future; here too various signal emotions mark the occurrence of PI (e.g., anxiety, fear, worry, yearning). Divergence increases as (a) the probability of an association (e.g., act and consequence, object and characteristic) increases and the value of the association becomes more negative or (b) the probability of an association decreases and the value of the association becomes more positive (Babrow, 1992).

A second form of PI detailed in early statements of the theory is *ambiguity.* I initially defined *ambiguity* specifically and narrowly in terms of quantitative probability (Babrow, 1992): a situation in which a particular probability is to some extent hazy. For instance, you are experiencing ambiguity if you believe that you have a possibility of securing a particular job, but your specific chances or odds are not clear (e.g., having less than a 50–50 chance, but not knowing how much less). Of course, the more valued the job, the more difficult it would be to integrate the hazy possibility with the value. I have redefined ambiguity in more recent writings and will explain this change a bit later in this chapter.

The initial statement of the theory identified *ambivalence* as a third form of PI. Ambivalence can take several distinctive forms. We experience ambivalence most commonly when we face some object, person, or issue that we associate with both desirable and undesirable attributes. Many students feel this sort of ambivalence when they contemplate graduation, and some feel it in relation to commitment. For example, some college students experience ambivalence about their major or about a particular romantic relationship. We commonly say that we have "mixed feelings" in these situations. PI increases to the extent that the attributes are valued both positively and negatively. It is also worth noting that a single object of our thoughts or perceptions can evoke not merely positive and negative evaluations but what appear to be mutually exclusive contradictory responses. So, for instance, many students are both happy and sad about the prospects of graduation. "Love–hate relationships" (e.g., with parents, friends, coaches; with concrete objects such as food or addictive substances) also illustrate this form of ambivalence. And another subtype of ambivalence is when we encounter choices involving mutually exclusive, similarly (un)attractive alternatives. If we must choose, then everything we like about the option we forgo is problematic, as is everything we dislike about the option we choose (Festinger, 1957).

Finally, the original statement of the theory characterized impossibility as a fourth major form of PI. The most fundamental feature of impossibility is that it denotes certainty. To say that something is impossible is to say that it certainly cannot be. Such certainty commonly leads us to "rule out" or "dismiss" any further consideration of whatever seems impossible. However, it is clear that impossibility cannot be dismissed so easily when it entails something supremely valued. For example, think about how hard it would be to learn that a loved one has an incurable, fatal disease. In such situations we face the difficulties of deciding just how sure we are of the (im)possibility of our desire, as well as how we should value what is apparently impossible (see Babrow, 1992). Should you accept that the loved one's death is imminent? Should you want the person's life to be prolonged or let them go peacefully?

Evolving Reformulation.   Over time I have come to rethink the original framework's four fundamental types of PI. No theory is ever more than an abstraction of the world as conceived through the theory's lens. Bateson (1972), one of the most extraordinary communication theorists of last century, urged us to realize that "the map [theory] is not the territory." Every theory or map must necessarily evolve as it is used to engage with experience and the territory. I have discovered ways that the original formulation of the theory was inadequate as I have begun to apply it to concrete problems, most notably the challenges of communicating about uncertainties related to health and illness. I will discuss these applications in more detail later in this chapter. At this point it is important to note that this work shows clearly that "uncertainty" takes many different forms, and this has led me to reconsider the basic forms of PI.

Clearly we can be uncertain about any object in our world. For example, you might be uncertain about performance on a specific assignment, your overall course grades and GPA at the close of the semester, getting good letters of recommendation from teachers, the state of the job market when you graduate, securing a desired job, and so on. But my work also suggests somewhat less obviously that *uncertainty about any one object can take many different forms.* Sometimes uncertainty takes the form of a clear quantitative probability. This is the case, for instance, when we consider the results of a coin flip ("50–50") or the odds of a particular basketball team in the final four of the NCAA tournament winning the national championship (i.e., 1-in-4).

At other times uncertainty is experienced in the sense of a quantitative probability, but the quantity is not clear-cut. This is the case, for example, when considering your odds of getting a desired grade in a class you suspect to have a tough but unknown curve. Like the decision theorists I was studying at the time, this is what I meant by "ambiguity" in the original statement of the theory (Babrow, 1992). But further inquiry and reflection reveal that oftentimes, and perhaps most often, "uncertainty" takes a form that cannot be reduced to a quantitative probability judgment. For instance, it makes little sense to think about the quantitative probability, however hazily formulated, that God exists, that one day humans will visit another universe, that you have all the relevant information bearing on some decision, or that you have analyzed some problem thoroughly.

In short, we must expand our conception of uncertainty beyond quantitative judgment. For example, when considering what the job market will be like when you graduate, you may be uncertain due to the perception that a single piece of data can be interpreted as either a discouraging or encouraging predictor of the future market. This is what we more commonly term *ambiguity.* You can also be uncertain due to a simple insufficiency of information, being overwhelmed by too much information, doubts about the accuracy of available information or the relevance of available information, or doubting whether the stability of the job market can be predicted at all. A full exposition of the different forms of uncertainty is beyond the scope of this chapter (but see Babrow, 2001c; Babrow, Hines, & Kasch, 2000; Babrow, Kasch, & Ford, 1998). We can however briefly consider a map that draws together various important features of the territory surveyed in PI theory as it has evolved thus far (see Table 10.1).

With a bit of thought about this map, we can come to some useful insights that often counter assumptions about uncertainty that are common in both everyday thinking and in works by communication researchers and in other areas of scholarship (see Babrow, 2001c;

TABLE 10.1

Forms (or Meanings) of Uncertainty (Babrow, 2001c; Babrow, Kasch, and Ford, 1998; Babrow, Hines, and Kasch, 2000)

I. Ontological uncertainty: uncertainty rooted in the nature of the world[a]
    A. Causal indeterminacy (e.g., multicausality, contingency, reciprocity, underdeterminacy)
    B. Typological indeterminacy: Are there distinct types or classes, or is every object essentially unique?

II. Epistemological uncertainty: uncertainty rooted in the nature of human knowledge[a]
    A. Qualities and uses of information
        1. sufficiency (e.g., clarity, completeness, and volume—too little or too much to manage)
        2. reliability and validity (e.g., freedom from error, source expertise or trustworthiness, ambiguity [multiple meanings], applicability, consistency)
    B. The nature of associations (quantitative probabilities and qualitative senses of uncertainty)
    C. Processing information
        1. ordering information (e.g., relative weights of pieces; logical precedence)
        2. deriving inferences
    D. The nature of knowing: lay epistemologies, or everyday, nonscholarly assumptions about what it means to know (and hence, what it means to be uncertain)

---

[a]Ontological and epistemological uncertainties are interdependent in the sense that conceptions of the nature of the world and the nature of human knowing are interdependent

Babrow & Mattson, 2003). Most obviously, PI theory challenges the idea that (a) uncertainty has a single or narrowly homogeneous meaning, such as the notion that (b) it is necessarily bad (also see chap. 11, this volume) or that (c) it results from insufficient information. PI theory also counters the related common beliefs that (d) the main response to uncertainty is information seeking, (e) the aim and significant outcome of any encounter with uncertainty is its reduction (or frustration of this aim), and (f) certainty is usually possible. Moreover, (g) the theory overturns the exceedingly common assumption that uncertainty and its attendant problems are resolved exclusively by reducing uncertainty as opposed to, say, reappraising the value of whatever it is that we are uncertain about (see Babrow, 1992, 2001c).

The PI framework challenges other common ideas about uncertainty, but the preceding illustrations will serve to make the point that PI theory suggests a number of fruitful, often counterintuitive ways of thinking about uncertainty. It is also worth noting that these insights come about only in part by nuanced thinking about uncertainty; they also come about by careful thought about evaluative orientations, the integration of evaluative and probabilistic orientations, and PI. In short, coping with uncertainty is problematic to the extent that we have difficulty forming a probabilistic orientation and to the extent that we value (positively or negatively) whatever is at stake. These ideas are synthesized in Table 10.2, which summarizes my evolving view of different forms of PI. Moreover, the preceding ideas are developed further in the theory's additional propositions.

PI Processes

Changing Forms.   PI theory develops the preceding ideas in two additional, closely related claims. One is that *the experience of integrative dilemmas entails processes by which given problematic integrations are transformed in a variety of ways* (Babrow, 1992, 1995). In part this means that *an initially problematic form may be altered into another problematic*

TABLE 10.2
An Evolving Map of Problematic Integration Forms

1. Divergence
    a. Unlikely happiness
    b. Likely sorrow
2. Uncertainty (see Table 10.1)
    a. Ontological: nature of the world
    b. Epistemological: nature of knowing
3. Ambivalence
    a. Mixed feelings
    b. Mutually exclusive alternatives
4. Impossibility/Certainty

form. This occurs, for example, when we change the perception that something is impossible by convincing ourselves that there is hope. We then have to struggle to hold onto that slim hope (divergence) or learn to live with some form of uncertainty. For example, in political campaigns, some people passionately support candidates that have no meaningful prospect of being elected (i.e., impossibility). Supporters of Ralph Nader in the 2000 presidential election faced this dilemma perhaps by cultivating a hopeful divergence ("Nader is a long-shot, but he's got a chance"). Alternatively, they might have developed a hopeful uncertainty. They might have argued "What if both Al Gore and George W. Bush make major blunders?" "What if Nader gets to participate in the debates and demolishes the other candidates?" "The polls are often bought by the candidates' PR consultants, so polling data are biased and inaccurate," "Political campaigns are fundamentally unpredictable." Alternatively, Nader supporters might have accepted the impossibility of his election by reframing its meaning (see Babrow, 1992, 2001c). For instance, they might have reasoned that "Nader's campaign in 2000 will legitimize the Greens as a third party" or that "Nader's campaign is inherently noble, just, and therefore an invaluable enterprise regardless of its prospects for electoral success."

Changing Focus.   A second sort of transformation that occurs in the process of PI is a *shift in focus from one particular issue to another.* Returning to an earlier example, learning that we have little chance of being hired for a highly desired job will unsettle our expectation (and evaluation) of achieving the self-identity we associate with having that job (being an investigative journalist, lawyer, politician, entrepreneur), and perhaps the prospects of desired salary level, leisure pursuits, and so on. Here, our attention shifts from the original PI (getting the desired job) to other dilemmas linked to the first (e.g., self-identity). As another example, illness requires us to cope not only with physical challenges of the disease but also personal and social goals that might be challenged by being sick.

Levels of Experience.   A third form of transformation in the process of PI occurs when our *personal concerns are shared by others.* When this is the case, PI is transformed from an isolated, idiosyncratic struggle into interpersonal, group, organizational, societal, and historical-cultural processes and practices. These ideas are the focus of one more theoretical proposition.

PI as Communication Processes   In addition to the preceding claims, the theory makes one more fundamental assertion: *Communication is the primary medium, source, and*

TABLE 10.3
Main Propositions of Problematic Integration Theory

5.   Humans form probabilistic orientations to concrete and abstract features of their world.
6.   Humans form evaluative orientations to features of their world.
7.   Probabilistic and evaluative orientations are integrated in experience.
8.   Integration of probabilistic and evaluative orientations is often problematic.
9.   The experience of integrative dilemmas entails processes by which given problematic integrations are transformed in a variety of ways.
10. Communication is the primary medium, source, and resource in problematic integration experiences.

resource in PI experiences (see summary of claims in Table 10.3). In other words, communication forms or constructs and transforms PI. Much of what we communicate about, particularly discourse that is significant to us, is concerned with PI.

Communication in families and friendships, impersonal relationships, and private and public contexts gives us our perceptual categories and the substance of our cognitive and emotional processes. In so doing, communication creates, shapes, clarifies, obscures, challenges, and transforms probabilistic and evaluative orientations. In these very same ways, communication creates and shapes the experiences of PI that arise out of these orientations. In other words, communication is a constructive activity through which we come to understand situations as problematic (such as in hearing warnings and bad tidings).

Communication is not merely a neutral medium through which dilemmas are fabricated. It also is the root source of PI. For instance, when we are the bearer of bad news or warnings, we are likely to experience PI. We are discomfited by knowing that we have to do something that is likely to be unpleasant. In addition, we are uncertain about the reaction our message will evoke. Similarly, PI arises for both speaker and hearer of acts such as threats, complaints, criticism, and many others. More generally, the difficulty of achieving shared understanding (the problem of "intersubjectivity") evokes PI to the extent that we value authentic, meaningful connection to other people.

Communication also provides imperfect coping resources for dealing with PI. The imperfections themselves often become sources of PI. For instance, the conventional resources of politeness and tact, euphemism, and strategic ambiguity or equivocality are useful for managing PI in conversations. However, each of these resources also has clear limitations. Each gives rise to its own particular challenges. For instance, people may hold to different conceptions of politeness. A concrete example of this is the following dilemma: Should you verbally acknowledge someone else's pain, or does politeness demand that you avoid any direct reference to the other's suffering? PI is created when the strong desire to be polite must be integrated with uncertainty about how to be polite. In the previous example, there is some chance that the act intended to be polite may not be experienced as intended (hence the saying that "The road to hell is paved with good intentions"). In addition, conversational challenges are magnified when participants subscribe to different answers to the question, "Should I address the other's pain or should I not?" (Babrow, 1992).

Communication also creates, both directly and indirectly, more general resources for coping with PI. It does so by transmitting and enforcing societal norms having to do with "character," maturity, sanity, and sanctity (see Babrow, 1992, 2001c). In other words, we are socialized into some set of beliefs and values that define what it means to have personal "character," to be mature, to be sane, and to uphold sacred covenants. Once these systems of belief are in place, they can be used to determine how to communicate and otherwise manage particular problematic integrations. You can illustrate many of these sorts of messages by imagining what others might say to you about personal character, maturity, sanity, and divine faith if you were having difficulty letting go of a seemingly impossible desire.

Communication also provides the means for creating and managing social organizations for dealing with PI. For example, we use communication to organize and manage health care systems, the insurance industry, police and courts, churches, governments, armies, libraries, theaters, and universities (Babrow, 1992, 2001c; McPhee & Zaug, 2001). Each of these organizations and systems of organizations has its roots in enduring, profound, universal problematic integrations; each has evolved through time as these PI have been transformed or chained from one to another form and focus, and as complex, broadly constructed means of coping with these dilemmas have emerged.

In Summary

PI theory provides a general perspective on communication. It suggests that communication creates conceptions of our world, both its probable structure and meaning, particularly its values. It also suggests that communication shapes and reflects problematic formulations of these conceptions or orientations to experience. In these situations, communication gives rise to, conveys, and shapes difficulties in integrating probabilistic and evaluative orientations with one another and with related beliefs, attitudes, and intentions. When we cannot readily resolve these dilemmas (e.g., by changing probabilities, perceived or actual, or by reevaluation; see Babrow, 1992), the experience of PI chains through time, as the form and object of PI are changed, and as the experience connects private, idiosyncratic struggles to broader bodies of discourse and social organization.

IMPLICATIONS/APPLICATIONS AND CHALLENGES/POSSIBILITIES

Implications and Applications

The examples used to illustrate theoretical concepts in this chapter also suggest by their variety that PI theory is broad in scope. Its claims and implications should illuminate a wide variety of phenomena. The theory has been applied in empirical studies and tests, theoretical analyses of practical problems, critical studies of significant social practices, and in theorizing about theory (or what is often called "metatheory").

Empirical Tests. Two studies have tested PI theory in the context of social support, one investigation focusing on communicative support among breast cancer survivors (Ford et al., 1996) and the other in hospice care (Egbert, 2000). This work used PI theory to challenge an idea that received a lot of attention in communication scholarship during the preceding decade, the claim that social support is primarily a matter of helping someone to reduce her or his uncertainty about some stressor (Albrecht & Adelman, 1987). By contrast, PI theory and related perspectives suggest that uncertainty can be good or bad depending on a person's situation; therefore, social support functions by increasing, decreasing, or maintaining uncertainty (also see chap. 11, this volume; Mishel, 1988). The studies by Ford et al. and Egbert found that support messages were most likely to be uncertainty reducing (or certainty maintaining) when conveyed to people who had expressed confidence (certainty) that all is well.

By contrast, when the supportee had said that something bad is certain, support providers were most likely to design messages to introduce (or increase) uncertainty. Preliminary findings also suggested that support efforts are most variable and hence difficult to predict when the supportee is uncertain about something bad (Ford et al., 1996).

In one other relevant investigation, a 3-year participant observation study of a prostate cancer support group, Arrington (2003) found that group members "focused on matters about which [they] could generate certainty rather than on those areas in which they could help survivors manage uncertainty" (p. 19). Whereas the group was beneficial for men anticipating treatment (i.e., information sharing reduced or removed many specific treatment-related uncertainties), the group failed to consider possibilities for coping with rather than merely eliminating uncertainty for men who had completed treatment. Arrington argued that, because posttreatment men faced a future in which recurrence and a host of other issues would remain open questions, "many survivors perceived the group as less important for them after undergoing treatment" (p. 19). Hence, he concluded that an approach to social support guided by PI theory could be used to develop new perspectives from which survivors can "create new identitites that (allow) them to see themselves as not cured, but not sick, either—and as sexual beings, regardless of sexual potency" (pp. 18–19).

These findings are only the proverbial tip of the iceberg. Ford et al. (1996), Egbert (2000), and Arrington's (2003) studies were limited because they used the general term uncertainty rather than the more nuanced conceptualization of uncertainty that has emerged in recent work (recall Table 10.1; see Babrow, 2001; Babrow et al., 1998). Considered in full, PI theory suggests that social support messages facilitate coping with the various forms of uncertainty that make up stress experiences. Each of these various forms of uncertainty may be increased, decreased, or maintained by support messages. It also is possible that messages may be designed to increase some forms of uncertainty even while they decrease or maintain others (e.g., "The available information is highly credible, but its relevance is to your situation is unclear"). PI theory also suggests that social support messages facilitate coping with tensions between these forms of uncertainty and the person's desires or wishes. In other words, support does not merely help us to form probabilistic orientations but also to form evaluative orientations and to integrate the two. Finally, the theory suggests that support messages foster coping through the processes by which given worries are changed (a) from one to another form of PI, (b) from one to another focus of concern or worry, and (c) from personal, private struggles into shared dilemmas. (See chap. 11, this volume, for a compatible perspective and relevant empirical support in the area of HIV/AIDS.)

PI theory also has been tested in the area of advance care planning (such as preparing living wills) and end-of-life decision making. Here, too, the work has only begun to explore the possible implications of the theory. In general, the PI framework suggests that both doctors and patients will work together to avoid or minimize PI.

In end-of-life situations, doctors and patients collaborate in various ways. First, they postpone talk about deteriorating health. For example, Hines, Babrow, Badzek, and Moss (1997) noted that most cases of kidney failure can be predicted at least 1 year in advance. Despite this, most of the elderly dialysis patients they interviewed were not informed about the major medical response to such failures, dialysis, until 1 month or less before their kidneys failed; one third were informed less than 1 week before they began dialysis! Hines et al. also found that patients and doctors attempted to minimize or avoid PI by focusing conversation on relatively less problematic topics (e.g., various forms of dialysis, kidney transplant) rather than more challenging topics (e.g., a short-term dialysis trial, refusing dialysis and accepting death). Moreover, the study revealed that patients were generally satisfied with their conversations with doctors despite the limits on the time and range of issues considered in these weighty discussions.

In a second study, Hines et al. (2001) added texture to these findings by interviewing dialysis nurses. The researchers found that patients seek information that will help them cope with debilitating dialysis treatments rather than information nurses believe is necessary for patients to make informed choices about whether to even undergo such treatments. In short, the researchers concluded that "the tension between information patients want to successfully cope with life and information they need to intelligently decide about treatments that forestall death constitutes a key reason why communication about end-of-life issues is frequently flawed" (pp. 327–328).

Before moving to other areas, it is important to point out that the health communication studies reviewed previously should not be taken to indicate that the theory is relevant only to this area. The illustrations in the chapter's review of the theory suggest that it has the potential to apply across the areas of traditional interest to communication students, such as relationship development, identity, and cross-cultural and organizational communication (see Babrow, 2001a, 2001b, 2001c). Some of this potential is revealed in the other forms of application.

Theoretical Analyses of Practical Problems.   Aside from empirical tests, PI theory has been used in theoretical analyses of practical problems. In the first such application, it was used as a springboard to analyze the very nature of uncertainty in illness (Babrow et al., 1998; but see Babrow, 2001c). This work was motivated by two intersecting realizations. First, many have argued that illness is largely the experience of uncertainty. Second, a few researchers have come to the realization that the vast majority of work in this area (including the aforementioned applications of PI theory to social support) treats the word "uncertainty" like a linguistic catch-all term (Atkinson, 1995). Our analysis of the large literature on uncertainty in illness produced the framework represented in Table 10.1 and the revised framework for understanding forms of PI represented in Table 10.2. It also stimulated several further analyses.

One direct outgrowth of the analysis of forms of uncertainty was development of a theoretical framework for understanding the nature and challenges of illness explanations (Babrow et al., 2000; more generally, see Whaley, 2000). Among other things, we argued that illness explanations are challenging not merely because of the difficulties of conveying technical information to non-experts. Indeed they also are challenging for several other reasons. First, explanations are bedeviled by the integrative dilemmas that arise as one's physical problems are laid bare or their irreducible uncertainties are realized. Second, challenges arise because it is often necessary to face multiple forms of uncertainty that arise over the course of the explanatory process. Third, the instability of PI arising out of illness explanations also creates dilemmas for those wishing to provide those explanations. These ideas have most recently been applied in a case study of the challenges of physical therapy with recalcitrant patients (Babrow & Dinn, 2005). Clearly these ideas about explanation and decision making are relevant far beyond the context of illness. They apply whenever people are faced with constructing or comprehending explanations. They also apply when collaborative decisions challenge not only probabilistic orientations but also desires or values and the problematic integration of expectations and desires.

In a practical application of the uncertainty management framework, which can be considered either a component of PI theory (Bradac, 2001) or a complementary perspective (Brashers, 2001; chap. 11, this volume), Parrott, Stuart, and Cairns (2000) analyzed the practical challenges of living with a spinal cord injury. PI theory also has been used to understand medical decision-making (e.g., Gillotti, 2003), lung cancer patients' refusal of treatment (Sharf, Stelljes, & Gordon, 2003), and persons living with AIDS/HIV (chap. 11, this volume).

Critical Studies of Significant Social Practices.   PI theory also has been used in critical analyses of different sorts. In one, the framework was used to analyze the central segment in Milan Kundera's *The Book of Laughter and Forgetting* (Babrow, 1995). The study examined Kundera's struggle to live with his small country's domination by a super-power, personal exile from his homeland, and his underlying views about the uses and limits of communication as a resource for dealing with PI such as impossibility and diverging expectation and desire. Hence, the study illustrated how both the theory and a major literary text could be used to illuminate one another. Similar studies easily could be undertaken with other works of fiction because such writings routinely deal with PI. Indeed, much literature might be thought of as an artistic response to PI and a resource for readers who find meaning in the resonance of literary themes with their own struggles.

Taking a much different critical tack, Kim Kline and I used PI theory to build on her ongoing efforts to understand, critique, and enhance communication related to women's health (Babrow & Kline, 2000). Specifically, we used the PI framework to uncover what we termed an "ideology of uncertainty reduction" underlying medical, behavioral, and popular discourse related to breast self-exams. The ideology reflects the idea that uncertainty is bad, and hence something invariably to be avoided or reduced. We argued that the ideology paints an inaccurate picture of women's experiences with breast self-examination and sets them up to feel incompetent and powerless. Finally, we developed an alternative perspective, based on the PI theory of coping with uncertainty, that we believe will lead to better appreciation of women's experiences and improved health communication. Clearly, because the ideology of uncertainty reduction pervades the communication literature more generally (Babrow, 2001c), this line of criticism can be extended in many other directions.

In a new but related line of investigation, Buenger and Babrow (in press) analyzed breast cancer articles in popular women's magazines. The study used concepts drawn from PI theory, and developed complementary ideas, to identify, understand, and evaluate qualities of this important area of health communication. The investigation and critique culminated in various recommendations for the practice of popular writing on breast cancer.

In addition to these past critical applications of PI theory, several other projects are underway. One of these is research on the social construction of risk associated with the anthrax attack of 2001 (e.g., Babrow & Dutta-Bergman, 2003). This work is designed to ascertain foci and forms of uncertainty as well as coping strategies and patterns of behavior that foster unhelpful views of uncertainty as they are manifest in press coverage of the anthrax attacks and in the public communiqués of national public health officials.

Theorizing About Theory.   The PI framework also has stimulated works that scholars call "metatheory." For example, it has provoked a growing number of theory comparisons, works in which the PI framework has been compared to other more and less compatible perspectives (see Babrow, 2001a, 2001c). For instance, Bradac (2001) compared and contrasted PI to uncertainty reduction theory, and uncertainty management theory (chap. 11, this volume; Parrott et al., 2000). McPhee and Zaug (2001) compared PI to three different theoretical traditions in studies of organizational communication. Brashers and Babrow (1996) used PI and uncertainty management notions to respond to reinforcement expectancy theory, chaos theory, and a poetic and political analysis of identity work. And, I have used PI theory to suggest limits or challenges to politeness theory (Babrow, 1998a), conversation analysis (Babrow, 1998a), and narrative theory (Babrow, 1998b). A more recent chapter proposes ways of synthesizing narrative and PI theory (Babrow, Kline, & Rawlins, 2005).

In a different vein, the PI framework has stimulated development of a perspective on what I believe to be the kind of theory most suited to the study of human communication: "multiple-process theory" (Babrow, 1993, 1998a). In brief, I have argued that human communication is best understood as a complex interweaving of multiple, substantively distinct processes. To understand communication adequately, we must develop theories that recognize that these processes can be complimentary, redundant, and contradictory.[2]

My experience of eulogizing a beloved grandfather illustrates some of these ideas about multiple-process theory. My grandfather and I were very close. He also was the first close relative I had lost up to that point in my life. Hence, I was quite upset when arriving home from graduate school to attend his funeral. This upset was pushed along when my uncle asked that I give the eulogy. Although deeply distraught, I could not refuse this speech occasion, and so I spent the next 24 hr trying to pull together thoughts and feelings. The eulogy turned out to be more tears than prose, but the aftermath was quite important. After the funeral and for the next couple of days before I had to return to school, I seemed to be grieving alone in the middle of family. I felt like crying at the mere sight of family members and desperately wanted to share what I was experiencing and give and take support. By contrast, my family seemed to be in relatively good spirits. They joked about my grandfather (he was a fun-loving, funny person) and otherwise seemed more interested in visiting with one another than talking about their grief.

It took me several days to figure out what was going on. Eventually I realized what was happening and was struck by the contradictory processes making up communication. In forcing myself to prepare a eulogy, I was pushed quickly past initial reactions to the sudden loss; the intense effort of thinking about the loss forced me out of initial shock and into the reality of my grandfather's death. By contrast, other family members were able to remain longer in the initial state of shock. Hence, when we talked together after the eulogy, we spoke from completely different vantage points. The words and feelings we were ready to express jarred against one another. As a result, I could not satisfy a desire to support and be supported, and my family members could not simply rest as they needed to in a cocoon of shock as they gradually came to face the reality of our loss.

In sum, communication about grief and mourning necessarily entwined not only our individual psychological processes, but also the social processes of grief and customs associated with burial. These various processes coalesced in ways that made our individual and joint needs clash. The more general point is that, sometimes, as when people join together as a community in prayer or some other significant effort (e.g., mobilizing for or against war), these processes are complementary or redundant. At other times, for instance when we move through the process of grieving (or the decision to go to war or to protest against it) at different rates, these various processes can yield contradiction and, of course, PI. Hence, again, PI theory has been useful in both stimulating and illustrating metatheory, in this case, the analysis of "multiple-process theory", or what we might call theorizing about theory.

---

[2]In other words, traditional theoretical values such as parsimony (elegance) and consistency are intellectual conveniences. They almost certainly impede scholarly map-making, both by inhibiting fruitful connections and by otherwise distorting maps by forcing a world of meaning that is complex, overdetermined, and inconsistent to conform to arbitrary cartographic conventions. As the great attitude researcher William McGuire (1969) once remarked, we must have pretzel shaped theories when we are trying to describe a pretzel shaped world.

Challenges and Possibilities

Although there have been various uses of PI theory to date, I believe that the future will reveal not only more of the sorts of uses reviewed above but entirely new and substantially different uses as well. I want to conclude this chapter with a brief look at some of these as yet untouched possibilities and associated challenges.

The framework sketched in this chapter suggests that communication scholars and students must find ways of coming to terms with the complexity of multiple-process theory. Such theory will offer rich opportunities for theory development and illumination of communication. Of course, these efforts will also require that we grapple with the nature of multiple-process theory. Among other things, this form of theory recognizes the elusiveness of consistency, prediction, certainty, and control, among the most valued aims of traditional social science.

PI theory also prompts us to realize and fully appreciate that communication is essential to every distinctive aspect of our human being. Every moment of our existence reflects the basic elements of our being: probabilistic and evaluative orientations and their (at times, problematic) integration. Whether or not we are capable of appreciating it at any moment, our life is, moment by moment, a profound accomplishment.

Finally, we must realize the dialectic of indeterminacy and constraint that result from the deep interdependence between our individuality and sociality. These are the challenges and the possibilities envisioned by PI theory in its current form.

REFERENCES

Albrecht, T. A., & Adelman, M. B. (1987). *Communicating social support.* Newbury Park, CA: Sage.
Arrington, M. I. (2003). *Theorizing about social support and health communication in a prostate cancer support group.* Manuscript submitted for publication.
Atkinson, P. (1995). *Medical talk and medical work.* London: Sage.
Babrow, A. S. (1991). Tensions between health beliefs and desires: Implications for a health communication campaign to promote a smoking cessation program. *Health Communication, 3,* 93–112.
Babrow, A. S. (1992). Communication and problematic integration: Understanding diverging probability and value, ambiguity, ambivalence, and impossibility. *Communication Theory, 2,* 95–130.
Babrow, A. S. (1993). The advent of multiple process theories of communication. *Journal of Communication, 43,* 110–118.
Babrow, A. S. (1995). Communication and problematic integration: Milan Kundera's "Lost Letters" in The Book of Laughter and Forgetting. *Communication Monographs, 62,* 283–300.
Babrow, A. S. (1998a). Colloquy: Developing multiple-process theories of communication. *Human Communication Research, 25,* 152–155.
Babrow, A. S. (1998b). Review of *The silicone breast implant controversy,* by M. L. Vanderford & D. H. Smith. *Journal of Health Communication, 3,* 69–73.
Babrow, A. S. (2001a). Introduction to the special issue on uncertainty, evaluation, and communication. *Journal of Communication, 51,* 453–455.
Babrow, A. S. (Ed.). (2001b). Uncertainty, evaluation, and communication [Special issue]. *Journal of Communication, 51(3).*
Babrow. A. S. (2001c). Uncertainty, value, communication, and problematic integration. *Journal of Communication, 51,* 553–573.
Babrow, A. S., & Dinn, D. (2005). Problematic discharge from physical therapy: Communicating about uncertainty and profound values. In E. B. Ray (Ed.), *Case studies in health communication* (2nd ed., pp. 27–38). Mahwah, NJ: Lawrence Erlbaum Associates, Inc.
Babrow, A. S., & Dutta-Bergman, M. J. (2003). Constructing the uncertainties of bioterror: A study of U.S. news reporting on the anthrax attack of Fall, 2001. In C. B. Grant (Ed.), *Rethinking communicative interaction: New interdisciplinary horizons* (pp. 295–315). Amsterdam: John Benjamins.

Babrow, A. S., Hines, S. C., & Kasch, C. R. (2000). Illness and uncertainty: Problematic integration and strategies for communicating about medical uncertainty and ambiguity. In B. B. Whaley (Ed.), *Explaining Illness: Messages, strategies and contexts* (pp. 41–67). Hillsdale, NJ: Lawrence Erlbaum Associates, Inc.

Babrow, A. S., Kasch, C. R., & Ford, L. A. (1998). The many meanings of "uncertainty" in illness: Toward a systematic accounting. *Health Communication, 10,* 1–24.

Babrow, A. S., & Kline, K. N. (2000). From "reducing" to "coping with@ uncertainty: Reconceptualizing the central challenge in breast self-exams. *Social Science & Medicine, 51,* 1805–1816.

Babrow, A. S., Kline, K. N., & Rawlins, W. R. (in press). Narrative and the problematic integration of expectations and desires. In L. M. Harter, P. M. Japp, & C. M Beck (Eds.), *Constructing our health: The implications of narrative for enacting illness and wellness.* Hillsdale, NJ: Lawrence Erlbaum Associates, Inc.

Babrow, A. S., & Mattson, M. (2003). Health communication theory. In T. Thompson, A. Dorsey, K. I. Miller, & R. Parrott (Eds.), *Handbook of health communication* (pp. 35–61). Hillsdale, NJ: Lawrence Erlbaum Associates, Inc.

Bateson, G. (1972). *Steps to an ecology of mind.* New York: Ballantine.

Bradac, J. J. (2001). Theory comparison: Uncertainty reduction, problematic integration, uncertainty management and other curious constructs. *Journal of Communication, 51,* 456–476.

Brashers, D. E. (2001). Communication and uncertainty management. *Journal of Communication, 51,* 477–497.

Brashers, D. E., & Babrow, A. S. (1996). Theorizing health commination. *Communication Studies, 47,* 243–251.

Buenger, E. A., & Babrow, A. S. (in press). To hope or to know: Coping with uncertainty and ambivalence in women's magazine breast cancer articles. *Journal of Applied Communication Research.*

Cialdini, R. B. (2000). *Influence: Science and practice* (4th ed.). New York: Pearson Allyn & Bacon.

Csikszentmihalyi, M. (1975). *Beyond boredom and anxiety.* San Francisco: Jossey-Bass.

Csikszentmihalyi, M. (1990). *Flow: The psychology of optimal experience.* New York: Harper & Row.

Eagly, A. H., & Chaiken, S. (1993). *The psychology of attitudes.* New York: Harcourt Brace Jovanovich.

Egbert, N. (2000). *Volunteering to provide social support to hospice patients: A test of Problematic Integration Theory.* Unpublished doctoral dissertation, University of Georgia.

Festinger, L. (1957). *A theory of cognitive dissonance.* Evanston, IL: Row, Peterson.

Ford, L. A., Babrow, A. S., & Stohl, C. (1996). Social support messages and the management of uncertainty in the experience of breast cancer: An application of problematic integration theory. *Communication Monographs, 63,* 189–207.

Gillotti, C. M. (2003). Medical disclosure and decision-making: Excavating the ethics of physician-patient information exchange. In T. Thompson, A. Dorsey, K. I. Miller, & R. Parrott (Eds.), *Handbook of health communication* (pp. 163–181). Hillsdale, NJ: Lawrence Erlbaum Associates, Inc.

Greenwald, A. G. (1989). Why are attitudes important? In A. R. Pratkanis, S. J. Breckler, & A. G. Greenwald (Eds.), *Attitude structure and function* (pp. 1–10). Hillsdale, NJ: Lawrence Erlbaum Associates, Inc.

Hines. S. C. (2001). Coping with uncertainties in advance care planning. *Journal of Communication, 51,* 498–513.

Hines, S. C., Babrow, A. S., Badzek, L., & Moss, A. (1997). Communication and problematic integration in end-of-life decisions: Dialysis decisions among the elderly. *Health Communication, 9,* 199–217.

Hines, S. C., Babrow, A. S., Badzek, L., & Moss, A. (2001). From coping with life to coping with death: Problematic integration for the seriously ill elderly. *Health Communication, 13,* 327–342.

Lazarus, R. S. (1991). *Emotion and adaptation.* New York: Oxford University Press.

Lazarus, R. S., & Folkman, S. (1984). *Stress, appraisal, and coping.* New York: Springer.

Littlejohn, S. W. (1999). *Theories of human communication.* Belmont, CA: Wadsworth.

McGuire, W. J. (1969). The nature of attitudes and attitude change. In G. Lindzey & E. Aronson (Eds.), *Handbook of social psychology* (2nd ed., Vol. 3, pp. 136–314). New York: Random House.

McPhee, R. D., & Zaug, P. (2001). Organizational theory, organizational communication, organizational knowledge, and uncertainty management. *Journal of Communication, 51,* 574–591.

Miller, K. (2002). *Communication theories: Perspectives, processes, and contexts.* Boston: McGraw-Hill.

Mishel, M. H. (1988). Uncertainty in illness. *Image: Journal of Nursing Research, 20,* 225–232.

Parrott, R., Stuart, T., & Cairns, A.B. (2000). Reducing uncertainty through communication during adjustment to disability: living with spinal cord injury. In D. O. Braithwaite & T. L. Thompson (Eds.), *Handbook of communication and people with disabilities* (pp. 339–352). NJ: Lawrence Erlbaum Associates, Inc.

Sharf, B. F., Stelljes, L., & Gordon, H. S. (2003). A little bitty spot and I'm a big man: Patients' perspectives on refusing diagnosis or treatment for lung cancer. *Psycho-Oncology, 14,* 636–646.

Whaley, B. B. (Ed.). (2000). *Explaining illness: Research, theory, and strategies.* Mahwah, NJ: Lawrence Erlbaum Associates, Inc.

QUESTIONS TO PONDER

1. The air attacks on September 11, 2001, and the subsequent anthrax attacks later that fall forced the United States to confront the realities of terrorism. As a nation, we began the process of working out relevant policy. Whatever the policy might be today, debates about what we ought to believe, desire, and do will be a major element in national politics for the foreseeable future. What important beliefs have been expressed in this debate, and how strongly and widely held are each of these beliefs? How is the veracity of each belief disputed? Why do you think people hold strongly to one or another belief when others strongly dispute those beliefs? What does PI theory suggest?

2. Which of the beliefs you identified above embody diverging expectations and desires (likely sorrows, unlikely happiness)? PI theory suggests that these expectations and desires might influence each other, and that diverging expectations might "chain" or be transformed into other forms of PI (e.g., impossibility or uncertainty). What would be examples of these dynamics in the debates about terrorism? What does the theory suggest about the challenges of communicating when really important beliefs and values diverge?

3. Consider options for dealing with terrorism. Which options seem to involve both highly desirable and highly undesirable consequences (i.e., ambivalence)? How might people attempt to resolve or deal with their ambivalence about these options? What does the theory suggest about how ambivalence and ways of coping with ambivalence influence talk about possible options for dealing with terrorism? For example, how might ambivalence "chain" or be transformed into uncertainty or some other form of PI?

4. Recall the distinctions among forms of uncertainty (Table 10.1). One important distinction is that between "ontological" and "epistemological" uncertainties. Ontological uncertainty arises out of the very nature of the world; for example, we experience ontological uncertainty when what we are trying to understand and control is fundamentally irrational and unpredictable. By contrast, epistemological uncertainty is rooted in the nature of human knowledge, such as having too little information or conflicting information. For example, we may be trying to understand something fundamentally ordered and predictable (e.g., a well designed piece of computer software); epistemological uncertainty would arise if we're a novice user, or we've received conflicting advice from friends or advice from someone who's expertise we doubt, and so on (review Table 10.1). Once you have the distinction firmly in mind, consider the uncertainties characteristic of terrorism: Which are ontological and which are epistemological? Which sorts of uncertainties seem to characterize conversations and debates you've heard about terrorism? Which do you think are the more deeply important uncertainties associated with terrorism: ontological or the epistemological uncertainties? Why?

5. In the preceding questions, you've no doubt noticed that individual psychological processes are vitally important to even the broadest national discourse on terrorism. What are examples of this? What are some of the ways that communication molds these psychological processes and contents? Which do you think is more influential in debates on terrorism: basic psychological processes and contents or communication processes and practices? Why do you think so? What does PI theory say about this?

11

A Theory of Communication and Uncertainty Management

Dale E. Brashers
University of Illinois at Urbana–Champaign

COMMUNICATION AND UNCERTAINTY MANAGEMENT

Uncertainty is a major part of our lives that can affect how and when we communicate. Sometimes you are unsure about relatively small things (e.g., "Is rain or sunshine most likely today?"). Uncertainty about the weather might influence your decision about what you will wear or whether you will plan an outdoor activity. You often can deal easily with uncertainties of this type: You can ask your roommate if she knows about the weather forecast; you can go directly to sources of weather information, by turning on your television to The Weather Channel or by checking its Internet Website; or you can simply look outside to try to guess what the weather will be like. Soon you are likely to have enough information to decide what to wear or whether to plan a picnic.

Other kinds of uncertainty may be more complicated for us to assess and manage. For example, imagine that you possibly are interested in dating someone you just met. There are many things you will not know about a person when you are first introduced (e.g., religious beliefs, political interests, hobbies, occupation, favorite music, and so on). In addition, because you know that people are likely to be on their best behavior during an initial encounter, you are not sure if you can trust your first impression. Similar to the options for finding out about the weather, there are various communication and observation strategies you can use to learn more about your new acquaintance: You can ask the person questions about himself or herself; you can ask others about the person; or you can simply observe the person's behavior to make guesses about his or her personality and values. If you really want to develop a close relationship with your new friend, you might use all three types of information seeking to help reduce your uncertainty. It may, however, take you quite some time before you have gathered enough information to feel like you really "know" the person.

These are just two of the many sources of uncertainty that you may face in such day-to-day activities as making decisions, planning events, or interacting with others. We experience these complications for many major life events (e.g., "What career should I choose?" "Should I have a child now?" "Can I afford a house?") and for many small ones (e.g., "Should I go to class today?" "What should I wear?" "Where should I have dinner?" "Should I ask him out on a date?").

One thing that will become clear as you progress through this chapter is that communication has important connections to uncertainty management. Communication can help people manage uncertainty they have about other people or about events in their lives. Talking to others helps us answer our questions and find other means of coping with uncertainty. On the other hand, uncertainty about others and about events in our lives can affect how we communicate. Being unfamiliar with people may make us feel shy or anxious when we communicate with them. Finally, communication actually can lead to *increased* uncertainty—for example, if you hear different stories from your friends about a person you are considering asking out on a date, the contradictory information you receive might make you more uncertain than you were before you received any information.

My colleagues and I developed the theory described in this chapter to help explain how people communicatively manage uncertainty across different types of situations (Brashers, 2001). Our theory is based on research we have conducted (Brashers et al., 2000; Brashers, Neidig, & Goldsmith, 2004); however it also connects and extends a number of other theories, especially Mishel's (1988, 1990) uncertainty in illness theory; Babrow's problematic integration theory (Babrow, 1992; also see chap. 10, this volume); Berger and colleagues' uncertainty reduction theory (Berger, 1987; Berger & Bradac, 1982; Berger & Calabrese, 1975; also see chap. 8, this volume); and Lazarus and Folkman's (1984) stress, appraisal, and coping theory. The relevant parts of these theories, and some research that supports them, are described in this chapter.

Because of the important connections between uncertainty and communication, researchers have turned their attention to questions about the sources of uncertainty experienced in different contexts and the various options that people use to manage uncertainty. The theory elaborated by myself and my colleagues addresses questions about (a) the nature of uncertainty, (b) the functions of appraisal and emotion in uncertainty management, and (c) the range of behavioral and psychological responses to uncertainty. The following sections describe contributions of recent theory and research within each of these three areas. To conclude, I discuss strengths of the theory and propose directions for future research.

COMMUNICATION AND UNCERTAINTY MANAGEMENT

The Nature of Uncertainty

Babrow and his colleagues suggested that people experience uncertainty for a number of reasons (Babrow, Hines, & Kasch, 2000; Babrow, Kasch, & Ford, 1998). For example, uncertainty can arise because people perceive that they need information. Decision alternatives may appear equally attractive, or equally unattractive, if people lack the information needed to distinguish them. Imagine that you are asked to choose between two restaurants for dinner, but you know little about either one (e.g., you don't know much about the price or quality of the food, availability of seating, quality of service, and so on). Your uncertainty likely will make the choice difficult.

Other characteristics of information also lead to uncertainty. For example, imagine that you *do* have information about the restaurants that you are considering, but what you heard from some people contradicts what others have said. One friend said that Restaurant A is her favorite because the food is always excellent and the atmosphere is very romantic. Another friend told you that he and his date left before their meals were served on his last visit to Restaurant A because the service was slow and the dining room was noisy. You may be experiencing what researchers call *cognitive dissonance* (Festinger, 1957); that is, you know facts about Restaurant A that seem inconsistent with one another. And this complexity does not take into account what you know about Restaurant B. Uncertainty again makes your decision difficult, because the information you have does not help you choose between Restaurant A and Restaurant B. And notice that communication actually led to uncertainty in this situation—the more information you received, the more uncertain you became.

This example also shows that uncertainty is not necessarily related to the *amount* of information that you have. You may have a great deal of information about a topic, you may have an amount of information that other people will consider sufficient to make a decision or to predict another's behavior, and you even may have all the information that is currently available; yet you still may feel uncertain. You may be uncertain because of contradictory information (as in the preceding example), because you doubt the validity of the information that you have, or because you have so much information that you are overwhelmed by it.

Another reason that you may remain uncertain is that many events are probabilistic (Babrow, 1992). That is, you cannot know the outcome until it does or does not happen, so you must make predictions about the likelihood of the event (e.g., "Is it likely to rain this weekend?"). Uncertainty is lowest when the probability of occurrence is believed to be 0% or 100% and highest when the probability of occurrence is believed to be 50%. People who are certain are those who know an event will occur (e.g., "It will rain this weekend") or will not occur (e.g., "It will not rain this weekend"); however, most things cannot be predicted with complete certainty. Uncertainty increases as the likelihood of the event occurring or not occurring becomes equal (i.e., when it could just as likely rain as not). If multiple alternatives are possible (e.g., "Rain, snow, or sunshine is possible this weekend"), uncertainty is highest when all events seem equally likely.

Understanding different sources of uncertainty helps us to describe and explain its influences on communication behavior (Babrow et al., 2000). These ideas are useful in a variety of areas that interest communication scholars. The following paragraphs review various sources of uncertainty that researchers have explored in health, organizational, and interpersonal settings.

Health communication is one area in which researchers have explored uncertainty. People with chronic and acute illnesses experience many ambiguous, complex, and unpredictable events (Babrow et al., 1998; Fox, 1998; Mishel, 1997, 1999). My colleagues and I described personal, social, and medical sources of uncertainty for people who are infected with HIV so that we can better determine how they manage these aspects of life (Brashers et al., 1999; Brashers et al., 2003; Brashers, Neidig, Reynolds, & Haas, 1998). For example, people living with HIV can experience *subjective symptoms* (i.e., those that cannot be readily observed by others) that can be attributed to numerous causes. A headache can be associated with the stress of having the illness, with the medications that a person has to take, or with a serious infection or cancer of the brain. Medical testing, such as a CAT scan or a blood test, may help to eliminate some of the possible causes (by determining if there is a tumor or an infection in the brain). Other options may be harder to differentiate (e.g., it may be hard to distinguish between a headache caused by stress from one caused by medications) and treatment options may vary according to the suspected cause of the headache (e.g., using relaxation techniques to treat a stress-related headache versus stopping or changing a prescription to treat a medication-related headache). The uncertainty associated with not knowing the cause of a headache can be extremely stressful, especially if one believes the headache could be the sign of a serious illness or harmful side effects of medications.

Describing sources of uncertainty also helps us understand organizational communication (Kramer, 1999; McPhee & Zaug, 2001). Individuals experience uncertainty in their work life about how they should do their job, what they should expect in performance appraisals, and how they should manage their relationships with supervisors, coworkers, and subordinates in the workplace (Teboul, 1994). At the organizational level, decision making reflects uncertainties due to environmental risks and ambiguities. Important contingencies, including the stability of the economy or the possibility of competing innovations, can help determine the success or failure of an organization (Giarni & Stahel, 1989). A recent example comes from news about the airline industry. Representatives of the industry recently reported that two major airplane manufacturers plan different innovations: One will develop a larger, more luxurious plane (guessing that people want comfort when they travel long distances) and the other will develop a faster plane (guessing that people want to get to their destinations faster). The success of the companies may depend on their ability to accurately predict customer preferences and the state of the economy. If customers do not react favorably to the new airplanes or if people are unable to afford more expensive travel, the airline manufacturers may find that the costly innovations reduce their competitiveness, seriously damage their profit margins, and perhaps even bankrupt their companies. These possibilities should make the manufacturers very cautious before proceeding with their decisions to adopt new technologies.

Of course, uncertainty is key to interpersonal communication as well (Baxter & Montgomery, 1996; Berger & Bradac, 1982; Marris, 1996). People in relationships experience uncertainty about their interactions because of questions they have about their own and others' communication skills and abilities, goals, plans, emotional states, and beliefs (Berger, 1995). For example, people in conversations with new acquaintances may need to develop a sense of the other's communication style to determine the meaning of nonverbal behaviors. A person who does not talk much in a conversation may be shy, may feel angry or sad, or simply may be a naturally quiet person. Without some degree of familiarity with the person, it may be hard to determine which explanation best fits the situation. In close relationships, there are also many sources of uncertainty. Solomon and Knobloch (2003) noted that the transition point from casual dating to serious involvement for dating couples was a time of particular *relational turbulence and uncertainty*. In long-term relationships, intimate partners (i.e., spouses or significant others) may question why their relationship seems less close over time or whether their partner is being faithful to them (Planalp, Rutherford, & Honeycutt, 1988). Close friends potentially face uncertainty about the meaning of displays of affection or the possibility of sexual tension in their relationship (Afifi & Burgoon, 1998).

Across health, organizational, and interpersonal situations, uncertainty can form at different levels or layers of context (Babrow, 1992, 1995; Brashers & Babrow, 1996). For example, in interpersonal relationships, uncertainty can be about *the self* (e.g., one's own beliefs, values, abilities, and behaviors), *others* (e.g., others' beliefs, values, abilities, and behaviors), *relationships* (e.g., the quality and durability of relationships), and *other features of a context* (e.g., rules, social norms, and procedures; Berger & Calabrese, 1975; Knobloch & Solomon, 1999). For example, individuals in new relationships may question their own ability to manage the interaction (e.g., "Can I effectively let him know how much I like him without making him think I'm too needy?"), their partner's definition of the relationship (e.g., "Does he think our relationship is long-term and monogamous?"), the potential for long-term commitment (e.g., "Are we compatible enough to make this relationship last?"), or the appropriateness of suggesting sexual intimacy (e.g., "Are we close enough to suggest having sex?"). To make things more complicated, people can experience uncertainties at all of these levels at the same time. Uncertainty across these levels can be connected to one another (Babrow, 1995; Hines, 2001) and can occur over short or long periods of time (Mishel, 1988, 1990).

The literature across these areas demonstrates that the experience of uncertainty can be complicated. This complexity requires people to develop uncertainty management skills that are sensitive to multiple goals and tasks so that they can have productive and happy lives. The following sections describe how these skills develop.

Appraisal and Emotional Responses to Uncertainty

People judge the meaning of an event based on how it will affect them. Researchers call this *the appraisal process* (Lazarus & Folkman, 1984). Appraisals focus on a number of issues, including three (*relevancy, congruency,* and *coping skills*) that I will mention here: (a) "Is the event relevant to my goals?" (b) "Is the event congruent or incongruent with my goals?" and (c) "What resources do I have available for coping with the event?" (Lazarus, 2001). For example, imagine that you just heard that it might rain this weekend. If you plan to stay in your room and study over the weekend, the possibility of rain is not relevant to your goals, so you will appraise the event as not meaningful to you. But what if rain *is* relevant to your goals? If it is, then you will next consider if the event is congruent or incongruent with your objectives for the weekend. If you are planning an outdoor activity, such as a picnic and base-ball game, then the possibility of rain is incongruent with your goals. If you have just planted a garden, water will help it grow, so the possibility of rain is congruent with your goals. The meaning of the event (rain) depends on the context in which it will occur: You will be trou-bled by rain if you have planned outdoor activities, and you will be glad if it rains after you have planted a garden.

Finally, if you have decided that the event is both relevant to, and incongruent with, your goals (as in the case of the rain on the weekend you have planned a picnic and baseball game), then you are likely to consider what options you have to cope with the situation. For exam-ple, can you find an indoor location for your activities, or can you postpone them to a later date? If the answers to those questions are no (perhaps because it is a large group of relatives and many are coming from long distances for a family reunion), then you probably will have a negative appraisal of rain.

Emotional responses are connected to your appraisals of events (Lazarus, 1991; Scherer, Schorr, & Johnstone, 2001). A negative appraisal of rain on the weekend that you planned outdoor activities means that you believe you will be sad or disappointed if it rains. A posi-tive appraisal of rain on the weekend after you planted a garden means that you believe you will be happy if it rains.

When people appraise uncertainty, they have a corresponding range of emotional responses (Babrow, 1992; Brashers et al., 2000). *Negative emotional responses,* such as anxiety or fear, occur when uncertainty is viewed as a danger or threat based on a negative appraisal (Mishel, 1988). For example, workers in an organization may feel anxiety if they have had unclear job instructions, and they do not feel confident that they know how to do their jobs. People who are diagnosed with cancer may feel extreme fear if they are unsure about the availability of treat-ments for the disease. These responses (i.e., anxiety and fear) come about because of the nega-tive consequences that might be associated with remaining uncertain.

It may be more surprising to find that uncertainty also can be positively appraised. Because they often focus on uncertainty as a negative experience, many researchers have failed to examine how it might benefit people. *Positive emotional responses* result when uncertainty is framed as opportunity based on a positive appraisal (Mishel, 1988). For example, when a person is faced with a life-threatening illness (e.g., cancer, AIDS, or heart disease), uncertainty about the outcome can help the person feel hope or optimism. That is, if certainty is the belief that a person with the illness will likely die from it, then people may prefer uncertainty so they can avoid thinking about the possibility of death. Similarly, scholars who study interpersonal relations have suggested that some amount of uncertainty in a relationship can be important because people like the excitement of spontaneous or novel behavior (Baxter & Montgomery, 1996; Berger, 1987), such as when one partner brings home an unexpected gift or suggests arranging a trip together on the spur of the moment.

Other types of emotional responses are also possible. *Neutral emotional responses,* such as indifference, occur when uncertainty is judged inconsequential (e.g., when it is not relevant to one's goals or when it can be coped with easily). Imagine that you do not know how you did on your final exam before grades are posted, perhaps because you felt unsure about many of your answers. Nevertheless, you may not be concerned about this lack of information: Because you made As on all exams prior to the final, only a very poor grade on the final will lower your overall grade. Thus, the uncertainty of your final exam score is not really an issue for you because you do not feel it will negatively or positively affect you. *Combined emotional responses* (Lazarus, 1991) can arise when positive and negative emotions occur at the same time (Folkman, 1997). When uncertainty represents elements of both danger and opportunity, the emotional response may be thrill (a combination of excitement and fear), which characterizes high-risk activities like sky diving or bungee jumping.

Uncertainty Management

What people do to manage uncertainty is determined by their appraisals and emotional responses to the experience. People may want to reduce, maintain, increase, or adapt to uncertainty. Depending on the circumstances and the resources they have available, people can use many possible methods to reach these goals. The following sections review a few of these options.

Reducing Uncertainty.   If people experience uncertainty that causes them distress, they will try to reduce it. To decrease uncertainty, information can serve to distinguish options, making one appear more attractive or more likely than another. For example, in searching for information about a restaurant, you may find that one is reported to have good food at a reasonable price, whereas the other is thought to be overpriced and the quality of its food is inconsistent. Having this information increases your confidence that you can predict which restaurant will be better for your date.

Information also can decrease uncertainty when it allows people to develop meaning for an event (Brashers et al., 2000). People develop knowledge structures that help them organize and interpret information about the world around them (Kruglanski, 1989; also see chap. 4, this volume). When people have these frameworks for an event or a situation, they are better able to integrate new knowledge into their existing beliefs. Investigating another culture (e.g., reading about its religious and social practices) may help you better understand a friend's behavior and communication style. You may be able to make sense of why your friend does or does not eat certain foods, which days are set aside for religious observance, or how dating and courting rituals are carried out. If people do not have knowledge structures to help them relate to a situation (recall the first time you went to a wedding), things will seem strange and unfamiliar.

People can use a variety of sources to gather information—they can talk to others, read books and magazines, or "surf the Web." As a student, you may feel uncertain about some of the material covered in this class. To reduce your uncertainty, you can talk to your professor or to friends in the class, read your textbook, or go to the library to look for articles on the topic. Similarly, people with health concerns can communicate with physicians, nurses, pharmacists, friends, and family; use pamphlets and Internet sites of health care organizations; and attend to media coverage of health issues (Brashers, Haas, Neidig, & Rintamaki, 2002). On the job, people seek information from supervisors, coworkers, and subordinates, as well as from their family and friends (Teboul, 1994).

Researchers also have explored *how* people use these sources to seek information (e.g., Kramer, Callister, & Turban, 1995; Miller, 1996; Teboul, 1994). In uncertainty reduction theory, Berger and Calabrese (1975) said that people gather information about new acquaintances in at least three ways. An *interactive strategy* involves asking the person for information about himself or herself and an *active strategy* involves asking others (e.g., friends) about the person. People use a *passive strategy* by observing the behavior of the person to make inferences about unknown characteristics. Recall the examples from the beginning of this chapter: They show how Berger and Calabrese's ideas about uncertainty reduction can be applied to seeking information about a potential dating partner and how the categories can be extended to seeking information about the weather.

Also notice that these information-seeking methods are more or less direct (Miller & Jablin, 1991). Asking people questions about themselves is a more straightforward strategy than simply observing their behaviors. So why do people sometimes use less-direct strategies? Although it may seem that directness will always be the fastest and most effective way to gather information, there are reasons why we might choose not to be straightforward. Berger and Kellermann (1983) noted that people need to balance *social appropriateness* and *effectiveness* when asking questions of others. Sometimes information may be sensitive and, therefore, hard to ask about: Questions about a person's past relationships or views on subjects like religion or politics may be difficult to ask. People judge the appropriateness of their communication and may choose to be indirect to preserve the "face" of the other person (see chap. 12, this volume, on politeness theory), even if it results in a less efficient or effective means of information seeking (Brashers, Goldsmith, & Hsieh, 2002).

Researchers have investigated other less-direct communicative methods of seeking information. For example, Berger and Kellermann (1983) studied how people elicit information from others and found that reciprocation of self-disclosure was one technique. Baxter and Wilmot (1984) labeled this act a *secret test* that people use to determine the meaning of their relationships. Reciprocation of a communication behavior occurs when one person matches what the other person has done. For example, if you tell the person you have just begun to date your favorite stories about your childhood (including details about where you lived, where you went to school, what hobbies you enjoyed, and so on), he or she might reciprocate with similar stories of his or her own childhood. Likewise, if you talk about your expectations for a relationship (perhaps saying that you hope to find someone soon with whom you can settle down), you may get the other person to talk about his or her hopes to develop (or perhaps avoid) a relationship. In essence, rather than asking questions of (or interrogating;

Berger & Kellermann, 1983) the other person, you encouraged him or her to disclose by first disclosing information about yourself.

Another indirect method to seek information is determined not by *what* you say, but by *how* you say it. Speech that often is labeled by researchers as *powerless communication* can indicate a state of uncertainty and can be thought of as a form of passive information seeking (Johnson & Davis, 1980; Michael, 1994; Sherblom & Van Rheenen, 1984). This type of communication includes hedges, hesitations, tag questions, and expressing probabilities. Hedges are statements that contain qualifiers (e.g., "I'm not certain, but I think we should choose the first option."). Hesitations include things like verbal fillers (e.g., saying "uh" a lot while speaking). Tag questions ask for confirmation of the idea from the receiver (e.g., "He's really cute, don't you think?"). The expression of probabilities includes statements about the likelihood that an event will occur (e.g., "The exam is probably tomorrow"). Using these four elements in your communication can indicate that you are not confident (i.e., are uncertain) about what you are saying, which can lead others either to express their opinions about what you have said or to extend and elaborate with their own ideas. Haleta (1996) found that college students reported being uncertain about the information they learned in class when their professor used a powerless communication style, indicating that people may have more questions about information when it is delivered with verbal indicators of hesitancy.

Maintaining Uncertainty.   If people experience uncertainty that is comfortable for them, they will appraise it positively and want to maintain it. Avoiding information is one way to maintain the level of uncertainty that a person is experiencing. Avoidance can shield people from information that is overwhelming or distressing, helping a person avoid a negative certainty. Common terms for information avoiding include direct information avoidance (Mishel, 1988), selective attention (Ratneshwar, Warlop, Mick, & Seeger, 1997), and selective ignoring (Mishel, 1988). Brashers et al. (2000) also described social withdrawal as a form of information avoidance, in which people avoid talking to others who may raise issues that they don't want to hear about or to discuss. For example, imagine that you have a friend who has indicated that she has negative information about the person you are dating. You might avoid her so that you do not have to hear what she has to tell you. She may feel she is doing you a favor by giving you information, but you may prefer not knowing to knowing.

People also use psychological (or cognitive) mechanisms for information avoidance. Cohen (1993) argued that people sometimes discount negative facts as a form of indirect information avoidance. She noted that this type of avoidance includes discrediting the source (e.g., "I can't trust that story because she's such a gossip"); comparing the current situation to a past instance of failed prediction (e.g., "The last time I thought he was cheating on me, I found out he actually was working late at the fertilizer plant"); or believing oneself to be unique (e.g., "Even though I know he cheated on the last person he dated, I'm sure he won't cheat on me"). These methods help a person deny the validity or applicability of information that they find distressing, perhaps resulting in what researchers call *intentional forgetting* (Golding & MacLeod, 1998).

Afifi and Burgoon (1998) studied dating couples and cross-sex friends and found that, compared to dating couples, cross-sex friends experienced greater uncertainty and were less likely to talk about their relationship status. They also found low to moderate amounts of romantic interest in cross-sex friendships, particularly for the male friend. These results suggest that cross-sex friendships may be uncertain because friends sometimes question the status of the relationship ("Should we be just friends or could this be a romantic relationship?")

but that cross-sex friends avoid talking about the relationship in order to avoid negative information and potential harm to the relationship. Afifi and Burgoon (1998) concluded that cross-sex friendships can be "satisfying with moderate levels of uncertainty and that individuals are not always driven to reduce their uncertainty, but, instead, are willing to cope with uncertainty in cases where there is fear that the desired information will be negative" (p. 270).

People also may avoid seeking information when they are not particularly motivated to reduce their uncertainty (Kellermann & Reynolds, 1990). Ickes, Dugosh, Simpson, and Wilson (2003) studied people who were high or low in "motivation to acquire relationship-threatening information." Participants in their study answered questions about whether they would prefer to know or not to know a number of different pieces of information about their dating partner (e.g., would they want to know if their dating partner had flirted with or dated anyone while they were dating and had not disclosed it to them). In a follow-up study 5 months later, the researchers found that people who scored high on this measure (i.e., people who were more motivated to acquire relationship-threatening information) were more likely to have ended their relationships, especially when initial closeness was low. Those who were not likely to seek out negative information were more likely to stay in the relationships. A number of explanations are possible for these results: People who did not seek out negative information (a) may have failed to discover infidelity on the part of their dating partner, so they remained in their relationship; (b) may have had greater trust in their partner, which made the relationship more stable; or (c) may have had partners who were not as likely to cheat on them (i.e., people who were more suspicious might have had good reason to be). Whatever the reason, people in this study who were more motivated somehow to seek out negative information were less likely remain in the relationship.

Increasing Uncertainty.   If people are not comfortable with their state of certainty (i.e., they prefer to be more uncertain than they are), then they may engage in behaviors aimed at increasing uncertainty. People who want to increase uncertainty may intentionally seek information to contradict their current beliefs or to add new alternatives for consideration (Frey, Schulz-Hardt, & Stahlberg, 1996; Heyman, Henrikson, & Maughan, 1998; Kruglanski, 1989). For example, if you have asked several people about the person you are thinking about dating, and that information has been mostly negative, you may keep asking people until you have some positive information as well so that you can be more uncertain about the person (because you would prefer uncertainty over negative certainty).

The information-seeking behaviors used for increasing uncertainty are the same as those for decreasing uncertainty. People can seek information from a variety of sources, can use a number of different strategies for eliciting information, and may be more or less direct in their efforts.

Adapting to Chronic Uncertainty.   People also learn to live with chronic uncertainty. *Ongoing uncertainty* covers an extended period of time, such as across the experience of a chronic illness (e.g., "Will I be able to keep my diabetes under control with this medication?"), the lifecycle of a career (e.g., "How far will I be able to advance in this organization?"), or the duration of relationship (e.g., "Will we always love each other as much as we do now?").

Uncertainty also can fluctuate over time, increasing and decreasing as new events happen or new information is acquired. Solomon and Knobloch (2003) studied what they call *relational turbulence,* a phenomenon that accompanies a major transition in a relationship—for example, when couples move from casual dating to more serious involvement. In one study of people in dating relationships they found that uncertainty increased slightly and then decreased as people moved from moderate (e.g., casual dating) to higher levels of intimacy (Knobloch & Solomon, 2002b). Thus, it may be that people experience relatively low levels of uncertainty while they are casually dating, but experience increases in uncertainty at the point in which the relationship becomes more intimate (e.g., "Is my partner also feeling stronger romantic feelings?" "Are we doing the right thing by becoming more involved?"), and then subsequently uncertainty may decrease as the relationship stabilizes in a new level of closeness.

Across health, interpersonal, and organizational domains, people can learn to adapt by tolerating or valuing uncertainty. According to Mishel (1990), accepting uncertainty as a "natural rhythm to life" creates a "new ability to focus on multiple alternatives, choices, and possibilities; to reevaluate what is important in life; to consider variations in personal invest-ment; to appreciate the fragility and impermanence of life situations" (p. 260). People who understand that the world is complex and often unpredictable may be less stressed by uncer-tainty that is "just part of life."

Adapting to chronic uncertainty also includes changing the nature of tasks. If people can-not achieve predictability in their lives, they can change the way they plan or make decisions (Berger, 1995). Because they were uncertain about how long they would live, participants in our study of people with HIV said that they learned to plan for short-term goals and for events with immediate consequences, rather than planning for long-range goals or activities with long-term payoffs (Brashers et al., 2000). People in our study said that deciding to go back to school to take a few classes might be easier or less stressful, for example, than deciding on a financial plan for retirement. Short-term planning allowed them to feel productive and goal-oriented without focusing on objectives that they might not live to reach.

People also buffer the effects of uncertainty by developing structure and routines. Merry (1995) called this the "cocoon of certainty" (p. 128) that people use to shield themselves from the complexity of life. If people are unable to control changes in their environment or if they feel threatened, they look for ways to provide structure and stability in their day-to-day lives. Merry noted that people in organizations tend to respond to uncertainty by more strictly enforcing the rules and regulations. Organizations that respond to crisis situations (e.g., armies, emergency medical personnel, police, firefighters) commonly have clearly defined rules, regulations, and hierarchies that help them manage new and complex situations. These organizational constraints help people to feel that some aspects of their experiences are pre-dictable and to perform in times of crisis and stress. Similarly, Hines, Babrow, Badzek, and Moss (1997) studied physicians and their patients experiencing kidney failure who are engaged in highly uncertain end-of-life decision making. Hines et al. noted that "patients and doctors will minimize ambiguity by reverting to stereotypical roles in which it is the doctor's responsibility to make recommendations and it is the patient's responsibility to follow them" (p. 211). Both of these situations show that people confronted with uncertainty can develop routines to restore a sense of coherence or certainty.

Other People's Influence on Uncertainty Management

Other people also affect how we manage uncertainty. One of these influences occurs when people provide encouragement and assistance to help others through major and minor life hassles. We call this *social support* (Burleson, Albrecht, Goldsmith, & Sarason, 1994). People who provide support help with uncertainty management through messages and behaviors that increase and decrease certainty and uncertainty (Albrecht & Adelman, 1987; Ford, Babrow,

& Stohl, 1996). For example, supportive others help people manage uncertainty by providing direct or indirect assistance as (a) sources of information, (b) collaborators in information gathering, and (c) evaluators of information (Brashers, Neidig, & Goldsmith, 2004; Zook & Miller, 1993). Imagine you want to buy a new car. A friend who is very knowledgeable about cars volunteers to help you find information. There may be things that she already knows about certain models of cars, and she probably knows about Web sites and other places to find additional information. She probably will be able to help sort through the information you gather, helping you decide which claims to believe (perhaps those of product testing organizations like *Consumer Reports*) and which to discount (perhaps those of the automobile manufacturer). Your friend provides direct assistance by helping with information seeking. She also can provide indirect assistance through what we call *emotional support*, by being available and helping you control your emotions (e.g., helping you to stay calm and not let the process make you too anxious).

A second way that others influence uncertainty management is through intentional manipulation of uncertainty. Researchers have argued that people in organizations manage the uncertainty of others for strategic reasons. Messick (1999) said that organizations sometimes use "smoke machines" that are "designed to obscure, blur, confuse, distract, or otherwise direct attention away from some features of an issue, and possibly toward other, less unfavorable aspects of it" (p. 75). Similarly, Tyler (1997) found that organizations use *strategic ambiguity* (Eisenberg, 1987) when confronted with charges of unethical behavior, because of concerns about corporate liability and lawsuits. She argued that a straightforward apology for an incident (e.g., the financial scandals of companies like Enron and WorldCom) eliminates the ambiguity of whether the company is responsible for what happened—that is, if they apologize, they must be guilty.

Challenges to Uncertainty Management

Managing uncertainty is not always a straightforward task. Uncertainty management can be complicated by the nature of information or by the complexity of information seeking and avoiding (Brashers et al., 2000). For example, uncertainty cannot always be reduced (Berger, 1995). Sometimes people will want answers to questions for which no information is available. People with relatively new illnesses may find that scientific information about the illness or about treatments to help them advances slowly. In addition, as I noted earlier in the chapter, people may find uncertainty reduction difficult because information from different sources is inconsistent or contradictory. Finally, people who are trying to reduce their uncertainty by seeking information can unintentionally increase their uncertainty. When people search for "the answer" to their questions, they might encounter more complexity and ambiguity, perhaps because some information can be challenging and difficult to interpret (e.g., scientific information about an illness).

Uncertainty management also may be challenging because people vary in their information-seeking skills and abilities. For example, many students who are new to college find the library system confusing and difficult to use. It may take several semesters before a student is confident that he or she can use the computer databases to search for journal articles and books on a topic and can locate those articles and books in the library. Similarly, the social skills needed to seek or provide information vary from person to person. Compared to an outgoing person, a shy person probably will find it much more difficult to get information from others. A reticent student may find it hard to ask questions in class, talk to the professor after class, or ask others in the class for help.

Dilemmas in managing uncertainty also arise from difficulty coordinating the goals of support seekers and support givers (Brashers, Goldsmith, et al., 2002). For example, one person might focus on reducing uncertainty while the other focuses on increasing or maintaining uncertainty (Brashers et al., 2004). Supportive others may provide unsolicited information and advice to individuals they believe need or desire uncertainty reduction (Brashers et al., 2004; Kramer et al., 1995). Recall the example from earlier in this chapter about a friend who indicates she has negative information to tell you about the person you are dating. If she tells you this information and you don't really want to hear it, her goal (e.g., being a good friend) conflicts with your goal (e.g., remaining uncertain about the person you are dating).

Other people also may unintentionally affect a person's uncertainty management. In established close relationships, for example, we might expect that the relational partners would be relatively certain about each other (i.e., they know about each other's beliefs, values, attitudes, and behaviors). Sally Planalp and her colleagues have studied *uncertainty increasing events* that occur in established relationships. Respondents to a survey in two studies described events that led to greater uncertainty in their relationships (Planalp & Honeycutt, 1985; Planalp et al., 1988). Planalp et al. (1988, p. 527) classified these events as *competing relationships* ("The respondent's relational partner had another relationship, either romantic or friendship, that competed with his or her relationship with the respondent"), *unexplained loss of contact or closeness* ("The respondent's relational partner broke off contact or reduced closeness with the respondent without any explanation"), *sexual behavior* ("The respondent discovers information concerning the other's sexual acts, desires, or preferences that was unexpected"), *deception* ("The respondent discovers that the other has lied, concealed information, or intentionally mislead the respondent"), *change in personality or values* ("The respondent perceived a change in the other person's personality, value system, or characteristic ways of behaving"), *betraying confidence* ("The respondent discovers that the other has revealed confidential information about the respondent to an outside party"), and *more serious* ("The respondent discovers that his or her relational partner thought the relationship was more serious or closer than the respondent did or that the partner desired a more serious or closer relationship"). All of these factors have the potential to influence a person's state of uncertainty about a relationship, even after the relationship has become close and previous uncertainty has been resolved.

The means of coping with problems of uncertainty management correspond to these dilemmas (Brashers et al., 2000). Individuals managing uncertainty learn to be vigilant when information is not easily obtained. They can accommodate for their own and others' deficits in information-seeking and cognitive-processing ability in many ways (e.g., by using a friend to help them). Dilemmas of social support and uncertainty management can be dealt with by withdrawing from social situations, selectively allowing others to be support persons, and maintaining boundaries about topics of conversation (Brashers et al., 2004). Planalp and Rivers (1996) found that people who experienced uncertainty increasing events could gather additional data, test their theories about the relationship, consider alternative explanations, attempt to attribute causes to the event ("Was he too drunk to know what he was doing?"), or attribute responsibility ("Was it my fault or the other person's fault?").

EXPANDING THE THEORY OF UNCERTAINTY MANAGEMENT

It is fortunate that more communication researchers recently have agreed that people have both positive and negative appraisals of uncertainty (Afifi & Burgoon, 1998; Babrow et al., 2000; Babrow & Kline, 2001; Baxter & Montgomery, 1996; Berger, 1995; Parrott, Stuart, &

Cairns, 2000). There needs to be continued research in the area, to verify predictions about how people use information seeking, information avoiding, and psychological mechanisms for uncertainty management. Many questions arise as we consider why people might want to reduce, maintain, or increase their uncertainty. For example, should we teach people that reducing uncertainty is the best route to decision making? In our society, knowledge is considered a basic form of human wealth (Merry, 1995). Many theories of group and organizational decision making and problem solving emphasize a rational *optimizing strategy* (Simon, 1956) in which all available information is gathered and analyzed, decision alternatives are carefully weighed, and the best option is selected. Nevertheless, we need to understand that people may be distressed by information, which may lead them to avoid situations in which they will encounter it. When we decide that people do need potentially distressing information, we should develop strategies for providing it in ways that minimize anxiety and maximize processing ability (Bottorff, Ratner, Johnson, Lovato, & Joab, 1998).

A theory of communication and uncertainty management also should focus on possible cultural differences in the experience and management of uncertainty. Most communication research on culture and uncertainty has been conducted within the framework of Gudykunst's (1995) anxiety/uncertainty management theory. Goldsmith (2001) recently offered a promising alternative perspective. Based on studies from around the world, Goldsmith noted that other cultures have different perspectives on uncertainty. Research on Puerto Rican (Morris, 1981) and Malagasy (Keenan, 1974) communities revealed that those cultures appreciate ambiguity and uncertainty and that members of both societies communicate in ways that preserve or increase uncertainty. Studies of the Western Apache tribe indicated that silence is often a response to uncertainty (Basso, 1979). Goldsmith noted that when Western Apaches are beginning a courtship or first meeting a stranger, "instead of engaging in increased amount of information seeking, they are likely to remain silent in one another's presence for long periods of time until they feel comfortable speaking to one another" (p. 521). These examples led Goldsmith to call for a theory of communication and uncertainty that accounts for cultural differences in how people respond to uncertainty.

Goldsmith (2001) also suggested focusing on developing normative theories of uncertainty. Normative theories help to explain differences between what people *do* and what people *should do* to effectively manage uncertainty. Goldsmith's suggestion is particularly attractive given the application of uncertainty management to many basic human tasks and goals. She argued that

> As interest in uncertainty and communication expands beyond the boundaries of initial interaction, and as the theory is applied to practical problems (e.g., how to maintain a relationship, how to cope with illness, how to adjust to a new organizational setting, how to get along with someone from a different cultural background), then predicting and explaining what people do is not sufficient. We also need attention to how well various responses to uncertainty work. (p. 531)

Normative models can help account for the incongruence between goals and outcomes in uncertainty management situations. If those models are developed, communication scholars will be better equipped to offer advice about uncertainty management.

SUMMARY AND CONCLUSION

The theory I presented in this chapter is among the newest of the theories described in this book, but it has connections to several other important theories listed in the beginning of the chapter. The major strength of the current formulation of this theory is that it advances our thinking about uncertainty management processes, including information seeking and avoiding. Much of the research by communication scholars on uncertainty has focused exclusively on how and why people *reduce* uncertainty. Because they typically have only talked about reducing uncertainty, researchers often have failed to examine other options for uncertainty management processes (Babrow, 2001). Communication scholars should continue to focus on three connected areas: the experience and meaning of uncertainty; appraisal and emotional responses to uncertainty; and corresponding communication behaviors.

Uncertainty experiences and the corresponding appraisals, emotional responses, and behaviors that accompany them reveal a great deal about how communication functions in human action. In some instances, people may want to reduce uncertainty because they find it threatening. At other times, uncertainty allows people to maintain hope and optimism. Across contexts, people engage in or avoid communication so that they can manipulate uncertainty to suit their needs. Theories of uncertainty management that account for these factors have important consequences for the practice of health care, for functioning in organizations, and for developing and sustaining relationships. Learning to manage uncertainty is an important life skill that communication researchers can help people develop.

SUGGESTED READINGS

For good overviews of theories of uncertainty management, see the recent special issues of the *Journal of Communication* (2001, Volume 51, Issue 4) *and Human Communication Research* (2002, Volume 28, Issue 2). These special journal issues include many articles on the topics of uncertainty management and information seeking, including articles about health communication (Brashers et al., 2002; Hines, 2001) interpersonal communication (Bradac, 2001; Eisenberg, 2001; Knobloch & Solomon, 2002a), organizational communication (McPhee & Zaug, 2001; Morrison, 2002), and intercultural communication (Baldwin & Hunt, 2002; Goldsmith, 2001).

Other important articles and books about uncertainty management that will give you good background on these concepts include Babrow (1992, 2001), Berger and Bradac (1982), Berger and Calabrese (1975), Brashers (2001), Merry (1995), and Mishel (1990).

ACKNOWLEDGMENTS

This chapter is based on "Communication and Uncertainty Management" published in the *Journal of Communication* (Brashers, 2001). I am grateful to the National Institute of Nursing Research for their support of this research (1R29NR04376) and to I-Ling Hsieh and Lance Rintamaki for their helpful feedback on this chapter.

REFERENCES

Afifi, W. A., & Burgoon, J. K. (1998). "We never talk about that": A comparison of cross-sex friendships and dating relationships on uncertainty and topic avoidance. *Personal Relationships, 5*, 255–272.

Albrecht, T. L., & Adelman, M. B. (1987). *Communicating social support.* Thousand Oaks, CA: Sage.

Babrow, A. S. (1992). Communication and problematic integration: Understanding diverging probability and value, ambiguity, ambivalence, and impossibility. *Communication Theory, 2*, 95–130.

Babrow, A. S. (1995). Communication and problematic integration: Milan Kundera's "Lost Letters" in *The Book of Laughter and Forgetting. Communication Monographs, 62,* 283–300.

Babrow, A. S. (2001). Uncertainty, value, communication, and problematic integration. *Journal of Communication, 51,* 553–573.

Babrow, A. S., Hines, S. C., & Kasch, C. R. (2000). Managing uncertainty in illness explanation: An application of problematic integration theory. In B. Whaley (Ed.), *Explaining illness: Research, theory, and strategies* (pp. 41–67). Hillsdale, NJ: Lawrence Erlbaum Associates, Inc.

Babrow, A. S., Kasch, C. R., & Ford, L. A. (1998). The many meanings of *uncertainty* in illness: Toward a systematic accounting. *Health Communication, 10,* 1–23.

Babrow, A. S., & Kline, K. N. (2001). From "reducing" to "managing" uncertainty: Reconceptualizing the central challenge in breast self-exams. *Social Science and Medicine, 51,* 1805–1816.

Baldwin, J. R., & Hunt, S. K. (2002). Information-seeking behavior in intercultural and intergroup communication. *Human Communication Research, 28,* 272–286.

Basso, K. H. (1979). *Portraits of 'the whiteman': Linguistic play and cultural symbols among the Western Apache.* Cambridge, England: Cambridge University Press.

Baxter, L. A., & Montgomery, B. M. (1996). *Relating: Dialogues and dialectics.* New York: Guilford.

Baxter, L. A., & Wilmot, W. W. (1984). "Secret tests": Social strategies for acquiring information about the state of the relationship. *Human Communication Research, 11,* 171–202.

Berger, C. R. (1987). Communicating under uncertainty. In M. E. Roloff & G. R. Miller (Eds.), *Interpersonal processes: New directions in communication research* (pp. 39–62). Newbury Park, CA: Sage.

Berger, C. R. (1995). Inscrutable goals, uncertain plans, and the production of communicative action. In C. R. Berger & H. M. Burgoon (Eds.), *Communication and social influence processes* (pp. 1–28). East Lansing: Michigan State University Press.

Berger, C. R., & Bradac, J. (1982). *Language and social knowledge.* London: Edward Arnold.

Berger, C. R., & Calabrese, R. J. (1975). Some explorations in initial encounters and beyond: Toward a developmental theory of interpersonal communication. *Human Communication Research, 1,* 99–112.

Berger, C. R., & Kellermann, K. A. (1983). To ask or not to ask: Is that a question? In R. M. Bostrom (Ed.), *Communication yearbook 7* (pp. 342–368). Newbury Park, CA: Sage.

Bottorff, J. L., Ratner P. A., Johnson J. L., Lovato, C. Y., & Joab, S. A. (1998). Communicating cancer risk information: The challenges of uncertainty. *Patient Education and Counseling, 33,* 67–81.

Bradac, J. J. (2001). Theory comparison: Uncertainty reduction, problematic integration, uncertainty management, and other curious constructs. *Journal of Communication, 51,* 456–476.

Brashers, D. E. (2001). Communication and uncertainty management. *Journal of Communication, 51,* 477–497.

Brashers, D. E., & Babrow, A. (1996). Theorizing communication and health. *Communication Studies, 47,* 243–251.

Brashers, D. E., & Goldsmith, D. J., & Hsieh, E. (2002). Information seeking and avoiding in health contexts. *Human Communication Research, 28,* 258–271.

Brashers, D. E., Haas, S. M., Neidig, J. L., & Rintamaki, L. S. (2002). Social activism, self-advocacy, and coping with HIV illness. *Journal of Social and Personal Relationships, 19,* 113–133.

Brashers, D. E., Neidig, J. L., Cardillo, L. W., Dobbs, L. K., Russell, J. A., & Haas, S. M. (1999). "In an important way, I did die." Uncertainty and revival among persons living with HIV or AIDS. *AIDS Care, 11,* 201–219.

Brashers, D. E., Neidig, J. L., & Goldsmith, D. J. (2004). Social support and the management of uncertainty for people living with HIV. *Health Communication, 16,* 305–331.

Brashers, D. E., Neidig, J. L., Haas, S. M., Dobbs, L. K., Cardillo, L. W., & Russell, J. A. (2000). Communication in the management of uncertainty: The case of persons living with HIV or AIDS. *Communication Monographs, 67,* 63–84.

Brashers, D. E., Neidig, J. L., Reynolds, N. R., & Haas, S. (1998). Uncertainty in illness across the HIV/AIDS trajectory. *Journal of the Association of Nurses in AIDS Care, 9,* 66–77.

Brashers, D. E., Neidig, J. L., Russell, J. A., Cardillo, L. W., Haas, S. M., Dobbs, L. K., et al. (2003). The medical, personal, and social causes of uncertainty in HIV illness. *Issues in Mental Health Nursing, 24,* 497–522.

Burleson, B. R., Albrecht, T. L., Goldsmith, D. J., & Sarason, I. (1994). Introduction. In B. Burleson, T. Albrecht, & I. Sarason (Eds.), *The communication of support: Messages, interactions, relationships, and community* (pp. xi–xix). Newbury Park, CA: Sage.

Caughlin, J. P., & Golish, T. D. (2002). An analysis of the association between topic avoidance and dissatisfaction: Comparing perceptual and interpersonal explanations. *Communication Monographs, 69,* 275–295.

Cohen, M. H. (1993). The unknown and the unknowable: Managing sustained uncertainty. *Western Journal of Nursing Research, 15,* 77–96.

Eisenberg, E. M. (1987). The strategic uses of ambiguity in organizations. *Communication Monographs, 51,* 227–242.

Eisenberg, E. M. (2001). Building a mystery: Toward a new theory of communication. *Journal of Communication, 51,* 534–552.

Festinger, L. (1957). *A theory of cognitive dissonance.* Stanford, CA: Stanford University Press.

Folkman, S. (1997). Positive psychological states and coping with severe stress. *Social Science and Medicine, 45,* 1207–1221.

Ford, L. A., Babrow, A. S., & Stohl, C. (1996). Social support and the management of uncertainty: An application of problematic integration theory. *Communication Monographs, 63,* 189–207.

Fox. R. C. (1998). *Experiment perilous: Physicians and patients facing the unknown.* New Brunswick, NJ: Transaction.

Frey, D., Schulz-Hardt, S., & Stahlberg, D. (1996). Information seeking among individuals and groups and possible consequences for decision making in business and politics. In E. H. Witte & J. H. Davis (Eds.), *Understanding group behavior* (pp. 211–225). Mahwah, NJ: Lawrence Erlbaum Associates, Inc.

Giarni, O., & Stahel, W. R. (1989). *The limits to certainty: Facing risks in the new service economy.* Dordrecht, The Netherlands: Kluwer.

Golding, J. M., & MacLeod, C. M. (Eds.). (1998). *Intentional forgetting: Interdisciplinary perspectives.* Mahwah, NJ: Lawrence Erlbaum Associates, Inc.

Goldsmith, D. J. (2001). A normative approach to the study of uncertainty and communication. *Journal of Communication, 51,* 514–533.

Golish, T. D., & Caughlin, J. P. (2002). "I'd rather not talk about it": Adolescents' and young adults' use of topic avoidance in stepfamilies. *Journal of Applied Communication Research, 30,* 78–106.

Gudykunst, W. B. (1995). The uncertainty reduction and anxiety-uncertainty reduction theories of Berger, Gudykunst, and associates. In D. P. Cushman & B. Kovacic (Eds.), *Watershed research traditions in human communication theory* (pp. 67–100). Albany: State University of New York Press.

Haleta, L. L. (1996). Student perceptions of teachers' use of language: The effects of powerful and powerless language on impression formation and uncertainty. *Communication Education, 45,* 16–28.

Heyman, B., Henrikson, M., & Maughan, K. (1998). Probabilities and health risks: A qualitative approach. *Social Science and Medicine, 47,* 1295–1306.

Hines, S. C. (2001). Coping with uncertainties in advanced care planning. *Journal of Communication, 51,* 498–513.

Hines, S. C., Babrow, A. S., Badzek, L., & Moss, A. H. (1997). Communication and problematic integration in end-of-life decisions: Dialysis decisions among the elderly. *Health Communication, 9,* 199–217.

Ickes, W., Dugosh, J. W., Simpson, J. A., & Wilson, C. L. (2003). Suspicious minds: The motive to acquire relationship-threatening information. *Personal Relationships, 10,* 131–148.

Johnson, F. L., & Davis, L. K. (1980). Hesitation phenomena and conversational style: Indications of uncertainty in family situations. In S. Fiddle (Ed.), *Uncertainty: Behavioral and social dimensions* (pp. 347–368). New York: Praeger.

Keenan, E. (1974). Norm-makers and norm-breakers: Use of speech by men and women in a Malagasy community. In R. Bauman & J. Sherzer (Eds.), *Explorations in the ethnography of speaking* (pp. 125–143). Cambridge, England: Cambridge University Press.

Kellermann, K., & Reynolds, R. (1990). When ignorance is bliss: The role of motivation to reduce uncertainty in uncertainty reduction theory. *Human Communication Research, 17,* 5–75.

Knobloch, L. K., & Solomon, D. H. (1999). Measuring the sources and content of relational uncertainty. *Communication Studies, 50,* 261–278.

Knobloch, L. K., & Solomon, D. H. (2002a). Information seeking beyond initial interaction: Negotiating relational uncertainty within close relationships. *Human Communication Research, 28,* 243–257.

Knobloch, L. K., & Solomon, D. H. (2002b). Intimacy and the magnitude and experience of episodic relational uncertainty within romantic relationships. *Personal Relationships, 9,* 457–478.

Kramer, M. W. (1999). Motivation to reduce uncertainty: A reconceptualization of uncertainty reduction theory. *Management Communication Quarterly, 13,* 305–316.

Kramer, M. W., Callister, R. R., & Turban, D. B. (1995). Information-receiving and information-giving during job transitions. *Western Journal of Communication, 59,* 151–170.

Kruglanski, A. W. (1989). *Lay epistemics and human knowledge: Cognitive and motivational bases.* New York: Plenum.

Lazarus, R. S. (1991). *Emotion and adaptation.* New York: Oxford University Press.

Lazarus, R. S. (2001). Relational meaning and discrete emotions. In K. R Scherer, A. Schorr, & T. Johnstone (Eds.) *Appraisal processes in emotion: Theory, methods, research.* New York: Oxford University Press.

Lazarus, R. S., & Folkman, S. (1984). *Stress, appraisal, and coping.* New York: Springer.

Marris, P. (1996). *The politics of uncertainty: Attachment in private and public life.* New York: Routledge.

McPhee, R. D., & Zaug, P. (2001). Organizational theory, organizational communication, organizational knowledge, and problematic integration. *Journal of Communication, 51,* 574–591.

Merry, U. (1995). *Coping with uncertainty: Insights from the new sciences of chaos, self-organization, and complexity.* Westport, CT: Praeger.

Messick, D. M. (1999). Dirty secrets: Strategic uses of ignorance and uncertainty. In L. L. Thompson, J. M. Levine, & D. M. Messick (Eds.), *Shared cognition in organizations: The management of knowledge* (pp. 71–88). Mahwah, NJ: Lawrence Erlbaum Associates, Inc.

Michael, M. (1994). Discourse and uncertainty: Postmodern variations. *Theory and Psychology, 4,* 383–404.

Miller, V. D. (1996). An experimental study of newcomer's information seeking behaviors during organizational entry. *Communication Studies, 47,* 1–24.

Miller, V. D., & Jablin, F. M. (1991). Information seeking during organizational entry: Influences, tactics, and a model of the process. *Academy of Management Review, 16,* 92–120.

Mishel, M. H. (1988). Uncertainty in illness. *Image: Journal of Nursing Scholarship, 20,* 225–232.

Mishel, M. H. (1990). Reconceptualization of the uncertainty in illness theory. *Image: Journal of Nursing Scholarship, 22,* 256–262.

Mishel, M. H. (1997). Uncertainty in acute illness. *Annual Review of Nursing Research, 15,* 57–80.

Mishel, M. H. (1999). Uncertainty in chronic illness. *Annual Review of Nursing Research, 17,* 269–294.

Morris, M. (1981). *Saving and meaning in Puerto Rico: Some problems in the ethnography of discourse.* Oxford, England: Pergamon Press.

Morrison, E. W. (2002). Information seeking within organizations. *Human Communication Research, 28,* 229–242.

Parrott, R., Stuart, T., & Cairns, A. B. (2000). Reducing uncertainty through communication during adjustment to disability. In D. O. Braithwaite & T. L. Thompson (Eds.), *Handbook of communication and people with disabilities: Research and application* (pp. 339–352). Mahwah, NJ: Lawrence Erlbaum Associates, Inc.

Planalp, S., & Honeycutt, J. (1985). Events that increase uncertainty in interpersonal relationships. *Human Communication Research, 11,* 593–604.

Planalp, S., & Rivers, M. (1996). Changes in knowledge of personal relationships. In G. O. Fletcher & J. Fitness (Eds.), *Knowledge structures in close relationships: A social psychological approach* (pp. 299–324). Mahwah, NJ: Lawrence Erlbaum Associates, Inc.

Planalp, S., Rutherford, D. K., & Honeycutt, J. M. (1988). Events that increase uncertainty in relationships II. *Human Communication Research, 14,* 516–547.

Ratneshwar, S., Warlop, L., Mick, D. G., & Seeger, G. (1997). Benefit salience and consumers selective attention to product features. *International Journal of Research and Marketing, 14,* 245–259.

Scherer, K. R., Schorr, A., & Johnstone, T. (Eds.) (2001). *Appraisal processes in emotion: Theory, methods, research.* New York: Oxford University Press.

Sherblom, J., & Van Rheenen, D. D. (1984). Spoken language indices of uncertainty. *Human Communication Research, 11,* 221–230.

Simon, H. A. (1956). Rational choice and the structure of the environment. *Psychological Review, 63,* 129–138.

Solomon, D. H., & Knobloch, L. K. (2003, May). *A model of relational turbulence: The role of intimacy, relational uncertainty, and interference from partners in appraisals of irritations.* Paper presented at the annual meeting of the International Communication Association, San Diego.

Teboul, J. C. B. (1994) Facing and coping with uncertainty during organizational encounter. *Management Communication Quarterly, 8,* 190–224.

Tyler, L. (1997). Liability means never having to say you're sorry: Corporate guilt, legal constraints, and defensiveness in corporate communication. *Management Communication Quarterly, 11,* 51–73.

Zook, E. G., & Miller, K. I. (1993). The role of care partners in managing AIDS patients' illness: Toward a triadic model of health care delivery. In S. Ratzan (Ed.), *AIDS: Effective health communication for the 90s* (pp. 55–70). Washington, DC: Taylor & Francis.

QUESTIONS TO PONDER

1. As mentioned in the beginning of the chapter, uncertainty is a common everyday experience. What uncertainty have you experienced lately? Has uncertainty affected any major decisions you have had to make? What did you do to manage your uncertainty?

2. Some people think that it's always good to have lots of information. Have you ever received information that you wished you had not? What did you do in response? Can you think of other situations in which you might not want information?

3. Genetic testing is one area of medical research that has received a lot of attention recently. People can be tested to see if they are more or less likely to have certain illnesses. Some argue that this information is useful because people who are at higher risk can monitor themselves more closely for signs of disease. Others argue that genetic testing causes unnecessary worry, because the tests are not definitive (you can't tell for sure if people will get the disease, just if they are at increased risk). Would you ever consider genetic testing? Why or why not?

3. Recall the example about the two airline manufacturers that are planning innovations (one company will make a more luxurious plane and the other company will make a faster plane). What uncertainty management strategies might they use? What information will they want to seek? Can they completely reduce their uncertainty? Why or why not? If not, how should they proceed with decision making?

4. Afifi and Burgoon (1998) studied the kinds of topics about which dating partners and close friends avoid talking. Similarly, Golish and Caughlin (2002) and Caughlin and Golish (2002) studied topic avoidance in families. Have you ever intentionally avoided talking about a topic in a close relationship? Are there things that you and your family don't talk about? Are there things that you and your friends don't talk about? Are there things that you and your relational partner don't talk about?

5. If you are interested in dating a person, what information-seeking strategies would you most likely use to find out more about the person (interactive, active, or passive)? Why? Can you think of questions or methods of observation that you would use for each category?

6. Planalp's studies of close relationships revealed a number of things that increase uncertainty in an established relationship. Have you or anyone you know ever experienced any of these sources of uncertainty: competing relationships, unexplained loss of contact or closeness, questions about sexual behavior, deception, change in personality or values, betraying confidence, and the other person wanting to be more serious. How did you or the other person handle these uncertainty increasing events? Did you use any interactive, active, or passive strategies? If so, what were they?

12

Brown and Levinson's Politeness Theory

Daena J. Goldsmith
University of Illinois, Urbana–Champaign

Imagine yourself slipping into a lecture hall just as the bell is ringing. As you take a seat, you notice with relief that the professor is running late today too—she's just finishing a chocolate bar and looking through a folder for her notes. As she begins lecturing, you notice she has a huge smear of chocolate across one side of her face. You laugh a little and turn to see if your neighbor has noticed. As you look around, it seems just about everyone has noticed except the professor, and as she moves closer to the front row, a hushed ripple of whispers and nervous laughter runs through the class. You wonder why none of the teaching assistants are doing anything to get the professor's attention. You feel sorry for her but you're also finding it very distracting. Finally, someone raises a hand and says, "Excuse me, professor, but I think you might have a little bit of something on your face." At first, everyone is completely silent, and then the class bursts into laughter and chatter as the professor wipes her face with a tissue.

If you found yourself in this situation, how would you react? When I have staged this demonstration in my classes, most students say that they feel embarrassed, distracted, and unsure what to do. They don't want to cause me even greater embarrassment by pointing out my mess so they sit and watch, hoping I will notice and wipe off the chocolate so that we can all pretend that nothing has happened. I hope you can identify with this example and see how it is similar to other embarrassing incidents that occur in everyday life. In fact, the reactions of students in my class may seem normal and natural to you. However, if you stop to think carefully about this example, it poses several puzzles.

Notice that having chocolate on my face didn't interfere with my ability to complete the communicative task of giving an informative lecture. So why did anyone pay any attention? If it was distracting for students, why didn't they just ask me to wipe my face—students in my classes ask me questions if something is unclear or if they can't read the overhead, so why should this be any different? Why did so many students say *they* felt embarrassed when *I* was the one with food on my face? Why would many students feel it was more appropriate for a teaching assistant to act than for a student to say something? If the person with chocolate on her face were a good friend sitting nearby, many students say it would be less awkward to just say "hey, you've got chocolate on your face." Why is that? Why should we feel more embarrassed for a relative stranger than we would for someone we know well, whose feelings might be of greater concern to us?

Answers to these questions can be found in theories of face and face work. Concerns for face are especially noticeable in embarrassing situations, but face and face work are apparent in all of our everyday interactions. Every time we communicate, we are not only engaging in some task (e.g., giving a lecture, asking a favor, passing the time pleasantly), but we are also enacting identities. Theories of face work help us to understand how identities are enacted, protected, and threatened, and noticing these processes explains many things we do in interactions with others.

There are many theories of identity and face but in this chapter, I focus on one especially well-known theory: P. Brown and Levinson's (1987) politeness theory. I begin by discussing the concept of "face." Then I summarize the main ideas in P. Brown and Levinson's politeness theory. Next, I discuss three different ways researchers have studied politeness theory. I conclude by describing some of the strengths and limitations of politeness theory.

DEFINING "FACE"

Although the chocolate in the previous example is smeared on the professor's *physical* face, the "face" we are discussing in this chapter has to do with *symbolic* face. It's the face we refer to when we say that someone is trying to "save face" or that someone has "lost face." Face is an image or identity we enact in our interactions with other people. Erving Goffman was a sociologist whose writings have had a great influence on theories of communication and especially on theories of face and face work. Through close observation of ordinary interactions, Goffman developed frameworks that help us understand the taken-for-granted communication processes that produce social roles, relationships, and structures. He often used a theater metaphor to describe communication, drawing parallels between everyday interaction and the ways actors take on roles or bring scripts to life. Goffman defined face as "the positive social value a person effectively claims for himself [or herself] by the line others assume he [or she] has taken during a particular contact. Face is an image of self delineated in terms of approved social attributes" (1967, p. 5). Goffman's work highlights several characteristics key to our understanding of "face."

Face Is Social and Public

Face happens in interactions with other people and this is one way the concept differs from related ideas such as self-image or self-esteem. Face does not refer to how you think about or value yourself but rather to what kind of image is revealed in your own and others' actions. Face is related to your ability to successfully take a "line" or play a role. For example, if I am trying to enact the role of professor in front of a class, I will have a difficult time sustaining that line if the students ignore me, continue talking to their friends, don't take notes, or if someone else stands up and begins giving a simultaneous lecture! Part of my image has to do with how I behave, but it also depends on the actions of others. Face is public in that it is located in observable actions, and it is social in that it involves the actions of all the participants and not just the individual whose face we are considering.

Face Is Situated

We adopt different identities in various interactions (e.g., over the course of a day, I might be a professor, daughter, mother, friend, customer, wife). Losing or saving face has to do with our ability to stay in character and behave in a way that fits with expectations for our role. We lose face when our own behaviors don't fit or because others say or do things that challenge our role. Some ways of losing face have to do with basic violations of civilized behavior, such as having food on your face, falling down, or leaving your fly unzipped. There may be a few situations in which these actions are an expected part of a role (e.g., being a 1-year-old, playing a clown, or joking around) but, for most identities we play as adults, these actions spoil our performance. In contrast, there are other ways of losing face that are more specific to a particular role. For example, if I am presenting myself as an "expert on politeness theory," and I don't know the answer to a simple question about the theory, I would risk losing face. However, if you are just learning about the theory and you ask a simple question, you probably wouldn't lose face, because knowing all about the theory isn't a part of the line you would be taking as "someone just learning about the theory." Some actions are face threatening in just about any situation and, other actions are threatening to a particular role. It's never just a behavior that sustains or loses face but the meaning of that behavior for the lines you and others are taking in a particular context.

Face Is Claimed

As you read about roles, you may be thinking of them as simply given by a relationship, family, group, institution, or society. For example, you might think the role of daughter or son is something you *are* by virtue of birth, or you may think of student and teacher roles as defined by having or not having a degree and position in a university. However, face has to do with our ability to *play* roles. You might be someone's daughter or son by birth and yet not behave in ways that enact that role. I might be designated as the teacher and yet lose face because I fail to act like a teacher. Face is something we claim when we *enact* the characteristics that go along with some line in an interaction and when others *act toward us* in ways that sustain that image. That's why it's possible to lose face, save face, or threaten face.

We're Emotionally Invested in Face

In all of this talk about playing roles it may appear that face is just an act, something distanced from who we really are and what we care about. On the contrary, face evokes emotional reactions. We feel good when we're in face and we feel bad when we're out of face. How good or bad we feel can vary. Sometimes we just feel normal for being in face and sometimes we feel a noticeable sense of accomplishment when we pull off a difficult role performance and others play along. Sometimes losing face involves minor awkwardness or hurt feelings, whereas other instances of face loss cut us deeply. The type of emotional reaction we feel may also vary, including shame, embarrassment, guilt, anger, regret, or anxiety.

There Is a Cooperative Motivation to Honor Face

Each of the preceding four characteristics of face provides a basis for an unspoken social contract in civilized society: I'll save your face and you save mine. Because face is social and public, you can't maintain it by yourself—you have to have the cooperation of others.

Because face is situated and claimed, you can't assume that you'll have it—both parties have to enact it and do things to avoid threatening it. Because we are emotionally invested in face, we have an incentive to want to save face and to sympathize when others lose face. Consequently, much of the time we interact with others under the assumption that all involved will take whatever steps necessary to sustain one another's face. This assumption is so pervasive, that most of the time we don't even realize we are doing it. This is why most people notice and feel embarrassed when they see someone else lose face and why most of us go to great lengths to pretend to ignore someone else's loss of face.

You can probably think of counterexamples to this principle. You may know individuals who rarely pay attention to face, and there are interactions in which we don't want to save face (e.g., in an emergency or other situation in which a message is urgent or the speaker needs to communicate as efficiently as possible) or we actually attack face (e.g., courtroom interaction, Penman, 1990; calls to 911, Tracy & Tracy, 1998; army boot camp, Culpepper, 1996). Although there are exceptions, the unspoken agreement to honor one another's face is a basic operating principle in most of our everyday interactions. It's noticeable and memorable when you have an interaction in which people don't try to honor face and if you know individuals who seldom pay any attention to face, it's likely that many people consider them to be socially unskilled.

Different Aspects of Face

In any interaction, we may be concerned with four different aspects of face. One set of distinctions has to do with *own* versus *other's* face. Any action simultaneously reflects on the speaker's own face (either upholding or undermining my line) and on the hearer's face (either upholding or undermining the lines of others). In addition, there are two different ways actions can threaten or honor face. One way is to undermine or fail to accept the identity being enacted. When we fail to receive validation, this is a threat to face and this desire for approval is referred to as *positive face* wants (because it's a desire *for* approval of identity). The second way to threaten or lose face is when someone fails to show proper respect for the degree of autonomy that is appropriate to an identity. Intrusions or impositions show disrespect for face and this desire for autonomy is referred to as *negative face* wants (because it's a desire for something *not* to happen, namely a desire *not* to be imposed on). The concepts of positive and negative face are integral aspects of politeness theory, which is the focus of this chapter.

POLITENESS THEORY

Imagine that despite your best efforts, you find you can't complete a class paper by the assigned deadline and you need to ask your instructor to accept a late paper. The following are five ways of approaching the situation. Notice what is similar and what is different in these responses:

1. "Let me turn this paper in late."
2. "Hey, Chris, you're really going to laugh when you hear this. You know how you brought the wrong handouts to class last week? Same thing–I finished my paper yesterday afternoon and was gonna print it between classes. I get to the lab, pull out the disk, no file— I brought the wrong disk! I go running back home, back here, up to the lab, down to 244, and the door is locked tight. What can we do about turning this in now so that I can at least get some credit for the paper?"

3. "Professor Rosa, I'm really sorry to bother you with this because I know the policy on late papers. Do you have just a minute? I had the paper finished in time but I brought the wrong disk to campus and by the time I discovered this, I was unable to get the right disk and print the paper in time to meet the deadline. I understand if there is a point penalty but if you could help me out and take this paper I would really really appreciate it!"
4. "I was wondering, is there a policy on late papers in this class?"
5. Decide to take a zero on the assignment rather than ask for special treatment.

We can view these examples as different ways of performing the same basic act: a request to turn in a late paper. Response 1 comes right out and makes the request without saying much of anything else. Responses 2 and 3 eventually make the request but also include a lot of other material. Response 4 doesn't ever say the request explicitly, though it's possible to read between the lines and infer the request. Response 5 chooses not to make the request. Imagine yourself in this situation and consider the following: Which of these responses is the best way to handle the situation? What additional information would you need (e.g., information about the paper assignment, about the instructor, about the student, about the class) to say which response is the best?

Now put yourself in the position of an observer. What kind of student would say something like Response 1? How about Response 4? What inferences would you draw about the instructor to whom these requests are addressed? For example, as you read Response 2, do you envision "Chris" as male or female? Older or younger? A teaching assistant or a full professor? An instructor who teaches a small, informal seminar or a world-renowned lecturer in a large class? When you read Response 3, do you envision a different kind of instructor? Finally, what kind of paper assignment do you imagine this is and what kind of class policy is there about late papers? For example, do some of these messages seem more appropriate for a term paper assigned on the first day of class? Are other messages more likely for an optional one page essay assigned just 1 week ago?

Finally, consider these questions: Why should our language practices provide us with so many different ways of making a simple request? Why wouldn't we just say what we mean when we make a request? Politeness theory grew out of this kind of close attention to the details of language and it suggests a way of answering these kinds of questions. P. Brown and Levinson (1987) are sociolinguists who noticed that three very different languages (the English language spoken in the United States and Great Britain, the Tamil language spoken in an area of South India, and the Tzeltal language spoken in the Chiapas region of Mexico), had some striking similarities in the options they provided for speakers to make requests, give criticisms, respond to compliments, give advice, issue offers, make apologies, and so on. In each of these languages, it was possible for a speaker just to come right out and say what he or she had to say. And yet in each of these languages, there were also a wide variety of alternative ways of saying the same thing.

Face Threatening Acts

P. Brown and Levinson (1987) proposed that our desire to honor face is one reason we don't always say exactly what we mean in the most direct and efficient way possible. Many actions in our everyday conversations have the potential to threaten face. Orders, requests, advice, and warnings threaten negative face, whereas criticism, complaints, or disagreement threaten positive face. Some "face threatening acts" (FTAs) threaten your own face (e.g., apologizing), whereas others threaten your hearer's face (e.g., criticizing). Politeness theory (and most research using the theory) focuses on how we respond to threats to the hearer's face.

We can use the late paper scenario to illustrate the notion of FTA. P. Brown and Levinson (1987) would classify the request to turn in a late paper as a threat to the hearer's negative face. This is because the very definition of a request involves asking a hearer to do something he or she wouldn't otherwise do and so this is an imposition on his or her autonomy. In this particular example, we can also think of other specific ways this request might impose on the instructor. Asking the instructor to make an exception may open up the door for other students to complain or to want to turn their papers in late. The instructor's deadline may have been necessary to give him or her time to grade all the papers, and therefore, a late paper may be an inconvenience. This particular request could also threaten the instructor's positive face. When a student misses a deadline, the instructor might feel the student thinks the class isn't a very important priority. Or the instructor might feel that a request for an exception to a class policy undermines his or her authority to set deadlines and have them taken seriously.

Strategies for Committing FTAs

Anytime we have an FTA to commit, there are a wide variety of ways to do it. *Politeness* refers to all of the verbal and nonverbal resources available in a language for making an FTA less face threatening. This is a broader use of the term than most of us consider in our everyday under-standing of politeness. For example, we might equate politeness with saying "please" or "yes sir" or with making sure you don't take more than your share of a dish that is passed around the table or with saying you enjoyed an outing even if you were bored stiff. These actions do fit within the larger notion of politeness but P. Brown and Levinson (1987) have more in mind than just good manners with strangers in formal situations. Politeness theory encompasses many features of lan-guage use in all kinds of relationships and situations. One of the main contributions of politeness theory is a system for identifying and categorizing different forms of politeness.

One way of committing an FTA is to say it directly and bluntly or *bald on record. On record* refers to the way in which the action is clearly stated—it's there in the actual words that are said. An action is "bald" when you don't say much else. In the previous examples, Response 1 is bald on record. The request is plainly there, and there isn't much else to the message.

A second way of committing an FTA is to do it *on record with positive face redress*. Like bald on record, you do say the FTA (e.g., if you're making a request, you do ask for what you want or if you're giving criticism, you say what's wrong). However, the way you do the FTA also includes various appeals to positive face wants. Positive face redress uses the language of solidarity to stress the speaker's similarity to and approval of the hearer. This may include claiming common ground (e.g., using in-group language, stating you have something in com-mon, joking, seeking to agree or avoid disagreement), conveying that the speaker and hearer are cooperators (e.g., showing you know and care about the hearer's wants, offering or promising something to the hearer, including both people in the activity, giving reasons for cooperation), and fulfilling some wants of the hearer (e.g., promising goods, offering sympathy, showing understanding). Response 2 includes many kinds of positive redress. The speaker calls the instructor by first name and uses informal language (*hey, gonna*). The speaker attempts to make the story of the late paper entertaining by using immediate, action-oriented language. The speaker emphasizes similarity with the hearer by comparing the late paper to the instructor forgetting handouts and portrays the speaker and hearer as cooperators (what can *we* do?).

A third way of committing an FTA is to do it *on record with negative face redress*. The FTA is stated in a way that tries to minimize disrespect or intrusion. Negative face redress speaks the language of deference in order not to offend or impose on the hearer. One common negative face strategy is to be conventionally indirect. For example, when you make a request by saying "Can you do this for me?" the literal meaning of your statement only asks about the hearer's ability to do something but, by convention or custom, we know this is a way of asking the hearer to actually do something as well. Other negative face strategies include the following: don't presume (e.g., asking questions or using hedges), don't coerce (e.g., giving options or explicitly acknowledging your lack of power or right to ask), communicate a desire not to impinge (e.g., apologizing, distancing yourself from the FTA), and explicitly give attention to negative face wants (e.g., giving deference to the other person, acknowledging you are indebted to him or her). Notice how these kinds of strategies give Response 3 a different feel than Response 2. The speaker addresses the instructor by title and last name, apologizes for bothering the instructor, asks if he or she may have a moment, and acknowledges that he or she is imposing by violating the late paper policy. The speaker's description of events in Response 3 is much more formal than the narrative in Response 2, and the speaker acknowledges that he or she would be indebted to the hearer.

A fourth way of committing an FTA is to do it *off record*. In contrast to the first three options, this strategy avoids actually saying the FTA. Instead, the speaker uses hints or ambiguity to get the FTA across. Notice how Response 4 is literally a request for information and not a request to accept a late paper. To interpret Response 4 as a request to accept a late paper, the hearer has to assume that the reason for asking is because the speaker has a late paper and wants to have that paper accepted. If the instructor were to take offense at this implied request, the off record FTA gives the speaker the possibility of denying that he or she really meant to do the FTA. The student could try to save face by replying, "Oh I wasn't asking to turn my paper in late, I just wanted to know what the policy was." Off record strategies also allow the hearer to get the point of the FTA while pretending that his or her face wasn't really threatened. Notice how the instructor responding to Response 4 doesn't have to say "no" to the student's request and create an awkward refusal; instead, he or she can play the helpful role of explaining a class policy and the reasons behind it. The instructor could even respond by asking the student if he or she was having trouble and volunteering to accept the late paper. The indirect request gives the instructor and student lots of leeway to define a closer or more distant relationship and thus provides room to negotiate face and identities. However, it runs the risk of not having the request recognized.

The final option for doing an FTA is not to do it. This strategy usually can't be observed in a conversation, but it is included because silence or choosing not to do an action is another option for handling a situation in which you might commit an FTA.

P. Brown and Levinson (1987) claimed these actions form a continuum from most face threatening (bald on record) to least face threatening (don't do the FTA). Bald on record is most face threatening, because there is no attempt to tone down the face threat or compensate for it. Doing an FTA with redress is less threatening, because the speaker adds material to show respect for face. Positive redress is considered less polite than negative redress because it presumes the other person would be pleased by your gesture of solidarity. The off record option is more polite than any of the on-record options. Face is a symbolic feature of our interactions, one that is public and social. Consequently, it makes a difference whether an FTA is stated or not. If a request to turn in a late paper will inconvenience the instructor, the amount of inconvenience is the same, regardless of whether you ask on record or not. However, by avoiding saying the FTA you have avoided making the threat public and preserved the option of backing away from the FTA. Finally, avoiding the FTA is least threatening because no face threat occurs.

One of the most useful aspects of politeness theory is the way in which it helps us formulate an answer to a practical question: Which option should I use to commit an FTA? Politeness theory says the reasonable thing to do when you need to commit an FTA is to use the form and amount of politeness that is appropriate to the situation. If you go through life afraid to ever commit an FTA, you won't be very successful! If you never made requests or only made them indirectly, you would risk not being able to do many things you need to do in everyday life. At the other extreme, it would be ineffective always to be completely direct and blunt. Others would know exactly what you meant but you would unnecessarily create hard feelings in situations in which greater diplomacy was required. P. Brown and Levinson (1987) say a rational speaker will take into account how much face threat is involved in a particular FTA and then formulate the FTA accordingly. For very large FTAs, a speaker would use the more polite strategies (e.g., don't do the FTA or do it off record). For very minor FTAs, a speaker could be bald on record or add a little positive redress. For medium sized FTAs, speakers can add positive or negative redress.

How do you know whether an FTA is large or small? Politeness theory poses three features of a situation that help to determine the weight of an FTA. One consideration is the *power* (P) of the hearer relative to the speaker. For example, it's a bigger FTA for a subordinate to criticize a superior than it is for a superior to criticize a subordinate. Coworkers who are peers fall somewhere in between. A second consideration is the *distance* (D) between speaker and hearer. D includes social distance and commonality. Imagine you're a dime short at the parking meter and there are two strangers nearby. If one stranger is similar to you in age, sex, and race it would probably seem less threatening for you to ask him or her than to approach a second stranger who is very different from you. D also includes relational closeness. Politeness theory suggests we tolerate FTAs from our intimates that we would find offensive from others. For example, although criticism is seldom enjoyable, politeness theory predicts we find it less difficult to hear from a close other who cares about us than from a stranger. Finally, the size of an FTA depends on its *rank* (R), which involves culturally shared ideas about how much different acts impose on us or undermine our image. For example, if another student you've just met were to ask you how much money you make, would you consider this a minor intrusion on your privacy, along the lines of asking what you study or your home town? Or would you consider this to be none of his or her business? Many Americans feel that as requests for information go, asking how much money someone makes is a fairly big intrusion compared to other kinds of requests for information (Berger, Gardner, Parks, Schulman, & Miller, 1976). However, in some other cultural groups, asking how much money someone makes may not be considered terribly intrusive (Lu, 1997). The request is the same, but the cultural assumptions about how much of an imposition it poses vary.

Taken together, P, D, and R affect the weight of an FTA, and this suggests a way of reasoning about how to commit the FTA. If you have the same request to make of two different people, you can afford to be less polite with a close friend (D) who is a peer (P) than with a stranger who has some power over you. In a close relationship, you can probably be fairly direct about requests or criticisms, but there may be some topics that are especially sensitive or some requests so large (R), that you need to be polite even though you know the other person well.

INTERPRETATIONS, TESTS, AND APPLICATIONS OF POLITENESS THEORY

Politeness theory originally appeared as a book chapter in 1978 (P. Brown & Levinson, 1978) and was so popular that it was re-released as a book in 1987. It continues to be an influential theory. Researchers in many fields have tested the theory and used it to explain many different features of communication. As you might expect when a theory is used by researchers in different fields and studying many different types of phenomena, the theory has been interpreted and used in different ways. This is a testimony to the importance of politeness theory, but it can also be a source of confusion when you read the many studies that purport to have tested or evaluated politeness theory. What counts as a test and what kinds of evidence support or refute the theory depend on how you interpret the goals of the theory. I find it useful to group research on politeness theory into three categories.

A Theory of Message Production

Some researchers use politeness theory to make predictions about what people are likely to say in various situations. For example, a study might examine whether knowing (or manipulating) the P, D, or R in a situation allows us to predict what politeness strategy people will use. Other studies test whether the kinds of messages people produce in response to some situation can be categorized according to the five types of politeness.

A common type of study presents participants with a hypothetical situation that involves an FTA and then asks them what they would say (e.g., Craig, Tracy, & Spisak, 1986; Holtgraves & Yang, 1992; Lambert, 1996; Leichty & Applegate, 1991; Morand, 1996; Roloff & Janiszewski, 1989; Roloff, Janiszewski, McGrath, Burns, & Manrai, 1988) or how likely they would be to use various strategies (Baxter, 1984; Holtgraves, 1986; Holtgraves & Yang, 1990). The kinds of hypothetical situations in these studies come from everyday life, including interactions with friends, family, professors, group members working on a project together, coworkers, and supervisors. Participants in the study read different scenarios (some might read about a person with high power, or closeness, who is committing a small FTA, whereas others would read about a speaker with low power, or closeness, who is making a large FTA). Another research strategy is to collect messages from a face-threatening situation and see if politeness corresponds to P, D, and R in the situation. For example, several studies examine politeness in business correspondence between people with varying P and D and for acts of varying R (Bargiela-Chiappini & Harris, 1996; Yeung, 1997).

Studies that have taken this approach have found partial support for predictions based on politeness theory: Some studies find support, some studies don't, and many studies find a mix of supportive and unsupportive findings. In studies of requests, P most often successfully predicts politeness and R is a fairly good predictor, but D has proven problematic (see Holtgraves, 1992, for a summary). In some studies, respondents are most polite to strangers and acquaintances, whereas in other studies, people are most polite with people they know well. For example, Holtgraves and Yang (1992) asked students to imagine making requests of people with whom they were completely unacquainted, acquainted but not well known to one another, or well-acquainted with each other. They found students wrote the most polite requests with hearers they knew least well and that this effect was strongest for the smallest FTA (asking for the time of day). In contrast, Baxter (1984) found students selected more polite strategies when they imagined interacting with a close friend than with someone they didn't know well. Baxter asked students to imagine they were working on a group project and had to ask another group member to redo his or her part of the project with only 3 days left to go before the project deadline.

Because studies using P, D, and R to predict politeness have had mixed success, some authors have concluded that politeness theory isn't especially useful as a predictive model of what people will say in a situation (Craig et al., 1986). Other researchers claim that with modifications, the theory could still be useful for prediction. One modification concerns whether P, D, and R each have independent influences on politeness (e.g., Holtgraves & Yang, 1990, 1992; Leichty & Applegate, 1991). For example, Holtgraves and Yang (1990) found that distance had the most effect on politeness when the speaker and hearer were peers (equal P); when there were power distances between speaker and hearer, distance didn't affect politeness. Similarly, power differences had the greatest impact on politeness among strangers and didn't have as much effect when speaker and hearer were in a close relationship. This is consistent with recent findings by Dillard, Solomon, and Samp (1996) suggesting we don't pay attention to both P and D simultaneously but rather tend to see one or the other dimension as more salient for understanding a situation.

Another proposed modification to politeness theory differentiates between social similarity and intimacy as part of D. Similarity may allow a speaker to be less polite, but closeness could create an incentive to be more careful of the other person's face (Baxter, 1984; R. Brown & Gilman, 1989; Leichty & Applegate, 1991; Slugoski & Turnbull, 1988). Lim and Bowers (1991) distinguished between two kinds of positive face wants and positive face redress: Desires for fellowship and inclusion can only be addressed by politeness forms that emphasize solidarity and commonality, whereas desires to have others respect our competence and abilities are best met by politeness forms that convey approbation or approval. They also suggest the effects of relational intimacy are different for small and large values of R: for FTAs of small R, we can address close others with less politeness but beyond some threshold, high R requires greater delicacy with close others to avoid damaging a valued relationship.

A Theory of Message Interpretation

Instead of trying to predict *what* people will say, some researchers focus on predicting how people will *interpret* what is said. In these studies, people may or may not behave politely but when a speaker does use redress or indirectness others are predicted to interpret that as more polite than a speaker who is bald on record.

A number of studies have compared the different politeness strategies to see if P. Brown and Levinson's (1987) ordering is correct, including studies of advice-giving (Goldsmith, 1994; Goldsmith & MacGeorge, 2000) and several studies of requests (Becker, Kimmel, & Bevill, 1989; Blum-Kulka ,1987, 1989; Holtgraves & Yang, 1990). Most find only partial support for the prediction that bald-on-record is more polite than positive redress, which is more polite than negative redress, and so on. For example, Holtgraves (1986) had students imagine situations in which they had to discuss a topic that reflected negatively on the hearer (e.g., wearing an ugly outfit or giving a poor presentation). The hypothetical person in the scenario either asked a direct question (e.g., "How do you like my new dress?"), an indirect question (e.g., "Did you notice my new dress?") or made a comment that might be interpreted as an off-record way of soliciting feedback (e.g., "I went shopping this weekend and bought this new dress"). The participants in the study then read several types of replies, including face threatening "direct and true" messages (e.g., "I don't think it looks very good on you"), face-saving false messages (e.g., "I think it looks very good on you") and several kinds of evasive or irrelevant responses. Contrary to what Holtgraves expected, direct questions were viewed as more polite than indirect questions. However, reactions to the potentially face-threatening replies were more consistent with politeness theory: Evasive replies were seen as more polite than direct and true replies. They were also seen as more polite than irrelevant replies.

Several studies find off-record strategies are not necessarily seen as more polite than negatively redressed strategies; however, this may be due to the difficulties of creating truly off-record strategies in questionnaire studies. Off-record strategies are genuinely ambiguous and rely heavily on contextual cues for interpretation, but studies of these strategies frequently use brief examples of off-record statements with little contextual information; moreover, they tend to show the off-record examples right next to on-record examples so that the off-record strategy is no longer ambiguous (Holtgraves, 1992).

Another type of message interpretation study uses politeness theory to predict how messages or speakers will be evaluated by others (Caplan & Samter, 1998; Carson & Cupach, 2000; Goldsmith, 1994; Goldsmith & MacGeorge, 2000; Holtgraves, 1997; Lee, 1999; Spiers, 1998). Politeness theory can be used to predict that when people commit FTAs in ways that match P, D, and R in the situation, they will be seen as behaving appropriately and they will be more effective in achieving their goals. For example, Carson and Cupach (2000) found when managers had to reprimand or correct an employee, subordinates perceived their managers as fairer and more competent when the reproach used redress instead of being direct or attacking face. The reprimanded employees were also less angry and more satisfied with the outcome of the interaction when their managers were polite. Likewise, Lee (1999) found that coworkers who used redress were seen as more likable, competent, and more desirable as colleagues. However, Becker et al. (1989) found that using more politeness strategies doesn't always lead others to perceive the speaker as more polite. In their study, when speakers with high power used highly polite strategies, they were likely to be viewed as being sarcastic rather than polite.

Findings from message interpretation studies have found somewhat better support for politeness theory predictions than message production studies. Nonetheless, one conclusion from this body of research is that the interpretation of politeness and effective use of polite strategies is not like painting by the numbers. Just because a speaker employs a particular polite form does not necessarily guarantee it will be interpreted similarly in different contexts. There is more to honoring face than simply matching a polite form to a predefined assessment of P, D, and R.

A Heuristic Framework

A third interpretation treats politeness theory as a conceptual framework for describing the competing goals that are relevant when we communicate FTAs, the linguistic resources available for addressing these competing goals, and a way of reasoning about making appropriate choices among different ways of communicating (e.g., Aronsson, 1998; Coupland, Grainger, & Coupland, 1988; Tracy & Baratz, 1994). This use of the theory doesn't try to predict what people will say or how people will interpret what is said. Instead, concepts from the theory are used descriptively to focus attention on how actions, identities, and relationships are constructed through the use of language. Politeness theory helps us see some of the communication resources and ways of reasoning that are available to social actors so we can understand how people are able to achieve goals and to explain why some people or some interactions are more successful than others.

Aronsson and Rundstrom's (1989) study of health care interactions is one example of this approach. They studied how a pediatrician's questions or directions might threaten a parent's face (e.g., appearing critical of how the parent cares for the child or imposing a difficult regimen), and they identified various ways of mitigating these threats, including not only strategies from politeness theory but also other interactional moves that were distinctive to this context. For example, they discovered sequences in which doctors employed indirect or negatively redressed politeness with the parent (to the mother of an allergic child, the doctor says "but then it's best to avoid cats, or what do you say?") but then delivering the same message in bald or positively redressed fashion to the child (saying "WHAT?! you SHOULD NOT do that" to the allergic child). The direct interaction with the child (often accompanied by playful positive redress appropriate to an adult–child relationship) ensures that necessary information is delivered clearly but without having to be so direct with the parent (to whom respect for parental authority is due).

Research in this tradition offers several important insights. First, it emphasizes that P, D, and R are not simply predefined qualities that then determine politeness strategies. Instead, there is a reciprocal relation between politeness and conversationalists' perceptions of P, D, and R. P. Brown and Levinson (1987, pp. 228–229) recognized that a speaker could use a more or less polite strategy than might be called for in a situation in order to try to redefine P, D, or R. For example, if a speaker wished to reduce the intimacy of a relationship that is moving too quickly, he or she might intentionally use negative redress strategies to convey to the hearer a desire for greater distance. Similarly, an ambitious employee might want to imply he or she has greater status by using less polite strategies. Aronsson and her colleagues (Aronsson, 1998; Aronsson & Rundstrom, 1989; Aronsson & Satterlund-Larsson, 1987) suggested a choreography metaphor for understanding this aspect of politeness: Polite forms are one of the ways we negotiate the kind of identity and relationship we have as an interaction proceeds.

Second, this way of viewing politeness theory focuses on how the general processes and concepts in politeness theory play out in specific kinds of communication situations. In a particular type of task or event, for what kinds of identities do speaker and hearer desire approval and what kinds of rights to nonintrusion are relevant? What aspects of power and distance are relevant? What kinds of acts are involved in completing the task and in what ways might these threaten face? How might some of the general kinds of linguistic forms described in politeness theory, as well as other situation specific features of communication, be used to achieve task and identity goals? For example, in my research I use concepts from politeness theory as a starting point for understanding how speakers can give advice to a distressed friend or loved one in a way that helps alleviate stress while simultaneously showing respect for face (Goldsmith, 1994, 1999, 2000; Goldsmith & Fitch, 1997; Goldsmith & MacGeorge, 2000). It is possible to make some predictions about what features of advice-giving situations shape participants' reactions to advice and to suggest what features of messages can be used to adapt to a situation to achieve participants' goals. However, it is necessary to combine the general concepts and reasoning in politeness theory with analysis of specific features of the advice-giving task. For example, there are many different bases for power differences in relationships (e.g., status, control of resources). Where advice-giving is concerned, expertise is an aspect of power that is especially relevant: If the advice-giver has little expertise, it is more likely that he or she will be seen as "butting in" by giving advice. In addition, expertise is not simply a characteristic of a speaker that exists apart from the interaction; it can be bolstered or damaged by what the speaker says in the course of giving advice. Specific aspects of how advice comes about in a conversation about a problem also shape perceptions of face threat. The same advice is likely to be seen as more face-threatening if a speaker gives advice unsolicited than if the advice-recipient brings up the topic, admits he or she has a problem, and asks for advice.

STRENGTHS AND LIMITATIONS OF POLITENESS THEORY

Much has been written about politeness theory and scholars differ in their interpretations of how well the original theory has held up to various kinds of tests and applications. I have already pointed to some problems in applying the theory and I hope you have begun to formulate your own questions and opinions about the theory. The following discussion points to some additional areas of controversy as well as some of the ways politeness theory has proven useful.

One controversy in research on politeness theory is its cross-cultural validity. P. Brown and Levinson (1987) suggested positive and negative face wants are a fundamental part of human experience in every culture and they show how the same politeness strategies exist in different languages. Yet they acknowledged that cultures vary in how often they use the different politeness strategies and this contributes to our perceptions of cultural differences in communication (e.g., some cultural groups seem friendlier whereas others seem more reserved). They explained this cultural variability by proposing that members of all cultures have face wants and take into account P, D, and R in reasoning about the appropriate level of politeness in a given situation. However, cultures differ in how they assess P, D, and R. The same situation (e.g., giving criticism to a friend) might be much more face threatening in some cultures than others and the frequency with which FTAs arise in daily life may differ from one culture to the next. In cultures in which power differences are highly salient or in which few relationships are seen as close, the overall tenor of interaction may be much more deferential than in cultures in which relationships tend to be viewed as egalitarian and social distance is minimized. P. Brown and Levinson suggested this variability in P, D, and R can also account for gender differences in politeness (see Shimanoff, 1994, for a review).

Many have questioned P. Brown and Levinson's (1987) views of cultural difference, and several alternative positions have emerged (e.g., Katriel, 1986; Scollon & Scollon, 1995; Ting-Toomey & Kurogi, 1998). These authors contended that the way people understand face, power, distance, indirectness, and the like are deeply embedded in larger systems of cultural knowledge and values. Consequently, these concepts may not be as relevant in other cultural groups or may take on different meaning and significance cross-culturally. For example, Katriel (1986) described situations in which Israeli Sabra engage in a mode of direct and face-threatening speech called *dugri*, which includes expressing blunt, direct disagreement or criticism. They value this *dugri* speech, not because it occurs in situations in which there is little threat to face but because it does threaten face. To engage in this speech in appropriate situations signals that the speaker respects the hearer as a fellow Sabra, one who is tough and committed to a shared value system in which direct talk about solutions to problems is more important than individual feelings. Is it useful to represent this culturally specific way of speaking within the parameters of politeness theory (e.g., *dugri* speech is an example of using a less polite strategy to define a relationship as having low D and equal P)? Or is it more useful to focus on how the Sabra people understand this practice in light of their distinctive history, experience, and beliefs?

Another controversy in politeness theory concerns the identification and categorization of the different types of politeness. One criticism is that the five types of politeness strategies aren't mutually exclusive. People frequently use positive and negative politeness together, and some of the same linguistic forms can be interpreted as performing both positive and negative face work (Craig et al., 1986; Dillard, Wilson, Tusing, & Kinney, 1997; Holtgraves & Yang, 1992). For example, is "do me a favor" a positive redress strategy because of the way it presumptively commands a favor, or a negative redress strategy because it acknowledges you would be doing something as a favor to me (Craig et al., 1986). The strategies in the theory also focus mainly on linguistic forms independent of their content (Goldsmith, 1999). For example, if you want to borrow someone's class notes, and you decide to use the positive redress strategy of complimenting your classmate, is an irrelevant compliment about his or her athletic ability just as good as a compliment specific to his or her note-taking abilities? Politeness theory also doesn't give much attention to the nonverbal aspects of communication that combine with verbal forms to influence perceptions of politeness (Trees & Manusov, 1998).

Third, the theory focuses on isolated speech acts and doesn't consider how the sequence in which an action occurs may influence its implications for face. For example, bald-on-record advice to a friend is less face-threatening if the friend first asked for advice than if the speaker simply volunteers the advice unsolicited (Goldsmith, 2000). Other researchers have examined the dynamics of politeness in sequences of requests for and refusals of sex (Afifi & Lee, 2000), self-disclosure and accounts (Holtgraves, 1992), doctor–patient interactions (Aronsson & Rundstrom, 1989), and business correspondence (Pilegaard, 1997). Face threats may not be intrinsic to particular acts but may instead unfold over a sequence of actions as participants in a conversation draw inferences about one another's broader goals and intentions (Goldsmith, 2000; Jacobs, 1994; Sanders, 1995; Wilson, Kim, & Meischke, 1991/92).

Finally, there is some evidence for individual differences in ways of communicating politeness. O'Keefe (see, 1990, for a summary) found individuals differ in how they reason about face threats and face work. Her theory of message design logic identifies several different ways of responding when a speaker must perform an FTA. She concluded that the pattern of reasoning captured in politeness theory represents but one way of designing a message to address competing needs for accomplishing a task while honoring face. Forgas (1999a, 1999b) explored how mood can alter perceptions of the appropriate degree of politeness in a situation. Both these lines of research explore how politeness behaviors and assessments are related to cognitive processes.

Although many of the claims in politeness theory have proven controversial or problematic, most scholars agree there are many strengths that make it worthwhile to know the theory and to continue to study the concepts and phenomena addressed in the theory. First, the theory has great heuristic value. Concepts from politeness theory help us to understand many different types of communication. By making bold, explicit statements about how concepts are related, the theory has inspired tests and applications that raise new questions about the linkages among language, identity, relational definition, and culture. A second strength of the theory is its broad scope. P. Brown and Levinson (1987) proposed that microscopic aspects of language were related to macroscopic variations in social power, distance, and culture and that language use resulted from a combination of culturally specific and universal processes. Although there are questions about the adequacy of their proposals, their theory encourages scholars to think about these linkages.

A third strength of the theory is especially important for communication scholars. Politeness theory is a different kind of model of communication than many of the theories we are accustomed to encountering in communication studies. In contrast to theories whose primary goal is to predict what people will say, politeness theory appears to be most useful as a model of how to communicate strategically. In this way, the theory can help us to generate different kinds of questions about communication. In contrast to thinking about what people usually do or are likely to do, the theory can help to redirect our attention to what people should do or can do if they want to be effective. It is likely to be most useful to us as a rational model (O'Keefe, 1992) or as a strategic inferential model (Jacobs, 1994) rather than a variable analytic predictive model. It can also direct our attention to the constructive and creative ways that communicators use language to enact identities and relationships over the course of an interaction, particularly if we recall the origins of the theory in Goffman's (1967) concepts of face and face work. Rather than treating the communication situation as a fixed set of factors that determines communication, the concepts and reasoning embodied in politeness theory can help us to focus on the reciprocal relations between communication tasks, identities, relationships, language forms, and sequences.

ADDITIONAL READINGS

Any reader with a deep interest in politeness theory should read the original work by P. Brown and Levinson (the 1987 reissue is especially useful because it includes a review of research and the authors' response). Other useful reviews may be found in R. Brown (1990) and Coupland, Grainger, and Coupland (1988). O'Keefe (1992) provided an especially useful interpretation of politeness theory.

The topics of face and face work are broader than the issues addressed in politeness theory. Goffman (see especially 1967) laid the conceptual foundation for much of the research on face work. Subsequent research is summarized in Cupach and Metts (1994), Meets (1997), and Tracy (1990). Edited books by Ting-Toomey (1994) and Watts, Ide, and Ehrlich (1992) include a variety of essays on face and politeness.

REFERENCES

Afifi, W. A., & Lee, J. W. (2000). Balancing instrumental and identity goals in relationships: The role of request directness and request persistence in the selection of sexual resistance strategies. *Communication Monographs, 67,* 284–305.

Aronsson, K. (1998). Identity-in-interaction and social choreography. *Research on Language and Social Interaction, 31,* 75–89.

Aronsson, K., & Rundstrom, B. (1989). Cats, dogs, and sweets in the clinical negotiation of reality: On politeness and coherence in pediatric discourse. *Language and Society, 18,* 483–504.

Aronsson, K., & Satterlund-Larsson, U. (1987). Politeness strategies and doctor-patient communication: On the social choreography of collaborative thinking. *Journal of Language and Social Psychology, 6,* 1–27.

Bargiela-Chiappini, F., & Harris, S. J. (1996). Requests and status in business correspondence. *Journal of Pragmatics, 26,* 635–662.

Baxter, L. A. (1984). An investigation of compliance-gaining as politeness. *Human Communication Research, 10,* 427–456.

Becker, J. A., Kimmel, H. D., & Bevill, M. J. (1989). The interactive effects of request form and speaker status on judgments of requests. *Journal of Psycholinguistic Research, 18,* 521–531.

Berger, C. R., Gardner, R. R., Parks, M. R., Schulman, L., & Miller, G. R. (1976). Interpersonal epistemology and interpersonal communication. In G. R. Miller (Ed.), *Explorations in Interpersonal Communication* (pp. 149–172). Beverly Hills, CA: Sage.

Blum-Kulka, S. (1987). Indirectness and politeness in requests: Same or different? *Journal of Pragmatics, 11,* 131–146.

Blum-Kulka, S. (1989). Playing it safe: The role of conventionality in indirectness. In S. Blum-Kulka, J. house, & G. Kasper (Eds.), *Cross-cultural pragmatics: Requests and apologies* (pp. 37–70). Norwood, NJ: Ablex.

Brown, P., Levinson, S. (1978). Universals in language usage: Politeness phenomena. In E. Goody (Ed.), *Questions and politenes: Strategies in social interaction* (pp. 56–289). New York: Cambridge University Press.

Brown, P., & Levinson, S. C. (1987). *Politeness: Some universals in language usage.* Cambridge, England: Cambridge University Press.

Brown, R. (1990). Politeness theory: Exemplar and exemplary. In I. Rock (Ed.), *The legacy of Solomon Asch* (pp. 23–38). Hillsdale, NJ: Lawrence Erlbaum Associates, Inc.

Brown, R., & Gilman, A. (1989). Politeness theory and Shakespeare's four major tragedies. *Language in Society, 18,* 159–212.

Caplan, S. E., & Samter, W. (1998). *Younger and older adults' evaluations of supportive messages: Two studies investigating the role of facework in evaluation of socially supportive communication.* Paper presented at the meeting of the National Communication Association, New York.

Carson, C. L., & Cupach, W. R. (2000). Facing corrections in the workplace: The influence of perceived face threat on the consequences of managerial reproaches. *Journal of Applied Communication Research, 28,* 215–234.

Coupland, N., Grainger, K., & Coupland, J. (1988). Politeness in context: Intergenerational issues. *Language in Society, 17,* 253–262.

Craig, R. T., Tracy, K., & Spisak, F. (1986). The discourse of requests: Assessment of a politeness approach, *Human Communication Research, 12,* 437–468.

Culpepper, J. (1996). Toward an anatomy of impoliteness. *Journal of Pragmatics, 25,* 349–367.

Cupach, W., & Metts, S. (1994). *Facework.* Thousand Oaks, CA: Sage.

Dillard, J. P., Solomon, D. H., & Samp, J. A. (1996). Framing social reality: The relevance of relational judgments. *Communication Research, 23,* 703–723.

Dillard, J. P., Wilson, S. R., Tusing, K. J., & Kinney, T. A. (1997). Politeness judgments in personal relationships. *Journal of Language and Social Psychology, 16,* 297–325.

Forgas, J. P. (1999a). Feeling and speaking: Mood effects on verbal communication strategies. *Personality and Social Psychology Bulletin, 25,* 850–863.

Forgas, J. P. (1999b). On feeling good and being rude: Affective influences on language use and request formulations. *Journal of Personality and Social Psychology, 76,* 928–939.

Goffman, E. (1967). *Interaction ritual: Essays on face-to-face behavior.* Garden City, NY: Anchor Books.

Goldsmith, D. J. (1994). The role of face work in supportive communication. In B. Burleson, T. Albrecht, & I. Sarason (Eds.), *The communication of support: Messages, interactions, relationships, and community* (pp. 29–49). Newbury Park, CA: Sage.

Goldsmith, D. J. (1999). Content-based resources for giving face-sensitive advice in troubles talk episodes. *Research on Language and Social Interaction, 32,* 303–336.

Goldsmith, D. J. (2000). Soliciting advice: The role of sequential placement in mitigating face threat. *Communication Monographs, 67,* 1–19.

Goldsmith, D. J., & Fitch, K. (1997). The normative context of advice as social support. *Human Communication Research, 23,* 454–476.

Goldsmith, D. J., & MacGeorge, E. L. (2000). The impact of politeness and relationship on perceived quality of advice about a problem. *Human Communication Research, 26,* 234–263.

Holtgraves, T. (1986). Language structure in social interaction: Perceptions of direct and indirect speech acts and interactants who use them. *Journal of Personality and Social Psychology, 51,* 305–314.

Holtgraves, T. (1992). The linguistic realization of face management: Implications for language production and comprehension, person perception, and cross-cultural communication. *Social Psychology Quarterly, 55,* 141–159.

Holtgraves, T. (1997). Yes, but … Positive politeness in conversational arguments. *Journal of Language and Social Psychology, 16,* 222–239.

Holtgraves, T., & Yang, J. N. (1990). Politeness as universal: Cross-cultural perceptions of request strategies and inferences based on their use. *Journal of Personality and Social Psychology, 59,* 719–729.

Holtgraves, T., & Yang, J. N. (1992). Interpersonal underpinnings of request strategies: General principles and differences due to culture and gender. *Journal of Personality and Social Psychology, 62,* 246–256.

Jacobs, S. (1994). Language and interpersonal communication. In M. Knapp (Ed.), *Handbook of interpersonal communication* (2nd ed., pp. 199–228). Newbury Park, CA: Sage.

Katriel, T. (1986). *Talking straight: Dugri speech in Israeli Sabra culture.* Cambridge, England: Cambridge University Press.

Lambert, B. L. (1996). Face and politeness in pharmacist-physician interaction. *Social Science and Medicine, 43,* 1189–1198.

Lee, F. (1999). Verbal strategies for seeking help in organizations. *Journal of Applied Social Psychology, 29,* 1472–1496.

Leichty, G., & Applegate, J. L. (1991). Social-cognitive and situational influences on the use of face-saving persuasive strategies. *Human Communication Research, 17,* 451–484.

Lim, T. S., & Bowers, J. W. (1991). Facework: Solidarity, approbation, and tact. *Human Communication Research, 17,* 415–450.

Lu, S. (1997). *Intercultural small talk: An ethnographic analysis of interactions among Chinese Americans.* Unpublished dissertation. University of Maryland, College Park, MD.

Metts, S. (1997). Face and facework: Implications for the study of personal relationships. In S. Duck (Ed.), *Handbook of personal relationships* (2nd ed., pp. 373–390). Chichester, England: Wiley.

Morand, D. A. (1996). Dominance, deference, and egalitarianism in organizational interaction: A sociolinguistic analysis of power and politeness. *Organization Science, 7,* 544–556.

O'Keefe, B. J. (1990). The logic of regulative communication: Understanding the rationality of message design. In J. Dillard (Ed.), *Seeking compliance: The production of interpersonal influence messages* (pp. 87–104). Scottsdale, AZ: Gorsuch-Scarisbrick.

O'Keefe, B. J. (1992). Developing and testing rational models of message design. *Human Communication Research, 18,* 637–649.

Penman, R. (1990). Facework and politeness: Multiple goals in courtroom discourse. *Journal of Language and Social Psychology, 9,* 15–38.

Pilegaard, M. (1997). Politeness in written business discourse: A textlinguistic perspective on requests. *Journal of Pragmatics, 28,* 223–244.

Roloff, M. E., & Janiszewski, C. A. (1989). Overcoming obstacles to interpersonal compliance: A principle of message construction. *Human Communication Research, 16,* 33–61.

Roloff, M. E., Janiszewski, C. A., McGrath, M. A., Burns, C. S., & Manrai, L. A. (1988). Acquiring resources from intimates: When obligation substitutes for persuasion. *Human Communication Research, 14,* 364–396.

Sanders, R. E. (1995). A neo-rhetorical perspective: The enactment of role-identities as interactive and strategic. In S. J. Sigman (Ed.), *The consequentiality of communication* (pp. 67–120). Hillsdale, NJ: Lawrence Erlbaum Associates, Inc.

Scollon, R., & Scollon, S. W. (1995). *Intercultural communication.* Oxford, England: Blackwell.

Shimanoff, S. B. (1994). Gender perspectives on facework: Simplistic stereotypes versus complex realities. In S. Ting-Toomey (Ed.), *The challenge of facework: Cross-cultural and interpersonal issues* (pp. 159–208). Albany, NY: SUNY University Press.

Slugoski, B. R., & Turnbull, W. (1988). Cruel to be kind and kind to be cruel: Sarcasm, banter, and social relations. *Journal of Language and Social Psychology, 7,* 101–121.

Spiers, J. A. (1998). The use of face work and politeness theory. *Qualitative Health Research, 8,* 25–47.

Ting-Toomey, S. (1994). *The challenge of facework.* Albany, NY: SUNY Press.

Ting-Toomey, S., & Kurogi, A. (1998). Facework competence in intercultural conflict: An updated face-negotiation theory. *International Journal of Intercultural Relations, 22,* 187–225.

Tracy, K. (1990). The many faces of facework. In H. Giles & W. P. Robinson (Eds.), *Handbook of language and social psychology* (pp. 209–226). New York: Wiley.

Tracy, K., & Baratz, S. (1994). The case for case studies of facework. In S. Ting-Toomey (Ed.), *The challenge of facework: Cross-cultural and interpersonal issues* (pp. 287–306). Albany, NY: SUNY University Press.

Tracy, K., & Tracy, S. J. (1998). Rudeness at 911: Reconceptualizing face and face attack. *Human Communication Research, 25,* 225–251.

Trees, A. R., & Manusov, V. (1998). Managing face concerns in criticism: Integrating nonverbal behaviors as a dimension of politeness in female friendship dyads. *Human Communication Research, 24,* 564–583.

Watts, R. J., Ide, S., & Ehrlich, K. (1992). *Politeness in language: Studies in its history, thought, and practice.* Berlin, Germany: Mouton De Gruyter.

Wilson, S. R., Kim, M. S., & Meischke, H. (1991/92). Evaluating Brown and Levinson's politeness theory: A revised analysis of directives and face. *Research on Language and Social Interaction, 25,* 215–252.

Yeung, L. N. T. (1997). Polite requests in English and Chinese business correspondence in Hong Kong. *Journal of Pragmatics, 27,* 505–522.

QUESTIONS TO PONDER

1. At the beginning of this chapter, I described some of the students' reactions to an in-class demonstration in which I show up for lecture with chocolate on my face. I posed several questions or puzzles about students' reactions on pp. 2–3. How would the theory answer these questions? Do you find these answers satisfying? Later in the chapter, I introduced the late paper request example and posed several questions on pp. 8–9. How would politeness theory answer these questions? Do you find these answers satisfying?

2. Imagine you want to ask your roommate to clean up the tower of dirty dishes in the sink. Can you generate examples of requests that illustrate each of the five politeness strategies? Now imagine these messages being used in a situation in which the two people are brand new roommates. The speaker is a freshman who was lucky to get to room with the hearer who is a senior. Which strategy would you expect? If both roommates are seniors who have roomed together since freshman year, what would you expect?

3. What do you think about the cultural variability argument? Do the assumptions and propositions of politeness theory ring true to your socio-cultural experience or are there aspects of the theory that seem inconsistent? Can you explain cultural differences within the parameters of Brown and Levinson's theory (e.g., as differences in how power, distance, and rank are interpreted) or do the differences suggest a more fundamental revision to politeness theory? Is the theory useful for thinking about gender and communication?

4. Imagine you tell a friend about politeness theory and her reaction is, "It sounds to me like a theory that just wants people to conform to traditional manners and values. It sounds like you're supposed to be fake and not really express how you feel with people. I think true communication should involve just saying what's on your mind." How would Brown and Levinson respond? Do you agree or disagree?

5. Do you find that you tend to be less polite with those to whom you are closest? Are you more polite with strangers than friends? Does it depend on the FTA? What do your experiences suggest about the relationships between politeness, social similarity, distance, and rank?

6. How is the concept of "face" similar to and different from other concepts you may have encountered such as "self esteem," "self-image," or "self-concept"?

13

Accounts

Michael J. Cody
University of Southern California

Deborah Dunn
Westmont College

We all do it. We apologize to friends for not returning phone calls, we make excuses to our bosses for missing deadlines or meetings, and we justify breaking traffic laws when pulled over by police. We hope that people will accept our explanations and not think any less of us. In short, we regularly employ these linguistic devices called *accounts* "whenever an action is subjected to valuative inquiry" (Scott & Lyman, 1968, p. 46). *Valuative inquiry* is a request for an explanation of either an inappropriate or unexpected behavior, or a failure to engage in an appropriate or expected behavior. Sometimes we freely offer an account, without a request for one, when we realize that an explanation for our behavior is in order. Other times, people demand one of us explicitly ("Where were you?") or implicitly through a look of disgust or annoyance (McLaughlin, Cody, & O'Hair, 1983; McLaughlin, Cody, & Rosenstein, 1983).

There are many good reasons to study accounts. For one thing, if you can explain yourself well and minimize negative judgments of your performance and motives, you will probably obtain better jobs, better pay, and better relationships. Likewise, if you can accurately and empathetically judge the accounts offered by others, you can make better decisions in your personal and professional life. We decide whether or not we can trust people or their accounts in an instant; we size up the situation and what we know about the person, and then make a series of decisions. Should I trust him? Do I like her? Is he reliable? Is she competent? Another way to think about the importance of studying accounts is to actively create better relationships at home and at work. If you are knowledgeable about accounts and face needs, you may minimize threats to face and protect the other's self-image, thus minimizing negative reactions. Finally, on a more "macro" or narrative level, accounts help us construct coherent stories and identities when we find ourselves having to cope with traumatic loss like divorce, a failed relationship, or a death in the family (see Harvey, Orbuch, & Weber, 1992; Harvey, Weber, & Orbuch, 1990; Orbuch, 1997; Weber, Harvey, & Melinda, 1987; Weber,

Harvey, & Orbuch, 1992). In these kinds of situations, we don't just come up with one account; rather, we rebuild a self-concept and public image by communicating a story over time. Communicating portions of a larger narrative to friends, therapists, and colleagues solicits needed feedback, including a reality check on the accuracy or fidelity of the account, and garnishes social support (the movies *When Harry Met Sally* and *Living Out Loud* provide good examples of narratives). Sometimes the accounting process helps us understand events that are ongoing, cumulative and repetitive (rather than a traumatic event in the past). Because many long-term relationships and families have shared histories that are detailed, comprehensive, and filled with emotions and memories families develop their own narratives and "accounts" (see Bochner, Ellis, & Tillmann-Healy, 2000).

The focus of this chapter is on the communication and consequences of accounts in interactions. Specifically, we will summarize the literature of communicated accounts and their consequences, including "remedial" work and impression management functions served by accounts, and the theories used to explain their daily use. Multiple theories have emerged in this area, including politeness theory, conflict escalation theory, attribution theory, and impression management theory.

The communication of accounts in society has a long tradition in the social sciences, dating to works on how people "neutralize" offenses or questionable behaviors (Scott & Lyman, 1968; Sykes & Matza, 1957; Goffman, 1971). Much of the early research on accounts focused on what was considered "deviant" behavior (Scott & Lyman, 1968), and many early theories revealed a power bias—it seemed that only powerless individuals were called on to account for their behavior. Today, however, powerful individuals do not escape demands placed on them to apologize or otherwise explain their actions. Every week a politician or corporate leader provides an account for flawed tires, poorly designed cars, tainted meat, accusations of sexual harassment, records of drunk driving, or failed stock predictions. Accounts can even make for good television—from on-air apologies on Montel Williams to the Dutch television show that spotlights regrets for past actions or inaction (Zeelenberg, van der Pligt, & Manstead, 1998).

INTERPERSONAL ACCOUNTING

Types of Accounts

Scott and Lyman (1968) originally proposed two forms of accounts: *excuses* and *justifications*. When using an *excuse*, the communicator admits that the act in question occurred but claims that he or she is not actually responsible for the act. The four common forms of excuses include *appeal to accidents, appeal to biological drives, scapegoating,* and *appeal to defeasibility* (the account giver claims not to have been fully informed about an event and could not predict outcomes that surfaced because of his or her actions or inaction). In each of these forms of an excuse, the account giver's goal is to deny that he or she either intended or was able to control the action in question, and that he or she should not be fully blamed for the event. If the account giver is not blamed, he or she should not be penalized, no conflict should occur, and the interaction (and the relationship between account giver and hearer) should proceed normally.

When using a *justification*, the account giver accepts responsibility for the act in question but denies that it was harmful or tries to claim that it actually had positive consequences. Scott and Lyman discussed six forms of justifications. First, in the *denial of injury* (or "minimization of harm") the account giver claims that no harm came from the action, and thus no penalty should be assessed. In the *denial of victim* the account giver argues that the person who was hurt or affected by the action was not worthy of concern. When using an *appeal to loyalty*, the account giver asserts that loyalty to a group, organization, cause, or friend is more important than the rules that were violated or ignored. The *self-fulfillment* justification involves accepting responsibility for an action, but claims that the act had value due to increasing a person's maturity, growth, or fulfillment. The *condemnation of the condemner* justification involves the claim that because others break the same rules, the account giver should not be personally reprimanded (everyone speeds on the freeway, litters, or fudges on taxes). Finally, in the use of the *sad tale*, the account giver may highlight a dismal, abuse-ridden childhood in order to explain current behaviors.

Some forms of justifications are more credible and influential if they appeal to the values shared by the hearer, fostering a loyalty to the organization or a worthy cause (also, see Hale, 1987). Compare these three accounts:

"I am late for work because I was working with a valued client across town."
"I am late for work because I helped my daughter with her science project this morning."
"I am late for work because I am in training to run the Marathon on Sunday."

Each is a higher loyalty justification, with the first probably eliciting more positive outcomes than the last, but the effectiveness of each depends in large part on the hearer sharing the values of promoting the organization, rearing children, and athleticism (relative to work punctuality).

The main limitation of the Scott and Lyman work is that when actions are called into question, an account giver has more options than merely excusing a behavior or justifying it. Schonbach (1980), first, followed by McLaughlin, Cody, and Rosenstein (1983) and McLaughlin, Cody, and O'Hair (1983), expanded the typology to include two other categories of responses: *refusals* and *apologies/concessions*. *Refusals* can be divided into certain types. First, a person can prove innocence by using logical argument or physical evidence ("There was no stop sign, as it had been blown down in the storm, and I have a photograph to prove it"), which can be effective in traffic court (Cody & McLaughlin, 1988). Alternatively, a person can challenge the authority of the person seeking an account ("You are not my boss anymore; I don't have to explain my actions to you"), or challenge labeling that the behavior was wrong or offensive ("My outburst was actually exactly what this team needed to give it a jump start, creatively"). Further, a person can simply deny the accusation ("I did not have sexual relations with that woman").

In a *concession*, the account giver simply confesses or admits to the act in question. Some concessions are nothing more than admissions of guilt ("Guilty, Your Honor"), but other forms of concessions contain any of several elements of apologies. Goffman (1971), and then Schlenker (1980) and Schonbach (1980), more fully developed elements of apologies. The five elements of a full apology that successfully performs remedial work are:

1. An expression of guilt, remorse, or embarrassment.
2. Clarification that one recognizes what the appropriate conduct would have been and acknowledgment that negative sanctions apply for having committed the failure event.
3. Rejection of the inappropriate conduct and disparagement of the "bad" self that misbehaved.
4. Acknowledgment of the appropriate conduct and a promise to behave accordingly in the future.
5. Penance, restitution, or an offer to compensate the victim(s).

To assess the use or consequences of apologies, research may compare "perfunctory" apologies or simple expressions of regret with "full" or "compensation" apologies (Holtgraves, 1989), or code the number of elements included in the apology/account (Gonzales, Manning, & Haugen, 1992; Gonzales, Pederson, Manning, & Wetter, 1990; also see Bennett & Dewberry, 1994; Scher & Darley, 1997; Schneider, 2000; Steiner, 2000, regarding elements of effective apologies).

Functions Served by Accounts

Accounts are used primarily to defend the "self" from accusation that one did something wrong, and/or engaged in inappropriate behavior(s). Accounts are communicated to satisfy other goals as well: to repair relationships, control emotions, manage or avoid conflict, avoid punishments, and to create or maintain a positive public image. The following sections review the application of theory to particular areas of account giving: (a) politeness theory, (b) Schonbach's theory of conflict escalation, (c) attribution theory, and (d) impression management theory.

THEORIES OF ACCOUNT GIVING

Politeness Theory

In assessing the relative merits of apologies, excuses, justifications and denials, researchers have relied on several theoretical rationales. Early works focused on "face work" or politeness forms (Brown & Levinson, 1978, 1987; Holmes, 1990, 1993; also see chap. 12, this volume), noting that apologies were preferred speech acts for receivers, while justifications and denials were not (McLaughlin, Cody, & O'Hair, 1983; McLaughlin, Cody, & Rosenstein, 1983). As Goldsmith (chap. 12, this volume) discusses in her chapter, this theory presumes two types of "face needs": positive face and negative face. Positive face needs refer to the desire to be liked and respected by others. Positive face occurs and is maintained when interactants communicate messages that reflect appreciation for one another and uphold each other's role during the interaction (usually as a competent, likeable individual). Negative face needs deal with one's desire to be free from constraints and obligations, reflecting the fact that one is autonomous, free to act as he or she desires, not constrained by others. A polite manner of behavior is expected as both interactants cooperate in maintaining face in interaction, and such cooperation is predicated on the notion of the "mutual vulnerability of face" (Brown & Levinson, 1987, p. 61). That is, both individuals need to cooperate to maintain face.

Polite language is generally used under three conditions. First, we are more likely to be polite with others who are more powerful and who might control more rewards and resources (relative to those who have less power and resources). Second, we are more likely to be polite when the type of offense or goal at hand is relatively more serious or important. Third, we are more likely to be polite when we are interacting with others who are socially distant—we are often more polite to our neighbors, friends, and strangers than to our own family members. Holmes (1990) found some exceptions to these rules, however, and named the exceptions the "bulge theory" of interaction. In her New Zealand sample, communicators were more likely to apologize when communicating with others who were neither strangers (a man on a train) nor intimates (spouses or siblings). Holmes believed that when relational definitions are less certain, and less predictable, account givers are more likely to communicate an apology. She found apologies combined with explanations occurred more often among friends when relational definitions might change, rather than among intimates or strangers (see discussion of cultural comparisons).

Nonetheless, the general argument made in the literature on accounts is that a concession, especially an apology, and a "full apology" at that, is more polite and is preferred by hearers. Apologies are more polite because they maintain a high degree of respect and appreciation for the hearer and, of course, pose little or no threat to a hearer's negative face. This assumes, of course, that the apology is not awkwardly or excessively communicated in a public setting, which could be embarrassing and perhaps even demeaning. For example, imagine that your friend just broke your favorite trophy while the two of you were throwing a ball indoors. Your friend recognizes his mistake, offers a full apology, and offers to have the trophy fixed. You may be disappointed about the trophy, but you accept your friend's apology. Accidents happen, right? But now imagine that you are at the office Christmas party, surrounded by dozens of your colleagues and people you want to impress. Your friend and coworker shows up and explains that he accidentally broke your favorite trophy from high school. He goes on and on about how sorry he is because he knows how much that trophy means to you. Plastering an understanding smile on your face you assure your friend that it's no big deal. Others in the group seem amused that you are so attached to your high school trophy. Now they want to know what the trophy was for. You want to scream at your friend to just "shut up!" The problem with this apology, of course, is that it is excessive and public, not to mention potentially embarrassing.

An excuse is considered the second most polite form of an account because the account giver communicates that he or she did not intend for the action to take place, or had no control over the causes leading to the questionable action. Justifications rank third in politeness. In theory, the account giver is not particularly polite because of a failure to support the hearer's positive face. This is so because a justification, by nature, implies that the account receiver has misjudged the situation, thereby threatening the face of the other. In addition, justifications are usually individualistic, or self-serving in some way. Finally, refusals or denials are the least preferred and least polite form of accounting, because no one likes to be challenged, proven wrong, or called a liar.

Politeness theory is relevant to the research on communicated accounts in three ways. First, research on the "account episode" indicates that how one asks for an account strongly influences the account provided by the account giver (Braaten, Cody, & Bell DeTienne, 1993; Cody & Braaten, 1992; Cody & McLaughlin, 1985, 1990; McLaughlin, Cody & O'Hair, 1983; McLaughlin, Cody, & Rosenstein, 1983; Schonbach, 1990; Schonbach & Kleibaumhuter, 1990). This makes sense if you think about it. Using particularly harsh language, a judgmental tone, or even a given relational context can seriously impact the nature of the account episode. The *account episode* is initiated when someone recognizes a *failure event* (a violation of expectations or norms) that needs to be explained. The communication sequence is initiated by a *reproach* (verbally or nonverbally) followed by the communication of an account, and the *evaluation* (honoring the account, rejecting the account, or partially honoring the account and requesting additional explanation). Reproaches can be communicated with varying levels of politeness by supporting the account giver's positive face needs and by avoiding threats to the account giver's negative face.

Originally, researchers contended that there would be a matching of reproach–account–evaluation sequences. Polite reproaches elicit polite accounts. Polite accounts include what are called *mitigating* accounts, including apologies and excuses, and often include a positive evaluation:

"Are you okay? I was worried about you when I got home first and the lights were out … ."
"Oh, I'm sorry about that, I ran into the Rabbi at Starbuck's on the way home and we talked."
"Good."

Reproaches that are less polite are called *aggravating reproaches*, and the more aggravating reproaches are especially threatening to a hearer's negative face. Aggravating reproaches elicit aggravating accounts.

"You're late again! Don't tell me you were shopping again!"
"I'm not late." (denial) (justification)

These aggravating accounts are often then rejected and result in escalation to conflict (see below, Schonbach's theory).

Although two studies found support for polite reproaches eliciting polite accounts (McLaughlin, Cody, & Rosenstein, 1983; Ohbuchi & Sachiko, 1996), others have found that the polite reproach simply allows the account giver freedom to communicate any account he or she wishes to communicate (Cody & McLaughlin, 1990). This conclusion does not contradict politeness theory, however, in that other factors (relational closeness, severity of the offense, status differences) impact on the use of mitigating-aggravating accounts (see below), and communicators are still bound to cooperate in maintaining face during interaction.

Although polite reproaches may not always elicit polite accounts, we do know that with very few exceptions (see Butney, 1993; Dindia & Steele, 1987), aggravating reproaches elicit aggravating accounts (including studies in Japan, see Ohbuchi & Sachiko, 1996). One explanation is that the threat to negative face ("Don't you have to be trained to work here?") elicits an equally aggravating or assertive statement in which the account giver claims or reclaims a desired public role, or face, in his or her defense. However, Schonbach (1990; Schonbach & Kleibaumhuter, 1990) made the same prediction using psychological reactance theory. An aggravating reproach is a threat to the account giver's freedom to behave as he or she desires, reducing the likelihood of behaving in a conciliatory fashion (using an apology or excuse) and increasing the likelihood of using a defensive reaction (denials, justifications). Suppose a teenager is assigned the role of babysitter and the child gets into the kitchen cabinet and plays with poisons and is then taken to the hospital. If the parents appear and simply ask, "What happened?" the teenager is free to communicate an account without restraint and is likely to offer an apology plus an excuse. If the parents appear and communicate a threat to the individual's self-image or self-esteem ("We had hoped that you would be more mature than this … ."), the teenager is less likely to use conciliatory accounts and more likely to defend the self with denials and justifications (see Schonbach, 1990; Schonbach & Kleibaumhuter, 1990).

Although we know of no formal test between the two theoretical explanations (psychological reactance theory compared to the consequences of threatening an account giver's negative face), it appears that not all "aggravating" reproaches are equally aggravating and restraining. Cody and Braaten (1992) assessed over 100 "aggravating" reproach forms sampled from a major bank in Los Angeles (Braaten et al., 1993) and concluded that the forms of reproaches that elicited anger and defensiveness included attacks on another's self-esteem or challenges to another's competency. Personal attacks were seen as more aggravating than when a reproacher was simply angry. If we rely on principles of attribution theory (see below), an account giver is likely to find reproaches aggravating if they involve personal attacks or threats to one's self-concept when the underlying causes of the reproacher's behavior is intentional, controllable, internally motivated, and stable (see below). It also implies that the more aggravating approaches are those that convey a particular social meaning—that the reproacher is derogating the accounter or elevating his or her own role in the encounter. Nonetheless, the general model is that aggravating reproaches elicit aggravating forms of accounts (denials, justifications), aggravating forms of evaluations (rejections), and result in higher levels of anger, stress, and dissatisfaction (see, e.g., Braaten et al., 1993).

The second application of politeness theory focuses on the way that accounts operate in performing *remedial work* in relationships. Apologies are generally thought to be more effective (followed by excuses, justifications, and lastly, denials) in neutralizing negative evaluations, reducing penalties, reducing the perceived seriousness of the offense, reducing anger and aggression, and helping to resolve disputes. A substantial body of literature supports this notion of mitigating or polite accounts in contrast with aggravating or less polite accounts (Barnlund & Yoshioka, 1990; Bean & Johnstone, 1994; Bennett & Earwaker, 1994; Braaten et al., 1993; Cody & McLaughlin, 1985, 1990; Hamilton & Hagiwara, 1992; Holtgraves, 1989; Hupka, Jung, & Silverthorn, 1987; Itoi, Ohbuchi, & Fukuno, 1996; McLaughlin, Cody, & O'Hair, 1983; McLaughlin, Cody, & Rosenstein, 1983; Ohbuchi, Kameda, & Agarie, 1989; Ohbuchi & Sato, 1994; Schonbach, 1980, 1990; Schonbach & Kleibaumhuter; 1990; Sell & Rice, 1988).

Sell and Rice (1988) can serve as an exemplar. Girls were interviewed about how they would respond to parents (higher status, authority) and friends (relationally close others) if they had committed a serious offense (took $5 from mother or friend) or a relatively less serious offense (took potato chips from mother's or friend's lunch). Young girls (first graders) provided only a simple statement of apology. However, fourth and seventh graders offered a variety of apologies, excuses and promises of restitution. As expected from politeness theory, the more serious the offense, the more elaborate the repairs. However, more elaborate repairs were communicated for friends, not mothers. Sell and Rice, like Holmes (1990), concluded that people are motivated and more likely to work on repairing relationships and tarnished images in situations where relationships can change quickly (as with school children), relative to relationships less likely to change (as with parents).

Many of the studies supporting the mitigating effects of apologies and excuses typically examine a single offense in which the severity involved has limited financial outcomes and no legal ramifications. That is, studies focus on taking small amounts of money, or potato chips, being tardy, being awkward (spilling drinks, bumping into others, "unintentional harm"). For long-term or stable, reoccurring offenses that harm others (like racial prejudice and sexual harassment; see Davidson & Friedman, 1998; Dunn & Cody, 2000; Hunter & McClelland, 1991; McClelland & Hunter, 1992), any number of excuses are more aggravating than mitigating. For example, in the area of sexual harassment, relying on an appeal to a biological drive, as in "boys will be boys" or denying intent ("Yes, I did proposition her, but I didn't mean to offend her—she should take it as a compliment!") are perceived as insensitive at best and are received with incredulity (see Dunn & Cody, 2000). Such statements are likely to result in a tarnished public image, being sent to counseling or training in sexual harassment awareness, and withheld promotions. Excuses also can result in a loss of credibility for a number of different reasons. First, the individual fails to grasp the severity of the offense as perceived by the audience members. Next, the individual tries to exonerate him or herself from blame for actions that are repetitive and occurred over time (the typical case for sexual harassment) and could have been altered earlier. Finally, the individual fails to understand the normative obligations and restraints in today's work environment.

The third and most important test of politeness theory is to discover just how universal it is. Itoi et al. (1996) found that when the severity of the offense was high, more elaborate mitigating accounts were required in order to elicit forgiveness. This supports politeness theory. In this study, however, there were some differences between Japanese and American participants. Japanese and Americans both preferred to use apologies, but the second most common strategy for Japanese respondents was to say nothing, or avoid confrontation, whereas Americans indicated a strong preference for using "direct" messages, such as justifications, excuses, and denials. Among Americans, relational closeness reduced the likelihood of using polite forms, like apologies (as politeness theory predicts). Among Japanese, however, relational closeness increased the likelihood that they would say something to their partners, whereas avoidance or saying nothing was preferred when communicating with relationally distant others. Sugimoto (1998) also found that Japanese were more likely to communicate apologies in private to relationally close others in one's in-group, thereby *relationalizing* the apology. She found that Japanese were more concerned with private apologies provided to a greater number of people in their in-group, compared with Americans, who focused more on communicating sincere apologies in public places. Japanese were more concerned with displaying the correct, or amenable, character, whereas Americans indicated that the apology should be spontaneous, original, and sincere.

There are some notable limitations to Brown and Levinson's (1987) politeness theory. Gonzales and colleagues (Gonzales et al., 1992; Gonzales, Pederson, Manning, & Wetter, 1990) found that when the offense was low in severity, high status account givers (relative to those of less status) expended significantly less effort in offering apologies and were less likely to acknowledge their personal responsibility explicitly (as expected in politeness theory). However, as the severity of the offense increased, there were no significant differences between high and low status account givers. Gonzales et al. (1992) also assessed the construction of accounts as a function of blameworthiness (contrasting negligent, accidental, and intentional acts) and gender (most studies support the conclusion that women offer more frequent and more full apologies than men). Although they did find partial support for Brown and Levinson's politeness theory, they basically concluded that the theory was too limiting and simplistic.

For example, imagine that you are in some way responsible for wrecking your friend's car. The severity of harm to your friend's care is great, so you would probably apologize, right? You wouldn't offer a perfunctory apology, "Dude, I'm sorry I wrecked your car." No, you would probably apologize effusely and offer to make restitution. Now imagine that the car you wrecked is your Dad's and you are 16 years old. Obviously, this is a serious offense, but you also want to escape punishment, so you might combine an apology with an excuse or justification (or perhaps deny it altogether!). You might say you're sorry you wrecked the car, but you would probably also combine that with a detailed explanation of the weather conditions, the irrationality of the driver in front of you, and the fact that you were on your way to pick up your little sister from soccer practice.

There are increasing studies that suggest that not all national cultures view accounts and facework in the same way. Ide (1998) completed a study of the use of *sumimasen*, which is a conventional expression of apology in Japanese and is also used to express gratitude. Apologies are so much a part of routine conversation that many Japanese might find it unremarkable.

Similarly, Wierzbicka (1996) questioned the ability of translating Western words like *criticize, self-effacement, apology,* and *thanks* into the Japanese cultural logic. Indeed, Wierzbicka, like Ide (1998) and others, argued that *apology* and *thanks* are intertwined. Japanese adhere to a correct linguistic "formula" type of apology containing many of the elements listed above as a "full apology," whereas Americans are more likely to voice hybrid statements, containing some elements of apologies coupled with statements of accounts (replicating Itoi et al., 1996; also see Sugimoto, 1997, 1998). Sugimoto (1998) also found that in communicating apologies Japanese are much more likely to repeat phrases than Americans ("I am sorry, sorry") and are much more likely to include self-castigation statements compared to the more individualistic Americans.

Politeness theory is predicated on the belief that interactants will jointly cooperate to maintain one another's public face. The theory applies to a set of common, daily experiences in which a single act of harm occurs, probably with minimal financial implications and no legal ramifications, and when a high level of severity (and other factors) elevates the need to reduce anger in the interaction. In examining the assumptions of politeness theory, threats to negative face when requesting the account often elicit less polite, more aggravating accounts; however, rival theories also explain the same finding, such as psychological reactance theory and attribution theory. Politeness behaviors appear to be most affected by the following three factors: status, level of harm or imposition, and relational closeness. We are convinced that increased harm does elicit more politeness of account givers, but the theory as a whole appears insufficient to explain the emergence of accounts for two reasons. First, the three proposed contextual variables interact with one another and the operation of the relational closeness variable has to be qualified. Second, the emergence of accounts in interactions is more complex and involves variables and goals beyond those originally specified by theory. Strong evidence suggests that the most polite accounts (full apologies) are often honored, and reduce anger. However, the relative "politeness" of excuses in the mitigating–aggravating continuum advocated some years ago do not appear to hold true for failure events involving severe harm.

Schonbach's Theory of Conflict Escalation

Schonbach's (1990) theory of conflict escalation (Braaten et al., 1993; Cody & Braaten, 1992; Cody & McLaughlin, 1990; Manusov, Cody, Donohue, & Zappa, 1994; Schonbach & Kleibaumhuter, 1990) relies on the assumption that self-esteem and control are interrelated, interactional variables in theories of account giving. According to Schonbach, the account episode begins with the recognition of a *failure event*, and extends through the reproach, account, and evaluation phases. Threats to one's sense of control or esteem prompt account givers to act defensively, communicating fewer concessions or apologies and more refusals and denials; this, in turn, prompts hearers to reject accounts and evaluate account givers negatively. Severely or harshly worded reproaches actually spur individuals (especially those scoring high on self-esteem and need for control) to act defensively, inspiring increased negative reactions and exchanges if no intervention is made (Braaten et al., 1993; Schonbach & Kleibaumhuter, 1990). For example, Manusov et al. (1994) found that in child custody mediation sessions, divorced parents could produce a series of spiraling, escalating account episodes if the mediator did not intervene early in the session. Once one partner inserted a personal reproach ("No one can trust a druggie … ") a spiral was begun. The account giver not only sought to present a defense of self but then escalated the conflict by taking the opportunity to challenge the public image of the reproacher (Manusov et al., 1994).

You will recall from the previous discussion that Schonbach relied on the theory of psychological reactance in proposing this model, but (as we have already discussed) there is a parallel to politeness theory, and specifically to negative face. By initiating an account episode with a hostile reproach or rebuke, the reproacher threatens the account giver's freedom of autonomy and independence. The limitations of the Schonbach theory include the emphasis on "reacting" to these threats to autonomy, rather than pursuing any other goals (reducing negative feelings, impression management) and the short-sighted nature of the selection of accounts. Most importantly, there is no explanatory mechanism within the Schonbach framework to explain why individuals (especially those with a high need for control) would apologize or otherwise take responsibility for a failure event. Additionally, Schonbach did not explore complex and hybrid forms of accounts (Gonzales et al., 1992) that are rated as difficult to communicate (Holtgraves, 1989). In short, Schonbach's theory is helpful in explaining conflict escalation (as it is designed to do), but it is not a full theory of account giving.

Attribution Theory and the Credibility of Excuses

Attribution theory (see chap. 4, this volume) is important to the research on accounts for two reasons. First, attribution theory deals with judgments concerning why people behave the way they do throughout the account episode. Second, excuses themselves suggest causes for questionable behavior, and certain types of excuses are effective in achieving remedial goals and in controlling the emotions of the audience. Weiner and his colleagues (Weiner, 1986, 1992; Weiner, Amirkhan, Folkes, & Verette, 1987) argued that the perceived underlying causes of behavior include stable (or unstable) causes, internal (or external) causes (or, sometimes, "personal" and "impersonal" causes), controllable (or uncontrollable) causes, and intentional (or unintentional) causes. Excuses citing causes that are unintentional, unstable, uncontrollable, and external are more effective in achieving interpersonal goals than excuses that are intentional, stable, controllable, and internal. For example, if your friend is late picking you up at the airport and on arrival breathlessly tells you that the traffic on the freeway prevented him from arriving on time, you are probably more likely to accept this account and still think highly of him than if your friend told you he got so caught up playing a video game he lost track of time and forgot about you. There is empirical evidence to support this hypothesis.

In the Weiner et al. (1987) study, psychology students acted as confederates and intentionally showed up late for a meeting. One student group was told to communicate a bad excuse, likely to evoke anger, whereas another group was told to communicate a good excuse. Students in the third group were simply told to communicate any excuse they wanted to communicate. Members in the fourth group were instructed not to communicate any reason for being late. The researchers found that 83% of the "good excuses" were ones that involved claims that the student was late due to a sudden, unexpected obligation ("I had to take my mother to the hospital"), a problem in transportation or arrival ("I could not find the room"), or a school demand that kept them from being prompt ("My midterm took longer than expected"). Students allowed to freely communicate any excuse they desired communicated ones just like those instructed to communicate "good excuses." "Bad excuses" were ones that communicated reasons that were internal, intentional, or controllable (i.e., "I ran into friends and stayed to talk to them for a while" or "I forgot"). Account givers who communicated good excuses avoided negative feelings and were rated as more positive, likeable, dependable, sensitive, and friendly than those relying on bad excuses.

This process, making attributions about people based on their accounts, takes place almost without our realizing it. It is important, however, to be conscious of it to achieve our interpersonal goals. Your short-term goal may be to avoid consequences, but probably long-term you want to be thought of highly by others, especially in important relationships and at work. What may get you "off the hook" in the present may actually come back to haunt you over the long haul. Braaten, Cody, and Bell-DeTienne (1993) discovered this in a study conducted among working adults in which they found that relying on excuses may immediately decrease penalties and negative attributions, but long-term reliance on excuses led to attributions of decreased competence and an inability to control one's life. In the workplace, if a manager doesn't believe you capable of being able to handle things that come up, you may get less attractive assignments or responsibility. Furthermore, Sitkin and Bies (1993) suggested that managers overusing explanations in the workplace may come to be viewed as less effective.

Another important element in the account and attribution process was demonstrated in a study by Folkes (1982) in which students used excuses strategically to avoid hurting another person's feelings. Students were asked how they turn down dates, and listed the "real" reason for rejecting the date offer, as well as the "communicated" reason for rejecting the date offer. For example, a woman might tell a man that she can't go out on Saturday due to a prior commitment, but she might actually have turned him down because she found him unattractive or unappealing. Folkes found that the communicated reasons for rejecting others were impersonal, uncontrollable, and unstable causes (she had to study for finals). Other common communicated reasons included impersonal, controllable and unstable causes (she would rather go to a dance than the movies). The true (private) reasons often involved personal, uncontrollable and stable reasons (the male was too old), or personal, controllable, and stable causes (they were of different religions). In short, citing personal reasons were avoided because they were more likely to cause hurt feelings. These findings, that external, uncontrollable, impersonal, or unstable causes operate as "good excuses" have also shown up in research in organizational settings, when dealing with explaining why people were not hired, or when budget requests were denied (Bies, 1987, 1989; Bies & Moag, 1986; Bies & Shapiro, 1988; Bies, Shapiro, & Cummings, 1988; Bies & Sitkin, 1992). Of course, one might ask whether the only goal is to avoid hurting someone else's feelings, or if we ultimately avoid hurting others to avoid negative attributions or consequences for ourselves!

Other researchers (Cody, Kersten, Braaten, & Dickson, 1992) expanded the applicability of attribution theory to accounts by exploring the credibility of apologies, rather than excuses. They examined relational problems that may or may not result in relational dissolution, and had students rate the credibility of apologies (expressing regret and a promise to change one's behavior). Credibility of apologies was high when the student raters believed that the cause was controllable, and therefore solvable. Credibility was low when they believed the cause was intentional. If the relational problems were difficult to control and intentional (public rudeness or anger, jealousy, possessiveness), then expressing remorse, and promising to change lacked credibility. Although support was found for the importance of underlying causes (intentionality, controllability, and stability), the correlations between these causes and the credibility of apologies were small (but significant), and other judgments were pivotal to predicting withdrawal from the relationship and proposed solutions. Social cognitive beliefs about the seriousness of the problem and the relative perceived solvability of the problem were stronger predictions of withdrawing and played a major role in the plans constructed to resolve the relational dispute.

Crisis communication theorists are also interested in understanding accounts in organizational contexts. Tyler (1997) examined the account provided by Exxon in the wake of the Valdez oil spill. She concluded that an outraged public rejected the Exxon account, at least in part, because Exxon could not properly apologize without increasing its blameworthiness and liability. In other words, Exxon had to provide an account not just to "Joe Public" but to stockholders, environmental groups, Alaskan residents, victims of the spill, and legal and governmental representatives and agencies as well. In short, Exxon needed to both take and evade responsibility. This theory of multiple audiences may hold true for individuals as well as organizations. How many times have you been aware of needing to please multiple people at once? A common colloquialism, "damned if you do, and damned if you don't" comes to mind!

Attribution theory is clearly relevant to the communication of excuses and apologies (see McLaughlin, Cody, & Read, 1992). What the application of attribution theory does in this literature base is inform us that communicators and evaluators rely on perceived underlying causes (or exploit alleged communicated causes) to reduce anger, control emotions, and promote a positive image. However, a more comprehensive model that incorporates more than simply the attribution of causes is needed.

Impression Management Theory

The final theoretical position reviewed here is impression management theory. In the domains of psychology, communication, sociology, and management, the term *impression management* may mean different things to different scholars. We emphasize two specific areas of research, including that by Schlenker and his colleagues, who have developed a main theoretical model as well as a "triangle model of accountability" (Schlenker, 1980; Schlenker, Britt, Pennington, Murphy, & Doherty, 1994; Schlenker & Weigold, 1989, 1992; Schlenker, Weigold, & Doherty, 1991; Sheer & Weigold, 1995), and the strategic self-presentation motivations advanced by Baumeister, Jones and Pittman, and colleagues (Baumeister, 1982; Baumeister, Tice, & Hutton, 1989; Jones & Pittman, 1982; Schutz, 1993, 1995, 1997, 1998; Vonk, 1998, 1999).

Work in impression management focuses on how individuals project an image and achieve particular goals through either "assertive" or "defensive" behaviors (Arkin & Sheppard, 1990); the defensive behaviors make this line of work directly relevant to research on accounts. This general approach provides a rich analysis of the communication of accounts and their outcomes, including when and why excuses and justifications are credible and the public images that are created and maintained by using all forms of accounts, from apologies to denials. First, we will review the main elements of impression management theory, followed by a brief description of the "triangle model of accountability." We conclude with a discussion of how impression management theory is applied to the communication of accounts in organizational settings involving fairly serious offenses. Such offenses are likely to motivate account givers to both avoid punishments and monitor public images.

Individuals use accounts to change the hearer's interpretation of events to maximize rewards or minimize punishments. According to the impression management approach, account givers prefer to communicate accounts that explain events in ways that are both beneficial to a desirable identity, and believable (conforming to beliefs hearers are likely to possess about behaviors and events). A "beneficial" identity within the literature on accounts involves not allowing the self to be linked to negative actions (Sheer & Weigold, 1995). Generally speaking, however, there are three main reasons for managing the "beneficial" identity: glorification (promoting and maintaining a positive public image), self-consistency (promoting and maintaining a consistent public image), and accuracy (promoting and maintaining an accurate self-image rather than one that is unrealistic).

According to Schlenker (1980), communicators generally engage in self-enhancing self-presentational styles within the framework of reality constraints and impression regulation constraints. By reality constraints, Schlenker meant that communicators will select a strategy they believe best fits the situation as it appears to be known to the audience; factors determining the reality of the situation include (a) the gravity of the situation; (b) the facts that are known about the situation by the audience members; and (c) the prevailing beliefs the audience has about such situations, as represented by the values and beliefs of a particular society or group. You may have noticed that when you feel terribly wronged, you often want more than an apology. You want the other party to acknowledge the seriousness of the offense and recognize why the act was wrong, and why you are justified in feeling offended. If the other party can communicate all of that to you, *and* apologize, you are not only more likely to be forgiving, you are also more likely to think positively of that person in the future. Judges, juries, and parole boards usually take into account not just the crime committed or time served, they also consider the legitimacy of remorse being expressed as well as empathy for the victims. Remorse, although helpful for the wronged party, may not always be evident, however, especially in potentially litigious situations. You may want a doctor to apologize, or a cop, or a person who discriminated against you at work, but savvy individuals understand that an apology or expression of regret can and will be used against them in a court of law.

Dunn and Cody (2000) compared the relative effectiveness of seven forms of accounts by persons accused of sexual harassment. Both a sample of students and a sample of employees rated excuses and denials low in credibility. The least credible explanation, and the one resulting in the lowest ratings of credibility, likeability, and competence, was a reliance on a *biological drives excuse* ("well, boys will be boys"). This kind of account implies at best that one does not understand or believe in the gravity of the offense, and at worst that one ascribes to cultural rape myths (see Burt, 1980). The most credible explanation was a justification message in which the male accused of sexual harassment accepted responsibility for the action, promised to correct the situation, and explained that he made a mistake in interpreting the woman's earlier behavior. Such a justification (adhering to beliefs about the gravity of the situation, male–female communication, and adopting a proactive stance) was rated as higher in credibility than a full apology, in which the accused male accepted responsibility, expressed regret and remorse, and promised compensation to rectify the situation. Of course, in the case of sexual harassment, a full apology might preserve a public image of being able to take responsibility, but would include an admission of guilt, thereby ultimately damaging one's credibility and, perhaps, longevity in the workplace.

Braaten et al. (1993) also found that accounts were rated more credible (more likely to be "honored") if they adhered to the gravity of the situation and the beliefs people have about the situation at hand. Data included actual interpersonal account episodes from hundreds of bank employees concerning performance evaluations, tardiness, poor judgments in decision making, and "lack of sociability" (not working well with others). The results concerning the honoring of accounts and judgments regarding credibility indicated that the honoring of accounts was strongly influenced by what the account communicated about the account giver's work motives. A full apology was honored often (53.1% of the time), but not a mere "perfunctory apology" (honored only 20.8% of the time), which may be perceived as not adequately adhering to beliefs about the gravity of committing errors at work. An excuse that appealed to "accidents" (events could not be controlled) were more likely to be honored (48.3% of the time) than a "denial of intent" (honored only 30.6% of the time). It is likely that hearers or evaluators may believe that people should be able to direct their intentions to achieve their work goals. Justifications appealing to higher involvement relevant to the work environment ("I was late to do X because I was working with P on Q") were more likely to be honored (39.4% of the time) than justifications that attempted to "minimize harm," again perhaps because such an argument treats work errors too lightly. "Logically proving" that one is innocent was honored 31.3% of the time, more so than other forms of "denials/refusals."

As mentioned previously, Braaten and colleagues (1993) also found that excuses might alleviate a problem initially, but an overreliance on them proved detrimental to long-term impressions of competence. Only a few studies have investigated correlations of accounts and different public images, however. Although excuses may be honored frequently because it is well known that accidents and unexpected circumstances tend to arise without notice, reliance on excuses over time communicates to others that the excuse maker is not able to control outcomes or is not able to achieve his or her intended goals. Hence, an excuse may result in a person being forgiven, but ultimately result in a public image of an ineffective individual. In fact, earlier studies found that workers using justifications (accepting responsibility for one's actions) and refusals were more likely to elicit leadership attributions than were workers relying on excuses (Giacalone, 1988).

In addition to the previous findings regarding the correlation between an account giver and his or her public image, Dunn and Cody (2000) demonstrated that an account giver also impacts the public image of others. In their study of sexual harassment accounts, the male was able to significantly impact the public image of the female, relative to the account provided. Based on four studies, Davidson and Friedman (1998) proposed that in responding to accounts involving injustice, people respond both to the plight of the victim and to the actions of the harm doer. Seiter and Dunn (2001) also found that physical cues (such as attractiveness and mode of dress) also impact attributions of guilt and public image. Furthermore, one's own experiences may impact the extent to which an account hearer empathizes with the victim or the harm doer.

Several projects have linked the communication of accounts to perceived types of self-presentations (Jones & Pittman, 1982). Results show that the communication of accounts influences perceptions of account givers as "ingratiators" (likeable), "exemplifiers" (dedicated, worthy), "self-promoters" (competent, effective, successful), "supplicators" (weak, indecisive, needing help), and "intimidators" (ruthless, strong, dynamic, to be feared). In the workplace study by Braaten and colleagues (1993) mentioned previously, account givers were perceived as more likeable if they apologized (fully) or used the "higher involvement" justification, followed by excuses and the minimize harm justification. Those using denials or challenges to authority were unlikeable. Account givers were rated as both "competent" workers and "dedicated" workers if they used a full apology, justified their actions, or used a "logical proof," demonstrating their innocence. On the other hand, excuse givers (and individuals only communicating a perfunctory apology) were perceived as weak or indecisive, especially if using the "appeal to accident" claim, and people employing excuses were generally rated as less dedicated and competent (compared to those using a full apology or a justification). Images of a person being strong, powerful, ruthless (an "intimidator") followed from challenging a reproacher's authority, or from using a denial.

In the aforementioned study, Dunn and Cody (2000; Study I) found that the accused male was rated most likable, dedicated, and competent if he relied on the "miscommunicated cues justification" (see previous discussion). He was rated lowest in liking, competence, and dedication if he had used excuses (appealing to biological drives or unintentional harm), or denied the accusation and attacked the credibility of the female accuser. In Study II, a sample of working adults confirmed that accepting responsibility for one's actions (miscommunicated cues justification) produced higher ratings of likability, competence, and dedication than skirting responsibility (excuses) or denying responsibility (denials).

As you can see, the evidence suggests that the account communicated directly impacts the impression we make on others. Generally, we are aware of our impressions, but we don't always exert a tremendous effort in this area. For example, you may care a great deal about how you are perceived by your boss or your romantic partner, but you may not care very much about how the grocery clerk sees you. Sometimes we simply want to avoid hurting others.

Folkes (1982) found in her study that individuals who rejected date offers listed a total of 207 private or "real" reasons for rejecting the offer, and the private "true" reasons included a wide range of underlying causes. However, the students actually communicated a total of 68 reasons, most of which focused directly on the causes underlying "good" excuses (impersonal, uncontrollable, unstable causes). Presumably it is more helpful and effective to communicate one "good" excuse to each rejected person, rather than several true reasons that may hurt a person's feelings. Ultimately, we weigh a variety of factors when making accounts to others, including (among other things) our desire to manage an impression, the amount of effort involved in managing that impression, and the audience we are addressing (see Schlenker & Weigold, 1992, pp. 137–158).

One model that is helpful in understanding the linkages between accounts and impressions is the *Triangle Model of Accountability* (Schlenker et al., 1994; Schlenker et al., 1991; Sheer & Weigold, 1995). The three elements in the triangle are *prescriptions, identity,* and *event.* A person is held accountable for actions if the linkages between prescription–event, prescription–identity, and identity–event are strong. Otherwise, if the account giver sought to be free from being held accountable, he or she would communicate messages that would weaken the links. The *prescription–event linkage* refers to whether or not there is a clear set of prescriptions that govern a person's behavior; are there clear traditions, rules, laws, or commandments that dictate behavior? Most colleges now have printed guidelines explaining and forbidding sexual harassment, discrimination, and plagiarism. This is used to hold people more accountable. The *prescription–identity link* refers to the extent to which an account giver is perceived to be bound by the prescriptions. Obviously, the link is strong if the account giver knows that the prescriptions apply to him or her and that there is an obligation, duty, or responsibility to follow the prescriptions. The *identity–event link* refers to perceptions that the account giver was perceived to be motivated to achieve an outcome and to have had some amount of control over the event.

Sheer and Weigold (1995) demonstrated the impact of these linkages in a study assessing two types of offenses—plagiarism and a failed business arrangement. They found that apologies were commonly communicated, followed by an excuse or a justification that focused directly on weakening a link:

"Your instructions were not clear" (prescription–event).
"I didn't think I really had to do exactly as others because of my learning disorder (prescription–identity).
"I had to do a rush job because I am taking six courses this semester to graduate on time" (identity–event).

Theoretically, it is clear that account givers utilize social knowledge about all of the links when claiming that they should not be held responsible; they apologize for the occurrence of the action or their part in it and claim that accountability and blameworthiness is reduced because of ambiguous prescriptions.

SUMMARY AND CONCLUSION

Theory development in the area of communicated accounts began with work on taxonomies of different types of accounts and focused on how accounts emerged in interactions. Early research emphasized whether or not a communicated account would "repair" an ongoing interaction such that two individuals would continue their conversation "normally," with no change or increase in negative feelings and no change in image of the account giver. After a quarter century of testing hypotheses generated from politeness theory, psychological reactance theory, and attribution theory, scholars have moved increasingly into social cognition areas of impression management and self-presentational theories because these theories offer more comprehensive and more detailed views of accounts communicated in a wider range of "failure events," and include more overall outcomes from the communication of accounts. A wider range of "failure events," requires the inclusion of more than simple, singular events of "unintentionally" bumping into others, but also acts of serious consequences (harassment, plagiarism), informed by the knowledge of contexts (organizational settings, traffic court, or other areas where there may be certain "prescriptions" for behavior). Similarly, "more overall outcomes," requires the inclusion of more than perceptions of blame, culpability, or the honoring of an account, but also the interactants' public images, ways of resolving disputes between hearer and account giver (see Braaten et al., 1993; Dunn & Cody, 2000), and ongoing relationships.

Politeness theory assumes that communicators will cooperate, mutually, in maintaining public faces, and the emergence of accounts in interactions is strongly affected by principles of politeness. However, as noted previously, politeness theory itself cannot account for the emergence of different forms of accounts during interactions, and it does not say much about creating or maintaining a public image other than being perceived as polite or impolite. Interactional goals of avoiding negative feelings, building a public image, and avoiding penalties all play a role, producing differential outcomes when the account giver seeks to avoid negative feelings, compared to avoiding penalties. Similarly, Schonbach's theory accounts well for conflict escalation and has been supported in research using the vignette approach, survey approach, and when observing communication in videotaped encounters, including transcripts of child custody mediation sessions. Principles of attribution theory are clearly relevant and applicable to the literature on accounts, and this work is subsumed into the larger literature base of "impression management theories."

Finally, as our work has advanced through the years, we have moved away from simple taxonomies of accounts to more thoroughly understanding the complex elements that comprise the communication and accounting process. In any given communication event, the possibility exists for multiple goals, multiple roles, and multiple audiences, especially as we study more intricate problems from sexual harassment to racism to plagiarism to infidelity. The tendency to simplify such complex interactions must be avoided, yet we must also guard against coming up with ever more specific and detailed models that are applicable only to a small number of contexts.

REFERENCES

Arkin, R. M., & Sheppard, J. A. (1990). Strategic self-presentation: An overview. In M. J. Cody & M. L. McLaughlin (Eds.), *The psychology of tactical communication* (pp. 175–193). Clevedon, England: Multilingual Matters.

Barnlund, D. C., & Yoshioka, M. (1990). Apologies: Japanese and American styles. *International Journal of Intercultural Relations, 14,* 193–206.

Baumeister, R. F. (1982) A self-presentational view of social phenomena. *Psychological Bulletin, 91,* 2–36.

Baumeister, R. F., Tice, D. M., & Hutton, D. B. (1989). Self-presentational motivations and personality differences in self-esteem. *Journal of Personality, 57,* 547–579.

Bean, J. M., & Johnstone, B. (1994). Workplace reasons for saying sorry: Discourse task management and apology in telephone interviews. *Discourse Processes, 17,* 59–81.

Bennett, M., & Dewberry, C. (1994). "I've said I'm sorry, haven't I?" A study of the identity implications and constraints that apologies create for their recipients. *Current Psychology: Developmental, Learning, Personality, Social, 13*(1), 10–20.

Bennett, M., & Earwaker, D. (1994). Victims' responses to apologies: The effects of offender responsibility and offense severity. *Journal of Social Psychology, 134,* 457–464.

Bies, R. J. (1987). The predicament of injustice: The management of moral outrage. In L. L. Cummings & B. M. Staw (Eds.), *Research in organizational behavior* (Vol. 9, pp. 289–319). Greenwich, CT: JAI.

Bies, R. J. (1989). Managing conflict before it happens: The role of accounts. In M. A. Rahim (Ed.), *Managing conflict: An interdisciplinary approach* (pp. 83–91). New York: Praeger.

Bies, R. J., & Moag, J. S. (1986). Interactional justice: Communication criteria of fairness. In R. L. Lewicki, B. H. Sheppard, & M. H. Bazerman (Eds.), *Research on negotiation in organizations* (Vol. 1, pp. 43–55). Greenwich, CT: JAI Press.

Bies, R. J., & Shapiro, D. L. (1988). Voice and justification: Their influence on procedural fairness judgments. *Management Journal, 31,* 676–685.

Bies, R. J., Shapiro, D. L., & Cummings, L. L. (1988). Causal accounts and managing organizational conflict: Is it enough to say it's not my fault? *Communication Research, 15,* 381–399.

Bies, R. J., & Sitkin, S. B. (1992). Excuse-making in organizations: Explanation as legitimation. In M. L. McLaughlin, M. J. Cody, & S. Read (Eds.), *Explaining one's self to others: Reason giving in a social context* (pp. 183–198). Hillsdale, NJ: Lawrence Erlbaum Associates, Inc.

Bochner, A. P., Ellis, C., & Tillmann-Healy, L. M. (2000). Relationships as stories: Accounts, storied lives, evocative narratives. In K. Dindia & S. Duck (Eds.), *Communication and personal relationships* (pp. 13–29). Chichester, England: Wiley.

Braaten, D. O., Cody, M. J., & Bell DeTienne, K. (1993). Account episodes in organizations: Remedial work and impression management. *Management Communication Quarterly, 6,* 219–250.

Brown, P., & Levinson, S. C. (1978). Universals in language usage: Politeness phenomena. In E. Goody (Ed.), *Questions and politeness: Strategies in social interaction* (pp. 56–289). New York: Cambridge University Press.

Brown, P., & Levinson, S. C. (1987). *Politeness: Some universals in language usage.* Cambridge, England: Cambridge University Press.

Burt, M. R. (1980). Cultural myths and support for rape. *Journal of Personality and Social Psychology, 38,* 217–230.

Butney, R. (1993). *Social accountability and communication.* Newbury Park, CA: Sage.

Cody, M. J., & Braaten, D. O. (1992). The social-interactive aspects of account-giving. In M. L. McLaughlin, M. J. Cody, & S. Read (Eds.), *Explaining the self to others* (pp. 225–244). Hillsdale, NJ: Lawrence Erlbaum Associates, Inc.

Cody, M. J., Kersten, L., Braaten, D. O., & Dickson, R. (1992). Coping with relational dissolutions: Attributions, account–credibility and plans for resolving conflicts. In J. H. Harvey, T. L. Orbuch, & A. L. Weber (Eds.), *Attributions, accounts, and close relationships* (pp. 93–115). New York: Springer-Verlag.

Cody, M. J., & McLaughlin, M. L. (1985). Models for the sequential construction of accounting episodes: Situational and interactional constraints on message selection and evaluation. In R. L. Street & J. N. Cappella (Eds.), *Sequence and pattern in communicative behavior* (pp. 50–69). London: Edward Arnold.

Cody, M. J., & McLaughlin, M. L. (1988). Accounts on trial: Oral arguments in traffic court. In C. Antaki (Ed.), *Analysing everyday explanation: A casebook of methods* (pp. 113–126). London: Sage.

Cody, M. J., & McLaughlin, M. L. (1990). Interpersonal accounting. In H. Giles & P. Robinson (Eds.), *Handbook of language and social psychology* (pp. 227–255). London: Wiley.

Davidson, M., & Friedman, R. A. (1998). When excuses don't work: The persistent injustice effect among Black managers. *Administrative Science Quarterly, 43,* 154–183.

Dindia, K., & Steele, D. J. (1987, May). *Account sequences in medical encounters.* Paper presented to the International Communication Association, Boston.

Dunn, D., & Cody, M. J. (2000). Account credibility and public image: Excuses, justifications, denials, and sexual harassment. *Communication Monographs, 67*(4), 372–391.

Folkes, V. S. (1982). Communicating the causes of social rejection. *Journal of Experimental Social Psychology, 18,* 235–252.

Giacalone, R. A. (1988). The effect of administrative accounts and gender on the perception of leadership. *Group and Organizational Studies, 13,* 195–201.

Goffman, E. (1971). *Relations in public: Microstudies of the public order.* New York: Basic Books.

Gonzales, M. H., Manning, D. J., & Haugen, J. A. (1992). Explaining our sins: Factors influencing offender accounts and anticipated victim responses. *Journal of Personality and Social Psychology, 62,* 958–971.

Gonzales, M. H., Pederson, J. H., Manning, D. J., & Wetter, D. W. (1990). Pardon my gaffe: Effects of sex, status, and consequence severity on accounts. *Journal of Personality and Social Psychology, 58,* 610–621.

Hale, C. L. (1987). A comparison of accounts: When is a failure not a failure? *Journal of Language and Social Psychology, 6,* 117–132.

Hamilton, V. L., & Hagiwara, S. (1992). Roles, responsibilities, and accounts across cultures. *International Journal of Psychology, 27,* 157–179.

Harvey, J. H., Orbuch, T. L., & Weber, A. L. (Eds.) (1992). *Attributions, accounts, and close relationships.* New York: Springer-Verlag.

Harvey, J. H., Weber, A. L., & Orbuch, T. L. (1990). *Interpersonal accounts: A social psychological perspective.* Oxford, England: Basil Blackwell.

Holmes, J. (1990). Apologies in New Zealand English. *Language in Society, 19,* 155–199.

Holmes, J. (1993). New Zealand women are good to talk to: An analysis of politeness strategies in interaction. *Journal of Pragmatics, 20,* 91–116.

Holtgraves, T. (1989). The form and function of remedial moves: Reported use, psychological reality, and perceived effectiveness. *Journal of Language and Social Psychology, 8,* 1–16.

Hunter, C., & McClelland, K. (1991). Honoring accounts for sexual harassment: A factorial survey analysis. *Sex Roles, 24,* 725–751.

Hupka, R. B., Jung, J., & Silverthorn, K. (1987). Perceived acceptability of apologies, excuses and justifications in jealousy predicaments. *Journal of Social Behavior and Personality, 2,* 303–313.

Ide, R. (1998). "Sorry for your kindness:" Japanese interactional ritual in public discourse. *Journal of Pragmatics, 29*(5), 509–529.

Itoi, R., Ohbuchi, K. I., & Fukuno, M. (1996). A cross-cultural study of preference of accounts: Relationship closeness, harm severity, and motives of account making. *Journal of Applied Social Psychology, 26,* 913–934.

Jones, E. E., & Pittman, T. S. (1982). Toward a general theory of strategic self-presentation. In J. Suls (Ed.), *Psychological perspectives on the self* (pp. 231–262). Hillsdale, NJ: Lawrence Erlbaum Associates, Inc.

Manusov, V., Cody, M. J., Donohue, W., & Zappa, J. (1994). Accounts in child custody mediation sessions. *Journal of Applied Communication, 22,* 1–15.

McClelland, K., & Hunter, C. (1992). The perceived seriousness of racial harassment. *Social Problems, 39,* 92–107.

McLaughlin, M. L., Cody, M. J., & O'Hair, J. D. (1983). The management of failure events: Some contextual determinants of accounting behavior. *Human Communication Research, 9,* 209–224.

McLaughlin, M. L., Cody, M. J., & Read, S. J. (Eds.) (1992). *Explaining one's self to others: Reason giving in a social context.* Hillsdale, NJ: Lawrence Erlbaum Associates, Inc.

McLaughlin, M. L., Cody, M. J., & Rosenstein, N. E. (1983). Account sequences in conversations with strangers. *Communication Monographs, 50,* 102–105.

Mongeau, P. A., & Blalock, J. (1994). Student evaluations of instructor immediacy and sexually harassing behaviors: An experimental investigation. *Journal of Applied Communication Research, 22,* 256–272.

Mongeau, P. A., Hale, J. L., & Alles, M. (1994). An experimental investigation of accounts and attributions following sexual infidelity. *Communication Monographs, 61,* 326–344.

Ohbuchi, K., Kameda, M., & Agarie, N. (1989). Apology as aggression control: Its role in mediating appraisal of and response to harm. *Journal of Personality and Social Psychology, 56,* 219–228.

Ohbuchi, K. I., & Sachiko, C. (1996). Mitigation of interpersonal conflicts: Politeness and time pressure. *Personality and Social Psychology Bulletin, 22*(10), 1035–1042.

Ohbuchi, K. I., & Sato, K. (1994). Children's reactions to mitigating accounts: Apologies, excuses, and intentionality of harm. *Journal of Social Psychology, 134,* 5–17.

Orbuch, T. L. (1997). People's accounts count: The sociology of accounts. *Annual Review in Sociology, 23,* 455–478.

Scher, S. J., & Darley, J. M. (1997). How effective are the things people say to apologize? Effects of the realization of the apology speech act. *Journal of Psycholinguistic Research, 26*(1), 127–140.

Schlenker, B. R. (1980). *Impression management: The self-concept, social identity, and interpersonal relations.* Pacific Grove, CA: Brooks/Cole.

Schlenker, B. R., Britt, T. W., Pennington, J., Murphy, R., & Doherty, K. (1994). The triangle model of responsibility. *Psychological Review, 101,* 632–652.

Schlenker, B. R., & Weigold, M. F. (1989). Self-identification and accountability. In R. A. Giacalone & P. Rosenfeld (Ed.), *Impression management in the organization* (pp. 21–43). Hillsdale, NJ: Lawrence Erlbaum Associates, Inc.

Schlenker, B. R., & Weigold, M. F. (1992). Interpersonal processes involving impression regulation and management. *Annual Review of Psychology, 43,* 133–168.

Schlenker, B. R., Weigold, M. F., & Doherty, K. (1991). Coping with accountability: Self-identification and evaluative reckonings. In C. R. Synder & D. R. Forsyth (Eds.), *Handbook of social and clinical psychology* (pp. 96–115). New York: Pergamon.

Schneider, C. (2000). What it means to be sorry: The power of apology in mediation. *Mediation Quarterly, 17*(3), 265–280.

Schonbach, P. (1980). A category system for account phases. *European Journal of Social Psychology, 10,* 195–200.

Schonbach, P. (1990). *Account episodes: The management or escalation of conflict.* Cambridge, England: Cambridge University Press.

Schonbach, P., & Kleibaumhuter, P. (1990). Severity of reproach and defensiveness of accounts. In M. J. Cody & M. L. McLaughlin (Eds.), *The psychology of tactical communication* (pp. 229–243). Clevedon, England: Multilingual Matters, Ltd.

Schutz, A. (1993). Self-presentational tactics used in a German election campaign. *Political Psychology, 14,* 469–491.

Schutz, A. (1995). Entertainers, expert or public servants? Politicians' self-presentation on television talk shows. *Political Communication, 12,* 211–221.

Schutz, A. (1997). Self-presentational tactics of talk-show guests: A comparison of politicians, experts and entertainers. *Journal of Applied Social Psychology, 27,* 1941–1952.

Schutz, A. (1998). Assertive, offensive, protective, and defensive styles of self- presentation: A taxonomy. *The Journal of Psychology, 132*(6), 611–628.

Scott, M. B., & Lyman, S. M. (1968). Accounts. *American Sociology Review, 33,* 46–62.

Seiter, J. S., & Dunn, D. (2001). Beauty and believability in sexual harassment cases: Does physical attractiveness affect perceptions of veracity and the likelihood of being harassed? *Communication Research Reports, 17*(2), 203–209.

Sell, M. A., & Rice, M. L. (1988). Girls' excuses: Listener, severity of violation, and developmental effects. *Discourse Processes, 11,* 357–371.

Sheer, V. C., & Weigold, M. F. (1995). Managing threats to identity: The accountability triangle and strategic accounting. *Communication Research, 22,* 592–611.

Sitkin, S. B., & Bies, R. J. (1993). Social accounts in conflict situations: Using explanations to manage conflict. *Human Relations, 46,* 349–370.

Steiner, C. (2000). Apology: The transactional analysis of a fundamental exchange. *Transactional Analysis Journal, 30*(2), 145–149.

Sugimoto, N. (1997). A Japan–U.S. comparison of apology styles. *Communication Research, 24*(4), 349–369.

Sugimoto, N. (1998). Norms of apology depicted in U.S. American and Japanese literature on manners and etiquette. *International Journal of Intercultural Relations, 22*(3), 251–276.

Sykes, G. M., & Matza, D. (1957). Techniques of neutralization. *American Sociological Review, 22,* 667–669.

Tyler, L. (1977). Liability means never being able to say you're sorry: Corporate guilt, legal constraints, and defensiveness in corporate communication. *Management Communication Quarterly, 11*(1), 51–73.

Vonk, R. (1998). The slime effect: Suspicion and dislike of likeable behavior toward superiors. *Journal of Personality and Social Psychology, 74,* 849–864.

Vonk, R. (1999). Impression formation and impression management: Motives, traits, and likability inferred from self-promoting and self-deprecating behavior. *Social Cognition, 17*(4), 390–412.

Weber, A. L., Harvey, J. H., & Melinda, A. S. (1987). The nature and motivations of accounts for failed relationships. In R. Burnett, P. McGhee, & D. Clarke (Eds.), *Accounting for relationships: Explanation, representation, and knowledge* (pp. 114–133). London: Methuen.

Weber, A. L., Harvey, J. H., & Orbuch, T. L. (1992). Communicating accounts of relational conflict. In M. L. McLaughlin, M. J. Cody, & S.J. Read (Eds.) *Explaining the self to others: Reason-giving in a social context* (pp. 261–280). Hillsdale, NJ: Lawrence Erlbaum Associates, Inc.

Weiner, B. (1986). *An attribution theory of motivation and emotion.* New York: Springer-Verlag.

Weiner, B. (1992). Excuses in everyday interaction. In M. L. McLaughlin, M. J. Cody, & S. J. Read (Eds.), *Explaining the self to others: Reason-giving in a social context* (pp. 131–146). Hillsdale, NJ: Lawrence Erlbaum Associates, Inc.

Weiner, B., Amirkhan, J., Folkes, V. S., & Verette, J. A. (1987). An attributional analysis of excuse making: Studies of a naïve theory of emotion. *Journal of Personality and Social Psychology, 52,* 316–324.

Wierzbicka, A. (1996). Japanese cultural scripts: Cultural psychology and "cultural grammar." *Ethos, 24*(3), 527–555.

Zeelenberg, M., van der Pligt, J., & Manstead, A. S. R. (1998). Undoing regret on Dutch television: Apologizing for interpersonal regrets involving actions or inactions. *Personality and Social Psychology Bulletin, 24*(10), 1113–1119.

QUESTIONS TO PONDER

1. Think about a recent argument or problem you experienced with a close friend or family member. How satisfied are you with the outcome? Now think back to some of the specifics. Did you receive an apology, an excuse, a denial? How satisfied would you be if you'd received a full apology right up front? Or a full-fledged denial? Could you have ended the argument or avoided it altogether if you'd apologized?

2. Americans like apologies to be sincere, and feel spontaneous. How would you react if you knew that your close friend or romantic partner "used" apologies in order to manipulate you?

3. Think back to a time when you had to decide who was telling the truth in a matter. Maybe you refereed a game, or an argument among children, or even between your parents. Perhaps you sat on a jury. How did you decide who was telling the truth, or who was at fault? Did you rely on their accounts? How much did their personal appearance, their demeanor, or their communication style impact your judgment?

4. Attribution theorists have noted this basic human tendency: When we are presenting an account, we typically reference the things that were beyond our control—we want others to give us a break and recognize that the traffic or the weather or our alarm clocks worked against us. Yet when we are evaluating someone else's account we typically think that their problem is more internal (they should have brought an umbrella, installed a back-up battery for their alarm clock, or left the house 15 minutes earlier). Have you noticed this tendency in your own interactions?

5. Imagine you are the president or leader of a large corporation. You are declaring bankruptcy. You have only been the leader for six months, and clearly the problems started long before you arrived. Do you take responsibility for the bankruptcy and apologize, or do you issue a statement pointing to all of the problems that existed before your arrival? During the Asian financial crisis of the late 1990s, some very strong Japanese institutions failed. It was not uncommon to see the leaders weeping and apologetic on the evening news, even when most analysts agreed that failure was not the individual's fault. Can you imagine an American CEO weeping and repeatedly apologizing in this manner? Why or why not?

14

Communication Privacy Management Theory

Mary Claire Morr Serewicz
University of Denver

Sandra Petronio
Indiana University-Purdue University, Indianapolis

In an episode of the television series *Ed* (Beckerman, Burnett, & Van Patten, 2003), Ed's new girlfriend, Frankie, is jealous of Ed's relationship with his friend Carol. One night, Frankie asks Ed to tell her about his history with Carol. Ed gives Frankie a brief, but accurate, account of their relationship. He tells her that, following the breakup of his marriage, he moved back to his hometown, asked out Carol (the girl he had had a crush on in high school), and she turned him down. Now they are good friends. Frankie is not satisfied with the story. The following night, while they are at a bar with Ed's friends, Frankie finds herself alone with the other women. She mentions to Carol that Ed told her their story. The women start to reminisce about all of the crazy things Ed has done to persuade Carol to go out with him. Over the past 3 years, he delivered flowers to Carol while dressed in a knight's suit of armor, hired a sky writer, made a music video, and threw frozen waffles at Carol's bedroom window. Frankie is furious, and, as they leave the bar, she accuses Ed of lying to her. She recounts all of the things the women said about Ed's behavior toward Carol. Ed argues that he did not lie—after all, the information he gave her was true. He just omitted a few things. Who do you think is right, Ed or Frankie? How much information does Frankie have a right to know about Ed's past relationships?

Although this example is fictional, the issue at stake is a common one for couples. How much information do people expect or feel they have a right to know about their partners' former relationships? Is Ed lying to Frankie, or is he protecting his privacy when he withholds information about his ex-girlfriend? What factors do people use to decide whether they share private information with a new partner?

The theory of Communication Privacy Management (CPM) provides a framework for understanding such issues of privacy and disclosure (Petronio, 2002). According to CPM, *privacy* is "the feeling that one has the right to own private information" (Petronio, 2002, p. 5). Because CPM is defined as a dialectical theory (see chap. 15, this volume), it argues that people feel forces pushing and pulling them to reveal information and to conceal information from others. Both opposing forces operate simultaneously, but at particular moments, one or the other may be more dominant. This means that both privacy and disclosure coexist. Even when people disclose, they never tell all that is private to them because limiting information that others know is one way people retain autonomy.

Consequently, people make decisions about handling information based on the simultaneous strength of their desires to disclose information and to protect their privacy. The decisions that people make can take a variety of forms. In the extreme, a person may keep information completely secret or tell another person every detail. However, there are innumerable ways that people may choose to manage their privacy that fall between those two extremes. In the previous example, Ed did not choose either extreme of telling Frankie every detail about Carol or of refusing to tell her anything at all. Instead, he chose the middle ground by telling her just some information (Beckerman et al., 2003).

In this chapter, we explain the principles of CPM theory. The theory presents five suppositions (basic assumptions or principles that make up the foundation of the theory) and argues that people use three main processes to manage their privacy through communication. After explaining the theory, we trace the way that CPM has developed over time. Finally, we will present some examples of the ways that researchers have used CPM to understand particular privacy management contexts.

THE BASICS OF CPM

CPM explains the ways that people control information that belongs to them (i.e., private information); it also takes into account the parallel needs people have to both share and withhold information (Petronio, 2002). Think of the information that you consider yours. This information probably includes such topics as your age, height, weight, family background, education, fears, hopes, personal goals, preferences, and beliefs. How do you handle this information? How do you decide when, to whom, and under what circumstances you reveal and conceal specific pieces of your personally private information? CPM gives us a theoretical perspective that helps to answer those questions.

Five primary theoretical suppositions form the basis of CPM. Those suppositions are (a) private information is the content of disclosures, (b) there is a metaphorical boundary or border between public and private, (c) people desire control over private information because they own this information and sharing it makes them vulnerable, (d) people use a rule-based system to manage private information in interaction, and (e) privacy-disclosure is a dialectical tension in relationships (Petronio, 2002).

Theoretical Suppositions

Private Information.   The first supposition of CPM places private information at the heart of disclosure. Other theories about disclosure have emphasized "self-disclosure" as the sharing of information about oneself (e.g., Altman & Taylor, 1973). In addition, some researchers tended to equate disclosure with intimacy, arguing that sharing information is the way that people develop closeness in their relationships (see Parks, 1982, for arguments against this view). CPM instead says that private information is the content of disclosure and revealing or concealing is the process with which people manage the information (Petronio, 2002). This statement differs from other researchers' ideas in two important ways.

First, according to CPM, *private information* is information that is inaccessible to others. In some cases, the information is about oneself, as when you tell someone the grade you received on your last exam. In other cases, though, the information might not belong to you alone. Instead, you might share ownership of information with significant relational partners, like a best friend or a spouse, with members of groups to which you belong, like your family or a club, and with entire organizations, like members of your religious group or students at your university. Information about your family relationships might not belong just to you, but also to the members of your family. Suppose that Jane were to tell Dan about the fight that she had with her sister last night. This information does belong to Jane, but it also belongs to her sister. Because the conflict happened while Jane and her sister were alone, it is not public or accessible to others. However, there are two owners of the information. Therefore, Jane's disclosure to Dan does not fit neatly into the definition of "self-disclosure" because the information is not about Jane alone. However, it does fit the definition of private disclosure according to CPM (Petronio, 2002). Because Jane owns the information (even though she shares ownership with her sister), and the information is not readily accessible to others, her statement to Dan is a disclosure of private information.

Second, defining disclosure as the sharing of private information separates the process of disclosing information from the process of developing intimacy with another person. Disclosure might have the result or means of increasing intimacy between two people. Nevertheless, there is more to intimacy than revealing information about oneself. Take, for example, the phenomenon of the "stranger on the train" (Jourard, 1970). According to this principle, people who have close contact with another person and do not expect to see him or her again might disclose large amounts of information to that person. For example, Victoria found herself sitting next to a stranger named Steve on a long plane flight. In the course of the flight, Steve told Victoria how he and his female friend had decided to have a baby together. After the child was born, Steve's friend married another man and moved across the country. Steve revealed to Victoria that he misses his son and is jealous of the relationship that his son has with his stepfather, whom the boy calls "Daddy." This man revealed plenty of personally private information that might make him feel vulnerable. However, that disclosure by itself does not create an intimate relationship between Steve and Victoria. There is more to intimacy than just sharing information about the self.

In addition, sharing private information might increase intimacy in some situations, but, in others, the effect of disclosure may be different (Orrego et al., 2000). Once again, take this situation between Jane and Dan. What would happen if Jane revealed to Dan that the fight with her sister was about how Dan—who is her sister's husband—is interfering with the sisters' relationship? Jane's statement is a private disclosure, but it is unlikely to bring Dan and Jane closer together. There are also cases in which individuals would rather not have others disclose to them. For instance, people whose jobs make them targets of disclosure, such as bartenders and hairdressers, have customers who often disclose excessive amounts of private information to them. In these cases, disclosure does not result in closeness between the discloser and the confidant (Petronio, Scheibel, & Snider, 1991). Instead, we would expect that the customer feels relief in sharing troubling information; yet, bartenders or hairdressers often feel the burden of having to deal with another person's troubles (see Petronio, 2002, for a more detailed explanation). Although increased intimacy is one possible consequence of private disclosure, disclosure is not sufficient to create intimacy, and intimacy does not automatically result from disclosure.

Privacy Boundaries.   CPM uses a metaphor of boundaries to represent the border around private information that a person or group owns (Petronio, 1991, 2002). Think about the kinds of physical boundaries that people use to separate private and public space. Children put "Keep Out" signs on bedroom doors, homeowners build fences around their property, and countries put up barbed wire and station guards at their borders. These boundaries can differ in the ease with which a person can gain access to the space inside the border. Neighbors can look through chain-link fences at the property next door but cannot so easily look through a stone wall around the house down the street.

In a similar fashion, people mark the borders of information that should be private. Some people have large boundaries, retaining ownership of large amounts of information for themselves. Others have small boundaries, considering very little information to be theirs alone. Boundaries around private information also differ in their permeability, that is, people allow differing levels of information to flow in and out of their privacy boundaries. Some people and groups have highly permeable boundaries, so that information flows through easily to people outside the boundary. Others have highly impermeable boundaries, and outsiders will have great difficulty in gaining access to the information inside. Young children, for instance, usually have small, highly permeable boundaries. Their parents have access to most information about them, meaning that their boundaries are very limited. In addition, young children typically do not vigilantly guard the information about themselves from others, resulting in more highly permeable boundaries. Parents often have to teach their children the benefit of learning how to regulate accessibility in reaction to the children freely disclosing their less complimentary observations about the way someone looks. Teenagers, on the other hand, are capable of keeping more information private from their parents than are small children. They also might be more careful in the way they share information about themselves. As a result, teenagers are likely to have larger and less permeable boundaries than are younger children. This tendency to restrict private information for teens is part of a process called "deindividu-ation" in which adolescents build more and more autonomy (Youniss & Smollar, 1985).

The example of children and teenagers illustrates how an individual's privacy boundaries may change over time. The same is true for adults as well as large groups of people. For instance, the Freedom of Information act changed the nature of the U.S. government's privacy boundaries. Because ordinary citizens gained access to information that was previously with-held from them, the government's boundaries became more permeable. On an interpersonal level, a newly dating couple might initially keep the status of their relationship private from their families and friends until they see whether the relationship is working out. As a result, the couple's shared privacy boundary is highly impermeable. However, after they have been dating for a while, and the relationship seems to be going well, they decide to make their boundary more permeable by beginning to tell others about being in a relationship.

Although privacy boundaries are not tangible, physical structures, they still serve some of the same purposes as physical structures in providing protection and regulating outside access. In the case of privacy boundaries, these borders indicate who does and does not have rights of ownership to the information inside the boundary, and they help to manage the access that outsiders have to the information.

Control and Ownership.   The next supposition of CPM concerns the principles of con-trol and ownership (Petronio, 2002). There are two primary reasons why people seek to con-trol private information. First, whether by themselves or with others, individuals feel they have the right to own the information. Second, disclosing private information can make them vulnerable, and controlling private information can protect them from vulnerability. As we can see, ownership and control are often intertwined. Feelings of ownership instigate the need for control as does anticipating vulnerability. However, the idea of ownership is more complex than one might think at first glance.

For example, issues of rights arise when people encounter questions about ownership of private information regarding their romantic partner's previous relationships. In the example at the beginning of this chapter, Frankie and Ed are having a dispute concerning the ownership of information about Ed's relationship with Carol (Beckerman et al., 2003). Frankie believes that she has a right to know about Ed's past, and so she perceives Ed's reluctance to share this information as deceptive. On the other hand, Ed believes that he has rights to ownership of this information, but Frankie does not. Therefore, he is within his "rights" to *share* whatever information he wishes to reveal to Frankie and to *conceal* whatever information he does not wish to share. Obviously, people can disagree about who belongs within a privacy boundary, that is, who has the rights of ownership to particular pieces of information. Those who feel that they own information are likely to believe they have the right to control that information.

However, control and ownership do not always go hand-in-hand (Petronio, 2002). Sometimes an individual both owns and controls private information. You probably own and control information about your finances or your grades in school, for instance. However, sometimes a person can own but not really have control over the information. In the previous example, Ed felt ownership over the information about his past with Carol but lacked complete control over how and when the information was disseminated, as illustrated by his friends exercising their control in telling Frankie the details that he had kept from her (Beckerman et al., 2003). Likewise, in another example, suppose a couple's daughter, Amy, was divorced and, with her child, had moved back in with her family. Although her parents and siblings shared ownership of information about her circumstances, the circumstances of the divorce were only discussed if Amy brought up the subject. In this case, Amy had shared ownership of the information with her family, but retained control of the information for herself alone. Conversely, people can exercise control over information they do not own. For instance, when celebrities sue tabloid newspapers for publishing rumors or unauthorized photographs, they are exercising control over information they do not own. Likewise, if Joe comes across a document that indicates the salaries of his coworkers and he tells others that information, he is seizing control over that information legitimately owned by his coworkers.

In addition to feelings of ownership, disclosure of private information makes people vulnerable. However, the relative vulnerability one feels with respect to private information can vary based on the circumstances and the particular kind of information (Petronio, 2002). Many people feel comfortable giving their credit card to the cashier in a store. However, those same people may feel uncomfortable buying something with a credit card on the Internet. The second circumstance makes these individuals feel more vulnerable. In making decisions about handling their private information, people consider the risks inherent in the disclosure along with the benefits they might gain. For instance, Jennifer might feel a risk inherent in submitting credit card information over the Internet, but she weighs that risk against the benefit that she would receive from purchasing a significantly discounted plane ticket at an Internet-only price. In relationships, the costs and benefits are not always so clear. In the example discussed previously, when Jane tells her brother-in-law, Dan, that he is interfering with her relationship with her sister, she probably recognizes the risks inherent in making this disclosure. For instance, Dan might get angry and interfere even more with the sisters' relationship, her sister might get angry that Jane shared this information with Dan, or Dan might decide that he does not like Jane anymore and treat her poorly at family functions. On the other hand, Jane may have also considered the possible benefits. Maybe, if she talks to Dan, they will be able to find a solution to the problem, or maybe the discussion will give Dan and Jane a chance to develop a stronger relationship, which will eventually improve Jane's relationship with her sister.

The issues of vulnerability and ownership are at the root of people's desire to control information that they view as private. People try to adjust the boundaries around private information to allow them the kind of control they would like to have over their private information.

Rule-Based Management System.   The fourth supposition of CPM articulates the idea that individuals and groups rely on a rule-based management system to handle their private information (Petronio, 2002). The system works both for individuals and for groups, but it is more complicated at the group or collective level because of the difficulty in coordinating privacy management among all members of the group. Coordination, the smooth handling of the forces pushing people toward disclosure and privacy, is the goal of privacy management at any level. For instance, at the group level, suppose that a couple's teenage niece, who lives in another state, has had a baby. The couple's younger children do not know about the new baby yet. However, because of an upcoming visit, the couple decides that their children should hear the news before they meet the baby in person and help them understand the sensitivity of talking about the baby's birth. In an attempt to coordinate management of this private information, the parents tell the children about the new baby, answer their questions, and tell them how to regulate discussing the information (e.g., what questions they can ask, what they can or cannot talk about, etc.). In this way, they set the rules and the children have a chance to clarify the parameters or perhaps even negotiate the depth and breadth of the information they discuss. If the children follow these privacy rules, coordination is achieved. Thus, coordination is often a combination of defined rules and negotiations, as we see in this example. The children reach an agreement with their parents about the way that the information should be handled, and then the entire family followed the privacy rules determined for that situation.

However, if the parents set rules disallowing this information to be shared outside the family, yet the children disobeyed the rule by telling their friends about the baby, then the system would be in a state of boundary turbulence. The processes of rule development and application, boundary coordination operations, and boundary turbulence make up the rule-based management system, and each process will be discussed in more detail in the next section.

Privacy Management Dialectics.   The final supposition of CPM was discussed briefly at the beginning of this chapter, when we explained what it means to say that CPM is a dialectical theory (Petronio, 2002). As you know from other chapters in this book, the basic idea of a dialectical perspective is that both opposing forces (in this case, the pressures to disclosure and to remain private) operate simultaneously. The relative strength of the forces at any given moment in time influences the type of management decisions that people make when they are controlling private information. In addition to these basic ideas, there are some other important characteristics of CPM's dialectical perspective.

First, it is virtually impossible for a person to disclose completely or to be totally private. Not only is complete privacy or complete disclosure highly improbable, but it would not be possible for us to understand the idea of privacy without understanding what it means to disclose or make something public. Would it make any sense at all to talk about privacy if everyone had complete control over his or her information? In addition, would it make any sense to talk about disclosure if everyone had access to information about every other person? In the practical world, people will deal with privacy and disclosure in degrees, not as absolutes.

Because we understand the meanings of both privacy and disclosure, we are able to make decisions about the information we wish to conceal and the information we wish to reveal. Have you ever been around a person who does not seem to understand the meaning of privacy? For example, suppose someone is visiting with friends, and one of those friends brings along a person who was not acquainted with the rest of the group. This new acquaintance, Gina, seems not to understand the meaning of privacy. She begins by asking intrusive questions of the group, and then proceeds to share progressively more intimate information about her marriage, her family background, and the way her sexual development as an adolescent related to her religious beliefs. These inappropriate disclosures make the other people feel uncomfortable. Because the others recognize the tensions between the simultaneous forces toward privacy and disclosure in this situation, they evaluate Gina's communicative choices as inappropriate. Instead of understanding that being too private or too open has negative consequences, Gina seems completely focused on her need to disclose, ignorant of the fact that her behavior is seen as violating the other people's expectation for more skillful regulation of a balance between privacy and disclosure.

A second point related to the dialectical nature of privacy and disclosure argues that people make decisions about addressing these opposing forces by striving for a goal of coordination. In other words, ideally, people will work to synchronize the privacy rules used to manage the private information. For instance, the parents who told their children about the niece's new baby considered their need to disclose (brought on by the impending family visit and their desire for the children to maintain their relationship with the extended family) and their need to keep the information private (influenced by their desire not to bring up the issue of teenage pregnancy with their young children and their uncertainty about the children's ability to handle the information in appropriate ways). The parents decided that the best option to achieve coordination would be to disclose the information to their children, to address their children's questions so that they would not need to ask outsiders about the information, and to explain to the children how the information should be handled. Therefore, the goal of privacy management is not to achieve a particular level of disclosure or privacy but to handle private information smoothly and competently.

Finally, people handle dialectical tensions at many levels concurrently. As we mentioned previously, a person has information that is personally private, owned by oneself alone. In addition, people share ownership of information with close relational partners, with group members, and with members of larger organizations. People deal with these multiple levels of private information all at once. Consider the situation in which a college student wants to confess to his sister that he is addicted to drugs. In deciding what to do, the student addicted to drugs deals with dialectical tensions at many levels. On the level of personal privacy, this addicted student considers his need to disclose about his drug abuse. He is feeling scared and wants to seek help but is worried that he might compromise his sister by telling her. Yet, his needs to disclose are strong and he tells her about the addition.

Once the disclosure is made, a dyadic privacy boundary is created around the information about the brother's drug addiction. On the dyadic level, after learning about her brother's addiction, the sister must consider whether her brother is granting her control over the information or if he is sharing ownership of the information with her but retaining the control himself. To address these issues, the brother and sister have a conversation about privacy rules so that they can coordinate how the information is communicated to third parties. This kind of coordination is necessary because the brother and sister are also part of a larger family system. The brother does not want his sister to tell other family members for fear that they will be ashamed of him. However, the control over this information is now being shared, and therefore the brother can only hope that his sister will abide by his wishes.

Although the sister has agreed to privacy rules stipulated by her brother about disclosing his addiction, she is in a family privacy dilemma (Petronio, Jones, & Morr, 2003). Her agreement to use his privacy rules to handle the information about her brother's drug addition is affected by two critical issues. One, there is pressure within the family to share all information relevant to the members' well-being. Two, she also feels that there is a possibility her family may be able to help her brother better than she can. However, part of her dilemma comes from the possibility that at the familial level, sharing the information with other members could result in negative reactions or alienate her brother from the family. Finally, at the societal level, the sister's decisions about handling this information are influenced by laws governing drug use. She also must consider the possible consequences that could affect her and her brother if his drug addiction were to become public knowledge. As this example illustrates, a single decision to disclose initiates a multiplex of choices and judgments by each person integrated into a privacy boundary. This example also demonstrates that everyone manages multiple levels of private information within expanding privacy boundaries.

The notion of dialectical tensions is complex. In addition to the claim that forces pushing people to disclose and to remain private operate simultaneously, CPM makes additional arguments about how dialectical forces work. First, neither privacy nor disclosure can exist without its opposite. In addition, people have the goal of coordination in mind when they make decisions about dealing with the forces pushing them to reveal and conceal information. Finally, dialectical tensions are present at multiple levels, which people must handle simultaneously.

Together, these five theoretical suppositions define the basis of CPM theory. Now that you have been introduced to the concepts and ideas that form the foundation of the theory, we will move on to describe the three management processes that people implement when they use communication to handle their private information: privacy rule foundations, boundary coordination operations, and boundary turbulence.

Rule Management Processes

So far, we have described concepts of privacy and disclosure, dialectical tensions, and boundaries, and we have emphasized the point that people make decisions about managing their private information. These decisions are made within the framework of rule management processes defined by CPM.

Privacy Rule Foundations. First, privacy management involves the development of rules, which have particular attributes. Rules are developed with reference to certain criteria, including *culture, gender, motivation, context,* and *risk-benefit ratios* (Petronio, 2002; Petronio & Martin, 1986; Petronio, Martin & Littlefield, 1984). That is, cultures have different definitions of and needs for privacy, and men and women appear to have different ways of defining their privacy boundaries. Moreover, people are motivated by a need for self-clarification that could lead them to disclose information to others or a need for control that could lead them to conceal information (Afifi & Guerrero, 2000). Factors within a context or environment may also influence decisions related to privacy and disclosure. For instance, while shopping in the grocery store, some people seem to believe that the contextual factor of speaking on a cellular phone affords them the privacy they need to speak about personal matters that they might not feel comfortable talking about if the other person were there in person. We have already alluded to the development criterion of risk-benefit ratios in discussing the effects of vulnerability on the need to control private information. People evaluate the relative rewards and costs of possible actions involving privacy and disclosure. Based on all of these criteria, individuals formulate rules for handling their private information.

Regardless of the criteria used to develop rules, the specific rules that result from the criteria have particular attributes related to the ways that people acquire the rules and the properties of the rules themselves. Rules are acquired either through socialization or through negotiation. Many groups tend to establish sets of rules for how they handle privacy. When a new member enters the group's collective boundary, he or she is socialized—that is, the person is expected to learn and abide by the group's existing rules. Do you remember how your family taught you its rules for handling privacy? Young children often make mistakes in learning the family's privacy rules. In her book, *Boundaries of Privacy: Dialectics of Disclosure*, Sandra Petronio (2002) told the story of a 3-year-old boy's accidental violation of his parents' privacy rules. Petronio and her husband were visiting friends for dinner, and their son was entertaining as his parents prepared the meal. After a while, sensing that he was losing the guests' attention, the boy blurted out "My mom and dad sleep naked." As his father led him up the stairs, he explained the family's rule that such matters were not to be discussed with company (Petronio, 2002, pp. 73–74). Families, organizations, and many other groups teach their new members existing rules, but in many disclosure situations, the people included within the boundary can negotiate rules (Petronio & Braithwaite, 1987). Such negotiations can take place explicitly or implicitly. In an explicit negotiation, the discloser states the rule to be followed, often in the form of *disclosure warnings* (Petronio & Bantz, 1991) and *time parameters* (Petronio, 2002). For instance, one of the participants in a study on newlyweds' relationships with their in-laws (Morr, 2002) described a situation when his wife told him that her sister-in-law was pregnant. She also instructed him not to let any of her family members know that he was aware of the pregnancy until the sister-in-law had shared the information herself. In this case, the disclosure warning outlined his wife's expectation that he would not let her family know that she had shared the information, and the time parameter indicated that the rule would apply until the sister-in-law's disclosure. When a rule is negotiated implicitly, the discloser may hint about the way the information should be handled, or the confidant might prompt the discloser to negotiate rules by asking a question like "Should I keep this information just between us?"

In addition to rule acquisition, rules vary based on how routine or unusual they are and on the consequences of following or breaking the rules. Sometimes a person or a group applies particular rules so often that they become *routinized* (Petronio, 2002). For instance, one family had a rule that financial matters were not discussed, so that when the oldest child was graduating from high school, she had no idea about information such as her parents' income that she needed for financial aid applications. Her parents still gave only general information, such as which category to check for certain questions. Because the rules were routinized, there was no need to negotiate new rules for every new piece of financial information— instead, every member knew that finances were not to be discussed. In other cases, a particular situation can force people to make decisions about new ways to manage their information, resulting in what CPM refers to as *triggered rules*. When you began college, you might have left home for the first time. Even if you did not leave home to begin college, think about the first time you left home or about what it will be like when you do leave home. Living in a new environment, and not having your daily life connected with your family, causes you to make new decisions. Because they are not around to observe what you are doing, how much information do you share with or withhold from them? In addition, if you are living with friends or roommates, how do you manage your privacy in these new relationships? Finally, living with privacy rules means experiencing *sanctions*. Sanctions are the consequences that people experience when they are held accountable for maintaining a group's privacy rules. If you abide by the rules, you might experience positive sanctions, such as the gratitude of group members and increased trust. If, however, you break the rules, you might experience negative sanctions, such as embarrassment, humiliation, or even having your access to the group's private information cut (Petronio, 2002).

Boundary Coordination Operations.   Managing privacy becomes much more complicated as more people are included within a boundary. When 7-year-old Courtney started to suspect that Santa Claus was not real, she decided to test him by telling no one else what she wanted for Christmas. She reasoned that she would get the desired gift for Christmas only if Santa were real and brought the gift himself. Courtney's mother, Mary, did not want Courtney to tell her younger brother, Matt, that Santa Claus was not real because he would be crushed. Mary called her mother, and together they hatched a plan. They called Mary's sister, Margaret, and asked Margaret to have her 9-year-old daughter, Kate, call Courtney and try to find out what she had asked for from Santa. Kate not only succeeded in her mission, but she also managed to talk Courtney down from her original request (a puppy) to a more reasonable request (a pet). Kate reported to Margaret, who reported to Mary, who surprised Courtney with a parakeet on Christmas Day. The secret was safe for another year. However, in the process of keeping the secret from Courtney, the whole extended family became involved in the process of coordinating the privacy boundary around this information. This complicated plan required the coordination of boundaries with all the family members—a much more daunting task than it had been in previous years, when Courtney did not question Santa's existence and only her parents were involved in keeping the secrets of Santa and the Christmas gifts.

In the process of including the extended family in the plan to convince Courtney of Santa's existence, the three boundary coordination operations of CPM were invoked. The first operation, *linkage*, involves the incorporation of information from personal boundaries into collective boundaries. Mary told her mother and sister about Courtney's test of Santa and when Courtney told Kate about her Christmas wish, which Kate passed through the family network, the boundary around that information was transformed from personal to collective. Many characteristics of linkage affect the nature of this boundary change. For example, the strength or weakness of ties between the group members influences the extent to which they can be expected to maintain the boundary rules developed by the group. In this case, the close family ties of the group made it easier to maintain privacy than if Mary had recruited a neighbor child, with weaker ties to the group, to learn Courtney's wish. Other factors also impact boundary linkage. For instance, how much information is shared or the proportionality of each individual's contribution to the boundary determines the extent to which someone is linked into a privacy boundary. A person's rules about timing, that is, when to link someone into a boundary, may have an impact on success of linkage. Depending on the topics of disclosure, one person may be selected for linkage into a boundary as opposed to someone else. Finally, who the targets of disclosure are affects boundary linkage.

Boundary *permeability*, the second coordination operation, involves the ease or difficulty with which information passes through the boundary. The permeability of the boundary can vary from highly permeable, when the information is shared easily with any confidant, to highly impermeable, when the information is a closely guarded secret from all outside the boundary. In this case, the boundary was permeable to most family members—after receiving disclosure warnings to keep this information from Courtney, Matt, and other young children in the family, information was given freely to the older family members. However, the boundary around the information was highly impermeable for the young children—under no circumstances did anyone share this information with Courtney, Matt, or their young cousins. The variable permeability of the boundary was controlled by privacy access rules, which granted access to all family members who were at least 9 years old, and privacy protection rules, which denied access to all family members under the age of 9.

Finally, boundary *ownership* can belong to an individual when one person retains information within a personal boundary. Nevertheless, when the information is shared within a collective boundary, they also share ownership. These co-owners are responsible for coordinating the management of the information within the collective boundary (Petronio, 2002). Coordination becomes more complicated because, as we stated earlier, people may not always recognize that control and ownership can operate independently from each other. For example, when Courtney disclosed her Christmas wish to Kate, she may have believed that she retained ownership and control of that information. However, although the family recognized that Courtney owned the information, they exercised control over that information to an extent that would have greatly surprised Courtney. Conversely, the family co-owned information about the surprise gift of a parakeet that Mary had planned. However, they recognized that Mary retained control over that information, and that no one but Mary could make a decision about when to share the information with Courtney.

Boundary Turbulence.   The final rule management process deals with what happens when attempts at coordination fail. As you have seen through this discussion, communicative management of private information is an extremely complex task. The inherent difficulty of handling the many parts of the process makes mishaps and failures quite likely. Petronio (2002) identified six factors that can lead to boundary turbulence. People may (a) violate rules intentionally, (b) make mistakes in following rules, or (c) experience uncertainty about ownership due to fuzzy boundaries. In addition, (d) boundary co-owners may have different orientations in the ways they generally handle privacy, (e) boundary definition predicaments occur when people treat public space as private space or have their privacy boundaries redefined (as when a person becomes famous), and (f) people may experience privacy dilemmas when they are forced to make unappealing choices to deal with private information they possess about another person (Petronio, 1990, 2002; Petronio, Olson & Dollar, 1989).

When a person betrays a secret, gossips about another person, or struggles to figure out what to do with the knowledge that a family member is in trouble, boundary turbulence exists (Cooks, 2000; Petronio, 1994). For instance, Jenny and Sam had met and started dating while they were in a club together in college. After they had been dating for about 6 months, Sam went out of town to visit Jim, the club's former advisor, and his family for a weekend. During the trip, Jim asked Sam if he and Jenny were having any problems. After they had been talking for a while, Sam admitted that he resented all the attention that Jenny got as president of the club. After Sam returned from the weekend, he had a long talk with the club's current advisor about the same topic, and their advisor told other students in the club. Jenny began to suspect that something was wrong because Sam was acting differently toward her. Finally, she convinced Sam to tell her what was bothering him. He told Jenny that he resented her and that he had not even realized that he was so angry until Jim had brought it up. Jenny was furious! She thought that Sam had violated the rules about how information about their relationship should be handled. In short, she felt as if Sam had betrayed her by telling others what she considered information belonging only to the two of them. The problem is best defined as one of fuzzy boundaries (Afifi, 2003). In other words, Sam perceived his resentment to be personally private information about his feelings. Consequently, he felt he had a right to share that information with anyone he might choose. However, Jenny defined the information as belonging to both of them because it concerned their relationship, so Sam should have told her first, and they should have decided together how to handle the information. Because Sam and Jenny did not agree on who owned the information, they experienced boundary turbulence. They had to renegotiate rules to make it clear how information like this should be handled in the future.

The processes that people use to manage their privacy show how the assumptions of CPM are set into practice. Understanding rule foundations, boundary coordination operations, and boundary turbulence can help to explain and predict how people will handle privacy in their actual interactions. Now that we have explained the basics of the theory, the remainder of this chapter will explain how CPM was developed and how it has been used to study specific situations.

Background and Development of CPM

To understand theory development there are at least four storylines that weave together telling the how's and whys of theory construction. Petronio (2004) argued that the storylines for CPM include the *intellectual history*, that is, how previous theorizing and research functioned as catalysts to give birth to CPM theory. Also relevant is the storyline that identifies *historic events* influencing the development of CPM. In the advancement of every theory, there is a *chronological history*. Finally, the stories about the *people* who participated through offering their ideas to the theory add the fourth dimension that laid the groundwork for CPM. A more complete explication of these four elements knitting the fabric of CPM theory may be found in Petronio's (2004) article. However, it is useful to take a quick tour in this chapter so we can identify some of more pertinent aspects of these theory building stories.

Starting in the middle to late 1960s Sidney Jourard (1970) began arguing that self-disclosure (a phrase he coined) was one of the most important processes in having a healthy self. From his persuasive arguments and influential research, Jourard convinced many people that talking about oneself was an important key to mental health. Historically situated, Jourard's research and theorizing coalesced with a movement during the 1960s and 1970s that capitalized on such ideas and stimulated encounter groups, sensitivity training for the practice of authentic communication, and revealing an inner self to others (Bormann, 1980). As a result, there was heightened interest in disclosure, both for the lay person and the researcher. Research on self-disclosure flourished and many studies resulted from this attention on disclosure.

By the late 1970s and early 1980s, there were literally hundreds of studies that investigated self-disclosure. Unfortunately, many investigations into self-disclosure tended to be atheoretical, using disclosure as one of many variables. The theory of Social Penetration by Altman and Taylor (1973), though not directly aimed at framing self-disclosure, featured self-disclosure as a dominate factor in building relationships. As a result, their theory of relationship development gave a grounding to help others understand the function of disclosure interpersonally. Within this context, Petronio began formulating ideas about CPM theory. She was frustrated with the lack of theoretical structure with which to understand the many studies on self-disclosure. She cast about looking for some way to make sense of the inconsistent findings and determined that, at least initially, a model might be useful to organize the research into a more informative diagram. In scouting to find a language to describe the phenomenon, Petronio naturally turned to Altman and Taylor's work. However, it was in Altman's theorizing on privacy and territoriality that she found a critical key.

Altman (1975) was interested in environmental psychology, particularly with regard to personal space, territories, and crowding. Within this sphere, Altman introduced the concept of boundaries to illustrate the way people defined space. Studying privacy regulation, Altman extended his earlier ideas and ultimately incorporated the notion of dialectics with that of social penetration and privacy regulation (Altman, Vinsel, & Brown, 1981). Petronio applied Altman's blending of privacy regulation, the notion of boundaries, and dialectics to untangle the contradictory research on self-disclosure. She elaborated on many of the basic issues proposed by Altman and his colleagues subsequently developing a preliminary theoretical draft of CPM then called, "Communication Boundary Management."

Some initial turns Petronio (1991) took capitalized on Altman's proposals but significantly extended them to lay the groundwork for CPM theory. Those turns were foundational to CPM theory. Most fundamental was the framing of disclosure itself. She reasoned that if we define disclosure as the process of revealing and define the messages disclosed as private information, we reorganize the way we understand the notion of disclosure. With this move, we can see two embedded definitional issues: (a) There is a process of revealing and (b) the nature of information revealed also needs to be defined—in this case, it is private. Once these two significant definitional questions were identified, many subsequent research projects followed contributing to the development of the grounded theory now known as CPM (Petronio, 2002).

From the initial model to the more elaborated theory presented in this chapter, several important things emerged. First, taking the lead from Altman, Petronio used a boundary metaphor to visually illustrate the way that people think about private information. Next, she argued that instead of trying to define the actual content of a disclosure that is private, it is better to think about private information as something we own: it is ours. Once this premise became clear, other factors emerged and needed to be explored. For example, Petronio realized she had to flesh out some way to explain people's behavior once they claim ownership over private information. She argued that when people believe they own information, they want to control it somehow. Consequently, Petronio proposed that people control their private information through a web of privacy rules.

The next theoretical move was critical. Derlega and his colleagues had made a case for the notion of a dyadic boundary (Derlega & Chaikin, 1977). The idea of dyadic boundaries was an important formulation that grew out of the work by Altman and Taylor. Petronio adapted this notion but customized the idea to theoretically fit within the conceptualization of CPM theory. Developing this notion of dyadic boundaries helped address how people manage disclosure to other people. This move was instrumental in birthing two new ideas. First, it gave rise to considering the confidant, a neglected feature of disclosure. Second, recognizing that disclosed information changes the nature of privacy boundaries means that there are possibilities for multiple privacy boundaries on many levels (e.g., personal, dyadic, and group). The introduction of multiple privacy boundaries and the confidant added important dimensions to CPM. As this chapter has already discussed, telling persons private information makes them a shareholder where the privacy rules used to manage boundaries need to be agreed on or synchronized. In her most recent book, Petronio (2002) explicated the ramifications of multiple privacy boundaries for all kinds of personal relationships within multiple contexts. This idea extends the early notion of "self" disclosure and propels it into becoming a multifaceted notion of "disclosure" not just about the self anymore.

At its most basic level, the page taken from Altman's foray into dialectical theory suggests that people really cannot have privacy without publicness to define it. This chapter articulates exactly what we mean and why it is important. For example, you could not be mad at someone for taking pictures of you in your pajamas through your living room window if you thought everything you did would be seen by everyone, anywhere. As you have already seen, the dialectical profile of CPM is fundamental to the theory. Everything flows from this base and the privacy rules used to manage boundaries stand on choices that manage revealing with concealing in a dialectical fashion. The complexity of the dialectical notion is seen most clearly within the multiple boundaries that are formed and the smoothness or turbulence that erupts when the coordination of these rules managing revealing and concealing are disrupted.

Today, CPM is in its early adulthood and continues to evolve. For Petronio, the theory must continue to change and grow to accommodate explanatory needs. The historical base was necessary, but the application of the theory is critical for it to be worth the energy of its creation.

RESEARCH APPLYING CPM

Many researchers have applied CPM (e.g., Yep, 2000) in a variety of contexts, some of which we listed in describing the development of CPM as a theory. Before we conclude this chapter, we will describe in more detail three examples of this research. We will describe the results of studies examining medical mistakes, disclosure of child sexual abuse, and family privacy dilemmas.

In Allman's (1995, 1998) research, 39 physicians described the difficulties they faced in managing their privacy regarding medical mistakes they had made. Because of the stringent penalties that medical doctors face if they make mistakes, disclosure of their mistakes would make physicians extremely vulnerable. Thus, the medical community has instituted a strict privacy rule restricting disclosure of medical mistakes from those outside the boundary (Allman, 1995). A further rule requires physicians to phrase any information they do disclose about mistakes very carefully in terms that minimize responsibility. Thus, they may refer to slip-ups, blunders, or making an honest error. One physician who participated in Allman's (1995) study stated, "as a serious and conscientious MD, you do not necessarily make any mistakes. You make better or worse decisions together with your patients" (p. 61). Physicians acquire these rules as part of their socialization from medical school on. However, maintaining the collective boundary around medical mistakes may cause problems for the physicians at the level of their personal boundary. The strong emotions, and even grief, that physicians may experience following a mistake might induce a keen desire to discuss the experience with someone in order to deal with the personally private information about their own emotions. When participants in Allman's (1998) study did disclose information about their mistakes, the confidants were usually other doctors, and the information was presented so that others could learn from the error. However, these physicians maintained highly impermeable privacy boundaries around their emotional reaction to the mistake (Allman, 1998). In other words, the silence required to maintain the boundaries of the medical community forced these physicians to live with the emotional consequences of their errors alone.

Another context in which people are likely to feel that strict secrecy is required exists in the highly traumatic experience of child sexual abuse. In their study, Petronio, Reeder, Hecht, and Mon't Ros-Mendoza (1996) interviewed 38 children and adolescents, all of whom had experienced child sexual abuse. The participants had all disclosed the abuse and were receiving treatment from a social worker. The researchers were concerned with discovering the rules that the children applied to decide whether to grant or withhold access to the information about the abuse. After analyzing the transcripts of the interviews, the researchers were able to identify three access rules that the children had applied when they chose to disclose and two protection rules that they used in deciding to withhold the information.

The children tended to disclose information to those who gave them *tacit permission* by showing concern them or by disclosing their own experience of abuse. For example, Lauren's close friend Theresa asked her why she was so often absent from school, and Lauren interpreted Theresa's concern as an invitation to share the information about abuse. The children also *selected the circumstances* for the disclosure by choosing a setting and activities that reduced their fears thereby making them feel more comfortable. Some common circumstances included asking a family member to watch TV together, asking someone to help do the dishes when no one else was present, or waiting until only the desired confidant was present. Finally, they tended to reveal information using a process of *incremental disclosure*, telling the details of the abuse a little bit at a time and waiting to see how the confidant responded before continuing with the disclosure. The children would often hint or make preview statements, as when Jennifer told her mother "Mom, I've got to tell you something. He's [stepfather] had been walking around the house with no clothes on" (Petronio et al., 1996, p. 191). After the mother responded positively by showing that she believed, trusted, and cared about her daughter, Jennifer was able to tell her mother that her stepfather had been abusing her.

In contrast, the children who participated in this study decided not to disclose to people who possessed particular *target characteristics*, such as an inability to understand or a lack of concern or trustworthiness (Petronio et al., 1996). If the *anticipated reactions* of a particular person were negative, the children also reported deciding not to disclose. For example, Patty did not tell her parents that her cousin had been abusing her because she was afraid of their possible reaction. Instead, Patty chose to tell her brother about the abuse. In combination, the access and protection rules revealed by the participants in the Petronio et al. study presented a powerful example of the ways that people make active decisions in managing the boundaries around their private information. Moreover, such information can be helpful to parents and others who need to recognize the ways that they can encourage children to feel comfortable disclosing such a serious matter.

Finally, Petronio et al. (2003) examined one of the six specific causes of boundary turbulence when they investigated privacy dilemmas in the context of family relationships. In their study, 121 college students described cases in which they came to possess private information about a member of their family that placed them in a dilemma. That is, the participants in this study had information about someone in their family that put them in the position of deciding between multiple unappealing options for handling the information. After analyzing the written descriptions that students provided, Petronio et al. identified three distinct types of dilemmas, classified according to the way that the participant came into possession of the private information.

In the first dilemma type, the *confidant dilemma*, a family member had explicitly disclosed the information to the participant (Petronio et al., 2003). These confidant dilemmas can be complicated by the tendency for the confidant and discloser to assume, rather than explicitly negotiate, the rules for managing the information. For instance, one participant recalled that, when he was 13 years old, his brother had told him in confidence that he was planning to steal the next-door neighbor's bike. Because the participant had a crush on the neighbor's sister, he told the sister about his brother's plan. She warned her brother, who got into a fight with the participant's brother.

The second type, the *accidental dilemma*, exists when a person stumbles on information about a family member. In an accidental dilemma, people may face challenges due to their lack of preparation to receive the information. Furthermore, pursuing the information further may lead to multiple discoveries. One participant in Petronio et al.'s (2003) study discovered accidentally that she had a different father than her siblings. Years later, she found her birth father on the Internet and met him in person. These multiple discoveries placed her in a difficult predicament and forced her to cope with the knowledge that she had a different father and that her mother kept the information from her.

Finally, *illicit dilemmas* occur when a person snoops, spies, or pries to discover information that places him or her in a difficult situation (Petronio et al., 2003). The difficulty in handling information implicated in a family privacy dilemma is compounded in this situation by the means used to gain the information. Interestingly, although participants in the study were asked to report on an instance in which *they* had information about another family member, most people who described an illicit dilemma told about a time when another family member had spied on them. For example, one participant described the situation in which her father read her personal journal. In the journal, this young woman had written about a conversation in which her mother said she did not love her father anymore.

These studies are only three examples of the many cases in which CPM has been productively used as a way to understand and explain communication phenomena (see also Sargent, 2003). Although this is a small sampling of research studies, the varied contexts of this research demonstrate that CPM can be applied to a wide range of situations.

CONCLUSION

In this chapter, we have presented the basics of CPM theory. CPM is based on five theoretical suppositions and three rule management processes. The theory is grounded in years of research conducted by Petronio and others, and the theory continues to inspire research and to undergo further refinement. Among the many studies that have been grounded in CPM, some examples have focused on medical mistakes, disclosure of child sexual abuse, and family privacy dilemmas.

SUGGESTIONS FOR FURTHER READING

To learn more about the current state of CPM theory, the best source for information is Petronio's (2002) book, *Boundaries of Privacy: Dialectics of Disclosure*. This book elaborates on all of the principles we discussed in this chapter and illustrates the ideas with interesting examples. To get an idea of the theory's development over time, read Petronio's (1991) original article on the theory and the book *Balancing the Secrets of Private Disclosures* (Petronio, 2000).

REFERENCES

Afifi, T. D. (2003). "Feeling caught" in stepfamilies: Managing boundary turbulence through appropriate communication privacy rules. *Journal of Social and Personal Relationships, 20,* 729–755.

Afifi, W. A., & Guerrero, L. K. (2000). Motivations underlying topic avoidance in close relationships. In S. Petronio (Ed.), *Balancing the secrets of private disclosures* (pp. 165–179). Mahwah, NJ: Lawrence Erlbaum Associates, Inc.

Allman, J. (1995). *Bearing the burden or baring the soul: Physicians' self-disclosure and boundary management regarding medical mistakes.* Unpublished doctoral dissertation, University of Oklahoma, Norman.

Allman, J. (1998). Bearing the burden or baring the soul: Physicians' self-disclosure and boundary management regarding medical mistakes. *Health Communication, 10,* 175–197.

Altman, I. (1975). *Environment and social behavior: Privacy, personal space, territory, and crowding.* Belmont, CA: Wadsworth.

Altman, I., & Taylor, D. A. (1973). *Social penetration: The development of interpersonal relationships.* New York: Holt, Rinehart, & Wilson.

Altman, I., Vinsel, A., & Brown, B. (1981). Dialectical conceptions in social psychology: An application to social penetration and privacy regulation. In L. Berkowitz (Ed.), *Advances in experimental social psychology* (Vol. 14, pp. 107–160). New York: Academic Press.

Beckerman, J. (Writer), Burnett, R. (Writer), & Van Patten, T. (Director). (2003, March 28). Second chances [Television series episode]. In T. Cavanagh, R. Davis, T. Dettmann, M. H. Karpf, K. McGill, K. Murphy, & A. Newman Producers), *Ed.* New York: NBC.

Bormann, E. G. (1980). *Communication theory.* New York: Holt, Rinehart & Winston.

Cooks, L. (2000). Family secrets and the lie of identity. In S. Petronio (Ed.), *Balancing the secrets of private disclosures* (pp. 197–211). Mahwah, NJ: Lawrence Erlbaum Associates, Inc.

Derlega, V. J., & Chaikin, A. L. (1977). Privacy and self-disclosure in social relationships. *Journal of Social Issues, 33,* 102–115.

Jourard, S. M. (1970). *The transparent self.* New York: D. Van Nostrand Company.

Morr, M. C. (2002). *Private disclosure in a family membership transition: In-laws' disclosures to newlyweds.* Unpublished doctoral dissertation, Arizona State University, Tempe.

Orrego, V. O., Smith, S. W., Mitchell, M. M., Johnson, A. J., Ah Yun, K., & Greenberg, B. (2000). Disclosure and privacy issues on television talk shows. In S. Petronio (Ed.), *Balancing the secrets of private disclosures* (pp. 249–259). Mahwah, NJ: Lawrence Erlbaum Associates, Inc.

Parks, M. R. (1982). Ideology in interpersonal communication: Off the couch and into the world. In M. Burgoon (Ed.), *Communication yearbook 5* (pp. 79–108). New Brunswick, NJ: Transaction Books.

Petronio, S. (1990). The use of a communication boundary perspective to contextualize embarrassment research. In J. Andersen (Ed.), *Communication yearbook 13* (pp. 365–373). Newbury Park, CA: Sage.

Petronio, S. (1991). Communication boundary management: A theoretical model of managing disclosure of private information between marital couples. *Communication Theory, 1,* 311–335.

Petronio, S. (1994). Privacy binds in family interactions: The case of parental privacy invasion. In W. R. Cupach & B. H. Spitzberg (Eds.), *The dark side of interpersonal communication* (pp. 241–257). Hillsdale, NJ: Lawrence Erlbaum Associates, Inc.

Petronio, S. (Ed.). (2000). *Balancing the secrets of private disclosures.* Mahwah, NJ: Lawrence Erlbaum Associates, Inc.

Petronio, S. (2002). *Boundaries of privacy: Dialectics of disclosure.* Albany, NY: SUNY Press.

Petronio, S. (2004). Road to developing communication privacy management theory: Narrative in progress, please stand by. *Journal of Family Communication, 4,* 193–208.

Petronio, S., & Bantz, C. (1991). Controlling the ramifications of private disclosure: "Don't tell anybody but … ." In M. Mayer & N. Dollar (Eds.), *Issues in group communication* (pp. 67–69). Scottsdale, AZ: Gorsich Scarisbrick.

Petronio, S., & Braithwaite, D. O. (1987). I'd rather not say: The role of personal privacy in small groups. In M. Mayer & N. Dollar (Eds.), *Issues in group communication* (pp. 67–79). Scottsdale, AZ: Prospect Press.

Petronio, S., Jones, S., & Morr, M. C. (2003). Family privacy dilemmas: Managing communication boundaries within family groups. In L. R. Frey (Ed.), *Group communication in context: Studies of bona fide groups (2nd ed.,* pp. 23–55). Mahwah, NJ: Lawrence Erlbaum Associates, Inc.

Petronio, S., & Martin, J. (1986). Ramifications of revealing private information: A gender gap. *Journal of Clinical Psychology, 42,* 499–506.

Petronio, S., Martin, J., & Littlefield, R. (1984). Prerequisite conditions for self-disclosure: A gender issue. *Communication Monographs, 51,* 268–273.

Petronio, S., Olson, C., & Dollar, N. (1989). Privacy issues in relational embarrassment: Impact on relational quality and communication satisfaction. *Communication Research Reports, 6,* 21–27.

Petronio, S., Reeder, H. M., Hecht, M. L., & Mon't Ros-Mendoza, T. (1996). Disclosure of sexual abuse by children and adolescents. *Journal of Applied Communication Research, 24,* 181–199.

Petronio, S., Scheibel, D., & Snider, E. (1991). *Unsolicited disclosure: Bartenders and their ability to cope with stressful information.* Paper presentation at the International Communication Association convention, Chicago.

Sargent, J. (2003, February). *Nonverbal boundary coordination: An exploratory examination of implicit disclosures.* Paper presented at the Western States Communication Association convention, Salt Lake City, UT.

Yep, G. A. (2000). Disclosure of HIV infection in interpersonal relationships: A communication boundary management approach. In S. Petronio (Ed.), *Balancing the secrets of private disclosures* (pp. 83–95). Mahwah, NJ: Lawrence Erlbaum Associates, Inc.

Youniss, J., & Smollar, J. (1985). *Adolescent relations with mothers, fathers, and friends.* Chicago: University of Chicago Press.

QUESTIONS TO PONDER

1. CPM states that private information is any information that an individual or group feels the right to own and control. What kinds of information are private to individuals, couples, groups, families, and organizations?

2. Think of a time when you tried to manage both personal and collective boundaries. What decisions did you make about how to handle the information? Was it possible for you to abide by your own personal privacy management rules as well as the rules for the group's boundary?

3. In this chapter, we explained that there are a range of options for managing the dialectical tension between privacy and disclosure. Other than total secrecy and complete disclosure, what other options exist?

4. The criteria used to develop rules include the stable features of culture and gender. What are your culture's and your gender's preferred rules for privacy?

5. How can people restore boundary coordination once they have experienced boundary turbulence?

15

Social Dialectics:
The Contradictions of Relating

Leslie A. Baxter
University of Iowa

Dawn O. Braithwaite
University of Nebraska

> *"I don't live with my dad and basically get to see him on weekends. I love him and love spending time with him, but it can be disruptive to my normal life with my friends and things. And sometimes, he'll call me in the middle of the week and I'll be watching my favorite TV program or something, and I just won't be interested in talking with him, even though I miss him a lot between visits."*

> *"I want to tell him what's been going on in my life, because he's my husband and even though he's in the nursing home, he wants to know what's going on in my life with the house and our family and friends. But with the Alzheimer's, it's really hard. He often gets confused or upset when I tell him things. So I must be very careful in what I say and what I don't say in his presence. Visiting him is exhausting."*

What is it that these two examples of the daughter and elderly wife share in common? Both capture the essence of relating with others as a dialectical experience; that is, a process in which parties must communicatively navigate the interplay of opposing tendencies or demands. The central assumption of social dialectical approaches is that all relationships are interwoven with multiple layers of contradictions like the connection–autonomy and openness–closedness dilemmas highlighted in these two examples. From a social dialectical perspective, the central research agenda scholars share is to illuminate the contradiction-ridden nature of communication in a given relationship.

We title this chapter "Social Dialectics" to differentiate the dialectical work discussed here from the dialectical materialism of Marx (1961). Although Marx, who lived in the 19th century, was arguably the first scholar to bring a systematic, social scientific perspective to bear in the study of dialectics (Mircovic, 1980), he was focused on the material conditions of production.

To meet the material needs of life, division of labor emerged with its alienating effects on workers and their exploitation by those who control the modes and means of production. By contrast, the dialectical theories discussed in this chapter focus on the social and symbolic practices of people in relationships rather than the material conditions of capitalism.

Throughout our chapter, we will stress that social dialectical theory is not a single theory, but instead is a family of theories. Like any family, the various dialectical approaches will share some common features and will differ in other ways (Baxter & Montgomery, 1998)—what we like to think of as a dialectical tree with multiple branches. We will examine social dialectics in this chapter by addressing three major points that form the premises and concepts common to all members of the dialectical family tree: the presumption that relating is a process of contradiction; the presumption that contradiction is central to relational change; and the presumption that communication occupies a central place in the enactment of contradiction. We will end by summarizing nine branches of the "family tree" of social dialectical theory.

RELATING AS A PROCESS OF CONTRADICTION

"You contradicted yourself!" If you've ever heard these words said about you, or directed them toward someone else, you probably understood this to be a criticism. However, to dialectical theorists contradiction is not negative. Instead, contradiction is intrinsic to social life and functions to keep a social system alive, adaptive, and ever-changing. Thus, to dialectical theorists, contradictions should be embraced, not denied or extinguished. But what exactly is a contradiction?

Definition of Contradiction

A contradiction refers to "the dynamic interplay of unified opposites." Three terms are important to understand in this definition: unified, opposites, and dynamic interplay.

Unified. Opposites are unified if they are interdependent in some way. Interdependence can take two basic forms, which Altman, Vinsel, and Brown (1981) referred to as the unity of identity and interactive unity. The unity of identity is a semantic or definitional unity. For example, we know what "cold" means only with an understanding of the concept of "hot." In the context of personal relationships, Baxter et al. (1997) illustrated this form of interdependence in discussing the concept of "loyalty." They argued that "loyalty" becomes meaningful to us only with an understanding of the opposite concept of "disloyalty."

Baxter et al. (1997) also presented data to illustrate the second form of unity, interactive unity. Social life is complex, they found. The very act of being loyal to one relationship partner or to one facet of the relationship with that partner simultaneously enacts disloyalty to other relationships in one's social network or to other facets of the relationship with one's partner. The most frequent enactment of loyalty and disloyalty grows out of the fact that we only have so many hours in each day. In being loyal by spending time with one relationship partner, we simultaneously position ourselves to be disloyal to others in our social network because we cannot spend time with them. Thus, loyalty and disloyalty go hand in hand in this instance.

Opposites. Central to the notion of opposition is mutual negation: opposites are in conflict and function to oppose, nullify, cancel, undo, or otherwise undermine one another. Opposition can take several basic forms and Montgomery (1993) identified three. First, oppositions can be mutually exclusive and exhaustive. For example, long-distance partners can be physically together or apart—these opposing conditions are exhaustive of all possible options and they cannot both apply at a single point in time. Second, oppositions can be mutually exclusive but not exhaustive. For example, open disclosure and deception are opposites that are mutually exclusive (if you are engaged in deception, you are not being open), but these two conditions do not exhaust all possibilities (you could not be engaged in deception and still not be open). Third, oppositions can be complementary; for example, dominance versus submissiveness.

Dynamic Interplay. Central to the concept of contradiction is the *interplay* of the unified opposites. Opposites are not simply copresent phenomena that exist in isolation of one another. Contradictory phenomena are tied together in interdependence at the same time that they negate each other. This simultaneous "both–and" dynamic produces an ongoing tension, one that keeps the relating process vibrant and alive.

This third component of the definition is often difficult for beginners to grasp when they first encounter dialectical theory. Often, people mistake a duality for a contradiction. A duality is a pair of opposites in the absence of any dynamic interplay. Thus, for example, in the context of long-distance couples, we could point to a basic duality between living apart and living together. These are opposite notions, to be sure. But if we were to conceive of them in isolation of one another, we would be framing them dualistically. From a dialectical perspective, we are interested in the ever-changing interplay of living together and living apart. We would ask how living apart works with and against living together, and vice versa. For example, one of the authors of this chapter and her partner of 20 years once worked in different states for 18 months, living together and apart. The dialectical theorist would be interested in the dynamic interplay of these two opposite living conditions. For example, while the return of the partner was longed for, when the two were together, they faced the contradictory interplay of mine and ours—"my bathroom" suddenly became "our bathroom" and "my phone line" suddenly became "our line" as they discovered one would be bumped off the Internet when the other would pick up the phone to make a call.

Types of Contradictions

Not all contradictions take the same form, and four basic distinctions are important to understand in order to grasp dialectical theory.

Binary Versus Multivocal Contradictions. In their approach to dialectical theory, Baxter and Montgomery (1996) distinguished binary from multivocal contradictions. Binary contradictions are characterized by two unified opposites, and multivocal contradictions are characterized by a web of multiple, interdependent opposites. For example, a binary contradiction can be seen in the openness–closedness example at the beginning of this chapter. The daughter wanted to be both open with her father and, at the same time, wanted to maintain her privacy with him. When we think of this as a multivocal contradiction, we appreciate that openness has many radiants just as closedness has many radiants. When considered as a unified whole, these various radiants provide us with a more complex view of how contradiction is enacted in relationships. Analytically, the issue is not a simple matter of being open or not; instead, there is a complex interweave of possibilities. With and against openness, for example, we can envision the opposite of closedness with respect to individual rights (e.g., the right to privacy), control (e.g., information is power), efficiency (e.g., the belief that silence "speaks volumes"), and so forth.

Antagonistic Versus Nonantagonistic Contradictions.   It is also important to understand that contradictions can take either antagonistic or nonantagonistic form (Baxter & Montgomery, 1996; Erbert, 2000). With antagonistic contradictions, the relationship parties are engaged in an interpersonal conflict in which each person aligns with a different dialectical tendency or pole. Imagine a conflict between dating partners, Juan and Sue. Juan is arguing for more freedom and independence from the relationship while Sue is arguing for greater exclusive commitment to the relationship—he thinks they should also be dating other people and Sue believes they should be dating one another only. In this conflict, Juan is aligned with the autonomy side and Sue is aligned with the connection side of a frequently identified contradiction of relating—autonomy.–connection. Now imagine a different exchange between Juan and Sue: one in which both Juan and Sue want greater freedom and autonomy *at the same time* that they both want greater relational connectedness. They may both desire to date one another exclusively, but they may also wish to see each other only 1 night per week. This second example illustrates a nonantagonistic contradiction, the interplay of united opposites in which the parties do not take opposing sides. Antagonistic contradictions involve interpersonal conflict, because each person is aligned with a different dialectical pole, whereas nonantagonistic contradictions are not enacted in interpersonal conflict between the parties.

Internal and External Contradictions.   Various dialectical scholars have drawn a basic distinction between contradictions that are located within the relational dyad versus contradictions located at the interface of the dyad and the society in which the dyad is embedded (e.g., Baxter, 1993; Montgomery, 1992; Rawlins, 1989; Werner & Baxter, 1994). Contradictory dilemmas that are embedded in interaction between the two relationship partners are internal contradictions. Contradictions that are located at the border of the relationship and the society are external contradictions. The same basic contradiction can surface both internally and externally for a given relationship pair. For example, relational partners negotiate between themselves how much discretion versus openness they will have with one another and with those outside of the dyad. Newly cohabiting partners must figure out what they will reveal to one another and what they will reveal to their friends, families, and others. How large a purchase can one make without discussing it with the partner first? How much information about the couples' joint finances should one reveal to parents or friends? Relationship closeness depends on the parties attaching value to complete openness and honesty between them and, at the same time, attaching value to privacy and discretion. Parties must negotiate how open and how closed to be with one another on an ongoing basis (e.g., Baxter, 1990; Rawlins, 1983b). In addition, partners constantly face the contradictory dilemma of how much to reveal and conceal about their relationship to third-party strangers, family members, and friends (Baxter & Widenmann, 1993). Although we know that relationship parties need to disclose their relationship to others to gain social recognition and legitimation of the relationship, on the other hand, close relationship parties usually hold an expectation that what happens in the relationship is private between those two people. This dialectic of expression–nonexpression thus exists both internally and externally for the relationship parties.

The distinction between internal contradictions and external contradictions is important for communication scholars to understand. If our focus is only on what happens between the two relationship parties within the boundaries of their relationship, our attention is directed toward internal contradictions. If, by contrast, we emphasize that relationships are embedded in the broader social webs of networks of friends and family, societal institutions, and cultural values, we will probably focus on external contradictions. Yet, both of these are important to understanding relationship communication. It is important to point out that relationship parties often experience the boundary between internal and external as somewhat fuzzy. For example, the married partners in a stepfamily often report that the solidarity of their marriage requires both separation from the larger stepfamily unit yet integration with the blended family (Cissna, Cox, & Bochner, 1990). The two of them need to concentrate on their new marriage and also function as part of the developing family. However, because the married couple is the central or linchpin relationship in the stepfamily, it is difficult to establish the boundary of what is internal and what is external to the family.

Frontstage Versus Backstage Contradictions.   Partners may have differing levels of awareness of relational contradictions, which we have labeled frontstage and backstage contradictions. When partners are aware of the contradictions they experience in their relationship, these are frontstage contradictions. When contradictions operate frontstage, we hear relationship parties often use such expressions as "feeling pulled in opposite directions," "feeling a tension," "feeling a dilemma," or they express a desire to "have their cake and eat it too." In this case, they are very aware that the contradictions exist. At the level of grammar, we may also hear relationship parties dealing with frontstage issues as reflected in such language as "on the one hand … on the other hand" or use qualifying phrases such as "but," "however," or "nonetheless" to note the oppositions that they perceive. In fact, several researchers study contradictions by asking relationship parties to describe the contradictions they experience in their relationship. However, dialectical tensions need not be consciously felt or expressed. As Montgomery (1993) noted, they "may work backstage in a relationship beyond the partners' mindful awareness or ability to identify and describe them, but still contributing to a sense of unsettledness or instability in the relationship" (p. 206). Obviously, not all occasions of instability are the result of contradictions. When contradictions work backstage, scholars must employ research methods that do not rely on the parties' perceptions of contradictions. For example, the researcher can, from his or her perspective as an outside observer to the relationship, detect the presence of contradictions in the parties' interaction even though the parties may be oblivious themselves to the contradiction.

The question raised in the backstage–frontstage distinction is the issue of whether all people are equally capable of identifying, understanding, and embracing contradictions in their personal relationships. Researchers who adopt a dialectical perspective have not studied systematically individual differences in people's awareness and acceptance of contradictions of relating. Some work in psychology suggests that such differences may exist. For example, Kramer and Woodruff (1986) found that persons' acceptance of contradiction in reasoning increased from young to middle-aged to older adults. Peng and Nisbett (1999) found cultural differences in dialectical thinking, with Chinese participants more accepting than European Americans of contradictions in argument. These findings are intriguing to us, because they suggest that people are not equal in their awareness and acceptance of the general concept of contradiction. Future researchers should study how dialectical awareness varies not only as a function of age and culture, but also as a function of other individual-level differences such as cognitive style and personality characteristics.

Some Primary Contradictions of Relating

As we were planning this chapter, we hesitated about including a list of the different contradictions that researchers have identified so far. In spite of our reservations, we decided to include a discussion of these different dialectical pairs. We realize that any presentation of a typology of contradictions can easily be viewed as a "cookie-cutter" analytical tool. Scholars and students who want to analyze dialectical contradictions may be tempted to simply look on the list of contradictions and try to pick out the pair(s) that seem closest to what they are observing. The dangers of a "cookie-cutter" approach are two-fold, in our view. First, it seduces us to believe that the list of contradictions contained in the typology is complete or exhaustive; it is too easy to ignore any additional contradictions that may animate a given social situation. Second, it seduces us to ignore subtle variations within a single contradiction category. With these cautions in mind, we will discuss some of the contradictions that many scholars have identified to date.

Baxter and her colleagues (Baxter, 1993; Baxter & Montgomery, 1996; Werner & Baxter, 1994) described three families of contradictions that have been identified by several dialectical scholars: the dialectic of integration–separation, the dialectic of expression–nonexpression, and the dialectic of stability–change. We will discuss each in turn.

The Dialectic of Integration–Separation.   The dialectic of integration and separation is a family of related contradictions, all of which share the family resemblance of necessitating both partner integration and partner separation in relationships. A relationship is a union of two distinct individuals; without union or integration, a relationship will cease to exist, but in the absence of separate individuals, there is nothing to integrate. Relating partners thus face an ongoing challenge of negotiating the oppositions of integration and separation. The communicative "dance" between these oppositions has surfaced in diverse vocabularies and labels by which various scholars have identified the integration–separation dialectic (for a summary, see Werner & Baxter, 1994). Although some of these labels are mere synonyms of one another, we would be remiss in arguing that these terms are fully interchangeable either. Instead, we think that many of these scholars are pointing to subtle, situation-specific variations of the integration-separation dialectic, or what we referred to earlier as radiants of meaning within a multivocal contradiction of integration and separation. Put more simply, the integration–separation dialectic can surface in many possible forms.

To underscore what we mean by the multivocality of the integration-separation dialectic, let's consider in a bit more detail some of the radiants of meaning that researchers have identified so far. The negotiation of integration–separation can be experienced by relationship parties at the mundane level of how much time to spend together versus how much time to spend with other people, or on meeting other individual obligations, such as work or school (e.g., Baxter et al., 1997). It can be experienced as a dilemma of rights and obligations, for example, the right to have one's own needs fulfilled by the relationship versus the obligation of goodwill to fulfill our partner's needs (e.g., Baxter et al., 1997; Rawlins, 1983a). The integration–separation dialectic can surface as a dilemma of identity construction, that is, constructing and sustaining an individual self-identity beyond the "we" of the relationship, while at the same time relying on the partner to help in constructing and sustaining the "I"—one's sense of who one is as a person (e.g., Baxter & Montgomery, 1996). Partners require both an individual identity and an identity as part of the couple, but they must take care that neither identity overtakes the other.

Related, the integration–separation dialectic is seen in the interplay of similarity and difference. Similarity between partners is essential to building and maintaining a relationship, yet at the same time partners grow as individuals through their differences (e.g., Baxter & West, 2003; Wood, Dendy, Dordek, Germany, & Varallo, 1994). Identity may be the site for the integration–separation dialectic in yet a different way, as parties grapple with competing bases of self-identity. For example, Williams and Guendouzi (2000) noted that personal relationships for residents of retirement homes are often complicated, as residents experience both the integration demands of joining the community of the retirement home, yet on the other hand, also experience separation in wanting to keep alive their relationships and lives on the "outside." The integration–separation dialectic also can be experienced at the emotional level, with emotional positivity, liking, and love integrally bound up with opposing emotions of negativity, dislike, and hatred (e.g., Baxter & Montgomery, 1996; Baxter & West, 2003; Brown, Werner, & Altman, 1998). This dialectic has been identified in research on the maintenance of relationships with people who are dying (Miller & Knapp, 1986). We have also seen this in our research with wives whose husbands have Alzheimer's disease. These men are still physically present but emotionally and cognitively absent; thus, their wives experience the integration–separation dialectic as living in a state of "married widowhood" (Baxter et al., 2002).

So far, our examples have illustrated only variations in the internal form of the integration–separation dialectic. But an external contradiction between integration and separation can be identified as well (Baxter, 1993; Werner & Baxter, 1994). Relationship pairs need couple time, time they spend apart from others, in order to build and sustain intimacy; in other words, couples need separation from others. At the same time, however, relationship well-being is contingent on others' recognition and legitimation of the couple as a social unit; such external validation comes only through the couple's integration as a pair with others. So, although a dating couple needs time away from others they also need the recognition as a couple and the support from the others in their lives, for example friends and coworkers.

This "sampler" from the research is far from exhaustive, but we hope it illustrates our point that the integration-separation dialectic can be experienced in many ways and at many levels by relationship partners. It is important not to gloss over these variations that are part of the broader dialectic of integration–separation; dialectical scholars appreciate that contradictions are experienced in very particular ways that are deeply embedded in the details of partners' relational lives.

The Dialectic of Expression–Nonexpression. In its internal manifestation, this dialectic captures the dilemma of candor and discretion, or openness and closedness, as the relationship parties communicate with one another. Relationship closeness is built on the scaffolds of open and honest disclosure. Yet, at the same time, relationship closeness also involves respect for each person's right to privacy and the obligation to protect one's partner from the hurt that can often result from excessive honesty (e.g., Altman et al., 1981; Rawlins, 1983b). In its external manifestation, the dialectic of expression–nonexpression revolves around issues of revealing and concealing details of the relationship to friends, family members, and strangers. For example, Ford and her colleagues (Ford, Ray, & Ellis, 1999) painted a very poignant portrait of the simultaneous agony of secrecy and agony of revelation that is experienced by adult survivors of sexual abuse by a family member.

As was the case with the integration–separation dialectic, we know that the expression–nonexpression dialectic can be experienced in many different ways by relationship parties (for a detailed discussion of this issue, see Baxter & Montgomery, 1996). For example, parties can frame expression and nonexpression around issues of the individual's rights to privacy and, simultaneously, their freedom of expression (Rawlins, 1983b). Alternatively, parties might frame the expression–nonexpression dialectic around issues of protection, in which the decision to disclose or not revolves around a concern to protect oneself from hurt or embarrassment versus a concern to protect the other from hurt (e.g., Dindia, 1998). The expression–nonexpression dialectic could also be framed by the parties' expectations about communication efficiency and appropriateness in their relationship. For example, one of us once experienced an exchange with her then 5-year-old daughter in which the child said "You don't always have to tell me to brush my teeth in the morning, mom. I'm a big girl now!" From the child's perspective, this parental directive was regarded as inappropriate and unnecessary and thus ought not to be expressed. However, from the mom's perspective, her expression of a request was deemed appropriate and necessary in getting the child to perform the task of brushing her teeth.

The Dialectic of Stability–Change.   This dialectic refers to a family of contradictions that revolves around the unified opposition of predictability, certainty, routinization, and stability with simultaneous uncertainty, novelty, spontaneity, and change. Relationships require both stability and change to establish and sustain their well-being (Altman et al., 1981; Baxter & Montgomery, 1996; Bochner & Eisenberg, 1987). Change is both inevitable and healthy for a relationship. Relationship parties are ever-changing as individuals, and this requires ongoing adaptation in their relationship. For example, college students often find that they undergo significant personal growth and change while away at college and, if they are going to maintain precollege friendships, this will require adjustments and adaptations in those relationships. Further, a relationship pair faces ever-changing circumstances as they adapt to the world around them. Braithwaite and Harter (2000) discussed the challenges couples face when one of them becomes disabled. For example, if one becomes a wheelchair user, the couple might adapt to the changes the disability brings about while also maintaining their relationship. The couple might keep up some of their joint activities, like going to the movies, but need to adapt others, like a morning jogging routine. Change functions to keep the parties "on their toes," always adapting to the relational needs of the moment.

Change and adaptation also function to renew a relationship, keeping the relationship vibrant and alive by offsetting boredom or stagnation. However, this ongoing change is tempered by a relationship's simultaneous need for stability, as unchecked change would be chaotic and de-stabilizing. Baxter and Montgomery (1996) use the metaphor of jazz in discussing the dialectic of stability–change in relationships. Jazz artists follow a basic melody; this provides a backdrop of predictability and certainty and functions as the center of a given performance. This backdrop enables wildly spontaneous musical departures, which are wonderfully surprising and unpredictable. Relating is like jazz, a performance that tacks back and forth between the stable "givens" of the relationship and the unpredictable "new."

This dialectic, like the others we have discussed, is multivocal in nature. Stability and change can occur in many ways, at many levels (for a detailed discussion, see Baxter & Montgomery, 1996). It might be experienced as a couple's reflections on the ways their relationship in the present is both the same as, yet different from, their relationship as it existed in the past. For example, in our study of long-term married couples who decided to renew their wedding vows, we found this theme of same-yet-different to feature prominently in the meaning of the marriage renewal ceremony (Braithwaite & Baxter, 1995). Several couples expressed how the ceremony allowed them to highlight how their relationship had changed over the years, and yet how their love for one another was enduring. The negotiation of the stability–change dialectic is experienced at the more mundane level whenever relationship parties leave each other's physical presence. As Sigman (1991) insightfully observed, whenever relationship parties experience physical separation, they communicatively sustain the continuity of their relationship through such activities as carrying token reminders of the partner (e.g., a photograph or a ring), saying how much they will miss each other, and discussing the particulars of their reunion (e.g., "see you at 7 o'clock."). The interplay of stability and change may be especially important to relationship parties during times of major transition in their relationship, as Stamp (1994) observed for married couples as they face parenthood for the first time. For example, some new parents cope with the changes the baby brings to their relationship by trying to preserve their regular "date night" for just the two of them. Braithwaite, Baxter, and Harper (1998) found that stepfamilies struggled with the interplay between the "old" family of origin and the "new" family that includes a stepparent and possibly stepsiblings. It is important to understand that our goal here is to illustrate the multivocality of the stability–change dialectic, as there is no way we can discuss all the ways in which the interplay between stability and change can be experienced by relationship parties.

Our examples of stability–change have emphasized the internal contradiction, and we want to note that issues of stability and change also can face relationship parties in the form of an external contradiction. For example, stability and order in any society are served by having institutionalized relationship forms in which expectations are fairly standard from one couple to the next; for example, the institution of marriage. At the same time, however, our society holds a strong expectation that every relationship is somehow unique from all others. Uniqueness is a source of unpredictability or novelty, and it is through the absence of standardization that potentially new relationship forms can emerge. Braithwaite and Baxter (1995) identified the conventional–unique contradiction as one of the salient features that made the marriage renewal ceremony so meaningful to long-term married couples. While they sought to celebrate the traditionality of marriage, each couple sought to have a ceremony that expressed their uniqueness as a couple, for example with special flowers, music, clothes, or food.

The vast majority of the dialectical research has been devoted to the identification of the contradictions that animate given relationship types or circumstances. However, some research activity has been devoted to two additional principles of dialectical thinking.

CONTRADICTIONS AND CHANGE

Dialectical scholars agree that the dynamic interplay of unified opposites results in ongoing change for relationship parties. The most common conception of change among dialectical theorists is a cyclical model, in which responsiveness to one dialectical pole creates pressure to attend to the opposite dialectical pole (e.g., Altman et al., 1981; Baxter & Montgomery, 1996; Conville, 1991; Cornforth, 1968). Although the interplay of opposed tendencies can be negotiated in temporary moments or periods in which all oppositions are fulfilled at once, it is much more common to see a pattern in which one pole is temporarily met at a cost to the other pole(s). The communicative actions that parties take at Time 1 in negotiating a given contradiction change how that contradiction is experienced at Time 2. For example, if parties emphasize their connectedness, pressure will build with the unmet demands for individual autonomy; at some subsequent point in time, the parties are likely to adapt their relationship to incorporate greater individual autonomy, but then pressure will build for greater connectedness. Thus, contradiction inherently functions as a source of ongoing change in a relationship.

Although this cyclic model, with its image of a pendulum swinging back and forth in an unending manner, is a useful one, dialectical scholars view it as too simplistic. First, the cycles of personal relationships do not occur with the regularity of a pendulum. Instead, relationship swings, or cycles, take place at irregular moments and in uneven amplitudes (e.g., Altman et al., 1981). For example, for most of us, developing a close friendship involves an unpredictable series of ups and downs; we may move closer and then suddenly something happens to drive us apart for a time. Several dialectical scholars (e.g., Baxter & Erbert, 1999; Baxter & Simon, 1993; Conville, 1991, 1998; Pawlowski, 1998) have argued that relationship change is an erratic process of up-and-down, back-and-forth motion propelled by pivotal turning-point events such as making a decision to make a commitment of exclusivity, experiencing a major fight that temporarily ruptures the pair's closeness, or experiencing sexual intimacy for the first time. When we experience positive turning points, a relationship is propelled toward greater closeness or commitment, whereas negative turning points produce a reduction in closeness or commitment. According to dialectical scholars, turning points are often moments of heightened dialectical struggle that are handled with varying degrees of effectiveness thereby resulting in a positive or negative effect on the relationship. When a dating partner says "I love you" for the first time, this may bring the relationship closer or create distance if the other party is not ready for greater commitment. Thus, contradictions can propel relationship change at major points or periods of crisis, transition, or transformation.

Second, the dialectical pendulum does not swing equally for all contradictions. In general, previous research suggests that not all contradictions are equally important in turning-point relationship change. Consistently, the integration-separation dialectic surfaces as the most central family of contradictions (e.g., Baxter, 1990; Baxter & Erbert, 1999; Pawlowski, 1998). Further, the salience of various contradictions appears to differ depending on whether the change takes place early or later in a relationship's history (e.g., Baxter, 1990; Pawlowski, 1998).

Third, the very meaning of a given contradiction shifts over time. Goldsmith (1990) nicely illustrated this point in asking romantic partners to reflect on issues of connection and autonomy in the development of their relationship. She found that what it meant to be connected and what it meant to be autonomous shifted over time as the relationship developed. For example, the autonomy–connection dialectic surfaced in the dilemma of whether to get involved with the partner in the first place, whether to make a commitment of exclusivity to the partner, and how to negotiate self versus partner wants and needs. Rawlins's (1992) work on the contradictions of friendship across the life cycle also demonstrates that contradictions surface in different ways over time as people grow older. Thus, each time a relating pair "cycles back" the meaning of the contradiction has likely shifted somewhat. For example, parents and children experience an ongoing negotiation of autonomy and connection as the child enters school, in adolescence, and in adulthood. This ongoing change in the meaning of a given contradiction has led dialectical scholars to propose either a helix (Conville, 1991) or a spiral (Baxter & Montgomery, 1996) as a substitute for the cycle image. In both a helix and a spiral, motion always swings full circle but one never returns exactly to the same place as before.

To date, most of the work on dialectics and relationship change has focused on major moments of change, what we have referred to as turning points of change. But we suspect that dialectics also produce smaller changes on a more microscopic level. For example, VanLear (1998) argued, based on his empirical work in monitoring openness and closedness behaviors in relationship pairs, that cycling is a complex dynamic. Cycles can vary in amplitude, with very large or very modest swings between dialectical poles. Further, shorter cycles of change can be nested in longer cycles of change; for example, as part of a general upswing in openness, smaller cycles of openness–closedness can be identified. The major changes captured in turning points probably reflect large amplitude changes only. More research attention is needed to understand smaller, day-to-day fluctuations as parties negotiate the ongoing interplay of unified opposites.

CONTRADICTIONS AND COMMUNICATION

What is the role of communication in a social dialectics theory? Basically, dialectical scholars argue that contradiction is produced in the communicative practices of the relating parties. It is through communication that contradictions gain a social life. How parties communicate and construct a given contradiction at one point in time holds implications for how that contradiction will emerge in their future interactions.

Baxter and Montgomery (1996) developed a typology of communicative practices by which parties construct, and negotiate, the contradictions of their relationship. We will summarize their typology here with the same cautionary note we raised earlier with respect to the typology of contradictions: (a) The communicative practices we discuss here are not exhaustive, and (b) it is important to pay attention to the details of each communicative enactment between parties in order to appreciate subtle variations in a given communicative practice.

Because of the cyclical (or more accurately, helical or spiraling) pattern that most commonly describes dialectical change, it is no surprise that researchers most often find communicative practices enable pendulum swings between dialectical polarities (e.g., Baxter, 1990; Baxter, Braithwaite, Golish, & Olson, 2002; Baxter & Simon, 1993; Baxter & Widenmann, 1993; Ford et al., 1999; VanLear, 1998). Baxter and Montgomery (1996) labeled these practices *spiraling inversion* and *segmentation*. When they enact *spiraling inversion*, relationship parties tack back and forth through time, alternating an emphasis on one dialectical pole with an emphasis on another dialectical pole. For example, a busy dual-career couple trying to manage the integration–separation dialectic might move back and forth between spending time together and spending time apart fulfilling individual obligations and desires. During particularly long workdays apart, they may connect via email, a quick phone call, or having flowers sent to their partner's office. In enacting *segmentation*, relationship parties negotiate by topic or activity domain, recognizing that in Domain A one dialectical pole will be emphasized whereas in Domain B another dialectical pole will be emphasized. For example, a relationship pair may reach agreement that certain topics are "off limits" for discussion, thereby privileging nonexpression, while at the same time the pair may agree that complete candor is expected on other topics. The busy professional couple may agree not to talk about work at the dinner table and, at the same time, agree that they will immediately discuss any work-related issues that would affect their relationship. Both *spiraling inversion* and *segmentation* allow a relationship pair to move in and out, back and forth, between oppositions. Over time and over multiple topic–activity domains, both dialectical demands are met.

Although a less common pattern of dialectical change is one in which both dialectical tendencies are fulfilled at the same time, it can occur in a given dialectical moment. Several communicative practices enable such "both–and" simultaneity. Baxter and Montgomery (1996) discussed three: *balance*, *integration*, and *recalibration*. When relationship parties enact *balance*, they basically strive for a compromise response, that is, a response in which both dialectical demands are fulfilled partially. For example, the pair struggling with the expression–nonexpression dialectic may agree that all topics are appropriately managed through partial disclosure, that is, revelation of some things but not everything. Such a practice is neither totally open nor totally closed, but somewhere in the middle.

The practice of *integration* involves a complete, not partial, fulfillment of both dialectical polarities at the same time. Given that the polarities and oppositions negate each other, the reader might wonder how this communicative practice is even possible. Several scholars have argued that communication rituals are one form of integration. As Roberts (1988) stated, "Ritual can hold both sides of a contradiction at the same time. … For instance, a wedding ceremony has within it both loss and mourning and joy and celebration" (p. 16). Roberts went on to say that what enables a ritual to enact integration is the fact that it is symbolically multilayered; at the same time, its many layers of meaning can collectively address both oppositions. For example, Braithwaite and Baxter (1995) found that the ritual of renewing marital vows celebrates marriage as *both* public and private, conventional and unique, and stable and changing. When they asked stepfamily members to talk about rituals that had been success-fully enacted in their respective blended families, Braithwaite et al. (1998) found further evi-dence of dialectical integration. Successful rituals managed to pay homage to both the "old" family (the family of origin) and the "new" family (the family of origin plus the stepparent and possible stepsiblings). So, a blended family may display a wreath from the original Smith family, a candle holder from the original Jones family, and each year they add a new Christmas tree ornament to celebrate the new Smith–Jones family.

Recalibration occurs when a relationship pair is able to reconstruct a contradiction so that the dialectical demands are no longer experienced as oppositional. For example, one of us once interviewed a person who described an instance of recalibration in her romantic rela-tionship. She told us that her boyfriend was beginning to feel smothered by their status as a couple, so she started to do more things individually—not as a way to fulfill her needs for autonomy but as a way to achieve a more secure closeness in the relationship with her boyfriend. She laughed and said that she was spending time on the relationship, alone. In appreciating that autonomous activity ironically fulfilled the demands for connection, this person described for us what recalibration looks like. This practice is a fleeting one which temporarily turns a contradiction on its head.

What is common to all these communicative practices is an appreciation of the dialectical nature of relating. All of them work well to help relational parties manage the dialectical ten-sions in their relationship. However, Baxter and Montgomery (1996) also described two com-municative practices that they regard as less functional in negotiating the dialectics of relating: *denial* and *disorientation*. In communicative *denial*, the parties attempt to extinguish one oppo-sition of a given dialectic, ignoring its existence or wishing it away. While a relational pair may delude itself temporarily, this practice is doomed to fail because relationships necessitate both oppositions of a given contradiction. It is only a matter of time before the pressure mounts for a response to the opposition that is denied or ignored. When the young daughter of one of us pronounces to her mother that "I can do it all by myself!" it is only matter of seconds (some-times minutes) before the futility of her denied interdependence becomes apparent and she needs to seek assistance from an adult. In enacting *disorientation*, parties construct contradic-tion as a totally negative problem, which they find overwhelming. When one of us was teach-ing social dialectical theory to a class, one student commented "Why do people even bother with getting involved in relationships, if all they are is one big dilemma after another!" This response illustrates a posture of disorientation, an attitude of doomed failure.

It is important to point out that dialectical scholars do not yet have a very good under-standing of dialectically functional or dysfunctional communicative practices. So far, only two studies have examined factors that relate to parties' dialectically oriented communication. Sabourin and Stamp (1995) compared abusive to nonabusive families, and found that abusive families have less functional ways than nonabusive families to negotiate the dialectics of integration–separation and stability–change. Bridge and Baxter (1992) reported that cohesion in the work group and equality in job status affect how work associates negotiate the contra-diction of their simultaneous status as both friend and coworker.

THE FAMILY TREE OF SOCIAL DIALECTICAL THEORY

As we stressed at the beginning of this chapter, social dialectical theory is not a single theory, rather, it is a family of theories. It is important to understand what different dialectical approaches share in common and how they depart from one another as well (Baxter & Montgomery, 1998).

In this last section of the chapter, we will briefly describe nine different branches on the family tree of social dialectics.

The first branch of the dialectical family tree was initially presented by Altman et al. (1981) over 20 years ago. As this theoretical branch has evolved, its developers have labeled it a transactional worldview. Research from this perspective has emphasized the physical and social context in which multiple contradictions are experienced (for a recent review of this approach, see Brown et al., 1998). The ethnographic study of Mormon polygamous families by Altman and Ginat (1996) characterized this approach to social dialectics. They observed families in polygamous households, studying their daily life, weddings, and other celebrations. The researchers painted a complex portrait of the contradictory nature of these families that are at once many distinct family units yet, at the same time, a single family.

A second branch of the dialectical family tree, centered in the work of Bochner and his colleagues (e.g., Bochner, 1984; Bochner & Eisenberg, 1987; Cissna et al., 1990), has roots in family studies. As this branch has continued to evolve, these scholars have adopted an autobiographical narrative method, in which the researcher attempts to capture, through individuals' in-depth personal stories, the complicated, contradictory, and dynamic process of everyday relational life (for a detailed summary, see Bochner, Ellis, & Tillmann-Healy, 1998).

A third branch of the dialectical family tree is represented by the work of Rawlins (e.g., Rawlins, 1983a, 1983b, 1992, 2000). Centered in the study of platonic friendship, this branch has displayed a commitment to the contradictions of friendship that occur over the life cycle, from the friendships of children, to adolescent friendships, to the friendships of adulthood.

A fourth family member is represented by the relational transitions approach articulated by Conville (e.g., 1991, 1998). Of the several dialectical branches, Conville's approach is tied most closely to the developmental course of a relationship. He argued that people in a relationship inevitably experience differences between them. When these differences reach crisis proportions, they are dialectical moments of change that bring a relationship to its next developmental stage. Conville's research approach is characterized by an interpretive method that he applies sequentially to the chronological events that relational partners tell about the history of their relationship.

A fifth branch of the dialectical family tree has been linked to the work of VanLear (e.g., 1998). Labeled dialectical empiricism, researchers adopt a quantitative approach in analyzing mathematically the cyclic patterning by which relating partners move back and forth behaviorally between actions that embrace opposite functions. In particular, VanLear identified smaller cycles of openness and closedness that function within larger pendulum swings between greater disclosure and greater discretion between partners.

A sixth branch of the dialectical family is characterized by the work of Dindia (e.g., 1998, 2000). Her work is focused the most narrowly of the several family branches on the single contradiction of openness–closedness. In addition, Dindia's approach also takes the most individualistic perspective. She concentrates on decisions individuals make to disclose (and not disclose) potentially stigmatizing information about themselves to others, for example, disclosing one's homosexuality or illness, such as HIV or AIDS.

The seventh branch of the dialectical family is relational dialectics (e.g., Baxter, 1988, 1990, 1993; Baxter & Montgomery, 1996; Montgomery, 1992, 1993). In their 1996 book, Baxter and Montgomery grounded their theoretical approach in the dialogism theory of Russian scholar Mikhail Bakhtin (1981, 1984). Bakhtin argued that social life should not be viewed as a monologue in which only one voice, theme, or perspective is heard. Instead, social life should be conceived as a dialogue in which multiple opposing themes or perspectives are given voice. "Dialogue" is a complex construct in dialogism and in relational dialectics, with at least five distinct meanings (Baxter, 2004). Space limitations do not permit us to elaborate on the richness of this concept, beyond the statement that selves and communication are positioned as social, not psychological, processes. Thus relationships, not individuals, hold contradictions. The communication practices by which contradictions are produced and negotiated are joint enactments of the two parties, not individual actions of each party acting in response to the psychological tension of a felt dilemma.

Two final branches of the dialectical family tree can be identified if we broaden our gaze beyond research on personal relationships to consider social relations in its broadest sense—any occasion of interaction between people. An eighth branch of the dialectical family can be identified in various discourse-analysis scholarship. Discourse analysis is a perspective devoted to the microlevel details of enacted talk—turn-taking, interruptions, pauses, and so forth. In their careful and detailed analysis of talk uttered in specific contexts, some discourse analysts have argued that communication is a dilemmatic undertaking, characterized by contradictory tensions and contrary themes. Whether the talk is that uttered in academic colloquium presentations (Tracy, 1997) or the ideologically laced talk of advocacy and justification (e.g., Billig, 1987; Billig et al., 1988), this work adopts a microscopic lens in viewing communication as riddled with contradictory themes.

The ninth, and final, branch of dialectical theory is centered in work on culture and communication (e.g., Carbaugh, 1996; Fitch, 1998). Carbaugh theorized a basic cultural dialectic of identification: a dialectical tension between commonality, on the one hand, and difference, on the other hand. Carbaugh argued that all cultural communication practices contain two accents, what he called "two sides of the same coin" (p. 201). On the one hand, cultural communication accomplishes a sense of shared identity among cultural members, and such sharing is essential for coherent communication. Yet, at the same time, cultural communication accomplishes the construction of social difference, with speakers behaving in different ways depending on their roles, positions, and relationships toward one another. Fitch agreed with Carbaugh in her claim that "the conversation of communal life is more a lively argument than a cozy chat" (p. 152). Fitch focused on the indigenous nature of contradictory dilemmas, emphasizing that the specific dilemmas will vary from culture to culture.

Why do these distinctions among branches of the dialectical theory family tree matter? We believe it is important as a matter of factual accuracy to understand that dialectical theorists view and study dialectics somewhat differently. If we imagine dialectics as a multifaceted diamond, each dialectical perspective functions as a different facet of the whole. Some dialectical theorists "specialize" in the contradictions of a particular type of personal relationship, whereas other dialectical theorists are not relationship-specific. Some dialectical theorists emphasize the fluidity of contradiction, whereas others emphasize the structure of contradiction. Some theorists emphasize the importance of locating contradictions in the details of a social and physical setting, whereas others focus on dilemmas that are located inside the heads of individuals. Some dialectical theorists emphasize the indigenous and idiosyncratic nature of contradictions, whereas other dialectical theorists emphasize a goal of generalizing contradictions across contexts, relationships, and cultures. Some scholars study contradictions quantitatively, some study contradictions qualitatively, and some move back and forth between both quantitative and qualitative approaches. In short, there are different nuances among the various branches of the dialectics family tree that should not be ignored.

The editors of this volume asked authors to address the issue of what type of theory they were describing. Given the nine-branch "family tree" metaphor we just described, it is easy to see why this is a difficult task for social dialectical theorists. In general terms, however, we will argue that dialectical theories are not focused on goals of prediction, explanation, and control.

Dialectical theorists as a group are not interested in questions of cause-and-effect. Instead, we think that it is more useful to think of dialectical theories as examples of what Turner (1986) referred to as descriptive–sensitizing theories, that is, "loosely assembled congeries of concepts intended only to sensitize and orient researchers to certain critical processes" (p. 11). Dialectical theories, then, are intended as heuristic, orienting our observational eye and directing our understanding of personal relationships down pathways that are not focused on prediction of behavior and the formulation of testable hypotheses.

At the same time that dialectical theorists occupy different branches of the dialectical family tree, they also share family membership and thus share certain theoretical premises and concepts in common. Our goal in this chapter was to focus our attention on these commonalties shared by dialectical theorists.

CONCLUSION

Our goal in this chapter has been to provide the reader with a "roadmap" of the basic tenets shared by the group of theories we have labeled "social dialectics." Our review is biased in its alignment with the relational dialectics branch of the social-dialectics family tree. However, regardless of which branch of the tree one perches on, certain key assumptions are shared in common: (a) relating is characterized by the dynamic interplay of unified opposites, or contradictions; (b) such dialectical interplay results in a pattern of ongoing change for relating partners; and (c) the contradictions of relating are constituted in the communication between partners. Future researchers need to devote more attention to an understanding of contradictions and relationship change. In addition, more scholarly attention is needed in understanding dialectically functional and dysfunctional communication practices.

ADDITIONAL READING

The reader interested in finding out more about social dialectics in general should read the Altman et al. (1981) essay. This essay is particularly strong in providing an historical overview of dialectical thinking and in differentiating dialectical from systems thinking. Early work published in communication by Rawlins (1983a, 1983b, 1989) is also important in marking the emergence of this perspective. Baxter and Montgomery's (1996) book provided an overview of how dialectical thinking can inform our understanding of all phases of relationship development; with the exception of the first overview chapter, the book articulates relational dialectics and its roots in dialogism theory. The edited volume by Montgomery and Baxter (1998) provided an overview of most of the branches of the social dialectics tree and provides the reader with sense of how these various perspectives are both similar to yet different from one another.

REFERENCES

Altman, I., & Ginat, J. (1996). *Polygamous families in contemporary society*. New York: Cambridge University Press.

Altman, I., Vinsel, A., & Brown, B. (1981). Dialectic conceptions in social psychology: An application to social penetration and privacy regulation. *Advances in Experimental Social Psychology, 14,* 107–160.

Bakhtin, M. (1981). *The dialogic imagination: Four essays by M. M. Bakhtin* (M. Holquist, Ed.; C. Emerson & M. Holquist, Trans.). Austin: University of Texas Press.

Bakhtin, M. (1984). *Problems of Dostoevsky's poetics* (C. Emerson, Ed. & Trans.). Minneapolis: University of Minnesota Press.

Baxter, L. A. (1988). A dialectical perspective on communication strategies in relationship development. In S. Duck (Ed.), *Handbook of personal relationships* (pp. 257–273). New York: Wiley.

Baxter, L. A. (1990). Dialectical contradictions in relationship development. *Journal of Social and Personal Relationships, 7,* 69–88.

Baxter, L. A. (1993). The social side of personal relationships: A dialectical analysis. In S. Duck (Ed.), *Social context and relationships* (pp. 139–165). Newbury Park, CA: Sage.

Baxter, L. A. (2004). Dialogues of relating. In R. Anderson, L. Baxter, & K. Cissna (Eds.), *Dialogic perspectives in communication* (pp. 107–124). Thousand Oaks, CA: Sage.

Baxter, L. A., Braithwaite, D.O., Golish, T., & Olson, L. (2002). Contradictions of interaction for wives of elderly husbands with adult dementia. *Journal of Applied Communication Research, 30,* 1–26.

Baxter, L. A., & Erbert, L. A. (1999). Perceptions of dialectical contradictions in turning points of development in heterosexual romantic relationships. *Journal of Social and Personal Relationships, 16,* 547–569.

Baxter, L. A., Mazanec, M., Nicholson, J., Pittman, G., Smith, K., & West, L. (1997). Everyday loyalties and betrayals in personal relationships. *Journal of Social and Personal Relationships, 14,* 655–678.

Baxter, L. A., & Montgomery, B. M. (1996). *Relating: Dialogues & dialectics.* New York: Guilford.

Baxter, L. A., & Montgomery, B. M. (1998). A guide to dialectical approaches to studying personal relationships. In B. M. Montgomery & L. A. Baxter (Eds.), *Dialectical approaches to studying personal relationships* (pp. 1–16). Mahwah, NJ: Lawrence Erlbaum Associates, Inc.

Baxter, L. A., & Simon, E. P. (1993). Relationship maintenance strategies and dialectical contradictions in personal relationships. *Journal of Social and Personal Relationships, 10,* 225–242.

Baxter, L. A., & West, L. (2003). Couple perceptions of their similarities and differences: A dialectical perspective. *Journal of Social and Personal Relationships, 20,* 491–514.

Baxter, L. A., & Widenmann, S. (1993). Revealing and not revealing the status of romantic relationships to social networks. *Journal of Social and Personal Relationships, 10,* 321–337.

Billig, M. (1987). *Arguing and thinking: A rhetorical approach to social psychology.* New York: Cambridge University Press.

Billig, M., Condor, S., Edwards, D., Gane, M., Middleton, D., & Radley, A. (1988). *Ideological dilemmas: A social psychology of everyday thinking.* Newbury Park, CA: Sage.

Bochner, A. P. (1984). The functions of communication in interpersonal bonding. In C. Arnold & J. Bowers (Eds.), *Handbook of rhetorical and communication theory* (pp. 544–621). Boston: Allyn & Bacon.

Bochner, A. P., & Eisenberg, E. (1987). Family process: System perspectives. In C. R. Berger & S. Chaffee (Eds.), *Handbook of communication science* (pp. 540–563). Beverly Hills, CA: Sage.

Bochner, A. P., Ellis, C., & Tillmann-Healy, L. (1998). Mucking around looking for truth. In B. M. Montgomery & L. A. Baxter (Eds.), *Dialectical approaches to studying personal relationships* (pp. 41–62). Mahwah, NJ: Lawrence Erlbaum Associates, Inc.

Braithwaite, D. O., & Baxter, L. A. (1995). "I do" again: The relational dialectics of renewing marriage vows. *Journal of Social and Personal Relationships, 12,* 177–198.

Braithwaite, D. O., Baxter, L. A., & Harper, A. M. (1998). The role of rituals in the management of the dialectical tension of "old" and "new" in blended families. *Communication Studies, 49,* 101–120.

Braithwaite, D. O., & Harter, L. (2000). Communication and the management of dialectical tensions in the personal relationships of people with disabilities. In D. O. Braithwaite & T. L. Thompson, (Eds.), *Handbook of communication and people with disabilities: Research and application* (pp. 17–36) Mahwah, NJ: Lawrence Erlbaum Associates, Inc.

Bridge, K., & Baxter, L. A. (1992). Blended relationships: Friends as work associates. *Western Journal of Communication, 56,* 200–225.

Brown, B. B., Werner, C. M., & Altman, I. (1998). Choice points for dialecticians: A dialectical-transactional perspective on close relationships. In B. M. Montgomery & L. A. Baxter (Eds.), *Dialectical approaches to studying personal relationships* (pp. 137–154). Mahwah, NJ: Lawrence Erlbaum Associates, Inc.

Carbaugh, D. (1996). *Situating selves: The communication of social identities in American scenes.* Albany: State University of New York Press.

Cissna, K. N., Cox, D. E., & Bochner, A. P. (1990). The dialectic of marital and parental relationships within the stepfamily. *Communication Monographs, 57,* 44–61.

Conville, R. L. (1991). *Relational transitions.* Westport, CT: Praeger.

Conville, R. L. (1998). Telling stories: Dialectics of relational transition. In B. M. Montgomery & L. A. Baxter (Eds.), *Dialectical approaches to studying personal relationships* (pp. 17–40). Mahwah, NJ: Lawrence Erlbaum Associates, Inc.

Cornforth, M. (1968). *Materialism and the dialectical method*. New York: International Publishers.

Dindia, K. (1998). "Going into and coming out of the closet": The dialectics of stigma disclosure. In B. M. Montgomery & L. A. Baxter (Eds.), *Dialectical approaches to studying personal relationships* (pp. 83–108). Mahwah, NJ: Lawrence Erlbaum Associates, Inc.

Dindia, K. (2000). Self-disclosure, identity, and relationship development: A dialectical perspective. In K. Dindia & S. Duck (Eds.), *Communication and personal relationships* (pp. 147–162). New York: Wiley.

Erbert, L. A. (2000). Conflict and dialectics: Perceptions of dialectical contradictions in marital conflict. *Journal of Social and Personal Relationships, 17,* 638–659.

Fitch, K. L. (1998). *Speaking relationally: Culture, communication, and interpersonal connection*. New York: Guilford.

Ford, L. A., Ray, E. B., & Ellis, B. H. (1999). Translating scholarship on intrafamilial sexual abuse: The utility of a dialectical perspective for adult survivors. *Journal of Applied Communication Research, 27,* 139–157.

Goldsmith, D. (1990). A dialectical perspective on the expression of autonomy and connection in romantic relationships. *Western Journal of Communication, 54,* 537–556.

Kramer, D. A., & Woodruff, D. S. (1986). Relativistic and dialectical thought in three adult age-groups. *Human Development, 29,* 280–290.

Marx, K. (1961). *Capital: Volume 1*. Moscow: Foreign Languages Publishing House.

Miller, V. D., & Knapp, M. L. (1986). Communication paradoxes and the maintenance of living relationships with the dying. *Journal of Family Issues, 7,* 255–275.

Mircovic, D. (1980). *Dialectic and sociological thought*. St. Catherines, Ontario, Canada: Diliton.

Montgomery, B. M. (1992). Communication as the interface between couples and culture. *Communication Yearbook, 15,* 475–507.

Montgomery, B. M. (1993). Relationship maintenance versus relationship change: A dialectical dilemma. *Journal of Social and Personal Relationships, 10,* 205–224.

Montgomery, B. M., & Baxter, L. A. (Eds.). (1998). *Dialectical approaches to studying personal relationships.* Mahwah, NJ: Lawrence Erlbaum Associates.

Pawlowski, D. R. (1998). Dialectical tensions in marital partners' accounts of their relationships. *Communication Quarterly, 46,* 396–416.

Peng, K., & Nisbett, R. E. (1999). Culture, dialectics, and reasoning about contradiction. *American Psychologist, 54,* 741–754.

Rawlins, W. K. (1983a). Negotiating close friendship: The dialectic of conjunctive freedoms. *Human Communication Research, 9,* 255–266.

Rawlins, W. K. (1983b). Openness as problematic in ongoing friendships: Two conversational dilemmas. *Communication Monographs, 50,* 1–13.

Rawlins, W. K. (1989). A dialectical analysis of the tensions, functions, and strategic challenges of communication in young adult friendships. *Communication Yearbook, 12,* 157–189.

Rawlins, W. K. (1992). *Friendship matters: Communication, dialectics, and the life course*. New York: Aldine de Gruyter.

Rawlins, W. K. (2000). Teaching as a mode of friendship. *Communication Theory, 10,* 5–26.

Roberts, J. (1988). Setting the frame: Definition, functions, and typology of rituals. In E. Imber-Black, J. Roberts, & R. A. Whiting (Eds.), *Rituals in family and family therapy* (pp. 3–46). New York: Norton.

Sabourin, T. C., & Stamp, G. H. (1995). Communication and the experience of dialectical tensions in family life. *Communication Monographs, 62,* 213–242.

Sigman, S. J. (1991). Handling the discontinuous aspects of continuous social relationships: Toward research on the persistence of social forms. *Communication Theory, 1,* 106–127.

Stamp, G. H. (1994). The appropriation of the parental role through communication during the transition to parenthood. *Communication Monographs, 61,* 89–112.

Tracy, K. (1997). *Colloquium: Dilemmas of academic discourse*. Norwood, NJ: Ablex.

Turner, J. H. (1986). *The structure of sociological theory* (4th ed.). Chicago: Dorsey.

VanLear, C. A. (1998). Dialectic empiricism: Science and relationship metaphors. In B. M. Montgomery & L. A. Baxter (Eds.), *Dialectical approaches to studying personal relationships* (pp. 109–136). Mahwah, NJ: Lawrence Erlbaum Associates, Inc.

Werner, C. M., & Baxter, L. A. (1994). Temporal qualities of relationships: Organismic, transactional and dialectical views. In M. L. Knapp & G. R. Miller (Eds.), *Handbook of interpersonal communication* (2nd ed., pp. 323–379). Newbury Park, CA: Sage.

Williams, A., & Guendouzi, J. (2000). Adjusting to "the home": Dialectical dilemmas and personal relationships in a retirement community. *Journal of Communication, 50,* 65–82.

Wood, J. T., Dendy, L. L., Dordek, E., Germany, M., & Varallo, S. M. (1994). Dialectic of difference: A thematic analysis of intimates' meanings for differences. In K. Carter & M. Prisnell (Eds.), *Interpretive approaches to interpersonal communication* (pp. 115–136). New York: SUNY Press.

QUESTIONS TO PONDER

1. Have you experienced the dialectics of integration–separation, expression–nonexpression, and stability–change in your own friendships, romantic relationships, and family relationships? Provide examples that highlight how you and your partner have experienced these contradictions simultaneously in a close relationship.
2. When experiencing contradictions in relating, how have you and your partner communicatively negotiated them? Provide examples. Have some ways of negotiating contradictions been more (or less) functional than other ways?
3. Cornforth (1968) said that contradictions do not exist in isolation of one another but instead are interwoven in complex ways which he calls a "knot" of contradictions. How might the dialectics of integration–separation, expression–nonexpression, and stability–change weave together? Discuss examples where you have seen these interrelated knots of contradictions.
4. Do you think that individuals differ in their capacity to identify and accept contradiction in their personal relationships? What individual factors (e.g., personality characteristics, cognitive styles, life experiences) do you believe might increase (or decrease) people's awareness and acceptance of the contradictions present in personal relationships? How might such awareness and acceptance relate to the ways partners communicate?
5. For theories that have prediction, explanation, and control as their main function, researchers will engage in a rigorous process of hypothesis-testing to determine the validity of these theories. How might a scholar establish the validity of a theory such as social dialectics, whose goal is heuristic understanding, rather than cause-and-effect explanation?

16

Communication Accommodation Theory

Howard Giles
University of California, Santa Barbara

Tania Ogay
University of Fribourg, Switzerland

INTRODUCTION

Imagine a conversation between an older male professor of British origin, a male African American undergraduate student, and a female postdoctoral student from Switzerland taking place in an American University. Think of the variety of social dimensions involved in this situation: gender, culture and ethnicity, social and occupational status, age, and so forth. How are the different personal and social identities negotiated during the interaction? Who changes his or her communicative style to accommodate whom? What are the outcomes of such accommodating behaviors on the relationship between the interactants? In what follows, we shall make frequent use of this scenario.

Communication Accommodation Theory (CAT) provides a wide-ranging framework aimed at predicting and explaining many of the adjustments individuals make to create, maintain, or decrease social distance in interaction. It explores the different ways in which we accommodate our communication, our motivations for doing so, and the consequences. CAT addresses interpersonal communication issues, yet also links it with the larger context of the *intergroup* stakes of an encounter. In other words, sometimes our communications are driven by our personal identities as Janet or Richard while at others—and sometimes within the very same interaction—our words, nonverbals, and demeanor are fueled, instead and almost entirely, by our social identities as members of groups; that is Janet now speaks not so much *as the individual Janet* but as someone who represents communication scholars to groups of chemists, biologists, and physicists.

Since its inception in the early 1970s, CAT has undergone several conceptual refinements and theoretical elaborations, as exemplified by moves from speech into the nonlinguistic (Giles,

Mulac, Bradac, & Johnson, 1987). Originally a sociopsychological model exploring accent and bilingual shifts in interactions (Giles, 1973; Giles, Taylor, & Bourhis, 1973), CAT has been expanded into an "interdisciplinary model of relational and identity processes in communicative interaction" (N. Coupland & Jaworski, 1997, pp. 241–242). Although language remains a central focus of the theory, other communicative symbols that people use to signal their identities (e.g., dress and hair styles, cosmetics, and eating patterns) can also be understood from a CAT perspective. Because the extensive amount of CAT research and theorizing can be somewhat overwhelming, predictive models have been developed in an effort to better organize and summarize thinking on these matters. In addition, recent theoretically driven reviews of research, engaged in a more textually flowing nonpropositional fashion, have emerged. References for specific work in these domains are presented at the end of the chapter. For now, we'll begin with a presentation of the basic principles and concepts of the theory, and thereafter we will review different areas where CAT has been applied and expanded.

BASIC PRINCIPLES AND CONCEPTS OF CAT

Basic Principles of CAT

- Communication is influenced not only by features of the immediate situation and participants' initial orientations to it, but also by the socio-historical context in which the interaction is embedded. For example, an isolated encounter between any particular police officer and citizen could be marred by alleged and past hostile relations between other members of these two groups in the neighborhood or on the media (as would be apparent probably for many citizens of color in the Rampant area of Los Angeles);
- Communication is not only a matter of merely and only exchanging information about facts, ideas, and emotions (often called referential communications), but salient social category memberships are often negotiated during an interaction through the process of accommodation. For example, when being quizzed by Howard Giles British relatives on some (for them, curious) aspect of American entertainment and media, his shift from a British into a more American dialect is meant to be far more telling than the overt answer provided. Being conveyed here is the feeling that he is no longer a recent immigrant to the United States, but now a fully fledged American citizen who has embraced many American ideals;
- Interactants have expectations regarding optimal levels of accommodation. These expectations are based on stereotypes about outgroup members as well as on the prevailing social and situational norms. Calibrating the amount of non-, under-, and overaccommodating one receives can be an important ingredient in continuing or withdrawing from an interaction;
- Interactants use specific communication strategies (in particular, convergence and divergence) to signal their attitudes towards each other and their respective social groups. In this way, social interaction is a subtle balance between needs for social inclusiveness on the one hand, and for differentiation on the other. As this last principle was the original cornerstone of CAT and spawned many of the empirical studies flowing from it, we shall move to a discussion of convergence and divergence studies next.

Strategies of Convergence and Divergence

CAT suggests that individuals use communication, in part, in order to indicate their attitudes toward each other and, as such, is a barometer of the level of social distance between them.

This constant movement toward and away from others, by changing one's communicative behavior, is called *accommodation*. Among the different accommodative strategies that speakers use to achieve these goals, *convergence* has been the most extensively studied – and can be considered the historical core of CAT (Giles, 1973). It has been defined as a strategy whereby individuals adapt their communicative behaviors in terms of a wide range of linguistic (e.g., speech rate, accents), paralinguistic (e.g., pauses, utterance length), and nonverbal features (e.g., smiling, gazing) in such a way as to become more similar to their interlocutor's behavior. For instance, during the (1973) Watergate Hearings, John Dean (counselor to then President Nixon) accommodated the formality of his language style to that of four of the Senators questioning him, presumably so as to sound convincing to them (Levin & Lin, 1988). Thomson, Murachver, and Green (2001) examined accommodation in communication via e-mail and found that, even in this rather "bare" context, women and men converged to the language style (more female- or male-like) of their Net-pals.

Conversely, the strategy of *divergence* leads to an accentuation of speech and nonverbal differences between self and the other. For instance, recently, Linford Christie (a Black British Olympic gold medal winner) was accused in the press of deliberately using divisive and incomprehensible Creole English by an influential fellow (White) athlete. Clearly, his motive for speaking in this manner was very different from the intent attributed by others to it; one possibility being that he was emphasizing the value of his ethnic identity in the context of this sport's administrative leadership being White, and perhaps exclusionary (see Bourhis & Giles, 1977). A phenomenon similar to divergence is *maintenance* whereby a person persists in his or her original style, regardless of the communication behavior of the interlocutor (Bourhis, 1979). One of us recalls the occasion in which he first went to a Heads of Physical Sciences Meeting attired in his typical casual manner. Our *hero* will never forget the aghast looks with which he was greeted by a dark-suited assembly upon entering the room! Yet sometimes our accommodations can be miscarried as the following week our dresser convergently—so he thought—wore a suit and tie to a complementary Heads of *Social* Sciences Meeting. Discomfort was again experienced for a couple of hours as he discoursed with his new colleagues, all of whom were (not uncharacteristically) sweatered and jeaned!

Another important conceptual distinction is whether the convergence or divergence is "upward" or "downward" in terms of its societal valence (Giles & Powesland, 1975). Upward convergence would be illustrated by an interviewee's adoption of the prestige patterns of an upper class interviewer. Upward divergence would be indicated by the adoption of a swifter speech rate and more cultured accent with someone nonstandard-sounding, whereas downward divergence could be seen in the emphasis of one's low-prestige minority heritage. A classic case of downward convergence has been documented with regard to the talk of Japanese Emperor Hirohito. Before the end of the Pacific War, the Emperor had never addressed his subjects. However, after the defeat, he traveled the countryside in an effort to bolster reconstruction and a revived sense of community. During this time and for a period of 8 years, rather than adopting the usual highly formal and distancing style of those considered "god-like," he assumed (often to apparent excess) a gentle, informal style typical of everyday people (Azuma, 1997). This counterintuitive tactic was received with overwhelming approval from the populous as it signified not only genuine camaraderie but, more particularly, mutually endured hardships.

We will now examine some of the principal motives that lie behind the strategies of convergence and divergence, consider their evaluative demeanor as well as the importance of stereotypes and social norms in defining participants' expectations about how much convergence or divergence a speaker should display.

Motives for Convergence and Divergence

An important *motive* for convergence is the desire to gain approval from one another. The premise is that of similarity attraction (Byrne, 1971): The more similar we are to our conversational partner, the more he or she will like or respect us, and the more social rewards we can expect. Converging to a common linguistic style also improves the effectiveness of communication, this, in turn, has been associated with increased predictability of the other and hence a lowering of uncertainty, interpersonal anxiety, and mutual understanding (see, e.g., Gudykunst, 1995). But convergence is not only rewarding, it may well entail some costs, such as the possible loss of personal or social identity. In our opening example, if the student converges towards the professor's communicative style, he may be rewarded by the professor who will perceive him as particularly competent, but the student may also feel deprived of his social identity. Members of his ingroup (i.e., other students) who happen to hear him might also perceive him as a "traitor" and label him derogatorily (Hogg, D'Agata, & Abrams, 1989).

This is where the strategy of divergence comes in: The motive lying behind divergence is precisely the desire to emphasize distinctiveness from one's interlocutor, usually on the basis of group membership. Following the premises of Social Identity Theory (e.g., Tajfel & Turner, 1986), this will likely occur when interactants define a situation more in "intergroup" than "interindividual" terms; the former activates one's shared social identity, the latter a personal identity. An intergroup interaction is when individuals treat each other entirely in terms of their social category memberships (e.g., when Jack and Jill communicate with each as "typical" males and females and their personal idiosyncracies are totally irrelevant at that time). An interindividual interaction is when interactants communicate with each other entirely on the basis of their individual differences in temperament and personality and where their ethnicity, gender, age, and so forth are not at a premium (e.g., rival team members discussing shared leisure interests at a bar after the game).

Intergroup theorists would contend that intergroup encounters are actually much more common than realized and that their interindividual counterparts are actually much more infrequent than we would perhaps have given them credit. Given that communication features (e.g., dress style, tattoos, earrings, slang, gait, and hand movements) are often core dimensions of what it is to be a member of a group (e.g., a gang member), divergence can be regarded as a very important tactic of displaying a valued distinctiveness from other. This not only reflects a sense of ingroup pride but also enhances a feeling of self-worth. As we belong to many different social groups (and or are put into them by others conversing with us), we have, then multiple social identities which are more or less salient across interactions (or in any one of them). The dynamics of communication are made even more complex by the fact that some of these social identities are shared between the interactants, and some are not. In our example, we have an interaction between two men and one woman, two English-speaking and one French-speaking, two of European origin and one of African origin, or also between one professor and two students! In this vein, Jones, Gallois, Barker, and Callan (1994) showed that the visible (and potentially potent) intercultural dimension of whether an individual was Anglo- or Chinese Australian was quite nonpredictive of their communicative behavior together; what was predictive, however, was their occupational group members as professors and students.

However, divergence can also be adopted in order to shape receivers' attributions and feelings. In our example, the French-speaking student could purposely say some words in French during the conversation, in order to remind her interactive partners that she does not belong to the same linguistic group. By so doing, she signals that her possibly unsubtle discourse should be attributed to her linguistic (in)competence rather than to deficient intellectual capacities. Divergence can also be an attempt to entice an interlocutor to adopt a more effective communicative stance. Again referring to our example, if the student is talking loudly and very expressively, the professor may exhibit a divergent response (e.g., speaking softly and with a neutral affect) in order to encourage the student to adopt a more reserved and seemingly thoughtful style. Note also that a strategy of maintenance can not only result from insensitivity to the others' styles, it can also be a deliberate attempt to affirm one's identity or autonomy in a low-key fashion without emphasizing it. All in all, it appears that satisfying communication requires a delicate balance between convergence—to demonstrate willingness to communicate—and divergence—to incur a healthy sense of group identity (see Cargile & Giles, 1996).

Evaluation of Convergence and Divergence

Attempts at social integration or identification by means of convergence have been generally accorded positive *evaluation* by receivers (Bourhis, Giles, & Lambert, 1975). In this sense, it validates the recipients' own ways of expressing themselves. Increasing similarity in communicative behavior such as speech rate increases both speakers' perceived attractiveness as well as their ability to gain addressees' compliance (Buller, LePoire, Aune, & Eloy, 1992). Converging speakers are generally viewed more favorably than diverging and maintaining speakers and are perceived as more efficient in their communication as well as more cooperative. Afterall, being the receiver of nonaccommodation tells you that the speaker dares not to value your approval—a stance we have difficulty applauding! However, there can also be negative outcomes for convergence too. Preston (1981) found that full convergence, in the case of foreign language learning, is not always desired by either the speaker or the addressee. He stated that full convergence, or native-speaker-like fluency, is often considered with distrust and seen as controlling by the addressee.

How listeners attribute motives for convergence is crucial to whether it garners positive or negative reactions. Addressees take at least three factors into account in making their inferences and ultimate evaluation: the other's language competence, the effort he or she engendered, and the external pressures impelling the speaker to act in a particular way (Simard, Taylor, & Giles, 1976). Hence, if a speaker is known not to have the necessary communicative competence and has been distracted by a close and recent bereavement, their nonaccommodative stance could be excused (if not justified). The power variable should not be left aside neither. It is generally expected that people in subordinate positions would converge to those in superordinate positions (called *upward convergence*). Returning once again to our example, it is very likely that both students will strive to speak an elaborate version of formal English and use scientific terms in order to persuade the professor that they are worthy interactional partners. In contrast, a higher status individual (like our professor) may converge by use of colloquial and lay language to the relatively lower status trainees gathered, that is, his students. This so-called *downward convergence,* however, might be perceived by the students as suspicious, inappropriate or even condescending.

Upward and downward convergence was demonstrated in a popular American TV talk show, where the presenter, Larry King, was found to change the pitch of his voice as a function of his guests' status (e.g., he would converge toward President Clinton). Conversely, guests of King that were held in lower social regard (e.g., Vice-President Dan Quayle) would accommodate more to Larry King than he would to them (Gregory & Webster, 1996).

Accommodative moves are also diversely appreciated by ingroup members, depending on the strength of their attachment to the group. In a study conducted in Hong Kong one year before its handover to the People's Republic of China, respondents with a strong identification to Hong Kong evaluated more favorably their ingroup members who, by using Cantonese, diverged from Mandarin-speaking Chinese people than did respondents who identified themselves with mainland China (Tong, Hong, Lee, & Chiu, 1999).

Communicative behavior as objectively measured, the intent that was behind it, and how the addressee perceives the behavior can be three different things. The latter two of these three levels has been termed *psychological* and *subjective accommodation*, respectively (see Thakerar, Giles, & Cheshire, 1982). Speakers may converge to their listener objectively (as assessed through direct observation of communication behavior); however, the intent behind this convergence may not be to show intimacy but, on the contrary, to indicate social distance. Woolard (1989) reported on a language norm in Spain at that time stating that Catalan should only be spoken between Catalans. Hence, Castillian speakers who attempted to speak Catalan often received a reply back in Castillian. At one level, the Castillians were recipients of objective convergence, but the psychological intent here was to keep them in their own social-linguistic space and hence was actually perceived and felt as a decisively divergent act. Likewise, subjective accommodation does not necessarily correspond with the objective behavior nor with the intent that was behind it. Returning to our example, the professor might interpret any converging behavior of the student not as a sign of competence, but as forwardness or a lack of modesty.

Expectations About Optimal Levels of Convergence and Divergence

As alluded to previously, accommodation can vary (e.g., as "full" or "partial") to the extent speakers approximate the communicative patterns of their receivers (Bradac, Mulac, & House, 1988; Street, 1982). Moreover, receivers have *expectations* about optimal levels of convergence and divergence. Violation of these expectations can result in a negative evaluation of the interlocutor. These expectations are based on *stereotypes* regarding outgroup members (and, in particular, their level of communicative competence). In our example, the Swiss student could have a stereotype of African Americans being forthcoming and sociable, and accommodate her behavior to become similarly expressive and outgoing. By so doing, she might offend the African American student who might, in fact, see such behavior as exaggerated and artificial, according to the situational norms and to his own stereotype of Swiss people. In this scenario, the Swiss student could be said to be *overaccommodating*. Other expectations regarding characteristics and behaviors of outgroups may similarly affect convergence. For instance, the fact that the professor expects the French-speaking student to experience linguistic difficulties may lead him to view nonconvergence on her part less negatively than if this nonconvergence could be attributed to a lack of effort.

Speakers' expectations about adequate levels of convergence and divergence are also based on societal norms for intergroup contact that determine, for example, what is the appropriate language to be used in the situation (Gallois & Callan, 1991). When groups coexist in a society for a long period of time, they establish norms about how members from the groups should interact with each other. A pervasive norm is that individuals will converge to the language of those who speak the standard or prestige variety of a language. Thus, it would be expected that Latino migrants converge to English speakers in the United States and Turkish Gastarbeiter and their families converge to their hosts in German. Interestingly, and in contrast, members of the German-dialect-speaking majority frequently converge to the French-speaking minority in

Switzerland more so than vice versa. This is so because members of the French-speaking minority do not learn the majority's localized *dialect* at school but, rather, standard German. Swiss Germans, then, would often prefer to risk speaking French than be converged to in a more prestigious variety of German than they themselves use as many Swiss Germans do not identify with this language variety. Standard German is the language of "their" dominant group and one from which they wish to distance themselves. This segueys appropriately into the next theme.

The Sociohistorical Context

Communication is embedded in a broader macrocontext, rather than a social vacuum. In our example, we do not only have *individuals* interacting, but also those who represent their differing social category memberships. Current, and particularly past, relations between these social groups build the sociohistorical context for the interaction. Its influence on accommodation attempts and their outcomes is a core concern of CAT, which posits that the relations between the social groups affect the degree to which the interactants accommodate to one another. In our example, it is not impossible that the heavy history of Black–White relations in the United States could play a role in the behavior of the interactants. A key construct for the analysis of the relations between cultural or ethnic groups is a comparison of their so-called *ethnolinguistic vitalities* (Giles & Johnson, 1987). Ethnolinguistic vitality can be understood and measured using three types of factors: status (economical, political, and linguistic prestige); demography (population numbers, birth rate, geographical distribution); and institutional support (recognition of the group and its language by public authorities, the educational system, and other agencies). The resultant comparison of the relative ethnolinguistic vitalities of the groups helps define which one is the more dominant. Moreover, having a high vitality could mean that groups have sufficient resources for it to be worthwhile and meaningful to invest energetically in their being good group members. In our context, this would mean that historically strong social collectivities will diverge in intergroup situations. For instance, when certain Native Americans became aware of their vitality (e.g., through casino business and the unique value of their histories and identities), many would wish not only to resurrect their heritage languages but adopt their distinctive dialect, phrases, and dress styles across all manner of interethnic contexts.

However, research has shown that *subjective* ethnolinguistic vitality is more influential in determining attitudes in the interaction than is the objective ethnolinguistic vitality (e.g., Harwood, Giles, & Bourhis, 1994). Here, subjectivity refers to the individual's perceptions of the ethnolinguistic vitality of the ingroup compared to the outgroup. In our example, ethnic identity could be salient for the African American undergraduate student. His perception of the ethnolinguistic vitality of African Americans at his own campus and in American society more widely could lead him to show loyalty to his heritage, for example, by emphasizing the speech and nonlinguistic markers of this group (i.e., Ebonics). CAT also suggests that such divergence will occur the more group members feel their status in the intergroup hierarchy is illegitimate and unfair (e.g., that they have been historically, and even currently, unfairly discriminated against because of their skin color. But threat is not the province of subordinate groups in society only. Barker et al. (2001) suggest that Anglo American support for the English-only movement—speech maintenance *par excellence*—is, at least in large part, due to the increasing perceived vitality of Latinos (especially in terms of the growing number of immigrants with political influence and the increasing amount of Spanish appearing on the linguistic landscape of shop, road, and other signs)—a process that clearly impacts Anglos' perceived distinctiveness and communicative superiority.

Thus far then, we have introduced some of the assumptions underlying CAT together with its major communicative strategies—convergence and divergence—and the motives underlying, as well as the attributions associated with, their enactment. After this, we discussed expectations regarding optimal levels of these strategies and emphasized the need to take into account the roles of the socio-historical context in which communication takes place for a truly comprehensive picture of how and why accommodation unfolds. In the remainder of this chapter, we look at how CAT has been applied to communication between members of various social groups (including interethnic, intergenerational, and between gender) and within different institutions such as in organizations and through the media.

SOCIAL APPLICATIONS OF CAT

The state of the theory as it stands now spans several disciplines, contexts, and language groups (see Meyerhoff, 1998). From its original roots in speech style modification, CAT has been expanded into a generalized model of communicative interaction. It has been applied to study communication between different social groups (cultures, genders, generations, and abilities), in different contexts (in organizations, in the healthcare system, in the courtroom, or simply in the streets), through different media (face-to-face interactions, but also radio, telephone, e-mail, etc.). Such research has occurred in different countries and been conducted by researchers of different cultural and language backgrounds. The rest of the chapter will provide an introduction to the variety of empirical investigations conducted under CAT's hat. These developments have not necessarily been systematically planned, and finding a post-hoc logic to why research has unfolded in the way they have is hazardous. This is why the following presentation of new areas of development does not pretend to give a coherent typology, and compelling overlaps between the areas (such as gender and the workplace) are unavoidable. The first three areas identify populations (communication between cultures, generations/ability groups, and genders), the fourth relates to a specific context of communication (organizations), and the last area considers media use.

Communication Between Cultures and Linguistic Groups

The intercultural context can be considered the most "natural" applied context for CAT, as the theory was first developed by studying interactions where linguistic markers (different languages, dialects, accents) defined membership to cultural groups. For example, Bourhis (1984) studied the strategies of convergence, divergence, and maintenance in Montreal by asking Francophone and Anglophone pedestrians about directions, either in English or in French. He found that 30% of Anglophones maintained English in their responses when they had been addressed in French, even when their linguistic skills would have been sufficient to answer in French. In contrast, only 3% of Francophone pedestrians used French in their answers to the English-speaking interlocutor. The difference in accommodative behavior displayed by the two groups of pedestrians is explained by the Canadian intergroup context. Traditionally, the Anglophone minority has higher status and power within the Francophone majority setting of Montreal. A similar research procedure was used by Lawson and Sachdev (2000) in Tunisia where Tunisian pedestrians were approached by either Arab Tunisians (speaking Tunisian Arabic) or White Europeans (speaking French) asking for directions to the post office. Although respondents generally converged to the language of the researcher, they were more likely to diverge if addressed in French. Thus, despite the prestige of French in Tunisia, Tunisians were likely to signal their distinctiveness from their former colonizers.

CAT's utility in explaining intercultural relations extends to macrolevel issues such as bilingualism, language maintenance and shift, and creolization (e.g., Burt, 1994; Lawson-Sako & Sachdev, 1996; Niedzielski & Giles, 1996). For example, Ross and Shortreed (1990) explain why, in Japan, a nonnative speaker of Japanese attempting to converge linguistically toward a Japanese partner may receive an answer in English rather than in Japanese (simultaneous convergence), even if the foreigner possesses excellent Japanese proficiency. As indicated with regard to the Catalan situation earlier, the intent of the Japanese speaker might be to sustain in-outgroup boundaries. The nonnative speaker's attempt to speak Japanese might be perceived as a threat to Japanese identity. However, another motive has to be considered: By converging to Japanese, the nonnative speaker is depriving his Japanese interlocutor of the opportunity to use the much-studied but (little used) English language, a code with high social prestige in modern urban Japanese society. Ross and Shortreed's study is another demonstration of how important it is to distinguish objective accommodation behavior from the intent that was behind it (psychological accommodation) and how it is perceived by the addressee (subjective accommodation).

A satellite model of CAT, the intergroup model of second language acquisition examines the sociopsychological variables influencing the attitude of subordinate group members towards learning the dominant group's tongue. According to this model, second language "failure" should not necessarily be attributed to incompetency, but could also be viewed in intergroup accommodative terms (e.g., Kraemer, Olshtain, & Badier, 1994). More specifically, learning another group's communicative code can be construed as convergence. When groups associate the acquisition of another tongue as an implicit loss of their own valued mode of communication, they can either infiltrate the target language with mother tongue words, syntax and pronunciation (let alone allied nonverbals), or not acquire it at all. In either instance, we have a "failure" (to master a second language) but attributed by the ingroup as *successful* maintenance, or even divergence from the communicative status quo. Put another way, the second language classroom is not purely about learning a "neutral" language code, but has sociohistorical implications for the very survival of an ingroup; the classroom can often become an emotionally-charged, intergroup laboratory.

Intergenerational and Interability Communication

Intergenerational communication is another area where CAT has made significant contributions, broadening out to health issues. Communication between younger and older adults is viewed as "involv(ing) different (internally differentiated cultural groups, who possess different values and beliefs about talk, different social and existential agendas, and different language codes" (Giles & Coupland, 1991, p. 159). In intergenerational conversations, older adults have been found not to make many accommodations to their younger partners (Kemper, Vandeputte, Rice, Cheung, & Gubarchuk, 1995) and may even *underaccommodate* them. On the other hand, younger communicators tend to *overaccommodate* or adjust too much, and often reluctantly so (Williams & Giles, 1996). They choose very simple topics, adopt a basic grammatical phrase structure with a very slow speech rate, and act overly polite or caring, regardless of their interlocutor's individualized capacities and personal needs; this is a telling example of the notion of "intergroup" encounter introduced earlier. Overaccommodative talk directed to the elderly has been called *patronizing speech* (see, e.g., Harwood & Giles, 1996) and, in its most extreme form, can be thought of as "baby talk." Such behavior is based on expectations about the communicative style of the elderly who are generally negatively stereotyped (e.g., frail, unattractive, slow, useless) in Western societies (Williams & Giles, 1996).

The elderly are not the only recipients of patronizing speech as data show that people with physical or mental disabilities are often spoken to in similar registers (for a review of "interability communication," see Fox, Giles, Orbe, & Bourhis, 2000). Even if patronizing speech usually proceeds from well-meaning intentions, its recipients generally find it demeaning. Fox and Giles (1996) reported that people with physical disabilities complained about three types of patronizing speech:

> (a) baby talk, such as "poor little dear" or "honey" spoken in a condescending tone; (b) depersonalizing language, such as "it's nice that you people get out of the house"; and (c) third-party talk, where a non-disabled person directs communication not at the person with a disability but to a disabled person who is with them, for example, "Does he take cream in his coffee?" (p. 267)

Patronizing speech is generally perceived, by those cognitively and socially active, as disrespectful and insensitive, and the majority of recipients feel less supported and less comfortable than when involved in nonpatronizing encounters. Ryan, Kennaley, Pratt, and Shumovich (2000) found that humor is a good compromise response style to patronizing speech, allowing the recipient to express opposition to being patronized, yet still maintaining an appearance of competence and politeness. Patronizing talk may even be damaging for recipients who would actually like to be nurtured communicatively, as it could encourage their dependence and passivity. It should be highlighted, however, that "patronizing talk" (as well as any form of under- and overaccommodation) is really a *social attribution* rather than a communicative given; what is deemed patronizing for one could be invited, reinforced, and believed appropriately caring by another.

If excessive accommodation can often be counterproductive (but see Azuma, 1997, earlier), a certain level of accommodation between health professionals and patients is clearly necessary. For example, Bourhis, Roth, and MacQueen (1988) found that physicians, nurses, as well as hospital patients considered it more appropriate for health professionals to converge to the patients' everyday language than to maintain their medical jargon. Doctor–patient interactions are characterized by differences in communicative roles, with greater dominance and control by the doctor. Complementary patterns of communicative exchange are created and accepted by both (e.g., both the doctor and the patient will agree that the doctor decides about the content and structure of the interaction). However, to ensure patients' satisfaction and compliance, it has been shown that doctors need to find a balance and behave neither too domineering and directive, nor too passive. Indeed, they need to take care of the patients' emotional needs as much as they provide patients with accurate information (Watson & Gallois, 1999; for more details on accommodation in medical consultations, see Street, 1991).

CAT research on communication in social gerontology and in the realm of health care underscores the position that accommodation has consequences not only along the information-exchange dimension, but also for self-esteem. Accommodative processes are important to health in the sense that adequate convergence is a core component of many supportive encounters. Indeed, feeling emotionally supported can often be a function of the degree of accommodation one receives. Social relationships (medical and nonmedical) affect our health in important and complex ways. If an older person is subject to being overaccommodated and condescended to in a variety of situations, it will take a very resilient person indeed not to accept this categorization of themselves as "old" and "past it." Indeed, such negatively framed nonaccommodations could be an important constituent in the social construction of aging and ultimate (and hence accelerated) demise—a process fundamental to another CAT—satellite theory, the "communicative predicament of aging" model (e.g., Ryan, Giles, Bartolucci, & Henwood, 1986). In this way, accommodation forms the linchpin to understanding the complex interrelationships of social support practices, psychological well-being, and physical health.

Communication Between Genders

Although a contentious empirical and ideological issue for some scholars, the idea that men and women speak differently has been widely acknowledged (for a review, see Coates, 1986). Compared to men, women have been described as more polite and cooperative speakers. They frequently take the role of the facilitator of conversation (e.g., by offering frequent and encouraging minimal responses like "mmmh") and their conversational goals and strategies focus on establishing affiliation with their partner. Women are also said to be more likely to emphasize solidarity and reduce inequalities in status and power (e.g., by attenuating criticisms and expressing appreciation). On the other hand, men have been described as more eager to hold the floor and control the topic of conversation. They use language to establish status and exchange information rather than to establish social connectedness. Men are reported to talk more than women in formal or public situations and to talk less in intimate relationships. Going back to our example, we could expect the male student to speak more than the female student who would wait to be offered the turn to speak and be less interruptive. However, given the context of the discussion, the influence of gender could be offset by the status dimension (the male is an undergraduate, whereas the student is a postdoctoral, student).

Interestingly, women and men do not have the same communicative behavior in same-sex situations and in mixed-sex situations. This means that they accommodate their communicative style to their interaction partners' gender. In fact, it appears that women are more prone to accommodate than are men (especially those who follow traditional sex roles), because of their concern for connectedness and societal power (Fitzpatrick, Mulac, & Dindia, 1995). However, Hannah and Murachver (1999) found that people accommodate to their conversants' speech style (more man-like or woman-like) more than to their *actual* gender. They trained female and male confederates to use a facilitative (which has been defined as more characteristic of women) or nonfacilitative (more characteristic of men) style of speech and examined the relative impact of gender and "gendered" speech style on the accommodation behavior. Their results showed gender differences in communication. Men and women responded differently to the same confederate's behavior, but the confederate's gender had a minor impact on participant behavior; what mattered was his or her "gendered" speech style. In less task-oriented situations and ones that have more *romantic* potential, a different pattern to the above can emerge. Men can accentuate their vocal masculinity by deepening their pitch (Hogg, 1985), whereas women can emphasize their femininity by doing the opposite as well as sounding softer (Montepare & Vega, 1988). Although these are, objectively, instances of mutual divergence, we would consider this to be "speech complementarity" as it can be driven by psychologically convergent motives and can be construed by some recipients as socially, if not sexually, appealing.

CAT provides a particularly powerful theoretical framework for studying how gender identities are negotiated during the interaction and their influence on the communicative behavior of the participants. Gender is a salient group membership that has been shown to have a major influence on communication in many Anglophone contexts. In his study of the impact of gender on linguistic accommodation in radio phone-in programs in Jordan, Al-Khatib (1995) demonstrated the importance of gender in the type of language used by the broadcaster and his or her interlocutors. But he also revealed that accommodation depends largely on the speaker's social knowledge and his or her ability to vary speech style. In this study, it was more the broadcasters who accommodated to their interlocutors than the reverse. The author explained this by virtue of the goals of the broadcasters who aim at pleasing their audience as well as by their greater ability to vary speech style; to work as a broadcaster, they are required to speak Modern Standard Arabic as well as its colloquial variety.

Communication in Organizations

Organizations offer a particularly interesting communicative context, oftentimes with strong situational norms and asymmetries in the status and power of the interactants. For most organizations, accommodation is also central to their relations with their customers and the public in general. Sparks and Callan (1992) applied CAT to the hospitality industry and showed how much a convergent style of communication with consumers is important for customers' satisfaction. This has been observed in a number of settings also where, for example, a travel agent accommodated her pronunciation to the different socioeconomically based language styles of her Welsh clientele (N. Coupland, 1984) and, in Taiwan, where salespersons converged more to customers than vice versa (van den Berg, 1986). These asymmetrical convergences are based on who holds economic sway at the time and are, of course, in accord with CAT predictions. Likewise, Cohen and Cooper (1986) showed that many tourists in the developing world (e.g., Thailand) do not expend much effort to acquire much, if any, competence in the language of the country visited, whereas locals in service industries (whose financial destiny is in many ways tied to tourism) often become convergently proficient in many foreigners' languages.

According to Bourhis (1991), the accommodation framework can be very helpful to researchers of the organizational field for their analysis of communication breakdown in such institutions. Invoking the notion of a "linguistic work environment" (with civil servants in New Brunswick, Canada), he showed how Francophone employees converge more to the first language of their coworkers than do their Anglophone counterparts, and how organizational status (sub- and superordinate roles) is also a factor in the convergent process in ways that CAT would predict.

In another organizational CAT study, this time in Australia, Gardner and Jones (1999) invited 216 superordinates (i.e., supervisers) and 142 subordinates to write down what they would say at "best" and at "worst" to their counterparts in a variety of communicative situations offered them (e.g., "you have an informal chat with your subordinate" or "you are negotiating a change in your working situation with your superior"). Analysis of the data showed that, for both organizational groups, the best communications were coded, as would be predicted, accommodative. For superordinates, this was indicated by taking the listener's position and knowledge into account and being clear and direct, while for subordinates it was manifest more in listening, asking for input, and being open. The worst communications were clearly *nonaccommodative*. For superordinates, such talk would be overaccommodative, manifest in being overly familiar whereas, for subordinates, it was more underaccommodative and expressed through being too demanding and aggressive. A similar kind of study of Australian student patients' past conversations with health professionals (Watson & Gallois, 1999) showed that satisfying encounters were remembered as accommodative (e.g., the health professionals show concern, provide information, and are reassuring) whereas codings of unsatisfactory exchanges included many instances of nonaccommodation (e.g., health professionals show displeasure, lack of information, and are unresponsive to their patients). Hence, CAT is very useful for our understanding of and analyzing occupational interactions—as these studies demonstrate well that lay participants holding different organizational roles do report varying conversations between them in accommodation terms.

An accommodation framework has also been applied to issues of organization miscommunication between men and women (Baker, 1991), a context known as the "gendered workplace". Toward this end, and with special reference to contexts where females are hired to take on occupation roles formerly reserved for men (e.g., fire-fighting), Boggs and Giles (1999) devised yet another CAT-satellite framework, the so-called "workplace gender nonaccommodation cycle model". In such settings, men may consider this social change as undermining their powers in the organization: If women can do the job, too, there is no reason to continue offering a greater share of rewards to the men who perform; a sense of threatened masculine identity can ensue. Moreover, if women are seen as benefiting from equal opportunity practices, then men may feel unjustly penalized by management through no fault of their own. Such men may choose to respond by adopting nonaccommodative behaviors (e.g., harassment, patronizing talk, non-inclusive networking, use of gendered jargon) to signal to the "interloping women" that their presence is unwanted. In return, the women may, understandably, reciprocate nonaccommodatively, such as by threatening to complain to supervisors, making written records of communication incidents, etc. Interpreting these as hostile responses, men may be even more inclined to nonaccommodate, thereby escalating nonaccommodation *cyclically*. Intergroup boundaries are now strengthened and communication breakdown can occur between the social factions. Consequently, women may quit their jobs or sue the organization for sex discrimination. This apparent failure of women to integrate into the male ingroup is then construed by males as data that women do not "have what it takes" to be successful in "men's" jobs, thereby further legitimating gender-biased organizational practices.

Communication Through Media

Face-to-face interactions, with direct verbal and nonverbal exchanges, are often what we think of when we hear the concept of communication. However, communication can also be "mediated" and accommodation tendencies are no less salient. This is illustrated by Bell's (1984) study of New Zealand broadcasters who read the news on a number of different stations. He found that these newscasters read the same material but radically accommodated their pronunciations to the *assumed* socioeconomic status of their listeners. These days, progress in technology keeps on inventing new communication media (e.g., the Internet and teleconferencing). Compared to face-to-face interactions, these media offer interesting features for communication studies. They can be audio or visual, oral or written. Moreover and particularly interesting for CAT, these media offer communicative situations where the addressee is unknown (press, radio, television, and, more recently, Web sites and chat groups), situations where context is reduced to its minimum, and situations where the exchange is nonsimultaneous or even absent (for accommodation in the mass media, see Bell, 1991).

For example, telephone-answering machines have become an everyday means of communication for most of us. This useful device is also very interesting for communication research. It allows us to record participants' reactions to messages manipulated by the researcher, and this in what is perceived by the participants as a natural setting. This was an idea of Buzzanell, Burrell, Stafford, and Berkowitz (1996) who studied accommodation of lower status callers (students) to higher status callees' (professors) answering-machine messages. Students were asked to telephone their professor in order to schedule an appointment. Their calls were directed to answering machines which played different types of messages (routine, humorous, jargonistic and a message requesting much more information than would be expected routinely). The results indicated that, even in this non-simultaneous, temporally limited and less information-rich communicative situation, convergence occurs and individuals modify their language choices as well as some message features in order to display similarity.

Like the above-mentioned research of Thomson et al. (2001), Crook and Booth (1997) studied accommodation in a rather new albeit increasingly used communication media: electronic mail (e-mail). Because feedback, if there is any, is slow in this written media (compared to face-to-face interaction in which additional questions, the use of gaze and silence as well as other signals provide the sender with cues to how the message is interpreted), accommodation from the writer to the recipient is crucial to increase communication effectiveness. According to these scholars, one dimension of diversity between individuals is their preference for a sensory system over the others: the three primary visual, auditory, and kinesthetic (body) senses. These preferred sensory system are reflected in language use through words like "see," "clear," "looks like" (visual style), "hear," "sound," "ringing" (auditory style), and "feel," "grasp," "touch" (kinesthetic style). Their results showed that individuals who received e-mails that matched their preferred representational system reported more rapport with the sender than those who received e-mails that did not match their preferred style. An implication of this finding is that, if one does not know the receiver's preferred sensory system in advance, one should take care to write a message that addresses the three styles.

CONCLUSION

In this chapter, we provided a flavor of the basics, as well as the inherent complexities, of Communication Accommodation Theory. As we have seen, many disciplines (besides Communication) have profited from its insights and herein we have selected an array of experimentally controlled laboratory and naturalistic studies from around the world designed to explore its dynamics. As readers will have gleaned from recurring treatments of our opening scenario, there are a plethora of communicative options for, and reactions of, people interacting (who have personal and many social identities). We contend that CAT—with its attention to macrocontextual forces, interpersonal and intergroup dynamics, motives, and social consequences—can handle these (and other) intricacies. That said, and although it could arguably be infinitely elaborated to take account of expectancy violations, arousal, cognitive schemas, relational development, and so forth, it was never conceived to be a theory for all interpersonal eventualities. Nonetheless, a person's accommodative resources and flexibility may make up a hitherto unrecognized statement about their "communicative competences," and CAT has the potential to be associated with a very wide range of individuals' uses of communicative actions (e.g., forms of address, politeness, cosmetic styles, car and interior design choices, etc.).

Space, of course, has precluded attention to all CAT's parameters, including the fact that in order to meet multiple conversational needs speakers can converge on some of their partners' communicative features and, simultaneously, diverge on others (Bilous & Krauss, 1988). In addition, we have not discussed the roles of awareness in forging and evaluating accommodative inclinations (see Williams, 1999), the dilemmas communicators can face in deciding what to accommodate to or not (Pittam & Gallois, 1999), and the discourse strategies by which speakers can accommodate their listeners' interpretive competences, emotions, patterns of control, and conversational needs (see J. Coupland, Coupland, Giles, & Henwood, 1988; Giles, Williams, & Coupland, 1990). We have also not talked to the roles of accommodation in other applied settings such as the courtroom (see Linell, 1991) and mental health clinics (see Hamilton, 1991), but leave it to the reader now to make links to these and other arenas (e.g., diplomacy, community disputes, leadership, counseling, mentoring, bargaining, etc.).

ADDITIONAL READINGS

Readers who are interested in CAT and might revel in the complexities of seeing it in proposition format are invited to consult the following resources: Giles et al. (1987) and Thakerar et al. (1982). For those with intercultural inclinations in this format, see also Gallois, Franklyn-Stokes, Giles, and Coupland (1988) and Gallois, Giles, Jones, Cargile, and Ota (1995). For a series of earlier empirical studies on CAT, see the collections of Giles (1984) and N. Coupland and Giles, 1988). Finally, for those particularly interested in sociolinguistic extensions and elaborated reviews in nonpropositional format, see the chapters in Giles, Coupland, and Coupland (1991) as well as Shepard, Giles, and Le Poire (2001).

ACKNOWLEDGMENTS

We thank the editors and their student editorial boards for their extensive and insightful comments on an earlier version of this chapter.

REFERENCES

Al-Khatib, M. (1995). The impact of interlocutor sex on linguistic accommodation: A case study of Jordan radio phone-in programs. *Multilingua, 14,* 133–150.

Azuma, S. (1997). Speech accommodation and Japanese Emperor Hirohito. *Discourse and Society, 8,* 189–202.

Baker, M. A. (1991). Reciprocal accommodation: A model for reducing gender bias in managerial communication. *Journal of Business Communication, 28,* 113–130.

Barker, V., Giles, H., Noels, K., Duck, J., Hecht, M., & Clément, R. (2001). The English-only movement: A communication perspective. *Journal of Communication, 51,* 3–37.

Bell, A. (1984). Language style as audience design. *Language in Society, 13,* 145–204.

Bell, A. (1991). Audience accommodation in the mass media. In H. Giles, J. Coupland, & N. Coupland (Eds.), *Contexts of accommodation: Developments in applied sociolinguistics* (pp. 69–102). Cambridge, England: Cambridge University Press.

Bilous, F. R., & Krauss, R. M. (1988). Dominance and accommodation in the conversational behaviors of same- and mixed-gender dyads. *Language and Communication, 8,* 183–194.

Boggs, C., & Giles, H. (1999). "The canary in the cage": The nonaccommodation cycle in the gendered workplace. *International Journal of Applied Linguistics, 22,* 223–245.

Bourhis, R. Y. (1979). Language in ethnic interaction: A social psychological approach. In H. Giles & B. Saint-Jacques (Eds.), *Language and ethnic relations* (pp. 117–141). Oxford, England: Pergamon.

Bourhis, R. Y. (1984). Cross-cultural communication in Montreal: Two field studies since Bill 101. *International Journal of the Sociology of Language, 46,* 33–47.

Bourhis, R. Y. (1991). Organizational communication and accommodation: toward some conceptual and empirical links. In H. Giles, J. Coupland, & N. Coupland (Eds.), *Contexts of accommodation. Developments in applied sociolinguistics* (pp. 270–303). Cambridge, England: Cambridge University Press.

Bourhis, R. Y., & Giles, H. (1977). The language of intergroup distinctiveness. In H. Giles (Ed.), *Language, ethnicity and intergroup relations* (pp. 119–135). London: Academic.

Bourhis, R. Y., Giles, H., & Lambert, W. E. (1975). Social consequences of accommodating one's style of speech: a cross-national investigation. *International Journal of the Sociology of Language, 6,* 55–72.

Bourhis, R. Y., Roth, S., & MacQueen, G. (1988). Communication in the hospital setting: A survey of medical and everyday language use amongst patients, nurses and doctors. *Social Science and Medicine, 24,* 1–8.

Bradac, J. J., Mulac, A., & House, A. (1988). Lexical diversity and magnitude of convergent versus divergent style-shifting: Perceptual and evaluative consequences. *Language and Communication, 8,* 213–228.

Buller, D. B., LePoire, B. A., Aune, R. K., & Eloy, S. V. (1992). Social perceptions as mediators of the effect of speech rate similarity on compliance. *Human Communication Research, 19,* 286–311.

Burt, S. M. (1994). Code choice in intercultural conversation: Speech accommodation theory and pragmatics. *Pragmatics, 4,* 535–559.

Buzzanell, P. M., Burrell, N. A., Stafford, S. R., & Berkowitz, S. (1996). When I call you up and you're not there: Application of Communication Accommodation Theory to telephone answering machine messages. *Western Journal of Communication, 60,* 310–336.

Byrne, D. (1971). *The attraction paradigm.* New York: Academic.

Cargile, A. C., & Giles, H. (1996). Intercultural communication training: Review, critique, and a new theoretical framework. In W. B. Gudykunst (Ed.), *Communication yearbook 19* (pp. 385–423). Thousand Oaks, CA: Sage.

Coates, J. (1986). *Women, men, and language: A sociolinguistic account of sex differences in language.* London: Longman.

Cohen, E., & Cooper, R. L. (1986). Language and tourism. *Annals of Tourism Research, 13,* 535–563.

Coupland, J., Coupland, N., Giles, H., & Henwood, K. (1988). Accommodating the elderly: Invoking and extending a theory. *Language in Society, 17,* 1–41.

Coupland, N. (1984). Accommodation at work: Some phonological data and their implications. *International Journal of the Sociology of Language, 46,* 49–70.

Coupland, N., & Giles, H. (Eds). (1988). Communication accommodation: Recent advances. *Language and Communication, 8*(3 & 4) 175–327.

Coupland, N., & Jaworski, A. (1997). Relevance, accommodation, and conversation: Modeling the social dimension of communication. *Multilingua, 16,* 235–258.

Crook, C. W., & Booth, R. (1997). Building rapport in electronic mail using Accommodation Theory. *Advances Management Journal, 62,* 4–14.

Fitzpatrick, M. A., Mulac, A., & Dindia, K. (1995). Gender-preferential language use in spouse and stranger interaction. *Journal of Language and Social Psychology, 14,* 18–39.

Fox, S. A., & Giles, H. (1996). Interability communication: Evaluating patronizing encounters. *Journal of Language and Social Psychology, 15,* 265–290.

Fox, S. A., Giles, H., Orbe, M. P., & Bourhis, R. Y. (2000). Interability communication: Theoretical perspectives. In D. Braithewaite & T. Thompson (Eds.), *Handbook of communication and people with disabilities: Research and application* (pp. 193–222). Mahwah, NJ: Lawrence Erlbaum Associates, Inc.

Gallois, C., & Callan, V. J. (1991). Interethnic accommodation: The role of norms. In H. Giles, J. Coupland, & N. Coupland (Eds.), *Contexts of accommodation: Developments in applied sociolinguistics* (pp. 245–269). Cambridge, England: Cambridge University Press.

Gallois, C., Franklyn-Stokes, A., Giles, H., & Coupland, N. (1988). Communication accommodation in intercultural encounters. In Y. Y. Kim & W. B. Gudykunst (Eds.), *Theories in intercultural communication* (pp. 157–185). Newbury Park, CA: Sage.

Gallois, C., Giles, H., Jones, E., Cargile, A. C., & Ota, H. (1995). Accommodating to intercultural encounters. Elaborations and extensions. In R. L. Wiseman (Ed.), Intercultural communication theory (Vol. 29, pp. 115–147). Thousand Oaks, CA: Sage.

Gardner, M. J., & Jones, E. (1999). Problematic communication in the workplace: Beliefs of superiors and subordinates. *International Journal of Applied Linguistics, 9,* 185–206.

Giles, H. (1973). Accent mobility: A model and some data. *Anthropological Linguistics, 15,* 87–109.

Giles, H. (Ed.). (1984). The dynamics of speech accommodation. *International Journal of the Sociology of Language, 46* 1–155.

Giles, H., & Coupland, N. (1991). *Language: Contexts and consequences.* Pacific Grove, CA: Brooks/Cole.

Giles, H., Coupland, N., & Coupland, J. (1991). Accommodation theory: Communication, context, and consequence. In H. Giles, J. Coupland & N. Coupland (Eds.), *Contexts of accommodation: Developments in applied sociolinguistics* (pp. 1–68). Cambridge, England: Cambridge University Press.

Giles, H., & Johnson, P. (1987). Ethnolinguistic identity theory: A social psychological approach to language maintenance. *International Journal of the Sociology of Language, 68,* 69–99.

Giles, H., Mulac, A., Bradac, J. J., & Johnson, P. (1987). Speech accommodation theory: The first decade and beyond. In M. McLaughlin (Ed.), *Communication yearbook* (Vol. 10, pp. 13–48). Beverly Hills, CA: Sage.

Giles, H., & Powesland, P. F. (1975). *Speech styles and social evaluation.* London: Academic Press.

Giles, H., Taylor, D. M., & Bourhis, R. Y. (1973). Towards a theory of interpersonal accomodation through speech: Some Canadian data. *Language in society, 2,* 177–192.

Giles, H., Williams, A., & Coupland, N. (1990). Communication, health and the elderly: Frameworks, agenda and a model. In H. Giles, N. Coupland, & J. M. Wiemann (Eds.), *Communication, health and the elderly* (pp. 1–29). Manchester, England: Manchester University Press.

Gregory, S. W., & Webster, S. (1996). A nonverbal signal in voices of interview partners effectively predicts communication accommodation and social status predictions. *Journal of Personality and Social Psychology, 70,* 1231–1240.

Gudykunst, W. B. (1995). Anxiety/uncertainty management (AUM) theory: Current status. In R. L. Wiseman (Ed.), *Intercultural communication theory* (pp. 8–58). Thousand Oaks, CA: Sage.

Hamilton, H. (1991). Accommodation and mental disability. In H. Giles, N. Coupland, & J. Coupland (Eds.), *Contexts of accommodation* (pp. 157–186). New York: Cambridge University Press.

Hannah, A., & Murachver, T. (1999). Gender and conversational style as predictors of conversational behavior. *Journal of Language and Social Psychology, 18,* 153–174.

Harwood, J., & Giles, H. (1996). Reactions to older people being patronized: The roles of response strategies and attributed thoughts. *Journal of Language & Social Psychology, 15,* 395–421.

Harwood, J., Giles, H., & Bourhis, R. Y. (1994). The genesis of vitality theory: Historical patterns and discoursal dimensions. *International Journal of the Sociology of Language, 108,* 168–206.

Hogg, M. A. (1985). Masculine and feminine speech in dyads and groups: A study of speech style and gender salience. *Journal of Language and Social Psychology, 4,* 99–112.

Hogg, M. A., D'Agata, P., & Abrams, D. (1989). Ethnolinguistic betrayal and speaker evaluations across Italian Australians. *Genetic, Social, and General Psychology Monographs, 115,* 155–181.

Jones, E., Gallois, C., Barker, M., & Callan, V. J. (1994). Evaluations of interactions between students and academic staff: Influence of communication accommodation, ethnic group, and status. *Journal of Language & Social Psychology, 13,* 158–191.

Kemper, S., Vandeputte, D., Rice, K., Cheung, H., & Gubarchuk, J. (1995). Speech adjustments to aging during a referential communication task. *Journal of Language and Social Psychology, 14,* 40–59.

Kraemer, R., Olshtain, E., & Badier, S. (1994). Ethnolinguistic vitality, attitudes, and networks of linguistic contact: The case of the Israeli Arab minority. *International Journal of the Sociology of Language, 108,* 79–95.

Lawson, S., & Sachdev, I. (2000). Code-switching in Tunisia: Attitudinal and behavioral dimensions. *Journal of Pragmatics, 32,* 1343–1361.

Lawson-Sako, S., & Sachdev, I. (1996). Ethnolinguistic communication in Tunisian streets: Convergence and divergence. In Y. Suleiman (Ed.), *Language and identity in the Middle East and North Africa* (pp. 61–79). Richmond, VA: Curzon.

Levin, H., & Lin, T. (1988). An accommodating witness. *Language and Communication, 8,* 195–198.

Linell, P. (1991). Accommodation on trial: Processes of communicative accommodation in courtroom interaction. In H. Giles, J. Coupland, & N. Coupland (Eds.), *Contexts of accommodation: Developments in applied international handbook of contemporary research* (pp. 332–342). New York: Cambridge University Press.

Meyerhoff, M. (1998). Accommodating your data: The use and misuse of accommodation theory in sociolinguistics. *Language and Communication, 18,* 205–225.

Montepare, J. M., & Vega, C. (1988). Women's vocal reactions to intimate and causal male friends. *Personality and Social Psychology Bulletin, 14,* 103–112.

Niedzielski, N., & Giles, H. (1996). Linguistic accommodation. In H. Goebl, P. H. Nelde, Z. Stary, & W. Wolck (Eds.), *Contact linguistics: An international handbook of contemporary research* (pp. 332–342). Berlin & New York: Walter de Gruyter.

Pittam, J., & Gallois, C. (1999). Negotiating a working consensus: Conversations about HIV and AIDS. *International Journal of Applied Linguistics, 9,* 207–222.

Preston, D. R. (1981). The ethnography of TESOL. *TESOL Quarterly, 15,* 105–116.

Ross, S., & Shortreed, I. M. (1990). Japanese foreigner talk: Convergence or divergence? *Journal of Asian Pacific Communication, 1,* 135–145.

Ryan, E. B., Giles, H., Bartolucci, G., & Henwood, K. (1986). Psycholinguistic and social psychological components of communication by and with older adults. *Language and Communication, 6,* 1–22.

Ryan, E. B., Kennaley, D. E., Pratt, M. W., & Shumovich, M. A. (2000). Evaluations by staff, residents, and community seniors of patronizing speech in the nursing home: Impact of passive, assertive, or humorous responses. *Psychology and Aging, 15,* 272–285.

Shepard, C. A., Giles, H., & Le Poire, B. A. (2001). Communication accommodation theory. In W. P. Robinson & H. Giles (Eds.), *The new handbook of language and social psychology* (pp. 33–56). New York: Wiley.

Simard, L., Taylor, D. M., & Giles, H. (1976). Attribution processes and interpersonal accommodation in a bilingual setting. *Language and Speech, 19,* 374–387.

Sparks, B., & Callan, V. J. (1992). Communication and the service encounter: The value of convergence. *International Journal of Hospitality Management, 11,* 213–224.

Street, R. L., Jr. (1982). Evaluation of noncontent speech accommodation. *Language and Communication, 2,* 13–31.

Street, R. L., Jr. (1991). Accommodation in medical consultations. In H. Giles, J. Coupland, & N. Coupland (Eds.), *Contexts of accommodation. Developments in applied sociolinguistics* (pp. 131–156). Cambridge, Engand: Cambridge University Press.

Tajfel, H., & Turner, J.C. (1986). The social identity theory of intergroup relations. In W. Austin & S. Worchel (Eds.), *Psychology of intergroup relations* (2nd ed., pp. 7–17). Chicago: Nelson Hall.

Thakerar, J. N., Giles, H., & Cheshire, J. (1982). Psychological and linguistic parameters of speech accommodation theory. In C. Fraser & K. R. Scherer (Eds.), *Advances in the social psychology of language* (pp. 205–255). Cambridge, England: Cambridge University Press.

Thomson, R., Murachver, T., & Green, J. (2001). Where is the gender in gendered language? *Psychological Science, 12,* 171–175.

Tong, Y.-Y., Hong, Y.-Y., Lee, S.-L., & Chiu, C.-Y. (1999). Language use as a carrier of social identity. *International Journal of Intercultural Relations, 23,* 281–296.

van den Berg, M. E. (1986). *Language planning and language use in Taiwan: A study of language choice behavior in public settings.* Taipei, Taiwan: Crane.

Watson, B., & Gallois, C. (1999). Communication accommodation between patients and health professionals: Themes and strategies in satisfying and unsatisfying encounters. *International Journal of Applied Linguistics, 9,* 167–183.

Williams, A. (1999). Communication accommodation theory and miscommunication: Issues of awareness and communication dilemmas. *International Journal of Applied Linguistics, 9,* 151–165.

Williams, A., & Giles, H. (1996). Intergenerational conversations: Young adults' retrospective accounts. *Human Communication Research, 23,* 220–250.

Woolard, K. A. (1989). *Double talk: Bilingualism and the politics of ethnicity in Catalonia.* Stanford, CA: Stanford University Press.

QUESTIONS TO PONDER

1. What aspect of CAT do you feel needs empirical attention the most, and why? Design both a qualitative and quantitative study toward this end.

2. Consider two people, on reflection, you believe to be the most and the least convergent people you know. Describe the ways they manage this communicatively. Why do you feel they act in this way, and what are the likely reactions of recipients to it?

3. Recall, in general fashion, your communications with your parents when you were a teenager. How would you describe your and their intergenerational behaviors in CAT terms? In what ways were these patterns typical or atypical of other families you knew or have observed since?

4. Again using CAT as an interpretive frame, how (in general) would you describe your interactions with elderly strangers? In what ways is your interpersonal communication in the foregoing different from that with elderly people you know very well (e.g., grandparents)?

5. Many nations around the world have more than one official language (e.g., Switzerland). Census 2000 indicates that the USA is becoming ever more ethnolinguistically diverse. Across a range of life's contexts, what accommodations should English-speakers make to other-language immigrants and vice-versa, and why should they do so?

17

Relational Communication: As Viewed From the Pragmatic Perspective

John A. Courtright
University of Delaware

Using the term *relational communication* in the title of this chapter causes me a bit of concern. So many theories of and approaches to interpersonal communication address the growth and maintenance (or, many fewer, the decline and termination) of relationships that the term refers to everything and, thus, to nothing. I have no doubt you've already read this term—perhaps several times—in this book, most likely associated with different meanings and definitions.

I ask that you momentarily put aside those other definitions. My use of *relational communication* will take on a much different meaning than has been used by the other authors in this book. The other meanings are not better or worse, right or wrong; rather, they are just different. The reasons for that difference, as well as my meaning for *relational communication* will emerge as we look at the history of this area of study.

Before launching into that history, let me offer a small conceptual appetizer, a nugget of information to sustain you for a few pages until we get to the main course. At the time I am writing this I have not read a single other chapter in this book, but I am willing to make a bold prediction: This chapter will be the only one to advocate the study of social interaction rather than the study of humans engaged in social interaction. Read the previous sentence again. The difference it describes is profound. In the pages to come, we will be talking about people's behavior, not the people themselves.

Also in the coming pages, I will attempt to explain what assumptions allow and prompt this exclusive focus on interaction. I will call this body of assumptions the Pragmatic Perspective. Students (and professors) who encounter the Pragmatic Perspective for the first time almost always have one of two, completely opposite reactions: (a) "this is utter nonsense; what kind of warped mind would accept this rubbish," or (b) "this is the most exciting and stimulating approach to interpersonal communication I have ever read; this really makes sense."

If you find yourself in the latter group, welcome aboard. You will have discovered a rich and interesting approach to the study of interpersonal communication, which is rich and interesting no matter how you study it. If you find yourself in the "utter nonsense" category, stick with me nonetheless. You may not find a new way for *you* to study interpersonal communication, but you will learn how *others* choose to study it. You will also learn that they're not "warped" at all.

The origins of what I am calling relational communication can be traced back almost 70 years to Gregory Bateson's (1935, 1958) writings about the Iatmul tribe in New Guinea. That's perhaps a bit too far. For our purposes, a more realistic starting place is the publication of the classic book, *Pragmatics of Human Communication*, by Watzlawick, Beavin, and Jackson (1967). Although most of this book was devoted to a discussion of "pathologies and paradoxes" (the authors were psychologists and psychiatrists), the first two chapters laid out an approach to interpersonal communication that was a radical departure from the dominant paradigms of the time (Fisher, 1978).

Gone was the study of individual communicators—we would study couples, families, or what Watzlawick et al. (1967) called "systems." Gone was the exclusive focus on the cognitive processes of these individual communicators—instead, we would focus on the actual behavior these communicators exhibited in an attempt to find "patterns" of behavior. And gone was the emphasis on the content of messages—in the pragmatic approach, "how" something was said had much more import for relationships than "what" was said. There were a few additional changes, but these should be enough to show you what a radical departure from orthodoxy this approach was and still is.

Over the next 5 years or so, there was a great deal of debate about the Pragmatic approach, but little actual research. That began to change quite dramatically in the early to mid-1970s with the introduction of several systems for coding and categorizing these interactional behaviors (Mark, 1971; Rogers & Farace, 1975). To study how interactional behaviors affect relationships, we have to be able to label and describe the various functions that those behaviors perform within an interaction. These coding systems allowed and prompted that to happen, thus paving the way for much of the research I will present later in this chapter.

Although there are many organizational strategies for presenting a body of information such as that associated with relational communication, the most logical would be to follow the historical pattern just outlined. Accordingly, I will first set the stage by describing the assumptions and tenets of the Pragmatic Perspective. Next, I will focus more specifically on relational communication and the coding systems used to describe this aspect of communication. Third, I will present some of the research findings about relational communication and attempt to put them in a larger context. Finally, I will conclude by discussing the importance of this entire paradigm.

THE PRAGMATIC PERSPECTIVE

Although the original use of the term *pragmatics* is often credited to Morris (1946), the use and development of this approach in communication research can be directly attributed to Watzlawick et al. (1967). Recall that these writers were psychiatrists and psychologists. Unlike their professional peers, their approach deemphasized the treatment of the individual person's problems, focusing instead on the larger social unit of which the individual was a member (e.g., the marital dyad, the entire family). They found that knowledge of the communicative context was extremely important for understanding and treating a person's psychological problems. They asserted that "a phenomenon remains unexplainable as long as the range of observations is not wide enough to include the context in which the phenomenon occurs" (Watzlawick et al., 1967, pp. 20–21).

When they observed the communicative behavior of these larger social units, they frequently discovered characteristic patterns of interaction that recurred time and time again. Moreover, they found that these recurrent patterns of interaction actually facilitated the continuance of an individual's psychopathology. Accordingly, the main thrust of their diagnosis and treatment involved breaking the cycle of these communicative patterns and substituting a nonpathological communication environment (see Watzlawick, Weakland, & Fisch, 1974).

As students of communication, we focus mostly on normal rather than pathological patterns of interaction. Accordingly, various researchers have interpreted and extended the theoretic principles suggested by Watzlawick et al. (1967) to a wider range of interpersonal communication contexts. These extensions of the Pragmatic Perspective involve combining two communication theories: systems theory and selected aspects of information theory.

Systems Theory

Systems theory suggests the importance of the social, communicative context. Within this theory, communication does not take place in isolation, but rather necessitates a communication system—the smallest of which must contain at least two members. Hence, to study the individual communicator and his or her behavior in isolation is to ignore the systematic processes characterizing this human activity. Watzlawick et al. (1967) commented:

> If a person exhibiting disturbed behaviors is studied in isolation, then the inquiry must be concerned with the nature of the condition and, in a wider sense, with the nature of the human mind. If the limits of the inquiry are extended to include the effects of this behavior on others, their reactions to it, and the context in which all of this takes place, the focus shifts from the artificially isolated monad [the individual] to the relationship between the parts of the wider system. The observer of human behavior then turns from an inferential study of the mind to the study of the observable manifestations of relationship. (p. 21)

To assume that Watzlawick and his colleagues incorporated all of the many elements of systems theory into their *Pragmatics* would be a mistake. They selectively chose several concepts, thus creating a coherent and workable, but certainly not exhaustive approach. Following their lead, I will confine our discussion to the basic principles of wholeness, openness, and hierarchical order.

Wholeness. The principle of wholeness is also referred to as the principle of "nonsummativity." This characteristic is so fundamental to a systems perspective that it has frequently been phrased as a maxim: "The whole is greater than the sum of its parts." This suggests that a communication system is more than two or more people who happen to be in physical proximity to each other. Rather, a communication system includes these people as well as *the relationships between and among these people*. The inclusion of the relationships is what makes the whole more than its parts. These individual humans have become *interdependent* with each other. Because this is a communication system, the reason for this interdependency— these relationships— is that these people exchange communication behaviors.

Stated differently, the behavior of one member of the system affects and is affected by the behavior of all other members. These interrelationships among the behaviors make the system, a separate entity, which cannot be recreated by the simple combination of the individual communicators. A "family," for example, is much more than several people of different ages who happen to live in the same house. The communication behaviors of each family member influence all of the others. Accordingly, to observe and study a single communicator (family member) in isolation would be to discard that person's linkages to or interdependencies with the other members of the system.

Openness.   Openness refers to the degree to which a system exchanges information or energy with the environment around it. All living organisms are open systems. They must take in nutrients, water, and oxygen from the environment, and in turn they must expel waste products. The term ecological balance is a systems term referring specifically to the natural and unimpeded (by pollution, civilization, etc.) exchange of energy among various living, open systems and their environments.

All human communication systems also are open, although the commodity of exchange in this instance is information, not energy. All normal people belong to various open systems—family, class at school, friends, work group, and so forth. As people enter and leave these various systems, they take information with them. In addition, even when people are not interacting in a system, they gain information by reading, watching television, or personally experiencing nonsocial aspects of the environment.

As you might imagine, the concept of an open system has an opposite, the "closed" system. A closed system has impermeable boundaries and thus is unable to exchange either information or energy with its surroundings. Everything that is needed for its functioning is contained within the system. Although the concept of a closed system makes an ideal contrast to openness, there is no perfectly closed system, no perpetual motion machine. All systems must be open to their environment to some extent, or they eventually will disintegrate. In systems jargon, this tendency to disintegrate is called "entropy."

The primary reason for introducing this distinction between open and closed systems is to suggest that human communication systems, because they are open and thus exchange information with their environment, are capable of self-regulation. The eventual fate of a closed system is disintegration, and this process can never be reversed. In contrast, the open system can sometimes restore itself by drawing resources from the environment. We constantly restore our bodies by eating and resting. Similarly, we regulate and restore social systems by communication. If you have ever had a serious argument with a friend, spouse, or family member, and if your relationship is still intact, then you have experienced the self-regulating process of an open system.

To overcome such an argument would almost certainly require information obtained from outside of the relationship (the system) itself. Perhaps you talked to a close friend, a family member, or even a professional counselor. Perhaps you found information in a book or magazine article to be helpful or comforting. Or perhaps you went to a religious service to obtain a different "take" on what had happened. Each of these possibilities involves obtaining information from outside of the system in an attempt to return the relationship to its former state. This process of self-regulation—that is, the members of the relationship using information to avoid disintegration—is a primary characteristic of an open communication system.

Hierarchical Order.   When systems theorists talk about hierarchical order, they mean that every system is a component of a larger *suprasystem*, while simultaneously being comprised of a number of smaller *subsystems*. As an example, let's consider the open communication system we usually call the family. As we move up the hierarchy, the family is part of the neighborhood, which is part of the city, which is part of the state, and so on until we reach the universe. If we move down the hierarchy, the family contains categories of members (parents, children, grandparents) as well as its individual family members. The individuals are made up of various biological systems (the cardiovascular system, the digestive system, etc.), which are comprised of various organs, which contain various cells, and so on.

This concept of hierarchical order implies that each system is a component in a vast set of interdependent linkages. Moreover, recall that the concept of wholeness suggested that we cannot appropriately and accurately study a member of a social system in isolation. Consequently, the appropriate study of any system involves locating it in its appropriate context, its suprasystem.

This is precisely what Watzlawick et al. (1967) meant when they wrote, "a phenomenon remains unexplainable as long as the range of observations is not wide enough to include the context in which the phenomenon occurs" (pp. 20–21). Whether that larger system, that context, is a family, a culture, an ethnic heritage or a work group (to name just a few), a communication system must be studied in the context of a larger, more encompassing suprasystem.

Information Theory

Physical systems and social communicative systems operate by similar processes, differing, however, by the way their component parts are linked. Physical systems operate via energy; social systems operate via information. As a result, certain implications of what is called "information theory" are an important aspect of the Pragmatic Perspective. We need to discuss two fundamental concepts that capture the essence of information theory: uncertainty reduction and redundant patterns.

Uncertainty Reduction.   Information theory begins with the proposition that people have the ability to choose from among a range of alternative behaviors. That is, as we enter into social interaction (more specifically, as we enter into each message exchange within a social interaction), we possess an extremely large number of communicative behaviors from among which we may choose. We have never chosen many of these behaviors and most likely never will (e.g., most of us have never sworn at a member of the clergy). Through a selection process, we reduce the number of available alternatives until we finally choose a single behavior.

Information theory can be applied to show that this selection process is not a random, haphazard, guessing game. Rather, people make purposeful choices. Moreover, we make these choices very rapidly, normally in a fraction of a second. What allows us to reduce systematically the number of alternatives and eventually select a single behavior is information. We make choices about our behavior based on the information we possess. In the absence of any usable information, the choice becomes a random selection, and we are required to "guess" which behavior to perform.

The situation in which no information exists is one of "maximum uncertainty." If we have no information by which to reduce the number of alternatives, then each of our choices has exactly the same probability of being selected, and we are totally uncertain about which to choose. As information is received and processed, however, certain alternatives can be eliminated, thus making some choices more probable and others less probable. As this happens, our uncertainty has been reduced. As even more information is received, the probabilities of selecting various options again change, and our uncertainty is reduced further until a single behavioral alternative is selected.

Information theory assumes, therefore, that we are constantly seeking to reduce uncertainty by a process (albeit most often unconscious) of asking questions. "Was that remark intended as an insult or a compliment?" "Are they laughing with me or at me?" "Was that a serious question or was she just wondering out loud?" Consequently, communication is seen as an ongoing process in which we are constantly seeking and obtaining information about which communicative behavior we should next perform.

Patterns of Behavior.   Now that we know that information is important in reducing our uncertainty about which behavior to perform next, we have to ask the following questions: What does that information look like? What form does it take? How do we know it when we see it? The Pragmatic Perspective assumes that interaction behaviors occur in a sequence. We've already looked at the question–answer sequence, so let me share another example. When I discuss this topic in my class, I casually walk over to someone sitting in the front row (remember, the entire time I'm talking about sequences of behavior), and without warning I put a smile on my face, stick out my hand, and say "My name's John. How are you?"

I've done this many dozens of times over the years, and no student has ever failed to shake my hand and say something along the lines of, "I'm fine." Let's think about this. Why wouldn't this person recoil and pull back from my attempt to touch them? At the very least, why wouldn't they think, "We're in the middle of class. This is some kind of setup. I'm gonna be embarrassed"? Instead, they invariably shake my hand and complete the greeting ritual.

From the perspective of information theory, the information contained in the behaviors of smiling, extending my hand, and asking a ritual question about the person's health was so overwhelmingly powerful that the individual immediately finished the sequence. She (momentarily!) forgot about class, forgot about what topic I was discussing and became absorbed in the sequence of behaviors we call a greeting ritual.

Information theory asserts that (a) we use information to decide what communication behavior to perform next in an interaction and (b) interaction behaviors occur in sequences. One more piece is required. Information theory maintains that many of these sequences occur over and over again. This is particularly the case when we interact with people we know well: friends, family members, coworkers, and so forth. We can easily recognize when one of these sequences is starting and, using that information, know with great confidence what behaviors to perform to complete our part of the sequence successfully.

In the Pragmatic Perspective, these sequences are referred to as "patterns," and because they tend to occur over and over, they are called "redundant patterns." On recognizing the start of a pattern of behavior (because it is so redundant), we then have the information we need to know what behavior we should perform. When this happens, information theory maintains that our past choices of behavior (because they occurred within these repeated sequences) have an impact on, limit, or "constrain" the large number of possible behaviors we have available to just those few that are appropriate to this sequence. We tend to process these patterns habitually with little conscious thought, reducing uncertainty in the same way again and again. In fact, in some instances, the recognition of the start of a sequence is so compelling (the extension of one's hand for shaking) that it actually overrides other events going on around us.

Implications

There are several implications that flow directly from these elements of the Pragmatic Perspective. I will simply list these with some explanation to follow each one.

All Communication Is Behavior.   A communication system is created because communication (interaction) creates relationships between and among the members of the system. Accordingly, the only way a person can affect other members of the system is to communicate, and the only way to communicate is to perform some behavior. By definition, therefore, in the Pragmatic Perspective, anything that we call communication must be enacted by behaving in some way. Wishing, hoping, and even dreaming will not make it so; the only way we can affect or influence another human being is to behave.

Watzlawick et al. (1967) expressed this same position in what is perhaps their most famous and most controversial axiom: "One cannot not communicate" (p. 48). Stated differently but not nearly so elegantly, it is impossible for members of a communication system not to communicate. If they are not communicating, they have not formed interdependencies, and thus their group of two or more people is not a communication system.

If that argument sounds somewhat circular, let's think of it a different way. The Pragmatic Perspective asserts that all communication is behavioral (i.e., one must behave to influence others). Accordingly, let's substitute the term *behavior* for *communication* in the axiom: One cannot not behave. Go ahead, try it. Even when you are sincerely trying not to behave, you're behaving. Have you ever watched the people in a doctor's waiting room as they try so hard to signal that they do not wish to communicate. But communicating they are. As Watzlawick et al. assert, "behavior has no opposite" (p. 48). Hence it follows that if one cannot not behave, then one cannot not communicate.

This axiom has been the topic of several critical essays, each trying to demonstrate how wrong it is (e.g., Motley, 1990a, 1990b). These writers, however, criticized the accuracy of this assertion from a perspective other than Pragmatics. Let's be clear: this axiom is true if and only if one first accepts all of the tenets of the Pragmatic Perspective. Within the logical context of Pragmatics, one cannot not communicate. If we were to adopt any other perspective on human communication (see Fisher, 1978) such an assertion is not merely incorrect, it becomes nonsensical.

Redundant Patterns Are Observable.   The next two implications are logical deductions from the first one. If all communication consists of behavior, then those behaviors are overt, out in the open, and visible. Moreover, the sequences or patterns of behavior are also capable of being observed. Such observations, of course, are precisely how we know that a pattern we have seen many times before is starting again: we observe its beginning.

Interactants and Observers Have Access to the Same Information.   We do not have the ability to read another person's mind, and others do not have the ability to influence us solely with their mental powers (e.g., telepathy). As I have claimed several times, the only way to influence others is to behave. By definition, that behavior is overt and observable.

Observable to whom? Certainly this behavior is observable to members of the communication system—those being influenced. What we don't think about very often is the fact that the same behavior can be seen by someone who is not a member of the system (i.e., an observer of the system). Every one of us has been in a public place and unintentionally overheard a family squabble or a lovers' quarrel. Had we wanted to pay closer attention, we could have observed every behavior—both verbal and nonverbal—that each member of the system made. As a result, we had access to exactly the same information that the interactants possessed.

Perhaps it is fitting that I attempt to explain this by creating a short interaction between you and me. You are a very good student in this dialogue, but not surprisingly, I get the last word.

You: You say that we have access to the same information as the interactants, but what about history? Don't these families, these lovers, in fact, don't all communication systems have a large body of past experiences that influences their communication behavior in many important ways?

Me: Yes, of course

You: References to unknown people and places, nicknames, taboo topics, and other types of communication shortcuts are all potentially influencing what's happening.

Me: You are absolutely correct

You: But we haven't observed those past experiences, so we don't really have access to the same information that the interactants do.

Me: Why haven't we observed all of those things in the past?

You: We haven't observed them in the past because we didn't know these people before now, and even if we did, they wouldn't let us observe all of their interactions in personal and intimate settings.

Me: Aha! Remember this quote? "A phenomenon remains unexplainable as long as the range of observations is not wide enough to include the context in which the phenomenon occurs" (Watzlawick et al., 1967, pp. 20–21).

The problem, it would seem, is not with the theoretic principles of the Pragmatic Perspective, but rather with our "range of observations." If we had observed that communication system from the first moment of its formation until right now, then we too would have observed all of that past experience. I fully recognize how difficult (okay, impossible) it would be to observe the entire behavioral history of a communication system, but that difficulty is not a theoretical issue. Rather, what we have is a shortcoming of our observational methods. We can't fault the Pragmatic Perspective because we don't have the ability to observe what it requires.

A Person's Intention Does Not Matter.   A person's intention to behave in a certain way cannot and does not influence the other members of a communication system. Remember, only behavior can affect others. I believe we can all agree that the vast majority of the time we behave as we intend. Occasionally, we do not—"Oh, I'm sorry, I didn't mean to sound so harsh." Whether our behavior matches our intentions or not, only our behavior affects other people. Accordingly, if we do not behave as we intend, then our intention is irrelevant. If we do behave as we intend, then our intention is superfluous.[1]

If pushed, I would probably make the same claim for almost every cognitive process you have read about in this book. Either they are consistent with our behavior or not. Either way, other people are not affected by cognitive processes which they cannot observe; they are affected by behavior. Accordingly, any reaction they display will be to our behavior, not our cognitive processes. Think about the previous example about sounding so harsh. The only way we knew that we sounded too harsh was that the other person reacted as if we were harsh. They did not react to our intention to sound pleasant and civil; they reacted to the words we spoke and the actual harshness in our voice. Their reaction, of course, is what allowed us to apologize and attempt to remediate the situation.

[1] I am not the original author of these two sentences and, as much as I would like to, I cannot take credit for them. Even though I have searched for a long time, I cannot locate the original source of this very elegant statement. I believe it was Aubrey Fisher, but I cannot be sure. If anyone reads it and recognizes the original author, please let me know.

This may be the most difficult implication for many of you to accept. Remember, however, I did not claim that intentions and other cognitive processes have no effect on our own behavior. Of course they do and to claim otherwise would be ridiculous. My claim was that those cognitive happenings cannot affect others unless and until they become enacted in behavior. Moreover, in the Pragmatic Perspective, we are not studying individuals, but rather communication systems. Consequently, "others" are the entire focus of our study.

INVESTIGATING RELATIONAL COMMUNICATION

Let me begin this section with a clarification: The Pragmatic Perspective and relational communication are not identical. The Pragmatic Perspective encompasses a set of assumptions and concepts that guide research and theory on relational communication. Relational communication, therefore, is a substantive topic area that is guided by the Pragmatic Perspective. Much earlier, I stated that I would offer a definition of relational communication, and now seems like a good time to make good on that promise. This definition, I believe, will also set relational communication apart from other topics that might easily be studied under the Pragmatic Perspective.

Content and Relationship Dimensions

The concept of relational communication began with Bateson (1958) and can be traced through the work of Watzlawick et al. (1967). More recent essays have tweaked the concept a bit (see Millar & Rogers, 1976, 1987), but not really changed its fundamental nature. The basic idea is that each time we send a message (i.e., behave to communicate) that message has two parts or dimensions: (a) a content dimension that contains the "what" of the message and (b) a relationship dimension that indicates how that content is to be taken.

Occasionally, this latter dimension is communicated verbally ("That was a joke, Susan"), but most often it is communicated nonverbally with paralinguistic cues such as vocal inflection, tone, intensity, and so forth. For example, the difference between a compliment and a sarcastic criticism is frequently not in the content ("That's really neat, John"), but rather in the tone of voice with which we deliver that content.

In early discussions of these two dimensions, they were referred to as the "report" and "command" aspects or operations of communication, respectively. Using those terms, Watzlawick et al. (1967) explained:

> The report aspect of a message conveys information and is, therefore, synonymous in human communication with the content of the message. It may be about anything that is communicable regardless of whether the particular information is true or false, valid, invalid, or undecidable. The command aspect, on the other hand, refers to what sort of message it is to be take as, and, therefore, ultimately to the relationship between the communicants. All such relationship statements are about one or several of the following: "This is how I see myself ... this is how I see you ... this is how I see you seeing me ... " and so forth. (pp. 51–52)

We should note how these writers quickly dismiss the content dimension as relatively uninteresting; after all, it's merely "about anything." In contrast, the command dimension is clearly where the action is. This is that aspect of communication with which relationships are formed, negotiated, maintained, and fall apart. No wonder the name became changed to the "relational" dimension or simply relational communication.[2]

In the previous paragraph, the key word to understanding much of the thinking and research on relational communication is the word "negotiate." In our everyday life, we tend to think of relationships as material, tangible things (e.g., "I have a new relationship" or "I'm having trouble with my relationship"). The fact that you can take these everyday comments about relationships and substitute "car" or "pet" or "kitchen sink" pretty much makes my point.

In relational communication, on the other hand, we assume that relationships are not fixed or static things that have material existence like cars or refrigerators. On the contrary, relationships are dynamic and changing; they are evolving or deteriorating; they are constantly being negotiated and renegotiated through every interaction we have with the other individual(s) in that relationship. As Duncan (1967) so aptly put it, "we don't relate and then talk, we relate in talk" (p. 249). How we relate to these other people in our life is precisely the question that relational communication seeks to answer.

Relational Control

This concept of negotiating or defining relationships could take many forms in actual research, but the most common has been to simplify the idea somewhat into three basic categories of relational behaviors: one-up ($\uparrow$) a behavior that asserts the right to define the relationship, to be in charge; one-down ($\downarrow$), a behavior that offers the other the opportunity to define the relationship, a submissive behavior; and one-across ($\rightarrow$), a behavior that extends the conversation without asserting or giving up any relational rights. Taken together, these relational definitions are referred to as the *relational control* dimension.

There have been several attempts to create a coding system that would capture these basic relational definitions, but the most widely used has been that of Rogers and Farace (1975). I will describe this coding system shortly, but first let's stop momentarily and consider briefly what we must do before we can apply any set of categories to human behavior. Remember: our goal is to do the same thing that the interactants do—observe—but to do so much more carefully and systematically.

First, we must have a permanent record of that behavior, usually a video or audio tape. Do not even think about trying to "code on the fly" in real time because the results will not be usable. In studies of relational communication, we have not usually focused on the visual components of nonverbal communication (e.g., facial expressions),[3] so a videotape can be transcribed into writing for easier use. Not having to rewind or fast forward to a certain point can save countless hours of time and much aggravation.

Second, in every endeavor where we attempt to code human communication behavior, we must decide what amount of such behavior constitutes a single unit. Depending on the nature of

---

[2]Watzlawick et al. (1967) referred to this relational dimension (recall, they referred to it as the "command aspect") as "communication about communication," which they go on to call "metacommunication." This is a truly fascinating concept, and we could spend many more pages discussing it; a temptation I must avoid. Let me just say that, as students of human communication, much of what we say, write, and think about might be thought of as communicating about communication or metacommunication.

[3]Choosing to omit facial expressions and nonverbal behaviors other than paralanguage strikes many people as unwise. Nevertheless, whenever researchers have conducted small pilot studies that attempted to compare relational control codes obtain both with and without the help of these nonverbal behaviors, the differences were so minimal that they did not warrant the tremendous effort needed to include these additional nonverbal dimensions.

TABLE 17.1
Three Digits Used to Code Interaction (Rogers & Farace, 1975)

1st Digit	2nd Digit	3rd Digit
1. Speaker A	1. Assertion	1. Support
2. Speaker B	2. Question	2. Nonsupport
	3. Talk-over	3. Extension
	4. Noncomplete	4. Answer
	5. Other	5. Instruction
		6. Order
		7. Disconfirmation
		8. Topic Change
		9. Initiation-Termination
		0. Other

the question, we might decide to code time units (every 30 sec) or grammatical units (every sentence or paragraph) or thought units. Some of these types of units can be quite subjective and require considerable training on the part of people who segment interactions into discrete units.

Fortunately, for studies of relational communication there are no such difficulties, because we use the same unit that real-world communicators use: the turn at talk. We all have learned long ago that a basic rule of interaction is that we take turns talking. Accordingly, you talk, I talk, you talk, I talk, and if we both talk simultaneously, we usually apologize for the interruption. Accordingly, we define a unit—the "turn"—as beginning when one interactant starts talking and lasting until the other interactant begins the next turn. No matter how long or how short, whether one word or a lengthy monologue, a turn is a turn is a turn. This task is so simple that anybody with normal hearing can segment interaction into turns.

Let's assume that we have an interaction written down and segmented into turns, using the labels Speaker A and Speaker B. The Rogers and Farace (1975) system assigns three codes to each behavior. The first is simply a Speaker code, in our case either A or B. In other studies, this might be husband–wife, or manager–subordinate, clerk–customer or some similar designation. The second code is intended to label the utterance descriptively, in terms of what it is. The third code is designed to label the utterance functionally in terms of what does (i.e., how it responded to the previous utterance). Table 17.1 shows the possibilities for these three codes.

To illustrate, a code of 121 would represent an utterance by Speaker A that was a question serving as support, for example, "Which house do you think it is?" In contrast, a code of 214 would represent Speaker B producing an assertion that served as an answer, for example, "It's that house on the right with the light on." Note that some combinations would not arise often (question as answer), whereas others might occur quite often (assertion as extension, e.g., "I understand" or "Mm-hmm").

Table 17.2 shows how the last two numbers are converted into relational control codes. Several features of this table are worth discussing. First, most of the control codes are obviously one-up (↑). Whenever an interactant is nonsupporting, provides an answer, instruction, order, or disconfirmation, or changes the topic, that person is seen as asserting the right to define the relationship *at that moment and for that moment only*. Despite the fact that these one-up codes dominate the table, we will see shortly that they do not occur in actual interaction with nearly the frequency we might expect.

TABLE 17.2

Assignment of Control Directions (Rogers & Farace, 1975)

	Support 1	Nonsupport 2	Extension 3	Answer 4	Instruction 5	Order 6	Disconfirmation 7	Topic Change 8	Initiate/ Terminate 9	Other 0
Assertion 1	→	←	↑	←	←	←	←	←	←	↑
Question 2	→	←	→	←	←	←	←	←	←	→
Talk-over 3	→	←	←	←	←	←	←	←	←	→
Noncomplete 4	→	←	↑	←	←	←	←	←	↑	↑
Other 5	→	←	↑	←	←	←	←	←	←	↑

Notice also that providing support to the previous speaker is always viewed as a one-down maneuver, thus offering control to that person's partner. Don't confuse one-down (or any other control code for that matter) with communication that is incorrect, bad, wrong, wimpish, or any other evaluative adjective. Although too much of any one kind of behavior may lead to relational problems, by themselves the control codes are meant to be descriptive, not evaluative.

Finally, the one-across codes do not occur very often in the table, and a couple of them (noncomplete as initiation or termination) seldom occur in interaction. Be that as it may, interactants use this code far more than any other. In fact, in most interactions—regardless of setting or status of interactants—one-across maneuvers constitute the majority (50% or more) of the behaviors we will observe.

Codes Into Sequences

Thus far, we have seen how we might code individual behaviors using this system. Remember, however, that the Pragmatic Perspective asserts that we should be looking for redundant patterns of behavior. To illustrate how this is done, let's look at the following example of an interaction between two classmates who are getting ready to study for an exam. From left to right the example identifies the speaker, the content of their message, the three digit code that would be assigned, and the single control code that would be generated. In the last column, the single codes are combined into two sequential behaviors to show a larger pattern. Following the terminology of relational communication, we will call the individual control code an "act" and the two sequential control codes an "interact."

A:	What do we need to do today?	123↑
B:	Can I ask a question about this relational communication stuff?	221↓
A:	Mm-hmm.	113→↓
B:	['cause I really don't get the sequences of behavior part]	233↑→↑
A:	Yeah. OK. . . . Uh.	143→↑→
B:	Maybe I'm reading it wrong, you know? Do you get how he puts this stuff together.	221↓→↓
A:	Yeah, I kinda do.	114↑↓↑
B:	You know, the part where he says sequences happen again and again?	221↑↓↑
A:	Yeah, that's when he talks about the redundant patterns.	114↑↓↑
B:	So these redundant patterns are just sequences that we see a lot of?	221↓↑↓
A:	You got it.	114↑↓↑
B:	So, then, like what are these redundant patterns supposed to mean?	221↓↑↓
A:	They mean that these people probably interact in the same way a lot.	114↑↓↑
B:	So, do you think people really talk that way?	221↓↑↓
A:	No, man, that's stupid. No one would talk like that.	114↑↓↑

Despite classmate A's doubts about how people talk, we can easily see a pattern develop in even this short bit of interaction. Of course, I invented this interaction to illustrate the concept of redundant patterns, so I made those patterns very obvious. From the content, we can see that this brief interaction turns into a series of questions and answers—B questions, A answers. This, in turn, results in a series of redundant interacts: B↓, A↑ and A↑, B↓. These patterns imply that A is in a dominant or one-up position, and B allows/invites A to assume that position. Read the content again. Is there any doubt about who's "in control"?

Although this is an obviously short and admittedly invented interaction, we would apply those codes and attempt to interpret their meaning in much the same way to much longer, real-world interactions. The primary difference is that the extremely large number of behaviors that comprise a real interaction (literally thousands) would require some organizational help from a computer. Real people would still carefully read each utterance and assign the appropriate 3-digit code, but the assigning and tabulation of control codes, because that merely requires the unthinking application of the codes in Table 17.2, is a perfect task for an unthinking computer.

With these ideas in mind, let's look at some of the findings these several procedures have discovered over the years.

SELECTED RESEARCH ON RELATIONAL COMMUNICATION

There are so many individual findings, both large and small, about relational communication that to list them all would require at least as many pages as you've already read. Neither you nor I am up for that task. Accordingly, let me attempt to summarize the most interesting and most provocative findings by dividing them into the several contexts in which they were discovered.

Married Couples

The bulk of the findings about relational control patterns in married couples comes from two, relatively large studies of marital interaction (Courtright, Millar, & Rogers-Millar, 1979; Rogers-Millar & Millar, 1979), containing 45 and 87 couples, respectively. Those sample sizes may not seem especially "large," but the people generated over 80 hours of interaction and a total number of behaviors exceeding 24,000. In addition, each couple filled out an extensive questionnaire in which they were asked about their happiness, satisfaction, understanding of their spouse, and a wide range of other personal and relational information.

Dominance and Domineeringness.   Some very interesting descriptions were derived from these interactions. For example, approximately half of those 24,000 communicative acts were coded as one-across, with one-up and one-down behaviors representing about 25% each. Recall that one-across messages do not assert (or give up) a relational definition, but rather are noncommittal, extending or carrying the conversation forward. This percentage of one-across maneuvers may seem striking, but if anything it is on the low side. In other samples (e.g., managers and subordinates in an organization), the percentage of one-across acts was well over 60%, approaching two-thirds of all relational behaviors (Fairhurst, Rogers, & Sarr, 1987). Finally, when we look at the percentage of interacts that contains one-across as one of the behaviors ($\uparrow\rightarrow, \downarrow\rightarrow, \rightarrow\rightarrow$, etc), we find almost 75% of these interacts contain one-across behaviors.

Two implications can be drawn from these findings. First, people in communication systems spend the majority of their time and effort extending the interaction (i.e., keeping the conversation moving forward). This seems true regardless of the social context or the status of the interactants. Interaction requires a reasonable degree of effort, but the bulk of this effort is not focused on relational definitions. Rather, we expend most of our effort on the basic maintenance and flow of the conversation. If you have ever interacted with a person who wasn't able or willing to keep a conversation flowing, you have experienced how awkward and frustrating such an interaction can be.

Second, because acts other than one-across and interacts that do not contain one across (there are only four—$\uparrow\downarrow$, $\downarrow\uparrow$, $\uparrow\uparrow$, and $\downarrow\downarrow$) occur much less often, their relevance as relational patterns is even greater. The frequent appearance of a particular pattern of behavior that does not occur very often tells us that something worth looking at is happening in the interaction. We may not always be able to determine actually what that "something" actually is, but these types of interacts are potentially important and should draw our attention.

Following these indications has led researchers to pay a good deal of attention to the one-up ($\uparrow$) act, as well as the interact in which a one-up is followed by a one-down ($\uparrow\downarrow$). In some senses, these behaviors (the first individual or "monadic," the other "dyadic") are the epitome of relational control. The one-up act asserts the right to define the relationship: "I'm in control right now." The $\uparrow\downarrow$ interact indicates that the person's relational partner has accepted that definition by submitting: "OK, you want to define, you've got it." Remember that all of this happens on the relational dimension of interaction; the content can be "about anything."

Although this act and this interact seem logically related, researchers have gone to great lengths to keep them conceptually separate. For example, the one-up act has been given the name domineeringness, implying that this behavior is an attempt to be dominant. When an interactant is actually successful in domineering because his or her partner accepted this relational definition, the resulting interact ($\uparrow\downarrow$) is referred to as dominance or sometimes "pure dominance." In practice, dominance is calculated as a percentage—given $\uparrow,\%\downarrow$. Domineeringness and dominance are calculated for both members of the married couple. Submissiveness ($\downarrow$) and pure submission (given $\downarrow,\%\uparrow$) are calculated similarly.

To be clear, attempts to be dominant are viewed as distinct from actual dominance. Several empirical findings indicate that this effort to keep dominance and domineeringness conceptually separate is important. Courtright et al. (1979), for example, found that the expression of a domineering, one-up message was unrelated to how often a spouse was actually in a dominant position. Stated differently, the frequency with which an interactant produced domineering ($\uparrow$) behaviors did not in any way predict how often they would actually be dominant ($\uparrow\downarrow$). This was the case for both husbands and wives.

Domineeringness by either spouse, however, did serve to decrease their partner's frequency of being dominant. Domineeringness, therefore, "says little about one's own dominance, but does decrease the likelihood of the other's dominance. If you do not want to be dominated, then you should increase your own domineeringness" (Courtright et al., 1979, p. 191). This is somewhat like the reverse of an old sports saying, "the best defense is a good offense." Sounds clever, but this is not a strategy I would encourage you to try in your own relationships.

Domineeringness is also related to several of the measures that these couples provided in their questionnaires. Not surprisingly, as domineeringness increases, satisfaction with one's marriage decreases. So too does one's satisfaction with marital communication decrease as domineeringness increases, which again is hardly a surprise.

In another study, Millar, Rogers-Millar, and Courtright (1979) examined the role that domineeringness and dominance might play in marital understanding.[4] Domineeringness was once again found to be detrimental: the more domineering messages expressed by one spouse, the less likely the other spouse was to understand. To be clear, however, we cannot assert any degree of cause and effect. Whether more frequent expression of domineeringness led to

---

[4]In this study, understanding was defined as a spouse knowing what behaviors he or she was to perform and not perform in a variety of family and household tasks: preparing meals, repairing broken objects, disciplining children, and so forth.

misunderstanding or, conversely, whether misunderstandings led to a perceived need to express more one-up behaviors simply cannot be established.

In that same study, Millar et al. (1979) calculated a slightly different index which they called the "pure dominance ratio." Recall that pure dominance was defined as: given $\uparrow$, %$\downarrow$. To construct an index for the couple, the husbands pure dominance was placed in a ratio with his wife's: PDh/PDw. Ratios that hover around 1.0 indicate relative equality in dominance by a husband and wife. When this ratio becomes larger or smaller than 1.0, one spouse dominates to a greater extent than his or her partner.

Millar et al. (1979) found that the more one spouse was clearly dominant (i.e., whenever their pure dominance ratio was well away from 1.0), the less accurately each spouse knew what behavior they were expected and not expected to perform. As pure dominance became more equal between the spouses, understanding increased and the partners "knew" what behaviors were expected of them.

Divorced Versus Married Couples

The previous findings—obtained from basically normal married couples—led to an intriguing set of results from a completely different sample. Courtright, Millar, Rogers, and Bagarozzi (1990) looked at a group of couples who were undergoing marital counseling for difficulties in their relationships. They identified eight of these couples who were very similar on a host of demographic variables (e.g., age, education, length of marriage, number of children). Moreover, as part of their counseling, each of the couples engaged in three interactions—before counseling, immediately after counseling, and two months later—that were taped and coded according to the Rogers and Farace (1975) coding system.

Having three separate interactions from couples in therapy would be interesting enough, but these couples offered another, extremely rare opportunity for study. After counseling, four of these couples resolved their marital problems and remained together, while four separated and obtained a divorce. What a unique opportunity to ask basic and fundamental questions about human interaction. Do couples that repair and stay together interact differently than couples who do not? What are those differences? Although eight couples is certainly a very small sample, their interactions represented data that had been previously described as "virtually impossible" to obtain (Fisher, 1987, p. 325).

As before, the number of differences that were discovered between these two types of couples, even in this one study, were so numerous that we could not discuss them all. Let me try to summarize the big picture. Recall that earlier studies had found that about 50% of the acts produced by marital dyads were one-across, whereas about 25% of these acts were labeled domineering (one-up) and submissive (one-down), respectively. In contrast, the counseled couples (perhaps as a result of their counseling) exhibited more domineering ($\uparrow$, 35%) and less extension ($\rightarrow$, 38%).

Courtright et al. (1990) suggest two patterns that clearly define the differences between these two sets of couples. Although both the together and separated couples decreased their use of domineeringness ($\uparrow$) over time, the together couples substituted more extensions ($\rightarrow$), while the separated substituted submissiveness ($\downarrow$). This difference extends into findings about interaction, with Separated couples displaying almost twice the percentage of complementary interacts ($\uparrow\downarrow$, $\downarrow\uparrow$) as did the together couples. They also exhibited significantly fewer interacts involving one-across: $\uparrow\rightarrow$, $\rightarrow\uparrow$, $\downarrow\rightarrow$, $\rightarrow\downarrow$.

These and many other, similar differences between these two types of couples led Courtright et al. (1990) to offer some general conclusions.

> Couples who terminated their relationships showed a marked tendency to display behaviors which were indicative of avoidance and indirectness, and which functioned to decrease the involvement between the spouses. ... The Together couples, on the other hand, produced much different patterns of behavior throughout these interactions—patterns which indicate more directness and more involvement in relational negotiations. ... These couples were significantly more structured, and hence more predicable to each other, in their interactional patterns.

Let's sum up: directness, involvement, and structure versus avoidance, indirectness, and less structure. General findings such as these could easily offer very useful suggestions and guidelines to counselors, physicians, clergy, and researchers, not to mention the couples themselves. And to return momentarily to the Pragmatic Perspective, at no time did anyone ask these couples what they felt, what they perceived, or what they were thinking. We communicate with our behavior, whether we intend to or not.

Organizations

A series of studies by Fairhurst and her colleagues (Courtright, Fairhurst, & Rogers, 1989; Fairhurst, Courtright, & Rogers, 1990; Fairhurst, Green, & Courtright, 1995; Fairhurst, Rogers, & Sarr, 1987) extended the investigation of relational communication into a variety of organizational settings. With a bit of reflection, we can see that organizations offer a potentially rich setting for such studies. People who work in organizations frequently come with prior designations of unequal status: supervisor, manager, or boss versus subordinate, employee, or labor. Accordingly, how these inherent status differences as well as other organizational features (e.g., does the organization use a hierarchical or a team-based approach to management) were reflected (or not) in different patterns of redundant communication behavior was the focus of these studies.

In the first of these studies, Fairhurst et al. (1987) investigated how closely patterns of relational control were related to several traditional, more cognitive-based indices of the relationships between managers and their subordinates.[5] The "central issue" surrounding all of the cognitive indices was "how much the manager will prescribe rather than negotiate role expectations and other job issues for the subordinate (that is, how much the manager will dominate)" (p. 397). This is a perfect context to examine whether actual behavior matches the managers' and subordinates' self-reported perceptions.

Fairhurst et al. (1987) employed a type of relational index we have not encountered previously, comparative dominance, which they defined as the proportion between the percentages of $\uparrow\downarrow$ and $\uparrow\uparrow$ (comparative dominance = $\%\uparrow\downarrow$ / $\%\uparrow\uparrow$). Using this ratio, Fairhurst et al. found that managers who were high in comparative dominance—that is, their subordinate submitted ($\downarrow$) much more than he or she resisted ($\uparrow$)—exhibited less understanding of that subordinate. Moreover, such managers perceived the subordinate to have less desire for involvement in decisions and, perhaps most important for all of us who have a supervisor, tended to give poorer performance ratings to their subordinates.

The researchers also discovered that the managers and subordinates used an excessive amount of one-across behaviors, reporting that a few of these dyads used one-across messages as much as 80% of the time. Although I earlier argued that extending the interaction is important,

---

[5]Descriptions of these several cognitive-based measures are not relevant to our current topic and a discussion or lengthy set of citations would detract from our present purpose. These indices are amply documented and ably discussed in Fairhurst et al. (1987).

such high frequencies of one-across messages are unlikely to lead to anything substantive in the interaction. Fairhurst et al. (1987) agreed:

> To use one-across, control-leveling messages exclusively is to avoid dominant-submissive interchanges altogether because neither the manager nor the subordinate asks questions, disagrees, offers support, or provides direction in any straightforward manner. Consequently, with this style it is hard to imagine that any communicative goal is effectively achieved (for example, problem solving, decision making). (p. 410)

The defining nature of one-across messages was made apparent once again in another study by Fairhurst and her colleagues (1990) using a totally different sample of managers and subordinates. This investigation examined the relationship between patterns of relational control and managers' evaluations of their subordinates' performance. The findings had much to say about the importance of making conversations flow in the work environment.

In this study, all interacts that a subordinate initiated with a one-across message (S→M↑, S→M↓, S→M→) were positively related to that subordinate's evaluation (i.e., more interacts, higher evaluation). In contrast, interacts in which a manager had to initiate with a one-across message (M→S↑, M→S↓, M→S→) were inversely or negatively related to that subordinate's evaluation (more interacts, lower evaluation). The moral of this story, it would seem, is that you should not make your manager carry the conversational load, or you will pay for it at evaluation time.

This stream of research was extended by Courtright et al. (1989), who compared the relational communication of managers and subordinates in two manufacturing plants, one organized by a self-managing team philosophy and the other by a mechanistic, authority-based philosophy.[6] Previous theory (Weick, 1987) had suggested that the primary characteristic of mechanistically managed organizations was argument. In support of that contention, Courtright et al. found that competitive interacts (S↑M↑) and one-up messages by the manager after a one-across (S→M↑) were significantly more likely in the traditional, mechanistic plant. Similarly, the data revealed the following:

> Managers and subordinates at the traditional plant were more likely to interrupt by talking over each other ... and follow each others' assertions with statements of nonsupport. ... In contrast ... managers of the self-managed plant exhibited fewer order-giving, decision-rendering, and other command-style forms of communication. (p. 797)

This might be a good time to tie the findings in the previous paragraph back to our much earlier discussion of "hierarchical order." Recall that systems exist within an encompassing suprasystem. In this example, manager–subordinate dyads exist within an organization. In the type of organization we call mechanistic or traditional, certain behaviors within the manager–subordinate system (namely, arguments) were functional, useful, and understandable. They made sense to both participants and observers. If we change the suprasystem to a "self-managed" organization, argumentative behaviors become dysfunctional and systems of managers and their subordinates exhibit an entirely different set of behaviors. This example illustrates why the understanding of a system's behavior is critically dependent of placing that system within the proper context.

---

[6]As before, a digression to discuss the very real and important differences between these two philosophies of organizational management would distract us from our central purpose. Courtright et al. (1989) reviewed these distinctions and offer citations to much of the original research in this area.

Let us look at one more brief report of research in this area. Fairhurst et al. (1995) examined the relational control of managers and subordinates in manufacturing plants that were converting from a traditional, authoritarian style of management to a team-based, self-managing style. These patterns of redundant communication behaviors were compared to managers and subordinates from similar plants that had adopted a team-based philosophy from the start of their existence. In short, "conversion" plants were compared to "startup" plants. Moreover, both types of plants had managers at various levels that were judged to be "autocratic" as opposed to managers who might be called "participative." Fairhurst et al. hypothesized that various combinations of these factors (e.g., autocratic managers trying to convert to a participative style of management) would exhibit much different patterns of relational control than other combinations.

The results certainly supported that hypothesis, as well as several other similar predictions. The authors reported:

> When both inertial forces [autocratic manager and conversion plant] were present, participation between manager and subordinates as equals was less (i.e., there were fewer challenges by subordinates of managers' statements, more manager led discussion, and more subordinate approval seeking). When these inertial forces were absent, subordinates assumed a more assertive, equal role in communication. Subordinates challenged manager assertions, more often led discussion that was copied by the manager, and experienced fewer control attempted by the manager in discussions led by the subordinates. (Fairhurst et al., 1995, p. 168)

In other words, subordinates in the team-based plants were allowed to be more challenging and assertive than those in the plants that had been converted from a traditional, hierarchical management style. Moreover, in these converted plants, managers who had previously been autocratic (i.e., they were the "boss") were by much more likely to attempt to maintain control and to dominate their subordinates in interaction. There's a lesson here about old dogs and new tricks, but I suspect you figured that one out already by yourself.

None of the findings in this section are presented solely to discuss various aspects of organizational communication. Although that topic may be interesting to some of us and not so intriguing to others, our focus here is on relational communication. All of these studies, as well as the research reviewed earlier, had two basic elements in common: (a) they focused squarely and primarily on actual communication behavior, and (b) they discovered linkages and provided insights that could not have been obtained through the exclusive use of paper and pencil, self-report questionnaires.

Let us keep these two elements in mind as we summarize and conclude our discussion of relational communication.

CONCLUSION

As we near the end of a lengthy chapter on relational communication, this becomes a good time to take stock, to ask ourselves what information this chapter has set forth and why is that information important. To no small extent, the latter question (Why is this important?) can only be answered by you, and some of you may well decide that, "it's not." Nevertheless, I suspect if you've read this far that you have found something interesting, intriguing, or disturbing about this material. Here are several major points I think we should take away from this chapter. All assume, without constant repetition, that we are viewing interpersonal communication from the Pragmatic Perspective.

- People interact in human communication systems.
- The only way to affect and influence other people in a communication system is to behave.
- People recognize and respond to redundant sequences of communication behavior.
- Because of this recognition, we know what behaviors to perform in interaction, that is, we know what is expected of us.
- People interacting in communication systems and those observing those systems (e.g., a researcher) have access to the same information.
- Every communicative behavior has two aspects or dimensions: a content dimension and a relational dimension.
- We negotiate the nature of our relationship primarily on the relational dimension.
- In research, the relational dimension has been defined primarily as relational control.
- Relational control has been simplified to three basic categories of relational behavior: one-up ($\uparrow$), one-down ($\downarrow$), and one-across ($\rightarrow$).
- Of all the research findings, the role and function of one-across messages is perhaps the most important and certainly the most intriguing.

I suspect you are a bit surprised that I didn't include quite a few more bullet items about the various research findings. From my point of view, the only purpose of those research findings was to illustrate all of the areas where applying the Pragmatic Perspective and studying relational communication has produced new and interesting insights. Besides, those reviews were so highly summarized that all I could possibly provide for you was a summary, an overview intended to tantalize not satiate.

At this stage of your progress as a student of communication, you will be much better served if you concentrate on the principles, the concepts, and the underpinnings of various approaches to interpersonal communication, rather than cramming your head full of detailed research findings. Those research reports will still be there when you are fully ready to tackle them. In the meantime, keep focused on the big picture!

A relatively common thing (for advocates of all perspectives) to do at this point is to launch into a sermon of sorts, using various persuasive tactics to encourage readers to adopt fully Pragmatics and relational communication and to carry them close to their hearts. Repent, oh ye believers in false cognitive constructs! Come to the True Way and find enlightenment!

I have no intention of doing any such thing. First, I don't preach very well and, second, I don't really believe in such evangelism. The study of relational communication from the Pragmatic Perspective offers a clear alternative to many other approaches in interpersonal communication discussed in this book. To say it is unique or different or a "radical departure" is to engage in understatement. For all of those reasons, it is an approach that is not for everyone.

If you decide that it's "for you," you should no longer rely on reviews and summaries such as this one, but begin to read the original works yourself. You are quite capable and the effort will be rewarding. At the end of this chapter, I have listed several suggested readings. Try those out. If you like them, follow their references, as well as those in this chapter, to new readings and other interesting insights.

Here's my final recommendation. Only after you have absorbed the content of those readings would I suggest that you delve deeply into various research findings. Empirical research—all empirical research, not just on relational communication—has numerous sections with many details (Procedures, Methods, Statistics, etc.) that will do nothing to further your understanding of relational communication. Wait until you are ready or you will fall prey to those methodological "trees" and never fully perceive the "forest" of relational communication. I wish you happy reading.

SUGGESTED READINGS

Millar, F. E., & Rogers, L. E. (1976). A relational approach to interpersonal communication. In G. R. Miller (Ed.), *Explorations in interpersonal communication* (pp. 87–103). Newbury Park, CA: Sage.

Millar, F. E., & Rogers, L. E. (1987). Relational dimensions of interpersonal dynamics. In M. E. Roloff & G. R. Miller (Eds.), *Interpersonal processes: New directions in interpersonal research* (pp. 117–139). Newbury Park, CA: Sage.

Parks, M. R. (1977). Relational communication: Theory and research. *Human Communication Research, 3,* 372–381.

Watzlawick, P., Beavin, J., & Jackson, D. D. (1967). *Pragmatics of human communication.* New York: Norton.

Watzlawick, P., Weakland, J. H., & Fisch, R. (1974). *Change: Principles of problem formation and problem resolution.* New York: Norton.

Wilder, C., & Weakland, J. H. (Eds.). (1982). *Rigor and imagination: Essays from the legacy of Gregory Bateson.* New York: Praeger.

REFERENCES

Bateson, G. (1935). *Culture contact and schismogenesis. Man, 35,* 178–183.

Bateson, G. (1958). *Naven* (2nd ed.). Stanford, CT: Stanford University Press.

Courtright, J. A., Fairhurst, G. T., & Rogers, L. E. (1989). Interaction patterns in organic and mechanistic systems. *Academy of Management Review, 32,* 773–802.

Courtright, J. A., Millar, F. E., & Rogers-Millar, L. E. (1979). Domineeringness and dominance: Replication and expansion. *Communication Monographs, 46,* 179–192.

Courtright, J. A., Millar, F. E., Rogers, L. E., & Bagarozzi, D. (1990). Interaction dynamics of relational negotiation: Reconciliation versus termination of distressed relationships. *Western Journal of Speech Communication, 54,* 429–453.

Duncan, H. D. (1967). The search for a social theory of communication in American sociology. In F. E. X. Dance (Ed.), *Human communication theory* (pp. 236–263). New York: Holt, Rinehart & Winston.

Fairhurst, G. T., Courtright, J. A., & Rogers, L. E. (June, 1990). *Interaction patterns and the prediction of performance.* Paper presented at the meeting of the International Communication Association, Dublin, Ireland.

Fairhurst, G. T., Green, S., & Courtright, J. A. (1995). Inertial forces and the implementation of a socio-technical systems approach: A communication study. *Organization Science, 6,* 168–185.

Fairhurst, G., Rogers, L. E., & Sarr, R. A. (1987). Manager–subordinate control patterns and judgments about the relationship. In M.L. McLaughlin (Ed.), *Communication yearbook 10* (pp. 395–415). Newbury Park, CA.: Sage.

Fisher, B. A. (1978). *Perspectives on human communication.* New York: Macmillan.

Fisher, B. A. (1987). *Interpersonal communication: Pragmatics of human relationships.* New York: Random House.

Mark, R. A. (1971). Coding communication at the relationship level. *Journal of Communication, 21,* 221–232.

Millar, F. E., Rogers-Millar, L. E., & Courtright, J. A. (1979). Relational control and dyadic understanding: An exploratory predictive regression model. In Dan Nimmo (Ed.), *Communication yearbook 3* (pp. 213–224). New Brunswick, NJ: Transaction Books.

Millar, F. E., & Rogers, L. E. (1976). A relational approach to interpersonal communication. In G. R. Miller (Ed.), *Explorations in interpersonal communication* (pp. 87–103). Newbury Park, CA: Sage.

Millar, F. E., & Rogers, L. E. (1987). Relational dimensions of interpersonal dynamics. In M. E. Roloff & G. R. Miller (Eds.), *Interpersonal processes: New directions in interpersonal research* (pp. 117–139). Newbury Park, CA: Sage.

Morris, C. (1946). *Signs, language and behavior.* Englewood Cliffs, NJ: Prentice Hall.

Motley, M. T. (1990a). On whether one can(not) not communicate: An examination via traditional communication postulates. *Western Journal of Speech Communication, 54,* 1–20.

Motley, M. T. (1990b). Communicating as interaction: A reply to Beach and Bavelas. *Western Journal of Speech Communication, 54,* 613–623.

Parks, M. R. (1977). Relational communication: Theory and research. *Human Communication Research, 3,* 372–381.

Rogers, L. E., & Farace, R. V. (1975). Analysis of relational communication in dyads: New measurement procedures. *Human Communication Research, 1,* 222–239.

Rogers-Millar, L. E., & Millar, F. E. (1979). Domineeringness and dominance: A transactional view. *Human Communication Research, 5,* 238–246.

Watzlawick, P., Beavin, J., & Jackson, D. D. (1967). *Pragmatics of human communication.* New York: Norton.

Watzlawick, P., Weakland, J. H. & Fisch, R. (1974). *Change: Principles of problem formation and problem resolution*. New York: Norton.

Weick, K. E. (1987). Theorizing about organizational communication. In F. M. Jablin, L. L. Putnam, K. H. Roberts, & L. W. Porter (Eds.), *Handbook of organizational communication* (pp. 97–122). New bury Park, CA: Sage.

Wilder, C., & Weakland, J. H. (Eds.). (1982). *Rigor and imagination: Essays from the legacy of Gregory Bateson*. New York: Praeger.

QUESTIONS TO PONDER

1. The author asserts that, within the Pragmatic Perspective, a person's intention to communicate something (as well as almost every other cognitive construct) is either irrelevant or superfluous. Explain his rationale for making this assertion. Do you agree or disagree? If you disagree, cite several examples from your own experience that clearly disprove this assertion.

2. One compelling finding from every study in relational communication is that the majority (sometimes the vast majority) of relational control maneuvers are one-across ($\rightarrow$) maneuvers that neither assert nor relinquish control, but rather extend the conversation. Why do you think these types of extensions occur so often in virtually every type of interaction? Now, think about a recent interaction you have had with someone who is not very good at keeping the conversation going. What was your reaction?

3. Here is a pure thought question. Could the tenets of the Pragmatic Perspective be used to study any of the communication phenomena that we usually associate with mass communication? Political debates? Soap opera interactions? Movie dialogues? There are a host of trivial issues that could be addressed (Will Bill and Laura's illegitimate baby use too few one-across maneuvers?), but can you devise several serious, substantive questions about mass communication that might be addressed from the Pragmatic Perspective?

4. As stated in endnote 3, several pilot studies have indicated that using nonverbal behaviors (facial expressions, gestures, etc.) to assist in coding the relational maneuvers ($\uparrow\downarrow\rightarrow$) produced very little improvement in accuracy over using a written transcript. On the surface, however, this would seem to contradict several things we have learned about the importance of nonverbal communication. How would you reconcile this seeming contradiction? Also, think of some types of utterances that simply could not be coded accurately if the nonverbal component was ignored. How often do these occur in everyday interaction?

5. Imagine a recent interaction you have had with a store clerk. Now imagine a similar interaction you've had with an authority figure; say, a physician or a police officer. Using the ideas associated with relational control maneuvers ($\uparrow\downarrow\rightarrow$), describe how these two interactions were different. What was the frequency of the three maneuvers? Was one type of maneuver obviously and considerably more prevalent? What was it about these status and authority differences that might have prompted those differences?

18

Conversational Interaction: Understanding How Family Members Talk Through Cancer*

Wayne A. Beach
San Diego State University

Consider the following excerpt of interaction, transcribed from a phone conversation between two family members discussing a mother's failing health due to cancer (see Appendix for explanation of transcription symbols):

Excerpt 1: SDCL: Malignancy#17:2 (S = son; G = son's wife)

G: (°W(h)ow−.°) How long (they) think she's gonna hold o::ut?
    She still in the hospital?=
S: =Ye:ah, yeah. She's still in the hospital. They don't
    kno::w. 'Could be a couple a weeks?

Because neither speaker knows how long mom might live, nor do medical staff ("they"), talking about the future is revealed as an inherently *uncertain* and *ambiguous* undertaking. Predicting the future is a fundamental quandary of everyday existence, particularly when attempting to assess the length of a person's life. Yet in Excerpt 1 (above) it is obvious that just as G devises ways to raise her questions, so does S respond by addressing her concerns (see below). But how does this communicative work get accomplished?

Alternative theoretical approaches to studying "communication in relationships" (e.g., see Casmir, 1994; Littlejohn, 2002; Sigman, 1995; Stamp, Vangelisti, & Knapp, 1994) would emphasize different yet related features apparent in Excerpt 1 (above). For example, during initial interactions and beyond, "uncertainty reduction theory" (e.g., see Berger, 1997; Berger & Calabrese, 1975; Gudykunst, 1988) gives priority to how communicators seek information to better explain, predict, and therefore minimize ambiguities about environments and relationships. Researchers utilizing "dialectical theory" (e.g., see Baxter, 1993; Montgomery & Baxter, 1998) would focus on apparent contradictions between opposing forces (e.g., "life and death," "closeness and distance"). Attention is given to how such "tensions" are experienced and managed by relational partners. Similarly, "relational theorists" (e.g., Millar & Rogers, 1976, 1987) address how interactants attempt to control and negotiate contiguous sequential messages. Patterns of interaction are therefore treated as communication activities individuals are incapable of producing.

The approach overviewed in this chapter, conversation analysis (CA), extends prior theoretical orientations by attending closely to details of (a) how speakers collaboratively organize naturally occurring interactional involvements and (b) how talk and embodied activities are sequentially organized. Before describing these fundamental assumptions of CA, and showing their relevance to how families talk through cancer, notice how Excerpt 1 (above) reveals an array of distinct features:

- At the beginning of G's utterance is "(°W(h)ow−.°)," one resource for displaying surprise—in this case, to having just been informed by S that his trip to visit with mom and family was cancelled (not included in Excerpt 1).
- G then proceeds to ask two contiguous questions, the second emerging before S is provided an opportunity to respond to her first query.
- G's references to "they" and "hospital" reflect her shared knowledge that mom is dealing with medical problems. Specifically, her "How long" and "hold o::ut" evidence a recognition that mom's death is imminent and inevitable. Asking whether mom is home or "still in the hospital?=" has implications for gauging how close mom actually is to dying.
- It is G's second, and immediately prior question, which son answers first with "She's still in the hospital." First, however, his repeated "Yeah, yeah." twice acknowledges, with emphasis, mom's being in the hospital.
- With S's next announcement "They don't kno::w," he returns to G's initial query. In so doing, he exhibits a reason for continued uncertainty but also frustration: Anonymous medical staff are not in a position to provide assurance about mom's unknown fate.
- By speculating "'Could be a couple a weeks?" it is not clear whether S was expressing his own (lay) or others' (experts') prognosis. But in either case, a time frame is socially constructed that provides a possible but not necessarily probable period for mom's dying.

By integrating these identified features, apparent in Excerpt 1 (above), it becomes possible to begin to identify the *interactional organization* of one set of key moments: How a wife displays surprise and solicits, from her informed husband (mom's son), *news updates* resulting in both basic uncertainties regarding mom's current health status, and S's apparent frustration with "not knowing."

Before examining additional excerpts revealing how family members talk through cancer, this chapter (a) overviews basic assumptions of CA research methods; (b) describes a research program designed to investigate communication and family cancer; (c) examines additional and selected data excerpts reflecting how family members deliver, receive, and update good and bad cancer news; and (d) concludes with a discussion of how this introduction to the study of conversational interaction reveals important procedures and implications for building fundamental communication theories addressing how family members interactionally talk about and through cancer.

AN OVERVIEW OF CA

It is difficult to briefly introduce and overview the history and assumptions of any research enterprise, and CA research is certainly no exception. Because introductions are essentially incomplete, readers are encouraged to independently read and reflect upon the citations included in this section, as well as those listed at the end of this chapter.

As noted, CA attends closely to *naturally occurring interactional data, that is, sequentially organized talk and embodied activities* (see Beach & Anderson, 2003, 2004). Attention is given to the direct examination of recordings and transcriptions of naturally occurring verbal, nonverbal, and nonvocal communication activities—interactions that would be occurring whether or not a recording device was present (Beach, 1990a). Data are thus not "idealized or hypothetical constructions" of communication, but records of actual interactional involvements (see Atkinson & Heritage, 1984, pp. 2–5; C. Goodwin, 1981; Heritage, 1984, pp. 234–238). Speakers' actions cannot be intuited, anticipated in advance, nor fully reconstructed (i.e., through self-reported information) following the occurrence of any given interaction or series of involvements. Observations about interactional phenomena thus emanate from contingently organized features of diverse ordinary conversations and institutional encounters involving bureaucratic representatives (e.g., in medical, legal, and corporate settings, see Drew & Heritage, 1992).

During communication, participants continually reveal their orientations to and understandings of moment-by-moment interactional involvements. In the precise ways speakers construct and respond to turns-at-talk, and related embodied actions (e.g., gaze, gesture, touch, and the use of objects), they demonstrate first for one another (and subsequently for analysts' inspections) their real-time and practical understandings of evolving conduct-in-interaction (e.g., see C. Goodwin, 1981, 1994; Heath, 1984, 1986). Exactly what gets achieved in communication is thus a result of how speakers construct and make available to one another their understandings of the local environment of which they are an integral part (see Beach, 1990a, 1990b, 1991, 1995; Jefferson, 1980; Pamerantz, 1990; Wootton, 1988).

A speaker's current turn at talk projects the relevance of a next turn because "talk amounts to actions" and "action projects relevance" (Schegloff, 1991, p. 46). Not just any response will normally suffice, since prior speakers project the relevance of some (not just any) range of appropriate and next actions. The range of possible activities accomplished by the second speaker display variations of "responsiveness" because talk is sensitive to "recipient design"—actions revealing how speakers hear and orient to specific social actions comprising prior speakers' utterances. By describing and explaining the precise ways participants organize and thereby shape their interactions, evidence is therefore provided about the inherent consequentiality of communication. And because "context" is not treated as external to or removed from communication (see Beach, 1990b; Goodwin & Duranti, 1992; Mandelbaum, 1991; Zimmerman, 1988), but *achieved through interaction*, social actions are both *context-shaping* as speakers tailor them to prior and immediate circumstances, and *context-renewing* as speakers contribute to evolving and subsequent actions.

Although considerably more issues could be addressed regarding basic working assumptions and verification procedures for CA research, and are available elsewhere (e.g., see Drew & Heritage, 1992; Heritage & Maynard, 2006; Maynard, 2003; Ochs, Schegloff, & Thompson, 1996), discussion next focuses on research conducted on family cancer, the phone call materials from which Excerpt 1 (above) was drawn, and a series of additional exemplars from these interactions.

COMMUNICATION AND FAMILY CANCER JOURNEYS

Cancer is considered the most ubiquitous and deadly disease in the world today (Kumar & Clark, 1990). Over 50% of all cancer patients cannot be cured (MacDonald, 1996), and three out of four families in the Western world are somehow impacted by cancer diagnosis and treatment (Biegel, Sales, & Schulz, 1991; Lichtman & Taylor, 1986). Not surprisingly, communication processes have been widely proclaimed as primary resources for managing understandings, relationships, and even outcomes throughout cancer diagnosis and treatment (e.g., see Benjamin, 1987; Bloom, 1996; Dunkel-Schetter & Wortman, 1982; Hilton, 1994; Keller, Henrich, Sesschhopp, & Beutal, 1996; Northouse & Northouse, 1987; Zerwekh, 1984). What is striking is how little remains known about basic communication patterns comprising family cancer journeys (see Kristjanson & Ashcroft, 1994).

In our review of overview of more than one hundred articles focusing on individuals' personal and social experiences with cancer (referred to as "psychoncology" and "psychosocial" dimensions of cancer (see Beach & Anderson, 2003), we reveal a *noticeable absence* of research on the social organization of naturally occurring interactions throughout cancer diagnosis, treatment, coping, and care. Our inquiry was guided by two basic questions:

- How do lay and professional persons work together to make sense of and deal with cancer journeys?
- In both clinical and home or work environments, what interactional patterns comprise these real-time communication events?

When considering the extended and rich history of research on communication cancer, these questions may be discounted as both odd and untimely. Yet we propose that because an empirical foundation for understanding ordinary social—and thus communicative activities of cancer journeys—is in its infancy, so too are any encompassing theories of communicative oncology.

In lieu of *interactional* research drawing attention to actual communication events—inquiries relying upon recordings and transcriptions of phone calls and face-to-face interactions between lay and professional persons—we have discovered that *investigations rely predominantly upon self-report and anecdotal data*. Research methods such as surveys, questionnaires, interviews, and direct observation (reconstructed through note-taking and diaries) offer rich insights into individuals' perceptions of and reported experiences about events and coping mechanisms. Yet such data can neither replace nor re-present details and contingencies of routine conversational and institutional interactions. Knowledge about how participants interactionally organize cancer-related care and treatment is thus lacking (see also Lutfey & Maynard, 1998).

But how do medical professionals, patients, and family members organize their interactional involvements? What specific communicative practices get enacted by speakers attempting to understand and somehow deal with complex issues throughout cancer journeys? Consider the following social activities:

- Delivering, receiving, and updating good and bad news.
- Managing uncertainty about cancer diagnosis, treatment, and prognosis.
- Remaining hopeful and optimistic in the midst of potentially despairing cancer circumstances.
- Attempting to understand, and talk about, what the "doctor" and other professionals have said about a patient's cancer.
- Absorbing, assimilating, and commiserating about cancer as a central and recurring quandary of everyday life.

Drawing attention to these (and related) social activities has not emerged from reading extant literature on cancer journeys. Rather, these questions have emerged as a result of our close and ongoing inspection of a series of 60 recorded and transcribed phone calls. These phone conversations focus on a woman (wife, mother, sister, daughter-in-law) who was diagnosed with lung cancer, leading to complications and her death nearly thirteen months later. This corpus of data is referred to as the "Malignancy Calls," and represent the *first natural history* (i.e., from initial diagnosis to death) of a families' ongoing interactional attempts, via local and long-distance telephone calls, to understand and deal with cancer and its consequences developmentally. Beginning with the son's first phone call to his dad, and throughout, these calls reveal the social and emotional impacts of family members (but also selected friends, acquaintances, and service representatives) as they deal with the uncertain (but often inevitable) trajectories of terminal cancer.

DELIVERING, RECEIVING, AND UPDATING
GOOD AND BAD CANCER NEWS

In the opening moments of the first phone call, dad informs son that mom's "tumor" is "malignant":

Excerpt 2: SDCL: Malignancy#1:1 (D = dad; S = son)

D: .hh The tum:or:: that is the:: uh adrenal gla:nd tumor
      tests positive.=It is: malignant.
S: O:kay? =

This pivotal moment is comprised of several noticeable features (see Beach, 2002). First, as dad announces news to son about mom's condition, he employs a series of technical terms not dissimilar to the "biomedical" language of medical practitioners. In this way, he portrays himself as having spoken with the doctors (and perhaps others) about mom's diagnosis, and is now attempting to update son (who is less informed) about the news.

Second, dad twice clarifies his delivered news for son: As "tumor" gets further specified with "adrenal gland tumor," and as "tests positive" is described as "malignant." By so doing, dad attempts to insure that son not only hears but understands the delivered news. Notice, however, that he does not state that mom has "cancer."

Third, son's "Okay" may be considered by some as a rather odd response to having just been informed that his mom's tumor is malignant (see Beach, 1993, 1995). Specifically, by withholding his emotions, and perhaps even appearing to initially accept dad's announcement, son's "Okay" also prefaces an upcoming clarification about the tumor's location. These actions begin to offer what evolves as a "stoic" (i.e., a serious yet enduring) response to bad news—news impacting not just mom as a diagnosed cancer patient, but family members as well, including how dad and son collaborate to understand (and eventually reveal their reactions to) news about mom's condition.

A more extended analysis of the interactional environment preceding and following Excerpt 2 (above) addresses how bad cancer news gets initiated, responded to, assimilated, and elaborated upon (see Beach, 2001b, 2002; Beach & Good, 2004, in press-a). By extending Maynard's (1997, 2003) analysis of "news delivery sequences" in everyday life to family interactions, this analysis confirms the "stoic" response as one altogether normal pattern enacted by those closest to and thus directly impacted by the news (i.e., consequential figures). It is not uncommon for such stoic patterns to be associated with a removed or even "objective" demeanor of medical professionals when delivering bad news to patients and family members—an interactional resource they often exhibit when navigating through difficult situations and keeping their emotions "in check" (Beach & LeBaron, 2002). In Excerpt 2 (above), it is seen that family members also have little choice but to somehow cope with bad news that is consequential for their daily relationships. Dealing with "family" cancer, then, involves actions similar to what Peräkylä (1993, 1995) referred to as "dreaded issues" that emerge when uncertain futures get discussed by HIV-positive patients, their significant others, and AIDS counselors.

Maynard (1997, 2003) identified a series of distinct patterns through which speakers organize the delivery and receipt of both good and bad news. Well over one hundred excerpts have been analyzed, drawn from dozens of interactional involvements, and across diverse speakers, topics, and occasions. Speakers have been shown to solicit specific kinds of news with an Itemized News Inquiry (INI; e.g., "How is Dez anyway?"), or more general information through a Topic Initial Elicitor (TIE; e.g., "What's new with you?"; Button & Casey, 1985). Such queries are routinely followed by four key actions: (a) announcement, (b) response, (c) elaboration, (d) assessment.

One example of a four-part news delivery structure (1→ - 4→) appears below, a discussion between J and L about an acquaintance apparently diagnosed with "cancer":

Excerpt 3: (H26B/Holt:088:1:8:4—Maynard, 1995, p. 5)

```
1 J:INI→      How is Gay Ma[rtin ]
2 L:1→                     [a-a-a-] Well she's (.) ʌ out' ʌ hospit'l
3 1→    ˅ no [:w,]
4 J:2→     [Is ] [she]
5 L:3→         [ a]nd uh- you know it is: it is I thin:k
        ˅ cancer
6 J:4→ .tch ˅(w)e-:-:-o:-:ll
```

This instance reflects how J and L display shared yet limited knowledge about "Gay Martin," a known individual but not a person with whom J and L are particularly close (Beach, 2001b). Here it can be seen that the good news L announces (1→) is responded to by J with mild surprise (2→). Next, in (3→) notice that L qualifies with an elaboration of bad cancer news, but with some uncertainty ("I thin:k ˅ cancer"). Clearly, as L displays that he is not sure whether Gay Martin's illness is cancerous or caused by some other problem, he also constructs his relationship as distant (i.e., non-intimate). Similarly, J receives and assesses this bad news with some concern (4→), but does not further reveal being affected by the news nor pursue elaboration about Gay Martin's condition.

FAMILY MEMBERS AS PRIMARY AND CONSEQUENTIAL FIGURES SHARING THE NEWS

In Excerpt 3 (above), J and L treat the news as a problem for someone else (Gay Martin), essentially a diagnosed condition having only minimal consequences for themselves. They do not share detailed knowledge about the illness, nor rely on such knowledge and background to claim ownership of the very illness circumstances being reported on. In these ways, J and L work together to treat their relationship with Gay Martin as variably "distant." In contrast, consider a more involved exemplar, in Excerpt 4 (below) between dad and son, where shared knowledge is displayed as speakers reveal themselves as primary figures within the news being reported upon. This excerpt involves the most complex set of interactional involvements discussed in this chapter. The moments below occurred shortly after the initial reporting and receipt of the bad news evident in the first phone call (Excerpt 2, above):

Excerpt 4: SDCL: Malignancy#1:4

S:INI→   [How did she far:e], through these pr[ocesses].
D:1→   [U::hmm]
         (1.5) pthh 'Think she did pretty we:ll. .hh She has been say:ing all alo:ng, that
         this is too ba:d to be something simple.
S:2→   Um hm[m]
D:3→   [pt].hh And she w [a:s]
S:2→   >[She's] never wrong is [she].<
D:3→   [Ye:]ah she's never wrong. .hhh And [she was] =
S: [((cough))]
D:3→   = f:alling apart (0.6) the ear:ly part of the week. That was the (.).h the fe::ar:
         etcetra. .hhh (.)
         Now at this point it's kinda of a combination of (.) a:nger and resignation. So .hhh
         I think she's doing pretty good. ((continues))
         ((9 lines deleted))
S:4→   [Yeah] having no course of action. (.) This has been just a nightmare of (.) not
         kno:wing.

Here, direct attention is initially given to how mom was personally dealing with the cancer diagnosis. These moments are particularly significant because they represent not only the first time in this phone call that mom's coping is addressed, but (it turns out) the first of a series of similar discussions throughout the entire body of phone calls as mom's cancer develops. The following observations reveal the intricate nature of family members talking through illness dilemmas.

Initiated by son's "How did she fare," and following an extended pause (1.5), dad produces two related actions in (1→). First, by announcing "'Think she did pretty well," dad proceeds as though he is adequately informed to answer son's prior query. Notice, however, that his report is not without some equivocation: He frames his assessment as what he "'Think[s]," not what mom had stated. And with "pretty well," what Jefferson (1988) described as a "premonitor" or preview of inevitable and upcoming trouble, dad forecasts that mom has also been experiencing some difficulties (which he later described in some detail, e.g., fear and anger).

Second, dad next reports what mom had been "saying all along," that it was "too bad to be something simple." By so doing, dad reveals his extended background with mom's illness journey, in part through an ability to report her speech and action (see Beach, 2000; Holt, 1996, 2000; Holt & Clift, 2006; Urban, 1984). These actions are an upshot of having directly interacted with her throughout the course of health difficulties, symptoms and problems only recently associated with the identification and medical–professional diagnosis of a malignant tumor.

Third, mom's reported assessment, "too bad to be something simple," reflects dad's version of her own "lay diagnosis" (see Beach, 2001a, 2001b; 2002; Beach & Good, 2004; Beach & Lockwood, 2003). Constructed in the form of a cliché or idiom, such commonplace figures of speech are frequently invoked during an assortment of troubling moments during conversations (see Beach, 1993, 1996; Drew & Holt, 1988, 1998). Without actual recordings of such reported events, it is of course not possible to discern just how (or even if) mom actually uttered "too bad to be something simple." But when such utterances do occur, they have been shown to be recruited as resources for (a) pursuing or soliciting withheld affiliation or sympathy and (b)shifting out of troubling topics. Either or both of these findings provide possible insight into what may very well have been a troubling interaction with mom invoked by dad in Excerpt 4 (above).

Following dad's preliminary announcement in (1→), son's reply (2→) briefly acknowledges with "Um hmm." Next, as dad begins to elaborate the news (3→, "And she was"), son overlaps and extends his response with "She's never wrong is she." Designed by son not to unduly interrupt dad's elaboration, but delay it briefly, he displays his shared knowledge with "never wrong." Offered as a statement of fact, not simply an opinion, son asserts his historical familiarity with mom's ability to accurately assess everyday situations. He also solicits alignment and thus agreement from dad (3→), which is quickly provided ("Yeah she's never wrong .hhh And she was"). As dad repeats son's assessment and recycles a portion of his turn with "she's never wrong," (see Schegloff, 1987), he reinitiates his elaboration of the news in (3→).

Yet there is something more occurring here between dad and son: the sharing of an enduring and endearing acknowledgment of wife's/mom's insight. In this way, the discerning and stable quality displayed by mom is celebrated by dad and son. As they continue to work through the convoluted news about mom's cancer, such a moment reflects a passing shift from bad to good news, essentially a "bright side" (see Holt, 1993) to this unfolding conversation. Though only a single instance, it should thus be clear that good and bad news are not only frequently interwoven (Maynard, 1997, 2003), but employed to balance and even manage ongoing difficulties (see Beach, 2003a, in press-a; Holt, 1993).

By continuing his elaboration with mom's "falling apart" (3→), dad's listing moves from "fear etcetra" → "a combination of anger and resignation" → "pretty good." From these descriptions, it is clear that dad relies upon "etcetra" and "combination" in attempting to capture the complex subtleties involved when characterizing how a loved one is dealing with bad cancer news. It is also notable that while "pretty good" (resembling "pretty well" in 1→, above) can be employed in reference to an apparent improvement from "fear" → "anger and resignation," it nevertheless embodies a troublesome dilemma. And once again, dad portrays himself as being in a position to figure out differences in mom's coping that would not be reportable by those less familiar with her evolving condition.

Following further elaboration by dad in (3→) that will be not addressed here (9 lines deleted), in (4→) son capsulizes his assessment of the situation: Given that "no course of action" has yet been proposed by medical professionals, "This has been just a nightmare of not knowing." Here "nightmare" is a revealing term, a depiction of the son's horrid experience dealing not only with mom's diagnosis, but simultaneously with the uncertainty of treatment options. As noted earlier, though all futures are inherently uncertain, the "not knowing" of one's own or others' illness can transform anticipated events into "dreaded" possibilities.

As Excerpt 4 (above) clearly reveals, *emotions* are not simply situated in individuals' experiences, but social constructed and thus collaboratively produced by interactants (see M. H. Goodwin & Goodwin, 2000; Sandlund, 2004).

Further Delicate Moments When Updating News

We now shift forward several months in time, from the first phone call to a series of moments within calls 35 through 38. One task faced by family members is to monitor how mom moves in and out of the hospital, activities related to the status of her illness. In the next example, son's gramma (GM) has called. Prior to this excerpt, gramma informs son that his dad had been trying to reach him, but was not able to leave a message on his voice recorder. This prompts the son to check his recorder, and he discovers that after recording a new message he had forgotten to "put it back on record calls." He informs gramma that he has just fixed the problem, and the following brief news delivery sequence gets initiated by the son:

Excerpt 5: SDCL: Malignancy#35:2 (GM = Gramma)

```
S: INI→    hh Is something up?
GM: 1→     Well your mother came home on Friday yesterday.
S: 2→      O::h.
GM: 3→     Uh- Friday.
S: 4→      Wow. Well that's good.
```

By querying "Is something up?" (INI→), it is obvious that son had concluded that dad was attempting to get in touch with him for a particular reason. In (1→) it is also apparent that gramma had not only spoken with dad, but now was in a position to deliver news that "mother came home on Friday yesterday." Notice that she does not describe what "came home" implies, and the son does not treat such a reference as requiring explanation. Rather, with "Oh" (2→) son responds to this news with mild surprise. After gramma clarifies with "Uh Friday" in (3→), however, son more fully assesses the news in a stronger fashion with "Wow. Well that's good." (4→)—a shift from mild to marked surprise that amounts to "good" news.

In Excerpt 6 (below), however, son's good news assessment gets transformed by dad into a problematic situation. Later that same morning, following his phone conversation with gramma, son calls his dad and queries dad about mom being home:

Excerpt 6: SDCL: Malignancy#36:4

```
S: INI→    Yes: .hh hh I understand mother is home?
D: 1→      Yes she is?
S: 2→      An:d how is that going.
D: 3→      A:::hhh (.) tough.
S: 2→      pt On everybody on her on you o:n who.
D: 3→      All of the above.
S: 4→      Oka:::y?
```

Earlier in this call son had informed dad that he had spoken with gramma, which is the source of his "I understand mother is home?" (INI→). It is curious that dad's "Yes she is?" (1→) confirms but does not further announce this occurrence. In response (2→), son pursues "how is that going," one specific feature not addressed in dad's prior utterance. And with "Ahh (.) tough." (3→), dad only briefly elaborates on what is hearably a difficult situation. Thus, again, son pursues a fuller explanation with a clarifying response "On everybody on her on you on who" (2→). In turn, after dad withholds fuller elaboration by reconfirming with "All of the above," son assesses the situation as troubling with a marked "Oka:::y?" (4→).

In these moments, dad appears reluctant (at least initially) to enter into a detailed discussion about his wife's return home from the hospital. My initial analysis of his reluctance focused on the possibility that wife/mom was within hearing of the phone call, and thus he chose not to elaborate on difficulties associated with caring for her. However, as the discussion continues, he does further disclose to son that because mom/wife was discharged from the hospital, he has little choice but to care for her (in unison with hospice staff). I thus concluded that it was not his wife's possible eavesdropping that was constraining his elaborations.

What, then, might dad be orienting to in his overly abbreviated responses to son's questions? On further inspection of this and related moments throughout the "Malignancy" phone calls, I have only begun to identify a series of moments when "few words are enough" (see Beach, 2003, in press-a). In Excerpt 6 (above), a displayed unwillingness to talk about an issue somehow gets associated with mom's illness. Such hesitation involves very few words, and appears to be connected with the fact that speakers who possess first-hand knowledge and experience in dealing directly with illness dilemmas—including mom, dad, and son—will at times invoke the right to refrain from talking about it: When there is so much to say, often very little is said (especially at the outset) of a News Delivery Sequence.

This is understandable in its own right, as serious illness can be a sensitive topic. But it is worth noticing that when directly confronted with such difficulties—as with dad dealing with his wife's return from the hospital—speakers possessing intimate knowledge about troubling illness events may position themselves to withhold talking about those same events. And no doubt for a wide variety of reasons. Yet in response others (like son in Excerpt 6, above) may pursue withheld information. This creates an environment where "knowing more about an event" becomes not only the focus of attention, but the displayed right of the informed party to regulate how talk about an issue may unfold (or not). These are delicate matters, embedded in News Delivery Sequences, which may be easily overlooked rather than inspected for specific practices enacted by speakers during each interactional occasion.

One final interactional example appears below, revealing how dad's caring for mom at home remains an issue for some period of time. Several weeks later, son again solicits a specific update about mom (INI→):

Excerpt 7: SDCL: Malignancy #38:1
((Son informs dad that he had just gotten out of the shower, and that dad needn't call back.))

```
S:        No: that's okay I can- I can dry. I'd already done my head so .pt it's okay I got the
          important part as long- there's not enough electricity in this thing to- to fry me if
          there was a problem.
INI→      So- .hhhh so what's up. HHhh
D:1→      Nothing I just called to say good morning and see how you were doing and ( ) and
          all that kind of stuff.
S:2→      .hh Well good h that's better than finding out there is something up I guess huh. heh
          heh [heh.
D:3→                                                                          [Yeah.
          No nothing's up. She's still- I'm gaining a new appreciation for hospital
          orderlies and home health care people.
S:4→      Oh:.
D:3→      (That's) what I'm doin'. Heh.
S:4→      I'll bet- I'll bet. You know they- .h they talk always about the uh the- the unsung
          heroes of the hospital.
```

Though it is implied in (2→) that son was soliciting information about mom, in (1→) dad informs him that he was just calling to "see how you were doing." That son was indeed preoccupied with mom's health status is evident in (2→), as his response—"that's better than finding out there is something up I guess"—confirms the popular belief that "no news is good news." Yet notice that even apparently good news is not without its problems: Son brings his utterance to a close with laughter ("heh heh heh"), itself a nervous display of the ongoing and inevitable trouble (see Beach, 2001a, 2002; Jefferson, 1984a, 1984b) family members are faced with (i.e., coping with mom's terminal cancer diagnosis, including the inherent uncertainty of future events).

This laughter is a delicate display of son's concerns, and is not designed to invite shared laughter (see Glenn, 1989, 2003; Haakana, 2001). Nor is such laughter provided by dad. Rather, in (3→) dad reports "No nothing's up. She's still-," and then shifts attention to himself: "I'm gaining a new appreciation for hospital orderlies and home health care people." While he earlier reported that it was "tough" to have mom home in Excerpt 6 (above), dad now makes clear that caregiving tasks are indeed reportable, noteworthy, and certainly not to be taken for granted. Following son's initial receipt with "Oh" (4→), dad clarifies with "That's what I'm doin'. Heh." Here the delicate and free-standing laugh token, "Heh," encapsulates dad's dilemma, the troubles he is experiencing while caring for mom at home, and his resistance to these troubles (see Jefferson, 1984a, 1984b).

Finally, son completes his assessment (4→) not by claiming first-hand knowledge of what dad is going through, but as something he can only speak indirectly about. His "I'll bet- I'll bet" minimizes his own experience, just as his reference to "they talk always about" attributes to others the ability to appreciate (like dad) "the unsung heroes of the hospital." These actions embody important distinctions between claiming knowedge anchored in "first-hand" experience, and avoiding such ownership by making clear that others (especially dad) are privileged to speak about caring for others' in ways son is not (see Beach, in press-a).

In essence, this is one set of moments reflecting the delicate interactional work involved when discerning and enacting how directly a speaker might identify with, understand, and perhaps even "take the credit for" caregiving activities.

CONCLUSION

Building theories to explain how family members talk through cancer requires a detailed understanding of how diverse interactions, like those examined herein, get organized and thus are "patterned" over time. Such insights, anchored in speakers' sequentially organized social actions, are not available through alternative theoretical approaches. Clearly, News Delivery Sequences (NDS's) are repeatedly enacted by family members to inform and update one another about issues related to mom's illness. As only a small sampling of over 100 NDS's identified within the "Malignancy" data have been briefly addressed in this chapter, readers can perhaps gain an appreciation for not only how frequently NDS's get utilized, but more importantly how they are delicately constructed to accomplish a wide variety of important communication activities. It may also have become clear how much time, effort, and attention CA requires to yield such important findings.

Based on frequency of utilization alone, any "theory" of how families talk through cancer must therefore address how NDS's get collaboratively produced. The goal of such "thick" descriptions and grounded explanations involves unpacking the patterned nature of specific interactional practices. Diverse "phenomena" were revealed as significant from the excerpts overviewed in this chapter.

First, regarding News Delivery Sequences (NDS's), it was initially shown how an NDS structure might be identified and verified. Numerous potential problems were identified within NDS's. For example, assessing news as "good and/or bad" is at times difficult for interactants, since a delicate balance often exists between "good and bad news" (Maynard, 2003).

Talk designed to clarify specific features of the "news" also involves a recurring set of problematic activities. Similarly, delivering and responding to bad news in a "stoic" fashion—that is, through initial withholdings of emotional reactions to bad news—creates environments where it may be difficult to express emotions about the news. What, then, is the role of emotion throughout NDS's? Clearly, deliverers and news recipients must work together as they manage their potential stoic, surprised (mild → marked), or emotional reactions to news dilemmas. So too must speakers adapt the news to both "primary or consequential" and more "distant" participants—which is consequential for how NDS's involve shared knowledge about events, "owning" of the news, and even how support and commiseration may be offered and withheld by those involved. Matters are further complicated when it is realized that news is routinely tracked and monitored though "updates" over time (i.e., across a series of phone calls). Thus, producing and subsequently analyzing the *cumulative and serial organization* of NDS's, an inherent part of longitudinal studies (which are themselves rare), is necessary when managing (and describing/explaining) everyday life activities (see Beach, in press-a).

Second, just as the word "cancer" was avoided, so too is the future often treated as inherently uncertain and therefore potentially "dreaded" (Peräkylä, 1993, 1995; Beach & Good, 2004). Central to describing upcoming and future events are repeated attempts to employ medical/technical language to describe a loved one's diagnosis, treatment, and prognosis. Thus, activities such as "speaking about and like the doctor" require reporting on what others' may have said or done. During these moments, it becomes necessary to understand what practices speakers recruit when attempting to inform others about the condition and status of own or others' illnesses. In so doing, various "troubles" may arise, including the following: how to "preview" the valence of news (i.e., as good or bad); how to speak with some confidence, and even authority, about technical matters which may not be very well understood; and even how to manage laughter and humor in the midst of troubling circumstances.

Finally, throughout discussions of potentially bad cancer news, speakers can be observed to "manage optimism" as they balance bad news with hope and optimism about the unknown future (Beach, 2003a). The task remains to understand how such activities as "doing being hopeful" (Sacks, 1984) emerge as social activities, not just individualized resources for coping with and navigating through the trials and tribulations of daily events.

It is striking that so many important social actions are embedded within even a limited number of selected NDS's. Ongoing work is attempting to expand this listing to empirically verify unique and generalizeable features of reporting, responding to, and assessing updated "family" news. When completed, it will be possible to advance an initial "theory" of how family members construct NDS's longitudinally, from initial diagnosis through death.

For several key reasons, such a "theory" will nevertheless be limited in scope: (a) Only one family has been systematically investigated, even though data are comprised of an extremely rich corpus of 60 calls over a 13-month period; (b) NDS's comprise a central but partial set of interactional resources for family members facing a terminal illness. Readers may recall that at the outset of this chapter, NDS's were listed among four other types of social actions: managing certainty, displaying hope and optimism, understanding and talking about the "doctor" (and other medical professionals), assimilating and commiserating about cancer. And however primary this collective listing of social actions might be, they are neither inclusive nor dichotomous.

From this brief chapter I hope that you, as communication students, can better grasp the fundamental research efforts involved in generating grounded understandings of ordinary interactional involvements. Historically, the alternative has involved proposing "theories" about interpersonal relationships and cancer care primarily from self-reported experiences about how family members manage their social lives (e.g., see Addington-Hall & McCarthy, 1995; Calman, 1987; Litman, 1974). For example, from self-reports it is clear that a need exists to be "open" and communicate "frequently" about the uncertainty and anguish associated with many cancer journeys (e.g., see Babrow, Kasch, & Ford, 1998; Bloom, 1996; Hilton, 1994; Northouse & Northouse, 1987). Similarly, regarding family caregiving, it is assumed that more enduring family relationships exist when "emotional–psychosocial support" occurs and less "stress" is experienced (e.g., see Gotcher, 1993; Keller et al., 1996; Rait & Lederberg, 1990). Reasonable as these claims may be, they do not reveal how being "open and supportive" are achieved together by participants in real (interactional) time. Nor are such matters as "stress" revealed as interactionally evident and thus enacted in negatively consequential ways, inhibiting the social organization of illness and relationships. Indeed, encompassing activities such as caregiving, quality of life, and healing outcomes are themselves awaiting empirical grounding as practical, interactional achievements.

ADDITIONAL READING

Perhaps the most useful point-of-departure for understanding the history and commitments of CA, including issues regarding methodological rigor and theoretical scope, is Harvey Sacks's (1992) *Lectures on Conversation*. Edited by Gail Jefferson, a compilation is provided of Sacks's transcribed lectures, unpublished and previously published papers prior to his untimely death in 1976. This is a remarkable collection of insights and identified/exemplified conversational phenomena (e.g., rules of conversational sequencing, turn-taking, topic organization, storytelling, laughter, and jokes). Also useful is Emanuel Schegloff's introduction, a rich historical reconstruction of the emergence of CA, its relationship with Harold Garfinkel and ethnomethodology (see also Heritage, 1984), other key contributors, as well as a variety of personal memoirs about the scientific, social, and cultural environments influencing (and shaped by) Sacks's work.

The volume edited by Atkinson and Heritage (1984) is fundamental reading, not only because of the quality of studies about ordinary conversational activities comprising the collection, but also the many and diverse linkages between these contributions and previous research. Slightly earlier work focusing on interactions between speakers and hearers (C. Goodwin, 1981) is also foundational. Related studies of ordinary conversations abound (e.g, see Beach, 1989; Button & Lee, 1987; Mandelbaum, 1993; Zimmerman, 1988), including telephone conversations (Hopper, 1992; Schegloff, 1968, 1986; gossip and storytelling activities (M. H. Goodwin, 1990; Bergmann, 1993), relationships with grammar and linguistics (Ochs et al., 1996), families and bulimia (Beach, 1996), and good and bad news in everyday life (Maynard, 2003)—to name only a few citations drawn from a rich tradition of research pursuing understandings of how naturally occurring interactional involvements are practical achievements.

CA inquiries also focus on relationships between *ordinary* and *institutional* interactions (see Boden & Zimmerman, 1991; Drew & Heritage, 1992; Maynard, 1998; ten Have & Psathas, 1995). A wide array of lay-bureaucratic encounters during courtroom interrogations (Atkinson & Drew, 1979), medical interviewing (Beach, 2001a, in press-b; Beach & Dixson, 2001; Heath, 1986, 1992; Maynard & Heritage, 2006), AIDS counseling (Peräkylä, 1995), radio talk shows (Hutchby, 1996), and news interviews (Clayman & Heritage, 2002) have been examined. Again, only a sampling of possible readings are listed here, but any combination of these publications will reveal the considerable reliance upon broad interdisciplinary citations of relevance to your interests.

ACKNOWLEDGMENTS

This research was made possible through funding provided by the American Cancer Society (ROG-98–172-01). Materials examined herein are copyrighted.

REFERENCES

Addington-Hall, J., & McCarthy, M. (1995). Dying from cancer: Results of a national population-based investigation. *Palliative Medicine, 9,* 295–305.

Atkinson, J. M., & Drew, P. (1979). *Order in court: The organization of verbal interaction in judicial settings.* London: Macmillan.

Atkinson, J. M., & Heritage, J. (Eds.) (1984). *Structures of social action: Studies in conversation analysis.* London: Cambridge University Press.

Babrow, A. S., Kasch, C. R., & Ford, L. A. (1998). The many meanings of *uncertainty* in illness: Toward a systematic accounting. *Health communication, 10,* 1–23.

Baxter, L. A. (1993). The social side of personal relationships: A dialectical perspective. In S. Duck (Ed.), *Social context and relationships: Understanding relationship processes* (Vol. 3, pp. 139–169). Newbury Park, CA: Sage.

Beach, W. A. (Ed.). (1989). Sequential organization of conversational activities. *Western Journal of Speech Communication, 53,* 85–246.

Beach, W. A. (1990a). Language as and in technology: Facilitating topic organization in a Videotex focus group meeting. In M. J. Medhurst, A. Gonzalez, & T. R. Peterson (Eds.), *Communication and the culture of technology* (pp. 197–220). Pullman: Washington State University Press.

Beach, W. A. (1990b). Orienting to the phenomenon. In J. Anderson (Ed.), *Communication yearbook 13* (pp. 216–244). Beverly Hills, CA: Sage. (Reprinted in *Building communication theories: A socio-cultural approach,* pp. 133–163, by F. L. Casmir, Ed., 1994, Hillsdale, NJ: Lawrence Erlbaum Associates, Inc.)

Beach, W. A. (1991). Avoiding ownership for alleged wrongdoings. *Research on Language and Social Interaction, 24,* 1–36.

Beach, W. A. (1993). Transitional regularities for 'casual' "Okay" usages. *Journal of Pragmatics, 19,* 325–352.

Beach, W. A. (1995). Preserving and constraining options: "Okays" and 'official' priorities in medical interviews. In G. H. Morris & R. J. Cheneil (Eds.), *The talk of the clinic: Explorations in the analysis of medical and therapeutic discourse* (pp. 259–289). Hillsdale, NJ: Lawrence Erlbaum Associates, Inc.

Beach, W. A. (1996). *Conversations about illness: Family preoccupations with bulimia.* Mahwah, NJ: Lawrence Erlbaum Associates, Inc.

Beach, W. A. (2000). Inviting collaborations in stories about a woman. *Language in Society, 29,* 379–407.

Beach, W. A. (Ed.). (2001a). Introduction: Diagnosing 'lay diagnosis' [Special issue]. *Text, 21,* 13–18.

Beach, W. A. (2001b). Stability and ambiguity: Managing uncertain moments when updating news about mom's cancer. *Text, 21,* 221–250.

Beach, W. A. (2002). Between Dad and Son: Initiating, delivering, and assimilating bad cancer news. *Health Communication, 14,* 271–298.

Beach, W. A. (2003) Managing optimism. In P. Glenn, C. LeBaron, & J. Mandelbaum (Eds.), *Studies in language and social interaction: In honor of Robert Hopper* (pp. 175–194). Mahwah, NJ: Lawrence Erlbaum Associates, Inc.

Beach, W. A. (in press-a). *A natural history of family cancer: Interactional solutions to medical problems.* Cresskill, NJ: Hampton Press.

Beach, W. A. (in press-b). *Handbook of patient-provider interactions: Raising and responding to patients' concerns about life, illness, and disease.* Cresskill, NJ: Hampton Press.

Beach, W. A., & Anderson, J. (2004). Communication and cancer? Part 2: Conversation analysis. *Journal of Psychosocial Oncology, 21,* 1–22.

Beach, W. A., & Dixson, C. (2001). Revealing moments: Formulating understandings of adverse experiences in a health appraisal interview. *Social Science & Medicine, 52,* 25–44.

Beach, W. A., & Good, J. S. (2004). Uncertain family trajectories: Interactional consequences of cancer diagnosis, treatment, and prognosis. *Journal of Social and Personal Relationships, 21,* 9–35.

Benjamin, H. H. (1987). *From victim to victor: The Wellness Community guide to fighting for recovery for cancer patients and their families.* New York: St. Martin's.

Beach, W. A., & LeBaron, C. (2002). Body disclosures: Attending to personal problems and reported sexual abuse during a medical encounter. *Journal of Communication, 52,* 617–639.

Beach, W. A., & Lockwood, A. (2003). Making the case for airline compassion fares: The serial organization of problem narratives during a family crisis. *Research on Language and Social Interaction, 36,* 351–393.

Berger, C. R. (1997). Producing messages under uncertainty. In J. O. Greene (Ed.), *Message production: Advances in communication theory* (pp. 221–244). Mahwah, NJ: Lawrence Erlbaum Associates, Inc.

Berger, C. R., & Calabrese, R. J. (1975). Some explorations in initial interaction and beyond: Toward a developmental theory of interpersonal communication. *Human Communication Research, 1,* 99–112.

Bergmann, J. R. (1993). *Discreet indiscretions: The social organization of gossip.* New York: Aldine de Gruyter.

Biegel, D. E., Sales, E., & Schulz, R. (1991). *Family caregiving in chronic illness: Alzheimer's disease, cancer, heart disease, mental illness, and stroke.* Newbury Park, CA: Sage.

Bloom, J. (1996). Social support of the cancer patient and the role of the family. In L. Baider, C. L. Cooper, & A. Kaplan De-Nour (Eds.), *Cancer and the family* (pp. 53–70). New York: Wiley.

Boden, D., & Zimmerman, D. (1991). *Talk and social structure.* Cambridge, England: Polity Press.

Button, G., & Casey, N. (1985). Topic nomination and pursuit. *Human Studies, 8,* 3–55.

Button, G., & Lee, J. R. E. (Eds.) (1987). *Talk and social organization.* Clevedon, England: Multilingual Matters, Ltd.

Calman, K. C. (1987). Definitions and dimensions of quality of life. In N. K. Aaronson & J. Beckman (Eds.), *The quality of life of cancer patients* (pp. 1–9). New York: Raven Press.

Casmir, F. L. (Ed.). (1994). *Building communication theories: A socio/cultural approach.* Mahwah, NJ: Lawrence Erlbaum Associates, Inc.

Clayman, S., & Heritage, H. (2002). *The news interview: Journalists and public figures on the air.* Cambridge, England: Cambridge University Press.

Drew, P., & Heritage, J. (Eds.). (1992). *Talk at work: Interaction in institutional settings.* Cambridge, England: Cambridge University Press.

Drew, P., & Holt, E. (1988). Complainable matters: The use of idiomatic expressions in making social complaints. *Social Problems, 35,* 398–417.

Drew, P., & Holt, E. (1998). Figures of speech: Figurative expressions and the management of topic transition in conversation. *Language in Society, 27,* 495–522.

Dunkel-Schetter, C., & Wortman, C. B. (1982). The interpersonal dynamics of cancer: Problems in social relationships and their impact on the patient. In H. S. Freidman & M. R. DiMatteo (Eds.), *Interpersonal issues in health care* (pp. 69–100). New York: Academic.

Glenn, P. (1989). Initiating shared laughter in multi-party conversations. *Western Journal of Speech Communication, 53,* 127–149.

Glenn, P. (2003). *Laughter in interaction.* Cambridge, England: Cambridge University Press.

Goodwin, C. (1981). *Conversational organization: Interaction between speakers and hearers.* New York: Academic.

Goodwin, C. (1994). Professional vision. *American Anthropologis, 96,* 606–633.

Goodwin, C., & Duranti, A. (1992). Rethinking context: An introduction. In A. Duranti & C. Goodwin (Eds.), *Rethinking context: Language as an interactive phenomenon* (pp. 1–42). Cambridge, England: Cambridge University Press.

Goodwin, M. H. (1990). *He-said-she-said: Talk as social organization among Black children.* Bloomington: Indiana University Press.

Goodwin, M. H., & Goodwin, C. (2000). Emotion within situated activity. In A. Duranti & M. A. Molden (Eds.), *Linguistic anthropology: A reader* (pp. 239–257). Oxford, England: Blackwell.

Gotcher, J. M. (1993). The effects of family communication on psychosocial adjustment of cancer patients. *Journal of Applied Communication Research, 21,* 176–188.

Gudykunst, W. B. (1988). The uncertainty reduction and anxiety–uncertainty reduction theories. In Y. Y. Kim & W. B. Gudykunst (Eds.), *Theories in intercultural communication* (pp. 123–156). Newbury Park, CA: Sage.

Haakana, M. (2001). Laughter as a patient's resource: Dealing with delicate aspects of medical interaction. *Text, 21,* 187–220.

Heath, C. (1984). Talk and recipiency: Sequential organization in speech and body movement. In J. M. Atkinson & J. Heritage (Eds.), *Structures of social action: Studies in conversation analysis* (pp. 247–265). London: Cambridge University Press.

Heath, C. (1986). *Body movement and speech in medical interaction.* Cambridge, England: Cambridge University Press.

Heath, C. (1992). The delivery and reception of diagnosis in the general-practice consultation. In P. Drew & J. Heritage (Eds.), *Talk at work: Interaction in institutional settings* (pp. 235–267). Cambridge, England: Cambridge University Press.

Heritage, J. (1984). *Garfinkel and ethnomethodology.* Cambridge, England: Polity Press.

Heritage, J., & Maynard, D. (in press). *Practicing medicine: Talk and action in primary care consultations.* Cambridge, England: Cambridge University Press.

Hilton, B. A. (1994). Family communication patterns in coping with early breast cancer. *Western Journal of Nursing Research, 16,* 366–391.

Holt, E. (1993). The structure of death announcements: Looking on the bright side of death. *Text, 13,* 189–212.

Holt, E. (1996). Reporting on talk: The use of direct reported speech in conversation. *Research on Language and Social Interaction, 29,* 219–245.

Holt, E. (2000). Reporting and reacting: Concurrent responses to reported speech. *Research on Language and Social Interaction, 33,* 425–454.

Holt, E., & Clift, R. (2006). *Reporting talk: Reported speech in interaction.* Cambridge, England: Cambridge University Press.

Hopper, R. (1992). *Telephone conversation.* Bloomington: Indiana University Press.

Hutchby, I. (1996). *Confrontation talk: Arguments, asymmetries, and power on talk radio.* Mahwah, NJ: Lawrence Erlbaum Associates, Inc.

Jefferson, G. (1980). End of grant report on conversations in which "troubles" or "anxieties" are expressed (HR 4805/2). London: Social Science Research Council, Mimeo.

Jefferson, G. (1984a). On stepwise transition from talk about a trouble to inappropriately next- positioned matters. In J. M. Atkinson & J. Heritage (Eds.), *Structures of social action: Studies in conversational analysis* (pp. 191–222). London: Cambridge University Press.

Jefferson, G. (1984b). On the organization of laughter in talk about troubles. In J. M. Atkinson & J. Heritage (Eds.), *Structures of social action: Studies in conversational analysis* (pp. 347–369). London: Cambridge University Press.

Jefferson, G. (1988). On the sequential organization of troubles talk in ordinary conversation. *Social Problems, 35,* 418–441.

Keller, M., Henrich, G., Sesschopp, A., & Beutal, M. (1996). Between distress and support: Spouses of cancer patients. In L. Baider, C. L. Cooper, & A. Kaplan De-Nour (Eds.), *Cancer and the family* (pp. 187–223). New York: Wiley.

Kristjanson, L. J., & Ashcroft, T. (1994). The family's cancer journey: A literature review. *Cancer Nursing, 17,* 1–17.

Keller, M., Henrich, G., Sellsschopp, A., & Beutel, M. (1996). Between distress and support: Spouses of cancer patients. In L. Baider, C. L. Cooper, & A. Kaplan De-Nour (Eds.), *Cancer and the family* (pp. 187–223). Chichester, England: Wiley.

Kristjanson, L. J., & Ashcroft, T. (1994). The family's cancer journey: A literature review. *Cancer Nursing, 17,* 1–17.

Kumar, P. J., & Clark, M. L. (1990). *Clinical medicine.* London: Bailliere Tindall.

Lichtman, R. R., & Taylor, S. E. (1986). Close relationships and the female cancer patient. In B. L. Andersen (Ed.), *Women with cancer: Psychological perspectives* (pp. 233–256). New York: Springer-Verlag.

Litman, T. J. (1974). The family as a basic unit in health and medical care: A social–behavioral overview. *Social Science & Medicine, 8,* 495–519.

Littlejohn, S. W. (2002). *Theories of human communication* (7th Edition). Belmont, CA: Wadsworth/Thompson Learning.

Lutfey, K., & Maynard, D. W. (1998). Bad news in oncology: How physician and patient talk about death and dying without using those words. *Social Psychology Quarterly, 4,* 321–341.

MacDonald, N. (1996). The interface between oncology and palliative medicine. In D. Doyle, G. W. C. Hanks, & N. MacDonald (Eds.), *Oxford textbook of palliative medicine* (pp. 11–17). Oxford, England: Oxford University Press.

Mandelbaum, J. (1991). Conversational noncooperation: An exploration of disattended complaints. *Research on Language and Social Interaction, 25,* 97–138.

Mandelbaum, J. (1993). Assigning responsibility in conversational storytelling: The interactional construction of reality. *Text, 13,* 247–266.

Maynard, D. W. (1988). Language, interaction, and social problems. *Social Problems, 35,* 311–334.

Maynard, D. W. (1997). The news delivery sequence: Bad news and good news in conversational interaction. *Research on Language and Social Interaction, 30,* 93–130.

Maynard, D. W. (2003). *Good news, bad news: Conversation order in everyday talk and clinical settings.* Chicago: The University of Chicago Press.

Millar, F. E., & Rogers, E. (1976). A relational approach to interpersonal communication. In G. R. Miller (Ed.), *Explorations in interpersonal communication* (pp. 87–105). Beverly Hills, CA: Sage.

Millar, F. E., & Rogers, E. (1987). Power dynamics in marital relationships. In P. Noller & M. Fitzpatrick (Eds.), *Perspectives on marital interaction* (pp. 78–97). Newbury Park, CA: Sage.

Montgomery, B. M., & Baxter, L. A. (Eds.) (1998). *Dialectical approaches to studying personal relationships.* Mahwah, NJ: Lawrence Erlbaum Associates, Inc.

Northouse, P. G., & Northouse, L. L. (1987). Communication and cancer: Issues confronting patients, health professionals, and family members. *Journal of Psychosocial Oncology, 5,* 17–46.

Ochs, E., Schegloff, E. A., & Thompson, S. A. (1996). *Interaction and grammar.* Cambridge, England: Cambridge University Press.

Peräkylä, A. (1993). Invoking a hostile world: Discussing the patient's future in AIDS counseling. *Text, 13,* 302–338.

Peräkylä, A. (1995). *AIDS counseling: Institutional interaction and clinical practice.* Cambridge, England: Cambridge University Press.

Pomerantz, A. (1990). Chautauqua: On the validity and generalizability of conversational analysis methods. *Communication Monographs, 57,* 231–235.

Rait, D., & Lederberg, M. (1990). The family of the cancer patient. In J. C. Holland & J. H. Rowland (Eds.), *Handbook of psychooncology: Psychological care of the patient with cancer* (pp. 585–597). New York: Oxford.

Sacks, H. (1984). On doing "being ordinary." In J. M. Atkinson & J. Heritage (Eds.), *Structures of social action: Studies in conversation analysis* (pp. 21–27). Cambridge, England: Cambridge University Press.

Sacks, H., (1992). *Lectures on conversation: Volumes I & II.* (G. Jefferson, Ed.). Oxford, England: Blackwell.

Sandlund, E. (2004). *Feeling by doing: The social organization of everyday emotions in academic talk-in-interaction.* Doctoral dissertation, Karlstad University, Sweden.

Schegloff, E. A. (1968). Sequencing in conversational openings. *American Anthropologist, 70,* 1075–1095.

Schegloff, E. A. (1986). The routine as achievement. *Human Studies, 9,* 111–152.

Schegloff, E. A. (1987). Analyzing single episodes of interaction: An exercise in conversation analysis. *Social Psychology Quarterly, 50,* 101–114.

Schegloff, E. A. (1991). Reflections on talk and social structure. In D. Boden & D. H. Zimmerman (Eds.), *Talk and social structure* (pp. 44–70). Cambridge, England: Polity Press.

Sigman, S. J. (Ed.). (1995). *The consequentiality of communication.* Hillsdale, NJ: Lawrence Erlbaum Associates, Inc.

Stamp, G. H., Vangelisti, A. L., & Knapp, M. L. (1994). Criteria for developing and assessing theories of interpersonal communication. In F. L. Casmir (Ed.), *Building communication theories: A socio-cultural approach* (pp. 167–208). Mahwah, NJ: Lawrence Erlbaum Associates, Inc.

ten Have, P., & Psathas, G. (Ed.). (1995). *Situated order: Studies in the social organization of talk and embodied activities.* Washington, DC: University Press of America.

Urban, G. (1984). Speech about speech in speech about action. *Journal of American Folklore, 97,* 310–328.

Wootton, A. J. (1988). Remarks on the methodology of conversation analysis. In D. Roger & P. Bull (Eds.), *Conversation: An interdisciplinary perspective* (pp. 238–258). Clevedon, England: Multilingual Matters.

Zerwekh, J. V. (1984). Understanding the patient experience. In A. G. Blues & J. V. Zerwekh (Eds.), *Hospice and palliative nursing care* (pp. 29–44). Orlando, FL: Grune & Stratto. Zimmerman, D. H. (1988). On conversation: The conversation analytic perspective. In J. A. Anderson (Ed.), *Communication yearbook 11* (pp. 406–432). Newbury Park, CA: Sage.

Zimmerman, D. (1988). On conversation: The conversation analytic perspective. In J. A. Anderson (Ed.), *Communication Yearbook 11* (pp. 406-432). Newbury Park, CA: Sage.

APPENDIX: TRANSCRIPTION SYMBOLS

In data headings, "SDCL" stands for "San Diego Conversation Library," a collection of recordings and transcriptions of naturally occurring interactions; "Malignancy #1" represents the title and number of call in the data corpus (see Data and Method section); page numbers from which data excerpts are drawn are also included. The transcription notation system employed for data segments is an adaptation of Gail Jefferson's work (see Atkinson & Heritage, 1984, pp. ix–xvi; Beach, 1989, pp. 89–90). The symbols may be described as follows:

:   *Colon(s)*: Extended or stretched sound, syllable, or word.

__   *Underlining*: Vocalic emphasis.

(.)   *Micropause*: Brief pause of less than (0.2).

(1.2)   *Timed Pause*: Intervals occuring within and between same or different speaker's utterance.

(( ))   *Double Parentheses*: Scenic details.

( )	*Single Parentheses*: Transcriptionist doubt.
.	*Period*: Falling vocal pitch.
?	*Question Marks*: Rising vocal pitch.
↑↓	*Arrows*: Pitch resets; marked rising and falling shifts in intonation.
° °	*Degree Signs*: A passage of talk noticeably softer than surrounding talk.
=	*Equal Signs*: Latching of contiguous utterances, with no interval or overlap.
[ ]	*Brackets*: Speech overlap.
[[	*Double Brackets*: Simultaneous speech orientations to prior turn.
!	*Exclamation Points*: Animated speech tone.
-	*Hyphens*: Halting, abrupt cut off of sound or word.
> <	*Less Than/Greater Than Signs*: Portions of an utterance delivered at a pace noticeably quicker than surrounding talk.
OKAY*CAPS*:	Extreme loudness compared with surrounding talk.
hhh .hhh*H's*:	Audible outbreaths, possibly laughter. The more h's, the longer the aspiration. Aspirations with periods indicate audible inbreaths (e.g., .hhh). H's within (e.g., ye(hh)s)parentheses mark within-speech aspirations, possible laughter.
pt*Lip Smack*:	Often preceding an inbreath.
hah*Laugh Syllable*:	Relative closed or open position of laughter
heh	
hoh	

QUESTIONS TO PONDER

1. What are the fundamental commitments and priorities of CA? How is CA similar to, yet different from, alternative methodological and theoretical approaches (e.g., those utilizing self-reported information)?

2. Describe the importance and advantages of studying naturally occurring interactions as communication activities?

3. How is communication critically important to family cancer journeys? What does this chapter summarize regarding the "noticeable absence of interactional research" when studying communication and cancer?

4. Describe the organization of a "news delivery sequence" (NDS). Provide examples of "delicate moments" apparent in the NDS's examined in this chapter.

5. How do "lay" persons report "technical/biomedical" information? What problems exist as family members talk about medical procedures and staff (including doctors)?

6. What other kinds of social activities occur throughout family members' attempts to understand cancer diagnosis, treatment, and prognosis?

7. What relationships exist between "basic" and "applied" research when studying how families talk about and through cancer? What potential problems arise when attempting to "improve" others' communicative behaviors?

19

Pragma-Dialectical Theory of Argumentation

Frans H. van Eemeren
University of Amsterdam

The study of argumentation is prospering. After its brilliant start in Antiquity, highlighted in the classical works of Aristotle, after an alternation of ups and downs during the following millennia, in the post-Renaissance period its gradual decline set in. Revitalization took place only after Toulmin (1958) and Perelman (1958) published their landmark works *The Uses of Argument* and *La nouvelle rhétorique* (coauthored by Olbrechts-Tyteca and translated into English in 1969), respectively. The model of argumentation presented by Toulmin and Perelman's inventory of argumentation techniques inspired a great many scholars in various ways to take up the study of argumentation in a serious way. Nowadays there are well-established (formal as well as informal) logical approaches to argumentation, but also social and socio-psychological, linguistic, juridical, and other approaches. In most of these approaches traces can be found of the influence of the classical and neoclassical argumentation theories just mentioned.[1]

One of the dominant contemporary approaches to theorizing about and investigating argumentation is the pragma-dialectical approach. The success of the pragma-dialectical approach is based on its comprehensive view of the study of argumentation and its integration of sound premises from other perspectives and that it considers argumentation as a form of communication. For these reasons, exposure to the pragma-dialect approach could be considered a foundational component in the students' academic study of communication. As such, this chapter addresses the nature of pragma-dialectics, its metatheoretical principles, the pragma-dialectical model of critical discussion, and some important empirical research regarding this perspective.

---

[1]For a more elaborate description of the history of the study of argumentation and the current state of the art, see van Eemeren et al. (1996) and van Eemeren (Ed., 2001).

NATURE OF PRAGMA-DIALECTICS

The most important characteristic of the pragma-dialectical approach to argumentation is that argumentation is studied from a communicative perspective. Argumentation is viewed as a type of communication aimed at resolving a difference of opinion by critically testing the acceptability of the standpoints at issue. Generally, this communication will take place by verbal means, whether oral or written, but nonverbal elements (such as gestures and images) may also play a part. In practice, the term *argumentation* is used in two ways at the same time: It refers to a process ("I am still in the middle of my argumentation") as well as to its result ("Let's examine what her argumentation amounts to"). Because argumentation is not just part of reality, but can, and should, also be judged for its quality, the study of argumentation has not only a descriptive but also a normative dimension. According to pragma-dialecticians, the quality of argumentation and its possible flaws are to be measured against norms of reasonableness that are suited to its purpose.

Logicians, whether they are in favor of a formal or an informal approach, tend to concentrate on the problems involved in the regimentation of reasoning. Social scientists and linguists, particularly discourse and conversation analysts, generally focus on empirical observation of argumentative discourse and its effects.[2] In the pragma-dialectical view, however, these two approaches must be closely interwoven. Both the limitations of nonempirical regimentation and those of noncritical observation need to be systematically transcended. Pragma-dialecticians make it their business to clarify how the gap between normative and descriptive insight can be methodically bridged. This objective can only be achieved with the help of a coherent research program in which a systematic connection—a *trait d'union*—is created between well-considered regimentation and careful observation.

Following a classical tradition, the study of the regimentation of critical exchanges is called *dialectics*. The study of language use in actual communication, which belonged in the past largely to the domain of rhetoric, is nowadays generally called *pragmatics*. Hence the choice of the name *pragma-dialectics* for the approach to argumentation that aims for a sound integration of insight from these two studies. Pragma-dialectics combines a dialectical view of argumentative reasonableness with a pragmatic view of the verbal moves made in argumentative discourse.[3]

Pragma-Dialectical Research Program

Because the pragma-dialectical research program is designed to achieve a well-considered integration of normative and descriptive insight, it is on the one hand aimed at developing a philosophical ideal of critical reasonableness and, grounded in this ideal, a theoretical model for acceptable argumentative discourse in a critical discussion. On the other hand, argumentative

---

[2]For protagonists of a purely normative or a purely descriptive approach, see Biro and Siegel (1992) and Willard (1983, 1989), respectively.

[3]The dialectical conception of reasonableness is inspired by critical rationalists and analytic philosophers, such as Popper (1972, 1974), Albert (1975), and Naess (1966), and by formal dialecticians and logicians, such as Hamblin (1970), Lorenzen and Lorenz (1978), and Barth and Krabbe (1982). The pragmatic conception of argumentative discourse as consisting of making regulated communicative moves is rooted in Austin (1962) and Searle's (1969, 1979) ordinary language philosophy, Grice's (1989) theory of rationality in discourse, and other studies of communication by discourse and conversation analysts. It is in the first place the combination of dialectical and pragmatic insight that distinguishes pragma-dialectics from "formal dialectics" as developed by Barth and Krabbe (1982) that incorporates dialectical insight in a formal (logical) approach.

reality is investigated empirically to acquire an accurate description of the actual processes of argumentative discourse and the factors influencing their outcome. Starting from the results achieved in these two enterprises, the conceptual tools are developed to analyze argumentative reality in light of the critical ideal of reasonableness. Then the individual and the procedural problems of the practical analysis, evaluation and production of argumentative discourse—the alpha and omega of the study of argumentation—can be tackled methodically. The research program thus includes five components: philosophical, theoretical, empirical, analytical, and practical.[4]

Philosophical Component. The fundamental question in the philosophical component is what it means to be reasonable in argumentation. As it happens, the conceptions of reasonableness entertained by argumentation scholars diverge from the outset, leading to quite different outlooks on what acceptable arguments are considered to be. Dialecticians maintain a critical outlook. For them, reasonableness does not solely depend on intersubjective agreement on the norms, as many rhetoricians think, but also on whether these norms are conducive to the goal of resolving a difference of opinion by way of a critical discussion. Because the ideal of reasonableness is linked to the methodic conduct of a critical discussion, the dialectical philosophy of reasonableness is *critical-rationalist.*

Theoretical Component. In the theoretical component the philosophical ideal of reasonableness is given a shape by designing a model of what is involved in acting reasonably in argumentative discourse. A theoretical model, like Toulmin's, aims at getting an adequate grasp of argumentative discourse by specifying modes of arguing and indicating when they are acceptable. The model serves as a conceptual and terminological framework that can fulfill heuristic, analytical, and critical functions in dealing with argumentative discourse. A dialectical model provides rules that specify which moves can contribute to resolving a difference of opinion in the various stages of a critical discussion. If this discussion is viewed, pragmatically, as an interaction of speech acts, the model is *pragma-dialectical.*

Empirical Component. Empirical insight is sought after in the actual processes of producing, interpreting, and assessing argumentative discourse and the factors that influence their outcome. Such insight is acquired by carrying out qualitative and quantitative research. Qualitative research consists primarily in making observations by means of introspection and case studies, the (sometimes connected) quantitative research in experimental and statistical studies. In pragma-dialectical empirical research the emphasis is on explaining how various factors and processes play a role in argumentative reality in resolving a difference of opinion. The interest centers on the aspects of argumentative discourse that affect its *cogency.*[5]

Analytical Component. The analytical component concerns a pragma-dialectical reconstruction of argumentative discourse to achieve an "analytic overview" of the discourse that constitutes a proper point of departure for a critical evaluation. In argumentative discourse things are not only not always immediately obvious, they even may be different from

---

[4]For an elaborated explanation of the research program, see van Eemeren and Grootendorst (2004, chap. 2).

[5]For pragma-dialectical research into the identification of argumentation that is cogency-centered see, e.g., van Eemeren, Grootendorst, & Meuffels, 1989; cf. for experiments concentrating on deductive reasoning Nisbett & Ross, 1980; Johnson-Laird, 1983.

what they seem. Sometimes a more or less complicated reconstruction is needed of what is said before an analysis can be justifiably made. Such a reconstruction always takes place from a perspective that focuses on specific aspects of the discourse, highlighting certain elements while ignoring others. A comparison with a stereotypical Freudian analyst may offer some clarification. Our Freudian analyst examines what is said from a psychological perspective, making use of the analytical tools provided by a particular theoretical background. She is, for instance, interested in mother fixation, signs of inferiority complexes, and the like. It goes without saying that she can only come to an analysis by examining carefully what has actually been said, or conspicuously left out, by her client. She cannot diagnose him as suffering from mother fixation right after the introduction. Neither can she do this on the sole ground that he has been singing the praise of his mother at every session. Nevertheless, after a careful reconstruction of certain things he said or implied, she might be justified to attribute a mother fixation to him because adding up a series of observations may warrant this analysis. Similarly, in a pragma-dialectical analysis of argumentative discourse a reconstruction of the discourse is carried out that starts from the theoretical model of a critical discussion, with its various stages and division of speech acts, and takes all knowledge gained by empirical investigation methodically into account. In pragma-dialectics, the central question in the analytical component is how argumentative discourse can be reconstructed in such a way that all those, and only those, aspects are highlighted that are relevant to resolving a difference of opinion on the merits. The resulting analysis can therefore be characterized as *resolution-oriented.*

Practical Component. Finally, in the practical component of the research program methods are developed for improving individual skills and specific argumentative procedures. Argumentative competence involves a complex of dispositions whose mastery is gradual and relative to specific communicative situations. This means that argumentative skills can only be measured adequately by applying standards relating to particular types of argumentative endeavors. To improve argumentative practice by way of education or otherwise, argumentation must therefore be studied in a diversity of institutionalized and noninstitutionalized contexts, ranging from the formal context of law to the informal context of a conversation with friends. In the practical component, pragma-dialecticians put their philosophical, theoretical, analytical and empirical insight to good use in developing methods for improving argumentative practice while taking account of circumstantial diversity. Because of its emphasis on furthering an awareness of the prerequisites for resolving differences of opinion and stimulating a discussion-minded attitude, the pragma-dialectical approach to the improvement of argumentative practice can be characterized as *reflection-minded.*

Metatheoretical Principles

In carrying out the pragma-dialectical research program, argumentation is approached with four metatheoretical premises. These basic premises are methodological in their concern about how one ought to set about studying argumentation. They constitute a basis for integrating the descriptive dimension of the study of argumentation with the normative dimension.[6]

Functionalization. Argumentation is usually studied as a structure of logical derivations, psychological attitudes, or epistemic beliefs rather than a complex of verbal (and nonverbal)

---

[6]The starting points are for the first time explained in van Eemeren and Grootendorst (1984).

acts that have a specific communicative function in a context of disagreement. As a result, argumentation is often described in purely structural terms, not only in formal and informal logical approaches, but also in studies of fallacies and practical argumentation. Such structural descriptions tend to ignore the functional rationale of the design of the discourse. The general function of argumentation is managing disagreement. It arises in response to, or anticipation of, a difference of opinion, and the lines of justification chosen in argumentative discourse are contrived to resolving the difference. The study of argumentation should therefore concentrate on the function of argumentation in the verbal management of disagreement.

Socialization. Especially in approaches concentrating on reasoning, argumentation is usually seen as the expression of individual thought processes. The central question then becomes assessing whether and how the elements that constitute the reasoning hold together in order to validate the arguer's position. But argumentation does not consist in a single individual privately drawing a conclusion and it is not put forward in a social vacuum. It is part of a communication process whereby two or more individuals who have a difference of opinion try to arrive at an agreement. Argumentation presupposes two distinguishable discussion roles, that of a protagonist of a standpoint and that of a—real or projected—antagonist. It reflects the collaborative way in which the protagonist in the fundamentally dialogical interaction responds to the questions, doubts, objections, and counterclaims of the antagonist. This is why argumentation should be put in the social context of a process of joint problem solving.

Externalization. To find out whether or not their opinions will be accepted, people put their standpoints by way of their argumentation to certification, submitting their reasoning to public scrutiny. Channeled by a system of public commitment and accountability, the beliefs, inferences and interpretations that underlie argumentation are expressed or projected in the discourse. Whereas the motives people have for holding a position might be different from the grounds they offer and accept in its defense, what they can be held committed to is the position they have expressed in the discourse, whether directly or indirectly.[7] For that reason, all efforts to reduce argumentation to a structure of attitudes and beliefs or a chain of reasoning are inadequate. Rather than speculating about the psychological dispositions of the people involved in argumentation, the study of argumentation should concentrate on their commitments as externalized in, or externalizable from, the way in which they have expressed themselves in a certain context and on the consequences these commitments have for the process of argumentation.[8]

Dialectification. Argumentation is appropriate for resolving a difference of opinion only if it is capable of accommodating the relevant critical reactions of the antagonist. Discourse and conversation analysts generally restrict themselves to describing argumentation as it occurs, without any regard for how it ought to occur if it is to be appropriate for resolving a difference of opinion. A theory of argumentation, however, must be attentive to critical standards for assessing a discussion aimed at resolving a difference of opinion. This can be achieved by considering argumentation to be subjected to a dialectical procedure for resolving differences of

---

[7]This does not mean that it is not important to find out to what extent and in which ways "internal" reasoning and "external" argumentation diverge, but this research can only be carried out methodically if the two concepts are kept separate.

[8]The principle of externalization is at odds with those rhetorical approaches that explain the effectiveness of argumentation by referring, without any further ado, to the presumed psychological states of arguers and their audiences.

opinion that is problem-valid as well as intersubjectively valid. The problem-validity of a procedure for conducting a critical discussion depends on how efficient and efficacious it is in furthering the resolution of a difference of opinion and excluding fallacious moves; its inter-subjective validity depends on its acceptability to the parties involved.[9] To transcend a merely descriptive stance, argumentative discourse should therefore be viewed from the perspective of a dialectical procedure for critical discussion that is valid in both respects.[10]

STATE OF THE ART IN PRAGMA-DIALECTICS

A Model of Critical Discussion

In pragma-dialectics, functionalization, socialization, externalization, and dialectification of argumentation are realized by systematically combining pragmatic and dialectical insight. *Functionalization* is achieved by making use of the fact that argumentative discourse occurs through—and in response to—speech act performances. Identifying the complex speech act of argumentation and the other speech acts involved in resolving a difference of opinion makes it possible to specify the relevant "identity conditions" and "correctness conditions" of these speech acts.[11] In this way, for instance, a specification can be given of what is "at stake" in advancing a certain "standpoint," so that it becomes clear what the "disagreement space" is and how the argumentative discourse is organized around this context of disagreement.[12] *Socialization* is achieved by identifying who exactly take on the discussion roles of protago-nist and antagonist in the collaborative context of argumentative discourse. By extending the speech act perspective to the level of interaction, it can be shown in which ways positions and argumentation in support of positions are developed. *Externalization* is achieved by identify-ing the specific commitments that are created by the speech acts performed in a context of argumentative interaction.[13] Rather than being treated as internal states of mind, in a speech act perspective notions such as "disagreement" and "acceptance" can be defined in terms of discursive activities. "Acceptance," for instance, can be externalized as giving a preferred response to an arguable act. Finally, *dialectification* is achieved by regimenting the exchange of speech acts aimed at resolving a difference of opinion in a model of a perfect critical dis-cussion. Such an idealized modeling of the systematic exchanges of resolution-oriented verbal moves, defines the nature and distribution of the speech acts that play a part in resolving a difference of opinion.

---

[9]This terminology was introduced by Barth and Krabbe (1982, pp. 21–22). In their usage, a discussion procedure that fulfills these requirements may claim "problem solving validity" and "(semi-)conventional validity." See Note 39.

[10]According to Wenzel (1979), a dialectical approach views argumentation as a "systematic management of dis-course for the purpose of achieving critical decisions" (p. 84). Its purpose is to establish how discussions should be carried out systematically in order to critically test standpoints. To avoid the dangers of absolutism (or skepticism) and relativism, a dialectical procedure for critical discussion that agrees with a "critical" philosophy of reasonable-ness incorporates both the product-oriented and process-oriented approaches to argumentation based on the "geo-metrical" (logical) and the "anthropological" (rhetorical) philosophies of reasonableness. For these philosophies, see Toulmin (1976).

[11]For a definition of argumentation as a complex speech act, see van Eemeren and Grootendorst (1984, pp. 39–46, 1992, pp. 30–33). For the speech act of advancing a standpoint, see Houtlosser (1994). And for the distinction between identity conditions and correctness conditions, see van Eemeren and Grootendorst (1992, pp. 30–31).

[12]The term *disagreement space* was introduced in Jackson (1992, p. 261).

[13]A kindred approach to argumentation in which commitments as well as other basic concepts of pragma-dialectics also play a crucial role is Walton and Krabbe (1995).

The pragma-dialectical model of a critical discussion is a theoretically motivated system for resolution-oriented discourse. Although the model is an abstraction, rather than merely serving as an ideal, it should provide people who wish to resolve their differences by means of argumentative discourse with vital guidance for their conduct.[14] The model must be constructed in such a way that it can serve not only as a paradigm for systematic reflection upon one's active oral and written participation in argumentative discourse, but also, and even more so, as a point of reference in analyzing and evaluating argumentative discourse. In addition, it can be a standard for guiding the methodical improvement of argumentative practice.

When developing a model of a critical discussion, one first needs to realize that resolving a difference of opinion is not identical with settling a dispute—the point of settling a dispute merely being that a difference of opinion is brought to an end.[15] A difference of opinion is resolved only if the parties involved have reached agreement on whether or not the disputed opinion is acceptable. This means that one party has either been convinced by the other party's argumentation, or the other party, realizing that its arguments cannot stand up to the first party's criticisms, withdraws the standpoint.[16] This is why a dialectical procedure designed for methodically resolving differences of opinion is a crucial part of the pragma-dialectical model of a critical discussion.

In a critical discussion, the parties attempt to reach agreement about the acceptability of the standpoints at issue by finding out whether or not these standpoints are defensible against doubt or criticism. The dialectical procedure for conducting a critical discussion is in the first place a method for exploring the acceptability of standpoints. In a critical discussion, the protagonist and the antagonist of a particular standpoint try to establish whether this standpoint, given the point of departure acknowledged by the parties, is tenable in the light of critical responses.[17] To be able to achieve this purpose, the dialectical procedure for conducting a critical discussion should not deal only with inference relations between premises and conclusions (or "concessions" and "standpoints"), but cover all speech acts that play a part in examining the acceptability of standpoints. In pragma-dialectics, the concept of a critical discussion is therefore given shape in a model that specifies all the various stages the resolution process has to pass and all the types of speech acts that are instrumental in any of these stages.

Stages in Resolving a Difference of Opinion

The stages that are to be distinguished analytically in the process of resolving a difference of opinion correspond with the different phases of argumentative discourse. Ideally, the discussion starts with a *confrontation stage*, in which a difference of opinion manifests itself

---

[14]In spite of their different philosophical roots, Habermas's (1971) ideal speech situation and the ideal model of a critical discussion are in some respects not dissimilar. In pragma-dialectics, however, instead of viewing communication as aimed at achieving consensus, intellectual doubt and criticism are seen as the driving forces of progress, and should lead to a continual flux of opinions.

[15]A dispute may also be settled by relying on the arbitration of a third party, such as an umpire, a referee or a judge, but then it has not really been resolved.

[16]A critical discussion reflects the Socratic dialectic ideal of rational testing of any conviction, not only of statements of a factual kind but also of normative standpoints and value judgments (Albert, 1975). Starting from the fallibility of all human standpoints, critical rationalists elevate the methodological concept of critical testing to the guiding principle of problem-solving.

[17]In accordance with their critical rationalist philosophy, dialecticians place great emphasis on the consequence of the fact that a proposition and its negation cannot both be acceptable at the same time. The testing of standpoints is thus equated with the detection of inconsistencies (Albert, 1975, p. 44).

through an opposition and nonacceptance of a standpoint. In real argumentative discourse, this stage corresponds with those parts of the discourse where it becomes clear that there is an opinion that coincides with—real or projected—doubt or contradiction, so that a (potential) disagreement arises. If there is no confrontation of views, then there is no need for critical discussion.

In the *opening stage* of a critical discussion, the initial commitments—procedural, substantive, or otherwise—of the participants in the dispute are identified and it is decided who will act as protagonist or antagonist. A protagonist undertakes the obligation to defend the standpoint at issue while an antagonist assumes the obligation to respond critically to this standpoint and the protagonist's defense.[18] This stage is manifest in those parts of the discourse where the parties express themselves as such and explore whether there is sufficient common ground. If there is no such opening for an exchange of views, having a critical discussion does not make sense.

In the *argumentation stage* a protagonist of a standpoint methodically defends this stance against critical responses of the antagonist. If the antagonist is not yet convinced of all or part of the protagonist's argumentation, he or she elicits new argumentation from the protagonist, and so on. As a consequence, the protagonist's argumentation can vary from very simple to extremely complex, and the "argumentation structure" of the one argumentative discourse may be much more complicated than that of the next.[19] The argumentation stage is gone through in those parts of the discourse in which one party adduces arguments to overcome the other party's doubts, and the other party reacts. If there is no argumentation and no critical appraisal of argumentation, there is no critical discussion and the difference of opinion will remain unresolved.

In the *concluding stage* the protagonist and the antagonist of a standpoint determine whether the protagonist's standpoint has been successfully defended against the critical responses of the antagonist. If the protagonist's standpoint has to be withdrawn, the dispute is resolved in favor of the antagonist; if the antagonist's doubts have to be retracted, it is resolved in favor of the protagonist. If the parties do not draw any conclusions about the result of their attempts to resolve a difference of opinion, no successful completion of a discussion has been reached. A completion of a critical discussion that is successful, however, does not preclude that the same parties embark upon a new discussion. This new discussion may relate to a completely different difference of opinion, but also to an altered version of the same difference, whereas the discussion roles of the participants may switch or remain the same. In any event, the new discussion that then begins must again go through the same stages—from confrontation to conclusion.

Distribution of Speech Acts in a Critical Discussion

Which speech acts can contribute in the various stages of a critical discussion to the resolution of a difference of opinion? To answer this question, it is useful to distinguish between

---

[18]The role of antagonist may coincide with that of protagonist of another—contrary—standpoint, but this need not be so. Expressing doubt regarding the acceptability of a standpoint is not necessarily equivalent with adopting a contrary standpoint of one's own. If the latter is the case, the difference of opinion is no longer "nonmixed", but "mixed" (van Eemeren & Grootendorst, 1992, pp. 13–25).

[19]For an analysis of how different types of argumentation structures can come into being, see Snoeck Henkemans (1992).

five basic types of speech acts that can be performed in argumentative discourse.[20] When pointing out the roles that several types of speech acts can fulfill in resolving a difference of opinion it is important to emphasize, right from the start, that in argumentative discourse a great many speech acts are performed implicitly or indirectly, so that a certain role in a critical discussion may be fulfilled by different speech acts. I shall return to this subject when I explain analysis as reconstruction.

A frequent type of speech act consists of *assertives*. The prototype is an assertion by which the speaker or writer guarantees the truth of the proposition being expressed: "I assert that Chamberlain and Roosevelt never met." Assertives, however, not only relate to the truth of propositions but also to their acceptability in a wider sense ("Baudelaire is the best French poet"). Assertives are, for instance, denying and conceding. In a critical discussion, assertives can express a standpoint at issue, be part of argumentation in defense of a standpoint, and establish a conclusion ("I can maintain my standpoint"). The commitment to a proposition expressed in an assertive may vary from strong, as in the case of an assertion or statement, to fairly weak, as in a supposition.

Another type of speech act consists of *directives*. The prototype is an order, which requires a special position of the speaker or writer *vis-à-vis* the listener or reader: "Come to my room" can only be an order if the speaker is in a position of authority, otherwise it is a request or an invitation. A question is a special form of request: It is a request for a verbal act—the answer. Other examples of directives are forbidding, recommending, and challenging. Not all directives can play a role in a critical discussion: Their role consists in challenging the party that has advanced a standpoint to defend this standpoint or in requesting argumentation to support a standpoint or (part of an) argumentation. A critical discussion does not allow for unilateral orders and prohibitions.

A third type of speech act is *commissives*. These are speech acts where the speaker or writer undertakes a commitment *vis-à-vis* the listener or reader to do something or refrain from doing something. The prototype is a promise: "I promise you I won't tell your father." The speaker or writer can also undertake commitments about which the listener or reader may be less enthusiastic: "I guarantee that if you walk out now you will never set foot in this house again." Other commissives are accepting, rejecting, undertaking, and agreeing. In a critical discussion, commissives fulfill a series of roles: (not) accepting a standpoint, (not) accepting argumentation, accepting the challenge to defend a standpoint, deciding to start a discussion, agreeing to take on the role of protagonist or antagonist, agreeing on the rules of discussion, and deciding to begin a new discussion. Some of the required commissives, such as agreeing on the rules, can only be performed in cooperation with the other party.

The next type of speech act consists of *expressives*. Here, the speaker or writer expresses feelings about something by thanking someone, revealing disappointment, and so on. There is no single prototypical expressive. Joy is expressed in "I'm glad to see you're quite well again" and hope is echoed by "I wish I could find such a nice girl friend." Other expressives include commiserating, regretting, and greeting. In a critical discussion, expressives, as such, play no constitutive role.[21]

A fifth type of speech act entails the *declaratives*. The performance of these speech acts creates a reality by calling a particular state of affairs into being. If an employer addresses an employee with the words "You're fired," he is not just describing a state of affairs but the words actually make a reality. Declaratives are usually bound to a specific institutionalized

---

[20]This typology is largely based on Searle (1979, pp. 1–29).

[21]This does not mean that they cannot affect the course of the resolution process: sighing that you are unhappy with the discussion, expresses your emotions, which distracts the attention from the resolution process.

TABLE 19.1
Distribution of Speech Acts in a Critical Discussion

I	CONFRONTATION
ASSERTIVE	Expressing a standpoint
COMMISSIVE	Acceptance or non-acceptance of a standpoint, upholding non-acceptance of a standpoint
[DIRECTIVE	Requesting a usage declarative]
[USAGE DECLARATIVE	Definition, specification, amplification, etc.]
II	OPENING
DIRECTIVE	Challenging to defend a standpoint
COMMISSIVE	Acceptance of the challenge to defend a standpoint
	Agreement on premises and discussion rules
	Decision to start a discussion
[DIRECTIVE	Requesting a usage declarative]
[USAGE DECLARATIVE	Definition, specification, amplification, etc.]
III	ARGUMENTATION
DIRECTIVE	Requesting argumentation
ASSERTIVE	Advancing argumentation
COMMISSIVE	Acceptance or non-acceptance of argumentation
[DIRECTIVE	Requesting a usage declarative]
[USAGE DECLARATIVE	Definition, specification, amplification, etc.]
IV	CONCLUDING
COMMISSIVE	Acceptance or non-acceptance of a standpoint
ASSERTIVE	Upholding or retracting a standpoint
	Establishing the result of the discussion
[DIRECTIVE	Requesting a usage declarative]
[USAGE DECLARATIVE]	Definition, specification, amplification, etc.]

context in which certain people are qualified to perform a certain declarative: "I open the meeting" only works if I am the chair. [22]

Usage declaratives, which regulate linguistic usage, are a special subtype of the declaratives.[23] Their main purpose is to facilitate or increase comprehension by indicating how speech acts that might be unclear are to be interpreted. Examples of usage declaratives are definitions, amplifications and explications. Only usage declaratives that enhance the understanding of speech acts play a role in a critical discussion. They can occur (and be requested for) in any stage of the discussion. In the confrontation stage, for instance, they can unmask a spurious dispute; in the opening stage they can clarify uncertainty regarding the rules of discussion. The speech acts that play a direct role in a critical discussion are listed in Table 19.1.

---

[22]Due to their dependence on the authority of the speaker or writer in a certain institutional context, declaratives can sometimes lead to a settlement of a dispute.

[23]This category of speech acts is introduced in van Eemeren and Grootendorst (1984, pp. 109–110).

Analysis as Reconstruction

For various reasons, argumentative reality does not always resemble the ideal of a critical discussion. According to the ideal model, for example, in the confrontation stage antagonists of a standpoint must state their doubts clearly and unambiguously, but in practice doing so can be "face-threatening" for both parties so that they have to operate circumspectly.[24] Analyzing argumentative discourse pragma-dialectically amounts to interpreting the discourse from the theoretical perspective of a critical discussion. Such an analysis is pragmatic in viewing the discourse as essentially an exchange of speech acts, and dialectical in viewing this exchange as a methodical attempt to resolve a difference of opinion. A pragma-dialectical analysis is aimed at reconstructing all those, and only those, speech acts that play a potential part in bringing a difference of opinion to a conclusion. In accomplishing a systematic analysis the ideal model of a critical discussion is a valuable tool. By pointing out which speech acts are relevant in the various stages of the resolution process the model has the heuristic function of indicating which speech acts need to be considered in the reconstruction.

Van Eemeren, Grootendorst, Jackson, and Jacobs (1993) further developed the analytical component of pragma-dialectics in *Reconstructing Argumentative Discourse.* They emphasized that it is crucial that the reconstructions proposed in the analysis are indeed justified. The reconstructions should be faithful to the commitments that may be ascribed to the participants on the basis of their contributions to the discourse.[25] To not "overinterpret" what seems implicit in the discourse, the analyst must be sensitive to the rules of language use,[26] the details of the presentation, and the contextual constraints inherent in the speech event concerned. So as to go beyond a naïve reading of the discourse, empirical insight concerning the way in which oral and written discourse are conducted will be beneficial.[27] The analyst's intuitions can thus be augmented by the results of (qualitative and quantitative) empirical research.[28]

In practice, the first question always is whether, and to what extent, an oral or written discourse is indeed argumentative. Sometimes the discourse, or part of it, is explicitly presented as argumentative.[29] Sometimes it is not, even though it clearly has an argumentative function. There may also be cases in which the discourse is clearly not argumentative—or at least not primarily. The most decisive demarcation criterion is whether or not argumentation is advanced, so that the discourse is, at least partially, aimed at overcoming the addressee's—real or projected—doubt regarding a standpoint. A discourse can only be justifiably analyzed

---

[24]Expressing doubt may also create a potential violation of the "preference for agreement" that governs normal conversation. See Heritage (1984, pp. 265–280); Levinson (1983, pp. 332–336); and van Eemeren, Grootendorst, Jackson, and Jacobs (1993, chap. 3).

[25]Only in exceptional cases, when interpreting a move as a potential contribution to the resolution process is the only charitable option left, an unsupported reconstruction may be warranted "for reason's sake." See van Eemeren and Grootendorst (2004, chap. 5).

[26]An integration of the Searlean speech act conditions and the Gricean conversational maxims in a set of "rules of language use" is proposed in van Eemeren and Grootendorst (1992, pp. 49–55, 2003, chap. 4).

[27]See, for example, Jackson and Jacobs (1980) and Jacobs and Jackson (1981, 1982, 1983).

[28]For a brief survey of the various approaches to the analysis of discourse and their empirical basis, see van Eemeren, Grootendorst, Jackson, and Jacobs (1993, pp. 50–59).

[29]Even a discourse that is clearly argumentative will in many respects not correspond to the ideal model of a critical discussion—or at least not directly and completely.

as argumentative, albeit not necessarily *in toto,* if, whether directly or indirectly, the complex speech act of argumentation is performed.

An Analytic Overview of Argumentative Discourse

To make it possible to evaluate argumentative discourse in a responsible way, an analytic overview is required of all elements in the discourse that are relevant to resolving a difference of opinion. Achieving such an overview is therefore the aim of the analysis. In an analytic overview the following points need to be attended to:

1. The issues that are at stake in the difference of opinion.
2. The positions the parties adopt and their procedural and material starting points.
3. The arguments explicitly or implicitly advanced by the parties.
4. The argumentation structure of the complex of arguments advanced in defense of a standpoint.
5. The argument schemes used in the individual arguments to justify a standpoint.

The terms and concepts referred to in the components of an analytic overview, such as *unexpressed premise, argumentation structure* and *argument scheme,* are defined from a pragma-dialectical perspective.[30] In dealing with unexpressed premises, for instance, first a differentiation is made between the "logical minimum" (i.e., the "associated conditional"—"if premise, then conclusion"), and the "pragmatic optimum"(i.e., a further specification or generalization of the associated conditional justified by the context and other relevant pragmatic considerations).[31] And in analyzing the argumentation structure, the multiple, coordinative and subordinative structures that are distinguished are associated with different kinds of responses to the critical questions the arguer anticipates, or responds to, when supporting a standpoint.[32] In turn, these critical questions are associated with the argument schemes that are used: They depend on whether the individual arguments and standpoints are connected by means of a causal, symptomatic or comparison relation.[33]

The elements included in an analytic overview are immediately relevant to the evaluation of argumentative discourse. If it is unclear what the difference of opinion is, there is no way of telling whether the difference has been resolved. If it is unclear which positions the parties have adopted, it will be impossible to tell in whose favor the discussion has ended. If implicit or indirect reasons and standpoints are not taken into account, crucial arguments may be overlooked and the evaluation is inadequate. If the structure of argumentation in favor of a standpoint is not exposed, it cannot be judged whether the arguments put forward in defense of the standpoint constitute a coherent and proper whole. If the argument schemes employed in supporting the various standpoints and substandpoints are not recognized, it cannot be determined whether the links between the individual arguments and the standpoints are equal to criticism.

Analytic Transformations in Reconstructing Argumentative Discourse

Generally, in argumentative discourse much remains implicit. Not only is there seldom any mention of the discussion rules or all the common starting points, but also other structural

---

[30]At an introductory level these terms and concepts are explained in van Eemeren, Grootendorst, and Snoeck Henkemans (2002). See also van Eemeren and Grootendorst (1992) and van Eemeren (2001).

[31]For the analysis of unexpressed premises, see van Eemeren and Grootendorst (1992, pp. 60–72).

[32]For a discussion of the argumentation structures, see van Eemeren and Grootendorst (1992, pp. 73–89).

[33]For a discussion of the argument schemes, see van Eemeren and Grootendorst (1992, pp. 94–102).

aspects of the resolution process are generally not indicated.[34] Because they are considered self-evident, but also for less honorable reasons, certain indispensable elements of the resolution process are often left unexpressed, including the exact nature of the disagreement, the division of roles, the relation between the arguments put forward in defense of a standpoint, the way in which the premises are supposed to support the standpoint, and even some of the premises. These elements usually are, sometimes in disguise, concealed in the discourse and need to be recovered in the analysis.

A reconstructive analysis of argumentative discourse as favored in pragma-dialectics entails a number of specific analytic operations that are instrumental in identifying the elements in the discourse that play a part in resolving a difference of opinion. Each type of transformation represents a particular way of reconstructing part of the discourse in terms of a critical discussion.[35] The transformations are analytic tools for the externalization of participant commitments that are to be taken into account in an evaluation of the merits and demerits of the discourse. Due to the transformations, the discourse as it is written down or transcribed from a tape and the discourse that is reconstructed may differ in several respects. Depending on the transformations that are carried out, these differences can be characterized as resulting from deletion, addition, permutation, or substitution.

The transformation of *deletion* entails identifying elements in the discourse that are not relevant to resolving the difference of opinion, such as immaterial interruptions and sidelines, and omitting these elements in the analysis. Any dysfunctional repetitions that merely repeat the same message are also omitted. This transformation amounts to the removal of information that is redundant, superfluous, or otherwise irrelevant to the resolution goal.

The transformation of *addition* entails a process of completion. This transformation consists in supplementing the discourse as it is explicitly presented with those elements that are left implicit but are immediately relevant to the resolution of the dispute. Addition amounts to making elliptical elements and presuppositions explicit and supplementing moves that are not made explicitly in the text but are necessary for the discourse to make sense, such as the implicit arguments that are usually called unexpressed premises.

The transformation of *permutation* entails ordering and rearranging elements from the original discourse in such a way that the process of resolving the difference of opinion is set down as clearly as possible. In a pragma-dialectical analysis, the elements that are directly relevant to the resolution of the difference are recorded in the order that is most appropriate for the evaluation of the discourse. Unlike a descriptive record, the analysis need not necessarily follow the order of events in the discourse. Sometimes, the actual chronology can be retained; sometimes a rearrangement is called for to portray the resolution process. Overlap between different stages of a critical discussion is readjusted, just as anticipatory moves and references to earlier phases of the discourse. In this endeavor, confrontational elements that in the discourse are postponed until the conclusion are moved to the confrontation stage and argumentative moves that are advanced during the confrontation are put in their proper place in the argumentation stage.

The transformation of *substitution* involves an attempt to produce an explicit and clear presentation of the elements that are potentially instrumental in resolving the difference of opinion.

---

[34]The implicit and unclear way in which the various stages of a critical discussion often appear in argumentative discourse, distorted and accompanied by diversions, should neither give rise to the premature conclusion that the discourse is deficient nor to the superficial conclusion that the ideal model of critical discussion is not realistic. The former is contradicted by pragmatic insight concerning ordinary discourse, the latter by dialectical insight concerning resolving differences of opinion. See van Eemeren and Grootendorst (1984, chap. 4, 1992, chap. 5); and van Eemeren, Grootendorst, Jackson, and Jacobs (1993, chap. 3).

[35]See van Eemeren, Grootendorst, Jackson, and Jacobs (1993, chap. 4).

Ambiguous or vague formulations are replaced by well defined and more precise standard phrases, giving elements that fulfill exactly the same function in the discourse but are phrased differently the same formulation. Different formulations of the same standpoint, for instance, are recorded in the same way and rhetorical questions that function as standpoints or arguments are noted as such. This process of translating elements from the discourse into standard phrases amounts to substituting pretheoretical formulations of colloquial speech with formulations that are theoretically meaningful in the technical language of pragma-dialectics.

In analytic practice, these reconstruction transformations are often carried out together in a cyclic process. For example, in reconstructing certain nonassertive speech acts as indirect standpoints, both the transformations of substitution and addition are carried out: A directive may thus first be reconstructed as an indirect assertive by means of the substitution transformation and then its communicative function of a standpoint is explicitly added by means of the addition transformation. Because it may become clear after a transformation has been carried out that some other transformation is also required and justified, the reconstruction process is recurrent and the analysis can be said to have a cyclic character.

Illustration of the Reconstruction of Indirectness

For an illustration of the use of transformations in cases of indirectness, we take a closer look at the transformations by means of substitution and addition. In speech act theory, it is a recognized fact that in ordinary discourse the communicative function—or, as Searle calls it, "illocutionary force"—of a speech act is not, as a rule, explicitly expressed. In many cases, this does not present much of a problem. The listener or reader is often directed to the desired interpretation by means of verbal indicators such as "since" or "therefore." In the absence of such indicators the verbal and nonverbal context usually provide sufficient clues. Indirectness, however, can pose a problem. The following piece of discourse is an example: Let's take a cab. You don't want to be late for the show, do you?

In a resolution-oriented reconstruction the analyst would without any doubt say that this is argumentation, but where is the standpoint and what constitutes the argumentation? The standpoint is to be found in the first sentence, the second contains the argumentation. At first sight, however, the first speech act has the communicative function of a proposal, the second speech act that of a question. How can the attribution of the function of a standpoint to the first sentence, and that of argumentation to the second, be justified?

As speech act theory indicates, performing a proposal presupposes that the speaker believes it to be a good proposal. According to the correctness conditions for the performance of a proposal, the speaker wants the proposal to be accepted by the listener; otherwise it would be pointless. One way to get the proposal accepted would be to show that it is in the listener's interest. By asking rhetorically whether the listener wants to be late for the show, the speaker indirectly provides a possibly conclusive reason: The speaker knows very well that the listener does not want to be late (assuming the unexpressed premise that not taking a cab would cause this unwanted effect). By adding the rhetorical question to the proposal, the speaker tries to resolve a potential dispute in advance. This explains how his proposal can be transformed into the standpoint that it is wise to take a cab, and his rhetorical question into the argument that otherwise they will be late for the show (which is undesirable).[36] This

---

[36]There is a difference between these two cases in the degree of "conventionalization." The rhetorical question is, as such, highly conventionalized, whereas the indirectness of the proposal is not. Only in a well-defined context indirectness can be easily detected and correctly interpreted. See van Eemeren and Grootendorst (1992, pp. 56–59).

reconstruction should suffice to show the merits of a pragmatic perspective in helping to get the transformations of substitution and addition carried out properly. Without speech act theory, no satisfactory analysis can be given.

Rules for Critical Discussion

In pragma-dialectics, the critical norms of reasonableness authorizing the speech acts performed in the various stages of a critical discussion are accounted for in a set of dialectical rules. Taken together, the model and the rules constitute a theoretical definition of a critical discussion. In a critical discussion, the protagonists and the antagonists of the standpoints at issue not only go through all four stages of the resolution process, but they must also observe in every stage all the rules that are instrumental in resolving a difference of opinion.[37] The dialectical procedure proposed by van Eemeren and Grootendorst (1984) in *Speech Acts in Argumentative Discussions* stated the rules that are constitutive for a critical discussion in terms of the performance of speech acts.[38] They covered the entire argumentative discourse by stating all the norms that are pertinent to resolving a difference of opinion, ranging from the prohibition to prevent each other from expressing any position one wishes to assume in the confrontation stage, to the prohibition to generalize the result of the discussion in the concluding stage.

Proposing an ideal model with rules for critical discussion may lead to running the risk of being identified with striving for an unattainable utopia. The primary function of the pragma-dialectical model, however, is a different one. By systematically indicating what the rules for conducting a critical discussion are, the model provides those who want to fulfill the role of reasonable discussants with a series of guidelines. Though formulated on a higher level of abstraction and based on a clearly articulated philosophical ideal, they may be to a great extent identical to the norms the discussants would like to see observed anyway.

The pragma-dialectical rules for critical discussion that are to be followed in order to conduct the discussion effectively are to be judged for their capacity to serve this purpose well—their "problem-validity." In order for the rules to be of practical significance, they must also be intersubjectively acceptable—so that they can acquire "conventional validity."[39] The claim that these rules are acceptable is neither based on metaphysical necessity nor derived from

---

[37]If the rules of the pragma-dialectical discussion procedure are regarded as first order conditions for having a critical discussion, the internal conditions for a reasonable discussion attitude can be viewed as "second order" conditions relating to the state of mind the discussants are assumed to be in. In practice, people's freedom to satisfy the second order conditions is sometimes limited by psychological factors beyond their control, such as emotional restraint and personal pressure. There are also external, "third order" conditions that need to be fulfilled in order to be able to conduct a critical discussion properly. They relate to the social circumstances in which the discussion takes place and pertain, for instance, to the power or authority relations between the participants and the discussion situation. Together, the second and third order conditions for conducting a critical discussion in the ideal sense are higher order conditions for resolving differences of opinion. Only if these conditions are satisfied critical reasonableness can be fully realized in practice.

[38]An improved version of the pragma-dialectical rules for critical discussion is to be found in van Eemeren and Grootendorst (2004, chap. 6).

[39]The notions "problem-validity" and "conventional validity", based on insight developed by Crawshay-Williams (1957), are introduced by Barth and Krabbe (1982). In van Eemeren and Grootendorst (1988a, 1988b, 1992) an account is given of the problem-validity of the pragma-dialectical rules; their inter-subjective validity is being investigated empirically (and has been to a great extent confirmed) in a series of experimental tests, for example, van Eemeren, Meuffels, and Verburg (2000).

any external authority or sacrosanct origin, but rests on their effectiveness when applied in resolving a difference of opinion. Because the rules have been drawn up to promote the resolution of differences of opinion, assuming that they are correctly formulated, they should be acceptable to anyone who has that aim in view. Viewed philosophically, the rationale for accepting the rules can therefore be characterized as pragmatic.

What sort of people will be willing to provide conventional validity to the discussion rules? They will be people who accept doubt as an integral part of their way of life and use criticism toward themselves and others to solve problems by trial and error. They use argumentative discourse as a means to detect weaknesses in viewpoints regarding knowledge, values and objectives, and eliminate these weaknesses where possible.[40] It should be borne in mind that the primary aim of a critical discussion is not to maximize agreement but to test contested standpoints as critically as possible.[41]

The pragma-dialectical procedure for conducting a critical discussion is too technical for immediate use in ordinary practice. For practical purposes, based on the critical insight expressed in this procedure, a code of conduct has therefore been developed for people who want to resolve their differences of opinion by means of argumentation. This code of conduct consists of ten basic requirements for reasonable behavior, profanely referred to as the Ten Commandments. I restrict myself here to presenting the succinct recapitulation of the rules for critical discussion given in the Ten Commandments.

Ten Commandments of Critical Discussion

The first commandment of the code of conduct is the freedom rule:
Discussants may not prevent each other from advancing standpoints or from calling standpoints into question.

Commandment 1 is designed to ensure that standpoints, and doubt regarding standpoints, can be expressed freely. A difference of opinion cannot be resolved if it is not clear to the parties involved that there actually is a difference and what this difference involves. In argumentative discourse the parties must therefore have ample opportunity to make their positions known. In this way, they can make sure that the confrontation stage of a critical discussion is properly completed.

The second commandment is the obligation to defend rule:
Discussants who advance a standpoint may not refuse to defend this standpoint when requested to do so.

Commandment 2 is designed to ensure that standpoints that are put forward and called into question are defended against critical attacks. A critical discussion remains stuck in the opening stage and the difference of opinion cannot be resolved if the party who has advanced a standpoint is not prepared to fulfill the role of protagonist of this standpoint.

---

[40]Such people, being opposed to protectionism of viewpoints and the immunization of any kind of standpoint against criticism, will reject all fundamentalist "justificationism" (Letztbegründung). In taking this view, pragma-dialectics connects with formal dialectics as developed by Barth and Krabbe (1982).

[41]See Popper (1971, chap. 5, note 6).

The third commandment is the standpoint rule:
Attacks on standpoints may not bear on a standpoint that has not actually been put forward by the other party.

Commandment 3 is primarily designed to ensure that attacks—and consequently defenses by means of argumentation—relate to the standpoint that is indeed advanced by the protagonist. A difference of opinion cannot be resolved if the antagonist criticizes a different standpoint and the protagonist defends a different standpoint.

Commandment 4 is the *relevance rule*:
Standpoints may not be defended by nonargumentation or argumentation that is not relevant to the standpoint.

Commandment 4 is designed to ensure that the defense of standpoints takes place only by means of relevant argumentation. The difference of opinion that is at the heart of an argumentative discourse cannot be resolved if the protagonist advances arguments that do not pertain to the standpoint or resorts to rhetorical devices in which pathos or ethos take the place of logos.[42]

Commandment 5 is the *unexpressed premise rule*:
Discussants may not falsely attribute unexpressed premises to the other party, nor disown responsibility for their own unexpressed premises.

Commandment 5 ensures that the antagonist can examine every part of the protagonist's argumentation critically—also those parts that have remained implicit in the discourse. A difference of opinion cannot be resolved if the protagonist tries to evade the obligation to defend elements that he or she has left implicit, or if the antagonist misrepresents an unexpressed premise, for example, by exaggerating its scope.

Commandment 6 is the starting point rule:
Discussants may not falsely present something as an accepted starting point or falsely deny that something is an accepted starting point.

Commandment 6 is intended to ensure that when standpoints are attacked and defended, the starting points of the discussion are used in a proper way. Neither may something be presented as an accepted starting point if it is not, nor may it be denied that something is an accepted starting point if in fact it is. Otherwise it is impossible for a protagonist to defend a standpoint conclusively—and for an antagonist to attack that standpoint successfully—on the basis of commitments that can be viewed as concessions made by the other party.

Commandment 7 is the validity rule:
Reasoning that in an argumentation is presented in an explicit and complete way may not be invalid in a logical sense.

---

[42]This does not mean that advancing argumentation cannot be combined with, or even include, the use of pathos and ethos, or that relevant arguments cannot be suggested by, or implied in, apparently irrelevant arguments. For an overview of (the history of) classical rhetoric, and an explanation of the role of logos, ethos and pathos, see Kennedy (1994).

It is possible for antagonists and protagonists to determine whether the standpoints defended do indeed follow logically from the argumentation that is advanced only if the reasoning that is used in the argumentation is indeed verbalized in full. Commandment 7 is designed to ensure that protagonists who reason explicitly in resolving a difference of opinion use only reasoning that is valid in a logical sense.[43] When the reasoning is valid, the defended standpoint follows logically from the premises that are used in the protagonist's argumentation. If not every part of the reasoning is fully expressed, commandment 7 does not apply.

> Commandment 8 is the argument scheme rule:
> Standpoints may not be regarded conclusively defended if the defense does not take place by means of appropriate argument schemes that are applied correctly.

Commandment 8 is designed to ensure that standpoints can indeed be conclusively defended if the protagonist and the antagonist agree on a method to test the soundness of the types of arguments that are used and are not part of the common starting point.[44] This implies that they must examine whether the argument schemes that are used are admissible in the light of what has been agreed on in the opening stage, and whether they have been correctly fleshed out in the argumentation stage.

> Commandment 9, bearing on the concluding stage, is the concluding rule:
> Inconclusive defenses of standpoints may not lead to maintaining these standpoints and conclusive defenses of standpoints may not lead to maintaining expressions of doubt concerning these standpoints.

Commandment 9 is designed to ensure that in the concluding stage the protagonists and the antagonists correctly ascertain the result of the discussion. A difference of opinion is resolved only if the parties are in agreement that the defense of the standpoints at issue has been successful or has not been successful.

> The tenth and last commandment is the general language use rule:
> Discussants may not use any formulations that are insufficiently clear or confusingly ambiguous, and they may not deliberately misinterpret the other party's formulations.

Problems of formulation and interpretation can occur in any stage of a critical discussion. Commandment 10 is designed to ensure that misunderstandings arising from unclear, vague or equivocal formulations are avoided. A difference of opinion can only be resolved if each party makes a real effort to express its intentions as accurately as possible in a way that minimizes the chances of misunderstanding. Equally, a difference of opinion can only be resolved if each party makes a real effort not to misinterpret any of the other party's speech acts. Problems of formulation or interpretation may otherwise lead to a pseudodifference or to a pseudosolution.

---

[43]What is meant by valid in a logical sense depends on the logical theory that is used.
[44]See van Eemeren and Grootendorst (1992, pp. 94–102).

Fallacies as Counterproductive Moves in Resolving Disagreement

A pragma-dialectical evaluation of argumentative discourse is aimed at determining the extent to which the various speech acts performed in the discourse are instrumental in resolving a difference of opinion. To achieve this goal, the evaluation needs to make clear which discussion moves hinder or obstruct a critical discussion. When an analytic overview has been compiled on the basis of a justified reconstructive analysis, a suitable point of departure has been created for such an evaluation of the discourse.

In principle, each of the pragma-dialectical discussion rules constitutes a distinct standard or norm for critical discussion. Any move constituting an infringement of any of the rules, whichever party performs it and at whatever stage in the discussion, is a possible threat to the resolution of a difference of opinion and must therefore (in this particular sense) be regarded as fallacious.[45] The use of the term *fallacy* is then systematically connected with the rules for critical discussion and a fallacy is defined as a discussion move that violates in some specific way a rule for critical discussion applying to a particular discussion stage.

This approach to the fallacies, fleshed out by van Eemeren and Grootendorst (1992) in *Argumentation, Communication, and Fallacies*, offers an alternative to the Standard Treatment of the fallacies that was criticized devastatingly by Hamblin (1970).[46] Rather than considering the fallacies as belonging to an unstructured list of nominal categories that happen to have been inherited from the past or considering all fallacies as violations of one and the same (validity) norm, the pragma-dialectical approach differentiates a functional variety of norms. Depending on the rule that has been violated, a series of other norms than logical validity are taken into account. In this way, many of the traditional fallacies can be characterized more clearly and consistently, while "new" fallacies are identified that went earlier unnoticed.

Violations of the Code of Conduct for Critical Discussion

When it comes to the detection of fallacies, a pragma-dialectical analysis proceeds in a number of steps. An utterance must first be interpreted as a particular kind of speech act performed in a context of discourse aimed at resolving a difference of opinion. Then it must be determined whether the performance of this speech act agrees with the rules for critical discussion. If the speech act proves to be a violation of any of the norms pertaining to a particular stage of the resolution process, the kind of violation must be typified by determining which specific criterion for satisfying the norm that has not been met.

The freedom rule (1) can be violated—in the confrontation stage—in various ways, both by the protagonist and the antagonist. A party can impose certain restrictions on the standpoints that may be advanced or called into question; a party can deny an opponent the right to advance a certain standpoint or to criticize a certain standpoint. Violations of the first kind mean that particular standpoints are declared sacrosanct or that some standpoints are in fact

---

[45]The pragma-dialectical identification of fallacies is always conditional. An argumentative move may be regarded as a fallacy only if the discourse is correctly viewed as aimed at resolving a difference of opinion.

[46]For an overview of the pre-Hamblin and post-Hamblin theoretical approaches to the fallacies, see van Eemeren (2001).

excluded from discussion. Violations of the first kind are directed at the opponent personally and aim at eliminating the opponent as a serious discussion partner. This may be done by putting pressure on the opponent, threatening that person with sanctions (*argumentum ad baculum*), or by playing on the opponent's feelings of compassion (*argumentum ad misericordiam*), but also by discrediting the opponent's expertise, impartiality, integrity, or credibility (*argumentum ad hominem*).

The obligation to defend rule (2) can be violated—in the opening stage—by the protagonist by *evading* or *shifting the burden of proof*. In the first case, the protagonist attempts to create the impression that there is no point in calling the standpoint into question, and no need to defend it, by presenting the standpoint as self-evident by giving a personal guarantee of the correctness of the standpoint (variant of *argumentum ad verecundiam*) or by immunizing the standpoint against criticism. In the last case, the protagonist challenges the opponent to show that the protagonist's standpoint is wrong (variant of *argumentum ad ignorantiam*) or that the opposite standpoint is right.

The standpoint rule (3) can be violated—in all stages—by the protagonist or the antagonist. In a discussion about a mixed difference of opinion they can do so by imputing a fictitious standpoint to the other party or distorting the other party's standpoint (*straw man*). The first effect can be achieved by emphatically advancing the opposite as one's own standpoint or by creating an imaginary opponent; the second by taking utterances out of context by oversimplification (ignoring nuances or qualifications) or by exaggeration (making something absolute or generalizing).

The relevance rule (4) can be violated–in the argumentation stage—by the protagonist in two ways: by putting forward argumentation that does not refer to the standpoint advanced in the confrontation stage (*irrelevant argumentation* or *ignoratio elenchi*), second, by defending a standpoint using nonargumentative means of persuasion. Playing on the emotions of the audience (variant of *argumentum ad populum*) and parading one's own qualities (variant of *argumentum ad verecundiam*) are examples. If the audience's positive or negative emotions (such as prejudice) are exploited, *pathos* replaces *logos*. For this reason, such violations of the relevance rule are sometimes called *pathetic fallacies*. If protagonists attempt to get their standpoints accepted by the opponent because of their authority in the eyes of the audience due to their expertise, credibility, integrity, or other qualities, *ethos* replaces *logos*; for this reason, such violations of the relevance rule are sometimes called *ethical fallacies*.

The protagonist can violate the unexpressed premise rule (5)—in the argumentation stage— by *denying an unexpressed premise* and the antagonist can violate this rule by *distorting an unexpressed premise*. In denying an unexpressed premise ("I never *said* that"), the protagonist in effect tries to evade the responsibility assumed in argumentation by denying a commitment to an unexpressed premise that is correctly reconstructed as such. Antagonists are guilty of the fallacy of distorting an unexpressed premise if they have produced a reconstruction of a protagonist's unexpressed premise that goes beyond the "pragmatic optimum" to which the protagonist can actually be held, given the verbal and nonverbal context.

The starting point rule (6) can be violated—in the argumentation stage—by the protagonist's falsely presenting something as a common starting point or by the antagonist's denying a premise representing a common starting point. By falsely presenting something as a common starting point, the protagonist tries to *evade the burden of proof*; the techniques used for this purpose include falsely presenting a premise as self-evident, enveloping a proposition in a presupposition of a question (*many questions*), concealing a premise in an unexpressed premise, and advancing argumentation that amounts to the same thing as the standpoint (*petitio principii*, also called *begging the question* or *circular reasoning*). By denying a premise representing a common starting point, the antagonist denies the protagonist the opportunity to defend his or her standpoint *ex concessis*, which is a denial of a *conditio sine qua non* for all successful argumentation.

The validity rule (7) can be violated—in the argumentation stage—by the protagonist in a variety of ways. Some cases of logical invalidity occur regularly and are often not immediately recognized. Among them are confusing a necessary condition with a sufficient condition (or vice versa) in arguments with an "If … , then … " premise (*affirming the consequent, denying the antecedent*). Other violations amount to erroneously attributing a (relative or structure-dependent) property of a whole to its constituent parts or vice versa (*fallacies of division* and *composition*).

The argument scheme rule (8) can be violated—in the argumentation stage—by the protagonist by relying on an inappropriate argument scheme or using an appropriate argument scheme incorrectly. The violations can be classified according to the three main categories of argument schemes: *symptomatic* argumentation of the "token" type, where there is a relation of concomitance between the premises and the standpoint ("Daniel is an actor [and actors are typically vain], so he is certainly vain"), *comparison* argumentation of the "similarity" type, where the relation is one of resemblance ("The measure I would like to take is fair, because the case we had last year was also dealt with in this way [and the one case is similar to the other]," and *instrumental* argumentation of the "consequence" type, where the relation is one of causality ("Because Tom has been drinking an excessive amount of whiskey [and drinking too much alcohol leads to a terrible headache], he must have a terrible headache").

Symptomatic argumentation is used incorrectly if, for instance, a standpoint is presented as right because an irrelevant or quasi-authority says so (special variant of *argumentum ad verecundiam*) or because everybody thinks it is right (populist variant of *argumentum ad populum* and also a special variant of *argumentum ad verecundiam*), or if a standpoint is a generalization based upon observations that are not representative or insufficient (*hasty generalization* or *secundum quid*). Comparison argumentation is used incorrectly, if, for instance, in making an analogy the conditions for a correct comparison are not fulfilled (*false analogy*). Finally, instrumental argumentation is used incorrectly if, for instance, a descriptive standpoint is being rejected because of its undesired consequences (*argumentum ad consequentiam*); a cause–effect relation is inferred from the mere observation that two events take place one after the other (*post hoc ergo propter hoc*); or it is unjustifiably suggested that by taking a proposed course of action one will be going from bad to worse (*slippery slope*).

The concluding rule (9) can be violated—in the concluding stage—by the protagonist concluding that a standpoint is true merely because it has been successfully defended (*making an absolute of the success of the defense*) or by the antagonist concluding from the fact that it has not been proved that something *is* the case, that it is *not* the case, or from the fact that something has not been proved *not* to be the case, that it *is* the case (*making an absolute of the failure of the defense* or special variant of *argumentum ad ignorantiam*). In making an absolute of the success of the defense, the protagonist commits a double error: First, the unjustified status of established fact, the truth of which is beyond discussion, is ascribed to the common starting points; secondly, in doing so, a successful defense is erroneously invested with an objective rather than intersubjective status. In making an absolute of the failure of the defense, the antagonist commits a double error: First, the roles of antagonist and protagonist are confused; second, it is mistakenly assumed that a discussion must always end in a victory for either a positive or a negative standpoint, so that not having the positive standpoint automatically means adopting the negative standpoint, and vice versa, ignoring the possibility of entertaining a "zero" standpoint.[47]

The language use rule (10) can be violated—in all stages—by the protagonist or the antagonist by taking undue advantage of unclearness (*fallacy of unclearness*) or ambiguity (*fallacy of ambiguity, equivocation, amphiboly*). Various sorts of unclearness can occur: unclearness resulting from the structuring of the text, from implicitness, indefiniteness, unfamiliarity, vagueness, and so on. Again, there are various sorts of ambiguity: referential ambiguity, syntactic ambiguity, semantic ambiguity, and so on. The fallacy of ambiguity is closely related to the fallacy of unclearness; it can occur on its own but also in combination with other fallacies (such as the fallacies of *composition* and *division*).

This brief overview may suffice to show that the pragma-dialectical analysis of the traditional fallacies as violations of the rules for critical discussion is more systematic than the Standard Treatment criticized by Hamblin. Instead of being given *ad hoc* explanations, all the fallacies are understood as falling under one or more of the rules for critical discussion. Fallacies that only were lumped nominally together in the traditional categories are either shown to have something in common or they are clearly distinguished. Genuinely related fallacies that were before separated are brought together. Distinguishing two variants of the *argumentum ad populum*—one a violation of relevance rule 4, the other of argument scheme rule 8—makes clear, for instance, that these variants are in fact *not* of the same kind. Analyzing one particular variant of the *argumentum ad verecundiam* and one particular variant of the *argumentum ad populum* as violations of the argument scheme rule makes clear that these variants *are* of the same kind when viewed from the perspective of resolving a difference of opinion.

The analytic overview also reveals that the pragma-dialectical approach makes it possible to identify so far nonrecognized and unnamed "new" obstacles to resolving a difference of opinion: *declaring a standpoint sacrosanct* (violation of freedom rule 1), *evading the burden of proof by immunizing a standpoint against criticism* (violation of obligation to defend rule 2) or *falsely presenting a premise as self-evident* (violation of starting point rule 6), *denying an unexpressed premise* (violation of unexpressed premise rule 5), *denying an accepted starting point* (violation of starting point rule 6), *falsely presenting something as a common starting point* (violation of starting point rule 6), *making an absolute of the success of the defense* (violation of concluding rule 9), and so on.

Making Use of Insight in Strategic Maneuvering

However justified it may be to view pragmatics as the modern version of rhetoric, certain attainments of classical rhetoric are then neglected that are vital to the study of argumentation. The pragma-dialectical method of analyzing and evaluating argumentative discourse can be enriched by a systematic integration of rhetorical insight in the dialectical theoretical framework (van Eemeren & Houtlosser, 1998, 1999, 2000a, 2000b, 2002). To remedy the existing separation between dialectic and rhetoric, it is necessary to realize that the two views are not incompatible, but can even be complementary.[48] Generally, in argumentative discourse it is not the arguers' sole aim to conduct the discussion in a reasonable way, but also to win the discussion by having their point accepted. The arguers' rhetorical attempts to have things

---

[47]A "zero" standpoint occurs in a non-mixed difference of opinion when the other party only has doubts about the acceptability of the standpoint. See van Eemeren and Grootendorst (1992, pp. 13–25)

[48]Regrettably, in academic practice there is still a yawning conceptual gap and lack of understanding between the protagonists of a dialectical approach and a rhetorical approach. As generally perceived, in Greek Antiquity the difference amounted initially to a division of labor. According to Toulmin (2001), after the 17th century's Scientific

their way are incorporated in their efforts to realize their dialectical aspiration of resolving the difference of opinion in accordance with the standards pertaining to a critical discussion.

Viewed pragma-dialectically, in argumentative discourse the parties are in every stage of the resolution process out for the optimal rhetorical result at the stage they are going through, but may at the same time be presumed to hold to the dialectical objective of that discussion stage. Thus the dialectical aim of each of the four stages of the resolution process may be taken to have its rhetorical analogue. To reconcile the simultaneous pursuit of these two different aims, the arguers make use of *strategic maneuvering* aimed at diminishing the potential tension between the two (van Eemeren & Houtlosser, 2002). The basic aspects of strategic maneuvering distinguished in pragma-dialectics are (a) making an expedient selection from the "topical potential" (i.e., the set of available alternatives in a certain discussion stage); (b) adapting one's contribution optimally to "audience demand" (i.e., the specific preferences and expectations of listeners or readers); and (c) using the most effective "presentational devices" (i.e., the various stylistic and other verbal and nonverbal means of conveying a message). If the selection results in a concerted succession of moves, in which the choices regarding the three aspects are coordinated, a full-fledged argumentative strategy is used.[49]

A pragma-dialectical analysis can benefit in several respects from using this conception of strategic maneuvering in reconstructing argumentative discourse. Taking the strategic maneuvering into account provides a clearer view of the rhetorical dimension of the discourse, so that a more comprehensive grasp is gained of argumentative reality. Through the more thorough and subtle understanding of the rationale behind the various moves made in the discourse the analysis becomes more profound. And by combining such rhetorical insight with the pragma-dialectical insight already achieved in the reconstruction process, the analysis can be better justified.[50]

Fallacies as Derailments of Strategic Maneuvering

The strategic maneuvering that takes place in argumentative discourse to maintain the balance between dialectical and rhetorical objectives may sometimes lead to inconsistencies and "derail." Such derailments generally coincide with the nonconstructive moves in argumentative discourse that are traditionally known as fallacies. One of the crucial problems in detecting fallacies is how sound and fallacious argumentative discourse can be distinguished. In pragma-dialectics, argumentative moves are considered sound if they are in agreement with the rules applying to the stage of a critical discussion in which they are made and fallacious if they violate any of these rules.[51] However, to be able to determine systematically for all stages of the resolution process whether or not certain argumentative moves violate a rule,

---

Revolution, the division became "ideological" and resulted in two mutually isolated paradigms, which were regarded incompatible. Rhetoric has become a field of study in the humanities for scholars interested in communication, discourse analysis and literature. Dialectic was first incorporated in the exact sciences and disappeared with the further formalization of logic in the nineteenth century for a long time almost altogether from sight. Until recently, rhetoricians largely ignored the results of dialectical theorizing, and the other way around. The papers in van Eemeren and Houtlosser (2002) are part of an effort to stimulate a rapprochement.

[49]What the best way of strategic maneuvering is depends in the last instance always on the contextual limits set by the dialectical situation, the audience that is to be persuaded, and the usable linguistic repertoire.

[50]The pragma-dialectical theory as originally developed by van Eemeren and Grootendorst (1984, 1992, 2004) can be seen as a dialectical approach to argumentation that keeps an open eye for rhetorical aspects of argumentative reality by studying argumentative discourse from a pragmatic perspective, but does not explicitly take insight from rhetoric into account.

[51]This approach differs from approaches to the fallacies, such as Biro and Siegel's (1992) and Johnson's (2000), that give precedence to—absolute—epistemological considerations, and Willard's (1995) and Leff's (2000), that rely on empirical—and relativistic—social considerations.

clear criteria are required for deciding when exactly a certain norm encapsulated in a particular discussion rule has been violated. The concept of strategic maneuvering can be of help in identifying such criteria.

In principle, all the moves made in argumentative discourse are motivated both by the aim of arguing reasonably and the aim of having things one's own way, but these aspirations are not always in perfect balance. On the one hand, speakers or writers may neglect their persuasive interests (e.g., for fear of being perceived as unreasonable); on the other hand, they may neglect their commitment to the critical ideal due to their assiduity to win the other party over to their side. Neglect of persuasiveness will harm the arguer but not the adversary, and is therefore not "condemnable" as being fallacious. However, if a party allows its commitment to a reasonable exchange of argumentative moves to become overruled by the aim of persuading the other party, the strategic maneuvering derails because the other party becomes the victim and the maneuvering is then condemnable for being fallacious.[52]

Each mode of strategic maneuvering is associated with a certain continuum of sound and fallacious acting and often the demarcation line between the two can only be determined contextually.[53] The criteria for determining fallacious strategic maneuvering can be more fully and systematically determined if we are able to rely on a well-motivated classification of the diverse modes of strategic maneuvering in the various discussion stages. If, for the confrontation stage, for instance, it can be established in which ways the parties may shape the issues on which they differ and the positions they assume to their own advantage, and the modes of strategic maneuvering can be specified that serve certain "local" and stage-related rhetorical aims, it becomes possible to investigate more precisely which soundness conditions apply. By relating the modes of strategic maneuvering concerned to the dialectical aim of the confrontation stage, appropriate criteria can be established that need to be taken into account in deciding whether or not a particular instance of strategic maneuvering has got derailed and a fallacy has been committed.

Illustration of the Boundaries of Strategic Maneuvering

To illustrate how the identification of criteria for demarcating fallacious and sound modes of strategic maneuvering may proceed, we take an example from an "advertorial" in which Shell defends its not pulling out of Nigeria's Liquefied Natural Gas project:

> If we do so now, the project will collapse. [...] A cancellation would certainly hurt the thousands of Nigerians who will be working on the project, and the tens of thousands more benefitting in the local economy. The environment, too, would suffer, with the plant expected to cut greatly the need for gas flaring in the oil industry.

Shell chooses its arguments for not pulling out of the project straight from its opponents' political concerns for the people of Nigeria and the environment, so that its strategic maneuvering

---

[52]Because a party who commits a fallacy will at the same time uphold a commitment to complying with the rules of critical discussion, an assumption of reasonableness is conferred on every discussion move (see also Jackson, 1995). This assumption is operative even when a particular way of maneuvering violates a certain discussion rule. This explains why fallacies are often not immediately manifest or apparent to others. Echoing the definition of a fallacy criticized by Hamblin (1970, p. 12), one can say that the maneuvering then still "seems" to obey the rules of critical discussion, although in fact it does not. The approach of fallacies as derailments of strategic maneuvering can thus be of help in explaining the deceptive character of (some of) the fallacies.

[53]There are some specific derailments of strategic maneuvering that can be generally pinned down as clear-cut violations of a certain rule applying to a particular discussion stage, but they are exceptional.

is characterized by the use of *conciliatio* (i.e., convincing the other party by exploiting its own views). In view of its opponents' professed concerns, at the proposition level Shell can be sure of acceptance. But how does the oil company proceed to ensure the opponents' acceptance of the justificatory potential of the two arguments for a standpoint that is precisely the opposite of their own? The company lends support to the view that the arguments of its opponents have an overriding justificatory potential for its own standpoint by claiming that there is a causal relation between Shell's pulling out of the project and a deterioration of the human and environmental circumstances. In spite of the use of the word "certainly," Shell does not really deter the reader from questioning the supposed causal link, so that it cannot be maintained that a derailment of strategic maneuvering has actually taken place, and there is no sufficient reason to accuse Shell of question begging. The use of conciliatio is a derailment of strategic maneuvering only if it is simply assumed that an argument that has been taken over has an unquestioning justificatory potential for the standpoint at issue and there is no room left for criticizing this presupposition.

Empirical Research Associated With the Pragma-Dialectical Theory

During the past two decades pragma-dialecticians have started to carry out several types of empirical research concerning the management of differences of opinion both in informal situations and in more institutionalized contexts. The research relates directly to the theoretical framework earlier described and is aimed at describing and explaining the way in which people produce, identify, and evaluate argumentative discourse. The issues that are investigated range from the principles that organize argumentative practice, to the cognitive processes and discourse structures that play a part in producing and interpreting argumentative discourse and the factors accounting for individual differences in argumentative competence.

As van Eemeren, Grootendorst, Jackson, and Jacobs (1993, 1997) showed, several empirically grounded claims can be made concerning the function, structure, and content of argumentative exchanges. A primary empirical grounding for these claims comes from ethnographic evidence. Other sources are found in comparative information about discourse in general and conventional structures and strategies of discourse. In cases of dialogue, another source of empirical grounding may come from various cues that indicate how the participants themselves understand the argumentative function of the discourse. Pauses, fillers ("uh," "well"), cut-offs and restarts are all characteristic vocal features of turns in conversation that go against the other party's preferences. None of the sources of empirical evidence works alone, and all need to be used against some knowledge of the cultural background of the speech event concerned and a trained intuition with respect to the conduct of argumentative discourse.

Reconstructing Argumentative Discourse provides, among other things, evidence from conversations during third-party dispute mediation that certain pieces of real-life argumentative discourse that seem, at first sight, just strikingly unreasonable may, at second sight, be understood as aimed at resolving a dispute, particularly when it is taken into account that certain higher order conditions for critical discussion were unfulfilled during the exchange. Focusing on problem-solving discussions, van Rees (1994, 2002) tried to establish whether the purposes of this type of discourse, as laid out in normative handbooks, are sufficiently in accordance with the purposes of critical discussion to warrant a pragma-dialectical reconstruction. She also used descriptive models for this kind of discourse in order to investigate the extent to which actual problem-solving discussions conform to these ideals. More recently, van Rees (1995) showed how the actual reconstruction of problem-solving discussions as a critical discussion can be accounted for by using insights from speech act theory, discourse analysis and conversation analysis, and, conversely, how the pragma-dialectical framework can be used in interpreting the function of an ordinary discourse phenomenon such as repetition.

Another qualitative contribution is made by Snoeck Henkemans (1992) in *Analysing Complex Argumentation*. She showed that multiple and coordinative argumentation result from different kinds of dialogical exchanges aimed at resolving a difference of opinion. Coordinative argumentation is put forward in an attempt to remove the opponent's doubt or criticism concerning the sufficiency of the argumentation. If the coordinative argumentation is used in a direct defense, it is "cumulative"; if used in an indirect defense, it is "complementary." In both cases, the arguments are interdependent. In multiple argumentation the arguments advanced in defense of a standpoint are separate and independent attempts to defend the standpoint, the one being motivated by the (potential) failure of the other. Later, Snoeck Henkemans (1995) examined the influence of stylistic properties of argumentative discourse on its comprehensibility and acceptability.

Another type of empirical research that pragma-dialectics brings to bear consists of (quantitative) experimental research. An important question that has been investigated is the extent to which people are capable of recognizing argumentation. The results suggest that verbal indicators of argumentation significantly facilitate the ease of recognition, whereas implicit and indirect presentations pose more problems, especially in the absence of sufficient contextual clues (van Eemeren, Grootendorst, & Meuffels, 1989). In the interpretation of indirect argumentation (and implicit argumentation in general), contextual indication proved to play a major part, assisting the interpretation of the communicative function of utterances by having a clarifying effect. Serious problems of interpretation only arise in "undefined" contexts devoid of helpful pointers.[54] van Eemeren, de Glopper, Grootendorst, and Oostdam (1995) investigated the performance of students in identifying unexpressed premises and argument schemes. The results of their tests clearly indicate that, in the absence of disambiguating contextual information, unexpressed "major" premises and "nonsyllogistic" premises are more often correctly identified than unexpressed "minor" premises. As Garssen's (2002) experiments showed, argument schemes of the causal type are more often correctly identified than symptomatic argumentation, but not more frequently than comparison argumentation.[55]

Pragma-dialectical insight is also brought to bear in providing guidelines for the construction of argumentative texts (van Eemeren & Grootendorst, 1999). The pragma-dialectical (re)writing procedure, which takes feedback from the primary text systematically into account, aims to ensure that the revised text is demonstrably better than the original text. On the basis of an analytic overview, which can also be designed as a plan for writing an argumentative text, a text can be (re)written in such a way that its comprehensibility and acceptability are not affected negatively by redundancy, lack of explicitness, poor arrangement, or unclearness. In this endeavor, four "presentation transformations" must be performed on the analytic overview, which "mirror" the reconstruction transformations. They roughly correspond to the questions of what can be left out ("presentational deletion"), what is to be added ("presentational addition"), which rearrangements are necessary ("presentational permutation"), and which reformulations improve the clearness of the text ("presentational substitution").

---

[54]Van Eemeren and Grootendorst (1992, chap. 5) argued that the degree of conventionalization of the verbal presentation required for indirect speech acts to be interpreted properly is inversely proportional to the degree of definition of the context in which they occur.

[55]For empirical research concerning the recognition of argument schemes, see also Garssen (1994).

Some Topical Research Themes

Presently pragma-dialectical research, which has become truly international,[56] concentrates in the first place on bridging the gap between philosophy and theory and the empirical, analytical and practical study of argumentative discourse. The following topical themes can be distinguished.

First, there is *dialectical and rhetorical analysis*, a cluster of ambitious projects that examine how joint insight from dialectic and rhetoric can be of help in developing more comprehensive tools for analyzing and evaluating argumentative discourse. As an illustration, an exemplarily analysis is prepared of a historical case of argumentative discourse, the *Apologie* [Apologia] (1581), a long pamphlet that justifies William of Orange's actions in the Dutch Revolt against the Spanish rulers (van Eemeren & Houtlosser, 2003).

Second, *broadening the scope of pragma-dialectics* encompasses projects aimed at widening the range, or "inclusiveness," of pragma-dialectics. Groarke (2002), for one, aimed to broaden the theory with an account of arguments that are wholly or partly conveyed by images. Jackson (2002) extends pragma-dialectics as a framework for "the engineering of argument." In the same vein, Aakhus (2002) modeled reconstruction in groupware technology.

Third, *conceptions of reasonableness* pertains to experimental empirical investigations aimed at testing the intersubjective acceptability of the critical normativity encapsulated in the pragma-dialectical rules (van Eemeren, Garssen & Meuffels, 2002; van Eemeren & Meuffels, 2002; van Eemeren, Meuffels, & Verburg, 2000).[57] The results provide insight in ordinary language users' reasonableness conceptions, their consistency, and the social, cultural and other differences between them.[58] They also provide an empirical basis for developing pedagogically adequate textbooks.

Fourth, *characteristics of argumentative discourse* concentrates on the pragmatic features of argumentative discourse and the commitments created by the use of certain expressions. For each stage of a critical discussion the expressions are identified that are available in ordinary language for indicating, directly or indirectly, the moves pertinent to the stage concerned, the kind of information conveyed by the use of particular indicators and the conditions justifying the analysis of certain expressions as indicators of specific discussion moves. Houtlosser (2002) examines indicators of a standpoint, taking not only the presentation into account, but also the responses of the interlocutor and the follow-up given by the original speaker or writer. Snoeck Henkemans (2002) concentrated on the clues for identifying the argument scheme of symptomatic argumentation.

Fifth, *interpersonal embedding of argumentative discourse*. Weger (2002) reconstructed problematic interpersonal behavior in conflicts as violating the rules for critical discussion. Polcar (2002) viewed question–answer argumentation as an attempt by questioners to elicit assertions from a respondent that represent standpoints and argumentation. By investigating empirically self-advocacy in the physician–patient context of HIV-treatment and AIDS, Brashers, Haas, and Neidig (2002) showed that social and cultural barriers cause deviations from the ideal of a critical discussion that must be accounted for.

---

[56]Whereas the overview pragma-dialectics given in van Eemeren and Grootendorst (1994) contained only essays by the Amsterdam group, its recent successor, van Eemeren (2002a), consists of contributions of an international group of scholars.

[57]O'Keefe (2002) made clear that a normative ideal, in this case argumentative explicitness, may also be persuasively effective.

[58]For the differences and relations between the norms pertaining to a critical discussion and those pertaining to a speech event such as bargaining in dispute mediation, see Aakhus and Jacobs (2002).

Sixth, *institutional argumentation* concerns a cluster of projects aimed at examining argumentation in the more or less conventionalized contexts of established procedures in institutional settings, taking due account of the way in which the conduct of a discussion is framed by the specific requirements of the type of discourse concerned. In a juridical context, Feteris (2002) investigated the use of pragmatic argumentation referring to the desirable (or undesirable) consequences of a legal decision.[59] Plug (2002) discussed the argumentation structures employed in the justification of judicial decisions (Plug, 1994) and maximally argumentative analysis of judicial argumentation. Hample (2002) studied control of the disagreement space in the institutional context of the Spanish Inquisition. Alford (2002) used pragma-dialectics in order to study the legal systems of the United States. Concentrating on a political context, van Eemeren (2002b) discussed the role of argumentation in democracy. Aldrich (2002) dealt with framing blame and managing accountability in congressional testimony in the congressional hearing of Oliver L. North.

CONCLUSION

In the pragma-dialectical approach, argumentation is studied from a communicative perspective by means of a comprehensive research program that has a descriptive as well as a normative dimension. The metatheoretical principles of functionalization, socialization, externalization, and dialectification are realized in the ideal model of a critical discussion that portrays the distribution of speech acts over the various stages of the process of resolving a difference of opinion. The rules for critical discussion pertaining to these speech acts constitute distinct standards for argumentative conduct that can be summarized as a code of conduct for critical discussion. Infringement of any of the rules is a possible threat to the resolution of a difference of opinion and must therefore be regarded as an incorrect discussion move, which can be analyzed as a fallacy. The problem validity of the rules is judged, pragmatically, by their theoretical contribution to the resolution of a difference of opinion. In order to be effective, however, the rules must also be intersubjectively acceptable to those people who wish to resolve their differences by means of argumentative discourse. The intersubjective validity of the rules has been tested empirically by experiments aimed at determining systematically the extent to which they agree with the norms favored by ordinary language users when evaluating argumentative discourse.

The pragma-dialectical method for analyzing argumentative discourse involves a systematic reconstruction of the discourse that results in an analytic overview containing all aspects of the discourse that are pertinent to the resolution of a difference of opinion. A recent crucial step in the development of this method was the introduction of the notion of strategic maneuvering, which refers to the perennial balancing between pursuing at the same time a resolution-minded dialectical objective and the rhetorical objective of having one's own position accepted. In the future, examining strategic maneuvering will no doubt lead to more refined and more thoroughly justified analyses. It will also lead to a better evaluation of derailments of strategic maneuvering. The criteria needed for identifying and evaluating potential fallacies must be determined in relation with the specific type of strategic maneuvering in which the potential derailment occurs. Future research will also be directed at determining the stylistic characteristics of the various

---

[59]For a pragma-dialectical perspective on prominent approaches to legal argumentation, see Feteris (1999). See also Feteris (1994).

ways of strategic maneuvering, thus substantiating the presentational dimension of strategic maneuvering. Focal points in future studies of argumentative discourse in institutional settings will certainly be the techniques that are used in strategic maneuvering in legal and political discussions. One of the main interests to be responded to is how politicians attempt to mask derailments of their maneuvering and respond to derailments of their opponents.

REFERENCES

Aakhus, M. (2002). Modeling reconstruction in groupware technology. In F. H. van Eemeren (Ed.), *Advances in pragma-dialectics* (pp. 121–136). Newport News, VA: Sic Sat/Vale Press.

Aakhus, M., & Jacobs, S. (2002). How to resolve a conflict: Two models of dispute resolution. In F. H. van Eemeren (Ed.), *Advances in pragma-dialectics* (pp. 29–44). Newport News, VA: Sic Sat/Vale Press.

Albert, H. (1975). *Traktat über kritische Vernunft* (3rd ed.). Tübingen, Germany: Mohr.

Aldrich, A. (2002). Framing blame and managing accountability in congressional testimony. In F. H. van Eemeren (Ed., 2002)*Advances in pragma-dialectics* (pp. 309–321). Newport News, VA: Sic Sat/Vale Press.

Alford, R. P. (2002). Improving the judicial review of common law argumentation. In F. H. van Eemeren (Ed.), *Advances in pragma-dialectics* (pp. 271–289). Newport News, VA: Sic Sat/Vale Press.

Austin, J. L. (1962). *How to do things with words*. Oxford, England: Clarendon.

Barth, E. M., & Krabbe, E. C. W. (1982). *From axiom to dialogue: A philosophical study of logics and argumentation*. New York: Walter de Gruyter.

Biro, J., & Siegel, H. (1992). Normativity, argumentation and an epistemic theory of fallacies. In F. H. van Eemeren, R. Grootendorst, J. A. Blair, & C. A. Willard (Eds.), *Argumentation illuminated* (pp. 85–103). Amsterdam: Sic Sat.

Brashers, D. E., Haas, S. M., & Neidig, J. L. (2002). Satisfying the argumentative requirements for self-advocacy. In F. H. van Eemeren (Ed.), *Advances in pragma-dialectics* (pp. 291–308). Newport News, VA: Sic Sat/Vale Press.

Crawshay-Williams, R. (1957). *Methods and criteria of reasoning. An inquiry into the structure of controversy*. London: Routledge & Kegan Paul.

Feteris, E. T. (1994). Rationality in legal discussions. In F.H. van Eemeren & R. Grootendorst (Eds.), *Studies in pragma-dialectics* (pp. 29–40). Amsterdam: Sic Sat, 4.

Feteris, E. T. (1999). *Fundamentals of legal argumentation. A survey of theories on the justification of judicial decisions*. Dordrecht, The Netherlands: Kluwer.

Feteris, E. T. (2002). Pragmatic argumentation in a legal context. In F. H. van Eemeren (Ed.), *Advances in pragma-dialectics* (pp. 243–260). Newport News, VA: Sic Sat/Vale Press.

Garssen, B. J. (1994). Recognizing argumentation schemes. In F.H. van Eemeren & R. Grootendorst (Eds.), *Studies in pragma-dialectics* (pp. 105–111). Amsterdam: Sic Sat, 4.

Garssen, B. (2002). Understanding argument schemes. In F.H. van Eemeren (Ed.), *Advances in pragma-dialectics* (pp. 93–104). Newport News, VA: Sic Sat/Vale Press.

Grice, H. P. (1989). *Studies in the way of words*. Cambridge, MA: Harvard University Press.

Groarke, L. (2002). Toward a pragma-dialectics of visual argument. In F. H. van Eemeren (Ed.), *Advances in pragma-dialectics* (pp. 137–151). Newport News, VA: Sic Sat/Vale Press.

Habermas, J. (1971). Vorbereitende Bemerkungen zu einer Theorie der Kommunikativen Kompetenz. [Preparatory remarks regarding a theory of communicative competence]. In J. Habermas & H. Luhmann (Eds.), *Theorie der Gesellschaft oder Sozialtechnologie. Was leistet die Systemforschung?* (pp. 107–141). Frankfurt, Germany: Suhrkamp.

Hamblin, C. L. (1970). *Fallacies*. London: Methuen.

Hample, D. (2002). A pragma-dialectical analysis of the Inquisition. In F. H. van Eemeren (Ed.), *Advances in pragma-dialectics* (pp. 229–242). Newport News, VA: Sic Sat/Vale Press.

Heritage, J. (1984). A change-of-state token and aspects of its sequential placement. In J. M. Atkinson & J. Heritage (Eds.), *Structures of social action. Studies in conversation analysis* (pp. 299–346). Cambridge, England: Cambridge University Press.

Houtlosser, P. (1994). The speech act "advancing a standpoint." In F. H. van Eemeren & R. Grootendorst (Eds.), *Studies in pragma-dialectics* (pp. 165–171). Amsterdam: Sic Sat, 4.

Houtlosser, P. (2002). Indicators of points of view. In F.H. van Eemeren (Ed.), *Advances in pragma-dialectics* (pp. 169–184). Newport News, VA: Sic Sat/Vale Press.

Jackson, S. (1992). "Virtual standpoints" and the pragmatics of conversational argument. In F. H. van Eemeren, R. Grootendorst, J. A. Blair, & C. A. Willard (Eds.), *Argumentation illuminated* (pp. 260–269). Amsterdam: Sic Sat, 1.

Jackson, S. (1995). Fallacies and heuristics. In F. H. van Eemeren, R. Grootendorst, J. A. Blair, & C. A. Willard (Eds.), *Analysis and evaluation. Proceedings of the third ISSA Conference on Argumentation* (Vol. II, pp. 257–269). Amsterdam: Sic Sat.

Jackson, S. (2002). Designing argumentation protocols for the classroom. In F. H. van Eemeren (Ed.), *Advances in pragma-dialectics* (pp. 105–119). Newport News, VA: Sic Sat/Vale Press.

Jackson, S., & Jacobs, S. (1980). Of conversational argument: Pragmatic bases for the enthymeme. *Quarterly Journal of Speech, 66,* 251–265.

Jacobs, S., & Jackson, S. (1981). Argument as a natural category: The routine grounds for arguing in natural conversation. *Western Journal of Speech Communication, 45,* 118–132.

Jacobs, S., & Jackson, S. (1982). Conversational argument: A discourse analytic approach. In J. R. Cox & C. A. Willard (Eds.), *Advances in argumentation theory and research* (pp. 205–237). Carbondale: Southern Illinois University Press.

Jacobs, S., & Jackson, S. (1983). Strategy and structure in conversational influence attempts. *Communication Monographs, 50,* 285–304.

Johnson, R. (2000). *Manifest rationality. A pragmatic theory of argument.* Mahwah, NJ: Lawrence Erlbaum Associates, Inc.

Johnson-Laird, P. N. (1983). *Mental models. Towards a cognitive science of language, inference, and consciousness.* Cambridge, England: Cambridge University Press.

Kennedy, G. A. (1994). *A new history of classical rhetoric.* Princeton, NJ: Princeton University Press.

Leff, M. (2000). Rhetoric and dialectic in the twenty-first century. *Argumentation, 14,* 241–254.

Levinson, S. C. (1983). *Pragmatics.* Cambridge, England: Cambridge University Press.

Lorenzen, P., & Lorenz, K. (1978). *Dialogische Logik* [Dialogic logic]. Darmstadt, Germany: Wissenschaftliche Buchgesellschaft.

Naess, A. (1966). *Communication and argument. Elements of applied semantics.* London: Allen & Unwin.

Nisbett, R., & Ross, L. (1980). Human inference: Strategies and shortcomings of social judgement. Englewood Cliffs, NJ: Prentice-Hall.

O'Keefe, D. J. (2002). The persuasive effects of variation in standpoint articulation. In F. H. van Eemeren (Ed.), *Advances in pragma-dialectics* (pp. 65–82). Newport News, VA: Sic Sat/Vale Press.

Perelman, C., & Olbrechts-Tyteca, L. (1958). *La nouvelle rhétorique. Traité de l'argumentation* [The New Rhetoric. A Treatise on Argumentation]. Paris: Presses Universitaires de France.

Plug, J. (1994). Reconstructing complex argumentation in judicial decisions. In F. H. van Eemeren & R. Grootendorst (Eds.), *Studies in pragma-dialectics* (pp. 246–253). Amsterdam: Sic Sat, 4.

Plug, J. (2002). Maximally argumentative analysis of judicial argumentation. In F. H. van Eemeren (Ed.), *Advances in pragma-dialectics* (pp. 261–270). Newport News, VA: Sic Sat/Vale Press.

Polcar, L. (2002). Non-straightforward answers in question-answer argumentation. In F. H. van Eemeren (Ed.), *Advances in pragma-dialectics* (pp. 215–228). Newport News, VA: Sic Sat/Vale Press.

Popper, K. R. (1971). *The open society and its enemies* (5th ed.). Princeton, NJ: Princeton University Press.

Popper, K. R. (1972). *Objective knowledge. An evolutionary approach.* Oxford, England: Clarendon Press.

Popper, K. R. (1974). *Conjectures and refutations. The growth of scientific knowledge.* London: Routledge & Kegan Paul.

Searle, J. R. (1969). *Speech acts. An essay in the philosophy of language.* Cambridge, England: Cambridge University Press.

Searle, J. R. (1979). *Expression and meaning. Studies in the theory of speech acts.* Cambridge, England: Cambridge University Press.

Snoeck Henkemans, A. F. (1992). *Analysing Complex argumentation. The reconstruction of multiple and coordinatively compound argumentation in a critical discussion.* Amsterdam: Sic Sat.

Snoeck Henkemans, A. F. (1995). *Anyway* and *even* as indicators of argumentative structure. In F. H. van Eemeren, R. Grootendorst, J. A. Blair, & C. A. Willard (Eds.), *Reconstruction and application. Proceedings of the third International Conference on Argumentation* (Vol. III, pp. 183–191). Amsterdam: Sic Sat.

Snoeck Henkemans, A. F. (2002). Clues for reconstructing symptomatic argumentation. In F. H. van Eemeren (Ed.), *Advances in pragma-dialectics* (pp. 185–195). Newport News, VA: Sic Sat/Vale Press.

Toulmin, S. E. (1958). *The uses of argument.* Cambridge, England: Cambridge University Press.

Toulmin, S. E. (1976). *Knowing and acting. An invitation to philosophy.* New York: Macmillan.

Toulmin, S. E. (2001). *Return to reason.* Cambridge, MA: Harvard University Press.

van Eemeren, F. H. (2001). Fallacies. In F. H. van Eemeren (Ed.), *Crucial concepts in argumentation theory* (pp. 135–164). Amsterdam: Amsterdam University Press.

van Eemeren, F. H. (Ed.). (2002a). *Advances in pragma-dialectics.* Newport News, VA: Sic Sat/Vale Press.

van Eemeren, F. H. (2002b). Democracy and argumentation. *Controversia, 1,* 69–84.

van Eemeren, F. H., Garssen, B. J., & Meuffels, B. (2002). The unreasonableness of the ad baculum fallacy. In T. Goodnight (Ed.), *Arguing communication & culture. Selected papers from the twelfth NCA/AFA Conference on Argumentation* (pp. 343–350). Washington, DC: National Communication Association.

van Eemeren, F. H., de Glopper, K., Grootendorst, R., & Oostdam, R. J. (1995). Student performance in identifying unexpressed premises and argumentation schemes. *Argumentation and Advocacy, 31,* 151–162.

van Eemeren, F. H., & Grootendorst, R. (1984). *Speech acts in argumentative discussions: A theoretical model for the analysis of discussions directed towards solving conflicts of opinion.* Berlin: Foris/Mouton de Gruyter.

van Eemeren, F. H., & Grootendorst, R. (1988a). Rationale for a pragma-dialectical perspective. *Argumentation, 2,* 271–291.

van Eemeren, F. H., & Grootendorst, R. (1988b). Rules for argumentation in dialogues. *Argumentation, 2,* 499–510.

van Eemeren, F. H., & Grootendorst, R. (1992). *Argumentation, communication, and fallacies: A pragma-dialectical perspective.* Hillsdale, NJ: Lawrence Erlbaum Associates, Inc.

van Eemeren, F. H., & Grootendorst, R. (Eds.). (1994). *Studies in pragma-dialectics.* Amsterdam: Sic Sat, 4.

van Eemeren, F. H., & Grootendorst, R. (1999). From analysis to presentation: A pragma-dialectical approach to writing argumentative texts. In J. Andriessen & P. Coirier (Eds.), *Foundations of argumentative text processing* (pp. 43–73). Amsterdam: Amsterdam University Press.

van Eemeren, F. H., & Grootendorst, R. (2004). *A systematic theory of argumentation. The pragma-dialectical approach.* Cambridge, England: Cambridge University Press.

van Eemeren, F. H., Grootendorst, R., Jackson, S., & Jacobs, S. (1993). *Reconstructing argumentative discourse.* Tuscaloosa: The University of Alabama Press.

van Eemeren, F. H., Grootendorst, R., Jackson, S., & Jacobs, S. (1997). Argumentation. In T. A. van Dijk (Ed.), *Discourse as structure and process. Discourse studies: A multidisciplinary introduction* (Vol. 1, pp. 208–229). London: Sage.

van Eemeren, F. H., Grootendorst, R., & Meuffels, B. (1989). The skill of identifying argumentation. *Journal of the American Forensic Association, 25,* 239–245.

van Eemeren, F. H., Grootendorst, R., & Snoeck Henkemans, A. F. (2002). *Argumentation: Analysis, evaluation, presentation.* Mahwah, NJ: Lawrence Erlbaum Associates, Inc.

van Eemeren, F. H., Grootendorst, R., Snoeck Henkemans, A. F., Blair, J. A., Johnson, R. H., Krabbe, E. C. W., et al. (1996). *Fundamentals of argumentation theory: A handbook of historical backgrounds and contemporary developments.* Mahwah, NJ: Lawrence Erlbaum Associates, Inc.

van Eemeren, F. H., & Houtlosser, P. (1998). Rhetorical rationales for dialectical moves: Justifying pragma-dialectical reconstructions. In J. F. Klumpp (Ed.), *Argument in a time of change: Definitions, frameworks, and critiques. Proceedings of the tenth NCA/AFA Conference on Argumentation* (pp. 51–56). Annandale, VA: National Communication Association.

van Eemeren, F. H., & Houtlosser, P. (1999). Strategic manoeuvring in argumentative discourse. *Discourse Studies, 1,* 479–497.

van Eemeren, F. H., & Houtlosser, P. (2000a). Managing disagreement: Rhetorical analysis within a dialectical framework. *Argumentation and Advocacy, 37,* 150–157.

van Eemeren, F. H., & Houtlosser, P. (2000b). Rhetorical analysis within a pragma-dialectical framework. *Argumentation, 14,* 293–305.

van Eemeren, F. H., & Houtlosser, P. (2002). Strategic maneuvering: Maintaining a delicate balance. In F. H. van Eemeren & P. Houtlosser (Eds.), *Dialectic and rhetoric: The warp and woof of argumentation analysis* (pp. 131–159). Dordrecht, The Netherlands: Kluwer.

van Eemeren, F. H., & Houtlosser, P. (2003). The rhetoric of William the Silent's *Apologie*: A dialectical perspective. In L. Komlósi, P. Houtlosser, & M. Leezenberg (Eds.), *Communication and culture. Argumentative, cognitive and linguistic perspectives* (pp. 177–185). Amsterdam: Sic Sat.

van Eemeren, F. H., & Meuffels, B. (2002). Ordinary arguers' judgements on ad hominem fallacies. In F. H. van Eemeren (Ed., 2002), *Advances in pragma-dialectics* (pp. 45–64). Newport News, VA: Sic Sat/Vale Press.

van Eemeren, F. H., Meuffels, B., & Verburg, M. (2000). The (un)reasonableness of the *argumentum ad hominem*. *Language and Social Psychology, 19,* 416–435.

van Rees, M. A. (1994). Analysing and evaluating problem-solving discussions. In F. H. van Eemeren & R. Grootendorst (Eds.), *Studies in pragma-dialectics* (pp. 197–217). Amsterdam: Sic Sat, 4.

van Rees, M. A. (1995). Functions of repetition in informal discussions. In C. Bazanella (Ed.), *Repetition in discourse* (pp. 141–156). Berlin: Walter de Gruyter.

van Rees, M. A. (2002). A new approach to problem-solving discussions. In In F. H. van Eemeren (Ed.), *Advances in pragma-dialectics* (pp. 83–92). Newport News, VA: Sic Sat/Vale Press.

Walton, D. N., & Krabbe, E. C. W. (1995). *Commitment in dialogue: Basic concepts of interpersonal reasoning.* Albany: State University of New York Press.

Weger, Jr., H. (2002). Violating pragma-dialectical rules in arguments between intimates. In F. H. van Eemeren (Ed.), *Advances in pragma-dialectics* (pp. 197–213). Newport News, VA: Sic Sat/Vale Press.

Wenzel, J. W. (1979). Jürgen Habermas and the dialectical perspective on argumentation. *Journal of the American Forensic Association, 16,* 83–94.

Willard, C. A. (1983). *Argumentation and the social grounds of knowledge.* Tuscaloosa: The University of Alabama Press.

Willard, C. A. (1989). *A theory of argumentation.* Tuscaloosa: The University of Alabama Press.

Willard, C. A. (1995). *Liberal alarms and rhetorical excursions. A new rhetoric for modern democracy.* Chicago: University of Chicago Press.

QUESTIONS TO PONDER

1. Why would it be important to reconcile the normative and the descriptive dimensions of the study of argumentation?

2. Explain why the four metatheoretical principles of pragma-dialectics can only be an adequate starting point for studying argumentative discourse when they are taken together.

3. What are the advantages of studying argumentative discourse in terms of speech acts contributing to the resolution of a difference of opinion?

4. Explain that the pragma-dialectical method of reconstructing argumentative discourse as a critical discussion results in an analysis motivated by theoretical considerations and grounded in empirical observation.

5. Explain how the study of derailments of strategic maneuvering contributes to substantiating the pragma-dialectical view of fallacies as violations of rules for critical discussion.

20

Tides in the Ocean: A Layered Approach to Communication and Culture

Sandra L. Faulkner
Syracuse University

Michael L. Hecht
Pennsylvania State University

Culture is a lens for viewing the connections and relationships that define the human experience. Just as physics has become more and more focused on the connections and relationships among energy and matter, so too have the human sciences come to focus on these sources of connectivity. We believe that the construct of "culture" provides a means for understanding and explaining the connections among people as well as between people and their environment. At the same time, it helps explain how people's various identities come together to create the self. We consider culture to be like a "lens" because it focuses us on these connections, helping us see more clearly something that, while containing material objects, is actually symbolic.

In this chapter we will attempt to describe and explain the lens of culture, and show you how it can be used to understand everyday occurrences as well as the more complex and enduring patterns of human experience. We hope to demonstrate how something can be both abstract and concrete, complex and simple. We invite you to look into our chapter through your own lens of culture and hope that the following will help you interpret this lens while lending understanding to those used by others.

But lenses are not passive or benign pointers. Rather, they may change the observation itself by bringing it closer or moving it further away, and by clarifying or distorting an image. Think of a camera lens that zooms in and out. Think also of what we mean by getting a camera lens "in focus"—we see more clearly what is in the middle of the picture while the edges or borders are fuzzy. In this way, the lens of culture calls our attention to parts of our experience, putting those parts in the foreground and center of our world picture. And what do we see most clearly through the lens of culture? We believe that culture highlights most clearly three concepts: *code*, *conversation*, and *community*. Culture helps us understand the codes of conduct and thought, the ways in people converse and interact, and the communities in which they live.

Gerry Philipsen (1987) was among the first to point out these three unifying concepts of culture. We use his approach as a starting point and offer definitions of cultural codes, conversations, and communities as well as discuss what it means to define culture as a code, conversation, and community. We will use Michael's culture to illustrate these concepts. Michael is of Eastern European Jewish American descent and was raised in New York City.

CULTURAL CODE

A *code* is a system of symbols, rules, meanings, beliefs, values, and images of the ideal. It is a world view or source of order. Geertz (1973) described culture as "webs of significance" (p. 5) and goes on to discuss the patterns of meanings and symbolic forms. Similarly, Carbaugh (1985) discussed culture as "a system of meaning or process of sense making" (p. 32), while Gudykunst and Kim (1992) referred to it as "a unified set of symbolic ideas" (p. 4). There are many ways to see these codes. One way is to examine the types of ceremonies that different cultures perform. These ceremonies reflect what is valued, and each has its own rules and customs. Think about the ceremonies you attend (e.g., weddings, funerals, graduation). What does a funeral mean to you? How do you behave at one? What clothing do you wear for it? In some cultures (e.g., Japan) white is preferred to show respect for death, and others (e.g., United States) prefer dark colors. Think about the rules for job interviewing. When starting a new job, what codes will you need to master to succeed as an employee? Cultures teach us about how to interpret events; how to behave; how to be. This is what we mean when we say, culture is a code.

Jewish American Code: Hebrew/Yiddish, Knowledge, Religion

Michael was encouraged to speak Hebrew, the language of the Jewish Bible when growing up. As eastern Europeans, his grand parents spoke Yiddish, a language combining Hebrew and German that had been used by previous generations of immigrants to assimilate to German culture. His parents, aunts, and uncles spoke this language, though all but the eldest of the next generation were discouraged from its use because of the belief it would interfere with learning Hebrew and would mark them as lower class and foreign.

But this marks only the "language code" of the culture. Remember, that in our definition we discussed code as meaning and values. One of the unifying values in this culture is knowledge—the quest for information and wisdom through study. Historically, Jewish culture has emphasized knowledge, reserving the Sabbath for study.

Finally, Judaism invokes a religious code. This more formal system is cataloged in the Jewish Testament, though it is not used as a rigid set of laws as much as a set of guidelines for life within Michael's cultural group.

CULTURE AS CONVERSATION

Conversation involves patterns of verbal and nonverbal interactions. Borman (1983) talked about culture as "the sum total of ways of living, organizing, and communing" (p. 100), while

E. T. Hall and Hall (1989) described it as a program for behavior. Hymes (1974) thought of culture as a speech community, in a sense combining culture as conversation with culture as community. For example, Black English represents a distinctive language code (Hecht, Jackson, & Ribeau, 2003). Culture tells us how to interact with others. Think about traveling to another culture as a salesperson. Who would you contact at a company to make the sale? How should you start the conversation? Now think about meeting people in another culture. Can you ask about personal topics? How quickly is it appropriate to invite someone to your home? Our cultures give us the answers to these questions about how to carry on a conversation.

Jewish American Conversation: Expressive, Aggressive, Political

The conversational style that Michael's culture invokes is a highly expressive and aggressive one. Conversations are animated and issues are engaged in a direct and sometimes provocative manner. Often, these discussions turn to political issues. Michael remembers family dinners becoming debates about the issues of the day, often between him and his elder sister with his father moderating. Just as Jewish religion and biblical interpretations are debated in religious practice, so to is this style of interaction pervasive in the group's cultural conversation.

CULTURE AS COMMUNITY

A *community* represents a group, shared identities, a sense of membership, who "we" are and the way people organize themselves. Linton (1955) defined culture as an organized group, and Winkelman (1993) talked about it as the people who share the culture. Carbaugh (1989) wrote extensively about "personhood"—what we consider a person to be and how they constitute part of a group. For instance, what does it mean to be a student and how does a student become part of a university student body? Many writers refer to culture as a "way of life," clearly implicating the community or collectivity. Nations are perhaps the most common way of thinking about a culture. Nations have a sense of place but, more importantly, are a group of people. We talk about the French culture, the Russian culture and the Chinese culture.

Jewish American Community: Temple, Other Jews

Being a Jewish American means feeling part of a group or community. This community is often defined locally around the Temple or Synagogue but more broadly includes all Jews. However, within Judaism there are sects or denominations (Orthodox, Conservative, Reform, and, recently, Reconstruction), and these may define the boundaries of group membership for some. Clearly, non-Jews are defined as outsiders and the pervasiveness of Yiddish words that mark this status is a clear sign of the importance of distinguishing Jews from non-Jews (see chap. 16, this volume).

Your Cultural Code, Conversation, and Community

Stop for a moment and think about your own cultural group membership(s). Do you feel aligned with a particular group? Or, perhaps, more than one? Choose a group and see if you can describe its code, conversation, and community. In our college classes, students sometimes describe their fraternity or sorority as a culture, or even the entire university (e.g., Here at Penn State there are people who consider themselves "Penn Staters"). Others choose their ethnic or racial group, religious group, or nationality. Still others define their group by sexual orientation.

USING THE CULTURAL LENS

Thus far, we have described culture as a lens for viewing the human experience and explained that the lens focuses us on code, conversation and community. We noted, however, that in addition to focusing on a particular picture (e.g, codes or conversations or communities) the lens also provides a perspective on the content—in a sense zooming us in on the details or zooming us out to see the overview.

We approach this issue from a layered perspective—that is, we assume that culture exists on different layers or levels. Some people define culture as only the group (e.g., African Americans) ignoring individuals. We believe that culture is present in individuals as well as shared by collectivities and communities. Philipsen (1987) commented that we need to understand how people manage the tension between the pull of communal life and the impulse of individuals to be free, and that we need a definition of culture that addresses this dynamic push and pull (or "dialectic" as Baxter and Braithwaite explained in chap 15, this volume).

Examining culture from this perspective allows one to consider the polarities and contradictions in social life, rather than viewing culture as simply the group or the individual, or even as existing at some point along a continuum from one to the other (Hecht, 1993). Using a layer metaphor lets us see that polarities are present in all interaction, and it broadens the view of contradictions as polar opposites between two elements (e.g., individual and society). This seems especially relevant to the examination of culture given that culture exists and is expressed on multiple levels. Culture is not only a characteristic of the individual or society; it is a characteristic of both the individual and society as well as the interrelationships between the two. The notion of layering is a metaphor used to represent people's experiences and how they understand their experiences. We experience our social worlds in many ways including behaviorally, emotionally, spiritually, physiologically, experientially, and cognitively. These various realms are like "tides in the ocean, each integrated into the whole ocean (i.e., human experience) and yet each with identifiable characteristics (i.e., a separable realm of the experience)" (Hecht, 1993, p. 77). Thus, the final characteristic of the cultural lens is to identify layers or levels at which culture can be viewed.

THE LAYERS OF CULTURE

The Layered Approach (Baldwin & Hecht, 1995, 2000; Hecht, 1993; Hecht & Baldwin, 1998; Hecht, Jackson, Lindsley, Strauss, & Johnson, 2001) identifies four layers of culture: the personal, enacted, relational, and communal.

The *personal layer* examines one's self-concept or spiritual sense of well-being. Culture can be conceptualized as a characteristic of a person—who they think they are and how they see themselves (self-concept). Above, we illustrated code, conversation, and community by showing how Michael saw himself, his personal take on his culture.

But culture is also expressed in the way people communicate. This is called the *enacted layer* and focuses on how messages express culture. There are both direct and indirect ways of expressing culture. For example, you telling someone directly you are Morman or you can mention specific Morman people who you know to express it indirectly. In addition, culture is enacted through specific practices such as putting up a Christmas tree, singing the National

Anthem, fasting during Ramadan, or wearing a dashiki. Not all communication is about expressing identity, but much in what we say and do expresses who we are.

The *relational layer* refers to how one's culture is *formed* through one's relationships, is *invested* in one's relationship to other people, and *exists* in relation to one's other identities. We learn about culture through our families and teachers—through our relationships. We practice our culture with other people (e.g., religious and cultural celebrations, national holidays). Sometimes we even define ourselves in terms of our relationships (e.g., as someone's relational partner, someone's father, someone's friend). Often our cultural groupings are defined in terms of others, a process labeled ingroup or outgroup distinction.

These group distinctions are commonly evoked in intercultural communication. Dividing the world into ingroups and outgroups or us versus them is a natural phenomenon and thus, necessary to consider in intercultural research and practice. In fact, this is one of the key concepts in intercultural communication theory. The "intergroup perspective" has been developed by authors such as Tajfel, Giles, and others, and focuses on how people make distinctions between groups in which they feel memberships and those in which they do not, as well as how people communicate across group lines. Our national cultures, for example, are often contrasted with other groups, particularly if they are traditional enemies and rivals (e.g., England and France). Other examples of ingroups include professions, families, religions, and social clubs. Among adolescents, they can include distinctions based on interests, like the skaters versus the jocks, or based on musical interests. Consider all of the world conflict that results from religious differences. These ingroup and outgroup distinctions play a major role in intergroup relations and underlie some of the most serious problems the world faces today (e.g., in the Middle East and the Balkans–Eastern Europe). At times, just the act of categorizing people into two groups fosters intergroup discrimination (Tajfel, 1981).

What determines the nature of intergroup conflict? Intergroup threats are present when individuals experience anxiety about interacting with outgroups (Tajfel, 1981). Individuals tend to experience high levels of anxiety if there has been little prior contact with or knowledge about outgroup members. Conversely, anxiety also results from a history of intergroup hostility and competition, especially if one group has been in a minority or low-status position. This is evident in recent international conflicts (e.g., Bosnia, Middle East) as well as interracial relations in the United States. Anxiety about interaction also is related to ethnocentricity. Being able to only see your own country or groups' point of view is ethnocentrism. When people want to show solidarity with an ingroup, communication tends to converge and when differences between ingroups and outgroups are being expressed, communication tends to diverge (Giles & Coupland, 1991). Research by Hecht et al. (2003) revealed that satisfaction in ingroup conversations depends on feeling you have some power or control over the conversation as well as the establishment of relational solidarity; satisfaction with outgroup conversations is contingent on establishing common ground through the communication of acceptance, shared world view, not stereotyping, and understanding.

Finally, the *communal layer* focuses on how a group of people or some particular community shares an identity, such as being Jewish or Gay. A community possesses its own identity and shared visions of personhood. This is perhaps the most common way to see culture—as a group of people. When we talk about "Japanese culture" we are not focusing on individual Japanese people but, instead, talking about the collective or group as a whole. This notion of collectivity or community is certainly important to how culture is defined and should not be neglected. In fact, the communal layer is probably the most common way of thinking about culture. Unfortunately, focusing on culture as communal can also be the source of problems because if you assume that members of the culture automatically share common characteristics, you will have stereotyped them. That's why it is important to remember that most of the time when we talk about culture we are talking about characteristics of the community or collectivity, not the individuals.

Connections Among Layers

These four levels, or layers, can work individually, in pairs, or in any combination. For example, you might ask about the values of a specific cultural group (communal level). Or, you might wonder how an individual's view of herself (personal level) effects how she interacts with members of the outgroup (relational level).

In addition, the layers may be in conflict with each other such as a person who feels pride in his or her own religious identity, yet does not wish to participate in religious practices. Another conflict may be a couple who come from two differing groups (e.g., Muslim and Christian)—they see themselves as possessing a relationship or relational culture of their own (relational level), though the larger collectivity (communal level) may not approve.

Moreover, the layers are considered to be interpenetrating, that is they can be found within each other. For example, relationships help shape personal understandings while at the same time relationships are formed out of a person's culture. Thus, the relational layer is in the personal layer and the personal is in the relationship.

When these four layers are considered, culture can be seen as a *negotiation* among the individual, the enacted, the relational, and the communal layers or any combination of the four. For example, think of how a gay Jew in a committed relationship with a non-Jew negotiates identity and culture at these various levels.

This ends our discussion about conceptualizing culture. Certainly, there are many other factors to consider. Culture is intergenerationally transmitted (e.g, handed down from generation to generation; Murphy, 1986); it is the human-made part of the environment (Triandis, 1990); it encompasses our practices and behaviors that signal our differences (Fiske, 1992). Some would argue that the most important aspect of culture are the power relations and hierarchies it creates (Hall, 1986). However, for our purposes the concepts of code, conversation, and community considered at personal, enacted, relational and communal levels is adequate for understanding of culture.

In the remainder of this chapter we will consider a theory of culture at each of the four layers. We hope this review will provide you with some idea about how culture and communication have been conceptualized (although it is not meant to be exhaustive). It should be clear that culture and communication are inseparable. There can be no culture without communication that constitutes and creates the code, is the conversation, and binds and organizes the community. Similarly, communication requires a code to give it meaning and is a set of cultural practices engaged in within and between communities.

Personal Layer

A number of writers have talked about how culture shapes or creates the individual or self. For instance, Hofstede (1991) focused on cultural values. While he was interested in describing the values of entire cultures, other writers have shown how individuals in cultures use these values and are influenced by them (e.g., Triandis, 1994). Communal values influence individual's (e.g., being Japanese in a collectivistic country) self-concepts and behavior. Space precludes a discussion of all such values, so here we focus on *Individualism/ Collectivism* and *Gender* as cultural characteristics of individuals.

Individualism/Collectivism. Individualism versus collectivism is one of the most basic cultural dimensions. According to Tomkins (1984), an individual's psychological makeup is the result of this cultural dimension. For example, he reported that human beings in Western Civilization have tended toward positive or negative self-celebration, and in Asian thought harmony between humans and nature is another alternative that is represented. Whether people live alone, in families, or tribes depends on the degree of individualism-collectivism in a culture (Anderson, 1985). An emphasis on community, shared interests, harmony, tradition, the public good, and maintaining face characterize collectivistic cultures. Collectivism "pertains to societies in which people from birth onwards are integrated into strong, cohesive ingroups, which throughout people's lifetime continue to protect them in exchange for unquestioning loyalty" (Hofstede, 1991, p.51). Societies in which people look after themselves and those in their immediate families and where ties are loose characterize individualistic cultures (Hofstede, 1991).

In individualistic Western cultures, people rely on personal judgments (Triandis, 1994), whereas an emphasis on harmony among people, between people and nature, and on collective judgement can be seen in people from Eastern cultures (Gudykunst et al., 1996). People living in the United States, for example, tend to place a very high value on individualism (Bellah, Madsen, Sullivan, Swidler, & Tipson, 1985; Kim, 1994). More traditional and collectivist cultures place value on the interdependence among individuals and conforming to social roles and norms whereas individualistic and less traditional cultures stress independence in the pursuit of personal goals and interests and self expression. The best and worst in U.S. culture can be attributed to individualism. If we think of some of the positive elements, we may consider individualism as the basis of freedom, creativity, and economic incentive. The majority of Americans believe "that a man [or woman] by following his [or her] own interest, rightly understood, will be led to do what is just and good" (Tocqueville, 1945, p. 409).

On the other hand, individual consciousness may disrupt the systemic nature of life on earth by pulling humans out of their ecological niche, that is separating humans from nature with the increasing isolation and industrialization (Bateson, 1972). The downside of individualism includes alienation, loneliness, materialism and difficulty interacting with those from less individualistic cultures (Condon & Yousef, 1983; Hofstede, 1991). Thus, our individualism leads us to value creative ways of expressing ourselves (e.g., the person who is the "life of the party") but may challenge our ability to work together as a team (e.g., sacrifice for the common good).

Even though the United States is the most individualistic country (Hofstede, 1984/1990), certain ethnic groups and geographic regions vary in their degrees of individualism. For instance, African Americans place a great deal of emphasis on individualism (Collier, Ribeau, & Hecht, 1986; Hecht et al., 2003; Hecht & Ribeau, 1984; Kochman, 1981), whereas Mexican Americans place greater emphasis on relational solidarity and their families (Hecht & Ribeau, 1984; Hecht, Ribeau, & Sedano, 1990). This translates into a general tendency for African Americans to "tell it like it is" in conversations in order to preserve authenticity and Mexican Americans to focus on the relational with others in conversations, sometimes avoiding negative information in the process. There is a tendency to relay on *simpatia*, a preference for harmony in interpersonal relations such that negative comments may be ignored in a conversation.

Of course, the very notion of individualism suggests that a person's own values may transcend his or her cultural group membership. In fact, there is evidence that personal individualism may transcend cultural differences for certain variables. Singelis (1996) urged us to examine the connection between context and individual variables. Schmidt (1983), for example, compared the effects of crowding on people from the United States (an individualistic culture) and Singapore (a collectivist culture). Schmidt hypothesized that similar psychological variables would underlie people's stress and annoyance responses to crowding. He studied students at a U.S. university bookstore during the first 3 days of the quarter (a typically crowded time) and Singaporean high school students in their places of residence and found similar perceptions for both cultures on the relationships among personal control on annoyance and stress about environmental crowding. What we conclude is that no culture or individual is completely individualistic or collectivistic. All have some conception of the person as well as the group. What differs is the relative value placed on each and how people work out the competing pressures (e.g., the role of sacrifice).

Gender.   Although gender is typically thought of (and investigated as) as an individual characteristic, it has been neglected as a cultural dimension. We conceptualize this dimension of culture as the rigidity and definition of gender roles. Cultures that are more rigid expect members to act within a narrow range of gender-related behaviors and stress traditional gender- role identification. Hofstede (1984/1990) described masculine traits within such a world view typically as attributes such as strength, assertiveness, competitiveness, achievement, and ambitiousness, whereas feminine traits are attributes such as affection, compassion, nurturance, and emotionality. More rigid societies prescribe masculine behavior for men and feminine behavior for women, although there is a tendency for women in masculine societies to be "tougher" than women in feminine societies (Hofstede, 1998). "The masculinity–femininity dimension relates to people's self-concept: Who I am and what is my task in life" (Hofstede, 1984/1990, p. 84). A cross-cultural study comparing advertisements from Japan, Russia, Sweden, and the United States suggests that countries can be characterized along these masculine feminine dimensions. Milner and Collins (2000) discovered that television advertisements from feminine countries (Sweden, Russia) compared with more masculine countries (Japan, United States) contained more depictions of relationships for male and female characters. They conclude that a feminine country's dominant orientation is reflected in media, specifically television advertising and the depiction of characters in relationships.

Cross-cultural research shows that while young girls are expected to be more nurturant than boys though there is considerable variation from country to country (E. T. Hall, 1984). An important area to explore are the kinds of goals individuals value in their lives. Hofstede's (1984/1990) work examined the degree to which people of both sexes in a culture endorse primarily masculine or feminine goals. Goals such as competitiveness, assertiveness, ambitiousness, and a focus on material success are considered masculine, whereas nurturance, compassion, modesty, and a focus on the quality of life are considered feminine goals (Hofstede, 1998). A cross-cultural study with male and female Israeli Arab students (more traditional collectivist culture) and male and female Israeli Jewish students (more individualistic less traditional culture) demonstrated the role that culture plays in discriminatory behavior (Lobel, Mashraki-Pedhatzur, Mantzur, & Libby, 2000). Lobel et al. (2000) presented students with candidates for class representative, one male with traditional feminine interests (ballet) and characteristics (slight build) and one male with masculine interests (football) and characteristics (broad-shouldered build). The study revealed that all participants discriminated against the feminine male, but the Arab students discriminate more explicitly. They were less likely to elect him, to believe that others would freely choose him, and to think that he should be elected. Additionally, they liked him less than the masculine candidate and compared with the masculine candidate were less likely to report engaging in activities with him. The authors conclude that any transgression against gender norms in Arab culture is looked upon more harshly because of the collectivist tradition while more individualistic Israeli Jews are judged less critically for deviating from gender norms.

Given all of the differences we have described, what goals should we adopt? Research suggests that androgyny (combinations of both feminine and masculine goals) results in more self-esteem, social competence, success, and intellectual development for both men and women. In other words, it is actually healthier for both male and females to adopt more androgynous patterns of behavior. For instance, males may harm their health by internalizing emotions rather than externalizing them as women are usually apt to do (Buck, 1984). It would be helpful for those used to a "masculine" style to express their emotions. Being concerned with both the task (traditionally "masculine" qualities) and emotional issues (traditionally "feminine" pursuits) is important in our intimate relationships. Inman's (1996) research on men's same sex friendships showed that self-disclosure and expressivity were as vital to men's friendships as "continuity, perceived support and dependability, shared understandings, and perceived compatibility" (p. 100). Self-disclosure and expressivity benefit friendships, both male and female (Jones & Dembo, 1989). Furthermore, over time romantic partners are more less satisfied if partners adhere to stereotyped gender role expectations (Ickes, 1993). Quakenbush (1990) discovered that in dating and sexual relationships, androgynous men compared with men with masculine and undifferentiated gender roles, reported the most comfort.

Jackson (1997) provided yet another argument for the advantageousness of androgyny when he speaks of the cultural crossroads Black masculinity occupies. Black men alternate between embracing and rejecting the more rigid gender roles of American mainstream culture and the more androgynous and interdependent gender roles with their own culture. He believes that androgyny is an approach that should be taken given the difficulty of separating masculine and feminine characteristics. Individuals need all characteristics to get a sense of a cultural self and to foster a strong community (Jackson & Dangerfield, 2003).

In short, we discussed the dimensions of individualism–collectivism and gender as part of how culture shapes or creates the individual or self. Individualism refers to cultures where individuals are more loosely connected and focus on personal achievement whereas collectivism references cultures were strong and cohesive groups are the norm. However, all cultures display characteristics of both. Similarly, we argue that displaying masculine and feminine qualities is advantageous, even though cultures can be characterized broadly as masculine and feminine and gender roles vary to a great extent.

Relational Layer

The relational level focuses on relationships between different elements of a culture (e.g., how it balances individualism and collectivism), how a culture defines relationships between people, and on the relationships between people that are culturally based (i.e., intergroup relations; relations between members of different cultural groups). For example, Hecht et al. (1993) talked about how African Americans attempt to balance the desire for sharing or commonality with the group and the value placed on individuality (i.e., the relationship between different elements of the culture). Gaines and his colleagues (1996; Gaines & Ickes, 1997) studied interethnic romantic relations, concluding that people in these types of relationships are often more romantic (i.e., relationships between people that are culturally based). Others have been concerned with prejudice and discrimination between groups (Hecht, 1998), that is how a culture defines relationships between people. Thus, the relational level can focus us on the relationships between individual members of groups or between and among the groups themselves. *Co-Cultural Communication Theory* is one example of a relational layer approach that focuses on the relationships between groups and their members. The *Dialectical Approach* (see chap. 15, this volume) focuses on how elements of a particular culture relate to each other (e.g., how competing values are balanced) as well as how the balances struck among the elements within one culture (e.g., individualism and collectivism) relate to the balance in a second culture.

Co-Cultural Communication Theory.   Co-Cultural Communication Theory examines an assortment of domestic co-cultures in the United States in terms of elements such as age, class, sex, education, ethnicity, religion, abilities, affection or sexual orientation. Orbe (1996, 1998a, 1998b) described this perspective as an examination of how those traditionally without societal power communicate "within oppressive dominant structures" (Orbe, 1998a, p. 1). The term co-culture is used in order to avoid negative connotations from terms that have been employed to describe the many cultures within the United States. The connotations of "subculture" and "minority communication" suggest that less importance is attached to a group member's communication among the variety of co-cultures that exist in our society (e.g., people of color, women, gays/lesbians/bisexuals). Orbe preferred co-culture "to signify that no one culture in our society is inherently superior over other co-existing cultures" (Orbe, 1998a, p. 2).

Co-Cultural Theory is predicated on the belief that some co-cultures have gained dominance in major social institutions over time. As a result, these co-cultural groups (e.g., European Americans and men) figure centrally in predominant social structures such as religion, corporations, and legal entities rendering other co-cultural groups marginal. Co-Cultural Communication Theory examines how dominant and underrepresented group members interact with each other and across groups and is based on the assumption that some co-cultural groups (e.g., people of color) have developed communication orientations in the United States to survive because of their marginalized positions. Orbe (1998a) identified two premises of the theory:

1. Although representing a widely diverse array of lived experiences, co-cultural group members including women, people of color, gays/lesbians/bisexuals, people with disabilities, and those from a lower socioeconomic status will share similar societal positioning that renders them marginalized and underrepresented within dominant structures, and;

2. To confront oppressive dominant structures and achieve any measure of success, co-cultural group members adopt certain communication orientations when functioning within the confines of public communicative structures. These communication strategies will be addressed later in the chapter.

These premises recognize the similarities in co-cultural group members' experiences of sexism, racism, heterosexism, ableism (i.e., discrimination against those who are not able-bodied), and classism, while acknowledging different experiences in the daily lives of co-cultural group members. For example, two women can both be African American, but one could also be lesbian and experience homophobia in addition to racism. Co-cultural group members may overhear racist and sexist comments in the workplace (e.g., "Since we hired more women, there has been more gossip around here." "You know how lazy Mexicans are ... ") and use an avoidance strategy with co-workers.

Dialectical Approach.   A Dialectical Approach, while not a theory, highlights another aspect of the relational nature of intercultural communication. Whereas, Co-Cultural Communication Theory is concerned with how members of groups as well as the groups themselves relate to each other, the Dialectical Approach focuses us on how the elements of culture are related. How does one cultural value relate to another value? For example, a fraternity may value good grades but also see itself as a "party" group. How does a member balance the need to study for an important exam with the pressure to party that night? A school may be trying to develop a strong sense of community that includes responsibility to the group at the same time it wants its students to be creative. How does a student balance the individuality needed for creativity with the need to be part of the collective whole?

Drawing on previous theory, Baxter and colleagues suggested that the elements of communication are dialectically related to each other (for a summary of this approach to communication and relationships, see Baxter & Montgomery, 1996; Rawlins, 1992). This means that concepts like academics and partying, and creativity and community are not separate from each other. That is, we don't focus on one or the other, or even a fixed combination of each. Instead, they are competing or opposite pressures that work at the same time. If the culture values both we are unlikely to escape their influence. In fact, one would not want to, from a dialectical perspective, because we are interested in multiple points of view that affect each other. Rather than looking for a resolution in a middle ground or compromise, the Dialectical Approach highlights the continuing need to balance and rebalance competing forces. In fact, these forces are seen as part of the same whole or entity rather than as separate and inconsistent with each other. Thus, the dialectics or contradictions cause tension in relationships and cultures, but this tension is necessary and not necessarily antagonistic (Werner & Baxter, 1994). For example, individual autonomy and interdependence with another person defines any relationship. A person desires to be an individual while at the same time establishing a connection with another person. Both elements are necessary even though they are in opposition.

The Dialectical Approach has been applied to the study of culture by a number of authors (e.g., Carbaugh, 1989; Hecht et al., 2003; Martin, Nakayama, & Flores, 1998). We can identify at least two additional implications for the study of communication and culture that the Dialectical Approach gives us. First, it implies that both culture and the members of the culture change are in process. When we communicate with others, we can not assume that if a person belongs to a particular culture he or she will have certain characteristics. Individuals change during their lifetime, as does the cultural environment in which they live. For instance, the United States in the 1980s is not the same as the United States in the 21st century.

Second, dialectics places an emphasis on the relational rather than individual characteristics of people and culture. Looking at culture dialectically means that we look at the holistic relationships, that we focus attention between the aspects of intercultural communication, individuals and individuals in relationship to other groups. Martin et al. (1998) asked "Can we understand culture without understanding communication and vice versa (p. 6)?" They provide an example of the former Yugoslavia by asking "Can we understand the conflict in the former Yugoslavia by only looking at the Serbian experience" (p. 6)?

Cultural studies have described a number of specific dialectics. Some of these are characteristic of a particular culture (e.g., the dialectic between sharing and individuality with African American culture described above), while others tend to be present in most, perhaps all cultures. We will discuss more of the general dialectics in greater detail.

The first of these is the *cultural–individual* dialectic which refers to the idea that intercultural communication contains elements of both culture and individuals, that is individuals may have behaviors that are not shared by anyone else (e.g., a certain, idiosyncratic way of using language), and they may share communication patterns with others whom they share cultural practices (e.g., family members). For instance, your younger brother may call a lemon a neebee, but he may also call your Aunt, Tante, like everyone else in your family.

A second dialectic, that of *present–future/history–past*, represents the need to balance our past with the present and future. What is the relationship between past, present and future? Does the culture value one more than the other? Or does the culture value the flow from one to another? For some, the past is viewed through the present. Think about the Israeli–Palestinian conflict. Both Israelis and Palestinians share an important tie to Jerusalem, their holy city. To understand the conflict, we need to know the history of each people, yet the current view of the conflict depends on the context of what occurs today.

The relational elements are also emphasized in the final two dialectics: personal–social and privilege–disadvantaged. The *personal–social* dialectic emphasizes the connection between an individual's social roles and his or her personal characteristics. When a police officer talks about certain topics he or she may be interpreted in certain ways depending on the context. Imagine how differently you would interpret what the officer was saying if it were uttered while writing a ticket versus while relaxing with you at a local pizza pub. The final dialectic, *privilege–disadvantage*, involves the role of power in intercultural communication. We have different types of privilege and power (e.g., social position and political preference) as individuals, which we carry with us into interactions. For instance, the intercultural interactions of a U.S. tourist in Africa will be influenced by economic power and this establishes a different relationship with the citizens of the country than if the visitor was a worker who came from a poor nation in Southeast Asia.

Enacted Layer

It is important to understand that culture is not merely an abstract way of understanding the world. Rather, an important element of culture are the ways it is enacted—that is, how it is expressed by behavior, particularly communication, and how these behaviors are themselves cultural practices. So, our messages can announce our culture to others. But at the same time, culture cannot exist without its being expressed. So when we communicate we create and recreate our culture. *Communication Accommodation Theory*, described in another chapter, provides an excellent example of culture as enactment. It examines the process of how identity may affect communication and references how individuals are motivated to move towards or away from others through language and nonverbal communication. In addition, *Co-Cultural Communication Theory*, introduced in the previous section, not only talks about the relationships between groups but also how these relationships get enacted in communication. We continue our discussion of this theory below and link it to research on ethnic similarities and differences in communication.

Orbe (1996, 1998a, 1998b) revealed six factors that influence how co-cultural group members communicate within dominant social structures by examining oral narratives of individuals possessing a wide variety of co-cultural experiences. These factors include preferred outcome, communication approach, abilities, perceived costs and reward, field of experiences, and situational context. The six interrelated factors affect the communication and communication orientation group members possess. Each of these factors is intimately connected to the others.

Preferred outcome refers to the goal that a person has for an interaction and may affect the *communication approach* an individual adopts, that is the voice that a person uses which can be assertive, aggressive, or nonassertive. "Each person asks herself or himself the following question, 'What communication behavior will lead to the effect that I desire'" (Orbe, 1998a, p. 5)? Consciously or unconsciously, co-cultural group members answer this question about how their communication behavior affects the relationship between themselves and dominant group members. Nonassertive behavior describes actions where a co-cultural member puts others' needs before his or her own by being inhibited and nonconfrontational. Aggressive communication includes hurtfully expressive actions that are self-promoting and controlling (Orbe, 1998a). Somewhere in the middle of these two is assertive behavior that is characterized by expressive communication that enhances the self and takes others into consideration. Orbe (1996) described 12 strategies that co-cultural group members use when communicating with dominant group members. These include:

1. Avoidance is maintaining a distance with others, not getting involved, and only communicating with people that are different from yourself when necessary. A young gay man described this:

   > "I don't get involved too much ... They will have these conversations...but I don't get involved because I don't want to lead them on one way or the other (concerning his closeted identity). I just communicate what has to be done" (p. 163)

2. Idealized communication refers to no change in communication when conversing with others different from yourself. The idea that "people are people," means a person emphasizes individuals' similarities and ignores differences.

3. Mirroring is like assimilation. This strategy is used when a person wants "to make their co-cultural identities less visible while adopting those behaviors of the dominant culture" (p. 163). This is when a person "talks white" and avoids the use of slang and ethnic idioms.

4. Respectful communication is marked by graciousness, being less threatening and less assertive, and the use of formal titles. When talking to male supervisors, a 20 year-old woman stated "I am very aware of their expectations of me and try to follow them."

5. Self-censorship occurs when a person says nothing and "swallows it." A person could be afraid of another's reaction to an open and honest response, so they "blow it off" and say nothing.

6. Extensive preparation entails cognitive rehearsal and research. An African American man talked about how he prepared talking with European American men so that "I am much more through and pointed" (p. 165). Before an encounter with someone outside of your group, you extensively prepare.

7. Countering stereotypes refers to the negation of existing stereotypes. "I guess you can say that I make more of an effort to be a positive person so that people can see that those qualities [black, lesbian, woman] are not negative ones" (p. 165). A person tries to set a positive examples through their behavior without debating dominant group members about stereotypical beliefs.

8. Manipulating stereotypes is a reaction to dominant's cultures stereotypes by conforming to these stereotypes for personal gain. For instance, crying, flirting, or sweet-talking to "manipulate men."

9. Self-assured communication occurs when a person simply is themselves. This means exhibiting positive self-esteem. "I let my accomplishments and personality speak for me," said a Mexican American man (p. 166).

10. Increased visibility means increasing other people's awareness of the self. Things such as wearing signs of your background and occupying space where others can see you are ways to increase visibility.

11. Utilization of liaisons is using other individuals when interacting with those from the dominant culture. Liaisons include friends, advisors, colleagues, and empathetic supervisors.

12. Confrontational tactics are using direct and belligerent "in your face" methods when interacting with the dominant culture. A European American gay man discussed how he liked confronting heterosexuals with his homosexuality, "Flaming was not the word for me, I mean I wanted everyone to know and deal with it" (p. 167).

Assimilation, accommodation, and separation are three major outcomes of these interactions. If a person "adopts" mainstream culture and eliminates cultural differences to fit in with dominant society, this is assimilation. On the other hand, if a person, rejects the idea of forming a common bond with dominant groups or even other co-cultural groups and limits the amount of interaction with "outsiders," the outcome is separation. Accommodation falls in the middle and refers to an insistence that the dominant cultural rules change to incorporate the life experiences of co-cultural group members. Orbe (1998a, 1998b) crossed the three outcomes with the three communication approaches described earlier to arrive at nine general communication strategies co-cultural members use shown in Table 20.1.

Research by Hecht and colleagues (e.g., Hecht et al., 2003; Hecht et al., 1990) focuses attention on what some co-cultural members, specifically Mexican Americans and African Americans, find to be satisfying communication with European Americans and with one another. Their work provides examples of what a co-cultural perspective would call preferred outcome. They (Hecht & Ribeau, 1984; Hecht et al., 1990) found that Mexican American's preferred a comfortable communication climate developed by both parties where individuals could honestly express themselves without fear of retaliation, judgment, or rejection. Work with African Americans revealed similar themes; acceptance, emotional expressiveness, understanding, authenticity, achieving desired outcomes, and not feeling controlled and manipulated were important (Hecht et al., 2003).

We do need to recognize that individuals will have different *abilities* to establish and enact strategies that work for their goals. A person may not have the skill to surmount a nonassertive orientation to communication in an organization, for example, when a more assertive approach may be warranted for success in promotions (Orbe, 1998b).

Individuals may consider the *costs and rewards* of different communicative practices before they engage in them. For instance, Orbe's (1998b) work in organizations shows that taking an assertive assimilation stance may bring benefits to co-cultural group members in the form of social approval and salary increases. These costs and rewards are often determined by *field of experiences* which are the sum of a person's lived experiences. Past experience helps individuals recognize the consequences and efficacy of certain strategies in different situations. Orbe (1998b) quoted a young Mexican American man who believes that "my father's influence and general background has a lot to do with the way I act in public" (p. 250). Finally, given that situations influence how an individual decides on communication choices, the notion of *situational context* plays a central role in co-cultural theory. The number of other co-cultural members present in a situation, for instance, may affect whether a person manipulates stereotypes in the work place.

Communal Layer

Finally, we come to the communal layer, the layer probably most commonly thought about as culture. Communities, or collectivities, are the groups that share a common culture. Culture can be defined as these groupings, although we prefer to see the community as one way of viewing culture in order to avoid defining culture exclusively as people rather than as codes, enactments, and relationships discussed above. The *Ethnography of Communication* approach provides an excellent example of the communal layer.

TABLE 20.1
Nine General Co-Cultural Communication Orientations

Strategy	Examples
Nonassertive assimilation	Emphasize similarities Develop positive face Self-censorship Avert controversy
Assertive assimilation	Bargaining Manipulating stereotypes Overcompensating Extensive preparation
Aggressive assimilation	Dissociating Mirroring Strategic distancing Self-ridicule
Nonassertive accommodation	Increasing visibility Dispelling stereotypes
Assertive accommodation	Communicating self Intergroup networking Using liaisons Educating others
Aggressive accommodation	Confronting tactics Power moves
Nonassertive separation	Avoidance Maintaining interpersonal barriers
Assertive separation	Communicating self Intragroup networking Exemplify strengths Embrace stereotypes
Aggressive separation	Exert personal power Verbal attacking Sabotaging dominant group efforts

Note. Adapted from Orbe (1998a, 1998b).

The ethnography of communication provides us with a useful way of describing the place of speaking for people from different cultures and misunderstandings that can arise when people from different social groups interact (Carbaugh, 1985, 1989, 1993; Fitch, 1998; Philipsen, 1975, 1987, 1998). This method focuses on collecting and analyzing information about how social meaning is conveyed. More specifically, it illuminates how distinct cultural groups instill styles of communication among themselves and interpret others' communication (Saville-Troike, 1989). "The ethnography of communication takes language first and foremost as a socially situated cultural form, while recognizing the necessity to analyze the code itself and the cognitive process of its speakers and hearers" (Saville-Troike, 1989, p. 3). The ethnography of communication would be useful for exploring the interactions of ethnic groups that use the same language such as English-speaking Cuban Americans and European Americans. It would also prove beneficial for the exploration of groups that share the same language (e.g., African and European Americans) but have different speech codes (Orbe & Harris, 2001). We can compare communication styles within groups as well as across groups.

The idea of a speech community is central to the ethnography of communication. A group of people is considered to be a speech community when they share goals and styles of communication in ways not like those outside of the group (Philipsen, 1998; Saville-Troike, 1989). There are four assumptions that ground the ethnography of communication (Philipsen, 1998). One is that meaning is created and shared among members of cultural communities. The differences in groups can be defined by geography and language and also by less visible boundaries such as class. Second, because speech codes are guided by a system or some order, those in a cultural group need to coordinate their actions, that is members of a group must share an understanding of what behavior means. Third, individual groups have particular meanings and actions, and fourth, the assignment of meaning is determined by each cultural groups' distinct resources.

Work by Philipsen (1975) and Carbaugh (1998) demonstrated these assumptions by showing how cultural orientations relate to living. For instance, Carbaugh (1998) found that silence in Blackfoot culture is considered to be a listener-active mode of nonverbal presence important for "communicating with animals and spirits." Silence allows one to maintain interconnectedness, a valued event in Blackfoot culture, while public speaking threatens to disrupt the harmony and is, therefore, considered risky. Philipsen's work in a community he called Teamsterville also demonstrated the importance of examining cultural meaning about the value and importance of talk from the participant's point of view. He found that a sense of place in terms of "marking a place for speech" was different from many other communities; front porches and street corners represented proper places for people to interact. "In Teamsterville it is the presence of such identity-matched personae in a location traditionally set aside for sociability among them, to the exclusion of others, that marks a place for speaking" (p. 224).

When we look at the four assumptions posited by Philipsen (1998), we can see how misunderstanding may arise, particularly when individuals fail to recognize that what they consider to be appropriate use of language or what people should and should not say may not be considered the same in another speech community. For instance, Carbaugh's (1993) analysis of a series of 1987 Phil Donahue talk shows from the former Soviet Union demonstrated that public discussion of sexual matters was not preferable. According to Carbaugh, Donahue brought a private matter to a public forum when he discussed sex in a rational, technical, and individual way. However, in Russian culture public talk with outsiders should be reserved, while private talk shows a greater expressiveness among insiders. This is in contrast to the values expressed in the United States, particularly on television talk shows.

The end result of the ethnography of communication are descriptions of how diverse communities use speech and other channels of communication. Hymes (1974) wrote that "One needs fresh kinds of data, one needs to investigate directly the use of language in contexts of situation, so to discern patterns of proper speech activity" (p. 3). The methods of inquiry include the ethnographic tradition of participant observation where a researcher spends extended periods of time observing and studying a community. What researchers strive to accomplish is a holistic picture of communication behavior in the context of the community or network, "so that any use of channel and code takes it place as part of the resources upon which the members draw" (Hymes, 1974, p. 4). The idea here is to examine all facets of life that may impact communication behavior such as social institutions, roles and responsibilities, cultural values and beliefs, and the history of a community. "The starting point is the ethnographic analysis of the communicative conduct of a community" (Hymes, 1974, p. 9). This includes paying attention to the participants, the topics of conversation, the setting, and the event.

One goal of the ethnography of communication is communicative competence, skills that a speaker needs to know in order to communicate appropriately within a given speech community (Saville-Troike, 1989). To be successful, an individual needs to know the rules of interaction, as well as the cultural rules that dictate the content and context of interaction. That is, what should be said to whom, when, and how. One simple question that a researcher can ask is, "What is being communicated" (Saville-Troike, 1989)? The ethnography of communication makes an important contribution in its focus on what a person needs to know to communicate appropriately in various contexts and the sanctions that may occur for violations of communicative competence in a speech community.

CONCLUSION

In summary, we began our discussion of culture by highlighting three key concepts, *code, conversation,* and *community.* A code referenced the rules, meanings, beliefs, values, and images of the ideal, such as an appreciation for knowledge in the Jewish culture. We wrote about conversation as verbal and nonverbal interaction, for example a highly expressive and aggressive communication style. Community is a shared identity and a sense of membership (e.g., European Americans). Next, we used a layered approach to describe some intercultural theories that operate at each of the four layers, personal, relational, enacted, and communal; at the personal level we discussed *Individualism/Collectivism* and *Gender*, at the relational level *Dialectics* was introduced, we referenced *Co-Cultural Theory* at the enacted layer, and the *Ethnography of Communication* at the communal layer.

Theories of communication and culture are a rich and diverse area. There is much more to say about communication and culture. Recent work has used the construct of *identity* as an explanatory mechanism (Hecht, 1993). People have identities—senses of who they are—some of which are group based. Complete the following sentences:

I am _____
I am _____
I am _____
I am _____
I am _____
I am _____

Now look at your answers—do any of them mention a group (e.g., religion, race or ethnicity, gender, nation, occupation, school)? If so, then it is a group-based or cultural identity. These new approaches are concerned with how our identities affect communication and relationships (Hecht et al., 2003; Jackson, 1999; Tajfel & Turner, 1986), and help us understand how cultures function and how problems in intercultural relations emerge. Some have suggested that we use the more general term, *intergroup,* to describe these processes.

We have tried to show how important culture is by presenting theories about a the wide range of experiences it affects. Culture tells us who we are (at least in part) by shaping our values, perceptions, beliefs, and interpretations. It also defines our society and defines us in relation to our society. It guides our communication and relationships. Of course, a chapter like this is just a beginning. Like culture itself, it is a "never ending story."

REFERENCES

Anderson, P. A. (1985). Nonverbal immediacy in interpersonal communication. In A. W. Siegman & S. Feldstein (Eds.), *Multichannel integrations of nonverbal behavior* (pp. 1–36). Hillsdale, NJ: Lawrence Erlbaum Associates, Inc.

Baldwin, J. R., & Hecht, M. L. (1995). The layered perspective of cultural (in)tolerance(s): The roots of a multidisciplinary approach. In R. Wiseman (Ed.), *Intercultural communication theory* (pp. 59–91). Thousand Oaks, CA: Sage.

Baldwin, J. R., & Hecht, M. L. (2000). The social construction of race. *Studies in International Relations, 20*, 85–115.

Bateson, G. (1972). *Steps to an ecology of mind.* New York: Ballantine.

Baxter, L. A., & Montgomery, B. M. (1996). *Relating: Dialogues and dialectics.* New York: Guilford.

Bellah, R., Madsen, R., Sullivan, W., Swidler, A., & Tipson, S. (1985). *Habits of the heart: Individualism and commitment in American life.* Berkeley: University of California Press.

Borman, E. (1983). Symbolic convergence: Organizational communication and culture. In L. Putnam & M. Pacanowsky (Eds.), *Communication and organizations: An interpretive approach* (pp. 99–122). Newbury Park, CA: Sage.

Buck, R. (1984). *The communication of emotion.* New York: Guilford.

Carbaugh, D. (1985). Culture communication and organizing. *International and Intercultural Communication Annual, 8,* 30–47.

Carbaugh, D. (1989). *Talking American: Cultural discourses on Donahue.* Norwood, NJ: Ablex.

Carbaugh, D. (1993). "Soul" and "self": Soviet and American cultures in conversation. *Quarterly Journal of Speech, 79,* 182–200.

Carbaugh, D. (1998). "I can't do that! But I can actually see around corners": American Indian students and the study of "public communication." In J. N. Martin, T. K. Nakayama, & L. A. Flores (Eds.), *Readings in cultural contexts* (pp. 160–172). Mountain View, CA: Mayfield.

Collier, M. J., Ribeau, S. A., & Hecht, M. L. (1986). Intracultural communication rules and outcomes within three domestic cultural groups. *International Journal of Intercultural Relations, 10,* 439–457.

Condon, J. C., & Yousef, F. (1983). *An introduction to intercultural communication.* Indianapolis, IN: Bobbs-Merrill.

Fiske, J. (1992). Cultural studies and the culture of everyday life. In L. Grossberg, C. Nelson, & P. Treichler (Eds.), *Cultural studies* (pp. 154–173). New York: Routledge.

Fitch, K. L. (1998). *Speaking relationally: Culture, communication, and interpersonal communication.* New York: Guilford.

Gaines, S. O., Jr., & Ickes, W. (1997). Perspectives on interracial relationships. In S. Duck (Ed.), *Handbook of personal relationships* (2nd ed., pp. 197–220). Chichester, England: Wiley.

Gaines, S. O., Jr., Rios, D. I., Granrose, C., Bledsoe, K., Farris, K., Page, M. S., et al. (1996, January). *Romanticism and resource exchange among interethnic/interracial couples.* Paper presented at the annual meeting of the Social Psychologists in Texas, Arlington.

Geertz, C. (1973). *The interpretation of cultures.* New York: Basic Books.

Giles, H., & Coupland, N. (1991). *Language: Contexts and consequences.* Pacific Grove, CA: Brooks/Cole.

Gudykunst, W. B., & Kim, Y. Y. (1992). *Communicating with strangers: An approach to intercultural communication.* New York: McGraw Hill.

Gudykunst, W. B., Matsumoto, Y., Ting-Toomey, S., Nishida, T., Kim, K., & Heyman, S. (1996). Influence of cultural individualism-collectivism, self-construals, and individual values on communication styles across cultures. *Human Communication Research, 22,* 510–543.

Hall, E. T. (1984). *The dance of life: The other dimension of time.* Garden City, NY: Anchor.

Hall, E. T., & Hall, M. R. (1989). *Understanding cultural differences.* Yarmouth, ME: Intercultural Press.

Hall, S. (1986). Gramsci's relevance for the study of race and ethnicity. *Journal of Communication Inquiry, 10,* 5–27.

Hecht, M. L. (1993). 2002: A research odyssey-Toward the development of a communication theory of identity. *Communication Monographs, 60,* 76–82.

Hecht, M. L. (1998). *Communicating prejudice.* Thousand Oaks, CA: Sage.

Hecht, M. L., & Baldwin, J. R. (1998). Layers and holograms: A new look at prejudice. In M. L. Hecht (Ed.), *Communicating prejudice* (pp. 57–84). Thousand Oaks, CA: Sage.

Hecht, M. L., Jackson, R. L., & Ribeau, S. (2003). *African American communication: Exploring identity and culture* (2nd ed.). Mahwah NJ: Lawrence Erlbaum Associates.

Hecht, M. L., & Ribeau, S. (1984). Ethnic communication: A comparative analysis of satisfying communication. *International Journal of Intercultural Relations, 8,* 135–151.

Hecht, M. L., Ribeau, S., & Sedano, M. V. (1990). A Mexican American perspective on interethnic communication. *International Journal of Intercultural Relations, 14,* 31–55.

Hecht, M., Jackson, R. L., Lindsley, S., Strauss, S., & Johnson, K.E. (2001). A layered approach to ethnicity, language and communication. In H. Giles & W. P. Robinson (Eds.), *Handbook of language and social psychology* (pp. 429–450). New York: Wiley.

Hofstede, G. (1984/1990). *Culture's consequences.* Beverly Hills, CA: Sage.

Hofstede, G. (1991). *Cultures and organizations.* London: McGraw-Hill.

Hofstede, G. (1998). Masculinity/femininity as a dimension of culture. In G. Hofstede (Ed.), *Masculinity and femininity: The taboo dimension of national cultures,* (pp. 3–28). Thousand Oaks, CA: Sage.

Hymes, D. (1974). *Foundations in sociolinguistics: An ethnographic approach.* Philadelphia: University of Pennsylvania.

Ickes, W. (1993). Traditional gender roles: Do they make, and then break, our relationships? *Journal of Social Issues, 49,* 71–83.

Inman, C. (1996). Friendships among men: Closeness in the doing. In J. T. Wood (Ed.), *Gendered relationships* (pp. 95–110). Mountain View, CA: Mayfield.

Jackson, R. L. (1997). Black "manhood" as xenophobe: An ontological exploration of the Heglian dialectic. *Journal of Black Studies, 27,* 731–750.

Jackson, R. L. (1999). *The negotiation of cultural identity: Perceptions of European Americans and African Americans.* Westport, CT: Praeger.

Jackson, R. L., & Dangerfield, C. (in press). Defining black masculinity as cultural property: An identity negotiation paradigm. In L. Samovar & R. Porter (Eds.), *Intercultural communication: A reader* (10th ed., pp. 120–131). Belmont, CA: Wadsworth.

Jones, G. P., & Dembo, M. H. (1989). Age and sex role differences in intimate friendships during childhood and adolescence. *Merrill-Palmer Quarterly, 35,* 445–462.

Kim, U. (1994). Individualism and collectivism: Conceptual clarification and elaboration. In U. Kim, H. C. Triandis, K. Cigdem, C. Sang-Chin., & G. Yoon, (Eds.), *Individualism and collectivism: Theory, methods, and applications* (pp. 19–40). Thousand Oaks, CA: Sage.

Kochman, T. (1981). *Black and White styles in conflict.* Chicago: University of Chicago Press.

Linton, R. (1955). *The tree of culture.* New York: Alfred. A. Knopf.

Lobel, T. E., Mashraki-Pedhatzur, S., Mantzur, A., & Libby, S. (2000). Gender discrimination as a function of stereotypic and counterstereotypic behavior: A cross-cultural study. *Sex Roles, 43,* 395–406.

Martin, J. N., Nakayama, T. K., & Flores, L. A. (1998). A dialectical approach to intercultural communication. In J. N. Martin, T. K. Nakayama, & L. A. Flores (Eds.), *Readings in cultural contexts* (pp. 5–15). Mountain View, CA: Mayfield.

Milner, L. M., & Collins, J. M. (2000). Sex-role portrayals and the gender of nations. *Journal of Advertising, 29,* 67–79.

Murphy, R. F. (1986). *Cultural and social anthropology: An overview.* Englewood Cliffs, NJ: Prentice-Hall.

Orbe, M. P. (1996). Laying the foundation for co-cultural communication theory: An inductive approach to studying "non-dominant" communication strategies and the factors that influence them. *Communication Studies, 47,* 157–176.

Orbe, M. P. (1998a). From the standpoint of traditionally muted groups: Explicating a co-cultural communication theoretical model. *Communication Theory, 8,* 1–26.

Orbe, M. P. (1998b). An outsider within perspective to organizational communication: Explicating the communicative practices of co-cultural group members. *Management Communication Quarterly, 12,* 230–279.

Orbe, M. P., & Harris, T. M. (2001). *Interracial communication: Theory into practice.* Belmont, CA: Wadsworth.

Philipsen, G. (1975). Speaking like a man in teamsterville: Culture patterns of role enactment in an urban neighborhood. *Quarterly Journal of Speech, 61,* 13–22.

Philipsen, G. (1987). The prospect for cultural communication. In L. Kinckaid (Ed.), *Communication theory: Eastern and Western perspectives* (pp. 245–253). New York: Academic.

Philipsen, G. (1998). Places for speaking in teamsterville. In J. N. Martin, T. K. Nakayama, & L. A. Flores (Eds.), *Readings in cultural contexts* (pp. 217–226). Mountain View, CA: Mayfield.

Quackenbush, R. L. (1990). Sex roles and social-sexual effectiveness. *Social Behavior and Personality, 18,* 35–39.

Rawlins, W. K. (1992). *Friendship matters: Communication, dialectics, and the life course.* New York: Aldine de Gruyter.

Saville-Troike, M. (1989). *The ethnography of communication: An introduction.* New York: Basil Blackwell.

Schmidt, D. E. (1983). Personal control and crowding stress: A test of similarity in two cultures. *Journal of Cross-Cultural Psychology, 14,* 221–239.

Singelis, T. M. (1996). The context of intergroup communication. *Journal of Language and Social Psychology, 15,* 360–371.

Tajfel, H. (Ed.). (1981). *Human categories and social groups.* Cambridge, England: Cambridge University Press.

Tajfel, H., & Turner, J. C. (1986). The social identity theory of intergroup relations. In S. Worchel & W. Austin (Eds.), *The social psychology of intergroup relations* (pp. 33–47). Monterey, CA: Brooks/Cole.

Tomkins, S. S. (1984). Affect theory. In K. R. Scherer & P Ekman (Eds.), *Approaches to emotion* (pp. 163–195). Hillsdale, NJ: Lawrence Erlbaum Associates, Inc.

Tocqueville, A. D. (1945). *Democracy in America* (Vol. 1, Bradley, Trans.). New York: Random House.

Triandis, H. C. (1990). Theoretical concepts that are applicable to the analysis of ethnocentrism. In R. W. Brislin (Ed.), *Applied cross-cultural psychology* (pp. 34–55). Newbury Park, CA: Sage.

Triandis, H. C. (1994). Theoretical and methodological approaches to the study of individualism and collectivism. In U. Kim, H. C. Triandis, K. Cigdem, C. Sang-Chin., & G. Yoon, (Eds.), *Individualism and collectivism: Theory, methods, and applications* (pp. 41–51). Thousand Oaks, CA: Sage.

Werner, C. M., & Baxter, L. A. (1994). Temporal qualities of relationships: Organismic, transactional, and dialectical views. In M. L. Knapp & G. R. Miller (Eds.), *Handbook of interpersonal communication* (2nd ed., pp. 323–379). Newbury Park, CA: Sage.

Winkelman, M. (1993). *Ethnic relations in the U.S.* St Paul, MN: West.

QUESTIONS TO PONDER

1. We say that "culture is enacted through specific practices such as putting up a Christmas tree, singing the National Anthem, fasting during Ramadan, or wearing a dashiki." What happens when someone whom you would not typically identify as a member of a culture enacts the practices of that culture? For example, what do you think of white people who wear dashikis? Non-Christians who put up Christmas trees?

2. Think about your own cultural values and choices. If your family was having a reunion or celebrating a holiday together at the same time you were planning a great vacation or had a concert to attend, what would you do? What your family say?

3. Some people reading about Co-Cultural Communication Theory will dismiss it as "political correctness." First, consider how this charge might have some validity. For example, is it useful to assume that all white males are empowered? Are there situations in which a particular white male might not be in power? What assumptions of the theory might distort his experience? Conversely, can you see how U.S. culture has historically favored this group? If a white male got into a certain college (e.g., Yale) because previous members of his family did at a time when the college was exclusively white and male (and probably Christian), does this give him an advantage? What does this tell us about being "PC" as a cultural lens?

4. Choose on approach to culture discussed in this chapter. What does this approach tell you about communicating effectively with members of other cultures?

5. Apply the ethnography of communication to prejudice and hate speech. What would using this approach offer? How would this approach illuminate these problems?

21

Historical Contexts and Trends in Development of Communication Theory

Jennings Bryant and Dorina Miron
University of Alabama

This chapter is designed to discuss the foundation for the material you just read—a volume on contemporary communication theory. As such, our approach undoubtedly will be quite different from those of our companion contributors. For the bulk of our exposition, we will rely on history as epistemology. Caveat emptor—our "history" certainly will not be comprehensive. It will of necessity be incomplete and selective, because we have chosen and emphasized events and personalities, issues and trends in order to illustrate and even dramatize the fascinating evolution of communication theory

MILESTONES IN HUMAN COMMUNICATION THEORY THE ORIGINAL POLARITIES: WEST–EAST AND GOAL–STYLE

The earliest traces of knowledge about human communication date from the 3rd millennium B.C. The oldest documents generally considered in academic circles as precursors of communication theory are an essay containing advice about effective speech for the use of a pharaoh's son and a treatise on effective communication (*The Precepts*), composed in Egypt around 3000 B.C. and 2675 B.C., respectively (McCroskey & Richmond, 1996). They reflect attempts to preserve and transmit knowledge with practical value for a very limited number of people who formed the political elite in the largest ancient state situated south of the Mediterranean. Given the absolutist, highly centralized power structure in Egypt, communication was not yet important enough and did not have a wide enough scope to call for an elaborate, full-fledged theory. That happened north of the Mediterranean in the 5th century B.C., in the radically different political context of the Greek and Roman states.

Greek theorizing about rhetoric began in the 5th century B.C., at Syracuse, in Sicily, when a democratic regime was established after the overthrow of the tyrant Thrasybulus and its citizens flooded the courts to recover property that had been confiscated during his regime. The "art of rhetoric" developed by Corax and his student, Tisias, was intended to help ordinary people prove their claims in court. They are credited with a concept of message organization and a theory of how arguments should be developed from probabilities (McCroskey & Richmond, 1996). The doctrine of arguing from probabilities was the outcome of the general distrust of direct evidence caused by experience-based knowledge that such evidence "could be faked or bribed" (Kennedy, 1980, p. 21).

The public nature of oratory was rather narrowly defined as court-related activity, serving individual interests. The role of an orator as a persuader emphasized the importance of victory and focused attention to the source or speaker. Because good, successful, influential orators came to enjoy special social status and power, oratory naturally began to be associated with the political power play in society. The increasing value socially attached to rhetoric made it worth studying, which triggered its development as a science and as an educational subject.

During the 5th century, itinerant teachers of rhetoric, the sophists, were disseminating the art of succeeding in the civic life of the Greek states (Kennedy, 1980, p. 25). Protagoras, the father of debate, taught persuasion for political and court use, and founded the science of grammar. Gorgias enhanced orator power by perfecting style. He borrowed speech forms from poetry and emphasized artificial stimulation of emotions for deceptive-persuasive purposes. The sophists advanced two directions of rhetoric: technical rhetoric (handbooks and the teaching of *techne* "art") and sophistic rhetoric ("literary oratory" involving stylistic refinement and the display of eloquence before an audience, for enjoyment and ceremonial purposes). The third direction evolved in opposition to sophistic rhetoric, which was perceived as frivolous cultivation of form and disregard of substance and moral values. The critics' concern with deeper and broader issues gave birth to philosophic rhetoric, which dealt with message validity and had close ties with logic, ethics, and what is now called audience psychology. Rhetoric can thus be considered a starting point for the differentiation of various areas of theorizing within philosophy and, more widely, within the domain of social sciences.

The illustrious Socrates was a rhetorician of the exclusively oral tradition. His death and fame were brought about by his self-defense discourse in the Athenian court, when he was on trial for corrupting the youth through his speeches, and he chose to value truth more than his own life. Socrates' theoretical contribution to philosophic rhetoric was the dialectic as a method of argumentation and truth finding. This was preserved through the writings of his contemporaries and disciples, especially Plato, who proposed a formal theory of dialectic as a process or method of discovering independently existing truths (as opposed to the sophistic subservience to predetermined persuasion goals that were indifferent to truth). In *Phaedrus,* Plato introduced the notions of audience analysis and speech adaptation to audience.

Aristotle, Plato's student at the Academy, was "the foremost theorist in the history of the study of human communication from the rhetorical perspective" (McCroskey & Richmond, 1996, p. 235). He founded the Peripatetic School in Athens and synthesized the communication knowledge of the time in a comprehensive, orderly, and creative treatise of *Rhetoric* (about 330 B.C.), which became "the most influential work on the topic" (p. 235). Aristotle's greatest contributions to communication theory often are considered to be in the area of persuasion theory. In his system, persuasion required adaptation to both situation and audience psychology. The means of persuasion could be inartistic (i.e., facts) or artistic: *ethos* (roughly corresponding to the modern concept of speaker credibility), *pathos* (emotionality), and *logos* (reasoning, proving truth). Aristotle (1954) agreed with Plato that the role of rhetoric was "to discover (*theoresai*) the available means of persuasion" (*Rhetoric*, 1.1.1355b25–6). Thus, the highest level of conceptualizing science reached in ancient Greece by Plato and Aristotle pictured truth as existing independently from theorists, whose job was to discover it for themselves and others by reasoning, using dialectic as a method. *Logos* was important as the means to develop knowledge/conduct Science, which at the beginning had no other method than reasoning through language. In this sense, early speech science coincides with the beginning of scientific methodology for other sciences.

At approximately the same time as the explosion in theorizing about rhetoric was blooming in ancient Greece, knowledge about communication was independently building up in the Far East. Broadly speaking, communication in ancient Asia was modeled on various philosophical systems, the most influential being Taoism and Confucianism, which emerged in China, and Buddhism, which emerged in India in the 6th century B.C. and then spread to other Asian countries. Communication principles in Asia were deduced from philosophy rather than induced from specific practical needs at particular moments.

The three major philosophies that developed in Asia in the 6th to 5th centuries B.C. established sets of beliefs that allowed for convergence toward a broad Asian model of communication oriented primarily inwardly rather than outwardly (as it evolved in the Mediterranean area). In China, Taoism promoted naturalism and simplicity, individualism and freedom, the search for harmony, and knowledge of the eternal through insight. It attacked formalities and artificialities. Confucianism started as a movement of social responsibility and social reforms, seeking harmonious social order, and propounding the doctrine of the mean.[1] It contributed the social component of philosophy that Taoism was missing, and placed it under the same overarching principle of harmony. Confucianism was very influential in China under the Han dynasty, when it became a state doctrine (136 B.C.). Its scholars and their disciples, whose prestige came from their knowledge of the classic texts, formulated social and moral concepts, controlled education, practically monopolized government, and even wrote and interpreted history in their light.

In India, *The Turning Wheel Doctrine* of Gautama Buddha advanced four basic truths: the pain, craving as the cause of pain, detachment as the way to cease pain, and the path that leads to the cessation of pain. Included in the path are the right view, right thought, and right speech (no lying, tale bearing, harsh language, or vain talk), right action, right livelihood, right effort, right mindfulness, and right concentration. Buddhist monks taught these principles of inner discipline to junior aspirants to salvation, but they also preached to laymen during the rainy season, which accounts for the massive impact of this system of thinking at the social level.

The primary goal of communication in Taoism and Buddhism was knowledge of the self and of the essence of the world, rather than informing and influencing others or manipulating the external world. As a consequence, communication took a "transcendental" form geared toward the eternal reality assumed to underlie all temporary events, including one's own individual existence. Such a form of communication was radically different from the transactional European type of communication. The method of transcendental communication involved intuitive interpretation (distinct from the rational conceptualization practiced around the Mediterranean).

---

[1] The European concept of "golden mean" was introduced in the Renaissance by Italian mathematician Luca Pacioli (1587/1980) in his treatise Divina Proportione, and represented an aesthetically satisfying ratio 8:13. Its impact was primarily on fine arts, where it influenced Leonardo da Vinci and Albrecht Dürer.

According to Kennedy (1980), "direct connection between the tendency toward conceptualization of rhetoric in India, China, and Greece is unlikely, even though the developments are roughly contemporary" (p. 7). Some consciousness of rhetorical method was evident in ancient India in the 6th century B.C. in the Buddha's advice to his followers about preaching, and a group of treatises and poetics in Sanskrit dealt with what in the Mediterranean area was called secondary rhetoric (see Oliver, 1966, pp. 94–96). Even greater interest in rhetorical methods can be found in ancient China in some writings by and about Confucius in the 6th and 5th centuries B.C. and in the treatise *Difficulties in the Way of Persuasion by Han Fei Tzu* (1940), composed in the 3rd century B.C. (see Oliver, 1966, pp. 100–104). Thus, in spite of geographic separateness and somewhat different timing, the broad polarization in theory development was similar in the West and the East: goal (persuasion) versus style (*letteraturizzazione*, poetics). As far as persuasion is concerned, in the Mediterranean, the emphasis on political and legal rhetoric preceded the flourishing of religious/missionary rhetoric.

The eastern philosophical systems played out slightly differently in various countries of Asia (Cushman & Kincaid, 1987). In Korea, Buddhism influenced communication in the same way as in India, cultivating skepticism of all knowledge based on categorizations of language and reliance on pure sensation and intuition. An instantaneous form of communication developed in which understanding was achieved in a fleeting moment as a "meeting of the minds," with no message stated, therefore no European-type distinction between source and receiver. Silence became full of meaning through implicitness and ambiguity (Cushman & Kincaid, 1987, p. 14).

Confucianism brought a new perspective on silence in Korean culture. Confucian morality assumed emotions to be the source of bad conduct. The goal of social cohesion was believed to be best served by accommodation, which required reduction of emotions. Consequently, taciturnity in interpersonal relations was preferred to verbal communication, and the effectiveness of communication came to depend on sensitivity to nonverbal cues. Other means of maintaining group cohesion were obligation and loyalty. Favors were done and obligations were created in order to increase interdependence (Cushman & Kincaid, 1987). The priority given to group-life optimization made communication an instrument of community building rather than a tool in the hands of separate individuals working competitively to attain their personal and often conflicting goals, as it developed to be in the West.

In Japan, the same Buddhist foundation discouraged reliance on verbal communication and emphasized sensation and intuition as methods of developing knowledge. What in Korea was instantaneous meeting of the minds, in Japan was *ishin-denshin*, traced to the search for truth between Zen masters and their disciples (Cushman & Kincaid, 1987). Concern with group harmony resulted in a similar tendency toward taciturnity. The distinctive Japanese nuance was *kuuki* (mood, consensus of feeling), a social-emotional atmosphere achieved without the use of language. The general Buddhist skepticism about language took a special twist in Japan later on, in medieval times, under severe restraint on communication imposed by feudal authorities for mostly political reasons. The special feature of communication that developed was indirectness, the "discrepancy between the meaning of the surface sentence uttered and the 'real' meaning intended by the speaker" (Cushman & Kincaid, 1987, p. 18). The latter had to be inferred with the help of traditional rules that had to be learned. Correct decoding and effective speech involved taking the role of the other.

Obviously, this is a selective exemplification of "geographic" variations within the Asian tradition of communication. Our purpose is to illustrate that in spite of many country-specific developments, human communication theory across Asian countries was originally very similar because of the common philosophical foundations of the model. On the other hand, we wanted to indicate how the different roots of the communication paradigms, political in the West and philosophical in the East, developed independently at about the same time (Kennedy, 1980) into two very different systems.

Over time, the differences in communication theory between the East and the West diminished somewhat with the expansion of commercial and cultural exchanges. Initially, the stronger influence was from the West towards the East: "The oratory of traditional societies has been subtly influenced by western conventions since the first contacts with Europeans, and the description of traditional rhetoric has been influenced by categories of Greek rhetoric" (Kennedy, 1980, pp. 7–8). Cushman and Kincaid (1987) suggested that in the long run the reciprocal influence is more balanced, because each system has adopted elements from the other, although some traditional forms of communication withered away in the historical process, leaving room for new imported forms expected to serve the needs of the day. As McCroskey and Richmond (1996) argued,

> It is not pragmatic … to conceive of these two [Western and Eastern] approaches to the study of communication as polar opposites. Rather, they represent differences in emphasis … . While individualism, competition, and straightforward communication are highly valued in most western societies, eastern societies have higher values for congeniality, cooperation, and indirect communication which will protect the 'face' of the people interacting. Maintaining valued relationships is generally seen as more important than exerting influence and control over others. (pp. 234, 238)

THE EAST–WEST POLARIZATION IN THE MEDITERRANEAN AREA: THE ATTIC AND THE ASIATIC SCHOOLS OF RHETORIC

The Hellenistic Age

The end of the classical Greek period is considered to be the second half of the 4th century B.C., marked by the death of Alexander the Great in 323, and of Aristotle and Demosthenes in 322 B.C.. The following three centuries in Greece are known as the Hellenistic Age, when the influence of the Greek school of rhetoric spread throughout the eastern Mediterranean, facilitated by *Koine*, a simplified form of the Attic dialect of Greek, which had become a universal language throughout Alexander the Great's empire. The geographic spread led to a stronger polarization among rhetoricians, who formed two competing groups, the Attic School, including those who preferred the style of the 5th and 4th centuries B.C. and such orators like Thucydides and Remoistens, and the Asiatic School, including those who preferred "an artificial and flowery style somewhat similar to that of Gorgias, mainly orators from Asia Minor" (Infante, Rancer, & Womack, 1990, p. 103). Neither group made major innovations, however.

The Roman Empire

The Romans vigorously upheld the Greek tradition of rhetoric, and their empire "helped to spread its use across the ancient world" (McCroskey & Richmond, 1996, p. 236). The 1st century A.D. was crucial. Cicero, often considered to be "the greatest orator," continued to support the Greek's view that rhetoric was a part of politics (*civilis ratio*). In *De Inventione*, Cicero (84 B.C./1949) established five canons or subdisciplines of rhetoric: invention, arrangement/organization, style, memory, and delivery. Invention and delivery were new emphases added to the classical Greek rhetoric. Cicero proposed three duties/goals of oratory—to prove, to delight, and to stir—and theorized on the three corresponding styles: the plain style (clear and moderate, similar to the Attic School style), the middle style, and the grand style (very ornamental, similar to the Asiatic School style).

Another great figure of the 1st century A.D. was Quintilian, considered by many to be "the greatest teacher" of oratory (McCroskey & Richmond, 1996, p. 236). He held an official chair of rhetoric paid for by government funds. Quintilian (94/1963) integrated rhetorical theories to form a complete system for the *Education of a Rhetor/Institutio Oratoria*. His treatise is the longest existing Latin work on rhetoric. Quintilian championed the classical Greek belief in the civic role of rhetoric. He believed that rhetoric was the centerpiece in the training of a citizen (Kennedy, 1980).

The Second Sophistic

Yet another great name in the 1st century A.D. was Longinus, a Greek rhetorician who critiqued the sophistic movement. His treatise On *Sublimity* (Longinus, 1554/1985) considered the sources of rhetorical power to be great thought and strong emotion. His emphasis on style and emotional effects paved the way for the emerging Second Sophistic (1st–4th centuries), a primarily Greek movement, imitated by the Romans. The Second Sophistic carried on the flourished-style tradition and influenced the Christian sophistry.

BEGINNINGS OF MASS ENTERTAINMENT

Not all early developments in communication theory were in rhetoric. As observed by Zillmann (2000), "from the onset of the first century A.D. to the beginning of the fourth century, the Roman Empire enjoyed enormous prosperity. Mostly as a result of its unprecedented wealth, leisure became an entitlement across all strata of Roman society" (p. 9). The luxuriousness in rhetorical style displayed by the Second Sophistic at the elite level was paralleled at the mass level by the luxury of popular entertainment in the form of games, chariot races, and gladiatorial fights. The proportion of this "mass" entertainment phenomenon is revealed by the capacity of theaters (e.g., Circus Maximus rebuilt in the 1st century B.C. to seat 150,000 spectators and in the 4th century A.D. to seat 250,000) and by the frequency of public holidays devoted to such games—93 during the reign of Claudius, and 200 by the middle of the 4th century (Zillmann, 2000). The Roman games were the first form of mass leisure in history. The massification of public spectacles involved a degradation of content from communicative events (drama) to primarily physical events. In spite of the fact that the Roman circus was unrelated to speech communication, it remains interesting as a mass phenomenon, because it seems to have created tremendous audience loyalty, perhaps even entertainment "addiction" (long before the age of television).

THE CHRISTIAN SOPHISTIC

The most prominent figure of the Judeo-Christian rhetoric was St. Augustine. He held the chair of rhetoric in Milan, then became a priest, then a bishop in Hippo. St. Augustine adapted rhetorical training, initially designed for secular use, to serve religious needs for preaching effectiveness. By doing this, he practically expanded the domain of public speech, originally limited to deliberative and judicial oratory, to include religious communication. According to Infante et al. (1990), the influence of Augustine is also important because it "permitted rhetoric to retain its role in education at a time when church writers mounted attack on virtually all elements of Greco-Roman culture" (p. 107) for introducing false gods.

St. Augustine's (1747) *De Doctrina Christiana* came close to being a rhetorical theory. It was based on Cicero's rhetoric. Like Plato's theory, it proposed that public speaking was the pursuit of absolute truth. The difference from Plato was that the source of the Christian truth was God's law. The task of the speaker was more modest than the Socratic working out of truth through dialectic. Preachers were vehicles through which God's message was expressed, but they still had some responsibility in acquiring and exercising persuasive skills. Cicero's three duties of an orator—to prove, to delight, and to stir—were replaced by St. Augustine with three functions: to conciliate those who are opposed, to arouse those who are remiss, and to teach those ignorant of his subject. St. Augustine's public was radically different from that of classical Greco-Roman rhetoric. Instead of legislatures and courts of law, the preachers typically addressed ordinary people. The arousing speech was supposed to elicit positive emotions and thus create an emotional connection to the source. The preaching was supposed to communicate scripts, to mobilize for action. All these principles can be found in modern advertising and public relations, which are not at all new as communication subdisciplines.

In addition, the students of Christian rhetoric were trained to address a more inclusive public, with different means at the grassroot and the elite levels. This enabled the movement to develop more control and political power. The strategy of audience inclusiveness and discourse differentiation became a rule in modern political campaigns.

Christian rhetoric was also creative in terms of forms. Innovation was driven by changes in the content and in the nature of the public. Some classical forms were adapted: The covenant speech involved reference to the past and was related to classical judicial oratory; the prophecy involved reference to the future and was related to deliberative oratory. However, the lack of education at the level of the masses made persuasion problematic. To make their messages clearly understood, preachers could no longer rely on dialectic reasoning; they had to resort to explanation in everyday language, exemplification, and illustration. They adopted proverbs from the secular lore, introduced homilies (informal interpretations of Scripture texts), and used dramatic visualizations (allegories and miracles) to convey abstract notions.

THE MIDDLE AGES: THE SECOND EAST–WEST POLARIZATION IN THE MEDITERRANEAN AREA

The end of the 4th and the beginning of the 5th century A.D. brought significant political changes in the Mediterranean space. Under increasing pressure from neighbors in the west and north, the Roman Empire moved its capital to Byzantium (324), which became Constantinople (330). On the death of Theodosius (395), the empire was permanently split into an eastern and a western half. The latter fell in 476, and three Germanic kingdoms became the centers of power in western Europe. Latin continued to be the international language of politics, religion, and scholarship (Kennedy, 1980), and was used more extensively in western Europe, whereas Greek was the official language in the eastern half of the Roman Empire (the Byzantine Empire).

According to Kennedy (1980), the barbarian attacks in the west put an end to orderly civic life. "Poverty, fear, poor communications became endemic; libraries were destroyed; books disintegrated and were not recopied; knowledge of Greek faded" (p. 174). A major shift occurred in western medieval rhetoric: The role of the speaker was de-emphasized, and the speech itself became central (though the speaker-centered tradition was preserved in the eastern half of the Roman Empire). "Some interest in the audience was also demonstrated by [western] writers on dictamen (letter writing) and on preaching" (Kennedy, 1980, p. 193).

During this time, the church finally defeated the Roman tradition of mass entertainment. Popular merriment "went underground" and "theater moved into the church" (Zillmann, 2000, p. 11). Christianity, in its desire to educate the mostly illiterate population, did not destroy theatre but put it to use in preaching the gospel. Gradually, the liturgical drama (miracles and mysteries, morality plays and allegories) came to include more secular interludes, clownery and sottish play (Berthold, 1972), which drew larger audiences, so that the dramas had to move out of the church building into the public square.

The medieval leisure class needed courtly diversions as a remedy for boredom. Strolling players were invited to perform at private festivities. Such histriones were trained in speech, dance, mime, music making, and acrobatics. They provided more or less impromptu entertainments with secular content that often incorporated gossip (Bucknell, 1979). Thus theatre as a communicative art differentiated significantly during the Middle Ages to meet the needs of the upper- and lower-class audiences. Its content polarized into religious-didactic and entertaining daily-life trivia. The former was conveyed in more formalized structures akin to religious rhetoric, but the latter came closer to everyday speech and, allowed for looseness and more creativity.

Throughout this era, the Byzantine Empire in the northeastern part of the Mediterranean area kept alive the ancient tradition of rhetoric. The empire was struggling to maintain "cultural stability and permanence in the face of destruction of the classical world and the dangers from the alien societies of Slavs to the north, Arabs to the south, Turks to the east, and a varied horde of semi-barbaric 'Latins' to the west" (Kennedy, 1980, p. 169).

However, it is now generally believed that the "Byzantine rhetoricians made no important contribution to rhetorical theory" and rhetorical studies did not significantly change throughout the Byzantine period because "there was little significant change in the need for rhetoric, its functions, or its forms, as perceived by the leaders of society" (Kennedy, 1980, pp. 169–170). The merit of medieval rhetoricians both in the Byzantine Empire and the western part of Europe was that they preserved classical rhetoric "as a living tradition for a thousand years" (Kennedy, 1980, p. 171) and made it available for more creative use when the economic and political situation began to change towards the end of the first millennium.

THE RENAISSANCE OF CLASSICISM AND THE PRINT REVOLUTION

Major changes in communication study began in the West, in the 8th century, when "the first glimmerings of a new civic life emerged in Italy" (Kennedy, 1980, p. 173). Venice, then Pisa, Pavia, and Bologna in the 9th and 10th centuries became important commercial centers. By the 11th century, the commune movement had created assemblies, councils, and courts of law with a jury system in many Italian municipalities. Opportunities for public speech increased and "Latin oratory reemerged as a major form of human communication" (Kennedy, 1980, p. 197), spurred by a new sense of civic responsibility and appreciation of liberty. "It was in this setting, not totally different from the city-states of antiquity, that rhetoric reemerged as a practical subject of study in Italian schools and communities" (p. 173) between the 11th and the 14th century and in the first universities founded between the 11th and the 13th century. The new life of Italian cities revived deliberative and judicial oratory, increased interest in the

Roman law, and gave prominence to dictamen (letter writing) and the associated arts of the notary.

Preaching continued to be emphasized as a branch of rhetoric by the new orders founded in the 13th century (e.g., Dominican, Franciscan). But it was the Reformation/Counter-Reformation propaganda in the 16th century, involving church and state authorities as well as individual thinkers (e.g., Calvin, Luther, Melanchton, Erasmus) that gave religious rhetoric brilliance and political prominence. The activities of the Counter-Reformation kept rhetoric within its classical boundaries. The Roman Inquisition established in 1542 to combat heresy cultivated judicial rhetoric, the anti-Reformation cooperation between the Roman Catholic Church and various states maintained a vigorous political tradition of oratory and dictamen, and the missionary activities of the Counter-Reformation continued the rhetorical tradition inaugurated by the Christian Fathers.

The increased opportunities for rhetorical practice during the Renaissance stimulated scholarly interest in the ancient sources. *Aristotle's Rhetoric* was recovered (1240) in Latin translation from Arabic. But, for communication science, the Renaissance was not a mere salvation and resurrection of the ancient rhetorical tradition, it brought a revolutionary change. The invention of the printing press by the German Gutenberg[2] in the 1430s–1450s opened the era of mass communication by introducing the first mass medium: the printed book. With the advent of printing, libraries grew and access to them expanded.[3] Beside the dramatic increase in the circulation of texts, printing gradually effected a change in content, which came to include secular, practical, and popular texts, not only in Latin and Greek, but also in vernacular languages.

The wider circulation and the more comprehensive content facilitated the dissemination of knowledge and made possible the enlightenment of the public, not only of elites. The extension into the public sphere of written communication, "an activity that had long taken place for governmental, diplomatic or commercial purposes," involved "struggle for freedom to publish" and an adversarial relation with the established power (McQuail, 2000, pp. 20–21). For authorities, printing represented a potential loss of control; for the population, it was a promise of emancipation and empowerment. A manifestation of the antiestablishment attitude and of the democratization process triggered by the invention of the press was the challenge of papal authority by the Protestant Church and the whole Reformation movement.

Printing also caused a change in the status of rhetoric. Originally a speech science, rhetoric expanded to include more and more written forms of communication, exercising authority even in the domain of language-based productive arts like poetry and theatre. A problem of boundary definition emerged during the Renaissance, and two divergent directions developed in the 15th century. One was of restricting or subordinating the domain of rhetoric. The second direction was one of expanding rhetoric. During the Renaissance, many saw rhetoric as no longer essentially civic and exclusively oral, no longer limited to speech and debate (i.e., expression through language); it came to be applied to painting and music. The blurring boundaries among arts contributed to an enrichment of speech with artistic qualities (e.g., visual images, sound). Francis Bacon, at the end of Renaissance, reintroduced the concept of imagination—treated in antiquity as invention—as rhetorically important (Kennedy, 1980).

Paradoxically, the wider practical application of rhetoric during the Renaissance did not significantly advance it much as a science. One limiting condition was education. "The elementary nature of most rhetorical studies in the Renaissance contributed to the failure of

---

[2]"Printing was invented in northern Asia long before Gutenberg." (Nordenstreng, 2000, p. 329)

[3]The concept of public library, funded by local government, did not appear until mid-19th century.

Aristotle's *Rhetoric* to become a major influence. … Cicero, the *Rhetorica ad Herennium*, and Quintilian remain the ultimate authorities behind the simpler handbooks" (Kennedy, 1980, p. 204). Another cause was the perception that rhetorical science had already covered all the major topics. Theoretical developments were rather rare and limited to form and to issues considered of secondary importance, like entertainment.

As far as entertainment is concerned, theoretical advances occurred in association with the changes undergone by theater. The shift from the predominantly secular content in ancient theater towards religious dramatization in the Middle Ages was gradually reversed during the Renaissance, when political topics and ordinary life prevailed once again (e.g., Shakespeare's historical dramas and *Romeo and Juliet*). In the Renaissance, theater became institutionalized entertainment, with its own quarters[4] and full-time professionals. The lengthy plays, written and produced to fill the leisure time of an increasingly large and devoted audience, including the new middle class, triggered a growing disregard for the rhetorical rules of antiquity and an emphasis on production for enjoyment. For instance, Italian Gian Giorgio Trissino (1529) elaborated a humor theory in *La Poetic*. In France, Montaigne introduced the notion that people, in the interest of their mental welfare, must escape from reality, and entertainment, as a provider of instant escape and relief, performed a therapeutic function (Zillmann, 2000, p. 15).

Another change with implications for communication science was a major split in scientific methodology. Trade, increased production, massive construction, and inventions focused entrepreneurial minds on getting things done in practice. This led to an applied, pragmatic, and inductive trend in science. The ancient rationalistic (Platonic–Aristotelian) way of doing science deductively, by reasoning from prior theories, was no longer adequate or sufficient in an environment of increasing novelty, where innovations and discoveries raised problems radically different from those of the ancient world. These and related developments led to clashing trends in the theory arena.

At the end of the Renaissance, Francis Bacon elaborated formally and systematically a new system of inductive science based on observation. His theory provided a foundation for natural sciences as a class, which split methodologically from humanities. Rhetoric remained within the humanities, but subsequent inquiry into social phenomena, including human communication, could choose between the two approaches, speculative-deductive and empirical-deductive.

THE ENLIGHTENMENT: RHETORIC LOSES GROUND

The Enlightenment period that followed (17th and 18th centuries) aggravated the discord between humanists and scientists and placed rhetoric in an ambiguous light. At a first glance, the neoclassical culture of the time appears to have carried on the ancient tradition. According to McCroskey and Richmond (1996), the European and American legislative and legal systems were modeled on the Greco-Roman and Judeo-Christian tradition because the Western world had essentially the same need in the 17th through 19th century as had ancient Greece and Rome: "The legislative and legal systems of these societies were devoted to the maintenance of the ruling class. It was important that the members of that class could resolve disputes and engage in coordinated action to maintain their power and control over the society. … The rhetorical orientation of the Speech Tradition was tailor-made for this society" (p. 238).

But the reality was not that neat and simple because neoclassicism shared the stage with other players. The new trend in science set by the Descartes' (1637/1982) *Discours de la*

---

[4]The first public playhouse, The Theatre, opened its doors in London in 1576.

méthode, the *Port Royal Logic* (Arnauld & Nicole, 1662/1869) and Pascal's *De l'esprit géometrique: L'Art de persuader* (1664/1980) in France, and by Locke and the British Empiricists in England, constituted a "radical departure from the philosophical assumptions of classical rhetoric" (Kennedy, 1980, p. 220). "The new logic claimed that the only sound method of inquiry is that of geometry, proceeding from self-evident axioms to universally accepted conclusions. The topics of dialectic and rhetoric are useless in discovering the truth or in demonstrating it, and the five traditional parts of rhetoric are a form of deception. The role of an orator seeking to dominate communication is inappropriate, and to stir the emotions of an audience is unacceptable" (Kennedy, 1980, p. 222). In his *Essay Concerning Human Understanding*, Locke (1690/1854) held that rhetoric was an art of deceit and error and proposed that all figures of speech and rhetorical devices be excluded from serious discourse (chap. 10, section 34). Speaking of *Eloquence*, Hume (1743/1987) concluded that the progress of eloquence was inconsiderable in comparison with the advances made in all other parts of learning.

Beginning in the 17th century, knowledge developed by the humanities in general was demoted to a lower position relative to the newly instated standard of truth. This forced subsequent studies of the human being and human society to emulate the new method of exact science and adopt the inductive empirical approach in order to regain "scientific" status. Even rhetoricians attempted to salvage their science by dressing it up à la mode. George Campbell (1776/1963), in his *Philosophy of Rhetoric*, presented rhetoric as a science of the mind by which the discourse is adapted to its end (in the tradition of the ancient sophistic). He accounted for its development in terms of observation and comparison of the effects of various forms of discourse, from which principles could be extracted. The method of theory development looked scientific, but the multiplicity of ends and ways could not meet the standard of truth (one correct way leading to one truth) imposed by the French mathematicians.

The new logic challenged rhetoric at the highest, philosophical level by reinstating the question of truth as the central issue, as it used to be in the Socratic–Platonic–Aristotelian tradition. On truth grounds, it attacked both political and religious persuasion and called for a new method of communication, needed for the new science, which was exact and unemotional. Banished from the front of truth finding now reserved for the new science, rhetorical theory gravitated more and more toward arts (literature and theatre). In the 18th century, Hugh Blair, Regius Professor of Rhetoric and Belles Lettres as the University of Edinburgh, integrated rhetoric into literature (belles letters) and saw a role for eloquence primarily in written form.

In addition to the migration of rhetoric toward the arts, several other movements shifted rhetoric away from the classical tradition. The first divergence was the Elocutionary Movement of the 18th century. Irish born actor and lexicographer Thomas Sheridan led the movement in England. Elocution had been a part of rhetoric since antiquity, as a subdivision of delivery. Sheridan reconsidered it from a theatrical perspective and made the first large-scale systematic attempt to describe and prescribe the oral delivery of written/printed discourses (poems, plays, speeches). Words were regarded as signs of ideas and tones as signs of passions. With the new treatment of eloquence, neoclassical rhetoricians began to discover psychology.

Other developments also led communication study in the direction of psychology. At the end of the Renaissance, Francis Bacon had touched on rhetoric in his writings and had called for a scientific approach to the study of gesture. The first to respond was John Bolwer (1644) with his *Chirologia*, followed by a host of studies of the physical, nonverbal expression of ideas and passions. Corneille, the "father of French classical tragedy" tried to account for entertainment by considering the psychology of the audience. He hypothesized that expectancy and impatience generate pleasure (Kennedy, 1980). Comedy playwright Molière rebelled against theory for dictating rather than explaining art. In *La Critique de L'École des Femmes*, Molière (1663/1962) elaborated on his own style that emphasized individual differences in the double vision of the normal and abnormal. Philosopher Hobbes (1651/1991), in *Leviathan*, outlined a very innovative superiority theory of humor. Campbell (1776/1963), in his *Philosophy of Rhetoric*, launched an even more unexpected theory of vivacity that made the loveliness of ideas responsible for attention and belief, thus anticipating the modern concept of message salience.

The Roman Catholic Church opened another direction in which the neoclassical rhetoric diverged from classicism. One of its efforts to counter the inroads made by the Reformation was a propagandistic program in which art was to serve as a means of stimulating faith through emotional and sensory appeal. The program included all arts and was addressed primarily to the consolidated middle class, which came to play a role in art patronage. The effectiveness of this policy came from its sensitivity to the characteristics of the target public. The naturalistic treatment made art accessible to a not-so-educated public; the vitality, sensuality, emotionality, and exuberant movement fit the middle class stamina and drive to enjoy life. The richness (exaggeration, overdecoration) and grandeur answered the aspiration for higher status. The departure from established rules and the irregularity of forms reflected the middle class disregard for or challenge of conventions. The result was the baroque art. The label was a term used by philosophers during the Middle Ages to denote an obstacle in schematic logic, and it came to mean contorted thought.

RHETORIC CHALLENGED BY ROMANTICISM

The era of Romanticism spans the late 18th to the mid-19th century. The Romantic movement was built around the concepts of genius and sublimity. It swept European countries and pre-Civil War America and demolished the classical precepts of order, balance, and harmony. In exchange, it resurrected the medieval taste for the mystic, transcendent, occult, and satanic, and exploited the taste for the exotic and remote that grew with the geographic discoveries of the Renaissance. The romantics brought front stage folk cultures and heroes, with strong personalities, moods, passions, inner struggles, and madness. The ultimate effect of the Romanticism was the Babylon of forms that characterizes modernity. But the worst blow dealt to rhetoric by the Baroque and the Romanticism was the fundamentally new concept that artistic form is a deformation (Popa, 1975), which made irrelevant the edifice of norms of "artful" communication and expression built and handed down for more than two millennia by the classical tradition.

In retrospect, we can speculate that the effort by sophists in late antiquity to take over poetry as a subdivision of epideictic, pushed poetry and literature in general toward more and more formal constrictions until as late as the 17th century (e.g., neoclassical tragedy and Corneille's rule of three unities). From such extremes, the language-based arts swung in the opposite direction. Creative powers gradually started to be liberated during the Renaissance and broke completely free in the era of Romanticism. The gradual emancipation from classical rules may be regarded as an emancipation of literary arts from rhetoric. This leaves rhetoric in the 19th century estranged from both science and arts.

MODERN TIMES: RHETORIC HITS NEW TERRITORIES

Although interest in rhetoric waned under the influence of Romanticism, belles letters, and the Elocutionary Movement (Kennedy, 1980), rhetoric gained ground geographically by developing a strong foothold in the United States. According to Wallace (1954), speech instruction reaches back to the colonial period. But modern academic structures, that is, speech departments, emerged in the 19th century (e.g., at Hamilton College in 1841, Boston University in 1873, and the University of Michigan in 1892).

In America, as it had been in ancient Greece, rhetoric was perceived as politically useful and important. According to McCroskey and Richmond (1996), because the political and social systems in American society "were very similar to those of Greece in the time of Aristotle, the Aristotelian rhetorical tradition was an excellent fit to the needs of the scholars of that era. The Aristotelian tradition soon became solidly entrenched as the dominant paradigm for the study of human communication" (p. 236). Infante et al. (1990) that "in 1806 at Harvard, nineteen years before he became President, John Quincy Adams was the first person to hold the Boylston Professorship in Rhetoric and Oratory" (p. 110). Adams set forth a thoroughly classical and conservative view of rhetoric, which confined the academic discipline and practitioners of rhetoric to teaching and applying old knowledge to current needs, or in Delia's (1987a) words, gave the field a "utilitarian and pedagogical focus" (p. 79).

Out of the ancient arts of communication, grammar, rhetoric, and dialectic, the first two were taught in English departments, which were dominated by the literary tradition (Delia, 1987a). Dialectic had already become a subarea of philosophy. According to Infant et al. (1990), the Elocutionary Movement had a substantial influence on the teaching of rhetoric in American universities in the 19th century, but it began to decline at the beginning of the 20th century. However, the invention and diffusion of radio, the second mass medium, in the 1920s boosted the demand for the oral performance of literature and not only saved elocution but gave it such strength that "entire departments of speech dedicated themselves to the theory and practice of literature in performance" (p. 111). Over time, many such departments split away from speech as autonomous theatre or radio–television departments.

The general empirical trend in science accounts for another offshoot from speech. The new science of language production, from which specialties such as audiology, speech pathology and therapy developed, emerged and gravitated towards medical sciences.

The expansion of speech science at the beginning of the 20th century into new areas of application and its growth and diversification had two effects on academic life. On the one hand, the speech faculty founded their own professional organization that helped change the academic structure. "Just before World War I, speech teachers separated from the National Council of Teachers of English to form an independent professional association, the National Association of Academic Teachers of Public Speaking" (Infante et al., 1990, p. 111), which became the Speech Association of America and, later, the Speech Communication Association, and then the National Communication Association. This "orality alliance" founded the *Quarterly Journal of Speech*, which catered to the needs of both traditional public speaking studies and emerging specialties.

Second, the new applications of speech disconfirmed John Quincy Adams's assessment at the beginning of the 19th century that theory in the field had reached its end. Research and theory oriented graduate studies in speech began with the first master's degree at the University of Iowa (in 1902), and the first Ph.D. at the University of Wisconsin (in 1922; Bryant & Thompson, 1999). In general, the traditional speech studies (oratory and secondary rhetoric) became more instrumental, applied to the understanding of politics. But research methods in the traditional areas remained essentially qualitative. The new territories of speech science (e.g., language production and speech pathology; mediated communication and, later on, interpersonal and group communication) were more open to interdisciplinary approaches and quantitative methods borrowed from other (medical and social) sciences.

THE INDUSTRIAL SOCIETY: COMMUNICATION VIA MASS MEDIA

In the 19th century and the first two decades of the 20th century, while rhetoric was struggling for survival and academic autonomy, it met a new challenge: mass communication, initially by print media and film, and, beginning in the 1920s, by the electronic media.

Communication became "mass" about 500 years after the invention of what we retrospectively call the first mass medium, print. The circulation of printed bills, pamphlets, and books certainly increased over time, but mass communication occurred only when large audiences got involved in technologically aided communication. This development occurred in the 19th century, when industrialism developed to the point where very large numbers of people left rural areas and came to live in big cities. Then, the available communication technologies—print (invented in the 15th century), then telegraph (mid-19th century), telephone and film (end of the 19th century), radio (beginning of the 20th century) provided solutions to the problem of social integration of heterogeneous populations (Fortner, 1994). Industrialism itself continually improved the means of communication. As observed by Fortner (1994), people had overly high, "messianic" (p. 221) expectations from technology in general and communication technologies in particular. But the intended beneficial uses were associated with some detrimental uses and effects that took some time to be realized, studied, and understood.

The first media of mass communication were printed periodicals, newspapers, and magazines. Papers had been around since the 17th century, but their circulation was restricted to religious and political elites for a considerable length of time. Large circulations and professional journalism developed in the second half of the 19th century (Nordenstreng, 2000), but the newspaper did not become a mass medium, "reaching a majority of the population on a regular basis" (McQuail, 2000, p. 21), until the early 20th century, when commercial and prestige newspapers were established. In America, national magazines rose to prominence after the Civil War, and commercial radio began after World War I (Delia, 1987a).

Media businesses were largely perceived to be commercial in nature and therefore were governed by existing market principles. This favored technological progress but generated problems related to media as an institution, its roles, uses, and effects. According to McQuail (2000), the ultimate source of the problems was the fact that mass communication was needed as a public rather than private service (i.e., it was considered socially important), and private ownership involved private interests that clashed with the perceived public interests.

The western mass communication philosophy emerged in Britain from the fusion of the liberal self-righting principle (free circulation of ideas and the triumph of truth), launched by John Milton (1644/1927) in *Areopagitica*, the British utilitarianism of the late 18th century, and Adam Smith's (1776/1976) "invisible hand" and laissez-faire economics propounded in *An Inquiry into the Nature and Causes of the Wealth of Nations*. This liberal/libertarian communication philosophy immediately crossed the ocean: The freedom of the press was endorsed, not without struggle, by the First Amendment to the United States Constitution (1791). As in ancient Greece, communication was politically important. The power of the press was perceived to be inherent in its informative capacity, which had two prongs: giving and withholding publicity, and the freedom to report and comment on acts of government. The former involved press latitude and the potential for manipulation. The latter was a right claimed for the population in the name of democracy, and was appealingly presented as a watchdog function. In reality, the press served the government for publicity and propaganda in exchange for access to information about government activities. The need of the government for press services was as strong as the need of the press for interesting and marketable government information, so a symbiotic relationship developed. This relationship has been greatly criticized throughout the second half of the

19th century and the 20th century by Marxist and post-Marxist schools of thought, who perceived the press–government tandem as being detrimental to the public, which both institutions were supposed to serve. But it was not until research and theory on political uses and effects of the media developed in the first half of the 20th century that a new normative theory of mass mediated communication could emerge.

Human communication research and theory construction developed at the confluence between the perceived communication needs and problems that arose from various events and changes in society and the resources that were available to examine and solve those problems. As we look back now at the human communication research and theorizing conducted over the past 100 years, it becomes apparent that the first half of the century was a period in which scholars defined the field and in which theories accumulated rapidly. A gradual qualitative change occurred about the middle of the century, when we entered a phase of complexity, sophistication, and tensions. We will examine select periods separately.

LAYING THE CORNERSTONES

Areas of Interest for Communication Research

Advertising.   Research and theorizing on mass media communication started in the area of print advertising, a practice that had begun in the 17th century with the placement of announcements in weekly newspapers in London. Although limited to elite publics, the circulation of newspapers expanded in the 18th century, so advertising kept growing. Towards the end of the 19th century and the beginning of the 20th century, the industrial boom brought about a similar explosion in advertising (Delia, 1987a), which became an industry. "The first vehicles for large-scale advertising were national magazines, which rose to prominence in America after the Civil War" (p. 46). According to Delia, 19th century advertising "was largely based on a philosophy of providing information" (p. 48). At the beginning of the 20th century, advertising agencies, besides placing advertisements in newspapers and magazines, started to produce ads and whole campaigns. This created a need for research, which intensified with the increasing competition among agencies. The exposure of advertisement recipients to competing messages made the consumer's choice between products or services the core problem in advertising, shifting the focus of research from information to persuasion (Curti, 1967; Kuna, 1976). Because advertising research, the parent of much mass communication research, was born to an industry, it was applied and pragmatic in nature. The nature of the most pressing questions in advertising took researchers beyond issues of information acquisition to concerns with competition for audience attention and to considerations of message features that via certain manipulations could make communication persuasive, thereby more effective.

The widespread diffusion of radio as a means of mass communication in the 1920s and of television in the 1940s added to the mass communication research agenda practical issues of effective channel features and of the nature of specific uses audiences made of media messages. These concerns, in turn, led to theoretical issues in uses, processes, and effects.

Propaganda and Elections.   While the practice of and belief in persuasion were growing, history continued to produce events of global magnitude and impact: World War I, the 1917 revolution in Russia and the establishment of the first communist state with a noncapitalist philosophy and economy, the Great Depression (1929–1939) and the rise of Nazism in the early 1930s, then World War II. These events often turned on the success or failure of human communication, especially at the elite, diplomatic levels but also at the mass level, through the media. Research on elite political communication evolved in the same direction as advertising studies, focusing on persuasion, and shifted emphasis from rhetoric towards psychology and sociology.

At the same time, interest in political communication in the context of mass media built up rapidly, fueled by alarming effects such as the success of the British propaganda in World War I (replete with images of Germans as murderers and credited with influencing Americans to enter the war on Britain's side); the success of Hitler's propaganda in Germany and the emergence of communist and fascist newspapers and magazines in many other western countries, including the United States; the political effectiveness of President Roosevelt's "fireside chats" on the radio (1930s); the popularity of the anti-Semitic discourse on American radio by the Roman-Catholic priest Charles Coughlin in 1936; and the mass panic inadvertently caused by Orson Welles' Halloween radio production of H. G. Wells' *War of the Worlds* in 1938. The effectiveness of propaganda and the perceived strong impact of mass mediated messages created a general feeling that media power was sufficient to mobilize large publics, create panic, or instigate mob behavior. Research took two directions: one of using this power for the benefit of society as a whole, for specific groups or private interests; the other direction was understanding and preventing deleterious uses of media power. In Fortner's (1994) view the result was a corpus of theory of "promise" and a corpus of "reactive theory" or a theory of disappointment (p. 214).

Once the western democracies came under Marxist ideological pressure, the political elites came to depend enormously on mass communication for maintaining control of the situation, and, more critically, for getting elected and reelected to positions of power. Consequently, electoral communication gained prominence in political communication research. Electoral discourse continued to be studied by rhetoricians, political scientists, and philosophers. But the campaigns, which involved journalism, advertising, and public relations, attracted researchers from all subareas of communication as well as from other fields, especially political science, psychology, sociology, and management.

Urban Socialization and Rural Diffusion of Innovations.   Another stage that opened to communication science in the first half of the 20th century was urban community life. The Industrial Revolution created agglomerations of very different and little related people, most of whom were relatively poor. The German sociologist Tönnies (1887/1955) described the difference as between *Community and Association/Society*—the old, traditional, rural, well organized small community and the new social-contract heterogeneous and loose urban society. Communication was perceived to be an important means for accelerating urban socialization, that is, for transforming discrete crowds into coherent, functional, and controllable communities. On the other hand, the old rural communities had to be infused with the products of industrialization and included in the new industrial market. The conservatism of rural constituents had to be broached and, again, communication research and theory was perceived to be a key solution to the problem.

Entertainment.   Last but not least, some form of happiness needed to be injected into the lives of hard-working urban dwellers to cure them from nostalgia for the families and small communities they had left behind; some new attractions had to give them pleasure to bond them to their cities. Technology responded to this need through inventions: Thomas Edison created the phonograph (1877), and the Lumière brothers in Paris produced the first commercially viable projector of motion pictures (1885). Added to books and printed periodicals, recorded music and cinema enlarged the range of popular pastime entertainments, and spread enormously at the beginning of the 20th century. When radio and television penetrated the market (1920s and 1940s, respectively), the content they carried already existed in various forms of entertainment; they merely brought theatrical and musical performances within the reach of the masses. The new media of communication made it easy to deliver simultaneously a large variety of amusements to large numbers of homes and neighborhoods at a relatively low cost.

The Intellectual Climate

Logical Positivism.   The theory landscape in which mass communication research began to be conducted at the beginning of the 20th century was dominated, both in Europe and the United States, by the rationalistic tradition. Theorizing developed within the inductive empirical framework outlined by Francis Bacon at the end of the Renaissance, and under strong influence from the 19th century French logic devoted to mathematical truth and method. Vienna Circle introduced the logical positivism (1920s), a "mechanistic world view" "characterized by the postulates of analyzability, lawfulness, and controllability" (Mue, 1999, p. 71). Wittgenstein's (1922) *Tractatus Logicus-Philosophicus* proposed the unity of science based on a common language (mathematical logic). Positivists promoted the analytic and experimental method and criticized all "knowledge" derived through natural language, thus undermining rhetorical, speculative, and critical approaches to truth. "Positivism was introduced into social science, including communication study, by American researchers, anxious to use it as a means of attaining the legitimacy for their work that was accorded to researchers in the physical sciences" (Fortner, 1994, p. 218). Neopositivism was adopted in the United States first in sociology (at Columbia University), from where it spilled to other social sciences, including communication. By the 1930s, neopositivism had a great influence at the University of Chicago, and it reached its pinnacle after World War II. The spreading of neopositivism is, to a large extent, because many European neopositivists moved to America at the outset of World War II.

Functionalism.   The social sciences were also still under the magic of functionalism, founded by French socologist Emile Durkheim around the turn of the century. The core idea of the functionalist approach was that all social phenomena have a function corresponding to specific needs of the social organism. From sociology, functionalism was readily adopted in many sciences and became a transdisciplinary paradigm. American economist and sociologist Talcott Parsons, educated in England and Germany, helped establish it long-term in the United States through his *Structure of Social Action* (1937) and *Social System* (1951).

Trends in Biology.   Other major influences on social studies came from the natural sciences. One was the Darwinian evolutionary conception (Darwin, 1859/1979), and the mechanistic classical conditioning on which Russian biologist Pavlov worked between 1890 and 1930. The latter was advanced in the West by the behaviorist movement in psychology, which became very popular immediately after World War I, pervaded other social sciences and, according to DeFleur (1966), became the first communication theory.

Pragmatism.   An American-born trend in the social sciences was pragmatism, which originated in philosophy, thrived during the first quarter of the 20th century and still plays a role in communication theory today (Perry, 2001). The pragmatic school championed the priority of action over doctrine, of experience over fixed principles, and proposed usefulness and practicality as criteria for assessing the merit of ideas. Pragmatism was founded by mathematician and logician Charles Sanders Peirce. Psychologist and philosopher William James contributed to the assimilation of pragmatism as a research method theory in psychology, from where it diffused to other social sciences including communication.

Progressivism.   Sociology exerted a particularly strong influence on mass communication research at the beginning of the 20th century. A major bridge that linked it to communication science was progressivism, a movement that emerged at the University of Chicago in response to the social problems associated with the industrial urban society and World War I. Progressivists saw the importance of interpersonal and mass communication in community and consensus building, democratic life, and the dissemination of the products of scientific progress.

Available Resources

Organizational Structures and Human Resources.   The expertise needed for communication research and theorizing was located primarily in academia. The Germans had introduced the system of postgraduate study, and American universities adopted the idea and placed research in graduate schools. The faculty who could address mass communication problems were housed in journalism, which, like speech, started as a subemphasis within English programs. When the speech and journalism sections broke away from English in the 1920s and 1930s, "the separation of interpersonal and mass communication was continued" (Delia, 1987a, p. 73) and separate journalism and speech departments were established.

The early journalism courses, offered in the second half of the 19th century by Washington College (1869), University of Missouri (1878), and University of Pennsylvania (1893), were designed for training professionals, so they were practical rather than theoretical. Unlike rhetoric, a discipline with very long academic tradition, whose 20th century emancipation was to a large extent a maneuver by professionally organized faculty, the setting up of journalism schools was pushed for by professionally organized journalists (Missouri Press Association, 1867). Journalism education was marked by patriarchal figures such as Walter Williams (University of Missouri School of Journalism, 1907), Joseph Pulitzer (Columbia School of Journalism, 1912), and Willard G. "Daddy" Bleyer, who started a course of journalism at the University of Wisconsin (1904).

In spite of the divergent academic paths of rhetoric and journalism after their emancipation from English departments, a positive outcome of that move is undeniable: Graduate programs developed and research became an important activity. The first doctoral degree in journalism was conferred at the University of Missouri (in 1934) and the first doctoral degree in mass communication at the University of Iowa (in 1943; Bryant & Thompson, 1999). "The doctorate became a requirement for hiring in many journalism schools" (Delia, 1987a, p. 75) and a strong research record became a selection criterion. Most problems were interdisciplinary and attracted attention from scholars in other, more mature fields such as psychology, sociology, anthropology, political science, or philosophy. Scholars from other disciplines "began systematic investigations into aspects of communication" (Infante et al., 1990, p. 111) and thus helped lay the foundation of communication science. They also applied theories from their fields to communication and affected transfers of research methodologies.

The crossbreeding that occurred early in the life of the mass communication discipline opened and enriched the field, which had been crippled by the divergence from speech when they both departed from English. The best example of crossbreeding is the communication research and theorizing conducted by the progressivists at the University of Chicago, in the School of Sociology and in the combined department of philosophy, psychology, and pedagogy. For instance, department chair John Dewey was interested in the creation and maintenance of publics; Robert Park studied the role of news. The configuration of expertise at the University of Chicago led to conceptual and methodological eclecticism, which resulted in interesting hybrids. In terms of methodology, the sociologists pioneered the application of ethnographic methods, borrowed from anthropology, to urban settings. In terms of theory, the close partnership between sociology, psychology, philosophy, history, and even economics created a uniquely favorable situation for a well-rounded approach to human communication. This led to original insights and theories, such as Mead's symbolic interactionism in the first half of the century, and Innis's technological determinism, launched at the beginning of the second half of the century.

Another phenomenon with significant consequences for the direction and style of mass communication research and theory was the exodus of Jewish European scholars to the United States occasioned by the growth of Nazism. This move affected a transfer of knowledge and research practices. Mathematician Lazarsfeld came from Austria in 1933 (Schramm, 1997). A few months after he arrived in the United States, Lazarsfeld was hired by the University of Newark, where he created a Research Center that soon joined forces with the Rockefeller-funded Radio Research Project (in 1937) headed by Hadley Cantril at Princeton University. That project moved to Columbia University (in 1938), where it was renamed the Columbia Office of Radio Research (later to become the Bureau of Applied Social Research). Lazarsfeld's centers were modeled on the institute for market and consumer research he had masterminded in Austria as a satellite rather than a part of the psychology department at the University of Vienna (Schramm, 1997). The American research centers set up by Lazarsfeld "cemented the emerging bridge between academic and commercial interests in communication research and established the theoretical relevance of communication research based on applied problems" (Delia, 1987a, p. 51). They became a model for the structuring of research institutes as externally-funded, semiautonomous units linked to university departments through their staff, which ensured the sharing of knowledge in the process of teaching and research and linked the academia to real-life problems. Lazarsfeld also set a positivist and pragmatist trend in American communication science that emphasized "value-free" (ideology-free) empirical research and statistical methods. The monies that fueled mass communication research in the first half of the 20th century came from a variety of sources including business, government, and non profit organizations.

Thus, the problem during this time was not so much one of competition for scarce resources as one of seeking projects that would advance the researchers' interests and simultaneously persuade potential patrons of the usefulness of communication research. Research questions abounded and the scholars could to some extent choose which to address. Therefore, the directions in which research and theory started to develop were a combination of societal demands and personal preferences of influential researchers and academic groups.

Mass Communication Theory in the First Half of the 20th Century

Naturally, the primary concern at the beginning of communication science was to establish the boundaries of the field and to define the objectives and methods of work. The industrialization of print as a carrier of information and advertising (periodicals) on the one hand, and as entertainment (books and magazines) on the other hand, helped dislodge print from rhetoric. The entertainment industry was shifted toward arts and the hugely increasing sector of mass mediated information and advertising was perceived or claimed to be new territory. The interest in mass communication manifested by scholars from already established social sciences made it imperative for researchers who were doing "just this" or "mostly this" to define their "turf."

The Linear Model.   The basic question that had to be answered was "What is communication as an object of study?" The researchers on the eastern coast of the United States took some time to come up with the "components," which they structured in the early 1940s in a typical functionalist way. The product was a linear/flow/transmission (sender–receiver) model traditionally attributed to Lasswell (1948). But, as shown by Bryant and Thompson (2001), the model was first stated by Waples (1942): "Who communicates what to whom by what medium, under what conditions, and with what effects?" (p. 907). This includes the conditions/context. This element indicates that from its very beginning the flow model was not simplistic, and the researchers who developed it had in mind contextual factors as mediators of media effects. Therefore, the flow model cannot be assimilated to the popular "hypodermic needle"/"magic bullet" theory.

The linear model of mass communication was reinforced by Shannon and Weaver's (1949; Weaver, 1949) information theory. The mathematicians were concerned with noise (distortions) occurring between sender and receiver and the informative quality of the message (affected by noise). Its full impact came in the second half of the century, when the communication field took a marked turn toward psychological investigation of message processing. What the information theory initially contributed was a "scientific" backing, which enhanced the credibility of the intuitive flow model.

The Two-Step Flow of Communication.   A serious problem with the flow model was the fact that it dealt exclusively with mass mediated communication, the underlying assumption being that the mass media were a new element (channel) added to interpersonal communication. Empirical research by Lazarsfeld and his associates in the 1940s in the area of political campaigns revealed the role of interpersonal communication in mediating the effects of messages carried by mass media. Thus appeared the two-step flow model, with community or opinion leaders as an additional link between sender and receivers (Katz & Lazarsfeld, 1955; Merton, 1949): The development stimulated interest in local community and in interpersonal communication networks on the eastern coast, but the angle was different from that of the Chicago studies on community-building and social construction of meaning. The findings of Lazarsfeld's circle coincided with those of Ryan and Gross (1943), whose independent research on rural communication in Iowa opened the new direction of diffusion-of-innovations studies.

The establishment of interdisciplinary links, the recognition of the inseparable nature of interpersonal and mass mediated communication, and the inclusion of mediating factors refined the flow model without changing its linearity, or its unidirectional transmissional pattern. In 1948, Hovland was still defining communication as "the process by which an individual (communicator) transmits stimuli (usually verbal symbols) to modify the behavior of other individuals (communicatees)" (p. 59). Nevertheless, Hovland's own research on communication effects (especially persuasion) related to and following World War II dealt a severe blow to the linear model by revealing the overwhelming importance of mediating factors (e.g., communicator credibility,[5] one- versus two-sidedness of the message,[6] emotional appeal, group membership, personality) and plunged communication research and theory into the psychology of message processing, so that "by 1970, American communication research was utterly dominated by social psychological approaches" (p. 65).

Limited Effects.   The discovery of mediating factors brought into discussion the size of media effects. The perception of direct and strong media effects gradually changed into one of limited and mediated effects. Berelson (1948)[7] presented a revised version of the linear model: "Some kinds of communication on some kinds of issues, brought to the attention of some kinds of people under some kinds of conditions, have some kinds of effects" (p. 172). This weak linear model accounts for the despondency of theorists struck around the middle of the century by the futility of attempting to predict the outcome of mass mediated communication. No predictability, no theory. Understandably, Berelson (1959) gloomily ruled that the field had reached its end.

Communication as a Continuous Process.   Beside the internal dynamics of research and theory, the communication discipline was also hit by a revolutionary change of vision that affected all social sciences towards the middle of the 20th century. The change was produced by mathematician Norbert Wiener's (1948) *Cybernetics*, which introduced the concept of feedback as a means of process control, and by Ludwig von Bertalanffy's work on systems theory (publications started in 1929). The impact of these thinkers on communication theory was enormous, but the switch from a covering laws perspective to a systems perspective (Infante et al., 1990) was gradual and slow: Schramm (1954) proposed a continuous loop (interactive) model, with communicators simultaneously sending and receiving messages; Westley and MacLean (1957) produced a corrected version of the linear model, including feedback loops; and Berlo (1960, 1977) finally imposed the notion that communication is a dynamic interactive process and communication cannot be isolated or separated from other events.

Roles of Communication.   In addition to elevating the field to more complex theoretical considerations, the systems perspective insidiously encouraged an older functionalist disposition in media research and theorizing. In a context of uncertainty about media effects, the fad of system functionality revived interest in the study of the media roles in society. Lasswell (1948) proposed a three-function model including surveillance, correlation, and transmission of social heritage. But from the very beginning, the media-functions model was asystematic, which allowed more and more functions (and dysfunctions) to be added.

---

[5]Hovland was a psychologist and very likely ignored classical rhetoric and the Aristotelian notion of ethos.

[6]Hovland's message sidedness is considered the basis of McGuire's (1964) inoculation theory (Infante et al., 1990), ignoring the classical sophistic notion of dialectic taught by Protagoras, the "father of debate" who contended that there were two sides to every proposition (a dialectic) and that speakers should be able to argue either side of the proposition equally well. Protagora's dialectic is commonly accepted as "the foundation in the United States for communication in today's legal and legislative systems" (McCroskey & Richmond, 1996, p. 235) but so far has not been acknowledged as the deepest root of inoculation theory, as possibility of sidedness manipulation.

[7]Bryant and Thompson (2001) indicated that the limited effects view had been expounded earlier by Beuick (1927), who believed that the effects of radio on society would be rather limited, and the greatest benefits would be to isolated individuals, and by Waples, Berelson, and Bradshaw (1940), who discussed limited effects of print on public opinion.

From Macro to Midrange Theories.   With the linear model largely rendered obsolete by systems theory and the endless number of mediating factors and perceived mass communication roles, any attempt to develop an all-encompassing map or macrotheory became vain and superfluous. Researchers and theorists had to resign themselves to covering just aspects of Human Communication, or Mass Communication, or Organizational Communication—or in Merton's (1957) formulation, theories of the midrange.

Symbolic Interactionism.   The pearl of the Chicago school was produced by pragmatist philosopher George Herbert Mead, regarded by his department chair, Dewey,[8] as one of the most fertile minds in American philosophy. Mead was interested in social psychology. His symbolic interactionism theory linked communication (symbols and language) with the concepts of social act and evolution. In his view, social interaction involves communication, through which individuals work out their purposes, direct and modify one another's activities, and transform their environments. While doing this, they acquire and modify knowledge. The process of knowledge development coincides with the evolutionary process. Mead's (1934) theory laid the foundation for the social construction of reality (instrumented by communication), which set a paradigm for linguistic and philosophical studies of meaning, group and social dynamics studies in social psychology, and the interactionist/transactional studies in communication in the second half of the 20th century.

TURNING THE TABLES

Berger and Chaffee (1987b) argued that the early development of communication science was dominated by the study of public and mass persuasion. The underlying assumption, expressed by the linear model, was that the mass media carried messages from centers of information and power toward the audience. In the second half of the 20th century, the interactionist-transactional perspective pioneered by Mead gained the ground lost by the linear unidirectional model. The change was a bottom-up revolution, starting from accumulations of knowledge in linguistics, semiotics, psycholinguistics, psychology, social psychology (dyadic and group dynamics, organizational behavior), and the study of media organizations. The evolving knowledge about what individuals, groups, and institutions (including the media) do in the communication process revealed their roles and power both as receivers and as originators of messages, in interpersonal and mass mediated communication. This made communication appear more like a game, and new research was needed to help reposition the players and remap the field. Once the unidimensional model of communication was discarded, researchers could "take angles" on issues. The pragmatic, logical-positivist research persisted, but qualitative, cultural, and critical approaches also flourished. This set the scene for a theoretical battle aimed at gaining control on decisions about the future of communication. Space limitations preclude a detailed presentation of developments in the battlefield.

Bridging the Gap: From Speech and Journalism to Communication

Fast technological progress in mass media technology increased visibility and made the content appear more realistic (closer to real life) and similar across channels (i.e., convergent). The

---

[8]Both Dewey and Mead came to the University of Chicago in 1894.

media gradually came to be perceived as alternative channels for delivering more or less the same fare (e.g., news stories, fiction, sports and music entertainment, commercials, propaganda). The electronic media in the West persistently cultivated their image as carriers in order to get industry status and market freedom (control over content). This detachment of content from carriers, that is, from technological and economic aspects, made the object of communication studies appear even more unified. On the other hand, the diversification of content categories and the increasing number of problems associated with each form paradoxically exerted pressure on researchers and theorists to make generalizations and establish common methodological and theoretical grounds. At the same time, theory development and circulation increased. Theories emerging in the field of communication or imported from other fields cut across big traditional barriers such as speech/journalism or information/entertainment.

One example is the Whorfian theory of linguistic relativity (Whorf, 1956), which empirically demonstrated that the structure of the language we use influences the way we understand the environment. It also postulated that all higher levels of thought depend on language. This theoretical event hinged communication effects on meaning (semiotics) and culture (anthropology and cultural studies). Interethnic friction around the globe enlarged the discussion of culture-determined communication and intercultural communication to include minority subcultures, and invited political considerations. The globalization of communication and trade increased attention to international advertising, the export of culture (information and entertainment), and international propaganda—all with political implications. The relativity of language also opened the door for interpretive studies that carried on the hermeneutical tradition started by the Christian scholars. The Whorfian theory is just one example illustrating how major theories helped unify thinking about a variety of communication phenomena traditionally studied by different scholars who specialized in segregated areas (e.g., advertising, rhetoric, or journalism).

These two tendencies—the perceived unification of the Object of study and of the Theory—created a trend toward the reunification of the discipline. The movement started in Speech, where public speaking was "no longer the sole, or even the most important, focus of the field" (McCroskey & Richmond, 1996, p. 240). Speech departments came to study interpersonal communication—often over the objections of rhetoricians, who opposed the introduction of social science into their field (Bochner & Eisenberg, 1985).

A new professional association for communication scholars was founded in 1950, the national Society for the Study of Communication, now known as the International Communication Association.

> This group was comprised of individuals disillusioned with studying communication exclusively from the rhetorical perspective. Some were general semanticists, others were primarily concerned with communication in organizations, and others in yet more applied communication settings. In the 1960s and 1970s this association attracted many scholars who were interested in interpersonal communication or the effects of mass media, particularly those who wished to study communication employing quantitative or experimental methodologies" (McCroskey & Richmond, 1996, pp. 238–239).

According to Delia (1987a), "A new brand of faculty member emerged in the years around 1960 with one foot in speech and the other in communication research" (p. 80).

At the same time, Journalism "needed the scientific legitimacy of the mass communication field" (Reardon & De Pillis, 1996, p. 401). Wilbur Schramm, "the most important figure in the development of mass communication within the journalism tradition" (Delia, 1987a, p. 73), was the first professor of communication so-designated. He started the first doctoral program awarding degrees in communication (1943) and presided over the first academic unit ("division") in the world (E. M. Rogers & Chaffee, 1997). But his greatest contribution may well have been that of institutionalizing communication research in American higher education (Delia, 1987a) by creating the Institute of Communications Research at the University of Illinois (1947) and the Institute of Communication Research at Stanford University (1956), subsequently imitated by many major schools. These institutes facilitated communication research within academia because they were more flexible than departments and allowed for interdisciplinary collaboration (E. M. Rogers, 1994).

CONCLUSION: BORN TO INTERDISCIPLINARITY

The second half of the 20th century brought a scientific revolution in the sense that most if not all sciences had proven their relevance to real life. That was a success of American pragmatism. The effect was a new faith, replacing the technological messianism associated with the industrial revolution at the beginning of the century: the faith in science, which came to cover aspects of life that had not previously been considered topics of scientific investigation, as well as new realities that were problematic just because they were new. The research methodologies applied in such new areas produced not only methodological refinements but also expansions of existing communication theories and often development of new insights.

Interpersonal and Group Communication Theory

One example is that of interpersonal and group communication theory, a new subarea of speech communication that developed at the crossroads of rhetoric, linguistics, communication, psychology, sociology, business and public administration, and political science. Research started on different problems from different angles. Then, interests, concepts, and findings were borrowed from one area to another and a joint mapping of the subarea gained momentum, with blank spaces calling for investigation and extant knowledge calling for integration. One of the pioneers was German social psychologist Kurt Lewin, who launched the Research Center for Group Dynamics at the Massachusetts Institute of Technology (1945). His work conducted within the Gestalt psychology framework brought attention to the communication aspect of group processes. For instance, Hovland built on Lewin's work and raised the problem of groupthink that is important in group decision making. Asch (1955, 1956) continued to conduct research on group pressure for conformity. Historic failures in political and military decision-making (e.g., Pearl Harbor, 1941; Bay of Pigs, 1961) prompted Janis (1972) to proceed to a thorough examination of group decision failures from a functionalist systems perspective. The outcome was a full-blown groupthink theory.

At the end of the 1940s, American psychologists became interested in communication from a consistency angle. Heider (1946/1988) proposed a balance model of communication advanced by Newcomb (1953) as a symmetry/coorientation model; Festinger (1957) developed the cognitive dissonance theory; and Osgood, Succi, and Tannenbaum (1957) contributed a congruity theory of attitude change.

Linguists, psycholinguists, and social psychologists began one-on-one communication research in the 1960s (from interactionist, functional-structuralist, and constructivist perspectives, combined with cultural and economic insights). Speech acts were defined in Watzlawick,

Beavin, and Jackson's (1967) *Pragmatics of Human Communication* and operationalized for empirical conversation analysis by L. E. Rogers and Farace (1975).

Various other approaches to interpersonal communication developed through the 1960s, 1970s, and 1980s. The relational approach (e.g., J. K. Burgoon, 1978; M. Burgoon & Bettinghaus, 1980; M. Burgoon, Dillard, & Doran, 1983; Millar & Rogers, 1976; L. E. Rogers, 1989; Wheeless, Barraclough, & Stewart, 1983) examined communication strategies (e.g., compliance gaining, empathy, persuasion schemata, expectancy violation). The social-cognitive approach (e.g., Berger, 1975, 1979, 1985, 1986, 1987; Berger & Bradac, 1982; Delia, 1987b; Irwin & Dalmas, 1973; Jacobs & Jackson, 1981; Sacks, Schegloff, & Jefferson, 1974) addressed the organization of communication and issues such as attribution, affect, or motivation. For instance, the uncertainty reduction theory (Berger & Bradac, 1982) hypothesized that conversation is conducted to alleviate anxiety by increasing knowledge. Berger and Calabrese (1975) also proposed a developmental theory of interpersonal communication. Grice's (1975) maxims of communication combined relational and social-cognitive aspects. The social exchange approach (e.g., Altman & Taylor, 1973) was inspired by cost-benefit considerations that were fashionable in economics.

In the 1950s, well-funded organizational communication research began in business and public administration, drawing on expertise from a variety of domains (e.g., British novelist George Orwell, psychologist Leon Festinger). The theoretical framework included structural functionalism, systems theory, and constructivism. The stating point was communication networks and flows (e.g., Bavelas, 1950; Granovetter, 1973; Leavitt, 1951; E. M. Rogers, 1973; Shaw, 1954). Other topics gradually emerged, such as communication roles (opinion leaders, gatekeepers, liaisons/boundary spanners; e.g., Carroll & Tosi, 1977; Mosher, 1982; Redding, 1972; E. M. Rogers & Agarwala-Rogers, 1976; Rourke, 1984; J. D. Thompson, 1967), message distortion and manipulation (e.g., Janis, 1972; Sebald, 1962; Zalkind & Costello, 1962), source credibility (e.g., Allyn & Festinger, 1961; Festinger & Maccoby, 1964; Jones & Davis, 1965), or jargon and style (e.g., Orwell, 1956). Theoretical gains from interpersonal communication were readily integrated, for example, Cushman and Whiting's (1972) rules theory of interpersonal relationships was adapted for organizational contexts as the theory of coordinated management of meaning (Pearce, 1976).

This bird's-eye picture of the modern field of interpersonal and organizational communication (excluding historical, speculative, and normative texts) reveals the power of socially important problems to generate research and theory. It also shows that individual efforts tend to converge and an amorphous mass of microtheories gradually structures into coherent chunks of knowledge that become midrange theories of specific problems (e.g., Janis's groupthink) or subarea theories (e.g., Organizational Communication Theory).

REFERENCES

Allyn, J., & Festinger, L. (1961). The effectiveness of unanticipated persuasive communications. *Journal of Abnormal Social Psychology, 62,* 35–40.

Altman, I., & Taylor, D. A. (1973). *Social penetration: The development of interpersonal relationships.* New York: Holt, Rinehart & Winston.

Aristotle. (1954). *Rhetoric.* New York: Random House

Arnauld, A., & Nicole, P., (1869). *La logique ou l'art de penser: Ouvrage connu sous le nom de logique de Port Royal* [Logic or the art of thinking: Work known under the name of Port Royal Logic]. Paris: C. Delagrave. (Original work published 1662)

Asch, S. E. (1955). Opinions and social pressure. *Scientific American, 193*(5), 31–35.

Asch, S. E. (1956). Studies of independence and conformity: I. A minority of one against a unanimous majority. *Psychological Monographs, 70,* 1–70.

Bavelas, A. (1950). Communication patterns in task-oriented groups. *Acoustical Society of America Journal, 22,* 727–730.

Berelson, B. (1948). Communications and public opinion. In W. Schramm (Ed.), *Communications in modern society: Fifteen studies of the mass media* (pp. 167–185). Urbana: University of Illinois Press.

Berelson, B. (1959). The state of communication research. *Public Opinion Quarterly, 6,* 54–73).

Berger, C. R. (1975). Proactive and retroactive attribution processes in interpersonal communications. *Human Communication Research, 2,* 33–50.

Berger, C. R. (1979). Beyond initial interaction: Uncertainty, understanding, and the development of interpersonal relationships. In H. Giles & R. N. St. Clair (Eds.), *Language and social psychology* (pp. 122–144). Oxford, England: Blackwell.

Berger, C. R. (1985). Social power and interpersonal communication. In M. L. Knapp & G. R. Miller (Eds.), *Handbook of interpersonal communication* (pp. 439–499). Newbury Park, CA: Sage.

Berger, C. R. (1986). Uncertainty outcome values in predicted relationships: Uncertainty reduction theory then and now. *Human Communication Research, 13,* 34–38.

Berger, C. R. (1987). Communicating under uncertainty. In M. E. Roloff & G. R. Miller (Eds.), *Interpersonal processes: New directions in communication research* (pp. 39–62). Newbury Park, CA: Sage.

Berger, C. R., & Bradac, J. J. (1982). *Language and social knowledge: Uncertainty in interpersonal relations.* London, England: Arnold.

Berger, C. R., & Calabrese, R. J. (1975). Some explorations in initial interaction and beyond: Toward a developmental theory of interpersonal communication. *Human Communication Research, 1,* 99–112.

Berger, C. R., & Chaffee, S. H. (1987). The study of communication as a science. In C. R. Berger & S. H. Chaffee (Eds.), *Handbook of communication science* (pp. 15–19). Newbury Park, CA: Sage.

Berlo, D. K. (1960). *The process of communication: An introduction to theory and practice.* New York: Holt, Rinehart & Winston.

Berlo, D. K. (1977). Communication as process: Review and commentary. In B. D. Ruben (Ed.), *Communication yearbook* (pp. 11–27). New Brunswick, NY: Transaction Books.

Berthold, M. (1972). *A history of world theater.* New York: Ungar.

Beuick, M. D. (1927). The limited social effect of radio broadcasting. *American Journal of Sociology, 32,* 615–622.

Bochner, A. P., & Eisenberg, E. M. (1985). Legitimizing speech communication: An examination of coherence and cohesion in the development of the discipline. In T. W. Benson (Ed.), *Speech communication in the 20th century* (pp. 299–321). Carbondale: Southern Illinois University Press.

Bolwer, J. (1644). *Chirologia, or, the naturall* [sic] *language of the hand.* London: Harper.

Bryant, J., & Thompson, S. (1999). Graduate communication programs. In W. G. Christ (Ed.), *Leadership in times of change: A handbook for communication and media administrators* (pp. 135–161). Mahwah, NJ: Lawrence Erlbaum Associates, Inc.

Bryant, J., & Thompson, S. (2001). *Fundamentals of media effects.* New York: McGraw-Hill.

Bucknell, P. A. (1979). *Entertainment and ritual: 600 to 1600.* London: Stainer & Bell.

Burgoon, J. K. (1978). A communication model of personal space violations. Explication and and initial test. *Human Communication Research, 4,* 129–142.

Burgoon, M., & Bettinghaus, E. P. (1980). Persuasive message strategies. In M. E. Roloff & G. R. Miller (Eds.), *Persuasion: New directions in theory and research* (pp. 141–169). Beverly Hills CA: Sage.

Burgoon, M., Dillard, J. P., & Doran, N. E. (1983). Friendly or unfriendly persuasion: The effects of violations of expectations by males and females. *Human Communication Research, 10*(2), 283–294.

Campbell, G. (1963). *The philosophy of rhetoric* (L. F. Bitzer, Ed.). Carbondale: Southern Illinois University Press. (Original work published 1776)

Carroll, S. J., & Tosi, H. L. (1977). *Organizational behavior.* Chicago: St. Clair.

Cicero, M. T. (1949). *De inventione. De optimo genere oratorum. Topica* (H. M. Hubbell, Trans.). Cambridge, MA: Harvard University Press. (Original work published 84 B.C.)

Curti, M. (1967). The changing concept of "human nature" in the literature of American advertising. *Business History Review, 41,* 337–345.

Cushman, D. P., & Kincaid, L. D. (1987). Introduction and initial insights. In L. D. Kincaid (Ed.), *Communication theory: Eastern and western perspectives* (pp. 1–10). San Diego, CA: Academic.

Cushman, D. P., & Whiting, G. C. (1972). An approach to communication theory: Towards consensus on rules. *Journal of Communication, 22,* 217–218.

Darwin, C. (1979). The origin of species: Complete and fully illustrated. New York: Gramercy Books. (Original work published 1859)

DeFleur, M. L. (1966). *Theories of mass communication*. New York: David McKay.

Delia, J. G. (1987a). Communication study: A history. In C. R. Berger & S. H. Chaffee (Eds.), *Handbook of communication science* (pp. 20–98). Newbury Park, CA: Sage.

Delia, J. G. (1987b). Interpersonal cognition, message goals, and organization of communication: Recent constructive research. In L. D. Kincaid (Ed.), *Communication theory: Eastern and western perspectives* (pp. 255–274). San Diego, CA: Academic.

Descartes, R. (1982). *Discours de la méthode & essais* [Discourse on method & essays]. Paris: Vrin. (Original work published 1637)

Festinger, L. A. (1957). *A theory of cognitive dissonance*. Standford, CA: Stanford University Press.

Festinger, L., & Maccoby, N. (1964). On resistance to persuasive communications. *Journal of Abnormal Social Psychology, 68,* 359–366.

Fortner, R. S. (1994). Mediated communication theory. In F. L. Casmir (Ed.), *Building communication theories: A socio/cultural approach* (pp. 209–240). Hillsdale, NJ: Lawrence Erlbaum Associates, Inc.

Granovetter, M. S. (1973). The strength of weak ties. *American Journal of Sociology, 78,* 1360–1380.

Grice, H. P. (1975). Logic and conversation. In P. Cole & J. Morgan (Eds.), *Syntax and semantics* (Vol. 3, pp. 41–58). New York: Academic.

Heider, F. (1988). *Balance theory*. New York: Springer-Verlag. (Original work published 1946)

Hobbes, T. (1991). *Leviathan* (R. Tuck, Ed.). Cambridge, England: Cambridge University Press. (Original work published 1651)

Hovland, C. (1948). Psychology of the communication process. In W. Schramm (Ed.), *Communications in modern society: Fifteen studies of the mass media* (pp. 58–65). Urbana: University of Illinois Press.

Hume, D. (1987). Of eloquence. In D. Hume, *Essays, moral, political, and literary* (pp. 97–110). Indianapolis, IN: Liberty Classics. (Original work published 1743).

Infante, D. A., Rancer, A. S., & Womack, D. F. (1990). *Building communication theory*. Prospect Heights, IL: Waveland.

Irwin, A., & Dalmas, A. T. (1973). *Social penetration: The development of interpersonal relationships*. New York: Holt, Rinehart & Winston.

Jacobs, S., & Jackson, S. (1981). Argument as a natural category: The routine grounds for arguing in conversation. *Western Journal of Speech Communication, 45*(2), 118–132.

Janis, I. L. (1972). *Victims of groupthink*. Boston: Houghton Mifflin.

Jones, E. E., & Davis, K. E. (1965). From acts to dispositions: The attribution process in person perception. In L. Berkowitz (Ed.), *Advances in Experimental Social Psychology* (Vol. 2, pp. 219–266). New York: Academic.

Katz, E., & Lazarsfeld, P. F. (1955). *Personal influence: The part played by people in the flow of mass communication*. Glencoe, IL: Free Press.

Kennedy, G. A. (1980). *Classical rhetoric and its Christian and secular tradition from ancient to modern times*. Chapel Hill: University of North Carolina Press.

Kuna, D. P. (1976). The psychology of advertising, 1896–1916 (Doctoral dissertation, University of New Hampshire, 1976). *Dissertation Abstracts International, 37,* 3048B.

Lasswell, H. D. (1948). The structure and function of communication in society. In L. Bryson (Ed.), *The communication of ideas* (pp. 37–51). New York: Harper & Bros.

Leavitt, H. J. (1951). Some effects of certain communication patterns on group performance. *Journal of Abnormal and Social Psychology, 46,* 38–50.

Locke, J. (1854). *An essay concerning human understanding: And a treatise on the conduct of the understanding*. Philadelphia: Hayes & Zell. (Original work published 1690)

Longinus. (1985). *On the sublime* (J. A. Arieti & J. M. Crossett, Trans.). New York: E. Mellen. (Original work published 1554)

McCroskey, J. C., & Richmond, V. P. (1996). Human communication theory and research: Traditions and models. In M. B. Salwen & D. W. Stacks (Eds.), *An integrated approach to communication theory and research* (pp. 233–242). Mahwah, NJ: Lawrence Erlbaum Associates, Inc.

McGuire, W. J. (1964). Inducing resistance to persuasion: Some contemporary approaches. In L. Berkowitz (Ed.), *Advances in experimental social psychology* (Vol. 1, pp. 191–229). New York: Academic.

McQuail, D. (2000). *McQuail's mass communication theory* (4th ed.). London: Sage.

Mead, G. H. (1934). *Mind, self, and society*. Chicago: University of Chicago Press.

Merton, R. K. (1949). Patterns of influence: A study of interpersonal influence and communications behavior in a local community. In P. F. Lazarsfeld & F. Stanton (Eds.), *Communication research* (pp. 180–219). New York: Harper.

Merton, R. K. (1957). *Social theory and social culture.* Glencoe, IL: Free Press.

Millar, F. E., & Rogers, L. E. (1976). A relational approach to interpersonal coomunication. In G. Miller (Ed.), *Explorations in interpersonal communication* (pp. 87–203). Newbury Park, CA: Sage.

Milton, J. (1927). *Areopagitica: A speech of Mr. John Milton for the liberty of unlicenc'd printing, to the Parliament of England.* New York: Payson & Clarke. (Original work published 1644)

Molière, J. B. P. (1962). La critique de l'école des femmes [Criticism of the school for women]. In *Oeuvres complètes* (Vol. 1, pp. 477–512). Paris: Garnier Frères. (Original work published 1663)

Mosher, F. (1982). *Democrary and the public service* (2nd ed.). New York: Oxford University Press.

Mue, J., de (1999). The informatization of the world view. *Information, Communication and Society, 2,* 69–94.

Newcomb, T. M. (1953). An approach to the study of communicative acts. *Psychological Review, 60,* 393–404.

Nordenstreng, K. (2000). Mass communication. In G. Browning, A. Halcli, & F. Webster (Eds.), *Understanding contemporary society: Theories of the present* (pp. 328–342). Thousand Oaks, CA: Sage.

Oliver, R. T. (1966). *Leadership in the 20th century Asia: The rhetorical principles and practice of the leaders of China, Korea, and India from Sun Yat-sen to Jawaharlal Nehru.* University Park, PA: Center for Continuing Liberal Education, Pennsylvania State University.

Orwell, G. (1956). Politics and the English language. In R. Rovere (Ed.), *The Orwell reader* (pp. 355–366). New York: Harcourt Brace Jovanovich.

Osgood, C. E., Suci, G. J., & Tannenbaum, P. H. (1957). *The measurement of meaning.* Urbana: University of Illinois Press.

Pacioli, L. (1980). *Divina proportione.* Paris: Jardin de Flore. (Original work published 1587)

Parsons, T. (1937). *The structure of social action: A study in social theory with special reference to a group of recent European writers.* New York: McGraw-Hill.

Parsons, T. (1951). *The social system.* Glencoe, IL: Free Press.

Pascal, B. (1664). De l'esprit géométrique: L'art de persuader [The spirit of geometry: The art of persuasion]. In *Oeuvres complètes* (pp. 348–359). Paris: Seuil. (Original work published 1664).

Pearce, W. B. (1976). The coordinated management of meaning: A rules-based theory of interpersonal communication. In G. R. Miller (Ed.), *Explorations in interpersonal communication* (pp. 17–36). Beverly Hills, CA: Sage.

Perry, D. K. (Ed.). (2001). *American pragmatism and communication research.* Mahwah, NJ: Lawrence Erlbaum Associates, Inc.

Popa, M. (1975). *Forma ca deformare* [Form as deformation]. Bucharest, Romania: Eminescu.

Quintilian, M. F. (1963). *The institutio oratoria of Quintilian* (H. E. Bultler, Trans.). Cambridge, MA: Harvard University Press. (Original work published 94 A.D.)

Reardon, K. K., & De Pillis, E. G. (1996). Multichannel leadership: Revisiting the false dichotomy. In M. B. Salwen & D. W. Stacks (Eds.), *An integrated approach to communication theory and research* (pp. 399–407). Mahwah, NJ: Lawrence Erlbaum Associates, Inc.

Redding, W. C. (1972). *Communication within the organization.* New York: Industrial Communication Council.

Rogers, E. M. (1973). *Communication strategies for family planning.* New York: Free Press.

Rogers, E. M. (1994). *A history of communication study: A biographical approach.* New York: Free Press.

Rogers, E. M., & Agarwala-Rogers, R. (1976). *Communication in organizations.* New York: Free Press.

Rogers, E. M., & Chaffee, S. H. (Eds.). (1997). *The beginnings of communication study in America: A personal memoir by Wilbur Schramm.* Thousand Oaks, CA: Sage.

Rogers, L. E. (1989). Relational communication processes and patterns. In B. Dervin, L. Grossberg, B. O'Keefe, & E. Wartella (Eds), *Rethinking communication: Paradigm exemplars* (pp. 280–290). Newbury Park, CA: Sage.

Rogers, L. E., & Farace, R. V. (1975). Analysis of relational communication in dyads: New measurement procedures. *Human Communication Research, 1,* 222–239.

Rourke, F. E. (1984). *Bureaucracy, politics, and public policy* (3rd ed.). Boston: Little Brown.

Ryan, B., & Gross, N. (1943). The diffusion of hybrid seed corn in two Iowa communities. *Rural Sociology, 8,* 15–24.

Sacks, H., Schegloff, E., & Jefferson, G. (1974). A simplest systematics for the organization of turn taking for conversation, *Language, 50,* 696–735.

Schramm, W. (1954). How communication works. In W. Schramm (Ed.), *The process and effects of mass communication* (pp.). Urbana: University of Illinois Press. Effort-reward model (in the 1965 edition, pp. 3–26)

Schramm, W. (1997). The forefathers of communication study in America. In S. H. Chaffee & E. M. Rogers (Eds.), *The beginnings of communication study in America* (pp. 3–20). Thousand Oaks, CA: Sage.

Sebald, H. (1962). Limitations of communication: Mechanisms of image maintenance in form of selective perception, selective memory, and selective distortion. *Journal of Communication, 12,* 142–149.

Shannon, C., & Weaver, W. (1949). *The mathematical theory of communication.* Urbana: University of Illinois Press.

Shaw, M. E. (1954). Some effects of unequal distribution of information upon group performance in various communication nets. *Journal of Abnormal and Social Psychology, 49,* 547–553.

Smith, A. (1976). *An inquiry into the nature and causes of the wealth of nations* (R. H. Campbell & A. S. Skinner, General Eds.; W. B. Todd, Text Ed.). Oxford, England: Clarendon Press. (Original work published 1776)

St. Augustine. (1747). *D. Augustini de doctrina christiana libri quattor: In quibus ad intelligendam Sacram Scripturam praecepta, et christiani oratoris official egregie traduntur.* Bergoni: Petrus Lancellotus.

Thompson, J. D. (1967). *Organization in action.* New York: McGraw-Hill.

Tönnies, F. (1955). *Community and association.* London, England: Routledge & Kegan Paul. (Original work published 1887)

Trissino, G. G. (1529). *La poetica di M. Gio van Giorgio Trissino* [The poetics of Mr. M. Gio van Giorgio Trissino]. Vicenza: Tolomeo Ianiculo.

Wallace, K. R. (Ed.). (1954). *History of speech education in America: Background studies.* New York: Appleton-Century-Crofts.

Waples, D. (1942). Communications. *American Journal of Sociology, 47,* 907–917.

Waples, D., Berelson, B., & Bradshaw, F. R. (1940). *What reading does to people: A summary of evidence on the social effects of reading and a statement of problems for research.* Chicago: University of Chicago Press.

Watzlawick, P., Beavin, J. H., & Jackson, D. D. (1967). *Pragmatics of human communication: A study of interactional patterns, pathologies, and paradoxes.* New York, Norton.

Weaver, W. (1949). Recent contributions to the mathematical theory of communication. In C. E. Shannon & W. Weaver (Eds.), *The mathematical theory of communication* (pp. 95–117). Urbana: University of Illinois Press.

Westley, B. H., & MacLean, M. (1957). A conceptual model for communication research. *Journalism Quarterly, 34,* 31–38.

Wheeless, L. R., Barraclough, R., & Stewart, R. (1983). Compliance-gaining and power in persuasion. In R. N. Bostrom (Ed.), *Communication Yearbook, 7* (pp. 105–145). Beverly Hills, CA: Sage.

Whorf, B. L. (1956). *Language, thought, and reality: Selected writings.* Cambridge: Technology Press of Massachusetts Institute of Technology.

Wiener, N. (1948). *Cybernetics.* New York: Wiley.

Wittgenstein, L. (1922). Tractatus logicus-philosophicus. New York: Harcourt, Brace & Co., Inc.

Zalkind, S. S., & Costello, T. W. (1962). Perception: Some recent research and implications for administration. *Administrative Science Quarterly, 7,* 218–233.

Zillmann, D. (2000). The coming of media entertainment. In D. Zillmann & P. Vorderer (Eds.), *Media entertainment: The psychology of its appeal* (pp. 1–20). Mahwah, NJ: Lawrence Erlbaum Associates, Inc.

Author Index

Subject Index

Made in the USA
Columbia, SC
18 December 2022

74267214R20261